Gender in Cross-Cultural Pe

This fully updated new edition of *Gender in Cross-Cultural Perspective* carefully introduces and responds to changes in anthropological approaches to and perspectives on gender. With two new editors and new authors from the Global South and underrepresented communities, it combines theoretically and ethnographically based chapters to examine gender roles and ideology around the world.

The book is divided thematically into five parts, with the editors opening each section with a succinct introduction to the principal issues. The book retains some of the classic chapters while offering new contributions and extended discussions throughout on methodology. It also has entirely new contributions that reflect more recent developments in the discipline, including more emphasis on LGBTQ+ communities, COVID, and migration. This new edition also features additional support for teaching and learning, including a film list and discussion questions, that are now offered as supplemental online materials.

The eighth edition of *Gender in Cross-Cultural Perspective* continues to be an essential resource for undergraduate and graduate students encountering the anthropology of gender for the first time.

Adrienne E. Strong is Associate Professor of Anthropology and Faculty Affiliate of the Center for African Studies and Department of Gender, Sexuality, and Women's Studies at the University of Florida, USA.

Richard Powis is Assistant Professor of Maternal and Child Health in the College of Public Health and has Faculty Affiliation in the Department of Women's, Gender, and Sexuality Studies at the University of South Florida, USA.

Gender in Cross-Cultural Perspective

Eighth Edition

Edited by Adrienne E. Strong
and Richard Powis

Routledge
Taylor & Francis Group

LONDON AND NEW YORK

Designed cover image: agsandrew, Getty Images

Eighth edition published 2025
by Routledge
4 Park Square, Milton Park, Abingdon, Oxon, OX14 4RN

and by Routledge
605 Third Avenue, New York, NY 10158

Routledge is an imprint of the Taylor & Francis Group, an informa business

First edition published by Prentice Hall 1993

Seventh edition published by Routledge 2017

British Library Cataloguing-in-Publication Data
A catalogue record for this book is available from the British Library

Library of Congress Cataloging-in-Publication Data
Names: Strong, Adrienne E., 1988– editor. | Powis, Richard (Professor of public health), editor.
Title: Gender in cross-cultural perspective / edited by Adrienne E. Strong and Richard Powis.
Description: Eighth edition. | Abingdon, Oxon ; New York, NY : Routledge, [2025] | Includes bibliographical references and index.
Identifiers: LCCN 2024005004 (print) | LCCN 2024005005 (ebook) | ISBN 9781032504131 (hardback) | ISBN 9781032504100 (paperback) | ISBN 9781003398349 (ebook)
Subjects: LCSH: Sex role—Cross-cultural studies.
Classification: LCC GN479.65 .G4634 2025 (print) | LCC GN479.65 (ebook) | DDC 305.3—dc23/eng/20240404
LC record available at https://lccn.loc.gov/2024005004
LC ebook record available at https://lccn.loc.gov/2024005005

ISBN: 978-1-032-50413-1 (hbk)
ISBN: 978-1-032-50410-0 (pbk)
ISBN: 978-1-003-39834-9 (ebk)

DOI: 10.4324/9781003398349

Typeset in Sabon
by Apex CoVantage, LLC

Access the Support Material: www.routledge.com/9781032504100

For the pathbreakers in the area of gender studies and to all those who work and seek to learn under conditions that make teaching and discussing the world's gender diversity still subversive actions.

Contents

PART 3
Gendered space and knowledge   229

PART 4
Gender and the state   339

About the editors

Adrienne E. Strong received her BS in biomedical science from the Ohio State University, her MA in anthropology from Washington University in St. Louis, and her PhD in anthropology jointly from Washington University in St. Louis and the University of Amsterdam. She also holds a graduate certificate in women's, gender, and sexuality studies from Washington University in St. Louis. She completed a National Science Foundation–funded postdoctoral position in the Heilbrunn Department of Population and Family Health at Columbia University's Mailman School of Public Health. She is an associate professor of anthropology and a faculty affiliate of the Center for African Studies and Department of Gender, Sexuality, and Women's Studies at the University of Florida. She served as a co-chair of the Council on Anthropology and Reproduction from 2019 to 2024. Her research interests are centered on critical global health and the study of maternal mortality, nursing, gendered personhood in hospitals, hospital ethnography, and biomedical healthcare systems. She is the author of *Documenting Death: Maternal Mortality and the Ethics of Care* (2020), the winner of the 2021 Eileen Basker Memorial Prize for research on gender and health from the Society for Medical Anthropology, in addition to a number of chapters in edited volumes and articles in journals such as *Social Science & Medicine*, *Medical Anthropology*, *Human Organization*, and *Health Policy and Planning*. She primarily conducts long-term fieldwork in Tanzania on maternal mortality in hospital settings and is currently conducting research funded by the National Science Foundation on pain care practices in two regions of the country.

Richard Powis received his BA degree in anthropology from Cleveland State University, his MA degree and PhD in anthropology from Washington University in St. Louis, and his graduate certificate in women's, gender, and sexuality studies from Washington University in St. Louis. He is an assistant professor of maternal and child health at the University of South Florida College of Public Health. He currently serves as a co-chair of the Council on Anthropology and Reproduction, and he is a research affiliate of the West African Research Center in Dakar, Senegal. His research interests focus on gender and kinship, labor and care, and the state. He teaches courses on the political economy of health, women's health, reproductive justice, and global maternal and child health, among others. At USF-COPH, he directs "The Entourage Lab," a collective of scholars and community members in both Tampa, Florida, and Dakar, Senegal, who conduct research and program evaluations on all things antenatal and postpartum support, fathers and expectant fathers, doulas, and others who care for and surround birthing people.

Contributors

James M. Adovasio is Director of Archaeology at the Heinz History Center in Pittsburgh, PA. He is a specialist in the analysis of perishable materials and the application of high-tech archaeological methods. He is the author of more than 500 publications, with his most recent book being "Strangers in a New Land."

Oğuz Alyanak is a postdoctoral researcher at Fairwork, Oxford Internet Institute, University of Oxford.

Caroline S. Archambault is Assistant Professor at Leiden University College, the Netherlands. Her current research focuses on human rights, international development, and demography in sub-Saharan Africa.

Tami Blumenfield is Kui Ge Scholar of ethnology at Yunnan University and Adjunct Research Assistant Professor in the Department of Anthropology at the University of New Mexico. She has researched social transformation, resilience, gender, and heritage in southwest China's Mosuo/Na, Naxi, and Nuosu communities since the early 2000s.

Andrea Bolivar is Assistant Professor of women's and gender studies and Faculty Affiliate of Latina/o studies at the University of Michigan, USA.

John R. Bowen is Dunbar-Van Cleve Professor at Washington University in St. Louis. He studies questions of Islam, law, and society in Indonesia and Europe. Awarded a Guggenheim prize in 2012 and named a Carnegie fellow in 2016, he is a fellow of the American Academy of Arts and Sciences.

Chad Broughton is Instructional Professor in the Social Sciences Collegiate Division of the Harris School of Public Policy at the University of Chicago. He is a sociologist interested in qualitative approaches to the study of policy and society.

M. Laetitia Cairoli is Director of Development at Oasis-A Haven for Women and Children in Paterson, NJ. She is the author of *Girls of the Factory: A Year with the Garment Workers of Morocco*.

Geoff Childs, Professor of anthropology at Washington University in St. Louis, is an anthropological demographer who studies the interplay of culture and population processes.

Siobhán M. Cully is Associate Professor of anthropology and Affiliate of the Feminist Research Institute at the University of New Mexico, USA. Her interests include non-normative kinship, demography, and health inequities.

Toyin Falola is Professor of history, University Distinguished Teaching Professor, and Sanger and Mossiker Chair of humanities, University of Texas at Austin.

Melvyn C. Goldstein, Distinguished University Professor, John Reynolds Harkness Professor, and Co-Director of the Center for Research on Tibet at Case Western Reserve University, is a sociocultural anthropologist specializing in Tibetan society and cross-cultural aging.

Alma Gottlieb is Professor Emerita of anthropology at the University of Illinois at Urbana–Champaign, USA, and Visiting Scholar in anthropology at Brown University, USA.

Ellen Gruenbaum is Professor Emerita in anthropology at Purdue University and Visiting Scholar at the University of California, Riverside, who specializes in cultural medical anthropology and gender research.

Lauren E. Gulbas is Associate Professor at the University of Texas at Austin. As a medical anthropologist, she studies the intersections of culture and mental health.

Barry S. Hewlett is Professor of anthropology at Washington State University, Vancouver, and has research interests in the anthropology of childhood and the cultural contexts of infectious and parasitic diseases.

Sharon Hicks-Bartlett is Associate Instructional Professor in the Department of Sociology at the University of Chicago. Her interests include urban and suburban poverty, ethnography, sociology of the family, gerontology, and race and critical race theory among others.

Jennifer S. Hirsch is Professor of sociomedical sciences at Columbia University's Mailman School of Public Health and Affiliated Faculty with the Institute for the Study of Sexuality and Gender. Her research examines gender, sexuality, and migration; the anthropology of love; social dimensions of reproductive health and HIV; gender-based violence; and undergraduate well-being, including sexual assault.

Adnan Hossain is Lecturer (Assistant Professor) in sociology at the School of Social and Political Sciences, University of Glasgow, UK. His research and activism concern gender and sexual diversity, race and ethnic relations, and reparatory social science.

Rosemary A. Joyce is Distinguished Professor of anthropology and Member of the Graduate Group of the Designated Emphasis in Women, Gender, and Sexuality at the University of California, Berkeley.

Ashley Thuthao Keng Dam is Medical Anthropologist, Ethnobotanist, and Food Writer. Their research interests lie in the entanglements of health, gastronomy, and bio(cultural)diversity. Currently, they are a lecturer in global health and global studies at Maastricht University (the Netherlands) and lead the project Plant Planet Plate on behalf of the National Geographic Society.

Scott F. Kiesling is Professor of linguistics and is Affiliated Faculty Member of the Gender, Sexuality, and Women's Studies Program at the University of Pittsburgh in Pittsburgh, PA, USA.

Gail Kligman is Distinguished Professor of sociology and Faculty Affiliate of the Center for European and Russian Studies and the UCLA Promise Institute for Human Rights at UCLA.

Nolan Kline, PhD, MPH is an Associate Professor in the Department of Population Health Sciences at the University of Central Florida College of Medicine. His research focuses on topics at the intersection of anthropology, public health, and law, with particular attention to im/migrants and sexual and gender minorities.

Sarah A. Lacy is Assistant Professor of biological anthropology at the University of Delaware, USA, specializing in paleoanthropology and bioarchaeology.

Louise Lamphere is a Distinguished Professor of Anthropology Emerita at the University of New Mexico and Past President of the American Anthropological Association. Her research interests include ethnology, social organization and kinship, political economy, gender, women and work, and urban anthropology in the U.S. Southwest.

Maria Lepowsky is Professor of Anthropology at the University of Wisconsin-Madison. She is also affiliated with Women's Studies. Her research interests include gender, environmental anthropology, exchange, ritual, medical/nutritional, and psychological anthropology in Oceania and the American West.

Margaret MacDonald is Associate Professor in the Department of Anthropology at York University in Toronto, Canada. As a medical anthropologist, her focus is on reproductive health in a range of settings: with midwives and their clients in Canada; within a global maternal health community of advocates, professionals, and policy makers; and in Senegal where non-governmental organisations work to improve maternal health in rural and remote communities.

Lawrence T. Monocello is T32 Postdoctoral Research Scholar in psychiatry and Lecturer in anthropology at Washington University in St. Louis, USA.

Cara Ocobock is Assistant Professor of anthropology, Concurrent Faculty in gender studies, Affiliated Faculty with the Environmental Change Initiative, and Affiliated Faculty with the Health, Humanities, and Society Program at the University of Notre Dame.

Shanti Parikh is Chair of African and African-American Studies and Professor of Sociocultural Anthropology and of African and African-American Studies at Washington University in St. Louis. Her research focuses on the intersections of race, gender, sexuality, and capitalism and the politics of state and global interventions that emerge to manage, protect, and mold populations.

Nancy Scheper-Hughes is Chancellor's Professor of medical anthropology at the University of California, Berkeley, USA. Her work concerns the violence of everyday life examined on the ground from a radical, existential, and critically engaged perspective. She is the author of *Death without Weeping* (1993), amongst other titles.

Sarah Sobonya lives in Marietta, Georgia.

Olga Soffer is Professor Emerita from the Department of Anthropology, University of Illinois. Her lifelong research interests focus on discovering and documenting the lives and lifeways of the diverse folk who peopled the Upper Paleolithic/Late Stone Age some 50,000–10,000 years ago.

Anubha Sood is Research Scientist at the University of Texas Southwestern in the Department of Psychiatry. She is a medical anthropologist specializing in psychological and psychiatric anthropology interested in the cultural practices in which people engage to resolve their suffering.

Chun-Yi Sum is Lecturer of social sciences at Boston University's College of General Studies and Faculty Affiliate at BU's Department of Anthropology. She conducts research on gender, ethnicity, and citizenship in China.

Rebecca L. Upton is Professor of global public and environmental health and African Studies Coordinator at Colgate University, USA.

Funda Üstek is a postdoctoral researcher and project manager at Fairwork, Oxford Internet Institute, University of Oxford.

Rine Vieth (they/them or iel avec les accords masculins) is an FRQSC Postdoctoral Fellow in the Department of Political Science at Université Laval in Québec City, Québec, and Part-Time Faculty in the Department for the Study of Religion at Saint Mary's University in Halifax, Nova Scotia. They also hold appointments as a postdoctoral affiliate at L'Observatoire des profilages at Université de Montréal in Montréal, Canada, and as an external affiliate at the Centre for Refugee Studies at York University in Toronto, Canada. They are a socio-legal researcher interested in migration, law, gender, and governance, and have a geographic focus on the UK, the EU, and Canada.

Puchung Wangdui, Member of the Tibetan Academy of Social Sciences, completed an MA in medical anthropology with a focus on aging at Case Western Reserve University.

Daphne Weber received her PhD from Washington State University in May 2024. Her research examines intersections of gender, religion, and bodily practices.

Marlene Zuk is Regents Professor of ecology, evolution, and behavior at the University of Minnesota, Twin Cities. Her research interests include animal behavior, especially the evolution of reproductive behavior, and the effect of parasites on host ecology and evolution.

Foreword

As we wrote in the preface to the first edition of *Gender in Cross-Cultural Perspective* (1993), the initial idea for the book came from the experience of teaching undergraduate courses on gender and anthropology. At that time, there were very few texts available, and the one that did exist, Michelle Rosaldo and Louise Lamphere's edited volume *Women, Culture and Society* (1974), while pathbreaking, had become outdated as feminist anthropologists began to challenge some of the theoretical assumptions outlined in that book. Thus, we began working to assemble an accessible reader that not only built on the classic contributions of the 1970s, when the field was formulated, but also incorporated more recent and diverse analyses of gender roles and ideology around the world.

In that first edition, we outlined our goals: to introduce students to the most significant topics in the field of the anthropology of gender; to provide broad cross-cultural coverage that would encourage comparative analysis of themes under discussion and that would encompass studies addressing issues of gender in industrial societies as well as in developing societies; to complement research on women's lives and experiences with research that dealt with masculinity and male gender roles; to combine theoretical and ethnographically based articles in each section of the book; and finally, to include introductions to each section that would review as clearly as possible some of the significant issues debated in particular subject areas in the anthropology of gender. We divided the volume into 11 sections, each with anywhere from three to five readings, and presented these sections in an order that made sense to us but with no requirement that instructors teach the book in that order. We also had a commitment to presenting the breadth of our discipline of anthropology by including a section on biology, gender, and human evolution, as well as one on prehistory and gender.

Over the seven editions that we co-edited between 1993 and the publication of the 7th edition in 2017, we retained much of the original structure, although we sometimes retitled the sections. For example, the final section, originally titled "Colonialism and Development," became "Gender and the Global Economy." Another section, originally titled "Gender and Sexuality," became "Gender, Sexuality, and the Body." Each time we tackled a new edition (and the publisher went from Prentice Hall to Pearson to Routledge), we chose new articles that spoke both to empirical and theoretical developments in the anthropology of gender since the previous edition. We often approached younger scholars to write original pieces for the volume, but we also held on, across all seven editions, to some of the theoretical classics (such as Lamphere's "The Domestic Sphere of Women and the Public World of Men: The Strengths and Limitations of an Anthropological Dichotomy," written originally for the first edition, or Nancy Scheper-Hughes's chapter "Lifeboat Ethics: Mother Love and Child Death in Northeast Brazil"). Over time, we expanded the number of articles dealing with the US context (on the suggestion of some of the instructors who used the volume), as well as with issues of masculinity and male roles. We also added articles that dealt with new topics – for example, gender and migration, or gay and lesbian parenthood.

Gender in Cross-Cultural Perspective has numerous unique features that have contributed to its value in the classroom. The volume is broad in scope, and the chapters present in-depth ethnographic detail. Depending on the interests of particular instructors, the wide range of chapter themes allows for designing a syllabus with a focus appropriate for the students, the professor, and the disciplinary orientation of the class. The section introductions also serve to orient students to the history of gender studies and its transformations since the first edition. To achieve this goal, we offer a continuous discussion in each section of new editions to highlight chapters that are no longer included but still important to the development of the field. The book, as a whole, emphasizes ethnography in broader social, political, and economic context, and the chapters represent classics and contemporary articles. This arrangement provides a trajectory of gender studies with provocative case studies set in global perspective.

The extensive references and list of films in each of the seven editions we co-edited have allowed students and professors to expand on themes of special relevance to the class and to prepare class assignments, whether essays or exams. We are grateful to the graduate students in our anthropology program at SMU who, over 30 years, contributed to the production of successive editions. Over this time period, competitors to this volume have emerged, but *Gender in Cross-Cultural Perspective* has remained successful, we believe, because of its breadth and flexibility. We are thankful that our first editor, Nancy Roberts (Prentice Hall and then Pearson), recognized the vision and promise of the project and offered unfailing support across six editions.

We are now both retired, and we think it is time to pass on this very successful collaboration and project to younger colleagues, who will give it their own imprint, direction, and authority. It is clear that they have rethought the volume for the third decade of the twenty-first century and identified the broader themes within which the study of gender around the world now proceeds. We have every confidence that our project is in very good hands and that this book will continue to be adopted by our colleagues in the profession who teach courses on gender in anthropology and our sister disciplines.

Caroline B. Brettell
University Distinguished Professor Emerita
Southern Methodist University

Carolyn Sargent
Professor Emerita of Anthropology
Washington University in St. Louis

December 1, 2023

Preface

Perhaps this is merely our perspective as academic anthropologists in the state of Florida, but speaking of "gender" as a meaningful concept worthy of scholarly attention feels a little rebellious – but then maybe it always has. As we write this, our home state is beginning a process of removing gender studies and related disciplinary curricula (e.g., women's studies, feminist studies, even sociology) from universities. The chapters in each section are selected either to represent readings of fundamental issues and concepts of the thematic subsection or to address new ways of thinking through the very problems that we face in our current moment.

It is an honor and a privilege to take over the editorship of this classic text in the anthropology of gender from Carolyn Sargent and her longtime collaborator, Caroline Brettell. Powis's first copy was given to him by his undergraduate mentor, Barbara Hoffman, at Cleveland State University. It was a beaten-up, outdated 4th edition that she had used in her Anthropology of Gender course years prior. That copy, which I still have, reference, and even teach from, was my introduction to gender studies, gendered labor, the state, and Marxist feminism in college. Strong came by the text as a graduate student as a grader for Carolyn Sargent's Global Gender Issues course. I have gone on to teach my own Global Gender Issues class every year since I started at the University of Florida, and I continue to utilize this textbook each time.

We deeply appreciate the previous editors' commitment to the analysis of gender in all four subdisciplines of anthropology, and we have sought to preserve that here. We have maintained some of the classic texts of previous editions while introducing ten new original chapters from our colleagues who are undertaking exciting scholarship in the anthropology of gender.

New in this edition

In some ways, the problems of gender that Brettell and Sargent would have hoped to help us think through in their previous editions have not gone away; rather, they find themselves re-emerging with new faces – new historical contexts, new political stakes, new media environments that ensnare a new generation of pundits and commentators into old conversations. It is our job to keep pushing back against patriarchal institutions, to keep busting myths about gender and biological determinism, to keep doing good science, and to keep speaking truth to power. To help accomplish these tasks, we've specifically sought out new chapters from junior colleagues who are doing cutting-edge work in the anthropology of gender. We've also engaged authors who bring us additional cultural and geographic diversity, while acknowledging there is always more we would like to cover and include, more peoples and lifeways we would want to explore and bring to the attention of students. However, we must stop somewhere; reviewers told us the previous edition was already quite long and sometimes difficult to teach in its entirety. With this in mind, we've reduced some of the older material, incorporated the new, and all the while, sought to maintain a balance of important, field-defining contributions and cutting-edge new work from around the world. We have also worked to update the terminology in the section introductions to reflect the changing lexicon of gender and sexuality. We acknowledge that there are some who will already consider us outdated even when the book is published – such is the rapidity with which these terms continue to proliferate and evolve. We view this linguistic diversity and change as an encouraging sign that more and more communities are able to self-identify with terms which they find most suitable – we're just trying to catch up. With that being said, we have left the language in all the chapters as the authors wrote it. In some cases, their use of binary language (i.e., *men* and *women*) is a result of the time period in which they were writing. In others, it is a result of how the communities with which they work would refer to themselves. For example, when teaching about pregnancy in the context of the United States, Adrienne refers to pregnant people to acknowledge that not everyone who becomes pregnant in the United States self-identifies as female. However, when talking or writing about her work on maternity care in Tanzania, Adrienne talks exclusively about pregnant women, reflecting what Tanzanians understand to be true in referring to this population (though Swahili, spoken in Tanzania, is a language without gender pronouns and a pregnant woman is called *mjamzito*, a term that does not include gender but which is locally understood to be gendered).

In a significant departure from the previous edition, we rearranged and condensed the sections, turning 11 into 5 thematic areas covering a wide range of topics. We have made this change in the hopes that this makes the present edition easily teachable, particularly for pedagogical techniques and approaches now much in favor, such as team-based learning and other so-called flipped classroom approaches.

Tips for teaching

Adrienne has been teaching with this textbook's previous editions at least once per year since she began teaching. Throughout this time, I've adjusted how I teach with the text, shifting from simply teaching the chapters in order start to finish to more recently grouping them into fewer, broader thematic sections that I use to structure my class throughout the semester. The new organization of this edition into fewer sections is a result of this approach, which has effectively helped me convert my teaching from lecture-based to more interactive, student-driven team-based learning. While, in my experience, some students new to the fields of anthropology or gender studies struggle with a lack of clear-cut answers to important questions presented in the chapters, our most productive classroom conversations have come from grappling with tensions that exist in the gray space of cultural relativism and some amount of personal discomfort encountered in the face of difference. Our hope is that these broader thematic sections provide the instructor with additional flexibility for teaching and lend themselves to creating modules for each term that encourage students to think across chapters to make connections across geographic location and time periods.

In teaching this textbook, it is important to emphasize the publication dates of the chapters. The 8th edition includes work originally published in the 1980s, with the fieldwork started even earlier, all the way through research still in progress and written in 2023 specifically for this edition. Students may connect more or less easily with topics they feel are old or outdated, but emphasizing that change is a constant is vitally important. The Sambia are no more frozen in time than are the Pulse nightclub victims or trans Latinas or men navigating masculinities in Spain or market women in West Africa, and so on.

Since we have moved the film list online for the first time, we hope you will also find it useful for teaching and engaging students with the broader topics, if not the specific stories, in each of the chapters. We have organized the films to correspond with the section they might best complement but also encourage you to use other films and resources to bring the content alive for your students, and many instructors surely already do.

Acknowledgments

Reading the acknowledgements in the previous edition of the text was reading the history of this textbook as it evolved over seven editions. Here, we thank all the many people who assisted Caroline and Carolyn in the production of those volumes, and we start fresh with our own thanks to those who have assisted us in compiling this 8th edition.

We first thank our graduate assistants, Alana Alexander and Assata Jasper, for their assistance with fielding numerous e-mails and formatting of the chapters. Alana, in particular, took on the incredible task of reorganizing the film list for the 8th edition.

Adrienne would like to thank Carolyn Sargent for her mentorship and for suggesting Adrienne take on this text as part of the next generation of editors. She would also like to thank all the students who have been in ANT 3302 Global Gender Issues over the last five years at the University of Florida whose conversations, comments, and critiques have shaped not only how Adrienne teaches the course but also this new edition of the text. Many thanks always to Jyoti, for his love, support, and partnership in all things, especially as I worked to complete this new edition while we tried to adjust to life with a new baby.

Dick's work on this project wouldn't have been possible without institutional support and sharp-witted mentorship from Ellen Daley. He also expresses an evergreen appreciation for Barbara Hoffman, Ellen Foley, and Carolyn Sargent's unwavering, enthusiastic teaching and mentorship in all things anthropology and gender.

Adrienne E. Strong
Richard Powis

Part 1

Gendering bodies

In this thematic subsection, we consider how bodies are gendered. Gendering is the process by which people and their bodies are coded with certain assumptions about what they are capable of or what they are supposed to do according to cultural values. (As we'll discuss in later sections, spaces, knowledges, institutions, and other things can be gendered too.) These values and assumptions are transmitted by our institutions (like schools and churches), beliefs systems (like religion and politics), families and relations, and media (like film and television). When these voices are nearly unanimous in their expression of what makes men and women who they are, it can seem like they are fully binary and biologically determined. This is where gender is often conflated with sex, which itself is not binary (Fausto-Sterling 2000). But when we, as anthropologists, examine these values in cross-cultural perspective, their cohesion and naturalness begin to fall apart. We have curated this collection of chapters to present a broad array of how anthropologists of gender think about the cultural values of what bodies are capable of, what societies expect from them, and what they are supposed to do.

Today, more than ever in recent history, trans health and politics are central in national conversations about the relationship between gender and the body. Since the publication of the 7th edition, trans and nonbinary issues have seemingly supplanted the liberal democratic debates around sexuality in ways that are both contiguous with and divergent from the theoretical perspectives that helped us understand these relationships in the past. We will look at some of these issues here and throughout this edition.

We begin with a brand-new chapter for the 8th edition in which biological anthropologist Sarah A. Lacy and human biologist Cara Ocobock re-examine the claims that men evolved to hunt and women evolved to gather. Based on evidence from exercise physiology and archaeology, they explain the important roles estrogen plays in endurance activities, such as ultramarathons and ancient hunting practices, as well as how we can learn from skeletal remains about what activities Neanderthals engaged in. Lacy and Ocobock firmly situate the "man the hunter" theory in its historical context, explaining some of the social landscape of the 1960s that first produced this theory. With Lacy and Ocobock's explanations, it's easy to see how researchers' own biases and time periods can heavily color what data they can collect, how they interpret results, and what data they might choose to overlook. Next, Rosemary A. Joyce demonstrates that recent archaeological research on biology and gender has challenged us to rethink assumptions about how we recognize sexual anatomical variation and how we explain it. Even the traits of the skeleton considered most diagnostic of sex can be ambiguous. In response

DOI: 10.4324/9781003398349-1

to this reality, some archaeologists call for increased use of DNA testing to determine the genetic sex of skeletons. But intriguingly, bone chemistry studies may show little difference between the sexes. Instead, we may find more pronounced differences between men and women of a privileged group and those less advantaged. The engendering of archaeology, Joyce argues, began with a search for women in the past (Ehrenberg 1989). That search has now definitively resulted in rich understandings of the roles of particular women, and of women as a group, which sometimes confirm – but also frequently contradict – the assumptions that archaeologists once made. Innovative archaeological explorations of gender increasingly investigate how embodied personhood, including differences in sexual anatomy and sexual practices, affected people's lives. In this way, we can hope to better understand the lives of women, men, and people of other genders across time and space.

Next, biologist Marlene Zuk takes up the question of animal models in gender studies, exploring the biological roots of sex differences. She argues forcefully that we should not succumb to stereotypes that would make us pawns of our evolutionary heritage. She cites current research that supports the idea of female preference for particular types of males as a major force in evolution. But she also stresses that there is a great deal of diversity and variation in sexual selection in the animal world and that this variation should offer lessons for how we understand the biological basis of sex differences and mating practices in humans. Even the nonhuman primate world is characterized by this variation. Zuk also warns us against imposing human characteristics or values (rooted in a particular sociocultural perspective) onto animals, thereby shaping our perceptions of the "naturalness" of gendered stereotypes, just as we should be careful to not uncritically extend present-day understandings of gender into the past.

Works such as Buckley's study of Yurok menstruation (1982) and Buckley and Gottlieb's (1988) classic collection on menstrual practices cross-culturally were groundbreaking in furthering our understanding of the diversity of women's bodily experiences and how body practices are shaped by culture and history. In her chapter in this book, Alma Gottlieb notes that most early anthropological writings on menstruation were overly simplistic in assuming that menstrual blood was necessarily a source of mystical contamination. Gottlieb describes the growing feminist literature that focuses on menstruation and on the body in general. Recent scholarship includes accounts by anthropologists who gained firsthand knowledge of women's menstrual houses by means of participant observation, something not possible when anthropologists conducting research were predominantly men. In addition, scholars have emphasized the agency of menstruating women – for example, their use of menstrual blood to engage in magical procedures to deceive their husbands or to attract sexual advances, the use of herbal and other methods to regulate menstruation, or the use of diverse techniques to induce abortions. For example, women in Bali use hormonal birth control pills to regulate the timing of their menstruation to ensure they are able to participate in important religious rituals closed to those who are bleeding. Gottlieb's analysis reminds us that people who menstruate shape their own menstrual experiences and are not bound to a solely biological or cultural script.

In some societies, people engage in or experience transformations of their bodies. In many cases, such transformations are related to issues of gender identity. These may occur as part of initiation rituals, through body art (tattoos, piercing, etc.), through dieting or skin lightening, or through cosmetic surgery (see Gulbas, this book). As Ellen Gruenbaum points out, female genital cutting (FGC) is a practice that has tested the limits of cultural relativism and generated continuing debate about how to respect cultural difference while taking a stance in accord with one's own moral position. There are various forms of female genital cutting practices (cliteridectomy, excision, infibulation/reinfibulation, etc.), and the age at which it is done is also different from one society to the next. These practices present serious biological or health risks, such as infection and hemorrhage at the time of the procedure and future risks to childbearing. And yet in many contexts, FGC is highly valued and is strongly defended by women who carry out the practice. The social risks of not being cut are still great in many communities. Gruenbaum observes that, in the past, efforts to reduce FGC focused on potential medical complications; these largely failed. New approaches focus on shifting, socially reinforced norms through mechanisms of community-based education. In implementing this approach, African states, including Sudan, have acted in response to broader international human rights agreements. They have passed laws against FGC as well as supported national campaigns aimed at reducing the practice. Of particular interest, in the Sudanese case, is the social marketing initiative launched by Sudanese activists with UNICEF to develop a new term for the uncircumcised girl – *saleema* (which means healthy and whole). You can find videos from the Saleema campaign on YouTube, and we encourage you to check those out.

Lauren E. Gulbas explores the high rates of cosmetic surgery in Venezuela, a country known for producing stunning competitors for the Miss Universe and Miss World competitions. Gulbas tries to find an explanation for why men and women, especially those from poor families, allocate scarce resources to the pursuit of an ideal feminine or masculine body. She links these body ideals with notions of self and with the psychological significance of looking good and feeling good within gendered frames of reference. While not included in this text, there is significant research being conducted within anthropology and gender studies on surgery for trans people as they pursue bodies that reflect their selves and are legible to others as ideally gendered bodies (e.g., Plemons 2017).

In a new chapter for this edition, Adnan Hossain builds on the work of Nanda and Reddy (previous editions of this text) to give us updated insight into the lives of *hijras* in Bangladesh. HIV/AIDS campaigns, in particular, have recast hijras a third gender/third sex. However, Hossain explains why it's more complicated than that and that hijra identity is also related to religion and class. Many of the hijras with whom Hossain worked considered their hijra identity to be more of a profession or occupation than a sexuality or gender identity. Likewise, how the general population views hijras and how hijras transform their bodies (or not) varies by location, complicating some outsiders' views of this population.

Reproductive labor is an obvious societal expectation put upon the body, and it's one that Margaret MacDonald examines through the lens of midwifery practice in Canada. As she argues, feminist scholarship and midwifery have shared a common goal in studies of the gendered body – to retrieve the "natural" facts of pregnancy and birth. Her research on the changing meanings of "natural birth" in contemporary midwifery in Canada suggests a significant shift away from essentialized interpretations of the category "woman." In conjunction with second-wave feminism, "natural childbirth" emerged as an alternative that represented birthing people as capable, strong, with competent bodies that do not require high-tech surveillance during pregnancy and birth. MacDonald argues that the concept of natural birth has complex meanings for Canadian midwives and women themselves. Rather than emphasizing the "natural" as birth without technological interventions, contemporary midwifery complicates the construct, including within its meanings the possibility of interventions such as pain medication or cesarean births. Midwives emphasized the importance of informed choice; natural childbirth, then, is about educating birthing people to validate their experiences of their bodies, and to foster personal responsibility. Resistance to medicalization is less central to the current Ontario midwifery paradigm, which, in turn, is nuanced in its approach to medical technology. Ultimately, MacDonald contends that these shifts in ideology and practice are linked to modernity and what is expected of the "modern woman."

Perhaps one of the most iconic images of maternity is that of the breastfeeding mother and her baby. As Sobonya observes, from Renaissance art showing a Madonna nursing infant Jesus to modern advertisements for breastfeeding supplies, breastfeeding is viewed as an intimate relationship between two people, a closed circle of mother and baby. Although most babies have a father, whether biological or social, they are usually left out of the breastfeeding narrative. This is a mistake, as Sobonya shows in her chapter on men's contributions to breastfeeding. A number of studies suggest that fathers can play a significant role in breastfeeding success, prompting programs designed to encourage fathers to join in the effort to increase their partners' likelihood of breastfeeding. Sobonya's own research in St. Louis demonstrates some of the ways fathers have become more visible in breastfeeding advocacy and support and identifies men's specific concerns about breastfeeding. In addition, she describes emerging research on transgender men and transmasculine individuals who breastfeed or "chestfeed" their infants, situating these fathers in current discourses about breastfeeding fathers.

In a new contribution to this edition, Lawrence T. Monocello presents a thorough background on anthropological engagement with eating disorders research and cross-cultural variation in body image. Using his own research with South Korean men, Monocello shows us that not only have men been missing from research on body image and eating disorders but that there also has been even less research on how locally desirable masculinities and what he terms muscularities are formed and shape the incidence of eating disorders. Variation rooted in historical and sociocultural processes can drive body image dissatisfaction and increases in eating disorders while also masking the extent to which men suffer from these conditions. Monocello's work is an important contribution to this text but may be difficult to engage with for those with a past or current history of eating disorders.

References

Buckley, Thomas. 1982. "Menstruation and the Power of Yurok Women: Methods in Cultural Reconstruction." *American Ethnologist* 9: 47–60.

Buckley, Thomas, and Alma Gottlieb, eds. 1988. *Blood Magic: The Anthropology of Menstruation*. Berkeley: University of California Press.

Ehrenberg, Margaret. 1989. *Women in Prehistory*. Norman, OK: University of Oklahoma Press.

Fausto-Sterling, Anne. 2000. *Sexing the Body: Gender Politics and the Construction of Sexuality*. New York: Basic Books.

Plemons, Eric. 2017. *The Look of a Woman: Facial Feminization Surgery and the Aims of Trans-Medicine*. Durham, NC: Duke University Press.

Chapter 1

The theory that men evolved to hunt and women evolved to gather is wrong

Cara Ocobock and Sarah A. Lacy

Even if you are not an anthropologist, you have probably encountered one of this field's most influential notions, known as "man the hunter." The theory proposes that hunting was a major driver of human evolution and that men carried this activity out to the exclusion of women. It holds that human ancestors had a division of labor, rooted in biological differences between males and females, in which males evolved to hunt and provide and females tended to children and domestic duties. It assumes that males are physically superior to females and that pregnancy and child-rearing reduce or eliminate a female's ability to hunt.

Man the hunter has dominated the study of human evolution for nearly half a century and pervaded popular culture. It is represented in museum dioramas and textbook figures, Saturday-morning cartoons, and feature films. The thing is, it's wrong.

Mounting evidence from exercise science indicates that women are physiologically better suited than men to endurance efforts, such as running marathons. This advantage bears on questions about hunting because a prominent hypothesis contends that early humans are thought to have pursued prey on foot over long distances until the animals were overheated. Furthermore, the fossil and archaeological records, as well as ethnographic studies of modern-day hunter-gatherers, indicate that women have a long history of hunting game. We still have much to learn about female athletic performance and the lives of prehistoric women. Nevertheless, the data we do have signal that it is time to bury "man the hunter" for good.

The theory rose to prominence in 1968 when anthropologists Richard B. Lee and Irven DeVore published *Man the Hunter*, an edited collection of scholarly papers presented at a 1966 symposium on contemporary hunter-gatherer societies (Lee and DeVore 1968). The volume drew on ethnographic, archaeological, and paleoanthropological evidence to argue that hunting is what drove human evolution and resulted in our suite of unique features. "Man's life as a hunter supplied all the other ingredients for achieving civilization: the genetic variability, the inventiveness, the systems of vocal communication, the coordination of social life," anthropologist William S. Laughlin writes in Chapter 33 of the book (Laughlin 1968: 320). Because men were supposedly the ones hunting, proponents of the man the hunter theory assumed evolution was acting primarily on men and women were merely passive beneficiaries of both the meat supply and evolutionary progress.

DOI: 10.4324/9781003398349-2

But man the hunter's contributors often ignored evidence, sometimes in their own data, that countered their suppositions. For example, Hitoshi Watanabe (1968) focused on ethnographic data about the Ainu, an Indigenous population in northern Japan and its surrounding areas. Although Watanabe documented Ainu women hunting, often with the aid of dogs, he dismissed this finding in his interpretations and placed the focus squarely on men as the primary meat winners. He was superimposing the idea of male superiority through hunting onto the Ainu and into the past.

This fixation on male superiority was a sign of the times not just in academia but in society at large. In 1967, the year between the "man the hunter" conference and the publication of the edited volume, 20-year-old Kathrine Switzer entered the Boston Marathon under the name "K. V. Switzer," which obscured her gender. There were no official rules against women entering the race; it just was not done. When officials discovered that Switzer was a woman, race manager Jock Semple attempted to push her physically off the course.

At that time, the conventional wisdom was that women were incapable of completing such a physically demanding task and that attempting to do so could harm their precious reproductive capacities. Scholars following man the hunter dogma relied on this belief in women's limited physical capacities and the assumed burden of pregnancy and lactation to argue that only men hunted. Women had children to rear instead.

Today these biased assumptions persist in both the scientific literature and the public consciousness. Granted, women have recently been shown hunting in movies such as *Prey*, the most recent installment of the popular Predator franchise, and on cable programs such as *Naked and Afraid* and *Women Who Hunt*. But social media trolls have viciously critiqued and labeled these depictions as part of a politically correct feminist agenda. They insist the creators of such works are trying to rewrite gender roles and evolutionary history in an attempt to co-opt "traditionally masculine" social spheres. Bystanders might be left wondering whether portrayals of women hunters are trying to make the past more inclusive than it really was – or whether man-the-hunter-style assumptions about the past are attempts to project sexism backward in time. Our recent surveys of the physiological and archaeological evidence for hunting capability and sexual division of labor in human evolution answer this question (Lacy and Ocobock 2024; Ocobock and Lacy 2024).

Before getting into the evidence, we need to first talk about sex and gender. "Sex" typically refers to biological sex, which can be defined by myriad characteristics such as chromosomes, hormone levels, gonads, external genitalia, and secondary sex characteristics. The terms "female" and "male" are often used in relation to biological sex. "Gender" refers to how an individual identifies – woman, man, nonbinary, and so forth. Much of the scientific literature confuses and conflates *female/male* and *woman/man* terminology without providing definitions to clarify what it is referring to and why those terms were chosen. For the purpose of describing anatomical and physiological evidence, most of the literature uses "female" and "male," so we use those words here when discussing the results of such studies. For ethnographic and archaeological evidence, we are attempting to reconstruct social roles, for which the terms "woman" and "man" are usually used. Unfortunately, both these word sets assume a binary, which does not exist biologically, psychologically, or socially. Sex and gender both exist as a spectrum, but when citing the work of others, it is difficult to add that nuance.

It also bears mentioning that much of the research into exercise physiology, paleoanthropology, archaeology, and ethnography has historically been conducted by men and focused on males. For example, Ella Smith of the Australian Catholic University and her colleagues (2022) found that in studies of nutrition and supplements, only 23 percent of participants were female. In studies focusing on athletic performance, Emma Cowley of the University of North Carolina at Chapel Hill and her colleagues (2021) found that only 3 percent of publications had female-only participants; 63 percent of publications looked exclusively at males. This massive disparity means we still know very little about female athletic performance, training, and nutrition, leaving athletic trainers and coaches to mostly treat females as small males. It also means that much of the work we have to rely on to make our physiological arguments about female hunters in prehistory is based on research with small human sample sizes or rodent studies. We hope this state of affairs will inspire the next generation of scientists to ensure that females are represented in such studies. But even with the limited data available to us, we can show that man the hunter is a flawed theory and make the case that females in early human communities hunted too.

From a biological standpoint, there are undeniable differences between females and males. When we discuss these differences, we are typically referring to means, averages of one group compared with another. Means obscure the vast range of variation in humans. For instance, although males tend to be larger and to have bigger hearts and lungs and more muscle mass, there are plenty of females who fall within the typical male range; the inverse is also true.

Overall, females are metabolically better suited for endurance activities, whereas males excel at short, powerful burst-type activities. You can think of it as marathoners (females) versus powerlifters (males). Much of this difference seems to be driven by the powers of the hormone estrogen.

Given the fitness world's persistent touting of the hormone testosterone for athletic success, you'd be forgiven for not knowing that estrogen, which females typically produce more of than males, plays an incredibly important role in athletic performance. It makes sense from an evolutionary standpoint, however. The estrogen receptor – the protein that estrogen binds to in order to do its work – is deeply ancient. Joseph Thornton of the University of Chicago and his colleagues (2003) have estimated that it is around 1.2 billion to 600 million years old – roughly twice as old as the testosterone receptor. In addition to helping regulate the reproductive system, estrogen influences fine-motor control and memory, enhances the growth and development of neurons, and helps prevent hardening of the arteries (Manolagas and Kousteni 2001).

Important for the purposes of this discussion, estrogen also improves fat metabolism. During exercise, estrogen seems to encourage the body to use stored fat for energy before stored carbohydrates. Fat contains more calories per gram than carbohydrates do, so it burns more slowly, which can delay fatigue during endurance activity (Besson et al. 2022). Estrogen does not only encourage fat burning but also promotes greater fat storage within muscles – marbling, if you will – which makes that fat's energy more readily available. Adiponectin, another hormone that is typically present in higher amounts in females than in males, further enhances fat metabolism while sparing carbohydrates for future use, and it protects muscle from breakdown (Nagai et al. 2016). Anne Friedlander of Stanford University and her colleagues (1998) found that females use as much as 70 percent more fat for energy during exercise than males.

Correspondingly, the muscle fibers of females differ from those of males. Females have more type I, or "slow-twitch," muscle fibers than males do. These fibers generate energy slowly by using fat. They are not all that powerful, but they take a long time to become fatigued. They are the endurance muscle fibers. Males, in contrast, typically have more type II ("fast-twitch") fibers, which use carbohydrates to provide quick energy and a great deal of power but tire rapidly (Haizlip et al. 2015).

Females also tend to have a greater number of estrogen receptors on their skeletal muscles compared with males (Wiik et al. 2005). This arrangement makes these muscles more sensitive to estrogen, including to its protective effect after physical activity. Estrogen's ability to increase fat metabolism and regulate the body's response to the hormone insulin can help prevent muscle breakdown during intense exercise. Furthermore, estrogen appears to have a stabilizing effect on cell membranes that might otherwise rupture from acute stress brought on by heat and exercise. Ruptured cells release enzymes called creatine kinases, which can damage tissues (Paroo et al. 2002; Enns and Tiidus 2010).

Studies of females and males during and after exercise bolster these claims. Linda Lamont of the University of Rhode Island and her colleagues (2003), as well as Michael Riddell of York University in Canada and his colleagues (2003), found that females experienced less muscle breakdown than males after the same bouts of exercise. Tellingly, in a separate study, Mazen J. Hamadeh of York University and his colleagues (2005) found that males supplemented with estrogen suffered less muscle breakdown during cycling than those who didn't receive estrogen supplements. In a similar vein, research led by Maughan et al. (1986) of the University of St. Andrews in Scotland found that females were able to perform significantly more weight lifting repetitions than males at the same percentages of their maximal strength.

If females are better able to use fat for sustained energy and keep their muscles in better condition during exercise, then they should be able to run greater distances with less fatigue relative to males. In fact, an analysis of marathons carried out by Robert Deaner and others of Grand Valley State University (2016) demonstrated that females tend to slow down less as the race progresses compared with males.

If you follow long-distance races, you might be thinking, *Wait, males are outperforming females in endurance events!* But this is only sometimes the case. Females are more regularly dominating ultra-endurance events, such as the more than 260-mile Montane Spine footrace through England and Scotland, the 21-mile swim across the English Channel, and the 4,300-mile Trans Am cycling race across the United States. Sometimes, female athletes compete in these races while attending to the needs of their children. In 2018, English runner Sophie Power ran the 105-mile Ultra-Trail du Mont-Blanc race in the Alps while still breastfeeding her 3-month-old at rest stations.

The inequity between male and female athletes is a result not of inherent biological differences between the sexes but of biases in how they are treated in sports. As an example, some endurance-running events allow the use of professional runners called pacesetters to help competitors perform their best. Men are not permitted to act as pacesetters in many women's events because of the belief that they will make the women "artificially faster," as though women were not actually doing the running themselves.

The modern physiological evidence, along with historical examples, exposes deep flaws in the idea that physical inferiority prevented females from partaking in hunting during our evolutionary past. The evidence from prehistory further undermines this notion.

Consider the skeletal remains of ancient people. Differences in body size between females and males of a species, a phenomenon called sexual size dimorphism, correlate with social structure. In species with pronounced size dimorphism, larger males compete with one another for access to females, and among the great apes, larger males socially dominate females. Low sexual size dimorphism is characteristic of egalitarian and monogamous species. Modern humans have low sexual size dimorphism compared with the other great apes. The same goes for human ancestors spanning the past two million years, suggesting that the social structure of humans changed from that of our chimpanzee-like ancestors (Carretero et al. 2023; Villmoare et al. 2019).

Anthropologists also look at damage on our ancestors' skeletons for clues to their behavior. Neandertals are the best-studied extinct members of the human family because we have a rich fossil record of their remains. Neandertal females and males do not differ in their trauma patterns (Berger and Trinkaus 1995; Trinkaus 2012), nor do they exhibit sex differences in pathology from repetitive actions (Lacy and Trinkaus n.d.; Fox and Frayer 1997). Their skeletons show the same patterns of wear and tear. This finding suggests that they were doing the same things, from ambush-hunting large game animals to processing hides for leather. Yes, Neandertal women were spearing woolly rhinoceroses, and Neandertal men were making clothing.

Males living in the Upper Paleolithic – the cultural period between roughly 45,000 and 10,000 years ago, when early modern humans entered Europe – do show higher rates of a set of injuries to the right elbow region known as thrower's elbow, which could mean they were more likely than females to throw spears (Sparacello et al. 2017). But it does not mean women were not hunting, because this period is also when people invented the bow and arrow, hunting nets, and fishing hooks. These more sophisticated tools enabled humans to catch a wider variety of animals; they were also easier on hunters' bodies (Holt and Formicola 2008). Women may have favored hunting tactics that took advantage of these new technologies.

What is more, females and males were buried in the same way in the Upper Paleolithic. Their bodies were interred with the same kinds of artifacts, or grave goods, suggesting that the groups they lived in did not have social hierarchies based on sex (Riel-Salvatore and Gravel-Miguel 2013).

Ancient DNA provides additional clues about social structure and potential gender roles in ancestral human communities. Patterns of variation in the Y chromosome, which is paternally inherited, and in mitochondrial DNA, which is maternally inherited, can reveal differences in how males and females dispersed after reaching maturity. Thanks to analyses of DNA extracted from fossils, we now know of three Neandertal groups that engaged in patrilocality – wherein males were more likely to stay in the group they were born into and females moved to other groups – although we do not know how widespread this practice was (Fox and Frayer 1997; Skov et al. 2022).

Patrilocality is believed to have been an attempt to avoid incest by trading potential mates with other groups. Nevertheless, many Neandertals show both genetic (Prüfer et al. 2014) and anatomical evidence (Trinkaus 2018) of repeated inbreeding in their ancestry. They lived in small, nomadic groups with low population densities and endured frequent local extinctions, which produced much lower levels of genetic diversity than we see in living humans. This is probably why we don't see any evidence in their skeletons of sex-based differences in behavior. For those practicing a foraging subsistence strategy in small family groups, flexibility and adaptability are much more important than rigid roles, gendered or otherwise. Individuals get injured or die, and the availability of animal and plant foods changes with the seasons. All group members need to be able to step into any role, depending on the situation, whether that role is hunter or breeding partner.

Observations of recent and contemporary foraging societies provide direct evidence of women participating in hunting. The most cited examples come from the Agta people of the Philippines. Agta women hunt while menstruating, pregnant, and breastfeeding, and they have the same hunting success as Agta men (Goodman et al., 1985).

They are hardly alone. A recent study of ethnographic data spanning the past 100 years – much of which was ignored by "man the hunter" contributors – found that women from a wide range of cultures hunt animals for food. Abigail Anderson and Cara Wall-Scheffler of Seattle Pacific University and their colleagues (2023) report that 79 percent of the 63 foraging societies with clear descriptions of their hunting strategies feature women hunters. The women participate in hunting regardless of their childbearing status. These findings directly challenge the "man the hunter" assumption that women's bodies and childcare responsibilities limit their efforts to gathering foods that cannot run away.

So much about female exercise physiology and the lives of prehistoric women remains to be discovered. But the idea that in the past men were hunters and women were not is absolutely unsupported by the limited evidence we have. Female physiology is optimized for exactly the kinds of endurance activities involved in procuring game animals for food. And ancient women and men appear to have engaged in the same foraging activities rather than upholding a sex-based division of labor. It was the arrival some 10,000 years ago of agriculture, with its intensive investment in land, population growth, and resultant clumped resources, that led to rigid gendered roles and economic inequality.

Now, when you think of "cave people," we hope, you will imagine a mixed-sex group of hunters encircling an errant reindeer or knapping stone tools together, rather than a heavy-browed man with a club over one shoulder and a trailing bride. Hunting may have been remade as a masculine activity in recent times, but for most of human history, it belonged to everyone.

Discussion questions

1. Think about what used to come to your own mind first when thinking about early hunter-gatherers. How does the evidence presented here help you rethink your previous images?
2. How can the re-reading of evidence presented in this chapter help us rethink other aspects of the past?
3. Think about systems in your own society that may have been built on the idea that men are physically superior (related to the "man the hunter" trope). How does this new understanding of women's physical abilities and the role of estrogen cast these systems in a new light?

References

Abigail, Anderson, Sophia Chilczuk, Kaylie Nelson, Roxanne Ruther, and Cara Wall-Scheffler. 2023. "The Myth of Man the Hunter: Women's Contribution to the Hunt Across Ethnographic Contexts." *Plos One*: e0287101–e0287101. https://doi.org/10.1371/journal.pone.0287101.
Berger, Thomas D., and Erik Trinkaus. 1995. "Patterns of Trauma Among the Neandertals." *Journal of Archaeological Science* 22(6): 841–852.

Besson, Thibault, Robin Macchi, Jeremy Rossi, Cédric Y.M. Morio, Yoko Kunimasa, Caroline Nicol, Fabrice Vercruyssen, and Guillaume Y. Millet. 2022. "Sex Differences in Endurance Running." *Sports Medicine* 52(6): 1235–1257. https://doi.org/10.1007/S40279-022-01651-W.

Carretero, José-Miguel, Laura Rodríguez, Rebeca García-González, and Juan-Luis Arsuaga. 2023. "Main Morphological Characteristics and Sexual Dimorphism of Hominin Adult Femora from the Sima de los Huesos Middle Pleistocene site (Sierra de Atapuerca, Spain)." *The Anatomical Record*. DOI: 10.1002/ar.25331.

Cowley, Emma S., Alyssa A. Olenick, Kelly L. McNulty, and Emma Z. Ross. 2021. "'Invisible Sportswomen': The Sex Data Gap in Sport and Exercise Science Research." *Women in Sport and Physical Activity Journal* 29(2): 146–151. https://doi.org/10.1123/WSPAJ.2021-0028.

Deaner, Robert O., Vittorio Addona, Rickey E. Carter, Michael J. Joyner, and Sandra K. Hunter. 2016. "Fast Men Slow More than Fast Women in a 10 Kilometer Road Race." *Peer Journal* (7): e2235. https://doi.org/10.7717/PEERJ.2235/SUPP-1.

Enns, D. L., and P. M. Tiidus. 2010. "The Influence of Estrogen on Skeletal Muscle: Sex Matters." *Sports Medicine* 40: 41–58.

Fox, Carles Lalueza, and David W. Frayer. 1997. "Non-dietary Marks in the Anterior Dentition of the Krapina Neanderthals." *International Journal of Osteoarchaeology* 7(2): 133–149.

Friedlander, Anne L., Gretchen A. Casazza, Michael A. Horning, Melvin J. Huie, Maria Francesca Piacentini, Jeffrey K. Trimmer, and George A. Brooks. 1998. "Training-Induced Alterations of Carbohydrate Metabolism in Women: Women Respond Differently from Men." *Journal of Applied Physiology* 85(3): 1175–1186. https://doi.org/10.1152/JAPPL.1998.85.3.1175.

Goodman, Madeleine J., P. Bion Griffin, Agnes A. Estioko-Griffin, and John S. Grove. 1985. "The Compatibility of Hunting and Mothering Among the Agta Hunter-Gatherers of the Philippines." *Sex Roles* 12(11): 1199–1209.

Haizlip, K. M., B. C. Harrison, and L. A. Leinwand. 2015. "Sex-Based Differences in Skeletal Muscle Kinetics and Fiber-Type Composition." *Physiology* 30(1): 30. https://doi.org/10.1152/PHYSIOL.00024.2014.

Hamadeh, Mazen J., Michaela C. Devries, and Mark A. Tarnopolsky. 2005. "Estrogen Supplementation Reduces Whole Body Leucine and Carbohydrate Oxidation and Increases Lipid Oxidation in Men during Endurance Exercise." *The Journal of Clinical Endocrinology & Metabolism* 90(6): 3592–3599. https://doi.org/10.1210/JC.2004-1743.

Holt, Brigitte M., and Vincenzo Formicola. 2008. "Hunters of the Ice Age: The Biology of Upper Paleolithic People." *American Journal of Physical Anthropology* 137(S47): 70–99.

Lacy, Sarah, and Cara Ocobock. 2024. "Woman the Hunter: The Archaeological Evidence." *American Anthropologist* 126(1): 19–31.

Lacy, Sarah A., and Erik Trinkaus. n.d. "Neandertal Paleopathology." In *Neandertal Skeletal Anatomy*, eds. Libby Cowgill and Scott Maddux. Cambridge: Cambridge University Press.

Lalueza-Fox, Carles, Antonio Rosas, and Marco de la Rasilla. 2012. "Palaeogenetic Research at the El Sidrón Neanderthal Site." *Annals of Anatomy-Anatomischer Anzeiger* 194(1): 133–137.

Lamont, Linda S., Arthur J. McCullough, and Satish C. Kalhan. 2003. "Gender Differences in the Regulation of Amino Acid Metabolism." *Journal of Applied Physiology* 95(3): 1259–1265. https://doi.org/10.1152/JAPPLPHYSIOL.01028.2002.

Laughlin, William S. 1968. "Hunting : An Integrating Biobehavior System and Its Evolutionary Importance." In *Man the Hunter*, eds. Richard B. Lee and Irven DeVore, 304–320. New York: Transaction Publishers.

Lee, Richard Borshay, and Irven DeVore, eds. 1968. *Man the Hunter*. New York: Transaction Publishers.

Manolagas, S. C., and S. Kousteni. 2001. "Perspective: Nonreproductive Sites of Action of Reproductive Hormones." *Endocrinology* 142(6): 2200–2204.

Maughan, R. J., M. Harmon, J. B. Leiper, D. Sale, and A. Delman. 1986. "Endurance Capacity of Untrained Males and Females in Isometric and Dynamic Muscular Contractions." *European Journal of Applied Physiology and Occupational Physiology* 55(4): 395–400. https://doi.org/10.1007/BF00422739.

Nagai, Saki, Kazuhiro Ikeda, Kuniko Horie-Inoue, Sachiko Shiba, Saya Nagasawa, Satoru Takeda, and Satoshi Inoue. 2016. "Estrogen Modulates Exercise Endurance Along with Mitochondrial Uncoupling Protein 3 Downregulation in Skeletal Muscle of Female Mice." *Biochemical and Biophysical Research Communications* 480(4): 758–764. https://doi.org/10.1016/J. BBRC.2016.10.129.

Ocobock, Cara, and Sarah Lacy. 2024. "Woman the Hunter: The Physiological Evidence." *American Anthropologist* 126(1): 7–18.

Paroo, Zain, James V. Haist, Morris Karmazyn, and Earl G. Noble. 2002. "Exercise Improves Postischemic Cardiac Function in Males but Not Females: Consequences of a Novel Sex-Specific Heat Shock Protein 70 Response." *Circulation Research* 90(8): 911–917. https://doi.org/10.1161/01. RES.0000016963.43856.B1.

Prüfer, Kay, Fernando Racimo, Nick Patterson, Flora Jay, Sriram Sankararaman, Susanna Sawyer, Anja Heinze, et al. 2014. "The Complete Genome Sequence of a Neanderthal from the Altai Mountains." *Nature* 505(7481): 43–49. https://doi.org/10.1038/nature12886.

Riddell, Michael C., Sara L. Partington, Nicole Stupka, David Armstrong, Courtney Rennie, and Mark A. Tarnopolsky. 2003. "Substrate Utilization during Exercise Performed with and Without Glucose Ingestion in Female and Male Endurance-Trained Athletes." *International Journal of Sport Nutrition and Exercise Metabolism* 13(4): 407–421. https://doi.org/10.1123/ IJSNEM.13.4.407.

Riel-Salvatore, Julien, and Claudine Gravel-Miguel. 2013. "Upper Palaeolithic Mortuary Practices in Eurasia." In *The Oxford Handbook of the Archaeology of Death and Burial,* eds. Liv Nilsson Stutz and Sarah Tarlow, 302–346. Oxford: Oxford Press.

Skov, Laurits, Stéphane Peyrégne, Divyaratan Popli, Leonardo N. M. Iasi, Thibaut Devièse, Viviane Slon, Elena I. Zavala et al. 2022. "Genetic Insights into the Social Organization of Neanderthals." *Nature* 610(7932): 519–525. https://doi.org/10.1038/s41586-022-05283-y.

Smith, Ella S., Alannah K. A. Mckay, Megan Kuikman, Kathryn E. Ackerman, Rachel Harris, Kirsty J. Elliott-Sale, Trent Stellingwerff, and Louise M. Burke. 2022. "Auditing the Representation of Female versus Male Athletes in Sports Science and Sports Medicine Research: Evidence-Based Performance Supplements." *Nutrients* 14(5): 953. https://doi.org/10.3390/NU14050953.

Sparacello, Vitale S., Sébastien Villotte, Laura L. Shackelford, and Erik Trinkaus. 2017. "Patterns of Humeral Asymmetry Among Late Pleistocene Humans." *Comptes Rendus Palevol* 16(5–6): 680–689.

Thornton, Joseph W., Eleanor Need, and David Crews. 2003. "Resurrecting the Ancestral Steroid Receptor: Ancient Origin of Estrogen Signaling." *Science* 301(5640): 1714–1717. https://doi. org/10.1126/SCIENCE.1086185/SUPPL_FILE/THORNTON.SOM.PDF.

Trinkaus, Erik. 2012. "Neandertals, Early Modern Humans, and Rodeo Riders." *Journal of Archaeological Science* 39(12): 3691–3693.

Trinkaus, Erik. 2018. "An Abundance of Developmental Anomalies and Abnormalities in Pleistocene People." *Proceedings of the National Academy of Sciences* 115(47): 11941–11946. https:// doi.org/10.1073/pnas.1814989115.

Villmoare, Brian, Kevin G. Hatala, and William Jungers. 2019. "Sexual Dimorphism in Homo Erectus Inferred from 1.5 Ma Footprints Near Ileret, Kenya." *Scientific Reports* 9(1): 7687.

Watanabe, Hitoshi. 1968. "Subsistence and Ecology of Northern Food Gatherers with Special Reference to the Ainu." In *Man the Hunter,* eds. Richard B. Lee and Irven DeVore, 69–77. Chicago: Aldine Publishing.

Wiik, A., T. Gustafsson, M. Esbjörnsson, O. Johansson, M. Ekman, C. J. Sundberg, and E. Jansson. 2005. "Expression of Oestrogen Receptor α and β Is Higher in Skeletal Muscle of Highly Endurance-Trained than of Moderately Active Men." *Acta Physiologica Scandinavica* 184(2): 105–112. https://doi.org/10.1111/J.1365-201X.2005.01433.X.

Chapter 2

The past is a foreign country

Archaeology of sex and gender

Rosemary A. Joyce

Original to a previous edition of this text. Courtesy of Rosemary A. Joyce.

Archaeology may seem to be hampered in understanding gender. Only archaeologists of the very recent past have the ability to ask people about their own ideas and views, and when they do, they still have to sort through how to reconcile what people say about the past and what actually happened (Wilkie and Hayes 2006). While some archaeologists work on time periods and societies that produced contemporary written records, these have to be translated, and often, the contexts that would help us relate them to lived experiences of sex and gender are poorly understood. The majority of archaeologists work on societies in the more distant past that did not use writing and so have to rely entirely on what can be said from the physical evidence alone.

Despite these challenges, there have always been archaeological interpretations of gender, even before feminist archaeologists began to insist that gender was a category of archaeological analysis (Conkey and Spector 1984). By the 1960s, when anthropological archaeology in North America was transformed by challenges to become more scientific, archaeologists could rely on cross-cultural surveys to support the assumptions they made about gender in the past. These allowed generalization from a sample of ethnographic studies: archaeologists could argue that if a majority of ethnographies showed that women carried out certain activities, like spinning and weaving, then that was sufficient ground to at least propose that spinning and weaving tools in the past were evidence of women's work.

Beginning in the 1970s, a new generation of anthropologists questioned the universality of many assumptions about gender. In the United States, an entire generation of budding archaeologists was exposed to studies questioning gendered assumptions. Many of these students wanted to know more about women's roles and experiences in the past and were unsatisfied with making broad assumptions that rested on arguing that the past was like the present, only a little less technologically advanced.

So began a revolution in archaeological investigations of gender that is still unfolding today (Claassen 1992; Conkey and Gero 1991). Today, archaeologists actively engaged in work on gender ask how people in the past understood variation in sexual anatomy, how people in the past understood diverse sexual desires and practices, how people in the past experienced different lives because of differences in their sexual anatomy or

DOI: 10.4324/9781003398349-3

sexuality, and what the hard work of trying to answer those questions can tell us about how we understand the same questions regarding humans living in the world today (Joyce 2008; Nelson 2006).

Biology and gender

Archaeologists used to say that gender was the culturally variable way of organizing people who differed in biological sex. Yet treating sex assignment as simply recognizing natural categories has been questioned by scholars outside and inside archaeology for a long time (Meskell 2005). While differences exist in sexual anatomy, how we recognize sexual anatomical variation, and how we explain it, is variable. If we employ two and only two categories, male and female, then everybody has to be assigned to one or the other. In the United States, gender assignment historically has relied on external anatomical differences: genitalia. These are intuited from other outwardly visible characteristics: the distribution of body hair, apparent muscularity, and height, to name three biological features.

Archaeologists, though, work for the most part with skeletal remains. These obviously no longer have sexual organs or hair. Specialists who work with skeletal remains, bio-archaeologists, categorize sexes from other characteristics: height and robusticity (bone size and thickness), for example. While popular culture is rife with forensic anthropologists easily identifying sex through relatively superficial examination, even the traits of the skeleton considered most diagnostic of sex can be ambiguous (Geller 2005). In practice, bioarchaeologists normally divide the skeletons they study into more than two simple groups. Younger people's bodies before puberty do not have easily identified sex-based variability, so it is uncommon to see children or juveniles classified as male or female. Sexually mature females show changes to the pelvic anatomy that when most pronounced are considered reliable signs that the pelvis came from a woman; but when these features are not as pronounced, the individual may be of less certain sex. So it is common for bioarchaeologists to divide their adult samples into a spectrum of categories: from clearly female to clearly male, with possible female, possible male, and indeterminate groups in between. Even this differentiation has a level of uncertainty, due to the fact that as women age, their pelvic anatomy continues to be remodeled, coming to look more like that of males.

In response to the reality that skeletal determination of sex is not as simple and objective as people might assume, some archaeologists call for increased use of DNA testing to determine the genetic sex of skeletons. This is not yet widely used as a method to "sex" skeletons. If it ever does become widespread, it will still not make it possible to assign all skeletons to two categories, male and female. Modern biologists know that a small but not inconsiderable number of human beings do not just have XX or XY chromosomes but may have a third-sex chromosome (XXY, for example). Such individuals may have differences in external or internal sexual anatomy as well. While in the modern United States surgeons were in the habit of operating to alter the bodies of infants they could not clearly assign as male or female, there is no reason to assume that such interventions were universal. Many populations in the past probably included people who were anatomically neither male nor female, meaning, that assigning all skeletons to one of two categories would distort the real population we are trying to understand.

Even when bioarchaeologists arrive at a satisfactory division of adult skeletons into a spectrum from certainly female to certainly male, their analyses often indicate that the experiences of the people whose bodies they are studying were not entirely explained by sexual differences. Bioarchaeologists have used analyses of chemical elements in bone to investigate everything from where the person grew up and if they migrated to what diet they were accustomed to eat and whether their protein came from plants, fish, or land animals. Many bone chemistry studies began with a separation of males and females, assuming that, as is true in many recent societies, men and women might have had different diets (Ambrose et al. 2003). Sometimes that assumption holds up and we find, for example, that men consumed more maize than women did in their own villages (Hastorf 1991). But just as often, these bone chemistry studies show little difference between the sexes. Instead, we may find that men and women of a privileged group, perhaps rulers and nobles, enjoyed a diet that most people in their towns did not (White 2005).

This kind of outcome is explained by using the concept of "intersectionality," meaning, that sex isn't always the most important factor in the kind of life people lived. Instead, intersecting forms of identity may be more important: wealth and power may group men and women together in classes, race may divide women from each other, or age may be more important in people's lives than sex, with older men and women facing similar challenges.

In recent years, bioarchaeologists have looked at human populations to ask whether things we take for granted as normal for males and females have always been the same. Osteoporosis, the loss of bone in aging accompanied by a tendency for bones to fracture easily is understood by most people today as an inevitable consequence of women's aging. Archaeological study of medieval Britain challenges that notion (Agarwal et al. 2004). Here, analyses showed that, in some places, tendencies of men and women toward bone loss and bone fracture were similar in old age; men sometimes had a higher risk than women did in the same population. Examining historical populations from different settings, the bioarchaeologist was able to determine that heavy work in agricultural villages helped women's bone health, and that women's reproductive cycles of childbirth and breastfeeding improved bone remodeling in ways not available to men in the same settings, whether rural or urban.

Contemporary archaeology of sex and gender has complicated the picture we have about how it was to be female or male in the past, even if we just limit ourselves to physical bodies and their experiences. When we shift our framework to look at the culturally mediated experience of sexual desire and sexual practices, archaeology again tells us that things have historically been more complex than we used to think.

Sexuality

When a group of archaeologists met to talk about sexuality in a session at the national archaeology meetings in 1998 (Schmidt and Voss 2000), few had actually ventured to write about the topic directly. Archaeology, in other words, was repressed. It would be difficult to say that now (Voss 2006). Yet how do we think we can know anything about something as personal as sexuality from the kinds of material remains we find?

A first line of evidence for ancient sexualities is imagery: whether carved in stone, modeled in clay, painted, or drawn, human beings have a long history of recording sexual acts. Archaeologists have almost as long a history of explaining these as symbolic. But even symbols need living practices for people to understand what the symbol is intended to convey. Archaeologists now can talk about and illustrate masturbation, anal sex, oral sex, different sexual positions, sex between men and men, men and boys, men and women, and men and men cross-dressed as women, although mutual sexuality between women remains underrepresented in archaeological studies.

Of course, simply having an image of a sex act does not help greatly in assessing what the status of such acts was, and it leaves us a long way from understanding the subjective experience of sexualities. Here, archaeologists draw on ethnographic and historical analogies, not so much to explain what sexuality *must have* been like in other times and places, but what the sexual activity seen in imagery *might have* implied for people in these societies. The main lesson we learn from comparative studies is that experiences of apparently similar sexual practices can be quite variable in different social settings.

Archaeologically, this point has been made very clearly by classical archaeologists, those who study the ancient Greeks and Romans. This is a perfect case study for sexuality in some ways. In addition to imagery, the Greeks and Romans left us a large documentary record. Scholars have been working to translate these texts and images and place them in context for a very long time.

For example, classical Greek art and texts both tell us that older men were expected to have sex with young boys. Yet at the same time, texts suggest that adult males were not expected to have sex with other adult males, and when young boys matured, they were not expected to continue their relations with older men. To call these cultural practices "homosexuality" would ignore the specific historical situation. First, for the ancient Greeks, men and women were not two biological sexes: they were different versions of a single sex (Laqueur 1990). Male anatomy was an externalization of what in women was anatomically interiorized. Maleness developed distinctly from femaleness, although both were based on the same organs, because males had more heat, while women were colder. Young males benefited from sex with older males because this helped develop the male state of the shared sexual anatomy. Continued sexual acts between adult males, however, would endanger sexual development.

Archaeologists have noted that all this philosophy of sexuality comes to us from texts referring to free citizens and cannot be applied to the large numbers of people who were not free, or to foreigners. Nor does it speak to us about women's views of these sexual practices, or the complicated lives of women married to men who engaged in these relationships. This is where archaeology has a unique role. Studies of classical Greek houses have demonstrated that normative models in which women were secluded in separate quarters don't hold up; house plans are highly variable (Goldberg 1999; Nevett 1994). Instead of evidence of male power over women, house plans suggest that men and women formed a group that prized its privacy and separated the family quarters from those the public could enter.

When we turn to a less-familiar society, the Moche of the north coast of Peru, the same kind of socially complicated approach is helpful. Moche pottery vessels present sexually explicit imagery, scenes showing males and females engaged in a variety of sexual acts. By drawing on historical and ethnographic analogies, scholars have recently been able to argue that the explicit sex scenes on Moche pots tell us about how the Moche understood people to be linked over generations through exchanges of body fluids (Weismantel 2004). Sexual acts of all kinds transfer fluids from one body to another and keep the substances that gave life to people moving from ancestors to adults to children who mature to become adults and continue the cycle. This does not tell us whether the sex acts we see on these pots were common or uncommon; it does tell us to be careful not to project a modern interpretation, in this case, of male sexual dominance, on ancient materials.

When archaeologists began to talk openly about sexuality, they also began to talk about the life experiences of people who chose voluntarily not to express their desires in physical acts. Cross-culturally, groups of men or women living in communities based on celibacy are not uncommon. A study of medieval nunneries in Britain argued that women's cloisters were more austere than monasteries, partly as a way to discipline women's sexuality, seen in Christian theology as less controlled than men's (Gilchrist 2000). At the same time, the precincts where the nuns lived were decorated with images that recall texts about their spiritual life that were expressed in highly physical terms. Women in these communities disciplined their bodies and internalized their desires, turning them to the divine.

The histories of sexuality that archaeology is exploring today are complex. Challenges based in contemporary "queer theory" argue that ignoring the abundant evidence of sexuality offered by archaeology allowed the creation of a very narrow story that made twentieth-century sexual norms seem inevitable (Joyce 2008; Perry and Joyce 2001; Voss 2006). The independent history of the Americas testifies to a much more fluid concept of sexuality and gender identities than that of Europe. What Native American activists and scholars call "two spirits" and archaeologists often refer to as third and fourth genders are people who occupied a separate status in their societies, neither male nor female (Hollimon 2006). Third- and fourth-gender people may sometimes have been biologically intersex but were not necessarily so. They were individuals who, in some way, exceeded the definition of either male or female in their societies. Often, they distinguished themselves in activities in which most people with similar sexual anatomy did not participate. They might have sexual relations with people of the same sexual anatomy or different sexual anatomy, or both. Rather than being based on a set of rigid categorical sexual or gender identities, third and fourth genders exemplified a more fluid way of responding to the individual preferences and abilities of members of these societies.

Difference

While archaeologists increasingly address sexuality directly and question the security of what once was a firm separation of biological sex as nature-given and cultural gender as social category, they have also continued to work on basic questions of gender difference and hierarchies in past societies. The multiplying of possible sexualities and gendered positions and the importance of intersectionality have been critical in moving forward what started as a search for women in the past. That search has now definitively resulted in rich understandings of the roles of particular women, and of women as a group, that sometimes confirm, but as often contradict, the assumptions archaeologists once made. Sensibly, contemporary archaeologists of gender no longer try to find some specific methods that can be used to "see" women or to see gender; instead, they insist that all methods archaeologists use be scrutinized so that any assumptions about gender that they contain are revealed and, if necessary, amended.

Many gender analyses in archaeology start by asking about differences in labor between males and females. Originally taking for granted a history of inequality between men and women, archaeologists now investigate the specific facts to show how variable economic relations have been (Pyburn 2004). Who did what activities? Where did people of different genders carry out their tasks? What relative value was placed on the labor of people of different genders? Under what circumstances did people have the ability to claim credit for the products of their work? Archaeology, which has a long history of materialist analysis, has developed a strong set of tools to address these questions.

Many studies began, and some still begin, by examining the distributions of tools, raw materials, and partially worked products across space within settlements. When clusters of tools, raw materials, and products are found, the archaeologist can then propose that evidence of a specific industry exists. The leap from industry to gender or sex of the participants is always indirect, often based on analogies. Archaeologists are comfortable with procedures for using analogies with better-documented historical or ethnographic settings and have created clear guidelines for how to do this. We consider analogies as being of two kinds. Some are historical: if you know that a particular contemporary society or historically documented group lived in an area, you can propose that older archaeological sites may represent the ancestors of the documented group. Many archaeological studies of the Mexica (Aztec) and classic Maya assume that spinning and weaving were carried out by women and so identify the tools of these tasks and the places they are found as evidence of women's work (Hendon 1997; McCafferty and McCafferty 1991). This is based on historical and ethnographic studies of the Nahuatl- and Maya-speaking peoples of Mexico and Central America, where women are normally spinners and weavers.

In contrast to such local or "specific" analogies, archaeologists may draw on what are called general analogies. These do not rest on the assumption of continuous historical identity between the inhabitants of an archaeological site and later people in the same area. Instead, a general analogy is created between a known case in a similar environment, with a similar level of technology, and a similar social scale, and the archaeological site under study. For example, understanding Paleolithic hunters of the European Ice Age does not rely on specific, local analogy with modern French, Spanish, or Germans. It may, however, draw on studies of hunters in northern latitudes, where cold weather and similar seasonality of herd animals provide somewhat-comparable conditions. Archaeologists have conducted original ethnographic or "ethnoarchaeological" studies (Weedman 2006) in order to produce general analogies from northern hunters. Such work has demonstrated that hunting parties are not automatically segregated by sex but may instead be organized by age, providing a mixed group with good physical abilities to travel out from base camps, hunt, process carcasses, and transport the products of the hunt back to the older and younger people waiting behind (Brumbach and Jarvenpa 2006). Drawing on this kind of analogy, archaeologists studying hunter-gatherer societies would not assume that men hunted while women gathered and instead would explore the specific range of tasks carried out and the skills necessary to complete them.

Whether general or specific, archaeologists today assess whether an analogy is well-developed by examining both how well the source of the analogy is understood and how well the society to which it is applied has been studied. Source-side critique often identifies gaps in ethnography, including gendered assumptions by ethnographers. In a study aimed at identifying the contributions of men and women to farming in classic Maya society (Robin 2006), the modern sources of analogy were found to be problematic, ignoring changes in farming techniques since the classic period and underemphasizing some agricultural tasks in favor of others. This had led to a model in which men were farmers and women were not. The alternative suggested was that men and women probably cooperated in the more complex farming systems that archaeologists have documented, which would have been unlike more recent farming techniques.

Sometimes, critical attention to analogy may result in questioning the very assumptions that have been used by earlier researchers to find evidence of women's lives. In the case of spinning and weaving in pre-Hispanic Mexico and Central America, while the evidence is good for these being female tasks for the classic Maya and postclassic Aztec, the evidence for gendered labor of this kind in earlier periods is weak. Aztec and Maya cases provide multiple lines of evidence to support the application of the modern analogy: images showing women doing these tasks, texts talking about them as women's work, and clusters of the tools of these tasks in household settings (Hendon 1997). When we turn to earlier time periods, though, none of these patterns is found. Tools for textile production in graves at one central Mexican site predating the classic Maya by more than 1,000 years are not found with females more often than with males (Joyce 2001). In fact, most evidence from this site fails to distinguish women's burials from those of men. Instead of sex, most variation is related either to age or to the specific house or neighborhood where the person was buried.

Instead of taking associations of gender and labor as consistent and unchanging, archaeologists working on Aztec and pre-Aztec sites examined the patterns of different tools during the period in which the Aztec conquered other towns, placing new demands for tribute on them, and during the period of Spanish conquest. Expecting to see evidence of reorganization of spinning to meet increased demands for cloth, they instead found evidence of changes in cooking, from an emphasis on stews that could not be easily transported to the fields by workers to tortillas that could be carried (Brumfiel 1991). Rather than see women only in textile production, these researchers were able to see how incorporation in empire affected daily cooking activities, also assumed to be carried out by women.

Other work inspired by the historical association of women and weaving in this region looked at patterns of distribution of spindle whorls, the tool used for producing thread, in late pre-Hispanic Cholula, south of the Aztec capital. Here, spindle whorls were found in the burials of males as well as females (McCafferty and McCafferty 2000). Rather than questioning the strong ideological association of spinning with women, we can suggest that ideology and pragmatism went side by side. The researchers noted that the one high-status woman in their sample was buried with textile tools, and that the men with spindle whorls appeared to be lower-status. Women's femininity was expressed in their talents as spinners and weavers, activities that had sexual connotations in everyday speech. When men spun thread, it wouldn't have had those associations for them. Their spinning was, however, economically valuable because it contributed to the production of cloth that was critical to political life in this society.

The suggestion that men could, in situations where thread was valuable, undertake a task typical of women without being feminized is an example of an argument made by archaeologists about masculinity. Almost more than women, men in the past have been imagined to be homogeneous, usually hypermasculine, creatures. Archaeologists examining masculinity suggest instead that we need to think in terms of masculinities, differences among men, as much as differences between men and women. Noting that rock art in Scandinavia shows some males with exaggerated leg muscles, often with erections, archaeologists suggest that scenes once thought to show normative males and females in fact depict varying masculinities, with other figures also males, but with a less-exaggerated masculine body (Yates 1993). Examination of medieval burials in Britain showed that some males buried with weapons had more robust skeletons than others buried without these objects, suggesting that we think in terms of a "warrior" masculinity juxtaposed with other forms of masculinity (Gilchrist 2004). Other archaeologists proposed that a material culture of male body care might tell us that a similar "warrior" masculinity was being cultivated in Bronze Age Europe (Treherne 1995).

For some, such new approaches threaten to make women disappear as a specific subject of analysis. After so much hard work has been expended to insist that women need to be treated as actors who may have had their own agendas and who may have caused historical change, it can seem like asking different questions about gender means abandoning the project of understanding specifically female forms of experience and agency. The solution to that is not to abandon studies of masculinity or ignore intersectionality: it is to ensure that every archaeological study begins by asking how embodied personhood, including differences in sexual anatomy and sexual practices, affected people's lives. Such a question cannot fail to illuminate the lives of women, but it will also, of necessity, help us understand the lives of men, and of people of other genders, from birth to death.

Discussion questions

1. What methods do bioarcheologists use to "sex" skeletal remains? And what are the challenges with these methods?
2. What forms of cross-cultural evidence have been found in the archaeological record to demonstrate fluid concepts of sexuality and gender identities?
3. What is "intersectionality," and how does it help us understand the structure of past societies?
4. What is the difference between a historical analogy and a general analogy? How do these concepts help us understand gendered labor in past societies?

References

Agarwal, Sabrina C., Mircea Dumitriu, George A. Tomlinson, and Marc D. Grynpas. 2004. "Medieval Trabecular Bone Architecture: The Influence of Age, Sex, and Lifestyle." *American Journal of Physical Anthropology* 124: 33–44.

Ambrose, Stanley H., Jane Buikstra, and Harold W. Krueger. 2003. "Status and Gender Differences in Diet at Mound 72, Cahokia, Revealed by Isotopic Analysis of Bone." *Journal of Anthropological Archaeology* 22: 217–226.

Brumbach, Hetty Jo, and Robert Jarvenpa. 2006. "Gender Dynamics in Hunter-Gatherer Society: Archaeological Methods and Perspectives." In *Handbook of Gender in Archaeology*, ed. Sarah Nelson, 503–535. Lanham, MD: AltaMira Press.

Brumfiel, Elizabeth. 1991. "Weaving and Cooking: Women's Production in Aztec Mexico." In *Engendering Archaeology: Women and Prehistory*, eds. Joan Gero and Margaret Conkey, 224–251. Oxford: Basil Blackwell.

Claassen, Cheryl, ed. 1992. *Exploring Gender through Archaeology*. Madison, WI: Prehistory Press.

Conkey, Margaret W., and Joan Gero, eds. 1991. *Engendering Archaeology*. Oxford: Basil Blackwell.

Conkey, Margaret W., and Janet Spector. 1984. "Archaeology and the Study of Gender." *Advances in Archaeological Method and Theory* 7: 1–38.

Geller, Pamela L. 2005. "Skeletal Analysis and Theoretical Complications." *World Archaeology* 37: 597–609.

Gilchrist, Roberta. 2000. "Unsexing the Body: The Interior Sexuality of Medieval Religious Women." In *Archaeologies of Sexuality*, eds. Robert A. Schmidt and Barbara L. Voss, 89–103. London: Routledge Press.

Gilchrist, Roberta. 2004. "Archaeology and the Life Course: A Time and Age for Gender." In *A Companion to Social Archaeology*, eds. Lynn Meskell and Robert Preucel, 142–160. Oxford: Blackwell.

Goldberg, Marilyn Y. 1999. "Spatial and Behavioural Negotiation in Classical Athenian City Houses." In *The Archaeology of Household Activities*, ed. Penelope M. Allison, 142–161. London: Routledge.

Hastorf, Christine. 1991. "Gender, Space and Food in Prehistory." In *Engendering Archaeology*, eds. Margaret W. Conkey and Joan Gero, 132–159. Oxford: Basil Blackwell.

Hendon, Julia A. 1997. "Women's Work, Women's Space, and Women's Status among the Classic-Period Maya Elite of the Copan Valley, Honduras." In *Women in Prehistory: North America and Mesoamerica*, eds. Cheryl Claassen and Rosemary A. Joyce, 33–46. Philadelphia: University of Pennsylvania Press.

Hollimon, Sandra. 2006. "The Archaeology of Nonbinary Genders in Native North America." In *Handbook of Gender in Archaeology*, ed. Sarah Nelson, 435–450. Lanham, MD: AltaMira Press.

Joyce, Rosemary A. 2001. "Burying the Dead at Tlatilco: Social Memory and Social Identities." In *New Perspectives on Mortuary Analysis*, ed. Meredith Chesson, 12–26. Alexandria, VA: American Anthropological Association.

Joyce, Rosemary A. 2008. *Ancient Bodies, Ancient Lives*. London: Thames and Hudson.

Laqueur, Thomas W. 1990. *Making Sex: Body and Gender from the Greeks to Freud*. Cambridge, MA: Harvard University Press.

McCafferty, Sharisse D., and Geoffrey G. McCafferty. 1991. "Spinning and Weaving as Female Gender Identity in Post-Classic Mexico." In *Textile Traditions of Mesoamerica and the Andes: An Anthology*, eds. Janet C. Berlo, Margot Schevill, and Edward B. Dwyer, 19–44. New York: Garland.

McCafferty, Sharisse D., and Geoffrey G. McCafferty. 2000. "Textile Production in Postclassic Cholula, Mexico." *Ancient Mesoamerica* 11: 39–54.

Meskell, Lynn M. 2005. "De/naturalizing Gender in Prehistory." In *Complexities: Beyond Nature and Nurture*, eds. Susan McKinnon and Sydel Silverman, 157–175. Chicago: University of Chicago Press.

Nelson, Sarah M., ed. 2006. *Handbook of Gender in Archaeology*. Lanham, MD: AltaMira Press.

Nevett, Lisa. 1994. "Separation or Seclusion? Towards an Archaeological Approach to Investigating Women in the Greek Household in the Fifth to Third Centuries B.C." In *Architecture and Order: Approaches to Social Space*, eds. Michael Parker Pearson and Colin Richards, 98–112. London: Routledge.

Perry, Elizabeth M., and Rosemary A. Joyce. 2001. "Providing a Past for Bodies That Matter: Judith Butler's Impact on the Archaeology of Gender." *International Journal of Sexuality and Gender Studies* 6: 63–76.

Pyburn, K. Anne, ed. 2004. *Ungendering Archaeology*. New York: Routledge.

Robin, Cynthia. 2006. "Gender, Farming, and Long-Term Change: Maya Historical and Archaeological Perspectives." *Current Anthropology* 47: 409–434.

Schmidt, Robert A., and Barbara Voss, eds. 2000. *Archaeologies of Sexuality*. London: Routledge Press.

Treherne, Paul. 1995. "The Warrior's Beauty: The Masculine Body and Self-Identity in Bronze-Age Europe." *Journal of European Archaeology* 3: 105–144.

Voss, Barbara L. 2006. "Sexuality in Archaeology." In *Handbook of Gender in Archaeology*, ed. Sarah Nelson, 365–400. Lanham, MD: AltaMira Press.

Weedman, Kathryn. 2006. "Gender and Ethnoarchaeology." In *Handbook of Gender in Archaeology*, ed. Sarah Nelson, 247–294. Lanham, MD: AltaMira Press.

Weismantel, Mary. 2004. "Moche Sex Pots: Reproduction and Temporality in Ancient South America." *American Anthropologist* 106: 495–505.

White, Christine D. 2005. "Gendered Food Behaviour among the Maya: Time, Place, Status and Ritual." *Journal of Social American* 5: 356–382.

Wilkie, Laurie A., and Katherine Howlett Hayes. 2006. " Engendered and Feminist Archaeologies of the Recent and Documented Pasts." *Journal of Archaeological Research* 14: 243–264.

Yates, Tim. 1993. "Frameworks for an Archaeology of the Body." In *Interpretive Archaeology*, ed. Christopher Tilley, 31–72. Providence, RI: Berg.

Animal models and gender

Marlene Zuk

The notion that biology, particularly evolutionary biology, can explain much about gender differences in humans raises hackles in many people. The fear is that science will be used to justify sexism, so that men are "naturally" dominant and women submissive, men natural philanderers and women naturally inclined to stop them from straying. These stereotypes are often said to arise from the animal kingdom, apparently leaving us with no other choices than to accept our evolutionary heritage and resign ourselves to a life of oppression, or reject the idea that biology has any relevance to explaining gender in modern-day humans.

In this chapter, I hope to counter this impression, both by explaining how biologists view the evolution of sex differences in animals and by showing how understanding the connection between our sexual behavior and that of other species can be liberating rather than restrictive. It is possible to use evolution to inform us about gender without either succumbing to the old stereotypes or substituting new ones; a caricature of a nature-girl is just as damaging as one that stays barefoot and pregnant. Much of the material here is discussed in more detail in Zuk (2002). Numerous other authors have attempted to link feminism and evolutionary biology and provide feminist critiques of biology from a scientific perspective, perhaps most notably Patricia Gowaty (1997, 2003), but also including Keller (1985), Hrdy (1986, 1997, 1999), Fausto-Sterling (1987, 2003), Liesen (1995), and many others. Here I focus on studies from animals, rather than examining the field of biology as a whole, and examine the use of animal models in studies of gender.

Sexual selection

Sex differences in animals are of much interest to biologists, and the body of theory commonly accepted as the explanation of how these differences evolve is called sexual selection. Like its relative natural selection, sexual selection relies on individual differences in the likelihood of leaving genes in succeeding generation, but unlike natural selection, the differential reproduction due to sexual selection occurs because of an individual's ability

DOI: 10.4324/9781003398349-4

to acquire the best and/or most mates, not because of survival ability. Thus, a bird with a long ungainly tail that attracts more females than his shorter-tailed counterparts is at a sexual selection advantage, even if he has a harder time flying and cannot escape predators as easily.

Also like natural selection, the theory of sexual selection has its origin in the work of Charles Darwin. When Darwin began to develop his ideas about the origin of species, he attempted to explain the evolution of traits that differ between the sexes but are not necessary for the physical act of reproduction, such as the mane of male lions or the antlers of male deer. Darwin devoted an entire book, *The Descent of Man and Selection in Relation to Sex*, published in 1871, to explaining such traits, which he called secondary sexual characteristics, and noted that in many cases, they simply could not seem to have arisen through natural selection because they are often costly to produce and make their bearers more conspicuous to predators.

Darwin suggested that secondary sexual characteristics could evolve in one of two ways. First, they could be useful to one sex, usually males, in fighting for access to members of the other sex, hence the antlers and horns on male ungulates, such as bighorn sheep, or on the aptly named male rhinoceros beetles. These are weapons, and they are advantageous because better fighters are presumed to get more mates and have more offspring. The second way was more problematic. Darwin noted that females often pay attention to traits like long tails and elaborate plumage during courtship, and he concluded that the traits evolved because the females preferred them. Peahens find peacocks with long tails attractive, just like we do. The sexual selection process, then, consisted of two components: male–male competition, which results in weapons, and female choice, which results in ornaments.

While competition among males for the rights to mate with a female seemed reasonable enough to Darwin's Victorian contemporaries, virtually none of them could swallow the idea that females – of any species, but especially the so-called dumb animals – could possibly do anything so complex as discriminating between males with slightly different plumage colors. Alfred Russell Wallace, who also independently arrived at some of the same conclusions about evolution and natural selection that Darwin did, was particularly vehement in his objections (Wallace 1889). He, and many others, simply found it absurd that females could make the sort of complex decision required by Darwin's theory; it would require the female to possess an aesthetic sense like that of humans, an idea they were unwilling to accept. According to the thinking of his time, even among humans, only those of the upper social classes could appreciate aesthetic things like art and music, so it seemed ridiculous to imagine that animals could do something many humans – particularly non-Englishmen – could not.

Largely because of this opposition to the idea of female choice, sexual selection as a theory lay dormant for several decades. This time lag meant that while sexual selection and natural selection were introduced at about the same time, sexual selection has not received the same continuous scrutiny by scientists. In some ways, therefore, the study of sex differences is a younger science than the study of species origin and diversity. It was not until the late 1960s that interest in the evolution of sex differences was revived, and the most important contribution to the new theory was a 1972 paper by Robert Trivers, who argued that selection acts differently on males and females because of how they allocate resources into succeeding generations. Females are limited by the number of offspring they can successfully produce and rear. Because they are the sex that supplies the nutrient-rich egg, and often the sex that cares for the young, they have an upper limit set at a relatively low number. They leave the most genes in the next generation by having the highest-quality young they can. Which male they mate with could be very important, because a mistake in the form of poor genes or no help with the young could mean that they have lost their whole breeding effort for an entire year.

Males, on the other hand, can leave the most genes in the next generation by fertilizing as many females as possible. Because each mating requires relatively little investment from him, a male who mates with many females sires many more young than a male mating with only one female. Hence, males are expected to compete among themselves for access to females, and females are expected to be choosy and to mate with the best possible male they can. In addition, females were often referred to as "coy," with the implication that the impetus for sex came largely from males, who fought among themselves to get to the females and allow the choices to occur.

This, of course, is the same division of sexual selection that Darwin originally proposed, and Trivers had given it a new rationale. What he did, too, was bring female choice back to the forefront of sexual selection and suggest a more modern underlying advantage to it. Furthermore, ideas about the evolution of behavior had advanced enough that scientists no longer worried about an "aesthetic sense" in animals; it didn't matter how females recognized particular males, just that if they did, and it was beneficial, the genes associated with the trait females were attracted to would become more common in the population than the genes of less-preferred traits. Evolutionary biologists, therefore, could ignore questions about motivation and get to the more testable issue of how discrimination among males might result in the evolution of ornamental traits that did not function either in day-to-day life or in male combat.

Current work on female behavior in many species of animals has confirmed Trivers's – and Darwin's – basic idea about female preference for particular types of males being a major force in evolution (Andersson 1994). Again and again, females have been shown to be able to distinguish small differences among available mates and to prefer to mate with those individuals bearing the most exaggerated characters. In some cases, those males are also more healthy and vigorous, so that ornaments appear to indicate not just attractiveness but the ability to survive.

One of the most well-known examples can be found in peacocks, often used as the symbol of sexual selection with their huge elaborate tails. English gentry have kept peacocks (more correctly, peafowl, as the term *peacock*, strictly speaking, refers only to the male) for many years, and British biologist Marion Petrie studied the behavior of flocks that were allowed to range freely in a park in England (Petrie 1994; Petrie and Halliday 1994). She discovered that females did indeed prefer males with greater numbers of eyespots on their tail feathers, and that this preference could be manipulated by cutting the eyespots off some males' tails and gluing them onto others; females lost interest in the dubbed peacocks and became attracted to the augmented ones. Even more interesting, she allowed females to mate with males that had variable numbers of eyespots and then reared all the offspring in communal incubators to control for differences in maternal care. The chicks fathered by the more ornamented males weighed more than the other chicks, an attribute usually connected with better survival in birds. Indeed, when the individually marked chicks were then released into the park and recaptured the following year, the ones with the more attractive fathers also were more likely to evade predators and survive in the seminatural conditions.

The notion that females are "coy" has not survived so well, as it has been amply demonstrated that females frequently seek out matings with multiple males, and that they often take an active part in many kinds of sexual interactions (Andersson 1994; Jennions and Petrie 1997, 2000; Gowaty and Buschhaus 1998). The reasons behind such behaviors are the subject of intensive study by biologists, and ideas are changing all the time. Nevertheless, the concept of sexual selection, and the core ideas of reproductive competition and mate choice, appears to explain a great deal about animal sexual differences.

The philandering male, the coy female, and other myths

What about humans? Does this mean that males are designed by evolution to be indiscriminate in seeking sex and females are forever conscribed by the need to raise children alone? The answer is an emphatic no, and to understand why, it is important to understand how animal models are used in biology.

First of all, even among animals, a great deal of variation exists in the manifestation of the basic principles of sexual selection. For example, male elephant seals come ashore at isolated beaches along the Pacific coast during late summer. The males can weigh up to three tons, more than twice the size of females, and spend several weeks fighting among themselves for dominance. Females arrive after the males, and after they come ashore, the dominant males attempt to sequester groups of females and keep them from rival males; the females themselves, although they do exert some degree of choice, are constrained in their movements by the males (Le Boeuf and Reiter 1988; Galimberti et al. 2002). The male competition aspect of sexual selection appears to prevail in this species.

In contrast, female bowerbirds have virtually total control over mating. This group of several species of birds is found in Australia and New Guinea. The males construct elaborate structures out of twigs, grass, and other objects and then decorate them with ornaments that can include plastic items as well as fruit, flowers, bones, and shells (Borgia 1995; Uy et al. 2001; Madden 2003). Each species has a characteristic bower type. After the bowers are made, males wait for females to visit; the bowers are generally rather widely separated, so males cannot hear or see each other when they are tending their bowers. A female generally visits the bowers of several males before choosing one of them. When a female arrives, the male courts her with elaborate vocal and visual displays, but he cannot prevent a female from leaving to sample additional males, something the females commonly do. Eventually, a female selects a male, mates with him, and leaves to lay her eggs and rear her chicks alone. The bower is not a nest, and males take no part in rearing offspring. Female choice, rather than male competition, is paramount among bowerbirds.

These two systems illustrate completely different "solutions" to the same problem of reproduction faced by all species. Other examples, including substantial male contributions to offspring, extreme female aggression and competition, and sexual behavior outside the fertile period, could also be cited. Among bonobos, small relatives of chimpanzees, sexual activity occurs between virtually all members of a social group, including members of the same sex. This point is an important one: although male competition and female choice are the basic elements of sexual selection, even among animals, tremendous diversity exists in how they are implemented. Those unfamiliar with the behavior of animals in the wild often do not realize that animal family life, or lack of it, is not a simplified version of human existence, even human existence in an imaginary early hunter-gatherer society. It is simply incorrect to suggest that finding a link between our gender-related behavior and that of other animals would inevitably mean a link to a male-dominated social system. A single animal model for the origin of sex roles does not exist, even if we were to accept that finding such a model would make it impossible to act outside of it.

Note that this diversity also precludes claiming that women are naturally caring, verbal, peace-loving, or sexually adventurous. Substituting one stereotype, that of a strong Amazon, for the more traditional one of a coy stay-at-home mom uninterested in sex does not solve the problem. We may like the previously unappreciated female bonobo, with her overt sexuality, more than another animal model, but it is important to remember that the animals are model systems for understanding a range of behaviors and not role models.

How, then, can we learn from animals about gender and sex roles? In what follows, I detail two examples of topics that are often discussed in the context of animal behavior: maternal instinct and mate fidelity. I hope to show that we can learn from biology without either succumbing to old stereotypes or substituting new ones for them.

Maternal instinct and mother love

One of the cornerstones of popular belief in a biological basis for gender-based behavior is that females instinctively care for their young. If maternal caregiving behavior is natural, then presumably all women want to do it, know how to do it without learning how, and feel deprived if they do not. A modern version of the maternal instinct is the mother–infant bond, this mysterious connection that supposedly naturally occurs between a woman and her child soon after birth.

How fixed is this bond, and how ingrained in a female's psyche is the ability – and even the desire – to care for her young? It would seem reasonable to assume that animals should show a behavior that women are supposed to have inherited, and it is therefore instructive to look at research from the 1950s and 1960s using rhesus macaques, the monkeys used in numerous medical and behavioral studies; the "Rh" in Rh-positive or Rh-negative blood types comes from the name of this species. Two psychologists, named Harry and Margaret Harlow, were interested in understanding the effects of social deprivation on humans, the kind of deprivation that arises through abuse, neglect, and warfare. The Harlows wanted to know how these problems arose and, thus, perhaps gain insight into correcting them. They could not, of course, perform controlled experiments on human children, and so they used an animal model and manipulated the early rearing environment of groups of macaques so that deprived youngsters could be compared to more normally raised controls. The Harlows' research is expertly analyzed by Deborah Blum (2002), who also raises some of the interesting ethical issues that arise from the treatment of the monkeys.

The infant macaques were taken from their mothers at birth and raised under one of several different sets of conditions. For example, some were allowed access to a monkey-sized, wire-covered model that had a bottle attached to it approximately where the nipple of a mother monkey might be. The bottle was filled with milk, and the cages cleaned at appropriate intervals by human caretakers who had no contact with the monkeys. Other baby macaques had the wire-covered model with the food and, in addition, were given another model covered with terrycloth. In some instances, the monkeys saw or contacted other equally deprived infants during their development, while in others, they were kept in isolation. As the monkeys grew up, they were used in a variety of tests to examine their social behavior and, eventually, their ability to mate and have offspring of their own.

To the surprise of a few, the socially deprived monkeys did not exhibit normal behavior. They were more fearful when new stimuli were introduced to their cages, did not interact with other juvenile monkeys the way that babies raised with their mothers did, and showed numerous other signs of psychological abnormality. Interestingly, however, the babies given the cloth-covered model "mother" were better adjusted than those given only the wire model, and when a novel and potentially frightening object was introduced into the cage, they ran not to the source of food but to the source of what the Harlows called "contact comfort." In other words, clinging to a soft object is more soothing than returning to the place where essential nourishment is found.

The Harlows went on from these studies to discuss a number of fascinating theories about the need for this contact comfort and its potential value in helping children with minimal resources develop more normally. Their ideas have been thoroughly dissected – and in some cases debunked – by developmental psychologists. For my purposes here, however, a more relevant finding was the discovery that females raised with the models had difficulties in mating with male monkeys once they reached sexual maturity. They simply did not know how to have sex – they didn't know the postures, the signals, the responses. Even more significant, if they were artificially inseminated and became pregnant, they were incapable of caring for the resulting young, and their infants had to be removed from their mothers, lest they be seriously injured. The mothers did get better with experience so that subsequent young fared better, but the early babies were as foreign as extra-terrestrials to their mothers.

These results seem to flatly contradict the notion of a simple maternal instinct. Even mother monkeys, animals very similar to ourselves, do not automatically feel bonded to their infants, much less know how to take care of them. The mystical mother–child relationship is shattered when the mother is raised without others of her kind. This situation is clearly unusual, of course. The monkeys are not usually raised by wire models, and under natural circumstances, they can relate to their offspring perfectly well. This, however, is precisely my point: even a behavior supposedly as sacrosanct as the love a mother will have for her child depends on the environment. And therefore, it is also clear that the evidence does not support assuming a particular behavior in humans is "natural," even one as supposedly biological as mothering.

The consequences of acknowledging this fact are many. If one is freed from the idea of the maternal instinct, one is also freed from equating being female to being a mother, as if no other role was possible or important. Examining female behavior, in humans or animals, is therefore enriched by abandoning the stereotype. Females can exhibit all kinds of behavior, and females, human or not, are not only defined by their relationship to their offspring. One can also start dissecting maternal behavior itself, asking questions about what kind and how much of an investment would benefit mothers under different circumstances. The "maternal–infant bond" becomes a malleable behavior rather than a fixed biological entity.

The idea of variable mothering leads to some interesting and sometimes startling predictions. For example, the eminent anthropologist Sarah Blaffer Hrdy has found that infanticide can be adaptive for monkeys and other mammals that exhibit it (Hausfater and Hrdy 1984). While I hasten to point out that this hardly justifies the behavior in humans, it does suggest that an analysis that does not focus exclusively on the stereotypical nurturing mother can be enlightening.

Adultery and philandering males

Infidelity, again whether in humans or animals, is a topic of great interest to those want-ing to understand whether animals show us our own biologically based behaviors. The classic stereotype of male nature is of the man seeking multiple sexual partners while the woman is content to remain with a single partner for her entire life. Infidelity has also recently become a subject of interest to scientists, because the advent of genetic testing has allowed us to sample the DNA from a set of chicks in a nest and compare it to the DNA of the male and female associated with the young. As it turns out, so-called extra-pair paternity is quite common among birds; estimates of the proportion of offspring sired by males other than the one attending a female and her nest range from 0 in snow geese to a whopping 90 percent in a species of fairy wren, brilliantly colored tiny birds from Australia (Griffith et al. 2002; Griffith and Montgomerie 2003). Although, fre-quently, only one male and one female are seen associating, including feeding and pro-tecting the young, it has become apparent that additional males fathered offspring in the nest. In mammals that have multiple young in a litter, the young may also have more than one father, though mammals are less likely to appear to be monogamous in the first place.

This discovery was quite a shock to scientists, because outwardly it had appeared that most birds were monogamous. If this were not the case, many questions arose. What are the advantages to females of having multiple fathers for her brood? Do males attempt to deter females from such multiple mating, since it is costly to them to help rear offspring not their own? Why, given the apparent disparity of investment of males and females in offspring, should females pursue quantity rather than quality of mates? Questions like these are currently the subject of ongoing research in a variety of species.

The occurrence of extra-pair mating is also rather surprising to non-scientists, perhaps because the birds unwittingly had served as something of a role model for human mar-riage. It is tempting to conclude that if warblers, robins, and other models of monogamy are doing it, we should admit that extra-pair copulation, or adultery – or whatever term you prefer – is natural, expected, and maybe we should stop making such a fuss about it and resign ourselves to our evolutionary heritage.

But the problem is that the birds are not "cheating"; they are just doing what they do, and they did not invent the rules about the pair bond between a male and female – *we did*. It isn't cheating if there are no rules to break. Some animals are monogamous, some are not, and one mating system is no more "natural," or "biological," than the other. Certainly, multiple mating appears to be favored in many species, more species than had previously been believed, but that does not argue for the death of fidelity. Instead, it suggests a re-examination of sexual selection theory, something that is already occur-ring among scientists. This brings up an important point about the use of animal models for human behavior. Animals are useful for showing us what kinds of solutions exist to the common biological problems involved in survival and reproduction. How does the environment influence the costs and benefits of multiple mating? This is an interesting and relevant question – whether human males are biologically destined to cheat on their wives is not. As with maternal behavior, in mating systems, multiple solutions are virtu-ally always the norm, and there is no single natural male or female role.

What about the primates, our closest relatives? Here, too, the sex-role stereotypes are crumbling. Male dominance was viewed as the major force in primate societies when most monkeys and apes were studied in the middle of the twentieth century (Strum and

Fedigan 2000), with females viewed as relatively uninterested in sex outside the time when they were most likely to become pregnant. However, probably not coincidentally with the growing numbers of women entering primatology, as more species were studied more intensively, it soon became clear that male–female relationships were more complex and, furthermore, that females often sought out sex (sometimes with both males and females) outside the period of maximum fertility (Smuts 1999; Strum and Fedigan 2000). In olive baboons, some males and females became what primatologist Barbara Smuts called "friends," with bonds of association that went beyond the brief act of sex itself (Smuts 1999). This complexity argues against the caricature of sex-crazed males and demure females that people sometimes think constitutes our heritage from other animals.

Studying a diversity of human cultures is also of interest once we recognize this multiplicity of solutions in other animals. What patterns of courtship and marriage seem to be universal, and what patterns depend on environmental attributes, such as food availability and distribution?

Model systems and role models

It is also important to remember not to substitute one stereotype for another; it would be just as fallacious to conclude that all women are sexual adventuresses as to adhere to the old model of the frigid female. Deciding that biology is relevant to understanding gender does not mean that we imitate the species we prefer; model systems, like the fruit flies used in genetics, are useful tools for generalizing because we understand a great deal about them, but as I mentioned earlier, they should not be confused with role models. Animals tell us that females can be assertive, but perhaps more important, they tell us that females are variable. Furthermore, like many other biologists, I urge caution in interpreting nature. The naturalistic fallacy holds that what is natural is good, but what is natural can't be inherently "good" any more than it can be inherently amusing, inherently painful, or more likely to keep your hair shiny. Finding out that some animals eat their young says no more about the ethics of infanticide than finding out that some animals are yellow says about fashion trends.

As a scientist studying animals, not humans, I am also concerned about how our verdict of cheating affects our views of the animals themselves. Some of the early papers on extra-pair paternity in birds are interestingly divided in who is portrayed as the active party in the behavior. Initially, there seemed to be two approaches, neither one particularly favorable to females. Either the males were roaming around, taking advantage of hapless females waiting innocently in their own territories for the breadwinner males to come home with the worms, or else, females were brazen hussies, seducing blameless males who otherwise would not have strayed from the path of moral righteousness into turpitude. One scientist refers rather peevishly to "female promiscuity" in blackbirds. Several papers, including one published in the prestigious journal *Nature*, call young birds fathered by males not paired with the mother "illegitimate," as if their parents had tiny avian marriage licenses and chirped their vows (Gyllensten et al. 1990; Hasselquist et al. 1995; Bjornstad and Lifjeld 1997). Scientists, of course, are subject to social influences, just like other people, but we should try not to allow our prejudices to influence our interpretation of what we see the animals doing. A paper on Tasmanian native hens, birds with a rather complex set of relationships between the sexes, discussed what appears to be polyandry, multiple males associated with a single female (Maynard Smith and Ridpath 1972). The paper refers to this behavior as "wife-sharing," but I have never seen multiple females associated with a male, its mirror image and a common mating pattern, called "husband-sharing." Making the males the active parties (they "share" the female as if she were a six-pack of beer) may reduce the likelihood of noticing what the females do, of seeing things from their point of view. Similarly, if we only see female baboons as mothers, we are less likely to notice that, in fact, their relationships, not those of males, determine troop structure and movement (Smuts 1999).

Conclusions

It is no surprise that many people get twitchy when they hear about any so-called biological explanations of behavior in humans. They are also nervous when scientists study behaviors in animals that seem to occur in humans, for the reasons I described earlier. Here I have tried to ameliorate this fear, though at least in part it should be replaced with caution and awareness. Biology has great potential for harming women, but it is through our misbehavior, not the science itself. Biology can extend the boundaries of our thinking about gender, as it can for so many other ideas. Contrary to popular belief, biology does not set limits; it demolishes them.

It is also important to remember that discoveries of mate fidelity, male tenderness, or female sexual violence do not argue for a human nature that includes or excludes them. Evolution is an important explanation for the origin and diversity of life on earth, including human life. It helps us understand how organisms are related to each other, how the species that occur on a coral reef got there, whether a reed warbler female is likely to have any surviving young in a given year, how the members of chimpanzee groups sometimes benefit by being kind to one another, and why diet may help determine the probability of getting heart disease. Suggesting that evolutionary biology is irrelevant to human lives is as foolish as suggesting that it is irrelevant to the lives of fruit flies. Men and women are not the same, both from the standpoint of physiology and evolution. Neither are male and female goldfish, or fruit flies, or weasels. But this does not mean that men and women inherit templates of irreversible behavior.

Discussion questions

1. What was Darwin's explanation for secondary sex characteristics in male animals, and how did some of his contemporaries argue against him?
2. Why does Zuk argue that animal models cannot be used to directly understand human gendered behavior?
3. What were the findings of Harlow's research with rhesus macaques in relation to the assumed "natural" mother–infant bond?
4. Why does the author argue that it is important to separate our own cultural prejudices from our interpretation of animal behavior when discussing "biological" explanations for gender differences?

References

Andersson, Malte. 1994. *Sexual Selection*. Princeton: Princeton University Press.
Bjornstad, Gro, and Jan T. Lifjeld. 1997. "High Frequency of Extra-Pair Paternity in a Dense and Synchronous Population of Willow Warblers. Phylloscopus Trochilus." *Journal of Avian Biology* 28(4): 319–324.

Blum, Deborah. 2002. *Love at Goon Park*. New York: Perseus Publishing.

Borgia, Gerald. 1995. "Why do Bowerbirds Build Bowers?" *American Scientist* 83: 542–547.

Fausto-Sterling, Anne. 1987. *Myths of Gender: Biological Theories about Women and Men*. New York: Basic Books.

Fausto-Sterling, Anne. 2003. "Science Matters, Culture Matters." *Perspectives in Biology and Medicine* 46: 109–124.

Galimberti, Filippo, Anna Fabiani, and Simona Sanvito. 2002. "Measures of Breeding Inequality: A Case Study in Southern Elephant Seals." *Canadian Journal of Zoology* 80: 1240–1249.

Gowaty, Patricia Adair, ed. 1997. *Feminism and Evolutionary Biology: Boundaries, Intersections, and Frontiers*. New York: Chapman and Hall.

Gowaty, Patricia Adair. 2003. "Sexual Natures: How Feminism Changed Evolutionary Biology." *Signs* 28: 901–921.

Gowaty, Patricia Adair, and Nancy Buschhaus. 1998. "Ultimate Causation of Aggressive and Forced Copulation in Birds: Female Resistance, the CODE Hypothesis, and Social Monogamy." *American Zoologist* 38: 207–225.

Griffith, Simon C., and Robert Montgomerie. 2003. "Why do Birds Engage in Extra-Pair Copulation?" *Nature* 422: 833.

Griffith, Simon C., Ian P. F. Owens, and Kathrine A. Thuman. 2002. "Extra Pair Paternity in Birds: A Review of Interspecific Variation and Adaptive Function." *Molecular Ecology* 11: 2195–2212.

Gyllensten, Ulf B., Sven Jakobsson, and Hans Temrin. 1990. "No Evidence for Illegitimate Young in Monogamous and Polygynous Warblers." *Nature* 343: 168–170.

Hasselquist, Dennis, Staffan Bensch, and Torbjörn von Schantz. 1995. "Low Frequency of Extra-pair Paternity in the Polygynous Great Reed Warbler Acrocephalus Arundinaceus." *Behavioral Ecology* 6: 27–38.

Hausfater, Glenn, and Sarah Blaffer Hrdy, eds. 1984. *Infanticide: Comparative and Evolutionary Perspectives*. New York: Aldine de Gruyter.

Hrdy, Sarah Blaffer. 1986. "Empathy, Polyandry, and the Myth of the Coy Female." In *Feminist Approaches to Science*, ed. Ruth Bleier. New York: Pergamon Press.

Hrdy, Sarah Blaffer. 1997. "Raising Darwin's Consciousness: Female Sexuality and the Prehominid Origins of Patriarchy." *Human Nature* 8: 1–49.

Hrdy, Sarah Blaffer. 1999. *Mother Nature*. New York: Pantheon.

Jennions, Michael D., and Marion Petrie. 1997. "Variation in Mate Choice and Mating Preferences: A Review of Causes and Consequences." *Biological Reviews of the Cambridge Philosophical Society* 72: 283–327.

Jennions, Michael D., and Marion Petrie. 2000. "Why do Females Mate Multiply? A Review of the Genetic Benefits." *Biological Reviews of the Cambridge Philosophical Society* 75: 21–64.

Keller, Evelyn Fox. 1985. *Reflections on Gender and Science*. New Haven: Yale University Press.

Le Boeuf, Burney J., and Joanne Reiter. 1988. "Lifetime Reproductive Success in Northern Elephant Seals." In *Reproductive Success: Studies of Individual Variation in Contrasting Breeding Systems*, ed. T. H. Clutton-Brock, 344–362. Chicago: University of Chicago Press.

Liesen, Laurette T. 1995. "Feminism and the Politics of Reproductive Strategies." *Politics Life Science* 14: 145–162.

Madden, Joah R. 2003. "Male Spotted Bowerbirds Preferentially Choose, Arrange and Proffer Objects That are Good Predictors of Mating Success." *Behavioral Ecology and Sociobiology* 53(5): 263–268.

Maynard Smith, John, and M. G. Ridpath. 1972. "Wife Sharing in the Tasmanian Native Hen, *Tribonyx mortierii*: A Case of Kin Selection?" *The American Naturalist* 106: 447–452.

Petrie, Marion. 1994. "Improved Growth and Survival of Offspring of Peacocks with More Elaborate Trains." *Nature* 371: 598–599.

Petrie, Marion, and Tim Halliday. 1994. "Experimental and Natural Changes in the Peacock's (Pave Cristatus) Train Can Affect Mating Success." *Behavioral Ecology and Sociobiology* 35: 213–217.

Smuts, Barbara B. 1999. *Sex and Friendship in Baboons*, 2nd ed. Cambridge, MA: Harvard University Press.

Strum, Shirley C., and Linda Marie Fedigan, eds. 2000. *Primate Encounters: Models of Science, Gender, and Society*. Chicago: University of Chicago Press.

Trivers, Robert L. 1972. "Parental Investment and Sexual Selection." In *Sexual Selection and the Descent of Man, 1871–1971*, ed. Bernard Campbell, 136–179. London: Heinemann.

Uy, J. Albert C., Gail L. Patricelli, and Gerald Borgia. 2001. "Complex Mate Searching in the Satin Bowerbird Ptilonorhynchus Violaceus." *The American Naturalist* 158: 530–542.

Wallace, Alfred Russel. 1889. *Darwinism: An Exposition of the Theory of Natural Selection with Some of Its Applications*. London: MacMillan Press.

Zuk, Marlene. 2002. *Sexual Selections: What We Can and Can't Learn about Sex from Animals*. Berkeley: University of California Press.

Chapter 4

From pollution to love magic

The new anthropology of menstruation

Alma Gottlieb

Adapted by the author from Alma Gottlieb, "Bloody Mess, Blood Magic, or Just Plain Blood? Anthropological Perspectives on the Menstrual Experience," *Ethnography* 41.4, pp. 381–390

Consider this story: a college student – we'll call him Eddie – is having difficulty in his love life. Girls are so keyed into feminism these days, Eddie has concluded, that they rarely consider boys worthy of their affection. How to seduce a girl of this feminist generation? One day, our frustrated student is inspired: even the staunchest feminist might be excited at the thought of a prospective boyfriend who himself professes an interest in feminist theory, he ventures. Eddie decides to make use of campus resources and scours the bookstores for the most unabashedly, even outrageously feminist book he can find. He chooses a scholarly tome called *Blood Magic: The Anthropology of Menstruation*, a collection of essays about the ways that women around the world experience their periods (Buckley and Gottlieb 1988a). Eddie buys the volume, brings it home, and places the unread prop strategically on his coffee table before inviting his next date to his apartment, then hopes for the book to have its anticipated effect.[1]

In planning his strategy, the model Eddie used was an old one, although he was undoubtedly unaware of its pedigree: he was relying on menstrual blood – or its textual representation – as a seduction technique, a form of "love magic." This use of menstrual blood to secure sexual favors (or fidelity) is well-documented in other cultural contexts (Hoskins 2002a, 2002b); in fact, a (semi-fictionalized) folk example from southern Illinois is even mentioned in the introduction to the very book Eddie was displaying on his coffee table.

However, most previously documented forms of menstrual-blood-as-love-magic involve women manipulating the substance either to seduce men or to bind straying husbands or lovers to them; Eddie had reversed the more usual gender pattern. Using cunning and deceit, he had acted as the initiator of the sexual relationship. In his plan, he upheld the usual patriarchal structure of Western gender relations of men taking advantage of women by exercising differential access to power of one sort or another. Thus, if Eddie's unexpected use of a feminist book about menstrual experiences spoke to a documented ethnographic practice, it also represented a violation of the feminist intention of the analytic project of understanding those practices. Eddie's story signals how far

DOI: 10.4324/9781003398349-5

scholars still have to go in furthering the widespread understanding of feminism and how it can lead us to understand women's lives and bodily based experiences.

When the book Eddie was using as a quasi-fetish in his flirtation repertoire was first published (Buckley and Gottlieb 1988b), anthropological works about menstruation were few and far between. Moreover, most early anthropological writings on menstruation tended to confirm a simplistic agenda, suggesting that menstrual blood is generally taken as a source of what anthropologists call symbolic pollution (Douglas 1966). In other words, menstrual blood was assumed to be seen as mystically contaminating, hence something to be avoided at all costs by anyone not menstruating – and especially by men.[2] Feminism had not yet made serious inroads into the comparative, cultural study of women's bodies in general. And systematic cross-cultural fieldwork with consultants concerning the topic of menstruation, let alone with menstruating women themselves about their own perspectives on their somatic lives, was still a rarity. In assembling our collection of anthropological essays about menstrual practices cross-culturally, Buckley and I hoped to be followed by a new generation of writings that would both add new data to our existing knowledge of women's experiences of their bodies and pose a range of new models inspired in one way or another by feminist theory. These future works would, we thought, investigate how women's experiences of the menstrual cycle – as with other body practices – are profoundly shaped by culture and history. For this to occur, we needed to be followed by a new generation of ethnographers committed to conducting fieldwork-based studies on somatic processes, such as menstruation, that seemed to belong exclusively to the domain of biology but that were nevertheless deeply defined by systems of cultural values and historical factors alike.

During the 15 years that have elapsed since *Blood Magic* appeared, feminism has, indeed, made exciting inroads into the comparative, cultural study of women's bodies in general. Accordingly, systematic cross-cultural fieldwork with consultants concerning the topic of menstruation in particular, and with menstruating women themselves about their own perspectives on their somatic lives, is no longer such a rarity. Indeed, in the past decade and a half, there has been a groundswell of published work, both within and outside anthropology, that focuses on menstruation as well as other aspects of reproduction in particular and the body in general. Originally, these writings emphasized *women's* bodily experiences. In many ways launched by Emily Martin's award-winning work *The Woman in the Body* (1987), a host of books and articles has brilliantly explored the culturally and historically produced nature of a wide gamut of reproduction experiences previously assumed to be regulated by biology alone.[3] Increasingly, scholars have begun to explore cultural and historical constructions of *men's* bodily experiences as well (e.g., Gardiner 2002; Gutmann 1996; Kimmel 1987; Lugo and Maurer 2000). Contemporary authors now writing about the menstrual experience cross-culturally are thus in conversation with a larger cohort of colleagues bringing fresh perspectives to the dynamic interface between body, person, gender identity, and society.

In this chapter, I will especially focus on one recent collection of essays that offers an especially rich selection of practices, beliefs, and values concerning menstrual cycle cross-culturally (Hoskins 2002a). Some important themes run through the essays in that collection. For example, the in/famous *menstrual hut* is drastically re-envisioned in this new writing. Long conceived as an architectural instantiation of female oppression, the "menstrual hut" in much classic anthropological literature was usually described as a lonely and flimsy structure in which women were consigned to spend their menstruating days alone – bored, self-loathing (allowed only to scratch an itch on their contaminated bodies using the infamous "scratching sticks" to avoid auto-pollution), and in virtual (if temporary) exile. This anthropologically vaunted, somewhat-mystical space was surrounded by decades of disciplinary speculation that was, however, rarely based on relevant fieldwork. The menstrual buildings described in current anthropological writings inhabit an entirely different universe.

Janet Hoskins (2002b) occupies an especially privileged position from which to understand the experiences of women while inside a menstrual residence. While living among the Huaulu people in eastern Indonesia, Hoskins herself was expected to spend time in the menstrual hut every month while she had her period. Her account runs parallel to that of another ethnographer, Wynne Maggi, who has recently conducted participant observation research in menstrual houses every month over the course of fieldwork with the (largely non-Muslim) Kalasha community in Pakistan and has written a first-person account of her experiences (Maggi 2001: 125–133). Having conducted fieldwork in societies with active menstrual shelters and a number of explicit menstrual expectations, both Hoskins and Maggi were afforded rare opportunities to gain firsthand knowledge of the occupants' activities and the general atmosphere inside the houses, and thus to demystify women's actual experiences.

Perhaps the greatest challenge posed by both the Huaulu and the Kalasha to the infamous image of the menstrual-hut-as-prison concerns the personnel. Due to the now fairly well-documented but still little-understood phenomenon of menstrual synchrony – the likelihood of coresident women starting their periods on the same day each month (often at the new moon or full moon)[4] – there is usually a lively gathering of several simultaneously menstruating women inside both Huaulu and Kalasha menstrual huts, rather than the stereotyped single, lonely woman. Moreover, among the Huaulu, beyond the menstruating women themselves, one is also likely to find some of their young children – both boys and girls – and, on occasion, some visiting women friends as well. Hoskins intrigues us with her account of all manner of pleasurable female activity occurring inside the collectivity temporarily inhabiting the hut. Singing and playing instruments, telling stories, doing craftwork, relaxing, breastfeeding, caring for young children – all these occur each month inside the menstrual residence. Indeed, the sociable nature of the chamber lends itself to charismatic personalities: one Huaulu woman even turned the hut into a performance space in which she recounted lively stories, building up political reputations village-wide from her narrative skills.

Elsewhere, women do not maintain a complete monopoly over the menstrual residence. Among the Pangia of the New Guinea highlands, such buildings may also legitimately shelter *men* (Stewart and Strathern 2002). This occurs on the rare occasion that a man is said by members of the local community to be pregnant because he inadvertently ingested menstrual blood. In such a disastrous situation, the unfortunate man is said to be cured by a ritual that he undergoes inside the menstrual hut shelter – now empty of women. Writing of less legitimate cases elsewhere in New Guinea, Stewart and Strathern (2002) also mention in passing the possibility of *menstrual adultery* occurring in the private space of the menstrual hut. This is an under-discussed but surely fruitful topic for comparative inquiry, especially where menstrual seclusion is practiced. Both these Melanesian cases serve as a powerful reminder to the outsider that, as anthropology so often teaches us about nearly every other aspect of social life, nothing may be assumed: in this case, in any given menstrual residence, even the gender of the occupants may be variable.

In Indonesia, Hoskins (2002b) further notes that the Huaulu menstrual building shelters women not only when they are menstruating but also while they are in labor. Such dual-use structures – for both menstruation and childbirth – are reported elsewhere as well (e.g., Maggi 2001). In such cases where the menstrual shelter also serves as the birth clinic, perhaps even the term "menstrual hut" (or "house") is misleading and ought to be replaced by a more culturally inclusive term – "women's reproduction house" or even just "women's house," echoing the "men's houses" that are documented among many groups in Melanesia, Africa, and South America. Such a semantic shift would be in keeping with the fact that menstruation may not always be singled out for special treatment, in complete contrast to all other bodily fluids and processes.

The emphasis on *agency* in contemporary works about menstruation extends beyond the menstrual shelter to the experience of menstruating women, whether or not they inhabit a special building reserved for the occasion. Thus, the agency of the individual woman-as-menstruator is stressed in several recent essays. From Hoskins (2002b), for example, we learn of Kodi women on Sumba in eastern Indonesia who deploy menstrual blood to deceive their husbands in a variety of disempowering ways, effectively manipulating the secret powers of menstrual blood at the expense of their men. The flip side to such actions is exercised by Huaulu women, who manage the more public powers of menstruation for the *protection* of their men.

Elsewhere in Indonesia, Balinese women may make use of menstrual blood in manufacturing more friendly forms of "love magic." At the same time, in a provocative narrative, Pedersen (2002) illustrates how the individual menstruator's own perceptions of her state can complicate seemingly simple ideologies of menstruation-as-pollution when she cites a Balinese consultant who claims that sitting on a garbage heap while menstruating makes her feel royal. Other Balinese women knowingly violate menstrual taboos by illicitly entering a temple while menstruating but apparently feel no remorse or guilt. As analyzed by Pedersen, such women employ psychological techniques to counterbalance the spiritual pollution they should, in theory, cause by their violation. Here we see how ideologies of pollution, where they exist, should be the beginning – not the end – of ethnographic analysis. Women's own views of a patriarchal ideology can strikingly offer an alternative reading of that ideology, sometimes affording women a form of personal resistance to a degrading cultural script, or allowing them to reinterpret it entirely.

The agency of the individual is explicitly stressed by Phyllis Morrow writing about the native American Yupik of central Alaska. Morrow (2002) explores how the Yupik generally emphasize individual responsibility in maintaining cultural expectations. Thus, the Yupik allow latitude for individuals to find their own comfort level in adhering to rules, or "teachings" (as Morrow sometimes translates the Yupik word), for personal behavior – including those that pertain to menstruation. This is an apt case of an Indigenous or "folk" model of social life pointing productively to an appropriate analytic model. The conjunction between Indigenous and analytic models serves as a humble reminder that local systems of knowledge exist on the same level as do "scientific" ones, and each can speak productively to the other (cf. Rosaldo 1989).

Another means to deploy agency in the menstrual experience involves the use of *emenagogues*: herbal and other practical methods that women throughout the world and throughout history have devised to regulate the timing of their periods. Sometimes, these techniques have been used to promote fertility; at other times, they have been used (usually furtively) to induce abortions. In either case, using such techniques may constitute a more secular effort by women to regulate their menstrual flow, thereby allowing them to exercise general control over their bodies.

Writing of Bali, for example, Pedersen (2002) mentions that women may prepare a dish with uncooked pig's blood to hasten the onset of their menstrual periods. This observation echoes abundant information contained in a new collection of essays (Renne and van der Walle 2001) reporting an impressive variety of emmenagogues cross-culturally and historically. Once again, we encounter the theme of agency, as women deliberately shape their own menstrual experience rather than seeing themselves as scripted actors reading from either a biologically *or* culturally mandated text.

All these cases demonstrate how close attention to individual perspectives deconstructs the classic, monolithic view of menstrual taboos and cultural expectations as pre-programmed models from which actual subjects may never diverge. Such testimonies are theoretically critical insofar as they challenge the image that anthropologists have long held of menstrual culture – perhaps as an extension of a more general model inherited from such early scholars as Lucien Lévy-Bruhl (1985) and others that cultural traditions in general exert a certain deadening, conservative force. This is a perspective that is very much challenged in the recent work on menstruation.

The individual manipulation of menstrual taboos and expectations speaks at another level to intracultural variation via subgroups with structurally divergent agendas or even ambiguity or ambivalence among members of a given society regarding women's menstrual activities. When Buckley (1988) first suggested that among the native North American Yurok of California, men and women, as well as aristocrats and commoners, may perceive menstruation differently from one another, it was a somewhat-novel proposal. Several recent essays provide extended studies of situations that are likewise complex in their own ways. Menstruation emerges from these societies as a process that is perceived differentially according to multiple subject positions.

Writing of Bali, for example, Pedersen charts how the deeply structured system of rank adapted from the Hindu caste system has a significant impact on how girls and women experience their periods. Whereas high-ranking Balinese women may find menstrual taboos to be empowering, low-ranking girls and women may experience menstrual taboos as simply one more painful sign of their inferior status. Social change adds further layers to the entanglements of rank. Pederson notes that "'modern' working women are more prone than any to 'take advantage' of the leverage provided by the exempting options." If such options are more available to higher-ranked women than to lower-ranked ones, this would perpetuate, and perhaps even magnify, the divide between women at different ends of the system of social hierarchy. Here we see the complexity of class and gender as they work against each other. Ironically, women's bodies – which might (seemingly) serve as a foundation for female solidarity – can be culturally manipulated in such a way as to divide rather than unite women of diverse class and prestige backgrounds. The menstrual experience speaks here to broader feminist concerns: sadly, the empowerment of some women often comes at the expense of the oppression of others.

Ironically, the opposite effects of the relationship between class and menstrual symbolism are found in Bengal. In this region of Hindu India, as analyzed by Hanssen (2002), the Brahmanic view is that menstrual blood is polluting. However, when men and women of the low-ranked leatherworker caste become "renouncers" through a particular religious sect – the Vaishnava Baul group – they embrace a major precept of the sect: that menstrual blood contains a life force or "seed" within it – as with other bodily fluids in the

Baul scheme of life, but even more so. Taking into account such symbolic potency, some of the "renouncers" with whom Hanssen conducted research may, on occasion, ingest menstrual blood so as to regain spiritual strength. Here we see the symbolic potency to menstrual fluid being harnessed not for nefarious goals, as is reported in much of the classic literature, but for regenerative purposes. Again, the menstrual pollution model is effectively challenged.

Another subgroup meriting particular attention is that of *unmarried girls*. The menstrual blood of this group – defined variously as virgins and/or unmarried – is held up for special ritual treatment in several societies that are the focus of the articles I have been discussing. For example, Stewart and Strathern (2002) report that the Duna people of Melanesia addressed societal disruptions that were said to be caused by a mischievous spirit by offering the spirit the menstrual blood of a virginal girl. The consequences to the girl chosen to supply this critical ritual ingredient were drastic: as an adult, she was not allowed ever to bear children. In exploring the individual nuances of such cases here and elsewhere, there may be a subject ripe for new, comparative analysis.

Indeed, the experiences of girls undergoing menarche in general are still underreported by anthropologists. Scholars in history, cultural studies, nursing, journalism, and other disciplines are embarrassingly ahead of anthropologists here, inasmuch as the menarcheal histories of girls in the United States are now well-documented by scholars in adjacent fields (e.g., Golub 1992; Houppert 1999; Lee and Sasser-Coen 1996). A few current works by anthropologists do address the issue, however. Thus, Pedersen (2002) recounts intriguing menarcheal histories of Balinese women that are at great variance from those reported for contemporary North American girls. Whereas, in the United States, many women and girls still feel great shame concerning their first periods (and regarding menstruation in general) and they attest to the continuing existence of a virtual taboo against discussion of the subject in most contexts, this is not the case in Bali. Intriguingly, Pederson reports that Balinese of all ages and both genders feel comfortable in discussing menstruation quite casually, and all females with whom Pederson conversed about the subject recalled that they enjoyed their first periods, even when they were surprised by or afraid of their first flow. Such discussions of the menarcheal experiences of non-Western girls remind us that the more negative experiences of contemporary North American and other Western girls, while now well-reported, cannot be taken as universal.

Surely, it is time for more anthropologists to conduct systematic fieldwork with menstruating – as well as pre-menarcheal – girls to hear their own perspectives on this crucial life passage. At a more structural level, such discussions may enable us to think about *deconstructing* the category of "menstrual blood" itself. Are we talking about a unified semantic field when we analyze the blood flow of young girls and that of married women in the same way, if a given society singles out the menstrual blood of unmarried/virginal girls as harboring special capacities that the menstrual blood of adult women does not bear?

In short, from recent work, it is clearer than ever that we can no longer talk of "the" (single or hegemonic) view or model of menstruation in a particular society. Rather, it is now clear that before assuming generality, we must interrogate the *range* of views and experiences that menstruation may produce across the social divides that structure women's lives.

Related to the previous points, one notices in the essays I have been discussing an insistence that the meanings of menstrual blood and menstruating women are decidedly *plural* in a given locale, depending on the particular context. The classic menstrual-blood-as-pollution model that permeated so much early writing by anthropologists is definitively discarded here in favor of much more situationally nuanced understandings. In particular, the symbolically constituted relation of menstrual blood to both *fertility and infertility*, as well as to other cultural matrices, emerges as an especially critical theme in these papers (for an earlier example, see Gottlieb 1988).

Thus, Stewart and Strathern (2002) propose a dramatic revisioning of the hegemonic, disciplinary model of menstruation-as-pollution as it was foundationally conceptualized. Taking us to the heartland of classical anthropological thinking about menstruation – the highlands of Papua New Guinea – they draw on A. Strathern's recent, stimulating book, *Body Thoughts* (1996), to ground their discussion of menstruation in broader issues relating the body and society. Their description (from Sainsbury) of the menarcheal Siane girl who is celebrated and courted for her induction into life as a menstruator is at striking odds with the classic pollution model that permeated much early anthropological writing about gender relations in New Guinea. Stewart and Strathern then produce, in effect, a counter-factual model, imagining what regional ethnography might have been like over the past three decades had Sainsbury's ethnography – rather than that of other Melanesianists, such as Mervyn Meggitt – prevailed as the orienting study.[5]

But Stewart and Strathern's *What if . . . ?* line of thinking is not purely conjectural: they argue that the Siane would, indeed, serve as a more appropriate model for the New Guinea highlands. Drawing on additional Melanesian ethnography, Stewart and Strathern (2002) propose that a complementary rather than antagonistic model of gender relations is more relevant to much of Melanesia than previous ethnography suggested. Stewart and Strathern's disarmingly reorienting survey should serve to reinscribe the anthropological imagining of that cultural region with new models steeped in subtlety well beyond the classic statements. Moreover, their proposed model of complementary gender relations resonates with contemporary discussions of complementary and egalitarian models of gender being developed for a variety of independent, non-Western groups elsewhere before state conquest (e.g., Du 2002). Here we see how menstruation theory can speak to, and even inform, gender theory more broadly. This is the case insofar as menstruation is deeply implicated in a wide array of social matrices, from religion (most obviously) to such disparate spheres as architecture, political economy, and beyond.

Indeed, the necessity for a contextual approach highlighting what anthropologist Victor Turner might have called *positionality* – an approach that would produce a wide-ranging analysis of how menstrual practices relate to other ritual and social forces at play in a given society – becomes quite pressing from all the work I have been discussing. Most of the societies that are the subject of the articles I have discussed – the Yupik of Alaska, several Melanesian groups, the eastern Indonesian Huaulu, and the Balinese – expect women to adhere carefully to culturally delimited menstrual restrictions; at the same time, the members of these societies orient these practices around conceptual models that are far from a simple pollution framework. Thus, all the authors of the works I have discussed remind us that menstrual restrictions are best seen as one of many types of ritual and/or somatic restrictions in the lives of all who practice them. Depending on the society, the proper context for understanding menstrual restrictions may necessitate understanding comparable restrictions in the lives of both males and females, old and young, laypersons and ritual specialists alike. The language of pollution misleads here, these authors all observe; as Morrow (2002) points out, Mary Douglas's early hypothesis that menstrual pollution indexes underlying sociological ambiguity concerning women does not necessarily apply.

At the same time, writing of the Kodi, Hoskins (2002b) points out that the *absence* of menstrual taboos belies a deep-seated conviction that menstrual blood is exceedingly *potent*. Her insight signals that a lack of explicitly religious *taboos* concerning menstrual practice does not necessarily signal a lack of culturally shaped thinking about menstruation. The current outpouring of ethnographies of modern urban life speaks powerfully to this point: secular culture is still culture, these ethnographies remind us – even science is grounded in a set of cultural assumptions that appeal to deeply held but unverifiable beliefs about the nature of reality.[6] As Clifford Geertz cautioned some time ago (1983), what passes for "common sense" is not necessarily common, as peoples everywhere forge their own distinctive notion of common sense as the basis for reality. A contextual approach to social life borrowed from Turner, highlighting positionality, offers a fruitful method for teasing out local nuances that seeming similarities across cultures might otherwise conceal.

As with other taboos, the long-standing anthropological and popular images alike of menstrual taboos is that they have somehow existed since time immemorial and that their origins are untraceable. In the recent writings I have been discussing, we learn otherwise. In taking into account the press of *history and social change*, it becomes clear that menstrual practices engage with a variety of modernities. Earlier studies tended to treat the body either as an artifact of biology – that is, more or less immutable, hence anthropologically boring – or, more recently, as cultural constructions that were nevertheless conceived as static. More recent discussions have taken up the insistence – persuasively argued by the French scholar Michel Foucault and others – that bodily regimes are as much subject to historical shifts as are political regimes. In keeping with this productive direction for scholarly research, in the essays I have been considering, the authors offer discussions of how menstrual practices have – or, in some surprising instances, have not – transformed within the recent past. Indeed, in some places, rather than insistent continuity, radical changes in menstrual practices have been documented.

Not only may their histories be knowable, but menstrual practices have also weakened in some places whereas – in contrast to what modernization theory would have predicted – they have intensified in other regions. Among the Pangia in Melanesia, for example, Stewart and Strathern (2002) inform us that menstrual huts, far from having existed since some primeval *ur-time*, were first introduced to the group along with performances dedicated to a regional female spirit cult. This spirit is widely respected as promoting fertility; Stewart and Strathern treat it as an index of a more general model of gender complementarity. The traceable co-introduction of female spirit cult performances and the practice of menstrual seclusion raises fascinating questions about changing gender roles during an earlier era of Pangia history. The case suggests that we might question the seemingly unchanging history of other menstrual practices elsewhere. Assuming that contemporary menstrual practices are a permanent feature of a given social landscape makes no more sense than assuming that any other aspect of a society – say, its political structure, or its economic base – has existed unchanged for millennia.

Moreover, in those cases where cultural continuity *is* demonstrable, its meanings are not necessarily transparent. On Bali, Pedersen (2002) tells us, menstrual taboos continue in strong force even in the face of available new menstrual technologies (industrially produced sanitary pads and tampons). However, the continuity of menstrual restrictions does not imply a thoroughgoing neglect of, or resistance to, modernity; the practices of menstrual culture can also acknowledge and even adapt to changing medical science. Thus, nowadays, some Balinese women take birth control pills in order to delay the onset of their periods; precisely timing the menstrual cycle in this way can allow women to participate in traditional temple rituals from which menstruating women are still actively banned. In this menstrual culture that persists in the face of active engagement with the Western world, even tourists are subject to regulations . . . as the English-language signs at Balinese temples forbidding entrance by menstruating women remind foreign visitors. The Balinese case teaches us that apparent cultural conservatism may be maintained self-consciously for reasons engaging with modernity. Contemporary factors such as ethnic pride and nationalism in the face of international pressure to Westernize may become as relevant as insistent maintenance of tradition might have been in a previous era.

In short, tracing menstrual histories can serve to remind us that, as with other current social practices, what we observe at any given moment in the field *may* represent continuity – but it may also be an aberration, a variation, or a rejection of what has occurred in the recent or distant past. In the colonized world in particular, the ravages brought by the triple invasion of soldiers, traders, and missionaries likely produced upheavals in the way that the body is culturally read and produced. *Precolonial* somatic regimes will, of course, be much more of a challenge to reconstruct, but oral histories, and, in some cases, colonial records, should help us understand pivotal moments in history when the gendered body may have been re-thought and re-experienced. Through such records, can we begin to account for *why* menstrual taboos have relaxed in some areas whereas they have rigidified in others under varying colonial and postcolonial regimes, as Indigenous populations endeavor to forge their own futures in the face of an increasingly engulfing modernity? This question contains a promising set of issues for researchers to continue to pursue.

The future of menstrual studies

For over 15 years, a pedagogical engagement with menstruation has allowed me to construct a classroom-based ethnographic portrait that affords some insight into contemporary US college students' perceptions and experiences of the menstrual cycle. At my home university, I have regularly taught an undergraduate course, "Cultural Images of Women," which always includes a section on menstrual practices in cross-cultural perspective. Learning of the obfuscatory terms by which American female students (who are largely but not exclusively female) still refer to their periods ("the curse," "Aunt Flo," "on the rag," and so on) – which are typically identical to terms that have been documented for the United States for much of the twentieth century – is a depressing exercise. For the striking continuity in such terms speaks to the continuing existence of strong menstrual taboos and a polluting image of menstruation at the heart of the supposedly rationalized and secular (and, dare one hope, decreasingly patriarchal) mainstream North American society.

However, another student exercise in this course often reveals a different, and more hopeful, portrait of the current generation of American students' attitudes towards toward menstruation. In choosing among several options for final exam essays, the most popular choice is often the essay question that invites students to design a new menstrual ritual for an imagined future daughter or niece, based on what students know from the menstrual experiences of their friends, relatives, and themselves, as well as what they have learned about women's menstrual experiences elsewhere from class readings. In writing their final essays, students year after year have proposed empowering rituals that harness the menstrual cycle to inspire menarcheal girls to feel pride rather than shame at their new, somatically acquired status. One student, for example, envisioned a long ritual process of educating her not-yet-conceived daughter into the wonders of the menstrual cycle. During one portion of the imagined ritual, the author and her future husband would, she planned, "throw confetti into the air in celebration" (Schroeder 2001: 2). This and other festive acts would serve to teach their future daughter to feel comfortable with her menstrual identity: "She would never once feel she had to hide the box of tampons in her bathroom or avoid the clerk's gaze while purchasing pads at the local grocery store" (Schroeder 2001: 6–7).

Year after year, imagined rituals such as these have testified to a hunger by my students to re-envision menstruation in general, and menarche in particular, from a stigmatized to a celebrated event in contemporary North America. If my students' responses are typical, menstrual experiences offer a rich site from which to understand the embodied subject as a place in which gender, power, and representation intersect in personally forceful ways. In particular, my students' writings suggest that at least some of the contemporary generation of young women is motivated to rethink their own menstrual histories and enjoys imagining menstrual futures offering ritualized revelry rather than secrecy and shame.

Meanwhile, current anthropological writings offer a range of models of menstrual practices that some of the world's women have forged. Together, these work constitute an exceedingly provocative set of writings that point to the exciting state that characterizes current comparative research into menstruation and that signal the fresh, *multiple* intellectual roads down which the anthropology of menstruation – as an exemplar of the embodied subject – is now traveling.

Discussion questions

1. Provide examples of ways women assert agency with regard to menstruation and how it can be seen as a form of personal resistance.
2. What are some methods that women have used throughout the world and across history to exercise control over their bodies?
3. What are some of the ways your own culture speaks about women's menstrual cycle? Is the subtext positive/negative?

Acknowledgments

A short version of this chapter was first presented at the 99th Annual Meeting of the American Anthropological Association (San Francisco, 2000), and a somewhat-different version was published in *Ethnology* 41(4) (2002) (special issue: "Blood Mysteries: Beyond Menstruation as Pollution," ed. Janet Hoskins). Many thanks to Janet Hoskins for comments on the earlier version.

Notes

1 The story was shared with me by my husband, writer Philip Graham, who heard it from a writing student of his who was "Eddie's" roommate. The writing student was visiting our home for a class party and, after noticing a copy of *Blood Magic* on my bookshelf, relayed the preceding narrative to his amused professor.

2 For a critical review of earlier works informed by this and other problematic perspectives, see Buckley and Gottlieb (1988a).
3 For an excellent review of earlier work, see Ginsburg and Rapp (1991). More recent works include: Bledsoe and Banja (2002), Davis-Floyd (1992), Davis-Floyd and Sargent (1997), Davis-Floyd et al. (2002), Davis-Floyd and Dumit (1997), Feldman-Savelsberg (1999), Franklin and Ragoné (1998), Ginsburg and Rapp (1995), Handwerker (1990), Héritier (1994, 1996), Inhorn (1994, 1995), Jordan (1993), Morgan (1999), Nourse (1999), Owen (1993), Ragoné (1994), Rapp (1999), Roth (2002), Sargent (1989), and M. Strathern (1992).
4 For ethnographic and historic examples of menstrual synchrony, see Buckley (1988), Knight (1988, 1991), and Lamp (1988).
5 Their fantasy reminds one of Mary Douglas's long-ago published work wondering what Africanist ethnography would look like had the British scholar Sir E. Evans-Pritchard studied the Dogon of francophone West Africa and the French scholar Marcel Griaule studied the Nuer of anglophone northeast Africa (Douglas 1975).
6 For some examples of ethnographic accounts of contemporary scientific culture, see Gusterson (1996), Haraway (1990), Martin (1994), and Toumey (1996).

References

Bledsoe, Caroline, and Fatoumatta Banja. 2002. *The Contingent Life Course: Reproduction, Time and Aging in West Africa*. Chicago: University of Chicago Press.

Buckley, Thomas. 1988. "Menstruation and the Power of Yurok Women." In *Blood Magic: The Anthropology of Menstruation*, eds. Thomas Buckley and Alma Gottlieb, 187–209. Berkeley: University of California Press.

Buckley, Thomas, and Alma Gottlieb. 1988a. "A Critical Appraisal of Theories of Menstrual Symbolism." In *Blood Magic: The Anthropology of Menstruation*, eds. Thomas Buckley and Alma Gottlieb, 1–53. Berkeley: University of California Press.

Buckley, Thomas, and Alma Gottlieb, eds. 1988b. *Blood Magic: The Anthropology of Menstruation*. Berkeley: University of California Press.

Davis-Floyd, Robbie E. 1992. *Birth as an American Rite of Passage*. Berkeley: University of California Press.

Davis-Floyd, Robbie E., Sheila Cosminsky, and Stacy Leigh Pigg, eds. 2002. "Daughters of Time: The Shifting Identities of Contemporary Midwives." *Special issue of Medical Anthropology* 20(3): 105–139.

Davis-Floyd, Robbie E., and Joe Dumit, eds. 1997. *Cyborg Babies: From Techno Tots to Techno Toys*. New York: Routledge.

Davis-Floyd, Robbie E., and Carolyn F. Sargent, eds. 1997. *Childbirth and Authoritative Knowledge: Cross-Cultural Perspectives*. Berkeley: University of California Press.

Douglas, Mary. 1966. *Purity and Danger: An Analysis of Concepts of Pollution and Taboo*. New York: Praeger.

Douglas, Mary. 1975. *Implicit Meanings: Essays in Anthropology*. London: Routledge & Paul.

Du, Shanshan. 2002. *"Chopsticks Always Work in Pairs": Gender Unity and Gender Equality among the Lahu of Southwest China*. New York: Columbia University Press.

Feldman-Savelsberg, Pamela. 1999. *Plundered Kitchens, Empty Wombs: Threatened Reproduction and Identity in the Cameroon*. Ann Arbor: University of Michigan Press.

Franklin, Sarah, and Helena Ragoné, eds. 1998. *Reproducing Reproduction: Kinship, Power, and Technological Innovation*. Philadelphia: University of Pennsylvania Press.

Gardiner, Judith Kegan, ed. 2002. *Masculinity Studies and Feminist Theory: New Directions*. New York: Columbia University Press.

Geertz, Clifford. 1983 [1975]. "Common Sense as a Cultural System." In *Local Knowledge: Further Essays in Interpretive Anthropology*, ed. Clifford Geertz, 73–93. New York: Basic Books.

Ginsburg, Faye, and Rayna Rapp. 1991. "The Politics of Reproduction." *Annual Review of Anthropology* 20: 311–343.

Ginsburg, Faye, and Rayna Rapp, eds. 1995. *Conceiving the New World Order: The Global Politics of Reproduction*. Berkeley: University of California Press.

Golub, Sharon. 1992. *Periods: From Menarche to Menopause*. London: Sage Publications.

Gottlieb, Alma. 1988. "Menstrual Cosmology among the Beng of Ivory Coast." In *Blood Magic: The Anthropology of Menstruation*, eds. Thomas Buckley and Alma Gottlieb, 55–74. Berkeley: University of California Press.

Gusterson, Hugh. 1996. *Nuclear Rites: A Weapons Laboratory at the End of the Cold War*. Berkeley: University of California Press.

Gutmann, Matthew C. 1996. *The Meanings of Macho: Being a Man in Mexico City*. Berkeley: University of California Press.

Handwerker, W. Penn, ed. 1990. *Births and Power: Social Change and the Politics of Reproduction*. Boulder: Westview Press.

Hanssen, Kristen. 2002. "Ingesting Menstrual Blood: Notions of Health and Bodily Fluids in Bengal." *Ethnology* 41(4): 365–380.

Haraway, Donna. 1990. *Primate Visions: Gender, Race and Nature in the World of Modern Science*. New York: Routledge.

Héritier, Françoise. 1994. *Les deux soeurs et leur mère*. Paris: Editions Odile Jacob.

Héritier, Françoise. 1996. *Masculin/féminin: La pensée de la différence*. Paris: Editions Odile Jacob.

Hoskins, Janet. 2002a. "Introduction: Blood Mysteries: Beyond Menstruation as Pollution." *Ethnology* 41(4): 299–301.

Hoskins, Janet. 2002b. "The Menstrual Hut and the Witch's Lair in Two Indonesian Societies." *Ethnology* 41(4): 317–334.

Houppert, Karen. 1999. *The Curse: Confronting the Last Unmentionable Taboo: Menstruation*. New York: Farrar, Straus, Giroux.

Inhorn, Marcia. 1994. *Quest for Conception: Gender, Infertility, and Egyptian Medical Traditions*. Philadelphia: University of Pennsylvania Press.

Inhorn, Marcia. 1995. *Missing Motherhood: Infertility, Patriarchy and the Politics of Gender in Egypt*. Philadelphia: University of Pennsylvania Press.

Jordan, Brigitte. 1993 [1978]. *Birth in Four Cultures: A Cross-Cultural Investigation of Childbirth in Yucatan, Holland, Sweden and the United States*. ed. Robbie Davis-Floyd, 4th ed. Prospect Heights, IL: Waveland Press.

Kimmel, Michael S., ed. 1987. *Changing Men: New Directions in Research on Men and Masculinity*. Beverly Hills, CA: Sage Publications.

Knight, Chris. 1988. "Menstrual Synchrony and the Australian Rainbow Snake." In *Blood Magic: The Anthropology of Menstruation*, eds. Thomas Buckley and Alma Gottlieb, 232–255. Berkeley: University of California Press.

Knight, Chris. 1991. *Blood Relations: Menstruation and the Origins of Culture*. New Haven: Yale University Press.

Lamp, Frederick. 1988. "Heavenly Bodies: Menses, Moon, and Rituals of License among the Temne of Sierra Leone." In *Blood Magic: The Anthropology of Menstruation*, eds. Thomas Buckley and Alma Gottlieb, 210–231. Berkeley: University of California Press.

Lee, Janet, and Jennifer Sasser-Coen. 1996. *Blood Stories: Menarche and the Politics of the Female Body in Contemporary U.S. Society*. New York: Routledge.

Lévy-Bruhl, Lucien. 1985 [1922]. *How Natives Think*. trans. Lilian A. Clare. Princeton: Princeton University Press.

Lugo, Alejandro, and Bill Maurer, eds. 2000. *Gender Matters: Rereading Michelle Z. Rosaldo*. Ann Arbor: University of Michigan Press.

Maggi, Wynne. 2001. *Our Women Are Free: Gender and Ethnicity in the Hindukush*. Ann Arbor: University of Michigan Press.

Martin, Emily. 1987. *The Woman in the Body: A Cultural Analysis of Reproduction*. Boston: Beacon Press.

Martin, Emily. 1994. *Flexible Bodies: Tracking Immunity in American Culture: From the Days of Polio to the Age of AIDS*. Boston: Beacon Press.

Morgan, Lynne, ed. 1999. *Fetal Subjects, Feminist Positions*. Philadelphia: University of Pennsylvania Press.

Morrow, Phyllis. 2002. "The Woman's Vapor: Yupik Bodily Powers in Southwest Alaska." *Ethnology* 41(4): 335–348.

Nourse, Jennifer W. 1999. *Conceiving Spirits: Birth Rituals and Contested Identities among Laujé of Indonesia*. Washington, DC: Smithsonian Institution Press.

Owen, Lara. 1993. *Her Blood Is Gold: Celebrating the Power of Menstruation*. San Francisco: Harper San Francisco.

Pedersen, Lene. 2002. "Ambiguous Bleeding: Purily and Sacrifice in Bali." *Ethnology* 41(4): 303–316.

Ragoné, Helena. 1994. *Surrogate Motherhood: Conception in the Heart*. Boulder: Westview Press.

Rapp, Rayna. 1999. *Testing Women, Testing the Fetus: The Social Impact of Amniocentesis in America*. New York: Routledge.

Renne, Elisha, and Etienne van der Walle, eds. 2001. *Regulating Menstruation: Beliefs, Practice, Interpretations*. Chicago: University of Chicago Press.

Rosaldo, Renato. 1989. *Culture and Truth: The Remaking of Social Analysis*. Boston: Beacon Press.

Roth, Denise. 2002. *Managing Motherhood, Managing Risk: Fertility and Danger in West Central Tanzania*. Ann Arbor: University of Michigan Press.

Sargent, Garolyn. 1989. *Maternity, Medicine, and Power: Reproductive Decisions in Urban Benin*. Berkeley: University of California Press.

Schroeder, Annica. 2001. "A 'Rite'ful Passage into Womanhood for Little Gabriella." *Paper for ANTH 262*, University of Illinois at Urbana-Champaign, December 6. Unpublished manuscript.

Stewart, Pamela J., and Andrew Strathern. 2002. "Power and Placement in Blood Practices." *Ethnology* 41(4): 349–367.

Strathern, Andrew. 1996. *Body Thoughts*. Ann Arbor: University of Michigan Press.

Strathern, Marilyn. 1992. *Reproducing the Future: Anthropology, Kinship, and the New Reproductive Technologies*. New York: Routledge.

Toumey, Christopher P. 1996. *Conjuring Science: Scientific Symbols and Cultural Meanings in American Life*. New Brunswick, NJ: Rutgers University Press.

Chapter 5

Female genital cutting

Moving forward on abolition?

Ellen Gruenbaum

Original material prepared for the 7th edition.

The international movement to abolish female genital cutting practices (known also as FGM/C or FGM) continues to accelerate, with demonstrable success. The governments of most African countries have passed laws to outlaw FGM/C and sponsored various educational programs to encourage people to discontinue the practices. But more significantly, there is evidence of actual change. Comparative statistics drawn from the Demographic and Health Surveys and Multiple Indicator Cluster Surveys show varying degrees of reduction in prevalence in all the 29 countries in Africa where the practices have been common (UNICEF 2013). Both DHS and MICS are population-based sampling surveys that provided measures of the prevalence of female genital cutting (all forms combined) in women ages 15–49, at approximately five-year intervals. Although figures must be interpreted cautiously, due to the reliance on self-report, nevertheless, it is the case that, for each country, the most recent iteration of the survey shows lower prevalence among women aged 15–49 than the previous iteration, demonstrating widespread decline, but at different rates for each country. Encouraging patterns are evident when the numbers are further disaggregated to compare two age cohorts for each country: in the UNICEF Statistical Overview, Figure 8.7 shows that in all 29 countries, prevalence rates reported by young women aged 15–19 are lower – and, in many cases, dramatically so – than reported by women in the cohort ages 45–49 (2013: 101). Keeping in mind that the older cohort's prevalence is due to circumcisions performed about 40–45 years before the survey while the younger cohort's would be circumcisions performed 10–15 years prior to the survey, the difference between the two would suggest a direction and rate of change over a 30-year interval. The country with the highest rate for the older cohort was Somalia, at 99 percent, and their 15- to 19-year-old daughters and granddaughters reported only a small prevalence decline, to 97 percent. While several other countries also showed only small declines, many had considerably larger declines. For example, Liberia went from 85 percent in the older cohort to 44 percent in the younger, Central African Republic from 34 to 18 percent, and Kenya from 49 to 15 percent. The overall pattern suggests that countries or regions with very high rates – where social expectations are presumably quite entrenched – are slower to change than where rates are already lower, and that once well-initiated, change can accelerate.

DOI: 10.4324/9781003398349-6

In this chapter, I make use of my own ethnographic research on how change is happening in Sudan (1974–1979, 1989, 1992, 2004, 2008, 2013, 2015, 2016), as well as my experiences consulting with international organizations and following the trends internationally, to argue for creative, positive, and multifaceted approaches. The theoretical model currently used in international organizations working to promote such change emphasizes socially reinforced norms and how norms can be shifted through community coordination, rather than individual decision-making, based on dissemination of health knowledge. In previous decades, the change efforts offered messages emphasizing fear of medical complications, which proved to be insufficiently persuasive to the populations where female genital cutting was valued culturally as a marker of virginity, honor, and cleanliness, and highly supported by social convention. When that health-risk approach did not result in widespread change, a supplementary human rights argument was introduced. The implementation of international human rights agreements also persuaded governments to enact laws against female circumcision, and at the same time, community-based education approaches were infused with the human rights message. Today, there is an exciting, new initiative utilizing positive messages and social marketing. Before examining how these change efforts have worked, we should be clear that there is quite a range of types of FGC and reasons for female genital modifications.

Terminologies and types

Cutting and the removal of tissues of genitalia of young girls and women are done to conform to social expectations in communities of many different ethnicities and religions. Although the term "female genital mutilation," or FGM, has been widely used to describe various forms of female circumcision, adding "cutting" as an alternative term has produced the label FGM/C. This is a way for reformers to reflect the removal of healthy tissues or organs ("mutilation") without invoking the connotation of intentional harm – the parents are intending just to do "cutting" (circumcision), with the usual intention to achieve an honorable purification based on traditional rituals and beliefs or perform a rite of passage to womanhood, membership in a women's society, or a status of marriageability. "Female circumcision" is still commonly used, but many activists and reformers prefer that it be abandoned so as to avoid association with the ritual removal of the foreskin in males. Using "female genital cutting," or "FGC," avoids disparaging the practitioners yet does not minimize the seriousness of the issue, but FGM/C works too. Whatever term is used, there are, in fact, many variations in what parts are cut, what it means to those who practice it, and what strategies might be most effective to encourage abandonment.

The form varies not only from one sociocultural context to another but even within a single village where different ethnic groups do different types of cutting, and there can be great variation in severity. Forms vary between families, too, with some preferring their ethnic group's traditional forms while other families seek less-harmful forms. Individual practitioners' techniques result in varying amounts of tissue taken and various levels of hygiene. Professional associations of medical doctors in the affected countries generally discourage practicing any form of FGC, and yet it is known to be practiced by many health personnel who believe they are protecting clients from the harm that might befall them at the hands of less-skilled practitioners. In some cultural contexts, it is very young children who are cut, including infants or toddlers (Toubia 1993, 1994; Jennings 1995:

48; Abdal Rahman 1997). Most commonly, it is done to young girls between the ages of 4 and 8. But in some cultural contexts (e.g., the Maasai of East Africa), cutting is delayed until a young woman is in her teens and about to be married (14–15 or even older). In West Africa, cutting has been part of the initiation into the Bondo women's secret society, with the preferred age of cutting in the teenage years, and people of various faiths (Christianity, Islam, and traditional African religions) participated. In some contexts, people associate FGC with their religious obligations (although many contemporary religious leaders argue they are ill-informed), and in Nile Valley and Northeast African countries, it has been part of the traditions of Jews, Muslims, and Christians. As you can imagine, this variation of reasons and audiences poses challenges for would-be reformers.

The World Health Organization developed a typology that technical experts use to categorize the types. People who practice female genital cutting have their own terms for different types in their many languages, of course, which may or may not fit well with the World Health Organization's four types. The following terms are commonly used.

Clitoridectomy

The World Health Organization's type I includes both the partial and total removal of the projecting tip of the clitoris, called clitoridectomy, and also the less-severe forms of the operations, such as the cutting away of part or all of the clitoral prepuce, or "hood," analogous to the foreskin removal of male circumcision. Removal of only the prepuce seems to be very rare. Since the anatomy of the clitoris includes substantial erectile tissue below the surface and extending near the vaginal wall, female genital cutting leaves most of the clitoral tissue in place, which probably accounts for the continuing sexual responsiveness reported by circumcised women.

Excision

In the World Health Organization's Type II, called "excision," the cutting goes further than clitoridectomy to include removal of the prepuce, the entire projecting tip of the clitoris, and partial or total excision of the labia minora (the smaller inner lips of the vaginal opening). In Sudan, in common parlance, there are just two basic folk terms for the types – pharaonic circumcision and *sunna* circumcision – the latter term suggesting it was based on the traditions of the Prophet Mohammed. While that association is disputed, nevertheless, it is common to use the " *sunna* " terminology for both clitoridectomy and excision (and perhaps even more severe gradations). Numerous other imprecise terms ("half," "sandwich," etc.) are used for in-between forms that would be included in type II.

Infibulation, reinfibulation

The most severe damage occurs with type III, or infibulation. It is the main type in Sudan, called pharaonic circumcision because of its presumed origin in the days of the pharaohs of the Nile Valley. In Egypt, where this severe infibulation is rare, it is called "Sudanese circumcision." In type III, part or all of the external genitalia – prepuce, clitoris, labia minora, and all or part of the labia majora – are removed, and the raw edges are infibulated (held together by stitching or another method of joining the two sides). When healed, infibulation leaves a smooth vulva of skin and scar tissue with a single tiny opening for urination and menstrual flow, preserved during healing by the insertion of a small object such as a piece of straw. In a variation of infibulation that is slightly less severe, the trimmed labia minora are sewn shut, but the labia majora are left alone. In either case, it is essential that a midwife be present for childbirth to make an incision in the tissue to deliver the baby. The new mother is then reinfibulated by the midwife, a practice that is repeated after each pregnancy (and by some women at intervals later in life). The new mother often asks the midwife to make the opening very small, "like a virgin," to enhance her husband's sexual pleasure. This is analogous to, although more severe than, what some North American obstetricians do: take an extra stitch, called "the husband's stitch," when doing an episiotomy, for the purpose of restoring tightness to the opening.

Other variations

Other practices that do not include tissue removal are grouped as type IV. This includes pricking, piercing, incision, stretching of the clitoris or labia, cauterization, cuts or scrapes on the genitalia, or the use of harmful or irritating substances (such as astringents for "dry sex") in the vagina. Labia stretching to pursue culturally preferred aesthetics of the body is not particularly harmful, but other variations can be painful or damaging. In Europe and North America, labia piercing or implants could be included as a type IV practice. The increasing popularity of vaginoplasty and labiaplasty, forms of elective genital cosmetic surgeries, has led to debate on whether these should be included in type IV.

Harmful effects

The harmful effects of these forms differ, but any form of cutting – from clitoridectomy to infibulation – creates risks for the girls at the time of cutting. Medical reports document cases of excess bleeding (hemorrhage), infections, blood poisoning (septicemia), retention of urine, or shock. Such complications can be life-threatening. Later on, the infibulated state sometimes results in retention of menses (if the vagina is blocked by scar tissue), difficulty in urination (if there is excess scar tissue around or over the urethra), and a high incidence of urinary tract and chronic pelvic infections. At first intercourse, the extremely small size of the opening created by infibulation presents a barrier that can make first sexual intercourse very difficult or impossible. Often, the scar tissue around the opening must be painfully ruptured or is cut by the husband, a midwife, or a doctor. During childbirth, the inelastic scar tissue of infibulation must be cut by the birth attendant at the right time so labor will not be obstructed. Not only is obstructed labor dangerous to the baby, but also the mother's internal tissues can be damaged, creating a fistula (opening in the tissue separating the vagina from the urinary bladder), which can result in an embarrassing condition with constantly leaking urine (Shandall 1967; Toubia 1994; Shell-Duncan and Hernlund 2000b: 14–18; Gruenbaum 2001).

The psychological effects are less well understood and clearly vary with context. Where FGC is the accepted social norm, many women accept the experience as simply part of becoming a woman or a much-anticipated, proud moment. But it can also be quite traumatic in other circumstances, as survivors attest.

Damage to sexual responsiveness is often assumed to be significant, and yet there is data that suggests the frequency and extent of problems vary greatly, with many circumcised women now reporting positive sexual experiences. Circumcised women do not necessarily lose sexual interest and can retain the ability to achieve sexual satisfaction and orgasms, even among the infibulated (Lightfoot-Klein 1989; Gruenbaum 2001, Chapter 5, "Public Policy Advisory Network on Female Genital Surgeries in Africa," 2012). Sexual responsiveness could be affected differently, depending on which tissues are cut and how they heal or scar, whether the surrounding or underlying tissues retain sensitivity, whether there is severe infibulation, and of course, whether the emotional attachment of the partners is strong and the relationship loving and supportive. Some midwives have been careful to avoid cutting too much of the sensitive tissue of the clitoris tip, hoping to preserve sensitivity but still make the result look like an infibulation by joining the labia across the opening. Since the erectile tissue of the clitoris is so extensive, with the unexposed (and, therefore, undamaged) part extending to areas stimulated during vaginal intercourse, the removal of the tip alone, while certainly unnecessary and also undesirable from a sexual response perspective, does not preclude a satisfying sex life. It is therefore erroneous to assume that all women who have been cut have lost their sexual responsiveness. Similarly, with so many different types of practices, there is great variation in the health consequences for women, depending on the circumstances.

But why?

Indeed, the world wonders how loving parents can allow their daughters to be held down and cut, usually causing fear, pain, and possible major damage to health and physical functions, immediate or long-term. It seems incongruous and shocking to imagine a 6-year-old girl enduring such pain and indignity, particularly at the hands of those she trusts.

Yet at least 200 million girls and women worldwide are living with FGC's lifelong effects, and the practices continue putting millions more girls at risk. While the practices are most known in 28 countries in Africa, they are also common in Indonesia, South Asia, and elsewhere, spread by immigration or due to adoption of genital cutting by those who believe it to be part of their religion. Why do women continue to arrange for these practices to be done to their daughters?

Is it the fault of any particular religion, as many in the US general public assume? No. The practices are found in many countries and among people of widely different ethnic groups and religions, including Judaism, Christianity, Islam, and traditional African religions. Yet religious communities have a role to play, since people who follow circumcision traditions often do associate the practices with their own religious beliefs, and religious leaders have a vital role in abolition efforts. Religious leaders who themselves support the practices create a particularly difficult situation, both because of their reluctance to support abolition and because the global community is apt to blame FGC on religion, fostering prejudice.

In Islamic contexts, for example, although many learned religious scholars have declared that infibulation has no place in Islam and others say that no form whatsoever should be permitted, a few teachers consider female circumcision as an "ennobling" act that is very proper for Muslims, so long as they do not go beyond clitoridectomy, which they call "*sunna* circumcision." Since the Arabic word "*sunna*" means "tradition" and usually connotes the traditions of the Prophet Mohammed, that is, those things that he did or advocated during his lifetime (570–622 CE), handed down through oral tradition and the writings known as the *Hadith*. Muslims believe the Holy Qur'an to be God's direct revelation and the first source of guidance for righteous living. The Qur'an is silent on female circumcision. But Muslims also respect the sayings and actions attributed to the Prophet Mohammed as a secondary source of guidance. Although disputes about which stories and quotations offer the most reliable versions of the Prophet's advice and how the sayings and stories should be interpreted, many Muslims have concluded that the Prophet Mohammed's words on the subject – "Reduce but do not destroy" – mean that there is no requirement to circumcise, but the least severe cutting is permissible. Others believe the Prophet meant to advocate cutting, making it either an obligation or at least a blessing to do it. Others believe Muslims should avoid female circumcision completely since it is not mentioned in the Qur'an. Those who use the term *sunna*, then, imply that it is expected of Muslims, and while the term may help convince Muslims to give up infibulation, it has reinforced their continuing clitoridectomy. This topic generates ongoing debates among Muslim religious leaders.

How about male dominance – is that the cause of this practice? Many analysts have noted that female genital cutting forms a part of the subordination of women where it is found: it is, indeed, embedded in the patriarchal structures of male domination of the lives of women and girls (Assaad 1980; El Saadawi 1980a, 1980b; Shell-Duncan and Hernlund 2000a; Gruenbaum 2001). But that is not to say that women do not have any control or influence on the decisions, types, and timing of the cutting. And that does not mean it is always men who are pushing for it. Rather, the conditions of women's lives often encourage their participation in and celebration of the cutting, their advocacy or their tolerance of the rituals, and their willingness to endure or accept the health risks.

In analysis of several case examples, including my Sudanese research, male dominance manifests itself in the unequal economic and social circumstances of women and men. In the African countries where FGC is practiced, women are economically productive (whether for the market economy or for subsistence), play vital roles in the home and family life, and hold social rights in their cultures. Still, the greater share of political and economic power often resides with men, especially older and more dominant and successful men, and women's access to economic resources is mediated by men. In Islamic law, Muslim women are entitled to own and manage property, but the inheritance rules favor men – a daughter receives half the share of a son – and wives inherit only a portion of a husband's property. In some ethnic groups, daughters are expected to relinquish their inheritance shares so that their brothers can be more secure, based on the idea that women are entitled to rely on husbands and male kin for support and should not need separate holdings. In other cultures, women may be dependent on men for access to land, livestock, foodstuffs, a share of a husband's income, and old-age support by sons. But women are vulnerable to divorce or polygyny, which might reduce their security. If economic security and socially approved reproduction are mediated by the dominant roles of men, women clearly need to conform to whatever rules the culture requires, including varying expectations for virginity, excision, or infibulation in order to have successful marriages and childbearing. Their enculturation process must prepare girls for their subordinate roles.

Globally, women's consciousness regarding their positions varies tremendously, from strong belief in the moral superiority of men, to wry acceptance of the role disparity, to powerful challenges to the status quo in favor of better futures. But in societies where social pressure is strong and the rewards of acceptance of female genital cutting are crucial – propriety, marriage, children, financial support, and old-age security – it should not be surprising that most women have been slow to pursue abandonment.

Identity is another factor. Female genital cutting often plays a role in gender identity. Some use terms like "male parts" for the clitoris and labia, saying removal of them results in a more feminine and aesthetically pleasing body. In the Nile Valley cultures of Egypt and Sudan, FGC was essential to defining feminine gender and considered an essential prerequisite to marriage.

Ethnic identity, too, can be influential, as a particular type of cutting may add to definition of a boundary between groups. Even within a single village, different ethnic groups do different types of cutting and regard each other's practices as less worthy. The Zabarma and Hausa minorities from West Africa – who settled in Sudan generations ago – have resisted adopting infibulation despite neighbors' criticism, yet some have adopted lesser forms along with other changes as part of their cultural and linguistic acculturation to the dominant Arab Sudanese culture.

Another reason (in some cultures) is to preserve virginity. In Sudan, not only is cutting expected to reduce some sexual sensitivity, thought to help girls and wives resist improper sexual relationships by taming what are thought to be overly powerful female sexual impulses, but also the infibulation is a barrier to penetration, preventing premarital pregnancy.

In short, the reasons for circumcising daughters are varied – a rite of passage, a religious belief or moral protection, an aesthetic preference, an identity preference, cleanliness beliefs, and so on. Further, the practices are embedded social norms, reinforced by normative expectations of others in the community, which requires wider social consensus for successful change.

The big day and the new day

Previously, I have described the work of Besaina, the midwife of Abdal Galil, Sudan, and the festive neighborhood and kin group celebrations associated with the circumcisions of young girls and boys, starting with my earliest fieldwork in Sudan in the 1970s. I followed Besaina's changing ideas and practices and what she and her community were exposed to during my field visits between the 1970s and 2016. Over that time, she moved from routinely doing the most severe and thorough type III infibulations in the 1970s to type I – with parental influence on how much to cut – in the early 2000s. She was influenced by specific life circumstances and personal experiences, some of the health information messages, and her growing interest in the opinions of religious leaders. She was only indirectly aware of the ideas and strategies promoted by the United Nations Children's Fund (UNICEF), the Sudan National Committee against Harmful Traditional Practices (SNCTP, an Inter-African Committee affiliate), the Babikr Bedri Scientific Association for Women Studies (at Ahfad University for Women), or the governmental policies. Yet by the time of our conversations together in 2015 and 2016, Besaina has completely discontinued all forms of FGC and become a committed advocate of abolition.

The idea that "human rights" might be an international imposition and should not be heeded unless these rights coincide with Islamic teachings has clearly engaged the urban intellectuals and is a key element of the human rights discourse in Sudan and elsewhere, something often overlooked internationally. But for Besaina, it was the religious opinions that mattered more in any case.

Although the ruling party and its Islamist commitment drive the whole government in Sudan in a strongly Islamist direction, the government has not issued religious pronouncements against FGC on its own even, since religious leadership in the country is not centralized. However, the various religious shaykhs who have strong loyalties from their followers play important roles in swaying not only the opinions and practices of their followers but also the political trends in the country. Thus, any efforts to enact laws that prohibit all forms of female genital cutting as well as support for movements to encourage not cutting must take these key figures into account. This is precisely what several human rights–oriented organizations have done: they respectfully courted the influence of major shaykhs. The result has been that several have written tracts, issued opinions, encouraged their followers, and even become public "ambassadors" of efforts to end FGC.

So what's being done about female genital cutting?

As you might expect, many outsiders who learn about female genital cutting practices respond with outrage against the practices. Outsiders often have evoked horrible stereotypes of malicious intent, condemning the people who practice such genital cutting of girls as intending to "torture" females or "deprive women of their sexuality."

Local reformers sometimes engage in similar strongly worded condemnations in international discourse. But grassroots change agents realize that inflammatory rhetoric and "preaching" alone are not likely to change strongly held values and traditions: voluntary abandonment will take more. Some Kenyan communities have successfully introduced alternate rituals that contribute to the social goals, for example, a rite of passage for maturing girls that substitutes for a traditional ritual of circumcision, but without the physical harm of cutting. Meanwhile, a large number of countries are also pursuing legal reforms and policy changes to criminalize or otherwise discourage the cutting of under-age girls. (See Rahman and Toubia 2000 for an international comparison of laws and policies on female genital cutting.)

Fundamental to changing social practices is better understanding what it means for people in the context where practiced, not only what they consciously think, but also how it impacts social relations in unspoken ways. Theoretical work and social sciences research offer important insights into why people have resisted change and why some are now pursuing change. Social scientists and public health researchers have continued to develop such knowledge to improve the understanding of people's reasons for genital cutting without condemning the people who have followed their traditional practices (El Dareer 1982; Gruenbaum 1982, 1996, 2001; Cloudsley 1983; Obermeyer 2003). Recognizing the value of this approach, some international organizations have both toned down their formerly more judgmental rhetoric (for example, using "female genital mutilation/cutting" or "cutting" instead of always "female genital mutilation") and explicitly recognized the need to engage the affected communities as partners in deciding how to move forward (as an example, see *The Saleema Communication Initiative*, National Council for Child Welfare, Sudan, 2014, a collaboratively produced manual with UNICEF Sudan).

In the Sudanese villages I studied, female genital cutting still persists, but change is in progress. In one village in northern Sudan where I lived for two weeks in 2016, no challenges to the norm of FGC with infibulation were in evidence – infibulation was clearly still the widely supported social norm. In contrast, in the Gezira area in central Sudan, over the past 30 years, female circumcision has made a major transition as awareness grew and opinions shifted. Already in the 1970s, a few families quietly arranged to have their daughters be cut less severely outside the village, moving from severe infibulation to preserving more of the tissue and not closing the opening as much. Others began to go further, dropping infibulation and doing only type II or type I, resisting the social pressure to conform. Eventually – by the 1990s – all the Arabic-speaking Sudanese of that community had shifted to the modified type as the accepted norm, and some were questioning why they needed to do even that. Today, the transition to non-circumcision for the young girls is fully embraced in that community, with no circumcisions having occurred after 2009. As this new cohort of fully uncircumcised girls reaches the age of marriage, further shifts in norms about marriageability can be anticipated there.

Besaina, the midwife of that community whom I have interacted with and interviewed repeatedly between 1977 and 2016, traces her own transition to embracing "saleema" as the norm to many factors. Although she herself transitioned to more minimal surgeries in the 1990s, her final action to stop entirely was facilitated by the involvement of the state Ministry of Health in summoning all the rural midwives for a training session. There, in addition to medical and religious information against FGC, they were asked to take an oath on the Holy Qur'an never to circumcise again. She did, and that became common knowledge in the community. The last several circumcisions done among local families (in 2009) involved a midwife from another community who came secretly to do private circumcisions. But when that was discovered, the medical assistant at the local health center "chased her out," I was told, and threatened that if she ever set foot in Abdal Galil again, he would report her to the state Ministry of Health and her right to practice would be revoked!

Accelerating change

Successful social change requires widespread support, not merely written laws and policies. How will that support be won? Reformers need to endeavor to fully understand people's reasons. As Gerry Mackie has noted, "[t]he followers of mutilation are good people who love their children; any campaign that insinuates otherwise is doomed to provoke defensive reaction" (Mackie 1996: 1,015).

But remaining detached and uninvolved with this serious problem tests the ethical limits of "cultural relativism" (the respect that anthropologists use to try to understand each culture in its own terms rather than to judge it ethnocentrically by the values of another culture). The World Health Organization, the United Nations Children's Fund (UNICEF), and the United Nations Population Fund issued a joint statement in 1996:

> It is unacceptable that the international community remain passive in the name of a distorted vision of multiculturalism. Human behaviours and cultural values, however senseless or destructive they may appear from the personal and cultural standpoint of others, have meaning and fulfill a function for those who practise them. However, culture is not static but it is in constant flux, adapting and reforming. People will change their behaviour when they understand the hazards and indignity of harmful practices and when they realize that it is possible to give up harmful practices without giving up meaningful aspects of their culture.

Both elements are necessary to a successful change effort aimed at a cultural practice: a deep understanding of people's reasons and motivations for keeping a practice, yet recognition of the flexibility of culture. People have demonstrated many times that cultures can adapt and people can make changes when convinced of the need without losing cultural identity and meaning. Ultimately, it is up to them to decide when the time is ripe, but can efforts within a cultural group and efforts from outside accelerate the process?

Obstacles to change: risk of *not* cutting

The social conditions that act as barriers to parents taking the risk of leaving their daughters uncircumcised help explain resistance to change (Gruenbaum 1996). No matter how clear the public health education message on the hazards of cutting, parents know that it *is* necessary if it is the prerequisite for their daughter's marriageability and long-term social and financial security. Even when the religious authorities speak against the practices and medical risks are known, these may not be sufficient reasons for parents to risk their daughters' marriageability and long-term security.

To counteract the social risks, policymakers and change agents are working to improve educational opportunities. This allows young women and their families to delay marriage to pursue education and careers, secure in the knowledge that although marriage is desirable, failure to marry or loss of spouse will not necessarily result in penury and dependence on male relatives. The teachers, professors, public health workers, students, and other activists now working on reform are, as a result of their awareness, literacy, and cosmopolitan outlook, better able to confidently state that female circumcision can be left behind, that it is both harmful to health and not Islamic. Such women are confidently deciding against the circumcision of daughters and are able to resist social pressures from the older generations while providing their daughters with the educational opportunities needed to be self-reliant. A social movement is in progress.

But even educated and confident women want their daughters to marry, and they cannot be certain their uncircumcised daughters will be marriageable. If the young men in the community remain committed to marrying infibulated brides, a daughter's education may preserve her from poverty, but it will not assure her of marriage and children. The risk is lessened if there are social and familial ties to progressive families where men prefer *sunna* or no circumcision.

But as this cultural debate unfolds (Gruenbaum 1996), it is encouraging that some young men are stating preferences for uninfibulated brides. One educated young man I knew in Khartoum told me he had insisted that the family not infibulate his sister, and he swore he would not marry an infibulated woman, even if she were a cousin. But will he or others like him actually refuse to marry a cousin the family expects him to marry? Or would he refuse to marry the young woman who has caught his eye simply because she is infibulated? And can young men effectively prevent their sisters' circumcisions? How do families cope with the risk that there may not be men like this for their daughters to marry?

Risk avoidance remains the most significant factor to explaining why otherwise well-informed families cling to female genital cutting practices. Gerry Mackie offered a provocative exploration of the risks involved in such social changes by comparing efforts to end infibulation and excision in Africa with the process of ending the painful, crippling foot-binding of girls (i.e., tightly binding their small feet so they would not grow) practiced in China for centuries. Foot-binding, which lasted until the early twentieth century, was also related to making daughters marriageable (Mackie 1996).

While there had been efforts to change foot-binding historically, parents were afraid to be the first to change, since men sought to marry women with tiny feet only. However, once a critical mass of people was persuaded of its harm through educational campaigns, they found they could take the risk of change when, with other parents, they pledged not to let their daughters' feet be bound or let their sons marry women with bound feet. The movement led to wholesale abandonment of foot-binding in a single generation (Mackie 1996: 1001). Pledge groups do function in African societies for various purposes, so now that there is growing awareness of the risks of female genital cutting, perhaps people will develop this pledge idea for female genital cutting as well.

Thus, despite the spread of female genital cutting and its tenacity, there is no reason to conclude that it cannot change rapidly in the coming years, when people have learned enough about the issue and when they believe the risks of not doing it are not too high. The conditions are ripe for change in infibulation and excision practices in Africa. The international activism, the efforts at culturally appropriate approaches, and the emergence of, and a degree of support for, indigenous leaders of the movement make this an excellent time, if the additional resources can be mobilized, for rapid change to occur. Indeed, the World Health Organization, UNICEF, and the United Nations Population Fund have announced a joint plan to "significantly curb female genital mutilation over the next decade and completely eliminate the practice within three generations" (Reaves 1997).

Mobilizing the Islamic religious arguments against infibulation – that is, claiming only *sunna* is permitted for Muslims – often results in people favoring *sunna*, allowing them to continue to reject total abandonment of all forms. Reformers debate the wisdom of this: although abandoning infibulation constitutes a definite improvement in the health of women and girls, what public health officials have often advocated as "harm reduction," it might result in even stronger belief in the Islamic rightness of the remaining form, clitoridectomy, which might delay the demise of *all* forms.

Positive approaches: alternative rites and social marketing

Even where circumcisions continue in Sudan, the celebration of it has lessened. Cutting is beginning to lose its symbolic power. In Kenya, reformers utilized the positive symbolic power of initiation rituals in a new way when they introduced "Circumcision through Words" (*Ntanira na Mugambo*). Groups of families participated in bringing together their appropriate-aged daughters to spend a week of seclusion learning their traditions concerning women's roles as adults and as future parents. The Kenyan national women's group Maende-leo ya Wanawake Organization worked with international collaborators to develop this program to include self-esteem and dealing with peer pressure, along with traditional values, as well as messages on personal health and hygiene, reproductive issues, and communications skills. At the end of the week of seclusion, a community celebration of feasting, singing, and dancing affirmed the girls' transition to their new status. In this way, the valued rite of passage was preserved while the cutting was not only not done but the initiates were also given a tool to be proud of the change and perhaps to help promote it. Such approaches recognize that female circumcision has deep cultural significance, and if that significance can be preserved while the actual cutting is discontinued, there is strong hope that change can be rapid.

In 2004, UNICEF Sudan decided to experiment with exploring the cultural significance of FGC and trying to develop programming that would affirm the positives while discouraging the cutting. The only words for girls who were not yet cut were negative: "not circumcised" or, worse, "ghalfa" (roughly meaning "slut"), which was recognized as a problem. Many of the health education posters and other tools featured ugly images of what struck me as being the "evil midwife" and razor blades along with a terrified girl. But in health communication, provoking fear is not enough to get people to change behavior. They must also see how they can do something that will be effective. So in 2006, Sudanese activists with UNICEF sponsorship convened a small conference of artists, scholars, poets, religious leaders, activists, and media people in Sudan to review and critique the imagery and messages of the past and to develop a new term for the uncircumcised girl. They came up with "saleema," a name and a word that means healthy and whole.

From this idea, a hugely promising social marketing initiative has been developed, featuring images of healthy girls and loving parents; a colorful design motif with swirling oranges and yellows; television spots; celebrity "saleema ambassadors" as spokespeople, including singers and actors, sports figures, and religious leaders; songs; a website (Saleema Initiative to Stop FGM/C in Sudan, saleema.net); and communication strategies. Rhyming couplets are a popular form of folklore in Sudan, so a memorable Arabic phrase was developed for use in the initiative: "Every girl is born saleema. Let her grow up saleema." The Saleema Initiative has been able to coordinate well with the efforts to engage with social norms and encouragement to people to make pledges of support for change.

More research will be needed to know if this is a successful approach. The initiative was introduced initially in a limited number of locations and, in 2013, expanded to more neighborhoods in Khartoum state. But the spots on national television and the wider dissemination of the imagery and marketing tools seem to have resulted in a somewhat self-perpetuating cultural message. In the Gezira community of Abdal Galil where the midwife Besaina lives and works, I found that despite there having been no organized programs to reach this area, by February 2015, the term "saleema" for an uncircumcised girls was well established linguistically. When Besaina smiled and told me she and the others now want all the girls to be "saleema, saleema," it was obvious she had come full circle. And so had her community.

Taking a stance?

As an anthropologist, I believe my first commitment is to research and promote understanding, but as a humanist, I also want to engage in fostering improvements of the human condition. Female genital cutting practices vary so much that they clearly are not equally harmful. But because they are performed on non-consenting children, the human rights stance of total opposition to all forms, based on a right to bodily integrity, is ultimately hard to refute. Yet that principle would also prohibit male infant circumcision and ear piercing of babies and toddlers, perhaps even extraction of a 12-year-old's teeth for orthodontia. At the same time, my cultural relativism leads me to respect the values people choose to live by, recognizing that people themselves will make their future and choose when and how to change. Outsiders can help most effectively by offering understanding, respect, and support for grassroots and international change efforts, not only on female genital cutting, but also on the *many* issues faced by the women and children of poor countries.

Thus, outsiders must remember that only the practitioners themselves are in a position to abandon female genital cutting. The global community should engender respect and understanding for dialogue to take place, starting from a respectful understanding on which to build the dialogue, or be allies in the change agendas that are already being pursued. Culture, as anthropologists recognize, is always contested and changing. Change is inevitable, and the world community should offer practitioners of female genital cutting not racist or ethnocentric condemnation but attention and collaboration. The international community can collaborate to ameliorate the underlying conditions that perpetuate the practices. Women and children living in poverty or marginal economic circumstances without clean water, decent housing, adequate food resources, educational opportunities, job opportunities, electricity, or immunizations and basic health services may have social change agendas for their lives that do not place abolition of female genital cutting as their top priority.

The international community – students, policymakers, and the general public interested in female genital cutting – would do well to understand African women's contexts, perspectives, and priorities to foster more effective collaborations for the future. Change efforts benefit from deep thinkers with passionate hearts, caring words, and images of a positive future.

Discussion questions

1. Why does the author argue that female genital cutting is not the result of any particular religion, despite the fact that people often associate it with their religion?
2. How is FGC related to women's subordination in patriarchal societies?
3. What efforts have been taken to change the practice of FGC in the past and more recently, and what are the respective roles of local activists, the state, and international organizations in these efforts?
4. How does FGC contribute to debates about cultural relativism and moral relativism?

References

Abdal Rahman, Awatif. 1997. "Member of the Sudan National Committee on Harmful Traditional Practices, Quoted in Reuter Report." *Sudan Tackles 'Silent Issue' of Female Circumcision*, February 20.

Assaad, Marie Bassili. 1980. "Female Circumcision in Egypt: Social Implications, Current Research, and Prospects for Change." *Studies in Family Planning* 11(1): 3–16.

Cloudsley, Anne. 1983. *Women of Omdurman: Life, Love, and the Cult of Virginity*. London: Ethnographia.

El Dareer, Asma. 1982. *Woman, Why Do You Weep? Circumcision and Its Consequences*. London: Zed Press.

El Saadawi, Nawal. 1980a. "Creative Women in Changing Societies: A Personal Reflection." *Race and Class* 22(2): 159–182.

El Saadawi, Nawal. 1980b. *The Hidden Face of Eve: Women in the Arab World*. London: Zed Press.

Gruenbaum, Ellen. 1982. "The Movement against Clitoridectomy and Infibulation in Sudan." *Medical Anthropology Newsletter* 13(2): 4–12. (Reissued in 1997 in *Gender in Cross-Cultural Perspective*, 2nd ed., eds. Caroline Brettell and Carolyn Sargent, 441–453. Upper Saddle River, NJ: Prentice Hall).

Gruenbaum, Ellen. 1996. "The Cultural Debate Over Female Circumcision: The Sudanese Are Arguing This One Out for Themselves." *Medical Anthropology Quarterly* 10(4): 455–475.

Gruenbaum, Ellen. 2001. *The Female Circumcision Controversy: An Anthropological Perspective*. Philadelphia: University of Pennsylvania Press.

Jennings, Anne. 1995. *The Nubians of West Aswan: Village Women in the Midst of Change*. Boulder, CO: Lynne Rienner.

Lightfoot-Klein, Hanny. 1989. *Prisoners of Ritual: An Odyssey into Female Genital Circumcision in Africa*. Binghamton, NY: Harrington Park Press.

Mackie, Gerry. 1996. "Ending Footbinding and Infibulation." *American Sociological Review* 61: 991–1017.

National Council for Child Welfare, Sudan (with UNICEF Support). 2014. *The Saleema Communication Initiative*. www.saleema.net.

Obermeyer, Carla Maklouf. 2003. "The Health Consequences of Female Circumcision: Science, Advocacy, and Standards of Evidence." *Medical Anthropology Quarterly* 17(3): 394–412.

Public Policy Advisory Network on Female Genital Surgeries in Africa. 2012. "Seven Things to Know about Female Genital Surgeries in Africa." *Hastings Center Report* 42(6): 19–27.

Rahman, Anika, and Nahid Toubia. 2000. *Female Genital Mutilation: A Guide to Worldwide Laws and Policies*. London: Zed Press.

Reaves, Malik Stan. 1997. "Alternative Rite to Female Circumcision Spreading in Kenya." *Africa News Service*, (November.).

Shandall, Ahmed Abu El Futuh. 1967. "Circumcision and Infibulation of Females." *Sudan Medical Journal* 5(4): 178–212.

Shell-Duncan, Bettina, and Ylva Hernlund, eds. 2000a. *Female "Circumcision" in Africa: Culture, Controversy, and Change*. Boulder, CO: Lynne Rienner.

Shell-Duncan, Bettina, and Ylva Hernlund. 2000b. "Female 'Circumcision' in Africa: Dimensions of the Practice and Debates." In *Female "Circumcision" in Africa: Culture, Controversy, and Change*, eds. Bettina Shell-Duncan and Ylva Hernlund, 1–40. Boulder, CO: Lynne Rienner.

Toubia, Nahid. 1993. *Female Genital Mutilation: A Call for Global Action*. New York: Women, Ink.

Toubia, Nahid. 1994. "Female Circumcision as a Public Health Issue." *New England Journal of Medicine*, September 15 331(11): 712–716.

United Nations Children's Fund (UNICEF). 2013. *Female Genital Mutilation/Cutting: A Statistical Overview and Exploration of the Dynamics of Change*, July. New York: UNICEF.

World Health Organization. 1996. *Female Genital Mutilation: A Joint WHO/UNICEF/UNFPA Statement*. Geneva: World Health Organization. www.unfpa.org/swp/1997/box16.htm.

Chapter 6

Surgical transformations in the pursuit of gender

Lauren E. Gulbas

Original to a previous edition of this text. Courtesy of Lauren E. Gulbas.

In May 2005, I found myself sitting in my neighbor Paola's living room, talking with her about the lengths that she was willing to go to in order to replace her breast implants.[1] I was living in Caracas at that time, starting a research project on the cosmetic surgery industry in Venezuela. My work focused on exploring the high rates of cosmetic surgery in a place with marked economic inequality and with rates of illness and death that are comparable with those of other developing nations. In a city whose residents had to confront high poverty, food shortages, and spiraling rates of violence and homicide as a part of everyday life, I was surprised by Paola's strong preoccupation with finding a way to undergo an aesthetic procedure, but she described her predicament – and her solution to it – as a common one. She did not have the money to purchase new implants but explained, "I am not going to buy new school uniforms for my children, and this way I can save up some more money. You know, this is how women are in Venezuela. There are women who do not feed their kids so that they can have cosmetic surgery. It is just the way things are here."

Throughout my anthropological fieldwork in Caracas between 2005 and 2007, I found that numerous individuals echoed sentiments similar to those of Paola. These anecdotes convey a powerful cultural stereotype about Venezuelan women: in their pursuit of "feminine" bodies, they prioritize cosmetic surgery as an important, if not necessary, practice, sometimes taking drastic measures to have their bodies surgically modified. Rationing food to save money, risking surgery with a cheap back-alley quack, or electing to have surgery without general anesthesia to avoid a long waiting list in public hospitals, women – and, to a more limited extent, men – hazard their bodies and lives to have cosmetic surgery. But why?

This chapter endeavors to uncover some of the reasons women and men allocate resources in particular ways to have cosmetic surgery, specifically cosmetic breast surgery.[2] Although individuals offer many different explanations for their behavior, I argue that the construction of gendered personhood figures prominently. This chapter will begin with an exploration of the body-as-self paradigm, which encourages individuals to formulate an understanding of self, or the subjective interpretation of one's personhood (Meyer 1987), as based on appearance. I suggest that the body-as-self paradigm enables

DOI: 10.4324/9781003398349-7

cosmetic surgeons to justify the importance of aesthetic procedures to their patients by laying claim to the psychological benefits of surgery. Then, I will contextualize the cosmetic surgery industry in Venezuela, both locally and historically. From this discussion, I will illustrate how cosmetic breast surgery is interpreted by patients as the only solution for correcting an ambiguously gendered body, allowing men and women to attain a normalized masculine or feminine self.

Selling the body-as-self

Throughout history, the cultivation of appearance has been a widespread practice in many societies. From makeup to corsets and cosmetic surgery, individuals use the body as a site for modification, actively crafting it to fit personal and social ideals of beauty. The practices individuals engage in to alter the body and its appearance vary across time and space, pointing to the importance of examining bodily practices as a way to uncover cultural meaning (Scheper-Hughes and Lock 1987).

Over the past decades, the meaning and purpose of bodywork has changed dramatically. Once a site to realize cultural ideals for beauty, the body has now become a vehicle through which individuals display the self (Becker 1994; Shilling 1993). This body-as-self paradigm both shapes and is shaped by an increasingly consumer-oriented society. Appearance-driven consumer markets promote the purchase of specific identities by encouraging individuals to buy products intended to transform the body (Mascia-Lees 2010). The cultivation of appearance requires that individuals become embedded within capitalist markets aimed at the manufacture and sale of face and hair products, body lotions, dieting supplements, and fashion (Malson 1998).

Consumption of these products is motivated by a global consumer industry that uses images of bodies to suggest how a given product enhances physical appearance. These images are constructed for a specific purpose: to enable an individual to develop a sense of what counts as "looking good" (Fraser and Greco 2005). In these images, the display of bodies – bodies that are retouched, airbrushed, and unlikely to exist in a natural state – creates an ideal against which individuals measure themselves and are measured by others (Rubin et al. 2003). The ability to lock people into these consumer markets is predicated on an ideological collapse of the outer body and inner self – if one *looks* good, then one *feels* good (Featherstone 1991).

Cosmetic surgery has capitalized on this perceived link between looking good and feeling good. In part, this reflects cosmetic surgery's relation to commercialism. It has, after all, turned the process of "looking good" into a multibillion-dollar industry. Yet for cosmetic surgery to be regarded as a legitimate medical practice, the field has had to demonstrate that modifying physical appearance can lead to improvements in overall patient health. Surgeons justify the practice of invasive surgery for aesthetic reasons by asserting the importance of the body-as-self paradigm: cosmetic surgery can improve a patient's image of self, promoting an enhanced sense of emotional and psychological well-being (Sullivan 2004).

In Venezuela, discourses of selfhood and psychological healing resonate deeply with cosmetic surgeons. The Venezuelan Society of Plastic Surgery describes *cosmetic surgery* as "absolutely necessary to maintain mental equilibrium and improve one's self-esteem" (Engel 2005: 3). The eager promotion of the body-as-self paradigm among Venezuelan surgeons provides a unique opportunity to explore the intersections of body, selfhood, and gender. As I will demonstrate later, cosmetic surgery has been central to the construction of contemporary beauty standards in Venezuela so that the industry contributes to the very problems in self-esteem that it claims to alleviate. This has not always been the case, and the local practice of cosmetic surgery in Venezuela can best be understood by considering the history of a growing symbiosis between cosmetic surgery and the ultimate symbol of female beauty: the beauty pageant contestant.

The evolution of an ideal: plastic Misses and cosmetic surgery in Venezuela

The Miss Venezuela pageant and the national cosmetic surgery industry share a parallel yet inexorably linked history. Both were established in the 1950s, in Venezuela's last years as a country dominated by more than a century of dictatorial regimes. The government of General Marcos Pérez Jiménez sought to build a modern nation and demonstrate to the developed world that Venezuela was its civilized equal (Coronil 1997). The Miss Venezuela pageant, initiated in 1952, operated as a symbol of this modernizing discourse. Venezuela would export the world's most beautiful women, evidence of its fulfillment of the qualities of an educated, cultured, and enlightened nation (Raidi 2005).

At the same time the pageant was beginning to export Venezuelan beauty, surgeons were importing Western aesthetic standards and medical techniques into an incipient professional cosmetic surgery industry. In 1956, Venezuela's first plastic surgery department was established, and the Venezuelan Society for Plastic and Reconstructive Surgery was founded later that year (García de Moral and Subero 2002). Even with these developments, physicians continued to travel to Europe and the United States, returning to their native country after completing their education to share the knowledge they gained in the hopes of modernizing Venezuelan medicine (Cisneros 1978).

The field of cosmetic surgery grew quickly after Venezuela became a democratic nation in 1958. No longer constrained by the educational mandates of dictatorial regimes, numerous public hospitals established residency programs in the 1960s. Cosmetic surgeons could be trained in Venezuela for the first time, but this medical instruction continued to be shaped by the global medical practices of Europe and North America, as Venezuelan medical schools continued to import English medical textbooks and teaching philosophies (SVCPREM 2005).

By 1975, cosmetic surgery began to creep into the Miss Venezuela pageant, marking the first year during which Misses are known to have undergone cosmetic surgery to enhance their chances of winning the crown (Rodríguez 2005: 143). In a matter of decades, the links between the Miss Venezuela pageant and the cosmetic surgery industry became so entrenched that the Miss Venezuela Organization, already staffed with numerous cosmetic surgeons, was dubbed "the house of dolls" and "a factory for the production of Misses" (Ortega 2005: 11). By 1992, every participant in the Miss Venezuela pageant had undergone at least one cosmetic procedure, and the winner that year, Milka Chulina, was proclaimed in the newspapers as the "most reconstructed Miss" in pageant history (Rodríguez 2005: 19).

The construction of "plastic" Misses through cosmetic surgery has produced a fundamental shift in cultural ideals of beauty: tall, extremely thin, with delicately curvaceous chest–waist–hip measurements. Although the average weight for Miss Venezuela has hovered around 123 pounds since the competition's inception, the height of contestant winners has increased dramatically over time. Prior to 1980, the median height of Miss Venezuela was 5 feet 5 inches, whereas the median height of contestants over the past three decades has been about 5 feet 9 inches. This has led to a shift in body shape, from one that "was fuller with wide hips" (Rodríguez 2005: 55) to a more emaciated physique. In fact, the average body mass index, a calculation used to measure body weight to height, is below 17.5 kg/m², making a typical Miss Venezuela from recent years categorically underweight.

The extreme thinness of Miss Venezuela makes the natural accomplishment of a lean yet curvy body more difficult, if not impossible. As contestant BMI has dropped, the aesthetic expectations for pageant winners have continued to focus on a curvy form that is unlikely to occur naturally on a body that has been stripped of its fat. According to the Miss Venezuela Organization, the ideal feminine body should possess chest–waist–hip measurements that approximate 90–60–90 cm (36–24–36 in) (Rodríguez 2005). Cosmetic surgery resolves the paradox of a declared preference for curvy bodies and the documented decline in BMI: successful pageant contestants strip their body of its natural curves through diet and exercise and then turn to cosmetic surgery to resculpt a body with 90–60–90 cm measurements. In this way, the ideal feminine body portrayed within the Miss Venezuela pageant has become, quite literally, a constructed one.

The opening of access: the practice of cosmetic surgery today

Today, cosmetic surgery is pervasive in the public view. Huge billboards line Caracas's congested highways, on which cosmetic surgeons promote their myriad services. These advertisements often feature a former Miss Venezuela, suggesting that although no one is born to look like a Miss, any woman can achieve the same transformation through surgery. In magazines, banks describe credit and loan options that enable customers to finance their aesthetic procedures. The profusion of print media operates to lure potential clients into the private, shiny, modern clinics of cosmetic surgeons. Yet the ubiquity of plastic culture is not without its critics. Newspaper comic strips often play on the excessive abundance of cosmetic surgery in cultural thought. For example, a comic published in a Caracas newspaper in December 2006 featured two little girls walking to school: one girl says that she is going to ask the baby Jesus to give her breast implants for Christmas; her friend responds that she will ask for liposuction (Estampas 2006). The underlying point of this satire is clear: How much further will the desire for cosmetic surgery among many Venezuelans go?

Ironically, a dramatic restructuring of the public healthcare system in 1999 has only helped fuel the demand for cosmetic surgery. In an effort to challenge immense inequalities in the distribution of wealth, President Hugo Chávez prohibited the collection of fees for all services rendered in public institutions, including the public healthcare system (PAHO 2006). These reforms effectively made cosmetic surgery free in all public hospitals and clinics. In theory, this mandate makes access to cosmetic surgery equitable to all Venezuelans regardless of means. In practice, however, many patients are denied access to an idealized body because resources and surgeons for carrying out aesthetic procedures are in short supply. Public hospitals are often unable to meet the high demand for cosmetic surgery, and access depends on how physicians prioritize the treatment of patients, as well as the training of residents – which is essential for a national program of medical training to thrive. Problems with capacity are compounded by the crumbling infrastructure at many public hospitals. For example, one public hospital once touted as

Table 6.1 Patient consultations for cosmetic surgery, July 2006 to July 2007

Procedure	Women	Men
Cosmetic breast surgery	924	9
Liposuction	267	8
Tummy tuck	170	3
Facelift	62	7
Eye lift	220	6
Nose job	265	57
Total	1,908	90

a symbol for medical advancement is now plagued by budget deficits and deterioration of its facilities. In weighing their options for having cosmetic surgery as quickly and cheaply as possible, patients often navigate public and private facilities as they seek procedures that will bring them closer to a body that conforms to their sense of self.

The majority of individuals who make this transformative journey are women. Although the president of the Venezuelan Society for Plastic Surgery told me that men are slowly making up a greater proportion of the population surgically modifying their bodies for aesthetic reasons, my own compilation of hospital data reveals that differences between rates of cosmetic surgery between men and women are still great. Women requesting cosmetic surgery outnumber men by 22 to 1 (see Table 6.1). Clearly, cosmetic surgery is an overwhelmingly gendered practice, and this is most evident in the case of cosmetic breast surgery.[3] Whereas women's requests for consultation for breast surgery far outnumber requests for any other procedure, men's consultations for breast surgery represent less than 1 percent of all consultations. Cosmetic breast surgery, then, is perhaps the most gendered procedure that patients seek. On the surface, the explanation for this difference seems quite simple: only women have breasts, and therefore, it is only women who have breast surgery. I assert that the diverse physical forms of male bodies, and their own narratives of surgery, defy cultural assumptions that breasts are an anatomical feature belonging solely to women. An examination of both women's and men's explanations for undergoing breast surgery reveals the powerful ways in which the breast operates as a symbol of a gendered subjectivity and how cosmetic surgery allows patients to overcome a "naturally" deficient body in order to reconstruct their sense of self.

Measuring up: women, breasts, and selfhood

In private clinics, approximately 60 percent of women who consult for breast surgery request breast implants. This is not the case in public hospitals, where departments of plastic surgery have suspended consultations for breast implants because hospitals are not structurally equipped to meet patient demand. Every morning, dozens of women line up outside the waiting room, hoping to have a consultation with a cosmetic surgeon for breast implants, and every morning, almost all these women are turned away. Only a fortunate few will be accepted for a consultation, usually because a resident in the program needs training in the surgical techniques.

Breast enlargement surgery may cost anywhere from $700 to $3,000 in a private clinic. In public hospitals, the cost of surgery is free, with one caveat: patients must purchase their implants from a local pharmacy. Depending on the type of implant, a patient may pay up to $560. Women carefully weigh the overall cost of surgical procedures, yet for many, the ability to purchase "the best" shapes decisions about which surgeons and breast implants to choose. Breast enlargement has become a symbol of consumer culture in Venezuela, wherein "what you buy is a major measure of your worth" (Young 1992: 224). By purchasing a specific body through cosmetic surgery, many women feel they can change how they feel about their bodies and themselves, constructing a self that is worthy of a feminine subjectivity.

Not surprisingly, metaphors of self-worth permeate narratives of decisions to undergo breast surgery. In a consumer culture where breasts become a symbol of womanhood, many women express feeling consistently judged about the size and shape of their breasts. Most women with whom I conversed were able to recall a specific moment in time when they realized they did not like their breasts. For some, this occurred during secondary school, when they were bullied by male and female classmates for having a chest "flat like a wall." These verbal torments were interpreted as a public rejection of individual womanhood. As one woman stated, the bullying at school left her feeling inadequate. She explained that she no longer felt "comfortable, because having breasts is part of being a woman. [She] felt like [she] was missing something, that [she] was incomplete."

Among older women, the change in breast shape over time is perceived as a symbol of inevitable old age and decline. One 46-year-old woman described her sagging breasts as making her feel "impotent." She recalled a period when she was younger and had many admirers, who would call after her in the street and remark on the beauty of her youthful womanhood. "[But] now I am old," she explained, "no one tells me anything anymore." Her breasts signify powerlessness and weakness as she approaches an age where she feels she is no longer useful for sex, reproduction, or work.

For other women, it is not necessarily about attaining or recapturing womanhood but about restoring it, usually after pregnancy and childbirth. Although motherhood is perceived by many as the cornerstone of femininity, it is often this very process that makes some individuals feel they are less womanly. A subtle irony exists in that the achievement of womanhood through reproduction becomes a factor that weakens a mother's gendered selfhood. Paola's narrative provides an illustrative example in the ways that motherhood and womanhood intersect in contradictory ways.

When I first visited Caracas in May 2005, I lived in the same building as Paola. At that time, she was in her late 30s and married with two children. My landlady had told me that Paola had breast implants, and one afternoon, I decided to ask her about her cosmetic surgery experience. I asked Paola if it was true, and she said yes. Lighting a Belmont cigarette, Paola began to tell me her experience of having breast enlargement surgery:

> I got my breast implants eight years ago, after the birth of my second child. Children change your body so much, so I decided to have breast implants. My breasts were gone because I gave milk to both my children. They sucked all my breasts away! The doctor told me after the surgery that I should not move my arms. I was not supposed to do any housework or carry my children. But I was a mother. What was I going to do? I had to take care of my children. And who was going to cook dinner and clean clothes if I was not going to? My husband? No! I had to work. And one day, maybe a week after the surgery, the wounds opened up. I had to go back to the doctor to have them sewn up again. Now I have big scars.

Paola construes her femininity as being subverted by motherhood. She constructs breast-feeding as a parasitic activity: her children literally sucked away her womanhood. Paola blames her children for her lack of breasts. Breast implants provide Paola with the means to reassert a feminine subjectivity: by making her body appear to be more feminine, Paola will *become* more feminine. It is interesting to note that having surgery poses a limitation on her ability to do what she perceives as "women's work," and because she must carry out her domestic responsibilities as a mother, she experiences complications after surgery. So strong is her desire to recreate a lost womanhood that in her determination to correct the scars and replace her implants, Paola expresses a willingness to withhold resources from her children, such as new uniforms for school.

My interpretation of women's decisions to have breast surgery reveals that breasts not only operate as a symbol of womanhood but also become part of a woman's experience of herself. The perceived failure to have "normal" breasts contributes to feelings of inadequacy, incompleteness, and many times, deterioration. The field of cosmetic surgery is complicit in the production of a normalized breast to which women feel they do not measure up: breasts that are too small (hypomastia), too big (hypermastia), or not perky enough after pregnancy (postpartum atrophy) are diagnosed as disordered, contributing to women's gendered experiences in terms of failure.

Men have breasts too

Cosmetic breast surgery is primarily conceived of as something requested by and performed on women. Men are rarely considered to be a part of this discourse, but in actuality, men have breasts too. The condition of "man-breasts" is referred to as *gynecomastia*, literally meaning "women-like breasts." It is surprisingly common among most men: an estimated 40 percent of men have breasts (Carlson 1980). But where women tend to seek surgery to create or restore their breasts, accentuating them to more closely approximate a cultural and medical standard, men elect breast reduction surgery in order to remove what is considered to be a shameful femininity that is not natural to the male body.

Guillermo's narrative reflects how experiences of a deficient masculinity become intertwined with perceptions of breasts and the normal male body. I met Guillermo in February of 2007 in one of Caracas's large public hospitals. He was waiting for an appointment with a cosmetic surgeon to discuss his options for breast surgery. He arrived at the hospital with his wife, but prior to entering the examination room, he asked his wife to stay behind in the waiting room. I found this to be curious, given that most of the women that I had observed and interviewed permitted their male partners to accompany them during the consultation. When I asked Guillermo why he asked his wife to stay outside, he whispered to me that his wife had never seen him with his shirt off. Not once – not even during sex.

During Guillermo's consultation, the cosmetic surgeon, a second-year male resident, provided Guillermo with an official diagnosis of gynecomastia. He explained to Guillermo that surgery would entail suctioning the subcutaneous fat that accumulated over his pectoral muscles, which created the appearance of having small breasts. The good news that surgery could treat this condition came with bad news for Guillermo – the surgical staff would not be able to perform the surgery because the hospital operating room was closed due to a bacterial contamination. The resident mentioned a possible solution: he could perform liposuction on Guillermo using local anesthesia. Guillermo replied with an emphatic yes, and his surgery was scheduled the following week.

After his consultation, Guillermo agreed to talk with me about his decision to have the procedure. He exclaimed that the risk of pain would be worth the opportunity to have surgery. He described the immense shame that he felt about his body, which forced him to feel as if he were not "truly a man." As he explained, a man is not supposed to have breasts. To disguise his chest, he often wore loose clothing and sometimes bandaged his chest when he felt that his shirt fit tightly. Whereas clothing provided a way to hide his ambiguously gendered body, his daily performance of masculinity allowed him to publicly display his manhood. Guillermo described acting like a "real" man: being dominant and assertive in the workplace, providing a substantial income so that his wife did not have to work, and going out with his friends in the evening to drink. Each of these behaviors corresponds to stereotypical notions of the Venezuelan man, in which the ideology of machismo continues to retain significant cultural capital. Yet his public performance of masculinity was ultimately challenged by a biological body that was coded as feminine. This inhibited what he described as the most important aspect of a masculine identity: the ability to engage in heterosexual intercourse without risking further shame about his body. His breasts, which prevented him from displaying his naked body, made it difficult for him to perform as a man in the bedroom.

For the few men who elect to have breast reduction, surgery offers the potential to recraft the male body into a more culturally acceptable form (Atkinson 2006). Yet given the prevalence of gynecomastia among men and the association of breasts with femininity, why is male breast reduction surgery not more popular? In part, this may be due to the fact that cosmetic surgery continues to be regarded as distinctly feminine. The increasing visibility of cosmetic surgery in Caracas, particularly in popular media, has contributed to widespread perceptions that aesthetic procedures are the domain of women.

Moreover, participation in practices designed to enhance appearance seem to contradict the dominant gender ideology of machismo in Venezuela. The ethos of machismo stems from a fear of being indistinguishable from the feminine, and manliness becomes that which contrasts with womanliness (Chant 2003). This includes attention to appearance, communicated through the expectation that a woman should take actions to pursue an accentuated femininity. Although many Venezuelans acknowledge that, in practice, both men and women pay attention to their physical appearance, for a man to do so risks attacks on his manhood. Thus, many men may shy away from the pursuit of an appropriately gendered male body through breast cosmetic surgery.[4]

Conclusion

Patients turn to cosmetic surgery for a variety of reasons. The choice to submit one's body to the knife may be perceived as desirable or necessary, as a way to improve self-esteem, or as a vain expense. Many patients will construct the process of having surgery as a positive experience, allowing them to transform not only how they look but also how they feel about themselves. Yet this process of transformation reveals that decisions to have surgery are shaped within a specific context, wherein ideas about attractiveness and the culturally ideal body contribute to a growing consumerism of plastic bodies. The cosmetic surgery industry has been able to profit on individual desires to recraft the body according to cultural notions of what constitutes the ideal body precisely because such notions contribute to low self-esteem.

This chapter has focused predominantly on how cosmetic breast surgery is offered to, and interpreted by, patients as a way to craft a gendered self by modifying insufficiently or ambiguously gendered body attributes. While this draws attention to the myriad ways individuals actively choose cosmetic surgery to overcome situations which are not of their own making (Davis 1995), we must also be mindful of how women and men become locked into consumer ideologies that reduce selfhood to physical appearance. In a global consumer culture that dictates that only certain bodies are available for consumption, the potential to experience one's body and self in terms of deficiency is great. As it pronounces its role in sculpting gendered bodies and promoting healthy minds, cosmetic surgery simultaneously promotes gendered differences in how individuals interpret their bodies and the potential to transform them through surgery.

Discussion questions

1. How has the Miss Venezuela pageant contributed to Venezuela's symbiosis between cosmetic surgery and female beauty ideal?
2. How did the restructuring of the healthcare system fuel the demand for cosmetic surgery?
3. What is the connection between self-worth, womanhood, and breast surgery? Provide narrative examples.
4. In what ways is manhood both restored and challenged through cosmetic surgery?

Notes

1 All names of individuals have been replaced with pseudonyms.
2 This chapter is based on conversations with a number of women and men living in Caracas, Venezuela. Altogether, I interviewed 499 individuals, in addition to having a number of informal conversations with people I met during the course of my fieldwork. I spoke with cosmetic surgeons, psychologists, pageant directors, employees in beauty salons and gyms, patients with cosmetic surgery or seeking consultation for surgery, and individuals without cosmetic surgery in order to gather their perspectives. I also spent hours observing cosmetic surgeons and residents in four private clinics and two public hospitals. I watched as patients interacted with their doctors and nurses during consultations and pre- and postoperative procedures, and I observed interactions among physicians and nurses during surgery. Additionally, I gathered clinic and hospital data on the prevalence of cosmetic procedures.
3 Cosmetic breast surgery includes surgical procedures aimed at the aesthetic modification of the breast and its underlying tissue and can include the enlargement, reduction, or lifting of the breast. This excludes reconstructive procedures, such as breast reconstruction after mastectomy.
4 This contrasts with other kinds of cosmetic surgery, such as rhinoplasty. Among men who have nose jobs, the procedure is described as reconstructive even when the benefits of surgery are purely aesthetic. By emphasizing the necessity of cosmetic surgery, men recast bodywork in a way that sublimates the aesthetic focus. Thus, the male pursuit of aesthetic surgery (excluding breast cosmetic surgery) is perceived as acceptable only insofar as it recapitulates the masculine trope of machismo: it is not viewed as *macho* to change one's appearances for aesthetic reasons. Rather, the necessity of the change is articulated as a way to correct a functional defect of the physical organ.

References

Atkinson, Michael. 2006. "Masks of Masculinity: (Sur)passing Narrative and Cosmetic Surgery." In *Body/Embodiment: Symbolic Interaction and the Sociology of the Body*, eds. Dennis Waskul and Phillip Vannini, 247–261. Aldershot: Ashgate Publishing Limited.

Becker, Anne B. 1994. "Nurturing and Negligence: Working on Other's Bodies in Fiji." In *Embodiment and Experience: The Existential Ground of Culture and Self*, ed. Thomas J. Csordas, 100–115. Cambridge: Cambridge University Press.

Carlson, Harold E. 1980. "Gynecomastia." *New England Journal of Medicine* 303: 795–799.

Chant, Sylvia H. 2003. "Gender and Sexuality." In *Gender in Latin America*, eds. Sylvia H. Chant and Nikki Craski, 126–160. New Brunswick: Rutgers University Press.

Cisneros, M. Zuñiga. 1978. *Historia de la Medicina, Toma III: La Medicina de los Tiempos Modernos y de la Epoca Contemporanea*. Caracas: Ediciones Edime.

Coronil, Fernando. 1997. *The Magical State: Nature, Money, and Modernity in Venezuela*. Chicago: The University of Chicago Press.

Davis, Kathy. 1995. *Reshaping the Female Body: The Dilemma of Cosmetic Surgery*. New York: Routledge.

Engel, Andrés Maroti. 2005. "La Cirugía Plática no es una Frivolidad." *Boletín Informativo de la Sociedad Venezolana de Cirugía Plástica, Reconstructive, Estética y Maxilofacial* 4: 3–4.

Estampas. 2006. "Humor de Rayma." *Estampas*, December 17.

Featherstone, Mike. 1991. "The Body in Consumer Culture." In *The Body: Social Process and Cultural Theory*, eds. Mike Featherstone, Mike Hepworth, and Bryan S. Turner, 170–196. London: Sage Publications.

Fraser, Mariam, and Monica Greco. 2005. "Introduction." In *The Body: A Reader*, eds. Mariam Fraser and Monica Greco, 1–42. New York: Routledge.

García de Moral, Margarita, and David Yaselli Subero. 2002. "El Servicio de Cirugía Plástica del Hospital Vargas: En sus 45 Años de Aniversario." *Archivos del Hospital Vargas* 44(1–2): 88–99.

Malson, Helen. 1998. *The Thin Woman: Feminism, Post-Structuralism, and the Social Psychology of Anorexia Nervosa*. London: Routledge.

Mascia-Lees, Frances E. 2010. *Gender and Difference in a Globalizing World*. Long Grove, IL: Waveland Press, Inc.

Meyer, John W. 1987. "Self and the Life Course: Institutionalization and Its Effects." In *Institutional Structure: Constituting the State, Society, and the Individual*, eds. George M. Thomas, John W Meyer, Francisco O. Ramirez, and John Boli, 242–260. Newbury Park, CA: Sage Publications.

Ortega, Nelson Hippolyte. 2005. "Casa de Muñecas: Así Fabricaron a Las Misses." In *Misses de Venezuela: Reinas que Cautivaron a un País: Crónicas, Reportajes y Testimonios del Concurso Miss Venezuela*, ed. Albor Rodríguez, 11–13. Caracas: Los Libros de El Nacional.

Pan American Health Organization (PAHO). 2006. *Mission Barrio Adentro: The Right to Health and Social Inclusion in Venezuela*. Caracas: PAHO/Venezuela.

Raidi, Aberlardo. 2005. "Venezuela País de Mujeres Bellas." In *Misses de Venezuela: Reinas que Cautivaron a un País: Crónicas, Reportajes y Testimonios del Concurso Miss Venezuela*, ed. Labor Rodríguez, 25–26. Caracas: Los Libros de El Nacional.

Rodríguez, Albor, ed. 2005. *Misses de Venezuela: Reinas que Cautivaron a un País: Crónicas, Reportajes y Testimonios del Concurso Miss Venezuela*. Caracas: Los Libros de El Nacional.

Rubin, Lisa R., Mako L. Fitts, and Anne E. Becker. 2003. "Whatever Feels Good in My Soul: Body Ethics and Aesthetics among African American and Latina Women." *Culture, Medicine and Psychiatry* 27: 49–75.

Scheper-Hughes, Nancy, and Margaret M. Lock. 1987. "The Mindful Body: A Prolegomenon to Future Work in Medical Anthropology." *Medical Anthropology Quarterly* 1: 6–41.

Shilling, Chris. 1993. *The Body and Social Theory*. London: Sage Publications.

Sociedad Venezolana de Cirugía Plástica, Reconstructiva, Estética, y Maxilofacial (SVCPREM). 2005. "Historia y Remembranzas de Nuestra Sociedad." *Boletín Informativo de la Sociedad Venezolana de Cirugía Plástica, Reconstructive, Estética y Maxilofacial* 4: 2–3.

Sullivan, Deborah A. 2004. *Cosmetic Surgery: The Cutting Edge of Commercial Medicine in America*. New Brunswick: Rutgers University Press.

Young, Iris Marion. 1992. "Breasted Experience: The Look and the Feeling." In *The Body in Medical Thought and Practice*, ed. Drew Leder, 215–231. Norwell, MA: Kluwer Academic Publishers.

Chapter 7

Revisiting the hijras

An alternate sex/gender in South Asia

Adnan Hossain

Original material prepared for this edition.

Hijras have long been an established trope as part of the various efforts at theorizing and compiling examples of alternate sex/gender categories across the world. The routine inclusion of hijras in various edited collections in the fields of lesbian and gay studies, sociocultural anthropology, gender and sexual rights has consolidated the hijras as an important figure in the cultural and social scientific analysis of gender and sexual diversity (see, for example, Abelove 1993; Aggleton and Parker 2010). Often described as a quintessential example of third sex/third gender in both international media and scholarly literature, hijras are culturally understood to be neither men nor women across South Asia, and especially in India, Pakistan, and Bangladesh. For a long time, hijras were predominantly associated with India in the Western imagination. However, a growing body of critical ethnographic scholarship based on Pakistan and Bangladesh has squarely challenged the India-centric spatio-intellectual bias in hijra studies (Hossain 2018; Hossain et al. 2022).

A plethora of anglophone terms, such as *homosexual, eunuch, transexual, transvestite,* or *hermaphrodite,* is in wide circulation as popular descriptors of hijras. More recently, hijras have been appropriated as a variant of transgender in the various HIV/ AIDS policies and interventions as well as in scholarly fields, including transgender studies. Part of the problem here is that the recent tendency to recast hijras as transgender is often oblivious to the fact that hijras not only predate the advent of transgender but also that hijras represent a complex subject position not reducible to transgender – a category that emanated from a very particular sociocultural and intellectual history and context in the USA (Valentine 2007; Dutta and Roy 2014). A lack of attention to such contextual specificities and differences works to obscure the global inequalities in intellectual and cultural exchanges and translations (Billard and Nesfield 2020; Chakrabarty 1992). This is, however, a problem not specific to the field of trans-hijra studies but more generally in relation to the tendency to assume that ideas and categories that originate in the Global North have universality in ways that their counterparts in global southern contexts do not (Chiang 2023).

This chapter seeks to revisit the hijras by taking seriously not only the power relations entrenched in cultural and intellectual translation of hijras but also the spatio-intellectual

DOI: 10.4324/9781003398349-8

inequalities shaping the dominant representations of hijras, primarily in the English language. Rather than seeing hijras as one of the examples of "transgender natives" (Towle and Morgan 2002) or reducing them to the category of transgender, attention will be focused on a range of factors, including social class, desire, gender, sexuality, religiosity, and transnational movement, through which the hijra subject is constructed and institutionalized in South Asian societies. The interpretations offered in this chapter are the result of my long-standing ethnographic engagement with hijras in Bangladesh starting in 2000. An ethnographic approach towards the dominant paradigms in hijra studies entails thinking of the various tropes, concepts, and categories with which hijras are examined and understood rather than taking those tropes, concepts, and categories for granted.

Third sex/gender paradigm

Hijras are often described as a third sex/gender both in scholarship and in popular media (Nanda 1999; Reddy 2005). Anyone encountering hijras in South Asia may often hear them say to the public that we are "neither men nor women," a liminal intermediate position that came to be construed as a third category in Western scholarship (Nanda 1999; Reddy 2005; Hossain 2017). Serena Nanda's *Neither Man nor Woman: The Hijras of India* (1999), based on her research in South Central India, serves as one of the pioneering ethnographic works in the field of hijra studies that introduced the hijra subject to the Western audience. Nanda argued that the cultural accommodation of hijras as an alternative third sex/gender in India is emblematic of Indian societal tolerance of sex/gender difference in ways unavailable in Western contexts. The social status of hijras in Indian society as auspicious beings with the ability to offer blessings and curse the public stems from societal ideas about putative hijra asexuality. Here, asexuality is ascribed to the hijra subject position because of the way hijras are assumed to be genitally ambiguous. Genital ambiguity is conflated with asexuality. Furthermore, hijras in India often undergo emasculation, that is, they remove their penises, scrotum, and the testes as a way to become an authentic hijra (Reddy 2005; Nanda 1999). The ritualized removal of the penis, scrotum, and testes is seen as a sacrifice, in return for which hijras obtain sacred power to bless and curse the mainstream populace. The public performances of *badhai*, the ritual practice of singing and dancing to mark various heteronormative social milestones, publicly mark these bodies as hijras.

Reddy's (2005) full-length ethnography further illustrates that hijra identity is too complex to be explained away as simply a third sex/gender. Disclosing the multiple hierarchies of religion, caste, class, gender, and sexuality within which hijras are located, Reddy explicates the contextual nature of thirdness and the "moral economy of respect" in terms of which various groups negotiate, contest, and assert their authenticity and solicit recognition as hijra. Reddy's ethnography unpacks how all thirdness is not alike and that the construction of hijra as a third sex/gender in Western imagination and scholarship represents the Global Northern academic and activist interest in challenging the binary two-sex/gender system (that dominated the Western context until recently) rather than what is at stake for those marked as third gender in the South Asian context.

As previously indicated, the construction of the hijras as a third gender/third sex has been entwined with the assumption about hijras being people with ambiguous genitals. Such an understanding is not only common but also in keeping with the lexical meaning of the word *hijra*, which includes ideas of impotency, asexuality, and the state of being emasculated. It is on account of such ideas about deficiency, defect, and failure that the category of thirdness is constructed (Hossain 2021). More importantly, such a thirdness is also not on an equal footing with either maleness or femaleness construed as first- and second-sex categories in this formulation, whereby those that fail to be either sufficiently first or second genders become the third by default. The bodily basis of hijra as third gender/third sex is further evident in the emasculation ritual that sets real hijras apart from fake ones in the Indian context (Reddy 2005; Nanda 1999). A substantial body of ethnographic work based in India points to the centrality of emasculation as the defining characteristic of hijra identity. Such a position, however, is not uncontested, as even when such a thirdness is accommodated, it comes at the expense of bodily sacrifice (Agrawal 1997; Cohen 1995).

Recent ethnographic research in Bangladesh (Hossain 2012, 2021) further critiques the third-sex/gender paradigm by challenging the centrality of emasculation to the production of the authentic hijra subject. There are both hijras with a penis as well as those without. Both these groups are indispensable to the successful conduct of *hijragiri*, the occupation of the hijra. *Occupation* of the hijra here refers to the various rules and rituals that mark people as hijras in public space. It is common for hijras with a penis to be embroiled in conflict with those without a penis. Trespassing of ritual jurisdiction within which each group is supposed or allowed to operate in line with unwritten hijra codes of conduct is often an occasion for such contestation over genital status. Hijra groups publicly denounce and, at times, beat up the putative transgressors as fake hijras, their fakeness being defined by their having penises, even though, in reality, hijra groups defending the jurisdiction are usually also composed of hijras with a penis.

More recently, the wave of legal recognition of hijras across South Asia has reactivated the social debate about the third-sex/gender paradigm despite sustained academic critique about third-sex/gender as indicated earlier. In my research with hijras in Bangladesh (Hossain 2017, 2021, 2022), I demonstrate that the process of legal recognition has necessitated a simultaneous mobilization of a discourse of disability in the constitution of hijra as citizens worthy of rights. While the international community views the recognition of a third gender as a progressive socio-legal advance in the obtaining of sexual rights in Muslim-majority Bangladesh, locally, hijra are understood as a special group of people born with "missing" or ambiguous genitals decoupled from desire. Unlike the Indian context described earlier, where emasculation is said to confer on the subject special power to bless and curse, hijras that undergo emasculation in the Bangladeshi context are seen as inauthentic and fake, and therefore unworthy of social commiseration and respect.

The eruption of a controversy over the genital status of hijras in 2017 in Bangladesh is a further testament to the contested public debate about hijras. A project to hire 14 hijras as government clerks in the aftermath of their legal recognition as a distinct sex/gender in 2013 was terminated after a medical examination concluded that all the candidates were male except one, since they all had penises. Even the hijra candidate without a penis was declared to be genetically male, since they had had their penis removed a few years ago. This controversy points to the widespread contestation over who hijras are and how they are understood across South Asia, with societally held ideas about genital ambiguity and thirdness often in conflict with a communitarian conceptualization of hijras that includes both those with a penis and those who rid themselves of penises.

Emasculation, asexuality, and desire

While the tendency to read the hijras through the prism of emasculation has been critiqued, emasculation is still widely practiced and forms one of the core rituals of the hijra community (Hossain 2021; Reddy 2005). Unlike sex reassignment surgeries (also described as gender reaffirmation surgeries), the hijra ritual of undergoing emasculation is called *nirban* – literally, *rebirth* and/or *salvation* – signaling its religious connotations rooted in various hijra cosmologies. In Bengal region (which comprises West Bengal, in the east of India, and Bangladesh), for example, hijras often explain their decision to undergo emasculation as a vocation in response to a calling from the mythic hijra ancestors. Several of my interlocutors who underwent nirban stated that they received messages and instructions in their dreams, and that once one gets such a calling, there is no avoiding such a process; one is empowered to subject oneself to this procedure and re-emerge stronger and purer. One of the tales often narrated by my interlocutors at different moments in my fieldwork is as follows:

> *It was the age of truth. In the first place, there was only one hijra, called Maya Ji, and they were alone. They were a true ascetic without any worldly lusts. They devoted their life to the service of gods and goddesses. Temples/shrines were their abode. They were a janana, that is, a hijra with a penis. Yet they were neither a male nor a female, as despite their having male genitalia, they were never a male at heart. They had the preternatural power to vanish their penis with three claps. They could also bring it back with the same. They lived alone for years, serving at the temples and shrines, and then one day, they implored the Creator to send them a companion. In response, the Creator sent Tara Moni as a disciple to them. Tara, too, was a janana and was blessed with magical powers. They would use roosters to traverse the length and breadth of the earth and entertain people. Roosters were their divine vehicle. Maya would lead the rooster while Tara would sit on its back. They would don saris and put on ornaments made of clay. Every day, while setting out for their destination, they would ask the clay to turn into ornaments and put them on. Upon return at dusk, they would break the bangles and the bracelets. They were purely asexual, and it was their asexuality that gave them the power to perform miracles.*
>
> *Once during their visit to a king's house, Tara Moni fell in love with the prince. Tara Moni was so enamored of the prince that they, by virtue of their magical power, turned the prince into a garland and left. Later, upon reaching home, as they sat to have food, Maya Ji found that though two plates were put in place whenever Tara served food, two plates magically broke into three plates. When it first happened, Maya put the food back and re-served the food, but this made no difference, and then they realized what their disciple had done.*
>
> *Having deciphered the sin Tara had committed, Maya convulsed with anger and asked the earth to split. Immediately the earth cracked open, and Maya entered into the hole to vanish from this earth [the place where they slipped into is now apparently the site of a temple somewhere in India – though an exact location was not specified]. While she was falling, Tara grabbed their hair and implored Maya to tell them about how they (Tara) should lead their life in their absence. Maya Ji then told her, "Since you have become debauched, you have lost all your powers, and from now on, you will lead a cursed and despised life. Now you are no longer asexual and pure. From now on, you have to get rid of your genitalia artificially, beg from door to door, dance for the newborn, and entertain the people for your livelihood."*

This mythic tale, one of the many versions in wide circulation among transregional hijra networks across South Asia, highlights not only the religious underpinnings of the emasculation ritual but also the discrepancy between the idealized asexuality and the active sexual desire for men that lies at the heart of hijra cosmology and lived life. Part of the problem here is that most representations of hijra shy away from granting sexual desire any central valence in conceptualizing hijras, precisely because emasculation, or the loss of the penis, is equated with the loss of desire (Hossain 2021). In another significant departure from the common understanding that emasculation renders the operated non-masculine, hijras in Bangladesh view emasculation as a route to attaining masculine vigor, as emasculated bodies become the repository of semen that can no longer be released easily. My hijra interlocutors generally maintain that once emasculated, while they lose the masculine bodily comportments (roughness, bodily hair, and so on), they attain a degree of intrepidness and aggressiveness that the wider society – including hijras – would culturally associate with the toughest of men (Hossain 2021).

Religious affiliation

Nanda (1999) positions hijra as a religiously inflected identity that derives its legitimacy and cultural salience from South Asian Hindu and Muslim traditions. The extraordinary abilities associated with hijras are said to derive from the practice of genital excision rooted in Hindu and partly Muslim ideals of sexual renunciation in South Asia. Once one loses the ability to be productive at an individual level, Nanda argues, one is able to paradoxically transform oneself into a source of collective fertility (ibid.). Importantly, scholars of Indian hijras have noted that hijras in India display a special bias for Islam, despite being born Hindus. Both Nanda and Reddy contend that hijras in India become Muslims by virtue of attaining the status of a hijra through emasculation. They suggest that such bias for Islam among Indian Hindu-born hijras is evident in how hijras perform certain Muslim rituals (Eid and Muharram) and address each other using the Muslim greeting, *salamalaikum*. Similar religious pluralism is also seen among hijras in Bangladesh who worship Hindu-marked goddesses as part of hijra cosmology despite being born Muslim. My own research indicates that Muslim hijras do not see their participation in Hindu-themed rituals as contravening their Islamic beliefs; rather, many were also devout Muslims who not only practiced Islam but also worked as voluntary preachers of the faith as part of Islamic religious groups (Hossain 2012). Hijras across South Asia often invoke and mobilize tales and references from both Hindu and Muslim traditions in a bid to justify and demand social respect from mainstream society. The creative ways hijras deploy various religious symbolisms and mythic tales in their everyday interactions with the public bring into view various forms of agencies that hijras exercise in navigating and negotiating South Asian public and private spaces (Hossain 2021, 2022).

Both Reddy and Nanda explain this special affinity for Islam among Indian hijras as a form of subaltern solidarity with minority Muslims in Hindu-majority India. Reddy further indicates that the hijras she did her research with in South India undergo both circumcision and emasculation. Since circumcision is a Muslim ritual, Reddy's hijra interlocutors claimed themselves to be doubly Muslim. In my work, I have critiqued the bodily basis of claiming a Muslim identity in the Indian context, where Muslims are routinely mocked as incomplete men because of their undergoing circumcision (Hossain 2012). The success of some hijras in various electoral politics in South Asia further complicates such suggestions of hijra alliance with minority religions. For example, research has also shown that hijras in India, despite their affinity for Islam, often highlight their Hindu connections in their electoral campaign in a bid to appeal to the mainstream, reinforcing existing forms of moral and political authority (Reddy 2003). In 2015, Laxmi Narayan Tripathi, a prominent transgender and hijra activist and celebrity in India, established Kinnar Akhara, a hijra religious organization, to assert hijra identity as an essentially Hindu religious identity, thereby questioning and contravening the long legacy of religious pluralism among the hijras (Bevilacqua 2022).

Pleasure and alternative erotic space

A formidable challenge to the dominant phallogocentric framing of hijras as emasculated and asexual third gender/sex is the recent centering of pleasure and desire in the formation of the hijra subculture (Hossain 2021). While public health interventions in the context of HIV/AIDS called into question the long-standing trope of hijra asexuality, hijras have often been represented in this framework as passive receptacles of male semen or victims of perverse male desire (Reddy 2006, Hossain 2017). However, more recent ethnographic research with hijras in Bangladesh indicates on the contrary that desire is not peripheral but central to the formation of the hijra subject position. It is, however, not just desire for men but its manifestation in the form of anal receptivity that is key to claiming a hijra identity (Hossain 2021). My interlocutors not only located their sexual desire in the anus but also argued that pleasures associated with anal receptivity are superior to penile penetration, so much so that once one takes up the hijra subject position, one has to adhere to this sexual protocol in the community context. This is, however, not to suggest that transgressions do not happen, rather that any deviation from this normative protocol of receptivity is often met with the strongest opprobrium and disgust.

While the opposition to the idea of hijras anally penetrating men is an absolute taboo, penetrating women is not, though it is not desirable either. This is not surprising, since many hijras are also heterosexually married householding men who function as hijras in a location away from their heteronormative families. While in mainstream heteronormative society, accessing anal pleasures is a taboo when one is male-bodied, seeking such gratification is normative within hijra space. Thus, erotic pleasures and sexual practices that are forbidden in the mainstream heteronormative social context become available to those that take up the hijra subject position. Those that join the hijra community do so not because they fail to be adequately masculine but, rather, because they wish to explore sexual pleasures that are otherwise unavailable to them. Instead of seeing hijras through the prism of failure, centering pleasures brings into view an active disavowal of normative heterosexual masculinity rather than a failure to live up to those ideals (Hossain 2021).

Social class and the construction of the hijra

In everyday settings across South Asia, the label *hijra* is also often used to mark and police deviations from the societally sanctioned protocols of masculinity. However, the invocation of hijra as a pejorative label has strong class connotations as it is a gender and sexual transgression associated with the working-class populace, whereby hijra becomes a problematic slur. The dominant middle- and upper-class social imagination often depicts the hijras as foul-smelling, dirty, and shameless – images typically associated with the working-class populace (Hossain 2017, 2021). Beyond such discursive demonization of hijras, hijra is also a working-class subculture in the sense that those that join the community emanate from working-class social backgrounds. The class-specific nature of the hijra subculture is further evident in the fact that hijras occupy the working-class and most squalid neighborhoods. Regardless of the amount of wealth one hijra group may have, it is because of hijra identity that hijras are not allowed to live in middle-class neighborhoods. During my fieldwork with hijras in Dhaka, my interlocutors often emphasized how it was people from the middle and upper classes that were hostile to them, while the working-class mainstream populace treated them like neighbors, to the extent that they shared food and utensils. This class-inflected nature of hijra interactions with the middle and upper classes is often evident in how the middle- and upper-class households are inaccessible to hijras in Bangladesh. While hijras in South Asia often perform songs and dance on various heteronormative social milestones, including the birth of a child and weddings, such performances are restricted only to working-class households (Hossain 2022).

Hijragiri: being versus becoming a hijra

For the mainstream majority, hijra is a liminal intermediate category to which one is relegated for gender failure. Among members of the hijra community, however, the word *hijra* has been appropriated as a self-affirming mode of identification. Importantly, from the hijra perspective, hijras are those who conduct hijragiri. *Hijragiri* here refers not only to various rules and rituals but also to the ability of the members to demonstrate mastery of those rules and rituals before both the mainstream public and fellow hijras. These rules and rituals cover issues ranging from how to wear a sari to how to address someone senior in the community to performing songs and dance in public places and households. It is through a systematic learning of these rules and rituals, as well as the acquisition of knowledge about the communitarian history and worldviews, that one can acquire the hijra subject position (Hossain 2012, 2021).

During my various stints of ethnographic fieldwork in Dhaka, Bangladesh, I was often struck by the way in which some hijras were able to establish their seniority and authority in public space by being able to invoke and tell various mythic tales in ways that junior hijras were unable to. Senior hijras could easily distinguish themselves from the junior ones by being able to produce flat-palmed thikri (clapping) in public, one of the signature gestures of hijras across South Asia. Different styles of clapping produce specific types of sound, and each style has a special meaning attached to it. Junior hijras are not allowed to clap in front of senior ones. There are elaborate rules about how such gestures are to be displayed, and it is only through training in a hijra household that a novice can eventually obtain the status of someone who is *pakki*, that is, possessing sufficient knowledge about hijra ways of life, rules and rituals, and worldviews. This emphasis on various doings through which one learns to claim and perform a hijra subject brings into view the fact that hijra is an acquired subject position rather than one that is ascribed, as is often commonly understood by society at large. This focus on active cultivation of hijra ways and acumen exemplifies agency on the part of hijra interlocutors who actively resist, negotiate, and navigate the mainstream heteronormative social world and have built the alternative social organization of hijras (Hossain 2021, 2022).

Based on her ethnographic research with language practices among hijras in North India, Kira Hall (1997) argues that it is not Indian society per se that is more accepting of hijras, as indicated by Nanda's previous ethnographic studies; rather, it is the hijras that continuously demand and actively negotiate with the mainstream society to gain social respect and recognition as hijras. Hall draws our attention to the way hijras use sexualized slurs in their conversation with the mainstream populace to challenge the heteronormative ideologies and respectability politics often used to marginalize them. In a similar manner, my most recent work on the impact of state legislative reform on hijras in Bangladesh brings into view how hijras navigate various governmental and NGO efforts at eradicating them through continued performance of badhai rituals in public (Hossain 2022). While the current state and civil society discourses in Bangladesh depict the hijras as a backward social group with communitarian baggage and a source of public nuisance engaged in extortion and begging, hijras resist such discursive demonization by underscoring the fact that the practice of badhai is imbued with religious significance and is part of a complex religious economic exchange that sets it apart from regular forms of begging (Hossain 2022). Elsewhere, I noted that the practice of hijras promenading through the bazaars in urban areas in Bangladesh engenders an atmosphere of carnivalesque conviviality, animating and lightening the moods of the clientele and the vendors. The use of slurs in their conversations with the public, accompanied by gestures of loud flat-palmed clapping and/or lifting up of their saris to expose their missing genitals, is an example of agentic acts through which hijras take control of the public space. Hijras' continuous challenging of the mainstream heteronormative and neoliberal ideologies in everyday life constitutes forms of resistance to various (post)colonial attempts to govern, contain, criminalize, and even eradicate them (Hinchy 2019; Hossain 2021, 2022).

Is hijra a gender or a sexual identity?

One of the challenges in writing about hijras is that neither gender nor sexuality is an adequate category capable of capturing the complexities characterizing their subject position. To frame hijras through the prism of gender is to erase critical dimensions of erotics and sexual desire that, as this chapter has indicated, are central to hijra identity. Thinking carefully about the hijra lifeworld, therefore, entails questions about the separation of gender and sexuality as analytically distinct domains, as these are often presumed to be in the provincial Euro-American model that dominates knowledge fields today (Valentine 2007).

For scholars interested in ethnographic methods and approaches, the tension between emic and etic perspectives may provide a fruitful avenue of reflective research. For example, in the context of my ethnographic fieldwork, hijras do not see their identity as either a form of gender or sexuality; rather, they position their own hijraness or identity as an occupation (*pesha pon*) bequeathed to them by the primordial hijra archetypes of Maya Ji and Tara Momni. It is only with the advent of HIV/AIDS activism and recent rights work that hijras are now recast as a (third or trans) gender. More importantly, the framing of hijra as gender works to obscure desires and pleasures that are central to the formation of the hijra subject position.

Rather than having any allegiance for either a disciplinary coda or theoretical framework, the ethnographic approach I adopt in my work allows me to locate and understand the tension between theory, method, data, and representation. Most importantly, an ethnographic approach has enabled me to see both how the discourses narrated by my hijra interlocutors interact with the practices they engage in and, thereby, the discrepancies that exist between how people speak about and how people may practice their lives. However, this should not be viewed as an example of people crafting lies but, rather, as evidence of the glorious messiness of lifeworlds in general.

More recent ethnographic research repositions the hijra as an alternative erotic space that offers possibilities to explore varied forms of erotic pleasure and desire that are otherwise unavailable to normatively masculine subjects across South Asia (Hossain 2021). Such a reading alerts us to the possibility that those that take up the hijra subject position and join the community do so not because of a lack of any other option but because they wish to access and explore otherwise transgressive and forbidden erotic pleasures. Instead of reading hijras through the tropes of failure, inadequacy, and lack often associated with expressions such as "neither men nor women," the active element of disavowal and repudiation of the mainstream heteronormative ideologies by those that join the hijra community should be central to our framing.

Discussion questions

1. Based on Hossain 's explanations, how does equating hijras with trans people in other contexts misrepresent this population? Why do you think people have gravitated toward translating hijras as trans?
2. What one question would you ask Hossain or the hijras with whom he works if you had the chance to speak with them?
3. Hijra identity has many parts. In thinking about these parts, which do you think has the potential to be most liberatory for this population as they seek recognition and respect from wider society? Why?

References

Abelove, Henry D., ed. 1993. *The Lesbian and Gay Studies Reader*, 1st ed. Abingdon, UK: Routledge.

Aggleton, Peter, and Richard Parker, eds. 2010. *Routledge Handbook of Sexuality, Health and Rights*, 1st ed. Abingdon, UK: Routledge.

Agrawal, Anuja. 1997. "Gendered Bodies: The Case of the 'Third Gender' in India." *Contributions to Indian Sociology* 31(2): 273–297.

Bevilacqua, Daniela. 2022. "From the Margins to Demigod: The Establishment of the Kinnar Akhara in India." *Asian Ethnology* 81(1/2): 53–82.

Billard, Thomas J., and Sam Nesfield. 2020. "(Re)making 'Transgender' Identities in Global Media and Popular Culture." In *Trans Lives in a Globalizing World*, ed. J. Michael Ryan, 66–90. Abingdon, UK: Routledge.

Chakrabarty, Dipesh. 1992. "Provincializing Europe: Postcoloniality and the Critique of History." *Cultural Studies* 6(3): 337–357. https://doi.org/10.1080/09502389200490221.

Chiang, Howard. 2023. "Trans without Borders: Resisting the Telos of Transgender Knowledge." *Journal of the History of Sexuality* 32(1): 56–65. muse.jhu.edu/article/878044.

Cohen, Lawrence. 1995. "The Pleasures of Castration: The Postoperative Status of Hijras Jankhas and Academics." In *Sexual Nature Sexual Culture*, eds. Paul R. Abramson and Steven D. Pinkerton, 276–304. Chicago: University of Chicago Press.

Dutta, Aniruddha, and Raina Roy. 2014. "Decolonizing Transgender in India: Some Reflections." *Transgender Studies Quarterly* 1(3): 320–337.

Hall, Kira. 1997. "'Go Suck Your Husband's Sugarcane!' Hijras and the Use of Sexual Insult." In *Queerly Phrased: Language, Gender and Sexuality*, eds Anna Livia and Kira Hall, 430–460. New York: Oxford University Press.

Hinchy, Jessica. 2019. *Governing Gender and Sexuality in Colonial India: The Hijra, c.1850–1900*. Cambridge, UK: Cambridge University Press.

Hossain, Adnan. 2012. "Beyond Emasculation: Being Muslim and Becoming Hijra in South Asia." *Asian Studies Review* 36(4): 495–513.

Hossain, Adnan. 2017. "The Paradox of Recognition: Hijra, Third Gender and Sexual Rights in Bangladesh." *Culture, Health and Sexuality* 19(12): 1418–1431.

Hossain, Adnan. 2018. "De-Indianizing Hijra: Intraregional Effacements and Inequalities in South Asian Queer Space." *Transgender Studies Quarterly* 5(3): 321–331.

Hossain, Adnan. 2021. *Beyond Emasculation: Pleasure and Power in the Making of Hijra in Bangladesh*. Cambridge: Cambridge University Press.

Hossain, Adnan. 2022. "Badhai as Dis/Ability: Meaning, Context, and Community in Bangladesh." In *Badhai: Hijra-Khwaja Sira-Trans Performance across Borders in South Asia*, eds. Adnan Hossain, Claire Pamment & Jeff Roy, 41–68. London: Methuen Drama.

Hossain, Adnan, Claire Pamment, and Jeff Roy. 2022. *Badhai: Hijra-Khwaja Sira-Trans Performance across Borders in South Asia*. London: Methuen Drama.

Nanda, Serena. 1999 [1990]). *The Hijras of India: Neither Man nor Woman*. London: Wadsworth.

Reddy, Gayatri. 2003. "'Men' Who Would Be Kings: Celibacy, Emasculation and the Reproduction of Hijras in Contemporary Indian Politics." *Social Research* 70(1): 163–200.

Reddy, Gayatri. 2005. *With Respect to Sex: Negotiating Hijra Identity in South India*. Chicago: University of Chicago.

Reddy, Gayatri. 2005. "Geographies of Contagion: Hijras, Kothis, and the Politics of Sexual Marginality in Hyderabad." *Anthropology & Medicine* 12(3): 255–270. doi: 10.1080/13648470500291410.

Towle, Evan B., and Lynn M. Morgan. 2002. "Romancing the Transgender Native: Rethinking the Use of the 'Third Gender' Concept." *GLQ: A Journal of Lesbian and Gay Studies* 8(4): 469–97.

Valentine, David. 2007. *Imagining Transgender: An Ethnography of a Category*. Durham: Duke University Press.

Chapter 8

Natural birth at the turn of the twenty-first century

Implications for gender

Margaret MacDonald

This chapter is based on material previously published by Vanderbilt University Press (VUP). The author gratefully acknowledges the permission of VUP to reproduce materials from Chapter 4 of the book *At Work in the Field of Birth* (2007).

The way I look at it is that we can make more decisions and we have more options, rather than, in the hospital, having somebody telling us how it's going to be. And that to me is natural. I'm not one that's into natural foods and all this kind of stuff. I'm not like that. But that's how I look at natural. It's natural in the hospital too, but what it means to me is making my own decisions.
Claudine (32, mother of two children born at home with midwives)

The notion of natural birth has long been used as a rhetorical strategy to counter the predominant biomedical or "technocratic" model of the pregnant and birthing body as inherently problematic and potentially dangerous to the fetus (Davis-Floyd 1994). Midwives, birthing women, and women's health writers and activists have often appealed to the authority of nature as a legitimizing basis for midwifery ideals and clinical practices. Natural birth at the turn of the twenty-first century, however, is not what it used to be. In this chapter, I explore the changing nature of natural birth in contemporary midwifery in Canada and argue that it is characterized by a fundamental shift away from essentialized understandings of female nature. I also discuss the implications of this shift for claims about gender.

Midwifery in Canada began as a radical social movement that grew out of the void left by the demise of traditional midwifery across the country in the nineteenth and early twentieth centuries. After a decades-long life in the margins, midwifery grew into an autonomous profession within the formal healthcare system, starting with the province of Ontario in 1994.[1] Ontario midwifery, on which the data for this chapter was gathered in the late 1990s, holds much in common ideologically and practically with radical midwifery in the United Kingdom and direct-entry and home-birth midwifery in the United States in terms of its opposition to the medicalization of birth and model of low-tech, women-centered alternatives. *Natural birth* is an idiom for what midwives now clinically refer to as normal or physiological birth, but it bears a cultural and political legacy that goes beyond these latter terms. Indeed, midwifery has long shared a common goal with feminist scholarship on the gendered body: to expose the fictions of science and

DOI: 10.4324/9781003398349-9

biomedicine built up about the female body in order to reveal its true nature – or, as one midwifery client said, "pregnancy and birth as it was meant to be" – underneath. Yet just as the universal female body as the basis for feminism has undergone a "destabilization," so has natural birth as a basis for midwifery. If we think of pregnancy and birth as gendered performances repeated within the "regulatory frames" of biomedical culture and institutions – rather than some prediscursive reality (Butler 1990; Lock and Scheper-Hughes 1990; Pasveer and Akrich 2001: 236) – then contemporary midwifery, I argue, is seeking to reconceive, rather than retrieve, the natural facts of pregnancy and birth. Natural birth, as a critical alternative, contains its own discursive intentions: to promote women as knowing, capable, and strong, their bodies perfectly designed to carry a fetus and give birth successfully without the high-tech surveillance and interventions of physicians in a hospital setting. New expectations of pregnancy and birth in midwifery, in turn, give rise to new gender performances – deeply personal, highly political re-articulations – that are *naturalized* in the body and which positively inform their sense of self as physical beings, as women and mothers, and as persons.[2]

Natural birth is a matter of choice

When asked directly about natural birth, midwives and the birthing women they attend to respond in predictable ways: "It means drug-free," "It means no interventions," "It means nonmedicalized, the opposite of a hospital birth." When probed, however, natural birth is often problematized by midwives and women themselves. Ada is a midwife who comes from rural Ontario. Her training began in the 1980s and was characterized by a mixture of formal education and apprenticeship. She worked for many years as a childbirth educator and a doula[3] before becoming a registered midwife. After offering me an initial definition of *natural birth* as the opposite of medical birth, Ada began to hedge.

> Well, I guess the obvious thing that comes to mind is nonintervention in the sense of augmentation, drugs, episiotomies, procedures, vacuum extractions – those kinds of things. It's a hard one in terms of the medication issue, because I would hate to say to a woman that she didn't have a natural birth because she required some pain medication. That's a hard one. On the one hand, she did have spontaneous vaginal delivery, and pain medication can be, in some cases, very positive for women. I guess I shy away from identifying what clearly is natural; maybe that's what got us into this trouble in the first place, is that feeling we have to have some model of what natural is and we have to have techniques to obtain that natural birth.

Having a specific ideal of natural birth necessarily means that some women will fail to accomplish it. Indeed, a young woman in the prenatal classes that I attended (herself a midwifery student at the time) said she would feel "ashamed" in front of her classmates and her instructors if she ended up in the hospital, and especially if she had a C-section. Another woman I met several times at a midwifery clinic and interviewed at her home after the birth of her baby was apologetic about the fact that she "couldn't cope" and had "cried for an epidural" during labor and had asked to go to the hospital. "Next time it will be different," she told me. "Next time I will do it naturally." The inevitability that some women will fail in the goal to birth "naturally" – at home, without drugs, without interventions, without screaming in pain and feeling like they have lost control – is one reason that Ada, like many midwives, avoids offering an absolutely fixed definition of *natural birth*. Ada went on to discuss how midwifery can provide the context for women to feel a sense of control even when interventions do occur.

> By stressing that she's actively participating in a lot of the decisions, that there are still options – whether they are as simple as rolling from one side to the other. But [the important thing is] that she feels somehow empowered by exercising those limited options, that she has *some* choices, *some* decision-making, and that those interventions occurred with her as the decision-maker. . . . [E]ven in the event that a woman has a cesarean – it happens lots of times in this practice – they are usually not bad experiences because of that aspect that she still controlled – not controlled – but she had input into the process.

Another longtime midwife, Isobel, asserts that natural birth is a myth that says that "if you are a together person, you can squat in the corner and have your baby by candlelight (and) you have to have a vaginal birth to achieve some sort of womanhood." The myth of natural birth has served, however, to counter another myth: "that childbirth is so horrible that you need to be knocked out in the hospital." Isobel explains how her thinking about natural birth in the context of her work as a midwife developed.

> I think that's really dangerous, when you are making people try to fit into little boxes. But I started out thinking like that. My goal was to prevent cesareans. But I have seen so many women feel a sense of strength and dignity and satisfaction after a cesarean birth. And I think it's because they have given birth and they've worked really, really hard. Even like [when a woman has] an *abruptio placenta* and you have to have an immediate cesarean, it doesn't take away from it if you have that feeling that you are in control.[4] I hear this all the time. Women consistently say on our evaluation sheets or I hear directly, "I felt I was the one making the decisions. Even though I would have preferred not to have to make that decision, I made it, and I was ready for it, and it was great that you guys were there, because I felt that I had a friend there, someone on my side to help me through that difficult time."

Making sure a woman has choices in labor may include where to labor, who to have with her, what to eat and drink, what position to labor in, how to manage pain and the progression of labor (including pharmaceuticals). Very occasionally, ensuring women have choices in childbirth means planning for an epidural early in labor – not exactly the kind of planning usually associated with natural childbirth. Even the midwives who think that natural birth *might* include epidurals are quick to elaborate how such preferences are negotiated in a prenatal visit and during labor. They don't want women making decisions based on fear of childbirth pain, peer pressure, or convenience. Midwives explain that if they do not have any pain medication, they are likely to have fewer interventions overall, feel better, and recover faster. Nevertheless, most midwives agree that when they have tried all the tricks in the book to relieve a woman's pain and exhaustion through physical and emotional support, an epidural can be "a blessed, wonderful thing." Other interventions, too, have their place in the realm of "natural." Isobel concludes that "natural childbirth [is about] making sure the woman makes her own choices. That's [Isobel's] goal, not natural childbirth *per se*."

The importance of informed choice in midwifery cannot be overstated. This inherently politicized notion is at the center of the philosophical and clinical practice of midwifery in Ontario; it is intended to foster a sense self-knowledge and personal responsibility among clients, and to create an egalitarian midwife–client relationship in which individualized, low-tech, even intuitive ways of knowing and doing are explored, valued, and acted upon. "The whole reason that midwifery arose in Ontario is because women wanted choice," one midwife asserts. Midwives explain *informed choice* as the act of conveying clinical knowledge to women and their partners in such a way that they can understand it and then make informed decisions about their own care. This may be something as simple as describing the importance of maternal nutrition on the developing fetus. Or it may involve citing the findings of a recent study on the effect of artificial rupture of membranes on fetal outcomes. Midwives also expect women to read on their own and generate their own questions. They stress that informed choice is about confirming and supporting women's own knowledge about their bodies and previous pregnancies. Trust in one's midwife as an expert is part of what makes women feel confident and helps them trust in their own bodies and what they can cope with or accomplish. Midwives do not offer informed choice on everything. Administering antihemorrhagic drugs for uterine bleeding after labor, for example, is not an informed-choice issue. Ada tells me this emphatically. "I wouldn't even ask her! If she was bleeding, I wouldn't ask her! It's not a choice. It's not a choice unless she wants to die. She's hired me to care for her. And that's my way of caring for her. And sometimes that means making decisions for her."

Negotiating medical technology through informed choice

One of the most basic understandings in midwifery is that routine biomedical interventions disrupt the normal or natural process of birth and, moreover, that one intervention begets another. For example, if a woman has her labor artificially induced or augmented with intravenous oxytocin – commonly referred to by its trade name, Pitocin, or simply as a "Pit drip" – her contractions may come on so fast and strong that she is more likely to need pain medication, which, in turn, makes her less likely to be able to push her baby out, which may result in prolonged third stage of labor, which may cause fetal distress and the need for an emergency C-section. A less extreme scenario is when a woman has an epidural, followed by an episiotomy, and then delivers a healthy baby vaginally, but her recovery time is much longer than if she had neither, and her baby is less alert and less likely to nurse right away. Evidence suggests that many of these interventions, when used routinely, are clinically unnecessary and do not change the health outcomes for either mother or baby; in some cases, these interventions are the source of measurable harm to mother and infant (Davis-Floyd 1992; Hartmann et al. 2005; Sleep et al. 1989; Thacker and Stroup 1999). Midwives and women receiving midwifery care often state the belief that our tendency to rely on – or be subjected to – medical technology has destroyed our natural instincts about pregnancy and birth.

Midwives do, of course, use technology during prenatal care and delivery both in hospital and at home. They use Dopplers – handheld ultrasound devices – to listen to fetal heartbeats. They order routine blood tests. They order sonograms to confirm gestational age or check for fetal anomalies. At home births, they carry oxygen for mother and baby, if necessary, as well as intramuscular oxytocin injections to stop uterine bleeding. At hospital births, they may administer fluids and some medications, such as antibiotics, intravenously, as ordered by a physician. (They can also do this at home births too, in some instances.) Some midwives are even seeking certification to manage laboring women with epidurals or to perform vacuum extractions (Kornelsen and Carty 2004: 5).

Giselle is a woman in her early 30s with two small children – the first born in a hospital with an obstetrician, and the second born at home with midwives. After we had chatted several times at the midwifery clinic where I volunteered, I went to meet her at her home just after the birth of her second baby. She and her husband – both professionals – live in a three-story Victorian house on a tree-lined residential street in a large city. Giselle sought out midwifery care for her second pregnancy because she was disappointed with the care she had received in the hospital with her first baby. She described being hooked up to a fetal monitor and recalled with frustration that everyone (including her husband) was focused on the monitor instead of her. She was unhappy with how her delivery was managed in other ways as well; she had delivered very quickly and sustained deep tears in her perineum. She felt her experience was typical of physician-attended hospital births, and did not want to repeat it. When she became pregnant with her second baby, a good friend recommended midwifery. Giselle was very happy with her care throughout the pregnancy, the delivery, and the postpartum period.

Giselle had maternal serum screening for both of her pregnancies, but she hinted to me that her midwife had discouraged her.[5]

> In the doctor's office [maternal serum] is routine, so I had it. But with my second baby, I was extremely well-informed, and I chose to have it. There was no need for me to have further tests, because my maternal serum came out fine. Had anything come up, I could have had more tests and determined whether the child was Down syndrome or spina bifida, and we would have had to make a decision at that point. Thank God we never had to make that decision.

What is interesting here is that Giselle contextualized her decision to use prenatal diagnostic technology in terms of the midwifery principle of informed choice. The difference, according to Giselle, is that with midwifery care, she was well-informed and acted on the basis of what was right for her, rather than having the test as part of a routine at the doctor's office. Giselle also elected to have one ultrasound because they were not sure about her dates, a detail that could affect the maternal serum. Again, she explained that the ultrasound was both necessary *and* her choice. She was satisfied with the ultrasound because it confirmed her dates. She was disappointed, however, with the image of the 15-week-old fetus – "We could hardly see her" – in contrast to the image of her 17-week-old fetus during her first pregnancy. Even so, because there was no reason for another ultrasound and her midwives, she knew, didn't like to do tests without a reason, she did not seek another one at a later gestational date, deciding she would just wait until the baby was born to see her again.

Clients like Giselle now make use of technology in a way that midwifery clients of the past seldom did – opting for maternal serum and longing for one more ultrasound yet planning a home birth and determined to avoid the alienating hospital experience of epidurals and fetal monitors. While it is clear that she prefers midwifery care generally, she is not beholden to it ideologically.

> There is a perception there that if you are going to a midwife, you are going to refuse medical treatment and only go to a naturopath, that you must be an extremist. But you don't have to be an extremist to go to a midwife. There is a good way of giving birth. There is no hard line between delivering safely and delivering comfortably. But some people feel that if you are going to go with a midwife, that you must be an extremist and you must be trying to make a statement. But I just learned from my first delivery, and from friends' stories who had midwives, that this is not right. It's not that I'm bucking the medical profession, but in my case, I don't think the medical profession knows how to handle a normal, uncomplicated birth. They want to complicate it. . . . [S]ome people just can't get the idea that [midwifery is] not a statement. It is just the natural way to go.

Giselle's "informed choice" use of technology might be seen to erode midwifery's political goal to resist the medicalization of birth and the social control of women's bodies by patriarchal institutions. Many midwives lament this trend and see it as a consequence of both their expanded scope of practice since being incorporated into the formal healthcare system and the influx of clients who are, in their view, "less committed" to the low-tech ideals of the past. Part of the problem for women making choices like Giselle's at this time is that midwifery care in Ontario is still a relatively uncommon choice – and public knowledge about midwifery is still somewhat limited.[6] Also, there is tremendous pressure to use medical technology because it has become so routinized in mainstream maternity care and the social consequences of not using it can be severe (Mitchell 1994; Rapp 1990; Rothman 1986). Giselle's decisions around the use of medical routines and technologies in her maternity care might be best understood in terms of pragmatism (Lock and Kaufert 1998: 208). Steering away from essentialist explanations that women are inherently opposed to technology by virtue of their closeness to nature or wholly oppressed by technology and the systems in which it is embedded, pragmatism focuses on women's agency: what women do, rather than what is done to them.[7] The notion of pragmatism adds a level of nuance to our understanding of midwifery, paying attention to the subtleties of everyday usage and not just the ideological basis encapsulated in such notions as medicalization versus natural birth.

Labor pains and women's power

> It's, like, who invented epidurals? The person should be shot. Because, you know, if they didn't exist, people would just shut up and grin and bear it. . . . And if there was nothing but the odd herb that would help you relax or something, then people would just do it.
> (Anna Lisa, *mother of three children born at home with midwives*)

How midwives think about the pain of labor is key to their view of pregnant and birthing bodies as naturally capable and competent. The vast majority of midwives recognize pain medication as having its place, but in the case of normal labor and delivery, they generally take the view that pain can and should be managed in nonpharmaceutical ways. The pain of labor is one of the main fears that women express in prenatal classes and appointments. Midwives do not pretend that labor is not painful, and they shy away from offering magic solutions, but they do offer clients another way to think about and experience it. One woman in my study said that her midwives helped her prepare for labor and birth by teaching "almost another worldview . . . more of an attitude than anything else." In the midwifery model of pain, a number of things are emphasized. One, the pain of labor is not continuous like most other pain: contractions are intermittent and build slowly in intensity, so one can learn to cope. Two, the pain of labor is "pain with a purpose": you are pushing out your baby. Three, labor pain is universal: "Women have been doing this for centuries. Our bodies are designed to do it well." Midwives work hard to naturalize the pain of birth even from the first minutes that a woman goes into labor. They advise women and their partners not to fuss too much in the early stages; they should do what they normally do – eat breakfast, do the dishes, go for a walk – so as to not give the woman the impression that she cannot cope. This kind of advice reflects an understanding that pregnancy is not an illness and labor and birth are not crises but, rather, normal physiological events.

Leigh's story is a good example of how midwifery works discursively to affect women's knowledge and experience of labor pain and how this becomes central (and desirable) to having a natural birth. When I met Leigh, a lawyer in her mid-30s, she had just had her second baby with midwifery care. The first one occurred before midwifery was a recognized part of the formal healthcare system. It was a planned hospital delivery, with the shared care of a midwife and a physician. The second was a planned home birth several years later, with the same midwife as her primary caregiver under the new regulated system. Leigh's experience of laboring without pain medication was profoundly empowering for her. She attributes this to midwifery's unique "worldview" of birth, which "has everything to do" with her confidence in her body during pregnancy and birth.

> One of the things that I was so fed up with was this stuff about how people in our society put a great deal of effort in making birth scary. . . . Most of the women I know are terrified of birth. Terrified of the pain. Terrified of the difficulty. Really competent, interesting, smart women are terrified of birth. It is terrible that they look at birth that way; it is a difficult experience, but it is also exhilarating. . . . I felt really powerful after I had Martha. I felt really powerful after I had Zoe. I felt fantastic. I felt like it was my marathon. It was something that I had done, and I found it intensely interesting too.

"Even in the moment? Even as you were laboring?" I asked her.

> Yes, even in the moment. When you are in labor and you are trying to figure out how you can go with the labor, how you can help yourself dilate, how you can carry on through it, how you can let it happen – there is a long time in labor when you are dilating when you have to do all that work. And it's work that you can do. I mean, your body helps you do it. And if you do it – at least for me – it is a very positive experience, and then at the end there is no more work because your body runs the show. But it's a very enriching experience because you end up thinking, "I did this! This was really hard, and I did this!" And you can do it because your body will help you do it. You don't have to doubt that you can do it, if you believe that about yourself.

Leigh's determination to give birth without pain medication was, for her, "a route to [her] power." She notes a clear difference between being in control of birth – something that she thinks is not totally possible on the physical level and something that midwives encourage women to give up – and being "in control of the circumstances of birth" – something that is possible to a great extent and something that Leigh and many other women cite as key to feelings of empowerment, strength, and even wisdom derived from midwifery care and birth. "The whole thing was a lesson to me. The pregnancy was a lesson to me, and the labor was a lesson to me. And it is a lesson in being almost someone not from our century," she concluded.

Natural interventions

Leigh concluded that, while in labor, she was "guided by something very primitive, but [she is] not just a primitive woman." When Leigh describes the situation during her second birth – the planned home birth that ended up in a hospital – her ambivalence about the definition of *natural birth* surfaces, and the line between nature and medical interventions becomes blurred. Because her first baby had meconium staining, Leigh was aware of the possibility of this happening again and refers to it in her description of how she labored at home with her second baby.[8]

> After six hours, I got [my midwife] to break the waters – partly because I had that meconium thing in my head and partly because I didn't want six more hours of labor. Frederick Leboyer would hate me, because he said that birth is violence and that breaking the waters would make birth more violent. I was worried about the meconium, and I didn't really care about Frederick Leboyer. And also [my baby] was seven days overdue. So that makes the risks higher. So it didn't seem to me to be a bad thing to do. . . . So I don't think that breaking the waters is terribly unnatural – people have been doing that for a really long time, you know? And if I feel like I want to break the waters because that labor is long and something else is niggling at me – which is what was going on – then I guess that's not unnatural.

As it turns out, Leigh was right. Her baby was taken to the hospital after the delivery at home, with meconium aspiration. Kelly's story echoes these sentiments. Kelly is in her early 30s, living in a medium-sized city in Ontario. Her first child, Clara, was born at home under the care of midwives. I met Kelly at her spacious apartment on the third floor of a suburban low-rise building. She says that she has always known that birth was meant to be "totally natural and joyous, not frightening," and she grounds this faith in a kind of biological determinism. "As females – it seems very simple to me – we are born with these parts, with this purpose of our biology, and that's it. It's a process that happens, and it's supposed to happen. It's just biologically natural." During pregnancy, she did not take any medication or undergo any prenatal tests. She was getting information from her midwife about nutrition, herbs, and natural remedies. She was thrilled. "For example," she tells me, "I was having heartburn and asked, 'What can I take?' and she said, 'You can eat almonds!'" During labor, she avoided interventions too. She explained why she did not have an episiotomy:

> [Because] it is unnatural unless it's absolutely necessary. And there *are* a very small number of cases where that would be necessary. So, in that case, if everything else was

dealt with without drugs or interventions – medical or technological types of interventions – then an episiotomy that is absolutely required would be. Now, for example, women who are dancers, their muscle tone and strength is so tight in that area of their body from dancing that they can't open up. Now they might need an episiotomy, and so if they went through the whole labor without any medicinal-type things, then I would say that she had a natural birth, even if she had an episiotomy, because that was just part of her, of who she is, her physiology as a dancer. But it goes beyond the physical sphere of things. It includes your state of mind too. And if you stay at home to have your baby, you can add to the naturalness of it.

In Kelly's view, if an intervention is done because it is absolutely necessary and not simply convenient or expedient, or done out of fear, then the birth could still be considered natural. Moreover, she is suggesting that there are degrees of naturalness.

One evening, at the prenatal classes I attended at a local midwifery practice, a discussion arose about tears that can occur in the labia and vagina when a woman is pushing her baby out. Ingrid, the midwife instructor, reported that scientific research had recently confirmed what midwives knew all along: that routine episiotomies were unnecessary and that most women did not require them. She then made a surprising comment: that most women tear during the pushing stage of labor. I suppose we were expecting to hear that most women do not tear during the pushing stage, a piece of information that would confirm the routine use of episiotomy as brutally unnatural. Her point was that most tears are small and either repair themselves or require just a few stitches. Even deep tears, in her opinion, are preferable to large episiotomies because the tissue tears only as far as it needs to and then heals more efficiently. One woman in the class asked her, "Are tears, then, a natural thing?" to which Ingrid responded, "I would have to say yes."

The room was quiet for a moment after that. The discussion then turned to what midwives do to prevent tears. It starts with perineal massage in the prenatal period, something that pregnant women and their partners do at home, to stretch the tissues that will have to stretch during birth. During the birth itself, midwives use hot compresses and apply pressure to the perineum to support it as the baby's head descends, crowns, and is born. They massage and stretch the tissues with olive oil to ease the baby's head out of the vagina. Midwives will often ask a woman to stop pushing altogether for a moment so that the baby does not come out too quickly. Many women in my study described such moments with awe and appreciation for the esoteric skills of their midwives. The intervention of the midwife in preparing the tissues with massage and lubrication and then averting the woman's instinct to push are all part of a natural birth.

Natural intentions

If some interventions are natural, they are nevertheless qualified. The case of artificial rupture of the membranes is a good example of how intention and context matter in the determination of the naturalness of birth. Although this intervention may be viewed as unnatural and recalled with anger or disappointment when experienced at the hands of a physician without being consulted, women in the care of midwives do not ordinarily regard it as a problem. In a clinic visit during my fieldwork, a couple – Marielle and Tom – came in with their newborn baby for a postpartum visit with their midwife, Isobel. The rapport between them was warm and sincere; Isobel had attended their first two babies' births and followed the pregnancy of their third, but she did not attend this newborn's birth.

As they discussed the birth, Marielle began to cry, recalling how, long into the labor, the alternate midwife had told her she was not working hard enough. "I know she just said it to inspire me, but it hurt my feelings, and it wasn't true." Marielle was even more upset that this midwife had insisted on breaking her waters to "get things moving." She described how different this was from the births of her first and second babies, when her waters had burst naturally in the pushing stage and the excitement of those moments inspired her and renewed her flagging energy. She felt that the alternate midwife had not respected her natural birth process. She was suspicious of her intentions, and this played a role in her evaluation of the artificial rupture of the membranes as an unnatural intervention. Thus, the exception to the trusting relationship between midwife and client reinforces the centrality of caring and trust in midwifery care itself as integral to natural pregnancy and birth.

Conclusion

Midwives in Ontario and the women they attend are engaged in culturally productive strategies (both discursive and clinical) to redefine natural birth in ways that no longer strictly fix nature against culture, nature against medical and technological interventions, and sometimes, nature against women themselves (in the case of the failure to birth "naturally"). Such flexibility reflects the growing comfort with the omnipresence of technology in our midst and, quite literally, in our bodies. The new professional context of midwifery and the influx of a more mainstream clientele have been factors as well. Yet this changing notion of natural birth still works to challenge the powerful discourses of science and medicine and the institutions of maternity care that have thus far shaped women's embodied subjectivity so much so that what midwives and their clients hope for and work for is often articulated in its terms. Natural birth seems to stand for midwifery itself and for a particular set of gender expectations inherent in these midwifery stories I have just relayed: that giving birth is hard but satisfying work that women are completely capable of performing; that, with proper support, women can handle the pain of labor and even find it empowering; and that women can trust their gut feelings in a context in which choice is paramount, interventions are negotiable, and trust characterizes the midwife–client relationship. This flexible rather than fixed construction and experience of natural birth strengthens rather than weakens its empowering potential.

The ideological foundation of such cultural work lies in modernity itself. Having choice is part of being a modern person, and making choices about sexuality and reproduction – from contraception to method of birth – is expected of the modern woman (Paxson 2002: 216). Thus, the importance of having knowledge, having a sense of control, and having a choice during pregnancy and labor is fundamental to the definition and experience of natural birth in a fully modern sense. Overall, midwifery in Ontario seeks to replace the predominant cultural version of pregnant and birthing bodies with what is, in their view, a better – but equally cultural – version. For indeed, as Marilyn Strathern has said, "[n]ature cannot survive without cultural intervention" (1992: 174).

Discussion questions

1. What is the problem identified by some of the midwives with having a specific ideal of what constitutes natural birth?
2. What is the importance of informed choice in childbirth as described in this chapter?

3. How do the midwives in this chapter attempt to present labor and childbirth as natural processes?
4. How do the women in this chapter see labor pains as empowering?

Notes

1   For detailed descriptions and analyses of this process, see Bourgeault (2006), Bourgeault et al. (2004), and MacDonald (2007).
2   Midwives argue that natural birth is empowering for families too, for example, by allowing fathers, other children, and even grandparents a greater role in the process.
3   *Doula* is the name given to the person who cares for the new mother after childbirth and who may also assist at the birth. It is a nonclinical but important role often taken on by close family members or friends who provide support for the new mother, particularly with breastfeeding. Since the 1980s, the role has become professionalized, with training programs in the United States and Canada and doulas charging fees for their services (Raphael 1993).
4   A condition that occurs during pregnancy or during labor in which the placenta pulls away from the uterus, causing bleeding and an emergency situation.
5   *Maternal serum* is a screening test performed at 15 to 18 weeks of pregnancy and is used to signal maternal risk for several fetal disabilities, including neural tube disorders and Down syndrome. It is not a diagnostic test, and thus, critics suggest that it creates anxiety and leads to increased use of other technologies (Blatt 1993: 237).
6   At the time I conducted the research for this work in the late 1990s, midwives attended approximately 6 percent of all births in the province; that figure rose to 8 percent by 2007.
7   For more work on the relationship of women to technology, see also Haraway (1991), Riessman (1983), Sawicki (1991), and Stabile (1994).
8   *Meconium* is the first stool excreted by the infant. Interuterine excretion (which can only be detected after the amniotic waters have broken) is associated with fetal distress. Meconium aspiration is a potentially dangerous situation for the baby and requires hospital-based intervention (Raines 1993: 244).

References

Blatt, R. J. 1993. "Maternal Serum Screening." In *The Encyclopedia of Childbearing*, ed. B. K. Rothman, 236–237. New York: Henry Holt.
Bourgeault, Ivy Lynn. 2006. *Push!* Toronto: McGill-Queen's University Press.
Bourgeault, Ivy Lynn, Cecilia Benoit, and Robbie Davis-Floyd, eds. 2004. *Reconceiving Midwifery: The New Canadian Model*, 46–66. Montreal: McGill-Queen's University Press.
Butler, Judith. 1990. *Gender Trouble*. New York: Routledge.
Davis-Floyd, Robbie. 1992. *Birth as an American Rite of Passage*. Berkeley: University of California Press.
Davis-Floyd, Robbie. 1994. "The Technocratic Body: American Childbirth as Cultural Expression." *Social Science and Medicine* 38(8): 1125–1140.
Haraway, Donna. 1991. *Simians, Cyborgs, and Women*. New York: Routledge.
Hartmann, Katherine, Meera Viswanathan, Rachel Palmieri, Gerald Gartlehner, John Thorp Jr., and Kathleen L. Lohr. 2005. "Outcomes of Routine Episiotomy: A Systematic Review." *JAMA* 293: 2141–2148.
Kornelsen, Jude, and Elaine Carty. 2004. "Challenges to Midwifery Integration: Interprofessional Relationships in British Columbia." In *Reconceiving Midwifery*, eds. Ivy Lynn Bourgeault, Cecilia Benoit, and Robbie Davis-Floyd, 111–130. Toronto: McGill-Queen's University Press.
Lock, Margaret, and Patricia Kaufert, eds. 1998. *Pragmatic Women and Body Politics*. Cambridge: Cambridge University Press.
Lock, Margaret, and Nancy Scheper-Hughes. 1990. "A Critical Interpretive Approach in Medical Anthropology: Rituals and Routines of Discipline and Dissent." In *Medical Anthropology: Contemporary Theory and Method*, eds. T. Johnson and C. Sargent, 47–72. New York: Greenwood Press.

MacDonald, Margaret. 2007. *At Work in the Field of Birth*. Nashville, TN: Vanderbilt University Press.

Mitchell, Lisa. 1994. "The Routinization of the Other: Ultrasound, Women, and the Fetus." In *Misconceptions*, eds. G. Basen, M. Eichler, and A. Lipman, Vol. 2, 146–160. Hull: Voyageuer.

Pasveer, Bernike, and Madeleine Akrich. 2001. "Obstetrical Trajectories: On Training Women's Bodies for (Home) Birth." In *Birth by Design*, eds. R. DeVries, C. Benoit, E. R. Van Teijlingen, and S. Wrede, 229–242. New York: Routledge.

Paxson, Heather. 2002. "Rationalising Sex: Family Planning and the Making of Modern Lovers in Urban Greece." *American Ethnologist* 29(2): 307–334.

Raines, Deborah. 1993. "Meconium." In *The Encyclopedia of Childbearing*, ed. Barbara Katz Rothman, 243–244. New York: Henry Holt.

Raphael, Dana. 1993. "Doula." In *The Encyclopedia of Childbearing*, ed. Barbara Katz Rothman, 113–115. New York: Henry Holt.

Rapp, Rayna. 1990. "Constructing Amniocentesis: Maternal and Medical Discourses." In *Uncertain Terms: Negotiating Gender in American Culture*, eds. F. Ginsburg and A. L. Tsing, pp. 28–42. Boston: Beacon Press.

Riessman, Catherine Kohler. 1983. "Women and Medicalization: A New Perspective." *Social Policy* 14: 3–18.

Rothman, Barbara Katz. 1986. *The Tentative Pregnancy: Prenatal Diagnosis and the Future of Motherhood*. New York: Viking Penguin.

Sawicki, Jana. 1991. *Disciplining Foucault*. New York: Routledge.

Sleep, J., J. Roberts, and I. Chalmers. 1989. "The Second Stage of Labour." In *A Guide to Effective Care in Pregnancy and Childbirth*, eds. Murray Enkin, Marc J. N. C. Keirse, and Iain Chalmers, 1129–1144. Oxford: Oxford University Press.

Stabile, Carol. 1994. *Feminism and the Technological Fix*. Manchester: Manchester University Press.

Strathern, Marilyn. 1992. *After Nature: English Kinship in the Late 20th Century*. Cambridge: Cambridge University Press.

Thacker, Stephen B., Donna F. Stroup, Man-huei Chang, and Sonja L. Henderson. 1999. *Continuous Electronic Fetal Heart Rate Monitoring versus Intermittent Auscultation for Assessment during Labor*. Cochrane Library. Issue 1. Oxford: Update Software.

Chapter 9

Making room for daddy

Fathers and breastfeeding in the United States

Sarah Sobonya

Original material prepared for the 7th edition.

It was hard to see her dedication to breastfeeding at all costs and not be able to do anything to help. She didn't want even a drop of formula to pass our kid's lips (and it never did), and that was not easy, what with her and myself working. I'd see her come home and slump down and start pumping for the next day at midnight or so. She looked exhausted and miserable. I would have given up.

44-year-old father of two, St. Louis, Missouri

Introduction: why breastfeeding matters

From Renaissance artwork showing a Madonna nursing infant Jesus to modern advertisements for breastfeeding supplies, breastfeeding is viewed as an intimate relationship between two people, a mother and infant in a closed circle, with no space for anyone else. Most research on breastfeeding is explicitly gendered, examining topics such as mothers' experiences combining breastfeeding with working outside the home or the maternal stigma attached to different infant feeding choices. Although most babies have a father, fathers are usually viewed as irrelevant to the breastfeeding narrative. This is a mistake: in a number of ways, fathers are directly and indirectly involved in breastfeeding, and because breastfeeding matters, this involvement matters. Drawing on existing scholarship as well as my own ethnographic research, this chapter addresses men's roles in breastfeeding, an important but often neglected dimension of the gendered aspects of infant feeding. I begin with a brief summary of the current research about breastfeeding and health, both globally and in the United States, and then look at two understudied but important issues: the role of non-lactating fathers in facilitating breastfeeding success and the emerging dialogue around how to support transgender fathers who choose to lactate.

Healthier babies, healthier mothers

Scientific evidence demonstrating the health benefits of breastfeeding has continued to accumulate over the past decades – or since breastfeeding is the biological norm, perhaps it is more accurate to talk about the health risks attached to *not* breastfeeding. Extensive

DOI: 10.4324/9781003398349-10

research links breastfeeding to a significant reduction in sudden infant death syndrome (SIDS) (Hauck et al. 2011), a reduction in both the incidence and severity of diarrheal and respiratory infections in infants and young children, and a substantial decrease in breast cancer rates in mothers (Victora et al. 2016). Other research strongly suggests that being breastfed confers some protection against SIDS, childhood leukemia and lymphoma, and asthma, and that breastfeeding a child reduces maternal rates of ovarian cancer, type II diabetes, coronary heart disease, and hypertension (Bartick 2013).

Breastfeeding is a global health issue. The United Nations Children's Fund (UNICEF) states that *breastfeeding* has the potential to save more lives than any other preventative health measure (2015). Worldwide, near-universal breastfeeding could prevent the deaths of 823,000 children under the age of 5, mostly from infectious diseases, and it could prevent 20,000 women from dying of breast cancer (Victora et al. 2016). Although most of these preventable deaths would occur in low- and middle-income countries, increased breastfeeding would also save lives in high-income countries, such as the United States. The American Academy of Pediatrics' most recent Policy Statement on Breastfeeding and the Use of Human Milk (2012) estimates that over 900 infant deaths would be prevented if 90 percent of US mothers breastfed for at least six months, mostly resulting from a significant reduction in SIDS rates.

Rates and disparities

Although breastfeeding was once almost ubiquitous, the introduction of commercial infant formulas during the latter half of the nineteenth century marked the beginning of a steady decline in US breastfeeding rates that would last for over a hundred years (Apple 1987). Breastfeeding fell to its lowest recorded level in 1972, when only 22 percent of infants were breastfed at all (Eckhardt and Hendershot 1984). Since then, however, both the initiation and duration of breastfeeding have climbed steadily. According to the most recent data available, 80 percent of infants born in 2012 were breastfed at least once, and 51.4 percent of infants were receiving at least some breast milk at 6 months (Centers for Disease Control and Prevention 2015).

However, these general statistics mask significant disparities in US breastfeeding rates. Although breastfeeding rates have continued to increase for US mothers in all demographic categories, they remain lower among women from marginalized groups. While 83 percent of non-Hispanic White mothers who gave birth in 2012 began breastfeeding and 56 percent were still breastfeeding at 6 months, only 66 percent of non-Hispanic Black mothers initiated breastfeeding and only 35 percent were still breastfeeding at 6 months. Household income is also strongly associated with breastfeeding: 91 percent of mothers with a household income of at least six times the federal poverty level initiate breastfeeding, while only 71 percent of mothers living under the poverty line do so.

Even mothers with the greatest resources struggle to meet current standards for breastfeeding. The World Health Organization and UNICEF recommend exclusive breastfeeding (meaning, that the baby receives no food or liquids other than breast milk and any necessary vitamins or medicines) for six months and breastfeeding with complementary foods for "up to 2 years of age or beyond" (World Health Organization 2016: para. 3). The American Academy of Pediatrics echoes the recommendation that mothers exclusively breastfeed for six months and advises that breastfeeding with complementary foods continue for "1 year or longer as mutually desired by mother and infant" (AAP Section on Breastfeeding 2012: e827–e828). Few American mothers attain these goals, however, which has opened the door for the development of healthcare programming and support organizations intended to increase breastfeeding rates.

Supporting breastfeeding

The Special Supplemental Nutrition Program for Women, Infants, and Children, known more generally as the WIC program, is the largest provider of breastfeeding help in the United States. Currently, WIC is required to spend $21 per pregnant or breastfeeding mother receiving services through the program on breastfeeding promotion and support (Oliveira and Frazao 2015). La Leche League, an international organization founded in 1956 to help breastfeeding mothers through education and support, is another key player in today's breastfeeding landscape, holding over 3,000 regular meetings in 68 countries (Wiessinger et al. 2010). Many hospitals also offer breastfeeding support to women who deliver at their facility, and an increasing number of lactation specialists (generally IBCLCs, or International Board Certified Lactation Consultants) either have their own private practice providing breastfeeding education and assistance or work with health professionals such as pediatricians or midwives. Finally, organizations have emerged to offer breastfeeding support specifically to mothers who they perceive as being poorly served by existing options. These include groups that specifically target African American mothers, such as Reaching Our Sisters Everywhere (ROSE) in Georgia and I AM: Breastfeeding in St. Louis, Missouri.

While these entities use varying models of support, one commonality is a primary focus on the "breastfeeding dyad": a mother and her nursing child (Pavill 2002; Mitchell-Box and Braun 2013). However, a number of studies suggest that fathers can play a significant role in breastfeeding success (Mitchell-Box and Braun 2013; Rempel and Rempel 2011; Bar-Yam and Darby 1997). In response, some healthcare providers and advocacy organizations in the United States have introduced programs specifically targeting fathers or encouraging fathers' participation in existing breastfeeding promotion activities in an attempt to increase their partners' breastfeeding rates. These are generally designed for social fathers, men who take a parental role and are often partnered with the infant's mother but may or may not be biological fathers, and I use the terms *father* and *mother's partner* interchangeably to refer to an infant's social father.

In the remainder of this chapter, I first describe some of the ways fathers have become more visible in breastfeeding advocacy and support and outline specific concerns fathers have about breastfeeding. For this, I draw on both existing literature and my own ethnographic study on breastfeeding praxis in and around St. Louis, Missouri, between 2013 and 2015, which examined the effects of race and socioeconomic status on the ways breastfeeding is conceptualized and practiced. I then introduce emerging research on transgender men and transmasculine individuals who breastfeed or "chestfeed" their infants, situating these fathers in current discourses about breastfeeding fathers.

Fathers promoting breastfeeding

Most mothers decide how they plan to feed their babies well before they give birth. Although, ultimately, this choice rests with the mother (except in the case of transgender fathers who give birth), a father can strongly influence this decision, and an early review of the literature noted that for most demographic groups, a father's outlook on breast-feeding mattered more in determining his infant's feeding choice than that of medical professionals or his partner's family or friends (Bar-Yam and Darby 1997). Interestingly, the mother's perception of the father's attitude was influential even when it differed from the father's actual attitude – that is, mothers were less likely to breastfeed when they thought their partners would disapprove, even when the partners themselves said they would support breastfeeding. One study found that mothers were not very accurate when reporting their partner's attitudes about breastfeeding, performing only slightly better than random chance (Freed et al. 1993).

A father's impact goes beyond influencing prospective mothers' plans for infant feeding. In their study of first-time mothers in Canada, Rempel and Rempel (2004) found that fathers affected not only whether the mother initiated breastfeeding but also the duration of breastfeeding. They documented two separate effects, one a function of how helpful and supportive a father was in facilitating breastfeeding, and a separate effect resulting from the father's attitudes and beliefs about breastfeeding. This suggests that interventions targeting fathers in an effort to increase maternal breastfeeding rates should focus on educating men about the benefits of breastfeeding, in an attempt to change attitudes, as well as on sharing information about how to best support a breastfeeding mother. For example, information about the health problems associated with formula feeding may convince a father to endorse breastfeeding, while more technical information about potential breastfeeding problems and the needs of a breastfeeding mother may allow him to feel more competent and involved with the process. One father told me that he knew it was important for breastfeeding mothers to drink enough fluids, so during the early days of his daughter's life, he held himself responsible for ensuring that his wife's large water cup was always by her side and never ran empty. Although he could not breastfeed his new daughter himself, this small task helped him feel that he was contributing in some way to the process.

Most formal intervention initiatives target the partners of low-income women, a demographic group with lower rates of breastfeeding initiation and duration (Centers for Disease Control and Prevention 2015). These programs generally focus on men with pregnant partners rather than fathers of infants, although some continue to work with men after their children are born. In addition to an educational segment, programs may also contain an affective component, asking fathers about their attitudes about breast-feeding and any concerns they might have. Some programs even provide ongoing support for fathers, which may include assisting them while they negotiate integrating breastfeeding into their relationships with their partners and their babies. Two such initiatives, one at a Flagstaff, Arizona, WIC clinic (Sciacca et al. 1995) and the other at a Baltimore hospital (Wolfberg et al. 2004), both found that the partners of fathers who attended prenatal educational classes about breastfeeding were more likely to initiate breastfeeding, and the Arizona program also found an increase in breastfeeding duration among these partners.

The first father-to-father breastfeeding promotion program was the WIC Peer Dad Program in Texas (Velarde 2014). Peer support or peer counseling refers to the provision of services by a non-professional who has firsthand experience and comes from the same community as those being served, and peer counseling has been an important part of many breastfeeding support programs. In 1990, WIC first involved women who had successfully breastfed their own children as WIC Peer Counselors serving breastfeeding mothers (Chapman et al. 2010). After successfully completing a 20-hour training course, women serving in this capacity today perform a variety of duties, including running informational classes and support groups and providing support and limited technical assistance to breastfeeding mothers, in person and by phone. In 2002, in response to the growing body of literature documenting the importance of fathers in breastfeeding, the Texas Department of Health piloted a Peer Dad program at two different WIC offices (Stremler and Lovera 2004). Four men at each location received eight hours of training about the advantages of breastfeeding, how to address men's concerns about breastfeeding, and basic counseling strategies. During the six-month pilot program, the men worked between 1 and 16 hours a week and were paid slightly above the minimum wage. Like WIC Peer Counselors, Peer Dads led educational classes for men and provided support for men via phone as well as in person. An evaluation of the pilot program found that contact with Peer Dads increased the likelihood that a man's partner would breastfed for six months or longer, although the difference was not statistically significant (Lovera et al. 2010), and that breastfeeding initiation increased in WIC clinics that employed Peer Dads (Stremler and Lovera 2004).

As of 2015, two Texas WIC clinics had long-standing Peer Dad programs, and two others were in the process of training Peer Dads (Hovis 2015). The Dallas program, which reaches over 700 fathers each month, is the larger program (Velarde 2014). Muswamba Mwamba is the coordinator of the Peer Dad program in Dallas, Texas, and is also an IBCLC, the highest credential available in the field of lactation. An outspoken breastfeeding advocate and African American man, Mwamba is particularly concerned about increasing breastfeeding rates in his community, noting that African American men may have no previous experience seeing a breastfeeding mother. A recent research study with low-income African American men in Cleveland, Ohio, echoed Mwamba's concerns, as Banks, Killpack, and Furman (2013) found that the men they interviewed wanted to be more involved and helpful to their partners but viewed their lack of knowledge about breastfeeding as a barrier. One of the men they interviewed expressed his feelings by saying: "They have all these programs for women but nothing to help us. It's frustrating. It hurts. Where's the program for us since we're trying to do our best? It's like we almost deleted" (2013: 507–508). A program like Texas's Peer Dad initiative would seem to be a good fit to serve the stated needs of these Ohio men.

Mwamba is not the only African American man advocating for breastfeeding. On June 22, 2015, an African American rap artist named George Moss posted a public photograph of himself on his Facebook page showing him standing in a bathroom, holding pieces of a breast pump. He captioned it: "If you ever wonder what Wrappers do when they get off stage, they clean breast pumps for their wives so their baby can eat. #thuglife" (Moss 2015). The post quickly went viral, with over 51,000 likes and over 9,000 shares, as well as coverage by a variety of news outlets (Bologna 2015). Many of the comments on the photograph praised Moss for his support of his wife's breastfeeding, as well as for publicly sharing the picture with his fans, sometimes phrased as "normalizing" breastfeeding. Moss stated in the comments on his photograph that he was initially taken aback by its popularity, but in the months following the initial picture, he has posted a number of other photographs depicting some aspect of breastfeeding on his Facebook page. In February of 2016, the Best for Babes Foundation interviewed Moss and Baltimore Ravens running back Justin Forsett, also an African American man, about their support for breastfeeding and the need for strong male voices in breastfeeding promotion (Best for Babes Foundation 2016). As noted previously, breastfeeding rates are significantly lower among African American women than among American women in general, which negatively affects the health of both African American women and their children. By advocating for breastfeeding, Mwamba, Moss, and Forsett are working to reduce this health disparity.

Over the past 20 years, healthcare providers and breastfeeding activists have begun to include fathers in the breastfeeding narrative, although programs that target men are still the exception to the rule. Although few programs are specifically intended for fathers, while doing research in St. Louis, I found that men were welcome to join their partners at many events for new and expectant parents. A number of men attended La Leche League meetings, for example, and the organization's calendar noted specifically that men were welcome at certain meetings. I attended a WIC Breastfeeding Café for pregnant and new mothers, and nearly a third of the women brought a male partner with them. Prenatal education classes in St. Louis, as in most US cities, are typically open to both expectant mothers and expectant fathers, and most include sessions on breastfeeding. While the choice of whether to breastfeed, and for how long, should ultimately rest with the parent whose body is actually breastfeeding, fathers also have an investment in the well-being of their children, and breastfeeding can make important contributions to that well-being. However, there are many reasons fathers may be reluctant to endorse breastfeeding wholeheartedly. In the next section, I describe some of the concerns men have about breastfeeding and the way they may influence their responses to their breastfeeding partners.

"I would have given up": fathers' concerns

Many fathers, like many mothers, have some degree of ambivalence toward breastfeeding. Wanting a healthy baby is a near-universal sentiment among parents, and breastfeeding's health benefits are a compelling reason for fathers to endorse the practice. However, most men find that breastfeeding also has drawbacks. Some fathers feel that breastfeeding negatively affects their ability to bond with and care for their infants, because they are not able to breastfeed themselves. Men may also feel trapped between supporting breastfeeding and being a caring partner, especially when breastfeeding appears exhausting, painful, or difficult. Finally, fathers may struggle to reconcile societal beliefs about the female breast as a sexual body part with the reality of breastfeeding, particularly in front of other people.

Breastfed babies nurse frequently, especially during the early weeks. One St. Louis mother of a 4-week-old baby told me that all her son did was "eat, poop, and sleep," a not-uncommon description of babies this age. When babies are fed via bottles, fathers and mothers can both participate equally, but breastfeeding requires the nursing mother. Some fathers report that they feel left out or superfluous during breastfeeding. In a study on male partners of WIC recipients in Hawaii, Mitchell-Box and Braun found that men complained of feeling like a "third wheel" (2012: E45) and explained that, when they offered to help, they were told that there was nothing they could do. Men perceived the things they actually could do to help, such as cleaning or cooking dinner, as unsatisfying when compared to being able to feed their babies. In an older study, Jordan and Wall (1990) interviewed a diverse group of expectant and recent fathers and found that many reported feeling frustrated and inadequate when they could not make their breastfed babies happy, noting that often the babies wanted only the breast and were not content when given anything else. One father stated that the only thing he could do that made his daughter happy was to change her diapers, certainly not a part of infant care that most people find enjoyable or fulfilling.

Being able to fully bond with their infants was an important concern for many fathers. In a study of middle- and upper-class Canadian fathers, Rempel and Rempel (2011) found that some of the men believed that their ability to bond with their infants was constrained by breastfeeding, although they attempted to mitigate this by bottle-feeding pumped breast milk or participating in feeding their infants solid foods once their children were old enough. Jordan and Wall also found that the men they interviewed were worried about bonding. One father said, "When you are breastfeeding that creates certain problems with both parents parenting. . . . I'm trying to do a bottle every night. I feel like I'm missing out a little bit on the bonding because we can't do that [breastfeed]" (1990: 211). This same concern was echoed by men I met during my own research. A St. Louis area father of two told me that he enjoyed giving his daughter bottles when he could, because this provided "a little more bonding time for [him]." As this theme has remained quite salient over the past 25 years, a focus on helping fathers find fulfilling ways to bond with their young breastfed infants is essential to any interventions targeting fathers, as is reassuring them that they can still be good fathers even if they are not able to have the close relationship they desire with their children until after their children are a few months old.

Men also expressed concern about the effects of breastfeeding on their partners. Especially during the early weeks, breastfeeding can be physically and emotionally exhausting as mothers try to adapt to the near-constant needs of a newborn. Most newborns wake frequently, and they may breastfeed as often as 10 to 12 times a day, or more. Even when everything is going well, many mothers experience nipple soreness and tenderness, and when mothers are experiencing breastfeeding difficulties, they may develop cracked and bleeding nipples, infections, painful clogged ducts, or other disturbing symptoms. While all these are signs of medical problems that should be treated by a competent lactation professional, many US healthcare providers lack the skill and knowledge to effectively diagnose and treat common breastfeeding problems (James and Berkowitz 2012). Although IBCLCs are specially trained to diagnose and remediate these problems, access to these specialists is limited: in the United States as a whole, there are fewer than four IBCLCs for every 1,000 births, and in some states, the rate drops to fewer than two per 1,000 births (Centers for Disease Control and Prevention 2014). This lack of knowledgeable care adds to the challenges that many women face while breastfeeding. Men often struggle to reconcile their support for breastfeeding with their own discomfort at seeing their partners' suffering, as they try to be both good partners and good fathers.

A number of the men I met during my research told me that because breastfeeding appeared so difficult or painful, they would not have continued breastfeeding as long as their partners did. The St. Louis area father of two quoted at the beginning of this chapter said quite clearly, "I would have given up," when he described his wife's exhaustion after the birth of their older child. Although he acknowledged that the choice to breastfeed was hers to make, he also felt frustrated when he was unable to make breastfeeding easier for her. "It wasn't easy watching that and not being able to help," he said. While he was able to do other things he viewed as part of being a good partner, such as supporting their family financially and cooking healthy meals, he felt "pretty useless" when it came to breastfeeding.

Another St. Louis father of two was concerned that breastfeeding would be emotionally trying for his wife, who had suffered from severe postpartum depression following the birth of their first child. Their first child was not breastfed, and he told me that when his wife decided she wanted to breastfeed their second, he was "concerned that she wouldn't feel confident in breastfeeding and that would alter her mood." He was somewhat reassured when the birth attendant, a certified nurse midwife (CNM), told him breastfeeding was actually associated with a decreased incidence of postpartum depression.[1] Still, he was aware that breastfeeding could be difficult and worried that his wife would struggle with the mechanics of the process, and that this would negatively impact her mental health. "My concern was that it would cause her mood to go down," he explained, "that if she didn't demonstrate an immediate competence . . . it would be more frustrating to her." Fortunately, breastfeeding did not have an adverse effect on her mental health, and she was able to breastfeed successfully.

A third man I interviewed was more circumspect when discussing his concerns about breastfeeding. His second child had been admitted to the hospital ICU when she was 3 days old, and breastfeeding had taken a back seat to more pressing health concerns, and once the infant was medically stable, his wife had struggled significantly with breastfeeding, including difficulty with poor latch (a term that references the way the infant sucks on the nipple), low supply, and pain. Although this father wanted to be supportive of his wife, he, in contrast to his wife, did not view breastfeeding as greatly important. When describing his response to his wife's injured nipples, he said, "I told her I would never breastfeed." When I interviewed him, his younger child was almost 4 months old, and he said that he thought 6 months old was a good time to "think about" or "start" weaning, even though the AAP and WHO guidelines described earlier and his wife all agreed that breastfeeding should last a minimum of a year. Although breastfeeding was no longer painful for his wife, he viewed it as interfering with her social life, saying it restricted her "interactions with family and friends." His wife disputed his statements, but he believed that if she was not breastfeeding, she would be freer to spend time away from her baby and this would improve her quality of life (and perhaps his as well).

The literature about male partners of breastfeeding mothers also supports the idea that men can find it challenging to fulfill their desire to protect their wives from discomfort or suffering while not undermining breastfeeding. Mitchell-Box and Braun (2012) found that a number of men they interviewed were very focused on the pain that their partners endured, which they found distressing to witness. One father talked about seeing his infant scratching and biting his partner while she was breastfeeding (or attempting to), and another also mentioned that his infant sometimes bit his wife, causing her to wince in pain. Similarly, based on their research in the United Kingdom, Datta et al. reported that men sometimes felt trapped between protecting their wives and supporting breastfeeding. One father explained that men should "do what they think they [mothers] need, which isn't always what you think" (2012: 159). According to the men interviewed, this should extend to supporting mothers in their choice not to continue breastfeeding, as well as their desire to continue. This reinforces the idea that the choice to breastfeed or not must ultimately reside with the breastfeeding mother, which in turn serves to clarify the partner's primary responsibility: respecting the mother's choices. While supporting breastfeeding and preventing the mothers' suffering are both worthy goals, they must remain secondary to supporting the mother's own autonomy and her rights to control her own body.

A third issue for many male partners is the sexualization of breasts in the United States and other Western countries. Murphy carried out a longitudinal research with British new mothers during the 1990s and found that these breastfeeding mothers were very aware of the societal association between sexuality and breasts and were therefore careful to characterize themselves as modest and discreet, distancing themselves from brazen exhibitionists who nursed their babies by "flashing [their] flesh" and "flicking it out" (2000: 203). Stearns (1999) also explored this juxtaposition of the maternal and the sexual within the same body part and the ways breastfeeding women experienced and negotiated this contradiction. Drawing on in-depth interviews with 51 women from Sonoma County, California, she wrote that some "women proceeded with their breastfeeding as though it were deviant behavior, occurring within a potentially hostile environment" (312). Exceptionally aware of the potential stigma against breastfeeding, most of Stearns's subjects emphasized breastfeeding discreetly when around other people, to avoid making anyone feel uncomfortable. They were especially diligent around men, believing that some men became sexually aroused when observing nursing women. Stearns's research participants were primarily White and middle- to upper-class, but for low-income African American women, stigmatization of breastfeeding as sexual deviance can be even more damaging. One woman in this demographic category told researchers Chin and Dozier about breastfeeding her infant on a bus, saying, "[Y]ou do not know how many people will stare at you and call you obscene names, and like, 'oh, that is so disgusting. Put your breast away'" (2012: 67).

My own more recent research found that a significant number of women were similarly concerned about breastfeeding in front of men, although there were also many who said this was not an issue. White middle-class mothers were most likely to feel unconcerned about the male gaze when nursing their children. However, it was common for women in this group to report that their husbands or male partners did not want them to breastfeed in front of others, including friends and family members. A number of women repeated that "breastfeeding isn't sexual," and many of these women said they did not find their own lactating breasts to be sexually responsive until sometime after they weaned their children. Although many breastfeeding mothers found that they did not enjoy having their breasts touched sexually, they frequently reported that their male partners still wanted to do so, suggesting that their male partners did not so easily separate the maternal and the sexual breast.

Other researchers have documented this as well. Mitchell-Box and Braun (2012) found this to be true for the men in their study, who expressed concern that breastfeeding could be viewed as immodest by others. More than two-thirds of their subjects did not think a woman should breastfeed in front of others, although half of those were willing to make an exception for women who were adequately covered. Some specified that they would not want their partners to breastfeed in front of other men, and one of these explained how it would be awkward for the man, saying, "If it was my friend's wife or something I would feel uncomfortable, thinking that maybe he's thinking I'm looking at her hooters" (2012: E46). For him, the act of looking at a woman's breast could not be innocent but must be lewd and inappropriate, so it was important to avoid putting men in situations where they might inadvertently perform this sort of act. In a larger study with a diverse group of men (not necessarily fathers), Pollock et al. (2002) reported that 29 percent believed that breastfeeding in public was not acceptable, and 34 percent found it embarrassing. African American men were significantly more likely than other men to view breastfeeding in public negatively, which is perhaps unsurprising, considering the lower breastfeeding rates in African American communities. Chin and Dozier (2012) noted that men in low-income African American communities described protecting their breastfeeding partners when they nursed in public, keeping them safe from other men who might gawk or ogle, as well as guarding against accidental breast exposure.

Cultural beliefs about breasts and sexuality are unlikely to change quickly, and the partners of breastfeeding women will thus continue to struggle to reconcile breastfeeding with both their own erotization of the female breast and their concerns about others doing the same. However, stories of fathers protecting their breastfeeding partners from others who might harass them are a hopeful addition to this discourse, creating a space for men to take an active part in supporting public breastfeeding. Of course, breastfeeding mothers can and do speak up for themselves when facing public harassment, but they may prefer to be able to simply focus on nursing their babies without needing to defend themselves from the reactions of others. If more fathers take on this role, they may aid in shifting societal attitudes about public breastfeeding.

Future directions: fathers who lactate

For centuries, discussions of breastfeeding have begun with the assumption that the person breastfeeding was a woman, usually but not always the infant's mother. Although fathers in a few societies are known to put their infants to their breasts for comfort (Raphael 1973; Hewlett and Winn 2014), the actual transfer of milk to an infant was considered only possible for women. However, new understandings of gender have gained traction during the past decade, including a greater awareness of transgender and genderqueer people who may not fit neatly into prescribed reproductive gender roles. For example, a person may be born with a female reproductive system, including a vagina, uterus, and ovaries, as well as breasts with a well-developed system of milk ducts, but identify primarily as male or masculine. A transgender man may decide against gender confirmation surgery and choose to retain the reproductive system he was born with, which often gives him the option of giving birth and nursing his babies, a process many call *chestfeeding* rather than *breastfeeding*.

The issue of transgender men and chestfeeding first entered popular discourse in 2012, when a transgender man named Trevor MacDonald published a short piece titled "How I Learned to Be a Breastfeeding Dad" on the popular Huffington Post news site. The piece, in which MacDonald describes the breastfeeding support he received from La Leche League support groups, was shared over a thousand times on Facebook. Later that year, MacDonald applied to become a La Leche League leader but was turned down by the organization because their rules required leaders to be mothers, not fathers (Tapper 2014). Public response to the decision from both breastfeeding advocates and the queer community was overwhelmingly negative, and after a period of review, La Leche League International reversed their decision and revised their guidelines to remove any mention of gender, opening the door for chestfeeding fathers to apply.

The medical community is also becoming more aware of the needs of chestfeeding men. Wolfe-Roubatis and Spatz (2015) recently published a set of case studies and clinical case guidelines for perinatal nurses caring for transgender men. Suggestions included creating gender-inclusive health forms and using the patient's preferred terminology for body parts, such as *chest* rather than *breast*. Another recent article (Berger et al. 2015) focused on barriers to good-quality healthcare frequently encountered by transgender men during pregnancy and the perinatal period, including professionals' lack of knowledge about the effects testosterone treatment or chest masculinization surgery can have on lactation. Despite these efforts, stigma and lack of knowledgeable care remain serious problems for transgender men who want to nurse their babies.

Perhaps the most encouraging development in this area is a new qualitative study by a diverse team of Canadian researchers (MacDonald et al. 2016). Interviews with 22 transmasculine individuals (a category that is inclusive of transgender men, or trans men, as well as other people who identify more strongly with masculinity than femininity) revealed that gender dysphoria related to the chest was an issue for a number of the individuals in the study, with two reporting this as the main reason they stopped chestfeeding. On the other hand, others found that they did not experience gender dysphoria while chestfeeding because they saw their mammary tissue as having a purpose (feeding their infants) but noted that, once their infants were weaned, they did experience gender dysphoria because of their chests, particularly when their chests caused them to be misgendered as female by others. This concern about being misgendered created other problems for study participants. For example, when meeting with a surgeon before chest masculinization surgery, some did not tell their surgeons of their plans to become pregnant and chestfeed in the future, out of fear that the surgeon would view this as a reason to deny them the surgery. For others, this concern made them reluctant to seek out lactation help after giving birth. The researchers suggested that healthcare providers make a point of bringing up these potential issues with patients ahead of time, in order to ensure that patients have the information necessary to make informed decisions. For instance, a surgeon might explain that mammary tissue may regrow during pregnancy and that chestfeeding after chest masculinization surgery may be possible, although supplementation will probably be necessary. While more research is still necessary, this growing consideration of the needs of lactating transgender men is a positive sign, suggesting that medical professionals are working to improve healthcare delivery to this population.

Conclusion: a place for Dad

Breastfeeding is an important public health issue in the United States as well as in low- and middle-income countries. While decisions about breastfeeding ultimately reside with the person whose body is lactating, fathers can play an important role in supporting and facilitating breastfeeding even if they do not lactate themselves. When men are knowledgeable about the benefits of breastfeeding, they are more likely to endorse the practice, which in turn influences their partners' attitudes about breastfeeding. Recently, a number of African American men have taken more active roles in promoting breastfeeding, an important step in reducing the disparity between breastfeeding rates among African American women and other women in the United States.

Fathers may struggle with some aspects of breastfeeding. Some feel left out and unable to bond with their nursing babies, especially during the early weeks, when infants breastfeed frequently. They may find it difficult to see their partners struggle or suffer due to breastfeeding. Because the female breast is sexualized in Western societies, men can feel uncomfortable when their partners breastfeed in front of others, and they may find it difficult to understand when their partners no longer see their own breasts as sexual objects. Some men have found ways to make meaningful contribution to breastfeeding, such as keeping a partner's water cup full or defending her from harassment.

While most fathers do not breastfeed their own infants, transmasculine men may do so, a process they usually refer to as chestfeeding. While more research on chestfeeding is still needed, researchers are beginning to investigate the phenomenon. Their work focuses on barriers that men who chestfeed may encounter and ways for healthcare providers to better serve their needs. While many of the challenges confronted by lactating men are different from those men face when their partners breastfeed, it is important to support all fathers in their efforts to improve the health of their children.

Discussion questions

1. What impact does a father's attitude or outlook on breastfeeding have on a woman's decision of whether or not to breastfeed?
2. What interventions does the author suggest might encourage men to support their partners to breastfeed?
3. What concerns do men have that may result in them being reluctant to encourage their partner to breastfeed?
4. How does the sexualization of breasts impact a father's perception of breastfeeding?
5. What issues did transgender men identify with regards to breastfeeding or chestfeeding?

Note

1   This is an oversimplification of the actual data on this issue, which suggests that postpartum depression is more closely linked to a woman not being successful at feeding her infant in the way she chooses. For more detailed information, see Borra et al. (2014).

References

AAP Section on Breastfeeding. 2012. "Breastfeeding and the Use of Human Milk." *Pediatrics: Peds* 129(3): 2011–3552.

Apple, Rima D. 1987. *Mothers and Medicine: A Social History of Infant Feeding, 1890–1950: Wisconsin Publications in the History of Science and Medicine.* Madison: University of Wisconsin Press.

Banks, Elizabeth, Steve Killpack, and Lydia Furman. 2013. "Low-Income Inner-City Fathers and Breastfeeding – Where's the Program for Us?" *Breastfeeding Medicine* 8(6): 507–508.

Bartick, Melissa. 2013. "Breastfeeding and Health: A Review of the Evidence." *Journal of Women, Politics & Policy* 34(4): 317–329.

Bar-Yam, Naomi Bromberg, and Lori Darby. 1997. "Fathers and Breastfeeding: A Review of the Literature." *Journal of Human Lactation* 13(1): 45–50.

Berger, Anthony P., Elizabeth M. Potter, Christina M. Shutters, and Katherine L. Imborek. 2015. "Pregnant Transmen and Barriers to High Quality Healthcare." *Proceedings in Obstetrics and Gynecology* 5(2): 1–12.

Best for Babes Foundation. 2016. "J & G: Breastfeeding Movement Needs Strong Male Voices." *Best for Babes.* www.bestforbabes.org/breastfeeding-movement-strong-male-voices/, accessed March 27, 2016.

Bologna, Caroline. 2015. "Dad Has Beautiful Response to Viral Breast Pump Photo." *The Huffington Post.* www.huffingtonpost.com/2015/06/29/george-moss-breast-pump_n_7688036.html, accessed March 27, 2016.

Borra, Cristina, Maria Iacovou, and Almudena Sevilla. 2014. "New Evidence on Breastfeeding and Postpartum Depression: The Importance of Understanding Women's Intentions." *Maternal and Child Health Journal* 19(4): 897–907.

Centers for Disease Control and Prevention. 2014. *Breastfeeding Report Card: United States.* Atlanta, GA: Centers for Disease Control and Prevention. www.cdc.gov/breastfeeding/data/reportcard.htm, accessed March 13, 2015.

Centers for Disease Control and Prevention. 2015. *Breastfeeding among U.S. Children Born 2002–2012, CDC National Immunization Surveys*. www.cdc.gov/breastfeeding/data/nis_data/.

Chapman, Donna J., Katherine Morel, Alex Kojo Anderson, Grace Damio, and Rafael Pérez-Escamilla. 2010. "Breastfeeding Peer Counseling: From Efficacy through Scale-Up." *Journal of Human Lactation: Official Journal of International Lactation Consultant Association* 26(3): 314–326.

Chin, Nancy, and Ann Dozier. 2012. "The Dangers of Baring the Breast: Structural Violence and Formula-Feeding among Low-Income Women." In *Beyond Health, Beyond Choice: Breastfeeding Constraints and Realities*. eds. Paige Hall Smith, Bernice Hausman, and Miriam Labbok, 64–73. New Brunswick, NJ: Rutgers University Press.

Datta, Jessica, Berni Graham, and Kaye Wellings. 2012. "The Role of Fathers in Breastfeeding: Decision-Making and Support." *British Journal of Midwifery* 20(3): 159–167.

Eckhardt, Kenneth W., and Gerry E. Hendershot. 1984. "Analysis of the Reversal in Breast Feeding Trends in the Early 1970s." *Public Health Reports* 99(4): 410–415.

Freed, Gary L., J. Kennard Fraley, and Richard J. Schanler. 1993. "Accuracy of Expectant Mothers' Predictions of Fathers' Attitudes Regarding Breast-Feeding." *Journal of Family Practice* 37(2): 148–153.

Hauck, Fern R., John M. D. Thompson, Kawai O. Tanabe, Rachel Y. Moon, and Mechtild M. Vennemann. 2011. "Breastfeeding and Reduced Risk of Sudden Infant Death Syndrome: A Meta-Analysis." *Pediatrics* 128(1): 103–110.

Hewlett, Barry S., and Steve Winn. 2014. "Allomaternal Nursing in Humans." *Current Anthropology* 55(2): 200–229.

Hovis, Amanda. 2015. "Peer Dad Program Expansion." *Memorandum*. www.dshs.state.tx.us/wichd/data15/15016.pdf, accessed March 27, 2016.

James, Jennifer Patricia, and Ruth Ann Berkowitz. 2012. "General Practitioners Knowledge of Breastfeeding Management: A Review of the Literature." *Public Health Research* 2(1): 12–19.

Jordan, Pamela L., and Virginia R. Wall. 1990. "Breastfeeding and Fathers: Illuminating the Darker Side." *Birth* 17(4): 210–213.

Lovera, Dalia, Maureen Sanderson, Margaret L. Bogle, and Martha S. Vela Acosta. 2010. "Evaluation of a Breastfeeding Peer Support Program for Fathers of Hispanic Participants in a Texas Special Supplemental Nutrition Program for Women, Infants, and Children." *Journal of the American Dietetic Association* 110(11): 1696–1702.

MacDonald, Trevor. 2012. "How I Learned to be a Breastfeeding Dad." *The Huffington Post*. www.huffingtonpost.com/trevor-macdonald/how-idearned-to-be-a-bre_b_1452392.html, accessed April 11, 2016.

MacDonald, Trevor, Joy Noel-Weiss, Diana West, Michelle Walks, MaryLynne Biener, Alanna Kibbe, and Elizabeth Myler. 2016. "Transmasculine Individuals' Experiences with Lactation, Chestfeeding and Gender Identity: A Qualitative Study." *BioMed Central – Pregnancy and Childbirth* 16: 106.

Mitchell-Box, Kristen, and Kathryn L. Braun. 2012. "Fathers' Thoughts on Breastfeeding and Implications for a Theory-Based Intervention." *Journal of Obstetric, Gynecologic, & Neonatal Nursing* 41(6): E41–E50.

Mitchell-Box, Kristen, and Kathryn L. Braun. 2013. "Impact of Male-Partner-Focused Interventions on Breastfeeding Initiation, Exclusivity, and Continuation." *Journal of Human Lactation* 29(4): 473–479.

Moss, George. 2015. "If You Ever Wonder What #Rappers Do When They Get off Stage [Photo]." *George Moss* [Facebook Page]. www.facebook.com/georgemossmusic/photos/a.153718837322.142409.30598712322/10153508583182323, accessed March 3, 2016.

Murphy, Elizabeth. 2000. "Risk, Responsibility, and Rhetoric in Infant Feeding." *Journal of Contemporary Ethnography* 29(3): 291–325.

Oliveira, Victor, and Elizabeth Frazao. 2015. "The WIC Program: Background, Trends, and Economic Issues, 2015 Edition." *SSRN Scholarly Paper, ID 2709086*. Rochester, NY: Social Science Research Network. http://papers.ssrn.com/abstract=2709086, accessed February 17, 2016.

Pavill, Brenda Condusta. 2002. "Fathers & Breastfeeding." *AWHONN Lifelines* 6(4): 324–331.

Pollock, Christine A., Rosa Bustamante-Forest, and Gloria Giarratano. 2002. Men of Diverse Cultures: Knowledge and Attitudes about Breastfeeding." *Journal of Obstetric, Gynecologic, & Neonatal Nursing* 31(6): 673–679.

Raphael, Dana. 1973. *The Tender Gift: Breastfeeding*. Englewood Cliffs, NJ: Prentice Hall.

Rempel, Lynn A., and John K. Rempel. 2004. "Partner Influence on Health Behavior Decision-Making: Increasing Breastfeeding Duration." *Journal of Social and Personal Relationships* 21(1): 92–111.

Rempel, Lynn A., and John K. Rempel. 2011. "The Breastfeeding Team: The Role of Involved Fathers in the Breastfeeding Family." *Journal of Human Lactation* 27(2): 115–121.

Sciacca, John P., David A. Dube, Brenda L. Phipps, and Michael I. Ratliff. 1995. "A Breast Feeding Education and Promotion Program: Effects on Knowledge, Attitudes, and Support for Breast Feeding." *Journal of Community Health* 20(6): 473–490.

Stearns, Cindy A. 1999. "Breastfeeding and the Good Maternal Body." *Gender and Society* 13(3): 308–325.

Stremler, Jewell, and Dalia Lovera. 2004. "Insight from a Breastfeeding Peer Support Pilot Program for Husbands and Fathers of Texas WIC Participants." *Journal of Human Lactation* 20(4): 417–422.

Tapper, Josh. 2014. "La Leche League International Removes Gendered Language from Leadership Requirements Accepts." *The Toronto Star*, April 25. www.thestar.com/life/health_wellness/2014/04/25/transgender_man_can_be_breastfeeding_coach.html, accessed April 11, 2016.

UNICEF. 2015. "Breastfeeding." *UNICEF.* www.unicef.org/nutrition/index_24824.html, accessed May 3, 2016.

Velarde, Kristie. 2014. "Fathers Hold Key to Breastfeeding Success." *National Institute for Children's Health Quality.* http://breastfeeding.nichq.org/stories/fathers-breastfeeding-support, accessed March 23, 2016.

Victora, Cesar G., Rajiv Bahl, Aluísio J. D. Barros, Giovanny V. A. França, Susan Horton, Julia Krasevec, Simon Murch, Mari Jeeva Sankar, Neff Walker, and Nigel C. Rollins. 2016. "Breastfeeding in the 21st Century: Epidemiology, Mechanisms, and Lifelong Effect." *The Lancet* 387(10017): 475–490.

Wiessinger, Diane, Diana West, and Teresa Pitman. 2010. *The Womanly Art of Breastfeeding.* 8 Rev Upd ed. New York: Ballantine Books.

Wolfberg, Adam J., Karin B. Michels, Wendy Shields, Patricia O'Campo, Yvonne Bronner, and Jessica Bienstock. 2004. "Dads as Breastfeeding Advocates: Results from a Randomized Controlled Trial of an Educational Intervention." *American Journal of Obstetrics and Gynecology* 191(3): 708–712.

Wolfe-Roubatis, Emily, and Diane L. Spatz. 2015. "Transgender Men and Lactation: What Nurses Need to Know." *MCN: The American Journal of Maternal/Child Nursing* 40(1): 32–38.

World Health Organization. 2016. "WHO | Infant and Young Child Feeding: N°342." *Fact Sheets.* World Health Organization. www.who.int/mediacentre/factsheets/fs342/en/, accessed February 17, 2016.

Chapter 10

Masculinities, muscularities, and eating disorders among young men in South Korea

Lawrence T. Monocello

Original material prepared for this edition.

Introduction

> If someone had told me in 1977 that in 1997 men would comprise over a quarter of cosmetic surgery patients, I would have been astounded. I never dreamed that "equality" would move in the direction of men worrying more about their looks than women worrying less.
>
> *Susan Bordo*, The Male Body (*1999*), p. 217

In this chapter, I explore body ideals among South Korean men as a means of challenging current narratives about masculinity and body image in eating disorders research. Eating disorders are the deadliest of all mental illnesses (Arcelus et al. 2011), and they are exploding in prevalence around the world. Despite this, little is known about the factors that predispose people to them across genders and cultures. Our understanding of eating disorders is based almost exclusively on the experiences of White Western-educated women from industrialized, rich, and democratic (WEIRD) countries, sometimes also referred to as "skinny White affluent girls" (SWAGs). Because eating disorders are among the most biosocial of mental illnesses (Becker 2018), attention to the intersectional cultural and gendered aspects of eating disorders risk is increasingly important.

Eating disorders

Anorexia nervosa is a well-known eating disorder characterized by restricted food intake, significantly low body weight, fear of weight gain, and distorted body image. It can be manifested as either restrictive or binge eating/purging type. Bulimia nervosa involves recurrent episodes of binge eating followed by compensatory behaviors like vomiting or excessive exercise, along with a fixation on weight or shape. Binge eating disorder is characterized by recurrent episodes of overeating without compensatory behaviors, accompanied by feelings of guilt or depression. The DSM-5 also includes categories for other specified and unspecified feeding or eating disorders, which encompass variations of the preceding disorders that do not fully meet the diagnostic criteria.

DOI: 10.4324/9781003398349-11

Of eating disorders, anorexia nervosa is also the deadliest. The crude mortality rate of anorexia nervosa is around 5 percent. Of survivors, 20 percent develop a chronic course and only 33 percent appear to fully recover (Steinhausen 2009). Recent reviews suggest that atypical presentations of eating disorders are almost equivalent to their typical presentations in their severity (Harrop et al. 2021; Walsh et al. 2022) and are especially prevalent among non-SWAG populations.

Theories of body image–eating disorder connections

Psychologist Thomas Cash, one of the pioneers in the field of body image research, especially body image research as distinct from eating disorders research, has defined *body image* as "the multifaceted psychological experience of embodiment, especially but not exclusively one's physical appearance. . . . It encompasses one's body-related self-perceptions and self-attitudes, including thoughts, beliefs, feelings, and behaviors" (Cash 2004: 1), which is the definition utilized in most body image research. While distinct from eating disorders, *body image* is thought to contribute heavily to disordered eating through the construct of body dissatisfaction.

Body dissatisfaction refers to negative feelings about, or even disgust with, one's body, especially as it relates to one's appearance (Polivy and Herman 2002). As a result, body dissatisfaction has been found to be the strongest predictor of eating disorders, with increased body dissatisfaction leading to a higher risk of developing eating disorders (Phelps et al. 1999). At the same time, body dissatisfaction is commonplace (sometimes referred to as a "normative discontent"), while eating disorders are relatively uncommon (Rodin et al. 1985; Tantleff-Dunn et al. 2011), suggesting that body dissatisfaction itself is insufficient for the development of eating disorders.

Most eating disorders research engages at least one of two theories about the body image–eating disorder connection. These are sociocultural theory and objectification theory.

Sociocultural theory

Sociocultural theory (Thompson et al. 1999) argues that current societal beauty standards present exacting body ideals that are difficult for most people to reach, and that these body ideals vary across time (i.e., different periods of history have articulated different body ideals) and cultures (i.e., different cultural groups assign values to bodies in different ways). Because the current ideal for women is the "thin ideal," women endeavor to approximate this body type, leading to disordered eating. Sociocultural theory also articulates a "tripartite influence model," which argues that ideals are reinforced by parents, peers, and the media, leading to women internalizing the thin ideal as correct and using means like dieting to achieve it. These behaviors then interact with other biological and psychological factors which erupt in full blown eating disorders (Tiggemann 2012).

Objectification theory

Objectification theory (Fredrickson and Roberts 1997) posits that women's psychological concerns are based on the ways in which they navigate engagements with men and patriarchal power structures throughout society. Specifically, since women's bodies are sexually objectified, they are treated as assemblages of parts valued primarily for their physical appearance and ability to reproduce (Bartky 2015). This happens not just in the individual moments of objectifying interactions but, more generally, within "sexually objectifying environments" (Szymanski et al. 2011), like the United States, where the thin ideal associates femininity and beauty with thinness. Women internalize that objectification and "self-objectify," coming to experience themselves as objects of scrutiny on the basis of their appearance (Tiggemann 2013). Self-objectification leads to women's increased surveillance of their own bodies, resulting in body dissatisfaction or body shame, the emotion that comes from failing to meet a cultural standard against one measures oneself (Moradi and Huang 2008). In objectification theory, self-objectification is the reason that body dissatisfaction and body shame increase women's risk for disordered eating (Murnen and Seabrook 2012; Schaefer and Thompson 2018).

Culture and body image

As long as eating disorders have been in the popular US imaginary (i.e., since the 1980s), anthropologists have also been interested in them. In the 1980s, medical anthropologists and transcultural psychiatrists thought about eating disorders as "culture-bound syndromes" (Yap 1951), bounded to "Western" cultures. The concept of "culture-bound syndromes" originated as an anticolonial critique of Kraepelinian psychiatry, which posed colonized populations' illness experiences as exotic aberrations from the European norm rather than themselves valid (Crozier 2018). However, the term was appropriated by biomedicine and used to essentialize illnesses of the "other" and imply that they were not psychiatrically legitimate (Prince 1985). Therefore, calling eating disorders "culture-bound syndromes" ironically critiqued this biomedical understanding by showing that "Western" people are also capable of having culture-bound syndromes – that culture was a quality of all humans, not just the "other."

But it was also not just irony: at that time, eating disorders were rarely found outside the English-speaking world (Prince and Thebaud 1983). Symptoms of eating disorders reflected ways of approaching and understanding women's bodies particular to the White Protestant Christian worldview prominent in the United States (Bordo [1993] 2003; Swartz 1985).

Yet this "eating disorders as culture-bound illnesses" hypothesis was being challenged by large numbers of cases being identified among ethnic minorities within the United States and UK as well as in Japan, later in Hong Kong, and increasingly around the world in places that did not share the Christian background associated with eating disorders in the West (Nasser 1997). At the same time, eating disorders were still highly associated with Western cultural norms and values. This led to the development of the "Westernization hypothesis," also known as "acculturation theory," to explain how a "Western" culture-bound illness could be cropping up in increasingly distant locales.

The Westernization/acculturation hypothesis holds that the worldwide ballooning in rates of eating disorders results from non-Western people's increasing interaction with Western (i.e., White, modern) culture, especially through globalized Western media. The acculturative process occurs among migrant or minority groups within Western countries (Berry et al. 1986), and the Westernization process occurs through contact with Western culture (mainly the media) within a non-Western country (Gordon 2001). Through this Western media, women are presented with the *thin* ideal (and men with the muscular ideal) and come to aspire to that body themselves. This exposure lays the groundwork for body dissatisfaction and, eventually, eating disorders (Chamorro and Flores-Ortiz 2000; Davis and Katzman 1999; Gunewardene et al. 2001; Kim and Han 2017).

The anthropological perspective does not completely reject Westernization as one of many factors related to the global rise in body image dissatisfaction and disordered eating; the dissemination of thin (and mesomorphic) body ideals to new locales has undeniably been a crucial undergird supporting the development of symptomologies that report these body types as goals. Rather, anthropologists emphasized that Westernization was nowhere near the entire story, or even a particularly interesting or explanatory part at that (Lester 2004).

Specifically, anthropologists were interested in the meanings, conditions, and power relations that led to disordered eating and shaped their locally particular manifestations. This is due to the ways in which anthropologists approach "the body." Scheper-Hughes and Lock (1987) describe a model of "three bodies," including the individual body-self, the social body, and the body-politic. The individual body-self refers to the body as individual experiences. The *social body* refers to a society's complex of symbolic and indexical meanings associated with bodies. The *body-politic* refers to the ways in which power is exerted over bodies in a Foucauldian sense. Often, this is concerned with how governments exert power over bodies, especially through biopolitical (the ways in which governments shape the process of living) and necropolitical (the ways in which governments decide who is worthy of life and death) endeavors (Foucault 2008; Mbembé 2003). Further, the body is not just something that culture happens to; the body is the means by which culture is possible: the body creates culture (Csordas 1990). Finally, the body is not simply a singular thing but is situational and contextual, emerging from and co-created in the particular cultural frames and practices in which they are enacted (Mol 2002).

Psychiatrist and anthropologist Anne Becker performed the foundational research in the cross-cultural anthropology of body image and eating disorders during her ethnographic fieldwork in rural Fiji in the late 1980s and early 1990s (Becker 1995) and has continued for the last 30 years. She was interested in how Fijians related to their bodies, and how their embodied experiences affected their vulnerability to disordered eating. She found in her early studies that Fijians were not particularly concerned with their own bodies, despite a clear preoccupation with others' body shapes and sizes. Moreover, rural Fijians' concern with others' bodies was not about personal considerations – for example, personal morality or self-presentation. Rather, their concerns reflected the ways in which body shape was a powerful index of social embeddedness and being cared for. Among rural Fijians, socially embedded and cared-for bodies, especially women's bodies, were robust bodies, well-fed and able to perform the demanding physical labor associated with their gender roles. On the other hand, thin bodies were seen as reflecting a lack of social care, or even falling victim to a local culture-bound illness or idiom of distress known as "going thin." Furthermore, the responsibility for a body's shape was not embodied in the individual, but in the community. As a result, there was little interest among Fijians in "working" on their own bodies, through exercise, diet, or any other means. Becker's data showed no contemporary evidence of disordered eating in this late-1980s, early 1990s research. Her work was an important early step in the direction of not just acknowledging "culture" as a factor in the global distribution of psychiatric disorders but also in doing the work of explaining what about a particular cultural group's beliefs and practices affected whether and how particular psychiatric phenomena do or do not manifest themselves.

By the publication of *Body, Self, and Society: The View from Fiji*, these rural Fijians received access to television, and individual concerns with body shape began to appear in its wake (Becker 1995). Research conducted in 1998, three years following the appearance of television in the community, demonstrated a marked increase in disordered eating. Particularly, women connected their newfound, thinner body ideals to goals for employment, social mobility, and lifestyle attainment through the emulation of characters they saw on television programs. Television became an avenue through which they could model their navigation of newly accessible cosmopolitan spaces. At the same time, they were interested not just in emulating television characters' body shapes but also in their physical capabilities (Xena from *Xena: Warrior Princess* was a popular example) and personality characteristics, focusing on concepts like gender parity and the ability to help others. Therefore, it was not just television, but television within the context of rapid social and economic change, that led to this profound transition in attitudes toward the body among rural Fijian women (Becker 2004).

Anderson-Fye's (2003, 2004) research challenged the conceptualization of the inevitability of eating disorders in the wake of globalization and exposure to Western media. Through her ethnographic account of Belizean schoolgirls' conceptions of and attitude about their bodies, in the context of ubiquitous beauty pageants and increased interaction with American fashion magazines and television shows, she explains how local body ideals (i.e., having curves) and a local ethnopsychology of "never leave yourself" protected Belizean girls from wanting to change their bodies drastically and from engaging the disordered behaviors that would make it possible. The only women in the community engaging in disordered eating behaviors were employed in the tourist industry and were encouraged to maintain an appearance preferred by American and British tourists but were not dedicated to the body ideal itself. Anderson-Fye (2004) points out that, as far as the globalization of body ideals is concerned, body ideals are not transferred whole cloth from one cultural group to another (i.e., the United States to the developing world) but are filtered through local ethnopsychologies such that certain messages are taken up while others are ignored.

It was not only body ideals that were different across cultures, but also the eating disorders themselves. Psychiatrist Sing Lee and colleagues noticed among their patients in Hong Kong that young women were presenting with all the symptoms of eating disorders *except* the drive for thinness. These women did not express a desire to be thin but were nonetheless starving themselves (Lee et al. 1993). Lee and colleagues noted that this "non-fat-phobic" presentation appeared to occur in 25–40 percent of women reporting for treatment in Northeast, Southeast, and South Asian communities. This, along with research on the "holy anorexia" recorded in medieval female saints (Bell [1985] 2014; cf. Bynum [1988] 2000), suggests that disordered eating behaviors existed prior to and without fat phobia. Anorexia and bulimia were culturally particular manifestations of a deeper human predilection to "[use] food to address conflicts about the self" (Lester 1995: 214) emerging within a specific sociocultural milieu and body-politic-enforced thinness as an ideal for White Western women (see Strings 2019), which act as ideological guardrails leading to fat-phobic presentations of eating disorders.

As the anthropology of body image and eating disorders evolved, it has become clear that the Westernization hypothesis is insufficient to explain why, by what means, and to what extent body ideals – and, therefore, eating disorder risk – change. This is because, to anthropologists, the Westernization and acculturation hypotheses, as well as sociocultural and objectification theories, are based on unsatisfactory – and even incorrect – treatments of culture. These theories tend to construct the process of Westernization/acculturation as US/Western culture being transplanted whole cloth from the West to the rest of the world. They also conflate processes of acculturation, Westernization, and modernization (Van Esterik 2001). The treatment of culture is shallow, monolithic, based on stereotypes, and approached through linguistic translations of popular research instruments without regard for local meaning systems that may lead respondents to interpret questions in unexpected ways, skewing results (Lee 2004). They also problematically reify culture as bounded and tied to geography (except American culture, which travels anywhere, unchanged, and with relative ease); portray eating disorders as "culture-bound syndromes" in the strict sense of boundedness in order to use them as evidence of Westernization, while also saying that Westernization is the cause of eating disorders; and overall use culture to represent whatever factors that are not strictly psychological or biological (Lester 2004).

Taking perspectives rooted in ethnography, anthropologists have continued to interrogate the contexts in which body ideals shift, are internalized, and instigate new forms of embodied praxis in response to rapid, global social change. These include studies of global shifts in body norms (Hruschka 2017; Dos-Santos et al. 2001), fat stigma (Anderson-Fye and Brewis 2017; SturtzSreetharan et al. 2021), cosmetic surgery (Edmonds 2010; Leem 2016), eating disorders treatment (Lester 2019; Warin 2010), and the intersectional ways in which race, gender, class, and size come to bear on young girls' bodily practices (McClure 2020). Overall, they show that, even as concepts like the thin ideal and fat stigma permeate global discourse, they do not also carry with them the entire systems of meaning which inform their manifestation in the United States. Rather, they are incorporated in ways unique to their particular local constellations of beliefs, histories, ecologies, and political economies.

A major oversight of this literature, however, is that this field has also focused almost exclusively on women's bodies, and the studies which included men (e.g., Dos-Santos et al. 2001) did not explore men's lived experience of their bodies.

Male body image

Men and eating disorders

The anthropology of body image and eating disorders reflects the body image and eating disorders field more broadly in that men's experiences have been largely excluded from the literature. Despite being among the earliest recognized cases (Morton 1694), men were excluded from research until the 1970s (e.g., Bruch 1971). The diagnostic requirement of amenorrhea – lack of menses when they would be otherwise developmentally appropriate – was the most common reason: men overwhelmingly lack uteruses and, therefore, cannot menstruate in the first place (Andersen 2014). Men were also excluded from research due to perceived rarity (Murray 2021), a problem which continues to manifest in the failure of studies to perform statistical analyses on men (Quadflieg et al. 2019). As a result of these factors, research on men makes up only 1 percent of the eating disorders literature (Murray et al. 2017).

This failure to include men in research is particularly troubling when evidence suggests that the number of men suffering from eating disorders is exploding globally. The DSM-5 (American Psychiatric Association 2013) notes that men make up 10 percent of cases of full syndrome eating disorders, but studies from Anglophone (English-speaking) countries indicate proportions like 25 percent (in Australia, Madden et al. 2009; in the United States, Hudson et al. 2007) and 33 percent (in the UK; Nicholls et al. 2011) would be more accurate. Epidemiological research suggests that prevalence rates are increasing among males to the extent that they will soon merge with those of women (Mitchison and Mond 2015). A recent review indicated that lifetime prevalence may be as high as 1 in 7 in men, compared to 1 in 5 for women (Ward et al. 2019). When considering atypical cases of eating disorders – those with all but one of the diagnostic criteria listed in the DSM-5, often being at higher weight – lifetime prevalence may be even higher in men than in women (Walsh et al. 2022; Masheb et al. 2021).

Despite a growing need for research, prevention, and treatment of eating disorders among men, little exists which is designed with men in mind. Because of the historical association of disordered eating with women and men's exclusion from the research, theories and research instruments have been developed based almost exclusively on women's experiences. As a result, research instruments often fail to consider the specific needs and concerns of men, for example, in their emphasis on thinness-related behaviors or concerns about bodily features more typically associated with women's body image (Reas et al. 2014; Stanford and Lemberg 2014; Strother et al. 2014). This leads to low estimates of male body image disturbance and disordered eating due not to an actual low severity of these disorders among men but rather reflecting low validity and reliability of these measures when men are confronted with them (Raevuori et al. 2014). This also suggests that population-level estimates of disordered eating and body image disturbance in men may be lower than their reality (Trompeter et al. 2021).

The unreliability of current research tools and current cultural understandings about eating disorders among men leads to men only being treated at later stages of their disorder. First, the popular association of body image disturbance and eating disorders with women means that men overlook their experiences, failing to consider the possibility that they are experiencing a women's disorder. Second, there is a lack of popularly available information directly and comprehensively addressing men's experiences of body image and disordered eating. Third, when presenting for treatment, providers, also biased by the popular gendering of eating disorders, may attribute symptoms of disordered eating or body image disturbance to a more gender-appropriate diagnosis (Räisänen and Hunt 2014). Often, this means that they only receive treatment at a much later and more severe stage of their disorder, leading to a higher mortality rate for male than for female patients (Coelho et al. 2018; Wooldridge 2016).

In treatment, men face issues of staff inexperienced in treating men, female-centric jargon and treatment strategies (e.g., encouragement to be vulnerable), and in in-patient programs, possibly being the only male in the entire facility (including patients, practitioners, and staff). These conditions may lead men to question the validity of their diagnosis and to self-stigma for having a "woman's disorder" (Bunnell 2021). Further, it is unclear whether treatments designed almost exclusively for women work equally well for men (Strobel et al. 2019); this is, again, due in part to existing measures' unreliability among men leading to concerns about whether treatments were actually effective.

Masculinity and body ideals

Presently, men's body ideals are understood to be oriented toward a physique characterized by large, lean musculatures within a V-shaped torso (i.e., a high shoulder–waist ratio), large biceps, and "six-pack" abs. This mesomorphic (muscular and low-fat body type) ideal for men re-emerged from a century of homoerotic connotations in the 1980s when (semi)nude and sexualized male forms entered eroticized media forms that had previously focused primarily on women (Grogan 1998). Male action figures portraying characters like G. I. Joe, Luke Skywalker, and Batman shifted from realistic proportions in the 1960s and 1970s to figurines with massive arms and miniature waists by the early 2000s (Baghurst et al. 2006; Pope et al. 2000). *Sports Illustrated*, *Men's Health*, *Men's Fitness*, and *Playgirl* magazines also all featured increasingly sexualized, exposed, and leanly muscular male bodies over this time span (Farquhar and Wasylkiw 2007; Labre 2005; Leit et al. 2001; Rohlinger 2002). These images continue to be promulgated, particularly through "fitspiration" posts on Instagram (Tiggemann and Zaccardo 2018) and increasingly on TikTok.

Early research into men's body ideals often did not find evidence of body dissatisfaction among men, because they tended to use measures designed for women and focused on skinniness. However, in reality, smaller men reported wanting to be larger, while fatter men reported wanting to be leaner. That is, men tend to emphasize both a desire for greater muscularity and low body fat, rather than an exclusive drive for thinness (McCabe and Ricciardelli 2004). In averaging difference scores between current and ideal bodies, the bidirectionality of men's body dissatisfaction would be collapsed into a score around zero (Holmqvist Gattario et al. 2014).

Desire among men to approximate the mesomorphic ideal, parallel to women and the thin ideal, has been associated with a type of body dysmorphic disorder known as "muscle dysmorphia." Other, more colloquial labels include "male anorexia," "bigorexia," and the "Adonis complex" (Pope et al. 2000). In muscle dysmorphia, the (typically male) sufferer views his own body as not muscular enough, usually in the form of being too skinny. He seeks to compensate for this by overexercise, with the goal of increasing muscle mass, and strict regulation of diet, with the goal of increasing muscle definition (Segura-García et al. 2010). However, these behaviors can also lead to nutrient imbalances, exercise-related injuries, bradycardia, and anabolic steroid use (Nagata et al. 2021).

The mesomorphic ideal has also been associated with "muscularity-oriented disordered eating" (Murray et al. 2012, 2013). *Muscularity-oriented disordered eating* refers to disordered eating beliefs and behaviors associated with a goal not of thinness, as tends to be the case for women, but with the goals of muscularity and leanness (Calzo et al. 2012). For example, men with a diagnosis of anorexia nervosa tend to fear weight gain rather than desire to lose weight, and their body concerns have more to do with maximizing muscular definition than with achieving a certain size or specific weight (Olivardia 2007). Because severity of muscle dysmorphia and that of muscularity-oriented disordered eating are highly correlated, Murray and colleagues (2012) suggest that muscle dysmorphia should be classified as an eating disorder.

As with women, however, muscularity-oriented disordered eating is not inevitable despite the pervasiveness of muscle dissatisfaction in (Western) men. While sociocultural theory has demonstrated fairly good evidence, objectification theory has been inconsistent in its ability to predict eating disorders in men (see Tylka 2021 for an overview). This may be because the zeitgeist of American heterosexist masculinity running in concert with advances in eating disorders research positions men's bodily value as coming from their function (sometimes called "instrumentality") rather than their appearance (or "ornamentality").

In her ethnographic study of fashion models in the United States and UK, sociologist Ashley Mears (2011) describes how male models are viewed, and view themselves, as transient within the field of modeling. Their aesthetic labor is devalued (they get paid about half as much as female models), they are mocked by their clients, and they themselves accept and often even repeat these tropes because to take modeling seriously – to actively pursue a career contingent upon being objectified – would compromise their masculinity. Clients also recognize the larger cultural attitudes toward objectified men and increasingly employ famous athletes to model brands, drawing on their muscles primary instrumentality to associate the product with masculinity (Mears 2011). Monocello and Dressler's (2020) interviews with American men about body ideals further evidenced the importance of the instrumentality–ornamentality divide in American thinking about men's bodies.

Exceptions to this pattern tend to include gay and bisexual men as well as bodybuilders. Gay and bisexual men are significantly more likely to report sexual objectification, self-objectification, and body shame than straight men (Engeln-Maddox et al. 2011; Martins et al. 2007), due perhaps to minority stress (Kimmel and Mahalik 2005) and the sexualization and social comparison (ornamentality) rampant in gay communities (Davids et al. 2015). Bodybuilders also demonstrate high levels of body dissatisfaction, drive for muscularity, and self-objectification compared to regular weight lifters and controls (Hallsworth et al. 2005), likely because bodybuilders are primarily driven by ornamentality rather than instrumentality (Monaghan 2014). Overall, however, men are assumed to understand their bodies through the lens of instrumentality, which may account for why eating disorders tend to be rarer among men than women (Franzoi 1995).

Masculinity hypotheses (Blashill 2011; Mishkind et al. 1986) provide another lens by which men's body dissatisfaction and disordered eating can be understood. The "threatened masculinity hypothesis" argues that as women increasingly enter domains historically associated with men, symbols used by men to project their status and differentiate themselves from women, such as their careers, no longer served that purpose. As a result, men retreated to their bodies, using their greater body mass and relative ease of developing muscularity to maintain their distinction (Mishkind et al. 1986). Similarly, the masculine norms hypothesis argues that men who endorse traditional norms of masculinity but who also cannot themselves approximate them in their own lives (e.g., for structural reasons) then try to compensate though something they believe they can control – their muscularity – which leads to body dissatisfaction and disordered eating (Blashill 2011; Griffiths et al. 2015).

Male body ideals and culture

Yet again, we confront the issue of culture in, or, rather, its absence from, the male body image/eating disorders literature. That 1 percent of the eating disorders literature which focuses on men focuses in particular on *White* men. Where the focus is on non-White men, research tends to focus on racially and ethnically marginalized men in the United States.

This is problematic, because neither body ideals nor norms of masculinity are universally shared across societies. They might not even be shared within societies. Hsu and Iwamoto (2014) conducted a study to determine if the Conformity to Masculine Norms Inventory (Parent and Moradi 2011), a 46-item scale designed to measure masculinity, especially to test the masculinity hypothesis, was equally valid for White American men (who comprised the majority of participants the scale was validated on) and Asian American men. They found significant differences between groups and suggested a truncated 29-item scale which includes the items indicated as relevant to both groups via factor analysis.

This solution, however, has a major flaw: it conflates cross-ethnic reliability with emic validity. *Emic validity* refers to the extent to which a measure actually reflects phenomena in a way meaningful to the population in question (Dressler and Oths 2014). Starting with a scale normed on White people and deleting items irrelevant to non-White people still centers the meaning systems of White people as the "valid" baseline. Moreover, it implies that non-White people's experience deviates from the White norm rather than incompletely overlaps. Rather, we should consider that the Asian American men in Hsu and Iwamoto's study do not have a *smaller* set of masculine ideals from White American men but a *different* one that is itself complete and valid in its own right.

Monocello and Dressler (2020) took this perspective in their study of White American and South Korean male body ideals. They found that White American and South Korean men overlapped in the ways in which they found many features of men's bodily presentation desirable or undesirable, but each group also highly valued certain features that the other ignored. That is, to start with a set of ideals developed in relation to the cultural models of White people and reduce the list to only those shared by both groups would excise features important to White Americans and entirely fail to consider features important to Koreans. To ignore these discrepant features in pursuit of a so-called "universalist" male body ideal would only serve to create a scale that, while reliable, would be meaningless to lived experiences in both groups.

Korean culture and men's body ideals

Therefore, my research attempts to advance psychological engagement with cultural variety in body image and anthropological engagement with men's body image through its focus on the body ideals and vulnerability to disordered eating of young South Korean men. Notably, South Korea evidences some of the highest levels of body dissatisfaction and eating disorders, as well as some of the highest per capita rates of cosmetic surgery, in the world, across genders (Pike et al. 2014; Lim and Paek 2016).

Cross-cultural research consistently demonstrates that Korean women have higher levels of body dissatisfaction and disordered eating than American women (Jackson et al. 2006; Jung and Forbes 2006; Jung et al. 2009; Ko and Cohen 1998). Jung and colleagues (2009) also found that Korean adolescent boys had higher levels of body dissatisfaction and drive for thinness than did American adolescent boys, and others (e.g., Hong et al. 2015) have found these attitudes prevalent among students, male and female, across all ages. Lim (2015) found that appearance anxiety was about equal between Korean men and women. Noh et al. (2018) found that Korean men were likely to overestimate their weight status, more so than Taiwanese men. Overweight boys were both more likely to bully and to be bullied verbally than girls and other boys (S.-G. Kim et al. 2016).

Masculinities and muscularities

Hegemonic masculinity refers to a dominant form of masculinity that is culturally valued. In Western societies, it is often associated with power, control, and aggression. It reinforces traditional gender roles and expectations, placing men in positions of authority and privilege while marginalizing those who do not conform to these ideals (Connell [1995] 2005). That is, in any society, there are multiple masculini*ties* hierarchized and differently valued insofar as they relate to culturally appropriate ways of doing-being a man. While Westernization hypotheses assume the global spread of the mesomorphic ideal as the body ideal to which men aspire, Korean male body ideals suggest that they approach masculinity and male body ideals distinctly from Western expectations.

In Korea, the hegemonic masculinity has been described as "soft" masculinity and is particularly embodied in a form of presentation known as the *kkonminam* (literally, a man who is as beautiful as a flower, heretofore called a "flower boy"). The *kkonminam* is marked by appearing "pretty," having perfectly styled hair, big eyes, and surgically altered "soft" features. His body is thin and sometimes has defined pectoral and abdominal muscles. Moreover, unlike the "macho" masculinity of the military dictatorship era (1970s–1990s), this "new male" showed an interest in fashion and makeup and deviated from previous models of masculinity in that he strove to impress and to be emotionally available to his partner (Maliangkay 2010, 2013; Moon 2005).

The *kkonminam* emerged in the late 1990s/early 2000s due to a combination of men's role as breadwinner being undermined following the 1997 Asian financial crisis (Jung 2011), middle-class women's increasing economic power due to their entry into the formal labor market (Cho 2009), targeted marketing by cosmetics, fashion, and toiletry companies to men (Lim 2008), and pressures of the precarious neoliberalized job market necessitating new strategies to stand out against other applicants (Elfving-Hwang 2017; Holliday and Elfving-Hwang 2012). In fact, Korean companies market lines of cosmetics specifically to men performing their mandatory military service, including sunscreens, face masks, moisturizers, and camouflage face paint formulated to be less harsh on the skin (Chae and Cheng 2018).

Importantly, *kkonminam* masculinity only subverts "traditional" masculinity when "traditional" masculinity is understood as the masculinity of the 1970s. In actuality, appreciation of male beauty has deep roots in Korean culture. During the Silla dynasty (668–935 CE), a group of poet-warriors selected from among the most handsome sons of the elites, called *hwarang* (also a term meaning "flower boy" or "flower of youth"), was valued for their beauty as well as their military and scholarly prowess (Rutt 1961). During the Chosŏn era, because there were fewer government appointments than male *yangban* (the Chosŏn-era upper caste) who could study, test, and work for them, many *yangban* were actually uneducated beyond a few aphorisms and projected their caste status through a particular attention to fashion and hairstyling in lieu of their knowledge of the Confucian classics (Gale 1975).

On this backdrop, the *kkonminam* is less of an anomaly than a continuation of Korea's cultural history of appreciation of male beauty; the masculinity promoted by the military dictatorship is the historically aberrant practice. That said, the *kkonminam* represents not a return to pre-modern beliefs about male presentation but a reformulation of these embodied ideals within the structures of South Korea's neoliberal service economy (Monocello and Dressler 2020). These practices are described as "feminine" (*yŏsŏngsŭrŏpta*), in that these are practices and aesthetics typically associated with women's practices and desires. However, they are not associated with femininity in a way that compromises a *kkonminam*'s masculinity or heterosexuality (Maliangkay 2013), and homosexuality remains heavily stigmatized.

Rather, the consumption and grooming practices associated with *kkonminam* aesthetics were subsumed into naturalistic narratives of "instinctive" masculine behavior rather than portrayed as deviant (Lim 2008). To present in line with *kkonminam* aesthetics is to project self-confidence, academic/occupational competence, mental well-being, care for others' feelings, and a commitment to social cohesion (An 2019). It is also an indicator of moral goodness: men are sometimes told that they are "wasting their face" (*ŏlgulgap mothada*) if their actions do not befit their appearance (*ŏlgul* refers to the anatomical face, not social face, which is *ch'emyŏn*). As a result, it is not uncommon to see young Korean men publicly primping themselves in reflective surfaces or applying makeup on the subway, showing off luxury accessories (not unlike the *yangban*) or having conversations with their other male friends about recommendations for eyebrow pencils, lip balms, and sunscreens. In fact, most Korean men with whom I spoke were surprised to hear that their standard appearance-maintenance practices – like using moisturizer, wearing sunscreen, and caring about their accessories – would call into question their masculinity and sexuality in other cultural settings.

Masculinities and muscularities

While some culture studies researchers have focused on the muscularity of the Korean male ideal as evidence of Westernization (e.g., Joo 2012), the kind of muscle to which Korean men typically aspire (if they aspire to muscularity at all) is known as *chan'gŭnyuk* ("small muscle"), muscle that is defined without significant muscle mass (Monocello and Dressler 2020). This is opposed to the large muscularity typical of depictions of Western male celebrities like Chris Hemsworth.

I have argued elsewhere that, just as there are multiple masculinities in a given society, there are also multiple *muscularities*. That is, beyond mere anatomy, there are multiple ways of doing muscularity which are recognized, hierarchized, and embodied with respect to the meaning systems of a given community (Monocello 2023). In the United States, these include instrumental muscularity (like that of athletes) and ornamental muscularity (like that of actors and models), where instrumental muscularity is more culturally valued in men. In Korea, muscularities are ornamental and distinguished as *chan'gŭnyuk* and *manŭn/k'ŭn kŭnyuk*, meaning "small muscle" and "large muscle," respectively, and are pursued and understood in relation to specific understandings of what men's bodies are "for."

Small muscle

If a *kkonminam* has muscle, he has "small muscle." *Small muscle* refers to defined muscles without much muscle mass. Clothes fit more attractively on men with small muscle, which is important in a society where body discrimination occurs not through discourses of health (healthism) but the way that they present their bodies for public consumption (*oemojisangju-ŭi*, "lookism") (Monocello 2020; Chae 2019).

Having small muscle also means that a man is diligent in going to the gym and dieting, in line with localized precepts of the neoliberal notion of *chagi kwalli* (self-maintenance). Therefore, small muscle – in concert with skincare, fashion, and sometimes even cosmetic surgery (Elfving-Hwang 2021) – indexes to potential employers that they are organized in other aspects of their life, making them a productive employee (Lim and Paek 2016). It is also a means of maintaining that image in the workplace once an increasingly scarce job is secured (Han et al. 2018).

Having small muscle is also a means of maintaining social relationships. Most Koreans view their bodies not as individual objects but as embedded in their larger social relationships (Kim 2009), termed "interrelational projection" (Kim 2008 in Choi 2019: 1007). As a result, not engaging in appearance maintenance indexes a lack of care or consideration for others, particularly for those with whom one is directly associated (Elfving-Hwang 2016). Importantly, self-maintenance is more about the process of making an idealized body than the idealized body itself (Lester and Anderson-Fye 2017).

Large muscle

Koreans also had strong feelings about large muscles, which were primarily negative. While I was conducting my research (2019–2021), the concept of the *helch'ang* (lit. "gym whore") was nascent but growing in popularity (Kŏmsaek-ŏ t'ŭrendŭ n.d.); however, many of the young Koreans I talked to did not like it.

In a larger survey, 82 young Korean men were presented with a nine-point Stunkard-like scale of male muscularity (Ralph-Nearman and Filik 2018), asked to indicate their ideal muscularity, and then describe why they chose that figure. Fifty-nine (72 percent) chose the fourth, fifth, or sixth figures. Of those 59 who did not just say "small muscle" or simply "muscular," the most popular reasons for their choice were that the figure looked "moderate" (11, 18.6 percent) and "not excessive" (10, 16.9 percent), with others using terms like "balanced" and "harmonious."

In interactions ranging from day-to-day conversations to semi-structured interviews, Koreans described men with large muscles to be "excessive" (*kwahada*), sexually immoral (*paramdungi*), unintelligent, antisocial, and possibly even mentally ill (Monocello 2023). Judgments about muscular men's bodies followed from this logic of the "moderate" and were rooted in beliefs that "large-muscled" men spent too much time in the gym.

This assessment is, in many ways, rooted in neo-Confucian understandings about appropriate ways of being a man. During the Chosŏn era (1392–1910), the *yangban* were at the top of the Korean caste system, consisting of the Confucian scholar-officials (*munban*) and military elites (*muban*) who populated the government. Under a belief called *mun-mu* (文武; *wen-wu* in Chinese, referring to the literati–military dichotomy), both the mental cultivation of the *munban* and the physical cultivation of the *muban* were important for men, but only the morality derived from deep scholarship of the Confucian classics entitled one to leadership (Śleziak 2013; Louie 2014). They were expected to devote their life to studying the Confucian classics and eschew worldly things like money and physical labor. *Yangban* caught performing manual labor would actually lose their status, along with their descendants, and may even be erased from family lineages (Abelmann 2002; Chung 1984; Kawashima 1989). There were also moments in history where it was illegal for *yangban* men to play sports (Chang 2002; Cho 2017).

Into the twentieth century, education remained a powerful form of cultural capital. Brandt (1971) described how poor rural families in the post-war development era would sacrifice the labor potential of a son for the prestige they would all garner for his being educated at a high school level. Even outside of the school year, he would be disallowed from assisting in physical labor. During the emerging democratic era, the Korean "middle class" was not defined on purely economic rationale. Rather, it was infused with *mun-mu* attitudes such that two families could be of comparable means, but the "middle-class" family would have reached it via education and subsequent white-collar professions, while the other family whose money comes from physical labor would be considered "working class." Likewise, university and college professors, physicians, and lawyers – those with doctorates – are viewed as modern *yangban* and count themselves culturally among the upper class, despite Korean professors in particular making little money in the form of direct salaries (Kendall 1996; Lett 1998).

In modern Korea, success is overdetermined by studying. Koreans sometimes describe their society as *sihŏm chiok* (exam hell), such that every step toward success is gatekept behind performance on hypercompetitive standardized tests. Many elite high schools have entrance exams, and Korea is famous for its *sunŭng* (university entrance exam), a once-per-year exam during which traffic around schools, and even flights, are minimized so as to prevent noise distractions. The *sunŭng* determines which university one may attend. Going to a SKY University (Seoul National University, Korea University, and Yonsei University) confers immense social and cultural capital on its graduates and makes it easier to land jobs post-graduation in an increasingly competitive job market; therefore, parents will often go into debt in order to support their children's exam preparation via private tutors and *hagwon* (cram schools). Even many companies use entrance exams to be considered for an interview. Continued studying to develop other skills is a crucial element of *chagi kwalli* as well.

Therefore, having small muscle indicated a balanced lifestyle. On the other hand, having large muscles ran counter to cultural norms and expectations, because the amount of time that one must spend in the gym to develop a large muscle physique is time not spent studying. Beyond that, the dieting required to achieve a muscular physique was also incompatible with the typical ways in which Korean male friends (and work colleagues and superiors) spend time together – eating pork belly and drinking beer and soju – suggesting that they deprioritize their relationships and career advancement opportunities.

Therefore, this imbalance of priorities led my interlocutors to draw several conclusions. First, they must not be stably employed. Second, they must not be smart enough to study. Third, they might have some traumatic past, such as bullying (*hakp'ok*), that makes them prioritize developing their muscles over their minds. Fourth, they may feel the need to compensate for some other deficiency, like their height, face, or penis size (I personally know examples supporting reasons 1, 2, and 4). While Koreans describe muscular men as having "masculine" (*namjadapta*) images, muscularity was in no way commensurate with locally valued ways of doing masculinity.

Korean male bodies and eating disorders

In this research, over 20 percent of the men surveyed evidenced a thinness-oriented eating disorder based on scores of 18 or above on the EAT-26, the cutoff for Korean men (Garner et al. 1982; Rhee et al. 1998). I also found that young men who have greater cultural consonance with the Korean cultural model of the ideal male body – that is, their appearance most closely aligns with the *kkonminam* ideal – have higher levels of thinness-oriented disordered eating symptomatology as measured by the EAT-26 than men with lower cultural consonance. I suggested that the pressures of class mobility and maintenance are particularly embodied through appearance maintenance practices. Therefore, thinness-oriented eating disorders emerge in this population as a means by which men attempt to achieve and maintain success through their appearance (Monocello and Dressler 2022).

Muscularity-oriented eating disorders are another story. Much of the theorizing around muscularity-oriented eating disorders assumes the large, instrumental muscles as the hegemonic muscularity in a society, as it is in the United States. Yet in the context of Korea, the desire for large muscles is, in many ways, itself disordered in that these men are finding themselves driven to a body ideal that is not just not socially sanctioned but also actively derided. This troubles sociocultural theory approaches to eating disorders, because it requires family, friends, and media to push men towards a body ideal; Korean society does not judge men against or push them towards large muscle presentations and, in many ways, pushes against it. It further complicates masculinity theory approaches in that, rather than providing a man whose masculinity is compromised in some way an alternative path to hegemonic masculinity, the pursuit of muscularity reinforces their position in a subordinated (*mu*) masculinity.

Further research is therefore needed to understand how Korean men become driven to muscularity, and what muscles mean to the men who develop muscularity-oriented eating disorders. If muscles are not particularly celebrated in a society, research and treatment modalities which assume that society pushes men toward muscularity or that developing large muscularity is a viable pathway toward hegemonic masculinity may be inadequate. As with women-centered paradigms failing to catch and effectively treat cases of eating disorders in men, leading to their increased severity and worse outcomes, efforts for men which are insufficiently culturally informed may continue this cycle of emic invalidity harming men.

Conclusion

As the prevalence of eating disorders continues to explode around the world, and especially as it has been accelerated by the coronavirus pandemic, deeper understandings of how to recognize and provide care for eating disorders in populations beyond "skinny White affluent girls" is increasingly urgent. They require attention to how gender, culture, and the body intersect in specific ways across communities which may be unanticipated by current paradigms. As the case of Korean men shows, exploring local muscularities and taking seriously their histories and meanings expose certain assumptions inherent in present theories that may not be valid across societies and that may compromise research and treatment strategies for different eating disorders which may emerge.

Questions for discussion

1. How does Monocello define *muscularities*? Describe the different muscularities you can identify in your own community/communities and society.
2. Which muscularities and masculinities seem to be hegemonic in your own context? How is this hierarchy reinforced in subtle and overt ways?
3. If you were in charge of a new initiative to study men's eating disorders, what would be the first thing you would focus on and why?

References

Abelmann, Nancy. 2002. "Women, Mobility, and Desire: Narrating Class and Gender in South Korea." In *Under Construction: The Gendering of Modernity, Class, and Consumption in the Republic of Korea*, ed. Laurel Kendall, 25–55. Honolulu, HI: University of Hawai'i Press.

American Psychiatric Association. 2013. *Diagnostic and Statistical Manual of Mental Disorders*, 5th ed. Washington, DC: American Psychiatric Publishing.

An, Chae-Yun. 2019. "Body Image Management Behavior, Self Respect, the Influence on Interpersonal Relations – For Adult Males-." *The Journal of the Korea Contents Association* 19(6): 620–631. https://doi.org/10.5392/JKCA.2019.19.06.620.

Andersen, Arnold. 2014. "A Brief History of Eating Disorders in Males." In *Current Findings on Males with Eating Disorders*, eds. L. Cohn and R. Lemberg, 4–10. New York: Routledge.

Anderson-Fye, Eileen P. 2003. "Never Leave Yourself: Ethnopsychology as Mediator of Psychological Globalization among Belizean Schoolgirls." *Ethos* 31(1): 59–94. https://doi.org/10.1525/eth.2003.31.1.59.

Anderson-Fye, Eileen P. 2004. "A 'Coca-Cola' Shape: Cultural Change, Body Image, and Eating Disorders in San Andres, Belize." *Culture, Medicine and Psychiatry* 28(4): 561–595. https://doi.org/10.1007/s11013-004-1068-4.

Anderson-Fye, Eileen P., and Alexandra Brewis, eds. 2017. *Fat Planet: Obesity, Culture, and Symbolic Body Capital*. School for Advanced Research Advanced Seminar Series. Santa Fe: SAR Press.

Arcelus, Jon, Alex J. Mitchell, Jackie Wales, and Søren Nielsen. 2011. "Mortality Rates in Patients with Anorexia Nervosa and Other Eating Disorders: A Meta-Analysis of 36 Studies." *Archives of General Psychiatry* 68(7): 724. https://doi.org/10.1001/archgenpsychiatry.2011.74.

Baghurst, Timothy, Daniel B. Hollander, Beth Nardella, and G. Gregory Haff. 2006. "Change in Sociocultural Ideal Male Physique: An Examination of Past and Present Action Figures." *Body Image* 3(1): 87–91. https://doi.org/10.1016/j.bodyim.2005.11.001.

Bartky, Sandra Lee. 2015. *Femininity and Domination: Studies in the Phenomenology of Oppression*. Abingdon, UK: Routledge.

Becker, Anne E. 1995. *Body, Self, and Society: The View from Fiji: New Cultural Studies*. Philadelphia: University of Pennsylvania Press.

Becker, Anne E. 2004. "Television, Disordered Eating, and Young Women in Fiji: Negotiating Body Image and Identity during Rapid Social Change." *Culture, Medicine and Psychiatry* 28(4): 533–559. https://doi.org/10.1007/s11013-004-1067-5.

Becker, Anne E. 2018. "Commentary." *Transcultural Psychiatry* 55(4): 572–577.

Bell, Rudolph M. 2014 [1985]. *Holy Anorexia*. Chicago: University of Chicago Press.

Berry, John W., Joseph E. Trimble, and Esteban L. Olmedo. 1986. "Assessment of Acculturation." In *Field Methods in Cross-Cultural Research*, eds. W. J. Lonner and John W. Berry, 291–324. Thousand Oaks, CA: Sage Publications.

Blashill, Aaron J. 2011. "Gender Roles, Eating Pathology, and Body Dissatisfaction in Men: A Meta Analysis." *Body Image* 8(1): 1–11. https://doi.org/10.1016/j.bodyim.2010.09.002.

Bordo, Susan. 1999. *The Male Body: A New Look at Men in Public and Private*. New York, NY: Farrar, Straus and Giroux.

Bordo, Susan. 2003 [1993]. *Unbearable Weight: Feminism, Western Culture, and the Body*. 10th Anniversary. Berkeley: University of California Press.

Brandt, Vincent. 1971. *A Korean Village: Between Farm and Sea*. Cambridge, MA: Harvard University Press.

Bruch, Hilde. 1971. "Anorexia Nervosa in the Male." *Psychosomatic Medicine* 33(1): 31–48.

Bunnell, Douglas W. 2021. "Psychotherapy with Men with Eating Disorders: The Influence of Gender Socialization and Masculine Gender Norms on Engagement and Treatment." In *Eating Disorders in Boys and Men*, eds. Jason M. Nagata, Tiffany A. Brown, Stuart B. Murray, and Jason M. Lavender, 197–213. Cham: Springer International Publishing. 3_14.

Bynum, Caroline Walker. 2000 [1988]. *Holy Feast and Holy Fast: The Religious Significance of Food to Medieval Women*. 1. paperback print., 8. print. The New Historicism. Berkeley, CA: University. of California Press.

Calzo, Jerel P., Kendrin R. Sonneville, Jess Haines, Emily A. Blood, Alison E. Field, and S. Bryn Austin. 2012. "The Development of Associations Among Body Mass Index, Body Dissatisfaction, and Weight and Shape Concern in Adolescent Boys and Girls." *Journal of Adolescent Health* 51(5): 517–523. https://doi.org/10.1016/j.jadohealth.2012.02.021.

Cash, Thomas F. 2004. "Body Image: Past, Present, and Future." *Body Image* 1(1): 1–4. https://doi.org/10.1016/S1740-1445(03)00011-1.

Chae, Jiyoung. 2019. "What Makes Us Accept Lookism in the Selfie Era? A Three-Way Interaction among the Present, the Constant, and the Past." *Computers in Human Behavior* 97: 75–83. https://doi.org/10.1016/j.chb.2019.03.012.

Chae, Yun-hwan, and Jonathan Cheng. 2018. "The Secret to Surviving Military Service: Moisturizer, Foam Cleanser, Cucumber Face Mask." *Wall Street Journal*, August 23. https://www.wsj.com/articles/the-secret-to-surviving-military-service-moisturizer-foam-cleanser-cucumber-face-mask-1535034194?mod=e2fb&page=1&pos=1.

Chamorro, Rebeca, and Yvette Flores-Ortiz. 2000. "Acculturation and Disordered Eating Patterns among Mexican American Women." *International Journal of Eating Disorders* 28(1): 125–129. https://doi.org/10.1002/(SICI)1098-108X(200007)28:1<125::AID-EAT16>3.0.CO;2-9.

Chang, Ju-Ho. 2002. "Korea: The Various Roles of Sport for All in Society." In *Worldwide Experiences and Trends in Sport for All*, eds. L. DaCosta and A. Miragaya, 133–174. Oxford: Meyer and Meyer Sport.

Cho, Joo-hyun. 2009. "Neoliberal Governmentality at Work: Post-IMF Korean Society and the Construction of Neoliberal Women." *Korea Journal* 49(3): 15–45. https://doi.org/10.25024/kj.2009.49.3.15.

Cho, Moongi. 2017. "Toward 'Sport for All': Jang Gwon and Sport Promotion by the Korean YMCA in the Japanese Occupation Era." *Sport History Review* 48(1): 91–105. https://doi.org/10.1123/shr.2016-0007.

Choi, Yoonso. 2019. "'One Is Not Born, but Rather Becomes, a Korean Woman': Gender Politics of Female Bodies in Korean Weight-Loss Reality TV Shows." *International Review for the Sociology of Sport* 54(8): 1005–1019. https://doi.org/10.1177/1012690218768751.

Chung, Young-Iob. 1984. "The Traditional Economy of Korea." *Journal of Modern Korean Studies* I(April): 21–52.

Coelho, Jennifer S., Tiffany Lee, Priscilla Karnabi, Alex Burns, Sheila Marshall, Josie Geller, and Pei-Yoong Lam. 2018. "Eating Disorders in Biological Males: Clinical Presentation and Consideration of Sex Differences in a Pediatric Sample." *Journal of Eating Disorders* 6(1): 1–12. https://doi.org/10.1186/s40337-018-0226-y.

Connell, Robert W. 2005 [1995]. *Masculinities*, 2nd ed. Berkeley, CA: University of California Press.

Crozier, Ivan. 2018. "Introduction: Pow Meng Yap and the Culture-Bound Syndromes." *History of Psychiatry* 29(3): 363–385. https://doi.org/10.1177/0957154X18782746.

Csordas, Thomas J. 1990. "Embodiment as a Paradigm for Anthropology." *Ethos* 18(1): 5–47. https://doi.org/10.1525/eth.1990.18.1.02a00010.

Davids, Christopher M., Laurel B. Watson, Johanna E. Nilsson, and Jacob M. Marszalek. 2015. "Body Dissatisfaction among Gay Men: The Roles of Sexual Objectification, Gay Community Involvement, and Psychological Sense of Community." *Psychology of Sexual Orientation and Gender Diversity* 2(4): 376–385. https://doi.org/10.1037/sgd0000127.

Davis, Cindy, and Melanie A. Katzman. 1999. "Perfection as Acculturation: Psychological Correlates of Eating Problems in Chinese Male and Female Students Living in the United States." *International Journal of Eating Disorders* 25(1): 65–70. https://doi.org/10.1002/(sici)1098-108x(199901)25:1<65::aid-eat8>3.0.co;2-w.

Dos-Santos, Jose Ernesto, Kathryn S. Oths, and William W. Dressler. 2001. "Socioeconomic Factors and Adult Body Composition in a Developing Society." *Revista Brasileira de Hipertensão* 8(1): 173–178.

Dressler, William W., and Kathryn S. Oths. 2014. "Social Survey Methods." In *Handbook of Methods in Cultural Anthropology*, eds. H. R. Bernard and C. C. Gravlee, 2nd ed., 497–515. Lanham: Rowman & Littlefield.

Edmonds, Alexander. 2010. *Pretty Modern: Beauty, Sex, and Plastic Surgery in Brazil*. Durham: Duke University Press.

Elfving-Hwang, Joanna. 2016. "Old, Down and Out? Appearance, Body Work and Positive Ageing among Elderly South Korean Women." *Journal of Aging Studies* 38(August): 6–15. https://doi.org/10.1016/j.jaging.2016.04.005.

Elfving-Hwang, Joanna. 2017. "Aestheticizing Authenticity: Corporate Masculinities in Contemporary South Korean Television Dramas." *Asia Pacific Perspectives* 15(1): 55–72.

Elfving-Hwang, Joanna. 2021. "Man Made Beautiful: The Social Role of Grooming and Body Work in Performing Middle-Aged Corporate Masculinity in South Korea." *Men and Masculinities* 24(2): 207–227. https://doi.org/10.1177/1097184X20976730.

Engeln-Maddox, Renee, Steven A. Miller, and David Matthew Doyle. 2011. "Tests of Objectification Theory in Gay, Lesbian, and Heterosexual Community Samples: Mixed Evidence for Proposed Pathways." *Sex Roles* 65(7–8): 518–532. https://doi.org/10.1007/s11199-011-9958-8.

Farquhar, Jamie C., and Louise Wasylkiw. 2007. "Media Images of Men: Trends and Consequences of Body Conceptualization." *Psychology of Men & Masculinity* 8(3): 145–160. https://doi.org/10.1037/1524-9220.8.3.145.

Foucault, Michel. 2008. *The Birth of Biopolitics: Lectures at the Collège de France, 1978–79*. In *Michel Foucault: Lectures at the College de France*, eds. Michel Senellart, Trans. Graham Burchell. Basingstoke: Palgrave Macmillan.

Franzoi, Stephen L. 1995. "The Body-as-Object versus the Body-as-Process: Gender Differences and Gender Considerations." *Sex Roles* 33(5–6): 417–437. https://doi.org/10.1007/BF01954577.

Fredrickson, Barbara L., and Tomi-Ann Roberts. 1997. "Objectification Theory: Toward Understanding Women's Lived Experiences and Mental Health Risks." *Psychology of Women Quarterly* 21(2): 173–206. https://doi.org/10.1111/j.1471-6402.1997.tb00108.x.

Gale, James S. 1975. *Korean Sketches*. Seoul: Kyung-In Publishing.

Garner, David M., Marion P. Olmsted, Yvonne Bohr, and Paul E. Garfinkel. 1982. "The Eating Attitudes Test: Psychometric Features and Clinical Correlates." *Psychological Medicine* 12(4): 871–878. https://doi.org/10.1017/S0033291700049163.

Grogan, Sarah. 1998. *Body Image: Understanding Body Dissatisfaction in Men, Women, and Children*. New York: Routledge.

Gordon, Richard A. 2001. "Eating Disorders East and West: A Culture-Bound Syndrome Unbound." In *Eating Disorders and Cultures in Transition*, eds. Mervat Nasser, Melanie A. Katzman, and Richard A. Gordon, 1–21. New York: Taylor & Francis.

Griffiths, Scott, Stuart B. Murray, and Stephen Touyz. 2015. "Extending the Masculinity Hypothesis: An Investigation of Gender Role Conformity, Body Dissatisfaction, and Disordered Eating in Young Heterosexual Men." *Psychology of Men & Masculinity* 16(1): 108–114. https://doi.org/10.1037/a0035958.

Gunewardene, Anoushka, Gail F. Huon, and Richang Zheng. 2001. "Exposure to Westernization and Dieting: A Cross-Cultural Study." *International Journal of Eating Disorders* 29(3): 289–293. https://doi.org/10.1002/eat.1020.

Hallsworth, Lisa, Tracey Wade, and Marika Tiggemann. 2005. "Individual Differences in Male Body-Image: An Examination of Self-Objectification in Recreational Body Builders." *British Journal of Health Psychology* 10(3): 453–465. https://doi.org/10.1348/135910705X26966.

Han, Seung-Yong, Alexandra A. Brewis, and Cindi SturtzSreetharan. 2018. "Employment and Weight Status: The Extreme Case of Body Concern in South Korea." *Economics & Human Biology* 29(May): 115–121. https://doi.org/10.1016/j.ehb.2018.01.002.

Harrop, Erin N., Janell L. Mensinger, Megan Moore, and Taryn Lindhorst. 2021. "Restrictive Eating Disorders in Higher Weight Persons: A Systematic Review of Atypical Anorexia Nervosa Prevalence and Consecutive Admission Literature." *International Journal of Eating Disorders* 54(8): 1328–1357. https://doi.org/10.1002/eat.23519.

Holliday, Ruth, and Joanna Elfving-Hwang. 2012. "Gender, Globalization and Aesthetic Surgery in South Korea." *Body & Society* 18(2): 58–81. https://doi.org/10.1177/1357034x12440828.

Holmqvist Gattario, Kristina, Ann Frisén, and Eileen P. Anderson-Fye. 2014. "Body Image and Child Well-Being." In *Handbook of Child Well-Being*, eds. Asher Ben Arieh, Ferran Casas, Ivar Frønes, and Jill E. Korbin, 2409–2436. New York: Springer.

Hong, Seong-Chul, Young-Eun Jung, Moon-Doo Kim, Chang-In Lee, Mi-Yeul Hyun, Won-Myong Bahk, Bo-Hyun Yoon, and Kwang Heun Lee. 2015. "Prevalence of Distorted Body Image in Young Koreans and Its Association with Age, Sex, Body Weight Status, and Disordered Eating Behaviors." *Neuropsychiatric Disease and Treatment*, April: 1043–1049. https://doi.org/10.2147/NDT.S82504.

Hruschka, Daniel J. 2017. "From Thin to Fat and Back Again: A Dual Process Model of the Big Body Mass Reversal." In *Fat Planet: Obesity, Culture, and Symbolic Body Capital*, eds. Eileen P. Anderson-Fye and Alexandra Brewis, 15–32. Santa Fe, NM: SAR Press.

Hsu, Kean, and Derek Kenji Iwamoto. 2014. "Testing for Measurement Invariance in the Conformity to Masculine Norms-46 across White and Asian American College Men: Development and Validity of the CMNI-29." *Psychology of Men & Masculinity* 15(4): 397–406. https://doi.org/10.1037/a0034548.

Hudson, James I., Eva Hiripi, Harrison G. Pope, and Ronald C. Kessler. 2007. "The Prevalence and Correlates of Eating Disorders in the National Comorbidity Survey Replication." *Biological Psychiatry* 61(3): 348–358. https://doi.org/10.1016/j.biopsych.2006.03.040.

Jackson, Safia C., Pamela K. Keel, and Young Ho Lee. 2006. "Trans-Cultural Comparison of Disordered Eating in Korean Women." *International Journal of Eating Disorders* 39(6): 498–502. https://doi.org/10.1002/eat.20270.

Joo, Rachael Miyung. 2012. *Transnational Sport: Gender, Media, and Global Korea.* Durham: Duke University Press.

Jung, Jaehee, and Gordon B. Forbes. 2006. "Multidimensional Assessment of Body Dissatisfaction and Disordered Eating in Korean and US College Women: A Comparative Study." *Sex Roles* 55(1–2): 39–50. https://doi.org/10.1007/s11199-006-9058-3.

Jung, Jaehee, Gordon B. Forbes, and Yoon-Jung Lee. 2009. "Body Dissatisfaction and Disordered Eating among Early Adolescents from Korea and the US." *Sex Roles* 61 (1–2): 42–54. https://doi.org/10.1007/s11199-009-9609-5.

Jung, Sun. 2011. *Korean Masculinities and Transcultural Consumption.* Hong Kong: Hong Kong University Press.

Kawashima, Fujiya. 1989. "The Way of the Sonbi: Local Yangban and the Korean Intellectual Tradition." *Korean Culture* 10(2): 4–14.

Kendall, Laurel. 1996. *Getting Married in Korea.* Berkeley, CA: University of California Press.

Kim, Eun-Shil. 2009. "The Politics of the Body in Contemporary Korea." *Korea Journal* 49(3): 5–14.

Kim, Myŏng-jin, dir. 2008. *Tong Kwa Sŏ: EBS Tak'yument'ŏri: Sŏro Tarŭn Saenggak Ŭi Kiwŏn.* Seoul, South Korea: Chisik Ch'aenŏl.

Kim, Seung-Gon, Ilhong Yun, and Jae-Hong Kim. 2016. "Associations between Body Weight and Bullying among South Korean Adolescents." *The Journal of Early Adolescence* 36(4): 551–574. https://doi.org/10.1177/0272431615577204.

Kim, Tae Hyun, and Euna Han. 2017. "Height Premium for Job Performance." *Economics & Human Biology* 26: 13–20. https://doi.org/10.1016/j.ehb.2017.01.002.

Kimmel, Sara B., and James R. Mahalik. 2005. "Body Image Concerns of Gay Men: The Roles of Minority Stress and Conformity to Masculine Norms." *Journal of Consulting and Clinical Psychology* 73(6): 1185–1190. https://doi.org/10.1037/0022-006X.73.6.1185.

Ko, Christine, and Henry Cohen. 1998. "Intraethnic Comparison of Eating Attitudes in Native Koreans and Korean Americans Using a Korean Translation of the Eating Attitudes Test." *Journal of Nervous and Mental Disease* 186(10): 631–636. https://doi.org/10.1097/00005053-199810000-00007.

Kŏmsaek-ŏ t'ŭrendŭ, [Searcher Trends]. n.d. "헬창 (helch'ang)." Naver DataLab. n.d. https://datalab.naver.com/keyword/trendResult.naver?hashKey=N_3b1794a96574fc999cd5d6 4ec5372975, accessed May 19, 2023.

Labre, Magdala Peixoto. 2005. "Burn Fat, Build Muscle: A Content Analysis of Men's Health and Men's Fitness." *International Journal of Men's Health* 4(2). https://doi.org/10.3149/jmh.0402.187.

Lee, Sing. 2004. "Engaging Culture: An Overdue Task for Eating Disorders Research." *Culture, Medicine and Psychiatry* 28(4): 617–621. https://doi.org/10.1007/s11013-004-1072-8.

Lee, Sing, T. P. Ho, and L. K. G. Hsu. 1993. "Fat Phobic and Non-Fat Phobic Anorexia Nervosa: A Comparative Study of 70 Chinese Patients in Hong Kong." *Psychological Medicine* 23(4): 999–1017. https://doi.org/10.1017/S0033291700026465.

Leem, So Yeon. 2016. "The Dubious Enhancement: Making South Korea a Plastic Surgery Nation." *East Asian Science, Technology and Society: An International Journal* 10(1): 51–71. https://doi.org/10.1215/18752160-3325203.

Leit, Richard A., Harrison G. Pope Jr., and James J. Gray. 2001. "Cultural Expectations of Muscularity in Men: The Evolution of Playgirl Centerfolds." *International Journal of Eating Disorders* 29(1): 90–93. https://doi.org/10.1002/1098-108X(200101)29:1<90::AID-EAT15>3.0.CO;2-F.

Lester, Rebecca J. 1995. "Embodied Voices: Women's Food Asceticism and the Negotiation of Identity." *Ethos* 23(2): 187–222.

Lester, Rebecca J. 2004. "Commentary: Eating Disorders and the Problem of 'Culture' in Acculturation." *Culture, Medicine and Psychiatry* 28(4): 607–615. https://doi.org/10.1007/s11013-004-1071-9.

Lester, Rebecca J. 2019. *Famished: Eating Disorders and the Failure of Care in America.* Berkeley: University of California Press.

Lester, Rebecca J., and Eileen P. Anderson-Fye. 2017. "Fat Matters: Capital, Markets, and Morality." In *Fat Planet: Obesity, Culture, and Symbolic Body Capital*, eds. Eileen P. Anderson-Fye and Alexandra Brewis, 193–204. Santa Fe, NM: SAR Press.

Lett, Denise Potrzeba. 1998. *In Pursuit of Status: The Making of South Korea's 'New' Urban Middle Class*. Cambridge, MA: Harvard University Asia Center.

Lim, In-Sook. 2008. "The Trend of Creating Atypical Male Images in Heterosexist Korean Society." *Korea Journal* 48(4): 115–146. https://doi.org/10.25024/KJ.2008.48.4.115.

Lim, In-Sook. 2015. "The Appearance Anxiety and Aging Anxiety in an Appearance-Discriminatory Society." *Korean Journal of Sociology* 49(4): 199–233. https://doi.org/10.21562/kjs.2015.08.49.4.199.

Lim, In-Sook, and Su-Kyeong Paek. 2016. "A Comparative Study on the Ideal Body-Shape and the Preference for Weight Loss." *Korean Journal of Sociology* 50(4): 169–202. https://doi.org/10.21562/kjs.2016.08.50.4.169.

Louie, Kam. 2014. *Chinese Masculinities in a Globalizing World*. New York: Routledge.

Madden, Sloane, Anne Morris, Yvonne A. Zurynski, Michael Kohn, and Elizabeth J. Elliot. 2009. "Burden of Eating Disorders in 5–13-Year-Old Children in Australia." *Medical Journal of Australia* 190(8): 410–414. https://doi.org/10.5694/j.1326-5377.2009.tb02487.x.

Maliangkay, Roald. 2010. "The Effeminacy of Male Beauty in Korea." *The Newsletter* 55: 6–7.

Maliangkay, Roald. 2013. "Catering to the Female Gaze: The Semiotics of Masculinity in Korean Advertising." Situations 7(1): 43–61.

Martins, Yolanda, Marika Tiggemann, and Alana Kirkbride. 2007. "Those Speedos Become Them: The Role of Self-Objectification in Gay and Heterosexual Men's Body Image." *Personality and Social Psychology Bulletin* 33(5): 634–647. https://doi.org/10.1177/0146167206297403.

Masheb, Robin M., Christine M. Ramsey, Alison G. Marsh, Jennifer L. Snow, Cynthia A. Brandt, and Sally G. Haskell. 2021. "Atypical Anorexia Nervosa, Not so Atypical after All: Prevalence, Correlates, and Clinical Severity among United States Military Veterans." *Eating Behaviors* 41(April): 101496. https://doi.org/10.1016/j.eatbeh.2021.101496.

Mbembé, Achille. 2003. "Necropolitics." *Public Culture* 15(1): 11–40. https://doi.org/10.1215/08992363-15-1-11.

McCabe, Marita P., and Lina A. Ricciardelli. 2004. "Body Image Dissatisfaction Among Males Across the Lifespan – A Review of Past Literature." *Journal of Psychosomatic Research* 56(6): 675–685. https://doi.org/10.1016/s0022-3999(03)00129-6.

McClure, Stephanie M. 2020. "Living Unembodiment: Physicality and Body/Self Discontinuity Among African American Adolescent Girls." *Ethos* 48(1): 3–28. https://doi.org/10.1111/etho.12266.

Mears, Ashley. 2011. *Pricing Beauty: The Making of a Fashion Model*. Berkeley, CA: University of California Press.

Mishkind, M. E., Judith Rodin, Lisa R. Silberstein, and Ruth H. Striegel-Moore. 1986. "The Embodiment Of Masculinity – Cultural, Psychological, and Behavioral Dimensions." *American Behavioral Scientist* 29(5): 545–562. https://doi.org/10.1177/000276486029005004.

Mitchison, Deborah, and Jonathan Mond. 2015. "Epidemiology of Eating Disorders, Eating Disordered Behaviour, and Body Image Disturbance in Males: A Narrative Review." *Journal of Eating Disorders* 3(1): 20. https://doi.org/10.1186/s40337-015-0058-y.

Mol, Annemarie. 2002. *The Body Multiple: Ontology in Medical Practice*. Durham, NC: Duke University Press.

Monaghan, Lee F. 2014. "'Postmodern' Muscle: The Embodied Pleasures of Vibrant Physicality." In *Challenging Myths of Masculinity: Understanding Physical Cultures*, eds. Lee F. Monaghan and Michael Atkinson, 15–37. Burlington, VT: Ashgate.

Monocello, Lawrence T. 2020. "Cultural Models of Male Body Image, Fat, and Acceptable Personhood among Euro-Americans and South Koreans." *Journal of Cultural Cognitive Science* 4(1): 73–86. https://doi.org/10.1007/s41809-019-00042-4.

Monocello, Lawrence T. 2023. "'Guys with Big Muscles Have Misplaced Priorities': Masculinities and Muscularities in Young South Korean Men's Body Image." *Culture, Medicine, and Psychiatry* 47(2): 443–465. https://doi.org/10.1007/s11013-022-09784-3.

Monocello, Lawrence T., and William W. Dressler. 2020. "Flower Boys and Muscled Men: Comparing South Korean and American Male Body Ideals Using Cultural Domain Analysis." *Anthropology & Medicine* 27(2): 176–191. https://doi.org/10.1080/13648470.2020.1742575.

Monocello, Lawrence T., and William W. Dressler. 2022. "Cultural Consonance, Body Image, and Disordered Eating among Young South Korean Men." *Social Science & Medicine* 314(December): 115486. https://doi.org/10.1016/j.socscimed.2022.115486.

Moon, Seungsook. 2005. *Militarized Modernity and Gendered Citizenship in South Korea*. Durham, NC: Duke University Press.

Moradi, Bonnie, and Yu-Ping Huang. 2008. "Objectification Theory and Psychology of Women: A Decade of Advances and Future Directions." *Psychology of Women Quarterly* 32(4): 377–398. https://doi.org/10.1111/j.1471-6402.2008.00452.x.

Morton, Richard. 1694. *Phthisiologia, or, a Treatise of Consumptions*. London: Sam. Smith and Benj. Walford.

Murnen, Sarah K., and R. Seabrook. 2012. "Feminist Perspectives on Body Image and Physical Appearance." In *Encyclopedia of Body Image and Human Appearance*, ed. Thomas F. Cash, 438–443. Oxford: Academic Press.

Murray, Stuart B. 2021. "A Historical Overview of Eating Disorders in Males." In *Eating Disorders in Boys and Men*, eds. Jason M. Nagata, Tiffany A. Brown, Stuart B. Murray, and Jason M. Lavender, 3–6. Switzerland: Springer.

Murray, Stuart B., Jason M. Nagata, Scott Griffiths, Jerel P. Calzo, Tiffany A. Brown, Deborah Mitchison, Aaron J. Blashill, and Jonathan M. Mond. 2017. "The Enigma of Male Eating Disorders: A Critical Review and Synthesis." *Clinical Psychology Review* 57(November): 1–11. https://doi.org/10.1016/j.cpr.2017.08.001.

Murray, Stuart B., Elizabeth Rieger, Tom Hildebrandt, Lisa Karlov, Janice Russell, Evelyn Boon, Robert T. Dawson, and Stephen W. Touyz. 2012. "A Comparison of Eating, Exercise, Shape, and Weight Related Symptomatology in Males with Muscle Dysmorphia and Anorexia Nervosa." *Body Image* 9(2): 193–200. https://doi.org/10.1016/j.bodyim.2012.01.008.

Murray, Stuart B., Elizabeth Rieger, Lisa Karlov, and Stephen W. Touyz. 2013. "Masculinity and Femininity in the Divergence of Male Body Image Concerns." *Journal of Eating Disorders* 1(1): 11. https://doi.org/10.1186/2050-2974-1-11.

Nagata, Jason M., Kyle T. Ganson, and Neville H. Golden. 2021. "Medical Complications of Eating Disorders in Boys and Men." In *Eating Disorders in Boys and Men*, eds. Jason M. Nagata, Tiffany A. Brown, Stuart B. Murray, and Jason M. Lavender, 3–6. Cham, Switzerland: Springer.

Nasser, Mervat. 1997. *Culture and Weight Consicousness*. London: Routledge.

Nicholls, Dasha E., Richard Lynn, and Russell M. Viner. 2011. "Childhood Eating Disorders: British National Surveillance Study." *The British Journal of Psychiatry* 198(4): 295–301.

Noh, Jin-Won, Young Dae Kwon, Youngmi Yang, Jooyoung Cheon, and Jinseok Kim. 2018. "Relationship between Body Image and Weight Status in East Asian Countries: Comparison between South Korea and Taiwan." *Bmc Public Health* 18(1): 1–8. https://doi.org/10.1186/s12889-018-5738-5.

Olivardia, Roberto. 2007. "Body Image and Muscularity." In *Textbook of Men's Mental Health*, eds. J. E. Grant and M. N. Potenza, 307–324. Washington, DC: American Psychiatric Publishing.

Parent, Mike C., and Bonnie Moradi. 2011. "An Abbreviated Tool for Assessing Conformity to Masculine Norms: Psychometric Properties of the Conformity to Masculine Norms Inventory-46." *Psychology of Men & Masculinity* 12(4): 339–353. https://doi.org/10.1037/a0021904.

Phelps, Leadelle, Lisa S. Johnston, and Kristine Augustyniak. 1999. "Prevention of Eating Disorders: Identification of Predictor Variables." *Eating Disorders* 7(2): 99–108. https://doi.org/10.1080/10640269908251189.

Pike, Kathleen M., Hans W. Hoek, and Patricia E. Dunne. 2014. "Cultural Trends and Eating Disorders." *Current Opinion in Psychiatry* 27(6): 436–442. https://doi.org/10.1097/YCO.0000000000000100.

Polivy, Janet, and C. Peter Herman. 2002. "Causes of Eating Disorders." *Annual Review of Psychology* 53(1): 187–213. https://doi.org/10.1146/annurev.psych.53.100901.135103.

Prince, Raymond. 1985. "The Concept of Culture-Bound Syndromes: Anorexia Nervosa and Brain-Fag." *Social Science & Medicine* 21(2): 197–203. https://doi.org/10.1016/0277-9536(85)90089-9.

Prince, Raymond, and E. F. Thebaud. 1983. "Is Anorexia Nervosa a Culture-Bound Syndrome?" *Transcultural Psychiatric Research Review* 20(4): 299–302.

Pope, Harrison G., Katharine A. Phillips, and Roberto Olivardia. 2000. *The Adonis Complex: The Secret Crisis of Male Body Obsession*. New York: Simon and Schuster.

Quadflieg, Norbert, Christine Strobel, Silke Naab, Ulrich Voderholzer, and Manfred M. Fichter. 2019. "Mortality in Males Treated for an Eating Disorder – A Large Prospective Study." *International Journal of Eating Disorders* 52(12): 1365–1369. https://doi.org/10.1002/eat.23135.

Raevuori, Anu, Anna Keski-Rahkonen, and Hans W. Hoek. 2014. "A Review of Eating Disorders in Males." *Current Opinion in Psychiatry* 27(6): 426–430. https://doi.org/10.1097/YCO.0000000000000113.

Räisänen, Ulla, and Kate Hunt. 2014. "The Role of Gendered Constructions of Eating Disorders in Delayed Help-Seeking in Men: A Qualitative Interview Study: Table 1." *BMJ Open* 4(4): e004342. https://doi.org/10.1136/bmjopen-2013-004342.

Ralph-Nearman, Christina, and Ruth Filik. 2018. "New Body Scales Reveal Body Dissatisfaction, Thin-Ideal, and Muscularity-Ideal in Males." *American Journal of Men's Health* 12(4): 740–750. https://doi.org/10.1177/1557988318763516.

Reas, Deborah L., Maria Øverås, and Øyvind Rø. 2014. "Norms for the Eating Disorder Examination-Questionnaire (EDE-Q) Among High School and University Men." In *Current Findings on Males with Eating Disorders*, eds. Leigh Cohn and Raymond Lemberg, 103–110. New York, NY: Routledge.

Rhee, Min-Kyu, Young-Ho Lee, Se-Hyun Park, Chang-Ho Sohn, Young-Cho Chung, Sung-Kook Hong, Byung-Kwan Lee, Philip Chang, and A.-Rhee Yoon. 1998. "한국판 식사태검사-26 (The Korean Version of the Eating Attitudes Test-26: KEAT-26) 표주화 연구 I: 신뢰도 및 요인분석 [A Standardization Study of the Korean Version of Eating Attitudes Test-26 I: Reliability and Factor Analysis]." *Korean Journal of Psychosomatic Medicine* 6(2): 155–175.

Rodin, Judith, Lisa R. Silberstein, and Ruth H. Striegel-Moore. 1985. "Women and Weight: A Normative Discontent." In *Psychology and Gender*, ed. T. B. Sondregger, 267–307. Lincoln: University of Nebraska Press.

Rohlinger, Deana A. 2002. "Eroticizing Men: Cultural Influences on Advertising and Male Objectification." *Sex Roles* 46(3–4): 61–74. https://doi.org/10.1023/A:1016575909173.

Rutt, Richard. 1961. "The Flower Boys of Silla (Hwarang): Notes on the Sources." *Transactions of the Korea Branch of the Royal Asiatic Society* 38(1): 1–65.

Schaefer, Lauren M., and J. Kevin Thompson. 2018. "Self-Objectification and Disordered Eating: A Meta- Analysis." *International Journal of Eating Disorders* 51(6): 483–502. https://doi.org/10.1002/eat.22854.

Scheper-Hughes, Nancy, and Margaret M. Lock. 1987. "The Mindful Body: A Prolegomenon to Future Work in Medical Anthropology." *Medical Anthropology Quarterly* 1(1): 6–41. https://doi.org/10.1525/maq.1987.1.1.02a00020.

Segura-García, Cristina, Antonio Ammendolia, Leonardo Procopio, Maria C. Papaianni, Flora Sinopoli, Carmelina Bianco, Pasquale De Fazio, and Laura Capranica. 2010. "Body Uneasiness, Eating Disorders, and Muscle Dysmorphia in Individuals Who Overexercise." *Journal of Strength and Conditioning Research* 24(11): 3098–3104. https://doi.org/10.1519/JSC.0b013e3181d0a575.

Śleziak, Tomasz. 2013. "The Role of Confucianism in Contemporary South Korean Society." *Rocznik Orientalistyczny* T.LXVI(1): 27–46.

Stanford, Stevie Chariese, and Raymond Lemberg. 2014. "A Clinical Comparison of Men and Women on the Eating Disorder Inventory-3 (EDI-3) and the Eating Disorder Assessment for Men (EDAM)." In *Current Findings on Males with Eating Disorders*, eds. Leigh Cohn and Raymond Lemberg, 76–92. New York, NY: Routledge.

Steinhausen, Hans-Christoph. 2009. "Outcome of Eating Disorders." *Child and Adolescent Psychiatric Clinics of North America* 18(1): 225–242. https://doi.org/10.1016/j.chc.2008.07.013.

Strings, Sabrina. 2019. *Fearing the Black Body: The Racial Origins of Fat Phobia*. New York, NY: New York University Press.

Strobel, Christine, Norbert Quadflieg, Silke Naab, Ulrich Voderholzer, and Manfred M. Fichter. 2019. "Long-Term Outcomes in Treated Males with Anorexia Nervosa and Bulimia Nervosa – A Prospective, Gender-matched Study." *International Journal of Eating Disorders* 52(12): 1353–1364. https://doi.org/10.1002/eat.23151.

Strother, Eric, Raymond Lemberg, Stevie Chariese Stanford, and Dayton Turberville. 2014. "Eating Disorders in Men: Underdiagnosed, Undertreated, and Misunderstood." In *Current Findings on Males with Eating Disorders*, eds. Leigh Cohn and Raymond Lemberg, 13–22. New York: Routledge.

SturtzSreetharan, Cindi, Alexandra Brewis, Jessica A. Hardin, Sarah Trainer, and Amber Wutich. 2021. *Fat in Four Cultures: A Global Ethnography of Weight: Teaching Culture : UTP Ethnographies for the Classroom*. Toronto, Buffalo, London: University of Toronto Press.

Swartz, Leslie. 1985. "Anorexia Nervosa as a Culture-Bound Syndrome." *Social Science & Medicine* 20(7): 725–730. https://doi.org/10.1016/0277-9536(92)90256-p.

Szymanski, Dawn M., Erika R. Carr, and Lauren B. Moffitt. 2011. "Sexual Objectification of Women: Clinical Implications and Training Considerations." *The Counseling Psychologist* 39(1): 107–126. https://doi.org/10.1177/0011000010378450.

Tantleff-Dunn, Stacey, Rachel D. Barnes, and Jessica Gokee Larose. 2011. "It's Not Just a 'Woman Thing': The Current State of Normative Discontent." *Eating Disorders* 19(5): 392–402. https://doi.org/10.1080/10640266.2011.609088.

Thompson, J. Kevin, Leslie J. Heinberg, Madeline N. Altabe, and Stacey Tantleff-Dunn. 1999. *Exacting Beauty: Theory, Assessment, and Treatment of Body Image Disturbance*. Washington, DC: American Psychological Association.

Tiggemann, Marika. 2012. "Sociocultural Perspectives on Body Image." In *Encyclopedia of Body Image and Human Appearance*, ed. Thomas F. Cash, 758–765. Oxford: Academic Press.

Tiggemann, Marika. 2013. "Objectification Theory: Of Relevance for Eating Disorder Researchers and Clinicians?" *Clinical Psychologist* 17(2): 35–45. https://doi.org/10.1111/cp.12010.

Tiggemann, Marika, and Mia Zaccardo. 2018. "'Strong Is the New Skinny': A Content Analysis of #fitspiration Images on Instagram." *Journal of Health Psychology* 23(8): 1003–1011. https://doi.org/10.1177/1359105316639436.

Trompeter, Nora, Kay Bussey, and Deborah Mitchison. 2021. "Epidemiology of Eating Disorders in Boys and Men." In *Eating Disorders in Boys and Men*, eds. Jason M. Nagata, Tiffany A. Brown, Stuart B. Murray, and Jason M. Lavender, 37–54. Switzerland: Springer.

Tylka, Tracy L. 2021. "Models of Body Image for Boys and Men." In *Eating Disorders in Boys and Men*, eds. Jason M. Nagata, Tiffany A. Brown, Stuart B. Murray, and Jason M. Lavender, 7–20. Switzerland: Springer.

Van Esterik, Penny. 2001. "Eating Disorders East and West: A Culture-Bound Syndrome Unbound: Commentary 2." In *Eating Disorders and Cultures in Transition*, eds. Mervat Nasser, Melanie A. Katzman, and Richard A. Gordon, 19–21. New York: Taylor & Francis.

Walsh, B. Timothy, Kelsey E. Hagan, and Carlin Lockwood. 2022. "A Systematic Review Comparing Atypical Anorexia Nervosa and Anorexia Nervosa." *International Journal of Eating Disorders*, no. Advance online publication (December). https://doi.org/10.1002/eat.23856.

Ward, Zachary J., Patricia Rodriguez, Davene R. Wright, S. Bryn Austin, and Michael W. Long. 2019. "Estimation of Eating Disorders Prevalence by Age and Associations With Mortality in a Simulated Nationally Representative US Cohort." *JAMA Network Open* 2(10): e1912925. https://doi.org/10.1001/jamanetworkopen.2019.12925.

Warin, Megan. 2010. *Abject Relations: Everyday Worlds of Anorexia: Studies in Medical Anthropology*. New Brunswick, NJ: Rutgers University Press.

Wooldridge, Tom. 2016. *Understanding Anorexia Nervosa in Males: An Integrative Approach*. New York and London: Taylor & Francis.

Yap, Pow Meng. 1951. "Mental Diseases Peculiar to Certain Cultures: A Survey of Comparative Psychiatry." *Journal of Mental Science* 97(407): 313–327. https://doi.org/10.1192/bjp.97.407.313.

Part 2

Gender, kinship, and family

Like gender and the body, there is nothing about family that presupposes gender. Yet historically, anthropologists (these two included) find it nearly impossible to talk about one without the other. Gender roles are so tightly bound to kin roles the two can seem as naturally intertwined as gender to the body. Unlike the ostensibly sudden rise of trans and nonbinary issues in the zeitgeist, debates about the gender, family, and the state have never stopped and are nothing new. The debates have changed, but the family is always a site of contentious disagreement and cultural innovation. For anthropologists, the family is a microcosm of what societies value in terms of gender, reproduction, care, labor, finance, and more. In many societies, the family is also the center of production and forms the basis for people's livelihoods. Therefore, the family may look or operate differently in places with different economic systems. Many scholars have argued that societies become less equitable in terms of gender relations as they move toward more capitalist means of production. For instance, hunter-gatherers, like the Aka (Hewlett, this text), experience low levels of gender division of labor, as do horticultural societies, such as the people of Vanatinai. On the other hand, pastoralists often have highly gender-segregated roles, as we will see in Archambault's chapter on the Maasai later in this text. We would argue that society's organization shapes the family and gender roles but that the reverse is also true. Economic systems do not dictate family structure and the degree of gender egalitarianism present, but it is important to examine how the two interact and reinforce each other.

We begin with Maria Lepowsky, who points to gender egalitarianism among the horticultural and matrilineal people of the Pacific island of Vanatinai. In this society, men are not dominant over women either in practice or ideologically. Like men, women on this island can gain both prestige and power through engaging in exchange activities and the sponsorship of feasts where valuable goods are distributed. As a result of these activities, they can become "big women," just as men can become "big men." Thus, Lepowsky argues that

> the prominent positions of women in Vanatinai exchange and other activities outside of household and subsistence indicate as well as reinforce generally egalitarian relations between women and men. Vanatinai women have access to power both through their control of the economic capital of land and the subsistence and surplus production of yams and through their accumulation of symbolic capital in exchange and mortuary ritual.
>
> (1993: 38)

DOI: 10.4324/9781003398349-12

We then turn to M. Laetitia Cairoli, who describes how young unmarried Moroccan women employed in the export garment industry in Fez, Morocco, reconcile some of the contradictions between the cultural values and role expectations for women and the reality of their industrial employment. Inspired by Aihwa Ong's (1991: 280) emphasis on the "experiential and interpretive dimensions of work relations," Cairoli discusses how these female laborers transform their workplace into an interior domestic space, operating in it as they would in their own household. "They model their position in the factory hierarchy on their role in the household and so are able not only to accept the domination of the factory, but to find in that domination their own sources of personal self-worth and power." Factory owners become like fathers who guard the virtue of their female workers. Fellow garment workers are like sisters, and thus the authority of a female supervisor is akin to the authority of the eldest sister. As in the Moroccan home, female space in the factory is separated from male space. Cairoli's work also asks us to critically examine how local values shape globalization, demonstrating that local concerns can create unique working environments within a global capitalist economic system.

Drawing on research that explores how gender and sexuality differ in two locations of a transnational Mexican community, Hirsch addresses questions central to the emergence, reformulation, and lived experience of the domestic–public dichotomy. She assesses this opposition both as an analytic tool and as a cultural construct that shapes people's own understandings of their social worlds. For her research populations in Mexico and in the United States, domestic–public is a salient distinction – a foundational principle of the gendered organization of space. She argues that this distinction predates the separation of the productive and reproductive domains and the spread of wage labor.

In their new chapter for this edition, Sum et al. introduce readers to the Mosuo people of Southwest China. The Mosuo are matrilineal and have long maintained a practice of "walking marriages," in which male partners do not live with the women with whom they engage in sexual relationships. Any children born of these relationships belong to their mothers' family, and Mosuo men are responsible for helping support their sisters' children instead of their own biological offspring. Using examples from three families with whom they have worked, Sum et al. add additional complexity and nuance to our understanding of Mosuo family organization. They show how people make decisions about whether to enter into formal marriages, engage in walking marriages, or other relationships as times are changing and under different political or economic circumstances. Through a discussion of Mosuo life and practices, the authors demonstrate how Mosuo values, not just walking marriage, have resulted in relative gender egalitarianism.

In their chapter, Childs, Goldstein, and Wangdui discuss the practice of fraternal polyandry (a group of brothers who marry the same woman) among rural Tibetans. This system has created a surplus population of unmarried daughters, who are viewed as a form of social capital by elderly parents, who may not be treated well by an in-marrying daughter-in-law. These daughters provide various forms of social support (financial, emotional, nursing, etc.) to parents and are much appreciated. This chapter also raises the important issue of how the responsibilities for eldercare are gendered and vary cross-culturally. In India, for example, such responsibilities often fall to the eldest son rather than to a daughter. In the Tibetan case, although there is a cultural preference for sons, parents have come to appreciate their daughters.

Megan Bond Hinrichsen discusses the impact of microfinance on poor urban families in Quito, Ecuador. She poses the question of whether providing microcredit to women elevates the status and well-being of a family more so than do loans made to men. Are women's goals more child-centered than those of men? What precisely is the impact of these small-scale loans on gender roles and household dynamics? The families that are the focus of Hinrichsen's research live on the edge, and microloans help them make ends meet. She discovers that both men and women are concerned about the well-being of their children, and hence, she challenges the orthodoxies of microfinance. Her research also contributes further to our understanding of gendered domestic and public spheres, but here in the context of global capitalism and finance.

Finally, we turn to surrogacy, which challenges the Euro-American emphasis on genetic relatedness and the biological basis of kinship and creates potential conflicts surrounding the claims of different kinds of biological and non-biological mothers and fathers. Surrogacy poses profound challenges to our understandings of kinship, family, and reproduction. In her chapter, Heléna Ragoné explores surrogates' stated motivations for becoming surrogate mothers, as well as the details of their actual experiences. She describes surrogates' explanations as a cultural script reflecting widely accepted ideas about reproduction, motherhood, and family. In contrast to popular opinion, surrogates in her study deny being motivated by financial gain; rather, they conceptualize surrogacy as a "gift," a priceless donation to the commissioning couple. The apparent "commodification" of women's bodies represented in surrogate motherhood remains a troubling issue, however. In addition, the recent shift from traditional surrogacy (in which the surrogate contributes an ovum) to gestational surrogacy, where the surrogate gestates the couple's embryo(s), raises important questions about what constitutes "real" parenthood. Surrogacy continues to pose ethical, legal, and social conundrums in countries globally. India, for example, once a leader in international commercial surrogacy, now has the 2021 Surrogacy Act, which bans commercial surrogacy, responding largely to concerns about exploitation of lower-class women. In the United States, not all states allow commercial surrogacy, and in those that do, legal fees are extremely expensive, reflecting the complexity of contracts and legal agreements meant to clarify parental rights.

References

Lepowsky, Maria. 1993. *Fruit of the Motherland: Gender in an Egalitarian Society.* New York: Columbia University Press.

Ong, Aihwa. 1991. "The Gender and Labor Politics of Postmodernity." *Annual Review of Anthropology* 20: 279–309.

Chapter 11

Gender, horticulture, and the division of labor on Vanatinai

Maria Lepowsky

Original to a previous edition of this text. Courtesy of Maria Lepowsky.

Gender and horticulture

"Women are the owners of the garden," Koita said early one morning. I probably looked startled, because she added, emphatically, "That is our custom; it's the way of the ancestors." Koita was my neighbor, a respected female elder on the small Pacific island of Vanatinai. She was stating, with no prompting from me, a fundamental principle of island gender ideologies, part of their overall worldview, their outlook on life.

I was studying relations between women and men in what I suspected would be at least a fairly egalitarian society. I chose the island for my research in part because I had read that cultures in this region of small islands had matrilineal kinship systems. People belonged to their mothers' clans. Matrilineality meant, I reasoned, that women were central to kinship systems, control of communally held lands, and inheritance patterns. This might translate, on Vanatinai, into egalitarian relations between the sexes.

The people of Vanatinai and their neighbors are primarily horticulturalists, practicing a nonintensive form of agriculture, which anthropologists sometimes refer to as gardening. The islanders actually have a mixed economy, fishing, hunting, and gathering wild plant foods, as well as planting and harvesting crops. Horticulturalists rely especially on root and tree crops. They use simple tools, such as digging sticks, rather than spending time and caloric energies on intensive, plow-based farming that uses draft animals (horses, mules, water buffalo) or machinery.

Social relations in horticultural societies vary, but they tend to be more gender egalitarian than in other agricultural societies or in large-scale industrial societies. Horticultural societies are often smaller in scale, with fewer people dependent on the resources of a particular territory. This leads to more possibilities for face-to-face negotiation, personal influence, consensus formation, and conflict resolution. All these factors can make for more egalitarian social relations overall: less hierarchy; fewer specialized roles and positions based on age, sex, rank, and/or training; and a greater overlap between the kinship system and the political system. Leaders or influential persons within an extended family or clan tend to be the political leaders as well, the most influential people in the community or region. Gender relations, the interactions between men and women and

DOI: 10.4324/9781003398349-13

the ideologies that shape them, are a key aspect of the potentially more egalitarian social relations found in many small-scale societies, where people make their living by horticulture, foraging, or a mixture of the two.

Vanatinai (whose European name is Sudest Island) is the largest island of an archipelago, a chain of islands, in a remote part of the Southwest Pacific, southeast of the great island of New Guinea by 200 miles, and 700 miles northeast of Australia. The island had never previously been studied by an anthropologist. I had hypothesized that the roles of women and men, and cultural ideologies of gender, were largely egalitarian. If so, women and men would have reasonably equal rights, privileges, personal autonomy, and influence over the actions of others. Women as well as men would be involved in prestige-generating activities. Here, that would mean exchanging ceremonial valuables and hosting elaborate feasts in honor of the dead. The region has been famous to anthropologists since the pioneering research of Bronislaw Malinowski (1922) on Trobriand Island *kula*. Kula is a remarkable system for the ceremonial exchange of shell valuables and stone axe blades. These prized objects circulate hundreds of miles among islanders who speak a dozen different languages and travel by sailing canoe to visit their exchange partners. They trade yams, pigs, clay pots, and other, more obviously practical goods at the same time. But in the Trobriands, kula is almost entirely a male prestige activity. Trobrianders also have chiefs, and they, too, are almost always male. Years later, anthropologist Annette Weiner (1976) showed that Trobriand women have their own system of wealth exchange, based on banana leaf skirts and the hosting of memorial feasts, and that it was closely articulated with kula.

On Vanatinai, 300 miles southeast, I found that there were no chiefs and no commoners. Women as well as men gained regional fame in the same way as men, by successfully exchanging the ceremonial valuables that circulate in kula as far as the Trobriands. Vanatinai women as well as men could, and did, host large-scale feasts commemorating the dead that drew hundreds of visitors from a half-dozen islands.

Both Vanatinai women and men, it turned out, describe island women as *ghuma tanuwagai*, owners, or bosses, of gardens. This is a philosophical statement. In actuality, men and women, sisters, brothers, mothers, maternal grandmothers, mother's brothers held land in common as matrilineal property. But it was a senior woman, or women, who tended to get everyone organized. Married men usually made gardens on their wives' matrilineal land, not that of their mothers, even though they retained the right to do so.

To a remarkable extent, the tasks considered appropriate for males and females, and for people of varying ages, were much the same. In other words, the sexual division of labor (sometimes called the gendered division of labor) was largely overlapping. This kind of overlap is a characteristic that anthropological theorists have long suggested is characteristic of a gender-egalitarian society.[1] On Vanatinai, women and men alike plant, weed, and harvest the large, white tropical yams that are one of the islanders' staple foods. Yams are the only annual crop, harvested just before the bright, tightly clustered stars of the Pleiades are visible once more on the eastern horizon. This marks the start of the new year. Both sexes also tend taro and banana patches and plant and harvest the easy-to-grow, drought-resistant sweet potatoes and manioc that were introduced in the colonial era. Every stage of the process of yam gardening is hedged with garden magic and ritual. I found that only a few people had the magical knowledge, derived from ancestor spirits and handed down from elders, to officiate at communal garden rituals. But these few people included both women and men.

Women and men, sisters and brothers, wives and husbands have to agree on which clan lands they are going to use for a garden. Sometimes this is a challenge. A big woman or big man, either for powerful emotional reasons or to enlarge a regional reputation, may want to host a feast the following year to commemorate someone who has died. That means clearing an especially big garden – cutting and then burning a clearing in the rainforest canopy – so as to have plenty of high-quality yams to feed off-island visitors, who may end up camped out in the hamlet for weeks.

It is the men, young and middle-aged, who do the work of cutting old-growth hardwood trees, while women cut understory trees and shrubs. A senior woman usually supervises the burning, which takes place about a month later, when the slash has had a chance to dry out. The ashes then fertilize the soil of the new garden. (This technique, characteristic of tropical horticulture, is called swidden, or slash-and-burn.) The population density on Vanatinai is quite low, only about four persons per square miles. In many parts of the island, land lies fallow for up to 40 years before it is again made into a garden. By then it resembles mature, closed-canopy rainforest.

Men are the ones, I was told, who use 8-foot-long wooden poles to loosen and aerate the soil of the new garden, forming it into mounds ready to receive yam seed. It is true that men do it most of the time. But women perform this hard labor as well. I saw a couple of my women neighbors hard at it and took their photo. The other villagers, men and women, commented admiringly that they were *ivurigheghe*, strong. They meant both physically and socially, a reference to their good reputations and influence over others.

Women do much of the preparation and planting of seed yams, removing them from storage in small stilted houses adjacent to the gardens, slicing off their growing tips, and stockpiling them in woven, coconut leaf garden baskets. The rest of each seed yam is boiled with coconut cream in a clay cooking pot and served for lunch to the communal working group. Women also tend to take primary responsibility for maintaining gardens. But this is only a general rule. Some men take great pride in their gardens. And some women are less ambitious gardeners, making more of their subsistence contribution by gathering shellfish or forest fruits rather than weeding under the tropical sun.

Women do much of the harvesting of garden produce, often several times a week. There is no refrigeration, and thin-skinned tubers will go rotten in a few days. The best way to store them is by keeping them under the soil, digging them up as needed for daily subsistence, feeding visiting in-laws, or contributing food to feasts. Yams are the only annual crop. Because of their tough, thick skins, these tropical yam varieties are the only root crop possible to store for many months, in baskets on high shelves in house rafters, or in a small yam house. Harvesting is an individual affair, private and secret. The gardener offers prayers to ancestor spirits as she or he digs loose the tubers from the tropical soil with a long digging stick, piling them into a garden basket. Inviting acquaintances and neighbors to observe could be unwise: it might arouse envy if the garden was especially prolific. Some islanders are said to know a special kind of magic that persuades tubers growing in a neighboring garden to travel underground to the garden of the magician. People know not to appear uninvited in someone's garden for another reason as well. A garden house or shelter (a wall-less, palm-thatch-roofed structure on wooden stilts) is where islanders take a work break, get out of the midday sun, and cook lunch, but is also the only place where a married couple has enough privacy during the daytime for sexual relations, after lunch, while it is too hot to work.

Men are strongly identified in island ideology with the production of sago, the almost-pure starch extracted from the trunk of a mature female palm. Sago is the other principal food in the island diet. Extensive sago palm groves grow wild in the swamps – dim, almost primeval-looking places that are also home to voracious clouds of mosquitoes. Islanders throughout the region count the sago swamps of Vanatinai as a source of great wealth. This is an enormous reservoir of potential food, not planted (although the occasional palm is transplanted closer to a village), but wild. The sago groves, and the tracts of swamp, are communally owned by island matrilineages.

Sago processing is not horticulture but a form of plant management. It is hard, concentrated work over the course of two or three days. But it requires far less time, caloric energy, and risk than planting a yam garden, guarding it from wild boars, dealing with drought or flooding by using weather magic to petition ancestors and place spirits, then digging up unknown numbers and sizes of tubers nine months later.

Men do most of the pounding of sago pith – the fibrous insides of the split-open palm – and the sluicing out the starch in a wooden trough, but the work party is usually mixed. Women supervise the drying of cakes of sago starch over a low fire, the cutting of long green sago leaves to use for wrapping the fresh bricks of starch, and the actual wrapping. The bundles are hung in pairs over long poles, then each is carried by two men or youths back to the village. Everyone who has joined the work party gets a share, and lines of sago bundles hang in pairs from the rafters in each house. They are ready for use at a moment's notice: to throw a chunk in a boiling pot of vegetables, prepare sago and grated coconut dumplings or pancakes, grilled on a broken shard of clay pot over the fire, or a sago and green coconut pudding. Bundles of sago are major items to barter to people who sail to Vanatinai from the smaller coral islands to obtain sago or yams for clay cooking pots or the smoked meat of giant clams.

Vanatinai women, men, and children are all diligent foragers, studying the growth patterns, seasons, and locations of a wide array of wild nuts, legumes, tubers, fruits, ferns, and edible leaves. The large grubs that live in decaying sago palms are a special treat, usually eaten on the spot. They are also a fine source of protein. In general, I observed that women spent more time foraging than men. Foraging, and being in the forest more generally, is something that men and women alike enjoy more than the tedious, sweaty work of weeding gardens.

Shellfish collecting is another subsistence activity practiced equally by men, women, and older children. It, too, is something people enjoy: going down to the shore, alone or with friends or relatives, to gather the small tasty oysters that cling to aerial roots of mangroves; hunting for blue mangrove crabs (taking care to avoid getting pinched by their giant front claws); or prying clams loose from the reef at low tide. Anyone who feels like it may fish in the lagoon, from a canoe, from shore, or by wading in the shallows. Men sometimes use metal-tipped spears to fish in the shallows, either from a canoe or on foot at low tide. The metal is often scavenged, washing ashore after a storm from some distant place.

Whole hamlets full of people troop down to the lagoon at neap tide, the lowest tides of the year. They use derris root, from a forest plant that contains a potent neurotoxin, to temporarily stun the fish that have collected in shallow pools in the coral, left behind by the falling sea. The fish are scooped up by hand, strung on a piece of cord made from a forest vine, and carried home. (Fortunately, stunning fish this way does not affect the human diner, although eating derris root directly would be fatal.) The islanders nowadays use monofilament for line fishing. But both men and women fish collectively, using nets woven by men from the fibrous aerial root of pandanus, a wild palm that grows in the rainforest.

Occasionally, young men, and less often young women, dive in the lagoon for black-lip pearl shell, or the larger, glowing gold-lip pearl that is used in other countries to make mother-of-pearl buttons. Shell can, in theory, be sold at the trade store at the end of the island, but the commodity price for it, set on the London market, has been extremely low for several decades now, a result of competition from the plastic button industry. Gold-lip pearl shell is rarer and harder to obtain, as it lives on reefs in deeper lagoon waters. Gold-lip shell is used by islanders themselves to make the translucent pendants that are attached to ceremonial shell-disc necklaces. Young or vigorous men and women some-times take a canoe to certain reefs where they dive for bagi, the red-rimmed shells used to make the discs for shell necklaces. The shells can be bartered or given to relatives. Discs to string into necklaces are manufactured, using pump drills with a metal bit, by island men and women, often middle-aged, who have chosen to specialize in this form of labor. Necklaces are strung together on bush cord, with mother-of-pearl pendants added to the larger ones. The deep reddish color of the shell discs should be set off pleasingly by the glossy black of wild banana seeds. These are bartered by visitors arriving by sailing canoe from larger islands near the mainland of New Guinea, 200 miles away; wild banana does not grow on or near Vanatinai. Newly made shell necklaces circulate through sets of exchange partners from island to island for hundreds of miles, as far as the Trobriand Islands, joining necklaces and other valuables that are 100 years and older in the kula system of interisland exchange that Malinowski made famous.

Sometimes, islanders successfully land a sea turtle by wrestling it into a canoe. Or they find a lonely beach where the female is laying eggs in the sand, turn her over, and drag her off. The eggs are scooped up as well. Once in a while, men spear a dugong, a sea mammal, cousin to the manatee of Florida and tropical South America, that grazes on the sea grasses of the lagoon. (Luckily for the dugong, they swim remarkably fast and often elude the hunters.) The islanders fish the inland streams for little silvery fish, sweet reddish prawns, and giant black eels. Every so often, parties of men, accompanied by the occasional young woman, hunt crocodiles late at night, using coconut-leaf torches and black-palm, metal-tipped spears.

It is up to the individual to decide how much time she or he wishes to spend fishing or collecting shellfish versus other kinds of subsistence activities such as gardening, gath-ering, or hunting. The variation in time and effort expended varies based on personal preference, not by sex.

Almost every adult, and some older children and adolescents, is the proud owner of at least one pig. Big women and big men own whole herds of them, and they snuffle around the hamlet, scavenging scraps of food. More dedicated owners cook their pigs a meal of sago pith (the part that is inedible to humans) at dusk, after the family dinner has been taken care of. Pigs go unfenced on Vanatinai, wandering into the forest to forage on their own during the day. They not infrequently find their way to someone's garden, where they enthusiastically dig up the sweet potatoes or yams the gardener has been carefully cultivating. Gardens, too, are unfenced. Islanders are always complaining about the seri-ous damage done to gardens by both wild and domestic pigs. But it would be too much work, they say, to fence off a whole garden. They have a point. Fences have to be made from tree limbs, laboriously cut in the forest, carried to the garden, then roped together with cord made from forest vines to form a sort of corral. Since wild and domestic pigs routinely commingle in one giant, island-wide herd, the wild boars are the ones that sire the piglets. In the hamlet, juvenile males are castrated. Domestic pigs often show affection for their owners. They also serve as watch pigs, growling menacingly and sometimes charging at strangers and visitors, who shout in alarm, on entering a hamlet, "Call off your pigs!"

There is one dramatic restriction on Vanatinai subsistence activities that is based on sex. It is taboo for women to hunt using spears. In earlier times, it was taboo for women to make war using spears, or using greenstone axe blades as hatchets. Young unmarried women did go into battle, elders told me, handing spears to their brothers and dragging them to safety if they were wounded. Mature women knew the special magic – petitions to powerful ancestor and place spirits – that was used to make war and to make peace. Senior women negotiated truces as experts in diplomacy.

Whenever I asked someone, of either sex, why women were not supposed to hunt with spears, or use weapons of war, the answer was always the same.

"Women are the life givers, and men are the death givers."

"And," the speaker usually added, "life giving is more important."

"But women hunt on Vanatinai," I would argue. "And some women are witches, or even sorcerers." In the supernatural domain of the island division of labor, most but not all witches are women, and most but not all sorcerers are men.

At this point, though, the elder I was talking to would add emphatically, "Ighabubu." It is taboo.

That always ended the conversation.

I learned firsthand from this conundrum that Vanatinai gender ideologies are multi-layered and occasionally contradictory. As is the case in all cultures, ideological statements of how people are supposed to behave are sometimes contradicted by individual actions.

Women do hunt on Vanatinai; they just don't hunt with spears.[2] They climb tall tropical hardwoods and coconut palms to capture opossum, flying foxes, and fruit bats. Young women are supposed to be the best at catching the slow-moving, 4-foot-long monitor lizards that resemble miniature Komodo dragons and frequent the tall mangroves lining the estuaries. Girls and women either climb the trees or set traps for them. The rough skins of monitor lizards, stretched by men and used for drum heads, are dark gray and whitish, abstractly patterned in a way that resembles the geometric designs of the fine coconut leaf baskets that island women weave, whose traditional colors are also gray (from being dipped in swamp water overnight) and off-white.

The climbing of trees by Vanatinai women and girls is telling in itself. In many Pacific societies, it is taboo for women to climb, or for her genitals to be higher than a man's head. Here, island women not only climb to hunt but agile younger women and girls also routinely climb areca and tall coconut palms to cut betel nuts (used daily as a stimulant and exported to other islands), brown ripe coconuts, and green drinking nuts. (The only issue, women told me jokingly, is to make sure there are no men or boys standing directly below a palm tree, looking up their skirts.)

This is another aspect of Vanatinai women's physical mobility, their freedom to roam around as they wish, just as men do. Island women are manifesting their freedom of movement when they disappear of their own accord, unchaperoned, into the forest or down the shore on some vague errand. Women also paddle and pole canoes, on subsistence tasks or to visit other coastal hamlets, and some are expert sailors. A few women know how to navigate a sailing canoe between islands single-handed, although navigating and crewing sailing canoes are mostly done by men and male youths.

Woodworking is a male specialization: chopping down hardwoods in the tropical forest to clear a garden, cutting down a mature sago palm, hauling a dense log of false mahogany out of the forest to carve out a canoe hull, or cutting and hauling timbers for housebuilding. The island houses are perched on tall hardwood stilts to catch cooling sea breezes, help defeat mosquitoes, and keep the pigs from wandering in the door. The walls, flooring, and roof come from the bark and leaves of the nipa and sago palms. Women gather sago leaves and weave them into panels that will overlap on the roof, and weave sago leaves together for a particular kind of wall. They also prepare cooked yams and other food for the male housebuilders.

Vanatinai men's woodworking specialty continues with the carving of large wooden, mushroom-shaped ceremonial spatulas, decorated with shell discs, another form of ceremonial valuable used in exchange and feasting. This kind of carving is done by only a few men, middle-aged or older, as is carving narrow ebony lime spatulas incised with representations of bird's heads. These master carvers also produce large, seven-shaped ceremonial axe handles from tropical hardwoods, featuring a stylized bird's head at the apex and abstract designs at the handle. These are valuable items in interisland exchange. Vanatinai men also carve tortoise shell into the rows of earrings worn by both sexes, as well as into smaller, mushroom-shaped lime spatulas, whose intricate curvilinear designs are outlined in the brilliant white of powdered coral lime.

Vanatinai island women are admired regionally for their fine, soft, tightly woven coconut leaf baskets, whose zigzag and chevron patterns are picked out in contrasting colors. These small round open baskets are used daily as purses by men and women. They are also essential objects at memorial feasts, circulating in interisland exchange. Women weave wild pandanus leaf sleeping mats and larger, coarse garden baskets of coconut leaf, and make skirts out of dried, shredded coconut fronds. The skirts, too, play a key role in the ceremonial exchanges of feasts honoring the dead.

The tasks of daily household maintenance are ideologically considered by islanders to be the domain of women: cooking, washing, fetching water from spring or creek, fetching salt water from the lagoon for seasoning food, gathering firewood, and sweeping the hamlet clean of debris and pig excrement each morning with a coconut-rib broom. The house itself is considered to be a woman's house, and the pigs are usually her pigs. It is a common sight every day, though, to see a man or boy performing one or more of these tasks, with the exception of sweeping the hamlet grounds.

Childcare is the primary responsibility of women, who customarily breastfeed on demand for up to 3 years. (A baby's diet is supplemented with other foods starting at around 6 months.) But it is common to see fathers, uncles, grandfathers, and older brothers carrying babies and toddlers around. Vanatinai women also make full use of that ancient institution, the babysitter, calling on older siblings – boys as well as girls – grandparents, and neighbors to watch a child while they are weeding a garden, collecting nuts in the forest, or gathering shellfish. Both fathers and mothers are loving and indulgent parents; island child-rearing is remarkably permissive. If a small child is frustrated and crying, that is, denied its desires, it may become angry and leave us, people say, meaning, it might die and rejoin the ancestors. Fathers as well as mothers often take an older girl or boy to the garden, gathering, or even on a long exchange voyage.

Exchange and the life course

In Vanatinai ideologies of gender, I learned, there is no principle of male superiority or female weakness or inferiority, no idea that women are supposed to defer to men. In fact, in customary and daily life, leaving aside colonial and postcolonial government and legal systems, no adult has the right to tell another adult what to do. The only options are to persuade, influence, shame, or work magic or witchcraft or sorcery on someone to get them to behave in a certain way: join a work party planting a large yam garden, agree to have sexual relations, offer a fine red shell-disc necklace to an exchange partner, or attend a feast, bringing a giant tusked boar as a contribution.

Vanatinai women and men are valued for the same qualities. The most admired individuals of both sexes were described to me as strong, wise, and generous. By *strong*, people mean hardworking, morally powerful, and successful in producing large gardens, obtaining valuables from their many exchange partners, hosting feasts, and persuading kinspeople and neighbors to work with them. *Wise* means practical knowledge, insight, and judgment, but also good relations with powerful ancestor spirits and place spirits, who are petitioned through magic and ritual learned over a lifetime from one's elders. *Generous* refers directly to giving things away – shell-disc necklaces, greenstone axe blades, pigs, yams – especially as contributions offered at the sequence of three to four feasts, increasingly large and elaborate, that honor the dead. These generous people, men and women alike, were called the *giagia*, a gender-neutral term which literally means "the givers." In other societies of the Southwest Pacific, this kind of influential and respected person is referred to by anthropologists as a big man. On Vanatinai, there are both big women and big men.

Neither every man nor every woman aspires to become known as a *gia*. But each person, from youth to elder, is expected to honor kinship obligations and respect the dead – who become powerful ancestor spirits – by contributing labor, valuables, or both at the increasingly elaborate feasts that mark a person's death. Death is an all-too-familiar visitor to every family: women die in childbirth, babies die suddenly, toddlers are carried off in a day by cerebral malaria, and strong, healthy adults are stricken with pneumonia or tuberculosis (Lepowsky 1990). This means each person learns firsthand from youth about mortuary obligations of the matrilineal kin group. The ceremonial rules are complex; there are different expectations, depending on whether the deceased is a member of one's own matrilineage, an in-law's, or the father's. Some of the heaviest responsibilities come at the death of the father himself, who, in a matrilineal society, is not a kinsman but a member of another matrilineage. His heirs need to be compensated – given valuables – by the deceased man's own children and widow. The father's kin bear the heaviest ceremonial burden at the death of the mother, his wife.

To document whether Vanatinai society is gender-egalitarian, in ideology and practice, we have to compare experiences, ideological principles, and expectations for each life stage, for girls and boys, men and women. Given islanders' cultural emphasis on ceremonial exchange, our comparison should highlight the ceremonial division of labor and access to the most important island domains of prestige and influence.

The life course on Vanatinai is not strongly marked by age categories. A person is referred to as child (*gama*) from birth to around puberty. There are no rituals of initiation for either males or females. A girl begins to be known as *gamaina* (literally "child woman") when her breasts start to show. She begins to menstruate a couple of years later, at around age 15 or 16, and to observe the taboo of not going to the garden during her period. Otherwise, people say, birds and animals, attracted by the blood, will eat the growing food plants (she is not considered unclean or polluting, and she may prepare and share food with others). An adolescent boy, around the time of his growth spurt and voice change, becomes known as *zeva*, or youth.

The period of youth, for both sexes, extends into the late 20s, well into what Westerners consider adulthood. (This cultural pattern of extended youth is traditional in many Pacific Island societies; see Lepowsky 1998). A person on Vanatinai is generally considered an adult (*wevo*, or woman; *ghomoli*, or man) when she or he is in a stable marriage and has a child. This is a gradual transition, as many early marriages end in divorce. Respected adults can soon earn the title of female or male elder (*laisali* for females and *amalaisali* for males), even as young as their mid-30s. But most individuals addressed as female or male elder range in age from their 50s to their 80s. The rights, privileges, constraints, and degrees of personal autonomy of both sexes are largely congruent throughout the life course, even though they are not perfectly symmetrical. This is a hallmark of a gender-egalitarian society, a society that tends toward equality (Lepowsky 1993).

Girls or boys as young as 10 or so may get their start in the interisland ceremonial exchange system with a parent's gift of a piglet to care for. When it is a portly, swaying adult, it is valuable enough to be exchanged for an impressive quantity of shell-disc necklaces, greenstone axe blades, or other shell valuables. The owner of the pig, regardless of age or sex, is the one who decides whether or not to accept a request for it from a kinsperson, or new or existing exchange partner. She or he alone decides whether to contribute the pig at a feast commemorating a deceased relative or in-law. People sometimes cry over the death of the beloved pig they have offered, sacrificed, to honor the deceased and the feast host. The owner never eats the meat from her or his own pig but instead eats pork from someone else's animal, a form of ritual sharing that emphasizes the close identity among human owner, deceased, and valued pig.

Youths of both sexes also earn a name as a hard worker and respected young person by producing yams, bundles of sago, skirts, baskets, and other goods to contribute to an upcoming feast. Some young adults go to kin, or a parent's exchange partner, to request a valuable to contribute. Eventually, they will have to replace it with another wealth object. Young people are expected to devote much of their energy to courtship and sexual intrigue: this is the stage of life for them to enjoy the cultural expectation of full premarital sexual freedom. But a young person who becomes known as lazy will be gossiped about, shamed by older kin, and spurned as a potential marriage partner.

Young people are enthusiastic attendees at feasts, working hard at the labor of provisioning hundreds of guests as directed by the host and food magician. They are sometimes gifted with a valuable, such as a greenstone axe blade, by the appreciative host. The last and largest feast, the *zagaya*, features at least one, and sometimes many, all-night sessions of drumming, singing, and traditional dancing. It is the perfect time for unmarried youths from small hamlets on far-flung islands to meet. They are expected to slip away discreetly and meet a lover in some dark corner of beach or forest. The final feast celebrates the lifting of the final mourning taboos, and the renewal and regeneration of life, the mending of ties of kinship and exchange after a death. Youthful sexuality is part of this celebration. Many marriages begin with flirtations and romances at feasts.

At feasts or occasions of communal labor such as planting a new yam garden or raising or re-roofing a house, men and women, girls and boys work diligently at the many tasks necessary to provide food and shelter for up to several hundred people for days or weeks, fetching huge quantities of firewood and water, grating mounds of coconut, cooking, and cleaning. Women are in charge of roasting vegetable food in the earth ovens, using superheated round river rocks wrapped in soft forest leaves. Men are responsible for preparing the ritual sago and coconut pudding, stirred with a special, 8-foot-long carved wooden paddle. Men also take charge of spearing, butchering, and boiling the pigs that visitors and exchange partners have brought to add to those of the feast host. There is generally one man who knows the secret magical spell for making the meat multiply itself to feed the multitudes. Women and men alike know some kinds of food magic, but a few individuals are experts. A senior female or male expert is selected by the feast host to say magical spells over piles of donated yams and bundles of sago – hidden in, or underneath, the host's house – so that they will extend far enough to feed the visitors and still have food left over. The food magician is simultaneously an experienced "kitchen" manager, directing all the food workers of both sexes for the duration of the feast.

Mature adults, male and female, are equally expected to honor ceremonial obligations. Rarely, individuals, scorned and feared as anti-social sorcerers or witches, refuse to participate. Some adults, of both sexes, contribute the bare minimum of labor or ceremonial valuables. The most common path is to work especially hard at ritual obligations when a spouse's parent, or one's own parent or matrilineal aunt or uncle, dies.

A minority of adult men and women whose children are already youths or adults (or who are childless) strive to exceed others in ceremonial exchange. They accumulate valuables, garden produce, sago, and other goods; host feasts; and contribute lavishly and publicly, in acts of ritual generosity, at the numerous feasts of exchange partners, kin, or in-laws. These people seek regional fame, prestige, and influence over others, striving to be admired as *giagia*, givers, big men or big women. This is a matter of individual personality and desire. It is also related to life stage. Along with the obvious childcare issues, children are placed at risk of death or illness by the destructive magic of a parent's envious rival, so it is unwise to strive for the status of *gia* when one has young children. Mature adults also have more supernatural and practical knowledge and greater stores of social capital through personal ties and exchange partners.

Established or aspiring *giagia* set off, on foot or by canoe, accompanied by kin or spouse, to request valuables from exchange partners. They attend and contribute to all the feasts in the region. They are admired, but also feared, for their supernatural knowledge: without the power of ancestor and place spirits, exercised through magic, witchcraft, or sorcery, a person cannot be successful in ceremonial exchange.

Vanatinai women as well as men can build personal fame and renown through active participation in the prestige and ritual economy of exchange and feasting. But they may also choose to gain respect in other ways: by nurturing families and gardens, practicing food magic or weather magic, or helping kin and neighbors through the spirit-directed practices of healing. Women and men have equivalent access to supernatural powers: to apprentice with an elder knowledgeable about certain kinds of magic and ritual. Choosing to do so is up to the seeker, not limited by sex or inherited position.

Vanatinai ideologies validate powerful beliefs in personal autonomy, control of one's own actions, and wide tolerance of personal idiosyncrasies. When I asked why a person behaved a certain way, people said, "We can't know their *renuanga*, their thoughts, emotions. It's up to them." This principle applies to both sexes. Yet in this small-scale subsistence society, people must be persuaded to cooperate, to share food, wealth, and knowledge, in order that all, or at least many, will survive and thrive. This ideological and practical tension underlies island life. Still, island ideologies grant all adults, female and male, equal opportunities to manage their own lives, and to influence others. The same personal qualities – strength, wisdom, and generosity – are valued in women and men.

Discussion questions

1. How is labor divided between men and women on Vanatinai?
2. How do the life experiences of Vanatinai boys and girls differ?
3. Why does the author argue that social relations in small-scale horticultural societies tend to be more egalitarian? Is Vanatinai truly egalitarian? Why or why not?

Notes

1 In a now-classic set of writings, Peggy Sanday (1974, 1981) hypothesized that if both sexes contributed equally to subsistence in a particular society, women's status would be higher. She was the first to suggest that when the sexes commingle in the labor of everyday life, this worked against the rise of male dominance. Albert Bacdayan (1977) suggests that what he labels "task interchangeability" between men and women is a key indicator of egalitarian gender relations. See Lepowsky (1993) for further discussion of characteristics that scholars have hypothesized are associated with gender-egalitarian societies. After research with the Lahu, matrilineal horticulturalists living in Yunnan, China, Shanshan Du (2002) has proposed that there are several different types, or cultural "schemas," of gender-egalitarian societies worldwide. She argues, for example, that the cultural emphasis in Lahu is "dyadic," organized around the wife and husband in subsistence and divine sister-brother twins in mythology. On Vanatinai, she continues (relying on my ethnographic reports), the cultural "schema" is, in contrast, based on "individual autonomy" and "collective cooperation." In other words, there are different viable ways to organize a gender-egalitarian society.

2 Female hunting is relatively rare worldwide, compared to hunting by males, but it has been documented in many societies. Examples include foragers such as Australian aborigines (Goodale 1971; Kaberry 1939), the horticultural Agta of the Philippines (Estioko-Griffin and Griffin 1981, 1985), and the Ojibwa, Montagnais-Naskapi, and Rock Cree, who hunt large game, such as moose and caribou, in the eastern woodlands and boreal forests of Canada (Brightman 1996; Landes 1938; Leacock 1978). In some, but not all, cases cross-culturally, women are ideologically restricted from hunting certain animals, using particular killing technologies (such as spears and greenstone axe blades in the Vanatinai example), or hunting when they are menstruating. See Brightman (1996) for a detailed discussion.

   The existence of contradictions between levels of gender ideology, the ideological positions of each sex, or between the ideal and the real, has long been pointed out by gender theorists (for example, Lederman 1990; Murphy and Murphy 1974; Ortner 1996; Sanday 2002; Schlegel 1990). The strands of gender ideology on Vanatinai are more congruent than those of most societies. I found no categorical difference between what men and women stated about gender philosophies, and not much individual or situational variation. This degree of congruence, I suggest, and the lack of a major gap between gender ideologies and social life as experienced, is characteristic of societies that tend toward gender egalitarianism (Lepowsky 1993: 34–35).

References

Bacdayan, Albert. 1977. "Mechanistic Cooperation and Sexual Equality among the Western Bontoc." In *Sexual Stratification: A Cross-Cultural View*, ed. Alice Schlegel, 271–291. New York: Columbia University Press.

Brightman, Robert. 1996. "Biology, Taboo, and Gender Politics in the Sexual Division of Foraging Labor." *Comparative Studies in Society and History* 38(4): 687–729.

Du, Shanshan. 2002. *Chopsticks Only Work in Pairs: Gender Unity and Gender Equality among the Lahu of Southwest China.* New York: Columbia University Press.

Estioko-Griffin, Agnes, and P. Bion Griffin. 1981. "Woman the Hunter." In *Woman the Gatherer,* ed. Frances Dahlberg, 121–140. New Haven, CT: Yale University Press.

Estioko-Griffin, Agnes, and P. Bion Griffin. 1985. "Women Hunters: The Implications for Pleistocene Prehistory and Contemporary Ethnography." In *Women in Asia and the Pacific: Towards an East-West Dialogue,* ed. Madeleine Goodman, 61–81. Honolulu: Women's Studies Program, University of Hawaii.

Goodale, Jane. 1971. *Tiwi Wives.* Seattle: University of Washington Press.

Kaberry, Phyllis. 1939. *Aboriginal Woman: Sacred and Profane.* London: Routledge.

Landes, Ruth. 1938. *The Ojibwa Woman.* New York: Columbia University Press.

Leacock, Eleanor. 1978. "Women's Status in Egalitarian Society: Implications for Social Evolution." *Current Anthropology* 19: 247–276.

Lederman, Rena. 1990. "Contested Order: Gender and Society in the Southern New Guinea Highlands." In *Beyond the Second Sex: New Directions in the Anthropology of Gender,* ed. Peggy Reeves Sanday, pp. 43–74. Philadelphia: University of Pennsylvania Press.

Lepowsky, Maria. 1990. "Sorcery and Penicillin: Treating Illness on Papua New Guinea Island." *Social Science and Medicine* 30(10): 1049–1063.

Lepowsky, Maria. 1993. *Fruit of the Motherland: Gender in an Egalitarian Society.* New York: Columbia University Press.

Lepowsky, Maria. 1998. "Coming of Age on Vanatinai: Gender, Sexuality, and Power." In *Adolescence in Pacific Island Societies,* eds. Gilbert Herdt and Stephen Leavitt, 123–147. ASAO Monograph 18. Pittsburgh: University of Pittsburgh Press.

Malinowski, Bronislaw. 1922. *Argonauts of the Western Pacific.* New York: Dutton.

Murphy, Yolanda, and Robert Murphy. 1974. *Women of the Forest.* New York: Columbia University Press.

Ortner, Sherry. 1996. "Gender Hegemonies." In *Making Gender: The Politics and Erotics of Culture,* pp. 139–172. Boston: Beacon Press.

Sanday, Peggy. 1974. "Female Status in the Public Domain." In *Woman, Culture and Society,* eds. Michelle Rosaldo and Louise Lamphere, pp. 189–206. Stanford, CA: Stanford University Press.

Sanday, Peggy. 1981. *Female Power and Male Dominance: On the Origins of Sexual Inequality.* Cambridge: Cambridge University Press.

Sanday, Peggy. 2002. *Women at the Center: Life in a Modern Matriarchy.* Ithaca, NY: Cornell University Press.

Schlegel, Alice. 1990. "Gender Meanings, General and Specific." In *Beyond the Second Sex: New Directions in the Anthropology of Gender,* eds. Peggy Reeves Sanday and Ruth Gallagher Goodenough, 21–42. Philadelphia: University of Pennsylvania Press.

Weiner, Annette. 1976. *Women of Value, Men of Renown: New Perspectives on Trobriand Exchange.* Austin: University of Texas Press.

Chapter 12

Factory as home and family

Female workers in the Moroccan garment industry

M. Laetitia Cairoli

Reproduced from "Factory as Home and Family: Female Workers in the Moroccan Garment Industry," *Human Organization* 57.2 (1998). Courtesy of the Society for Applied Anthropology.

Thus, one Fez clothing factory worker explained why she had remained at her job for four years, despite the notoriously low pay and constant overtime demanded there. In the past two decades, the Moroccan garment industry has developed into one of the country's most significant export trades, and Moroccan females have become the labor power for clothing manufacture. Although their role in the garment factories is widely regarded as exploitative and demeaning, the workers themselves continue to use the idiom of family to describe their relationships to factory owners, administrators, supervisors, and their fellow workers. In the course of a year of ethnographic research in the city of Fez, I began an exploration of how garment factory workers make sense of their labor on the shop floor.

Inside one Fez garment factory where I worked during a three-month period, I observed workers as they sought to impose their own assumptions and values upon the factory system and thereby render their labor meaningful. Nearly all of Morocco's garment factory workers are female, and most are unmarried.[1] They confront the factory with a set of cultural values that order their social world, central to which is their identity as kinswoman, a self-perception workers believe to be ordained by Islam. Despite their engagement with the factory, workers continue to perceive themselves first and foremost as daughters, sisters, and perhaps wives and mothers in a patriarchal family. As such, they presume that their rightful place is in the private sphere of the home, which is the arena of their most noble efforts. Thus, they transform the workshop floor into an interior space, recast factory staff into family, and operate in the factory as they would in the household. In this way, they retain their prized identity as kinswoman, even within the factory, and they convert factory labor into work that is significant to them.[2] In doing so, however, they render themselves more amenable to the factory's exploitation.

There are, of course, limits to the workers' re-creation of the factory: for Moroccan females, the garment factory is a new kind of public space with characteristics unlike the private arena of the home. In some instances, workers find that their efforts to impose the blueprint of home and family on the factory fall short, and they confront what they

DOI: 10.4324/9781003398349-14

recognize to be foreign work regimes and excessive domination. When this occurs, workers resist. I do not see this behavior as contradictory; rather, I assert that the workers' ability to comply with factory domination (which occurs far more frequently than does resistance) is rooted in their conversion of factory into home. Here I explore how this transformation is enacted.

The "global factory"

Any study of Moroccan female garment workers must be set in the context of the recent literature on the phenomenon of women's participation in factory production. Over the past two decades, this scholarship has explored the effects of global capitalism on the definitions and meanings of *gender*. Two central questions have been posed: the first concerns the impact of women's participation in industrialization on the women themselves, on the men, on the family, and on the local culture. The second question is whether this impact – and the very participation of women in factories worldwide – is intrinsic to factory technology itself and/or capitalism, or if it results from local culture (Warren and Bourque 1989). Researchers have sought to understand whether women's participation in these new forms of labor marks their liberation from local "patriarchy" or marks a new kind of enslavement to the demands of foreign capital. Those arguing the former possibility have pointed to ways in which factory work provided women an escape from the confines of home and new opportunities for personal autonomy (Lim 1983; Salaff 1981). Other researchers have emphasized, instead, the exploitation in modern production systems that is particularly detrimental to female status (Nash and Fernandez-Kelly 1983).

The literature on women and technology has demonstrated that women's entry into capitalist wage work affects the nature of gender roles and relations in complex and contradictory ways. As Nash (1981) notes, female participation in new forms of capitalist wage labor intensifies existing forms of gender subordination while simultaneously decomposing and recomposing them. The roots of these transformations are found both in local patriarchies and in global capitalism. While the literature on women in the global factory has illuminated critical aspects of gender transformations which accompany the movement of global capital, much of the early research was limited in scope.

A particular weakness in the literature is its relative lack of detailed cultural analysis of what Ong (1991: 280) calls the "experiential and interpretive dimensions of work relations." Much of the earliest research overlooked the unique ways in which workers transform capitalist work regimes and formulate their own kinds of meanings. This limitation in the literature was partly a result of the analysts' perspective on the nature of capitalism. Characterizing the capitalist system as powerful and deterministic, theorists often assumed that the methods and relations of production associated with high-tech factories would occur wherever these factories were established (Blim 1992). Theorists would then analyze the new industrialization as an effect of a standard logic, or as the result of the intersection of capitalism and a local patriarchal system.

More recent conceptualizations of the global capitalist system stress the flexibility of capitalist processes and allow for a new interpretation of the effects of industrialization (Blim 1992; Ong 1991). Capitalism (including its associated technology) is no longer seen as a homogenizing agent that flattens local systems into replicas of each other. Instead, *capitalism* is now understood to merge with indigenous values and practices and thus to proliferate new kinds of labor processes and relations.

If this particular perspective on capitalism is adopted, the phenomenon of the factory, and the lives of its workers, can be studied as a cultural process linked to other local cultural forms, rather than as a consequence of capitalist production (Calagione and Nugent 1992). With this perspective, the local particulars in the worker's experience of industrialization become central; indeed, they become the focus of the study. Here, I follow this approach and discuss the Moroccan clothing factory as another expression of specifically Moroccan cultural values. Workers experience their labor according to Moroccan categories already familiar to them and use their own cultural meanings to interpret the garment factory. The Fez garment factory is thoroughly "Moroccanized" despite imported technology and systems of production.

Inside the factory, the garment workers struggle to retain a notion of themselves as family members, specifically as daughters (or sometimes as wives) in patriarchal households. They have accepted a notion of themselves as subservient and dutiful long before they enter the garment factory. They model their position in the factory hierarchy on their role in the household and so are able not only to accept the domination of the factory but also to find in that domination their own sources of personal self-worth and power. Thus, workers transform colleagues into loyal sisters and factory owners into concerned fathers. They are able to accept the constraints that the factory imposes by assimilating the owners' dominance into other, more acceptable forms of relationships. This re-molding of relationships formed inside the factory to fit the prototypes of ties formed outside ultimately makes the workers available for increased exploitation. Persons with authority in the factory capitalize on workers' interpretations of their roles to maximize production and ultimately increase profit.

Research methods

I conducted the fieldwork for this study in the city of Fez from August 1994 to August 1995. The fieldwork involved intensive ethnography, which included formal interviews of Fez factory owners, formal and informal interviews of workers and their families, two random surveys carried out in separate garment factories in the city, and three months of participant observation inside one of those garment factories. The factory where I worked, which I call "Confection," employs some 150 workers and has been in operation for some six years. It is typical in size and operation of garment factories in Fez. At Confection, I worked in the packaging department, where finished garments are tagged and prepared for shipment. This experience provided me a position from which to observe everyday work routines, the nature of the work process, staff hierarchies, and personal interactions inside the factory. It was through "acting like a worker" that I began to understand something of what factory work means to Moroccan factory girls.

The economic context of garment production

Today, clothing manufacture is one of Morocco's chief export industries, and garments account for a quarter of the country's exports (Leymarie and Tripier 1992). Conservative estimates suggest that Morocco's garment factories employ close to a quarter of the country's factory workers: some 95,000 of the country's total 444,000 industrial workers produce garments. Virtually all these workers are female (Ministère du Commerce 1994).[3]

The importance of the garment industry to the Moroccan economy is a recent phenomenon. Before the 1980s, garment manufacture was relatively insignificant. Between 1981 and 1991 the production of garments more than quadrupled (Leymarie and Tripier 1992), and although males had formerly predominated in the garment factories, it was females who were hired, en masse, to staff the new enterprises.[4] The boom in the Moroccan garment business, and the concomitant employment of females, was fueled by several factors. These included the government economic readjustment program, trade agreements with the European Economic Community, and the movement of European production "offshore."

The Moroccan government economic readjustment program, instituted in 1983, was a primary catalyst of the new trend (Leymarie and Tripier 1992). Before the institution of the readjustment program, Moroccan industry consisted largely of state-owned, high-tech enterprises with little capacity for generating employment. These included such industries as phosphate mining and production of thread and cloth. The program sought to replace such industries with private, low-capital, labor-intensive ones. This change in Moroccan industry marked a shift in the gender of the country's workforce. As Morocco turned to light manufacturing for export, including garment production, food processing, and electronics manufacturing, females flooded into factories. This employment of female factory workers is characteristic of export-oriented industries across the globe (Nash 1981; Nash and Fernandez-Kelly 1983; Ong 1987, 1991; Rothstein and Blim 1992).

European subcontractors (predominantly French), motivated by favorable trade conditions and the desire for "offshore" production sites, became involved in the industry in the late 1970s. They sought out Moroccan enterprises that could supply them with low-cost labor, sent in raw materials needed for production, and exported the final products. These subcontractors encouraged the wide-scale employment of females, enjoying greater profits because women would accept far lower wages than the salaries men demanded (Joekes 1982a, 1982b, 1985). Thus, the nature and structure of the Moroccan garment industry are defined by the relationship between the European contractors and private Moroccan industrialists.

Moroccan garment factories are generally small, family-owned businesses with staff of 50 employees or less, flexible enough to respond to a foreign, somewhat-volatile market. Because of their relatively small size, they can, and often do, elude government regulation. The garment factories commonly do not heed Moroccan labor law, which, in part, accounts for their poor working conditions. The factories open and close rapidly and unexpectedly, with fluctuations in the external market. Thus, Moroccan females labor in an industry that provides them insecure positions and relatively poor conditions (Leymarie and Tripier 1992).

Originally, Morocco's garment factory workers, like all Moroccan factory hands, were predominantly male. Before the 1980s, female garment factory workers did unskilled work on the margins of production, but they did not operate sewing machines. Today, however, women and girls fill nearly all positions in the garment factories. The wide-scale employment of females as garment factory workers takes on new meanings in the Moroccan context.

The social context of garment production

In my research, I found that garment factory workers are, for the most part, unmarried young girls who live at home with their parents and unmarried siblings. This fact is widely recognized in Morocco. The workers are generally daughters of lower-class households which, in comparison with others of their class, are relatively poor and suffer high rates of male unemployment. (I hereafter refer to the households where garment workers live as "factory households.") The vast majority of garment workers contribute all or at least part of their earnings to household support and are significant wage earners.[5]

Despite their positions as breadwinners, factory workers retain a fierce hold on the value of the patriarchal family. Both in word and action, they revere the traditional hierarchy that establishes males as protectors and females as dependents. Garment workers speak of factory labor as a temporary aberration they must tolerate until a successful marriage places them in the position of non-working wife and mother (married workers, a minority, are often young and as yet childless; workers with children generally work because they are destitute).

In their homes, garment workers enact the rituals of subservience that confirm and reinforce their positions as daughters, or sometimes as wives, in either case female and junior members of the household. Despite their engagement with the factory, workers strive to maintain their identity as kinswoman because this identity is more central to them than their self-perception as workers.[6]

Local ideologies of gender, to which workers adhere, reinforce the patriarchal structure of factory households. Male authority in the family is legitimized by an ideology that defines women as economically dependent, subservient, and in need of control. According to the Moroccan gender code, a woman's proper role is that of wife and mother, a position that is essentially non-economic and properly played out in the privacy of the domestic sphere. Men appropriately take the position of breadwinner and operate in the economic sphere outside the home. Thus, women are symbolically associated with the home and with private, interior domestic space. A family's honor is embedded in its ability to keep women inside and protected, thus maintaining the divide between male and female that is at once a separation between inside and outside, private and public, kin and non-kin, home and business.[7]

The favored portrayal of female activities as homebound, kin-related, and non-economic obscures the fact that Moroccan women have always been active in the economy (Beneria 1984; Davis 1983). Today, the economic participation of Moroccan females represents 36 percent of national economic activity (Direction de la Statistique 1994), although it goes largely unrecognized. Still, the previously described gender code retains its position as an ideal, rooted in the popular understanding of Islam. The mass entry of Fez's women into the garment factories blatantly contradicts the pervasively held Moroccan notions of family and gender. In this chapter, I explore how factory workers live with this contradiction.

The factory in Fez

Fez is an ancient city, revered among Moroccans as a spiritual capital and regarded as a bulwark of Islam and Muslim society. Traditionally, Fez has been an important artisanal center. Today it is a textile town. At independence, the Moroccan government established its largest public cloth spinning and weaving factories in Fez, which were (and are today) staffed by men. During the 1980s, garment manufacturing emerged as the city's principal industry, and today the sewing factories of Fez employ more than a third of all Fez factory workers, nearly all of them women (Ministère du Commerce 1994). This is a vivid contrast to the situation that existed less than three decades ago, when the town's textile enterprises were the province of men.

Industrial enterprises are scattered throughout the city of Fez, although most industry is located in three industrial quarters. Small factories and artisanal workshops producing for the local market and the tourist trade are found in the ancient medina. Other modest-sized factories exist in the city's newer sections, including the Ville Nouvelle and the recently developed urban periphery. The bulk of Fez's industry, including the largest and most "modern" factories, many of which produce for export, is located in the city's industrial quarters. These include the oldest and largest, Quartier Industriel Sidi Brahim, the industrial quarter of Doukkarat, and the most recently created quarter in Ben Souda. Three-quarters of Fez's factory workers labor in these districts (Fejjal 1987).

The majority of Fez's garment factories are privately owned by a class of Moroccan elite known as the *Fassi*. The term "Fassi" is used throughout the country to describe a group of influential families originally native to the city of Fez who control much of Morocco's wealth and political power. The Fassi are at the top of the local class structure, which includes a middle level of educated bureaucrats and a lower level made up of the majority of city dwellers, who are relatively poor and uneducated. This lower class is the class with which garment workers identify.

The labor process and factory staff

The labor process in Fez garment factories involves six separate steps, which precede and follow upon the actual sewing of the garments. They include, in sequential order, the intake and inventory of fabric and supplies imported from Europe; the cutting of the fabric; the actual sewing of the garments, carried out by workers seated in rows ("sewing lines"); the ironing of finished products; the final inspection of completed garments; and packaging and shipment. This production sequence is carried out in the same manner, using the same kind of technology, in garment factories throughout the world.

These production tasks are carried out by factory staff who labor in a hierarchy of authority. At the top of this hierarchy are the factory owners, who are either upper-class Moroccans (generally the previously described Fassi) or Europeans; in both cases, those at the top of the factory hierarchy are most frequently men.[8] Owners generally leave the daily direction of the factory to be handled by administrators, the garment manufacturing technicians who plan and supervise production. Like the owners, these individuals are upper-class Moroccan men (often of the owner's family) or Europeans.[9] A workshop director, generally a Moroccan man, oversees the management of all factory staff on the workshop floor. Next in the hierarchy are the workshop supervisors, who manage each particular production process; there are, for instance, one or two line supervisors for each sewing line. These supervisors are generally Moroccan males or females, of the same class as the workers. Finally, at the bottom of the factory hierarchy are the mass of factory workers, who are Moroccan females of the lower class.

On the margins of production are the factory mechanics, transport bus drivers, secretaries, and maids. The mechanics and bus drivers are Moroccan lower-class men, the former considered relatively skilled. The secretaries are Moroccan females who, because they are literate and not engaged in manual work, hold relatively high status within the factory. The maids, unskilled and impoverished females in a demeaned occupation, occupy the lowest position in the hierarchy.

Factory staff relies on familiar and valued models of relationships to interact with each other and with those who control them. I will explore how local assumptions about home and family, assumptions that are themselves infused with ideas about gender, inform the workers' attempts to transform factory relations into meaningful intercourse.

Factory as home and family

I like this factory very, very much. The people here are nice; it is like a family. There are hardly any men working here . . . so it is like being in your own house. . . . If I ever left this job, I would go straight back home.

Research participant

The gendering of the workshop floor as female transforms what might have been a public and immoral space into a private and acceptable one. As Emen, a seven-year employee of the Confection, expressed it earlier, the fact that garment factories hire (nearly) only females makes the work that goes on in them somewhat more respectable. The factory is a private space, like a house, because it is a female space, a space free from the threat of illicit sexuality. Whatever transpires inside the factory is less morally questionable because the shop floor is imagined to be a private rather than a public arena. As one worker explained with pride, "one girl passes her cloth to another girl and we are at ease, because we are all girls."

Garment factory workers are generally demeaned by Fez inhabitants for their participation in factory labor. Factory labor is in itself poorly regarded because it is manual labor, neither autonomous nor artisanal, and participation in factory work connotes a low-class status. But for females, it also suggests a lack of family honor and the real or potential loss of personal virtue. Girls who engage in factory labor are assumed to be related to males who are unable to appropriately support and protect them. The glaring presence of factory girls on the streets of Fez is often cited as proof of the inability of families to control and monitor their daughters. In response to such deprecating images, garment workers take refuge in the fact that they work in a safe, protected, all-female environment.

The actual physical construction of the factories and the way workers approach and understand factory space express the notion of factory as home. The factories producing for export, situated in Fez's three industrial districts, are large, low-lying structures that look like warehouses. Rows of narrow windows parallel the factory roofs but are almost unnoticeable from outside. The windows are generally too high for a passerby to see inside and, unlike the male-staffed cement and construction factories (where metal doors are often left open and interior courtyards are visible to the outside), the garment factories in the same districts housing Moroccan girls are shut tight to the stranger's eye. They look at first glance as if they were unoccupied.

Large metal doors mark the entrance to the factories, and a guardian sits directly behind these doors. The doors open into a courtyard, where the trucks that transport materials to and from Europe load and unload. The factory men – the guardian, mechanics, and drivers – often remain in this open, transitional space. On arrival, workers file through the courtyard and directly into the workshop. This is an area separate from the courtyard, located behind it, or up a flight of stairs. Once they have arrived inside the factory, workers may not leave the building without permission (often written) from their supervisors. At the Confection factory, workers who became ill during the workday required written authorization to get past the guardian and walk out of the building. Even if a worker wished to quit the job permanently, she could not leave the premises with written permission. The factory is a private space, tightly enclosed and closely monitored.

Altogether, then, the garment factory is a concrete structure built around an open courtyard, monitored by a male guardian, in which women remain protected from view and separate from males. This description of place is reminiscent of the traditional Fez household (Mernissi 1994), in which a male slave prevented the entrance of strangers, and where women remained protected inside, carrying out the labor specific to them. While such households may have existed only rarely and for the wealthy few, the notion of the home as a private, enclosed, and specifically female space remains a Moroccan ideal. The female garment factory is modeled on this prototype.

Unlike Moroccan female bureaucrats who wear European business suits, or university students who wear Western-style skirts or jeans on campus,[10] garment factory workers do not don "professional" or Western dress to go to work. They travel to and from the factory in the modest jellaba, a long loose-fitting robe worn in public spaces by traditional Moroccan women. Their retention of the jellaba signals identification with conventional Moroccan womanhood, as opposed to "modern" working women or with university girls (two other groups of women in transition). Inside the factories, workers are dressed in the informal clothing Moroccan women wear in the privacy of the home: baggy, pajama-like dresses or skirts or blue jeans in distinctive Moroccan combinations of style and color (in some factories, workers must wear regulation smocks). Most wear plastic sandals on their bare feet, as they would at home. In summer, the workshops can be stiflingly hot, and workers who take pains to dress modestly in the public arena of the streets labor in a minimum of clothing in the factory, as if confident that they are not exposed to a stranger's view.

Inside this production center imagined as domestic space, factory owners and workers alike assert that they work together "as a family"; owners claim to treat workers "as daughters." Workers identify the owners in a protective role that their fathers might hold and assert that all fellow garment workers are "sisters."[11] Even where workers recognize the discontinuities between ties formed inside the factory and those formed at home, the analogy to family life is implicit. For example, one worker, who detested the factory, claimed she would prefer to stay at home because her mother, as she said, "would never yell at [her] the way this administrator does."

The factory is the home and family is the idiom through which factory personnel think about their relations to one another. The gendered dimension of family relationships is evident in the way female factory workers approach owners, co-workers, and supervisors, male and female.

In using the metaphor of family, workers quite consciously help owners in their achievement of production goals. Despite a skill hierarchy among them, they treat each other as "sisters" and thus with relative equality. Workers vehemently assert that they support each other in the accomplishment of factory tasks. Repeatedly, I was told stories of lines of machine operators who had stayed late in order to help one of their slower members, or of individual machine operators who had fallen behind in their own tasks in order to assist an inexperienced newcomer. Workers emphasized their willingness to work well with each other, taking pride in their ability to behave in a sisterly fashion. At Confection (as at many other Fez factories), workers ate lunch together from communal plates, just as they would at home, making evident their attempts to replicate the atmosphere of the home inside the factory.

The sisterly relations among workers is perhaps most evident in the way they interact with their supervisors, particularly in their defiance of factory demands. Females are increasingly being placed in supervisory positions inside Fez factories, and the majority of sewing line supervisors today are female. At Confection, workers were relatively free in directly challenging female supervisors; they seemed to fear these supervisors less than they feared supervisory males.

Disputes between workers and female supervisors were not uncommon and often took the form of loud and sudden outbursts of resistance from workers in response to unbearable production pressures. Before such exchanges became problematic, however, the defiant worker's co-workers would often intervene, attempting to assuage the stressed worker's feelings and encourage her compliance. In one such case, I watched as a put-upon worker argued with her supervisor, refusing to complete a particular task. When the other workers tried to calm this worker and urge her compliance, the worker asked, "Why should she be allowed to boss me?" In response, her colleague asserted, "If Hakima cannot boss us, then who will?" The annoyed worker ultimately complied.

Co-workers had reminded the rebellious worker of the validity of the hierarchy among them, one not foreign to the mode of control used within the family. An age hierarchy among siblings is accepted in traditional Moroccan homes, and it is recognized that the eldest sister has the authority to lead her younger sisters in the housework. Verbalization of defiance and argument is not uncommon among siblings in a household. Neither is the eventual cooperation attained through a common acknowledgement of, and respect for, a universally recognized hierarchy. The authority of the female supervisor gains validity because it is reminiscent of the authority of the eldest sister. This argument, like others between workers and their female supervisors, is reminiscent of arguments between sisters in a household. Arguments with male supervisors take on a different tone, as discussed later. First, however, it is necessary to discuss the position of males in the factory.

Workers and workshop-level supervisors are today nearly exclusively female. Still, there are some males present inside the factories and on the workshop floor. The men may be the factory owners, high-level administrators, the workshop director, supervisors, or the male service workers (who include the factory transport drivers, guardians, and mechanics). It is now rare to find men on the sewing lines; three was the greatest number of male sewing machine operators I could identify in any Fez factory, and most have none.

In general, the factory men attempt to separate themselves from the females. Factory guardians and transport drivers generally remain in the courtyard, separate from the workshop floor and the females there. The mechanics' duties compel them to be present on the workshop floor amidst the females. At Confection, they did not dally on the floor and remained in a separate room when possible. The factory men took lunch together, eating only after the mass of workers had left the lunchroom. Just as men in Moroccan homes often remove themselves after meals to retreat to the all-male public cafés and street corners, men in the factory did not linger with women in a space that was clearly female.

The men present on the workshop floor are most often the workshop director and the supervisors directing the labor of the female machine operators. As noted earlier, the majority of line supervisors in Fez factories today are female; still, most factories retain at least several men in the position of sewing line supervisor. Almost all factories have retained men in the position of cutting supervisor (a post requiring technical training largely unavailable to lower-class Moroccan females). All the Fez factories I visited retained a male as workshop director, the position of greatest authority on the workshop floor. Workshop directors are always men, one informant explained, because "a man can make the girls afraid, but a woman cannot."

This hierarchy of gender authority on the factory floor reflects the hierarchy within the domestic sphere, where women carry out the daily labor and men retain the authority. The organization and use of space inside the factory makes explicit a gender hierarchy taken for granted. The few men who are present on the workshop floor (either administrators, supervisors, or mechanics) are free to move about the factory at will. The female workers, however, are not permitted to leave their positions without authorization; a pass is required even to use the restroom. Workers must remain in place until production quotas are met and often do not know when the workday will end. Officially, they are not permitted to speak while they work.[12]

Thus, the very few males present on the workshop floor are upright figures standing and moving with relative self-control across a space in which females are fixed. It appears that males control females in an otherwise all-female space. The apparent immobilization of women in fixed places inside the factory parallels the limits placed on their freedom of movement in the culture generally. It also reiterates the local gender ideology, which defines women as subservient and men as in control.

Given this presumed hierarchy of authority between male and female, the female garment workers directly confront male supervisors less often than female supervisors do. In one case, I observed a young packaging worker carrying heavy boxes down a staircase while the male workshop supervisor stood by, watching her without assisting. When the task was done, the worker complained to her colleagues that the supervisor had done nothing to help. One colleague responded, "What business does a man have working in this factory?" and the other co-workers agreed that a man has no compelling interest in factory work. The demeaned labor in the garment factory is not worthy of a man's time or energy. It is common in Moroccan households to watch females toil while males relax, and factory families invariably defend this as natural. Just as a girl would not expect her father, or even her brother, to help her carry out her household tasks, so is a garment factory worker ought not to expect assistance from males on the workshop floor. Garment factory work is degraded work, and it is the work of females.

Nonetheless, workers do occasionally resist the authority of men in the factory; they are, however, sanctioned for it. In one case at Confection, a sewing line operator asked her male supervisor for permission to use the restroom. When he refused her, she stood up to leave her seat, nonetheless. He slapped her, and she, in return, slapped him. She was fired for her deed. In explaining to me why the worker was forced to leave, one girl said, "In Morocco, a man can hit a woman, but a woman must never, ever, hit a man. Even if he hits her, she must not hit him back." These customs prevail on the shop floor.

Factory owners, almost always male, are removed from everyday interactions on the shop floor and, thus, are not engaged in the quotidian labor process. According to the dominant metaphor, factory owners are fathers, and the mass of females who toil on the workshop floor are daughters. Cast in the role of fathers, owners take their positions as guardians of female virtue seriously. They provide transportation so that workers can travel to and from the factory in the protected space of factory vans (which are frequently all-female spaces; male workers often travel separately). In this way, owners curb the workers' wanderings on the streets of Fez, like fathers protecting their chastity.[13] In many factories, owners required the workers to remain inside while awaiting the arrival of the company vans, thereby preventing their unnecessary exposure on the street. At Confection, the owner instituted a rule forbidding workers from traveling to and from the factory on public transportation and requiring all workers to commute in the company vans. The rule was put in place when the owner discovered that young men were frequenting the local streets in the early evening, hoping to socialize with workers leaving the factory.

Thus, the owners' control of workers reaches beyond service inside the factory. The owners' efforts to monitor female comportment on the streets of Fez were approved by community members and workers as well. Owners themselves used the idiom of family to characterize their relations with workers. One owner described himself as the workers' "father, brother, uncle, friend." He reported that he gave extra money to the neediest workers, and he claimed to buy many of them the rams needed for the ritual annual sacrifice. Although it was impossible to corroborate his story, owners cultivated the loyalty of workers by presenting themselves as concerned and watchful fathers.

Typically, workers verbalized feelings of fondness and respect for the factory owners. Concerning the aforementioned transportation regulations at Confection, many workers defended the restrictions placed on their movements outside the factory, claiming that such controls helped maintain their reputations and assure the community that they were honorable girls. In a similar way, I found that Moroccan girls who chafed at the restrictions their fathers and brothers placed upon them would nonetheless defend these men against criticism and readily portray their influence as a form of protection or an expression of concern. Thus, workers justified the owners' increased control just as they might justify the limits placed on them by male kin as the men's attempt to guard and shelter them. Workers, perceiving themselves as "daughters," were compelled by a sense of family obligation to comply with the limits imposed on them.

This rich and meaningful basis for relationship binds girls to the factory in a sort of moral obligation that many workers acknowledge. Work becomes a commitment to the father, and through fulfilling it, a worker demonstrates her high moral standing as a female and as a member of the community. One worker at a Fez garment factory described the working of overtime as a kind of moral obligation, a burden necessary to bear. "If the boss needs us to stay and work till seven o'clock in the evening, we must stay. We have to help him keep his commitments with people overseas." She explained how a fellow worker got fired: one evening, when they were working overtime, the girl just got up from her machine and said to the owner, "Just give me my money for my hours worked." She then left the factory without waiting to be certain the export truck was ready to go, unwilling to help the owner meet his deadlines. "One must not speak like that," the first worker said, criticizing the actions of her colleague. "It sounds hard, as if you do not trust that the boss will give you what he owes you." Although workers frequently see little of the factory owners, the relationship between worker and owner is phrased as highly personalized and based on trust.

Another worker described an incident that forced her to miss the seven-day naming ceremony for her sister's firstborn child, which she sorely regretted. In recounting how this had come to pass, she emphasized the cooperative and dutiful quality of her own response:

> On the day of the naming ceremony, I went to the director and said, "Today is the seventh-day naming ceremony for my sister's first child. I want to leave early to attend." The director pleaded with me, "Please, we cannot let you go early today. Please don't go. You understand we need you, don't you?" I answered, "Yes, no problem."

In continuing, the worker explained that she could have feigned illness in order to be released from the factory that day, but she would not do so because she was an honest and trustworthy person. Although I prompted her, the worker would express no resentment or anger at this sequence of events. According to her interpretation, she was never forbidden to leave the factory but rather was begged to stay and help. And to this appeal she responded. She missed her sister's party because she was obliged to answer a higher duty.

This worker's description of loyalty to the factory is a familiar form of discourse among workers, and it precisely parallels the way in which relations with family are described. For instance, another worker described to me her premature departure from school, which came about when her father approached her and (by her account) said, "My little daughter . . . you can see the situation we are in. Please, can you leave school and try to get work to help us?" The worker emphasized that her father had never commanded her but rather had pleaded with her. As she recounted his words, the worker imitated her father's begging voice and placed her fingertips over her mouth and kissed them, mimicking the gesture her father had used to signal a request.

Within the family, workers do not experience authority simply as a gripping hold on their liberties and personal autonomy. Instead, in submitting to authority, they perceive themselves as providing a needed response to a call for service. The assistance they provide to the owners, and to their male kin as well, is in some ways a source of personal power, for it is these females alone who can answer the males' call for assistance. They interpret their own compliance as a moral obligation, and in cooperating, they display their own good character and worthiness as daughters or wives.[14]

As the worker–owner relationship gets carried out in terms of the code associated with father–daughter, parent–child, or possibly husband–wife, what might appear as domination or exploitation of workers by owners often gets reconfigured into something more acceptable. By thinking in terms of the family model, workers can experience owners and administrators not as dominating but as begging or pleading for their cooperation and assistance. In cooperating with the owner, they assert their own moral rectitude as loyal, principled individuals who understand the importance of preserving the social tie above all else.

Conclusion

It is young unmarried women who staff the garment factories of Morocco. Fez locals, and Moroccans generally, claim that the low pay, long hours, and unpaid overtime associated with garment factory labor are accepted by these young girls because they work "only for clothes and makeup." As daughters (or sometimes wives), workers are presumed to be supported by family males; they are believed to contribute minimally, at most, to household support. As noted earlier, contrary to public opinion, research indicates that garment factory workers are an important source of household support.

Nonetheless, the local understanding of women's participation in low-paid factory labor coincides with Marxist feminist explanations of female employment on the global assembly line (Elson and Pierson 1981). From both perspectives, it is women's role in reproduction, and their position as dependent daughters, wives, and/or mothers, that explains their vulnerability to and acceptance of low-wage work.

Here, I have attempted to explore how Moroccan understandings of home, family, and gender render females willing workers on the garment factory shop floor. Workers transform the public space of the factory into the private space of the home in an attempt to assuage the contradiction inherent in their presence inside the factory, outside the home, in a role ideologically reserved for men. They behave inside this "home" as kinswoman, using the assumptions and practices associated with family to regulate their comportment inside factory walls. They approach owners much like fathers, and supervisors like parents or elder sisters. They treat each other like siblings. They accept factory hierarchies based on their understanding of, and reverence for, the patriarchal family and the gender order it endorses.

Local meanings and values thus mediate the workers' approach to the factory. Their transformation of factory into a home allows them to accommodate the owners' power with little resistance. They willingly accept the factory administration's power as they would accept the authority of their own fathers, in their role as daughters, or that of their husbands in the role of wife. In this way, the owners are able to appropriate labor at a low cost without risking resistance. To some extent, workers and their families are willing accomplices in the factory's exploitation, because this exploitation gets phrased in terms that are not just accepted but revered.

Discussion questions

1. How can the capitalist Moroccan garment factory, and its workers, be understood as a cultural process linked to other local cultural forms?
2. How is gender hierarchy manifested on the factory floors?
3. In what ways do owners capitalize on the idiom of family to ensure profit and loyalty?

Notes

1   Here, the word "workers" refers to the female garment factory workers of Fez. I refer to the workers as "girls" rather than women because the vast majority of them are unmarried and thus defined, in Morocco, as girls, or *binet*. The residents of Fez, Moroccans generally, and the workers themselves refer to garment factory workers as girls.
2   Here I contrast the idea of "labor" with that of "work" as in Comaroff and Comaroff (1987) and Wallman (1979).
3   The accuracy of these numbers is questionable. The figures are based on government census materials and reflect only the factories officially registered with the government. It is widely understood in Morocco, however, that many industrial operations are unregistered and "hidden." Factory owners prefer to keep their operations unnoticed by the government to avoid the financial and legal implications that are inherent in official recognition. Even where the factory itself is recognized by the government, many of its workers may not be. Factory owners often regard even permanent, full-time employees as seasonal workers, temporary staff, or apprentices and thus deny them the work papers that would ensure them the benefits prescribed by law. Obviously, government data cannot account for such employees. One economist in Morocco suggested that government figures be doubled to arrive at a more accurate count of industrial workers in Fez. During one year in Fez, I met few garment workers who held work registration papers. None of the 150 workers in the factory where I worked had working papers.
4   Moroccan men were slowly replaced by women in the garment industry. Throughout the 1980s, females were hired to replace departing males in existing factories, and most workers hired in new factories were female. Females were frequently hired to replace males involved in labor unrest. Fez factory owners recounted that males working in Fez garment factories before the general workers strike of 1990 were replaced by females. Morocco suffers high rates of unemployment, and male joblessness has not been alleviated by the boom in the garment industry.

5 According to my survey research, 76 percent of workers surveyed were never-married females, 16 percent were married, and 8 percent were divorced. Nearly all the workers surveyed (92 percent) were between the ages of 13 and 25. Never-married and divorced workers (84 percent of the total) almost invariably lived as daughters in their natal households (divorced young women return to their natal homes when possible). Married workers lived either in their husband's natal home or in a separate conjugal home. The majority of married workers were newly married women who had worked in the factory before marriage. Most of the married workers who continued working after having children were destitute women whose husbands were unable to work. Workers earned anywhere from 300 to 800 dirhams per month, and 89 percent of workers reported contributing some of or all their salary to the family. These salaries were considered significant in lower-class households in which men found difficulty securing steady work.

6 Although I am not in any way suggesting a privileged relationship between Islam and women's subjugation to factory labor, other researchers have investigated women's participation in wage labor with focus on the Muslim context (Hijab 1988; Ibrahim 1985; Macleod 1991; Ong 1987; White 1994).

7 Abu Lughod (1986) provides a complex exploration of the notion of honor, and an early, comprehensive collection on the notion of honor is found in Peristiany (1966). See Combs-Schilling (1989), Dwyer (1978), Mernissi (1987), and Sabbah (1984) for discussions of specifically Moroccan notions of honor as they pertain to gender and gender relations.

8 Related women – the wives and sometimes daughters of the owners – are prominent in the operation of a few Fez factories. But it is most frequently men who play the day-to-day roles of factory owner and administrator.

9 It is interesting to note that many of the European technical directors are female, while Moroccan technical directors are almost exclusively male.

10 There is a growing number of university students who dress in distinctively Islamic robes, but I do not consider them here.

11 This situation is reinforced by the fact that many workers are related to each other through biological kinship. High-level factory staff are often relatives of the factory owner (Fejjal 1987), so that there is a sense in each factory that this is a family enterprise. Personal ties are key in the recruitment of new workers: factory owners and administrators give the relatives and friends of trusted workers preference in hiring. It is common for sisters, cousins, even mother and daughter to work in the same factory, either at the same time or sequentially. At Confection, 10 percent of the workers had sisters or cousins working contemporaneously with them; others reported that their relatives had worked there previously. Nearly 20 percent of the workers surveyed had sisters who worked in other garment factories in Fez. Biological kin ties among the workers help contribute to making the idiom of family a reality.

12 Moroccans, and men in particular, characterize women as "full of empty talk." Their propensity to be engaged in meaningless speech is prohibited on the factory floor.

13 There are economic reasons for providing transport as well: for many workers, the cost of public transportation to and from the factory would represent such a large percentage of the salary as to make working purposeless. The father of one former worker laughed wryly when he explained that his daughter's month of factory work had actually cost the family money; the girl's salary did not cover her bus fare to and from the factory. (She was considered an apprentice, which explains her absurdly low salary.)

14 Abu Lughod (1986) explores the dimensions of the authority relationship between Bedouin men and women.

References

Abu Lughod, Lila. 1986. *Veiled Sentiments*. Berkeley: University of California Press.

Beneria, Lourdes. 1984. "Women and Rural Development: Morocco." *Cultural Survival Quarterly* 8(2): 30–32.

Blim, Michael L. 1992. "Introduction: The Emerging Global Factory and Anthropology." In *Anthropology and the Global Factory: Studies of the New Industrialization in the Late Twentieth Century*. Eds. M. L. Blim and F. A. Rothstein, 1–30. New York: Bergin and Garvey.

Calagione, John, and Daniel Nugent. 1992. "Workers' Expressions: Beyond Accommodation and Resistance on the Margins of Capitalism." In *Worker's Expressions: Beyond Accommodation and Resistance*. Eds. J. Calagione and D. Nugent, 1–34. Albany: SUNY Press.

Comaroff, John L., and Jean Comaroff. 1987. "The Madman and the Migrant: Work and Labor in the Historical Consciousness of a South African People." *American Ethnologist* 14(2): 191–209.

Combs-Schilling, M. Elaine. 1989. *Sacred Performances: Islam, Sexuality and Sacrifice*. New York: Columbia University Press.

Davis, Susan S. 1983. *Patience and Power: Women's Lives in a Moroccan Village*. New York: Schenkman.

Direction de la Statistique de Maroc. 1994. *Femme et Condition Feminine au Maroc*. Rabat: Les Editions Guessous.

Dwyer, Daisy H. 1978. *Images and Self-Images: Male and Female in Morocco*. New York: Columbia University Press.

Elson, Diane, and Ruth Pierson. 1981. "The Subordination of Women and the Internationalisation of Factory Production." In *Of Marriage and the Market: Women's Subordination in International Perspective*. Ed. Kate Yound, 144–166. London: CSE Books.

Fejjal, Ali. 1987. "Industrie et Industrialisation à Fes." *Revenue de Geographie Marocaine Nouvelle Serie* 11(2): 55–70.

Hijab, Nadia. 1988. *Womanpower: The Arab Debate on Women at Work*. Cambridge: Cambridge University Press.

Ibrahim, Beth. 1985. "Cairo's Factory Women." In *Women and the Family in the Middle East*. Ed. Elizabeth Fernea, pp. 293–299. Austin: University of Texas Press.

Joekes, Susan. 1982a. "The Multifibre Arrangement and Outward Processing: The Case of Morocco and Tunisia." In *EEC and the Third World*. ed. C. Stevens, pp. 102–112. London: Hodder and Soughton.

Joekes, Susan. 1982b. "Female-Led Industrialization and Women's Jobs in Third World Export Manufacturing: The Case of the Moroccan Clothing Industry." *Brighton: Institute of Development Studies Research Reports* No. 15.

Joekes, Susan. 1985. "Working for Lipstick? Male and Female Labour in the Clothing Industry in Morocco." In *Women, Work and Ideology in the Third World*. ed. H. Afshar, 183–214. London: Tavistock Publications.

Leymarie, Serge, and Jean Tripier. 1992. *Maroc: Le Prochain Dragon?* Casablanoa: Editions Eddif Maroc.

Lim, Linda Y. C. 1983. "Capitalism, Imperialism and Patriarchy: The Dilemma of Third-World Women Workers in Multinational Factories." In *Women, Men, and the International Division of Labor*. Eds. June Nash and M. P. Fernandez-Kelly, 205–223. Albany: State University of New York Press.

Macleod, Arlene E. 1991. *Accommodating Protest: Working Women, the New Veiling, and Change in Cairo*. New York: Columbia University Press.

Mernissi, Fatima. 1987. *Beyond the Veil: Male-Female Dynamics in a Modern Muslim Society*. Bloomington: Indiana University Press.

Mernissi, Fatima. 1994. *Dreams of Trespass: Tales of a Harem Girlhood*. New York: Addison-Wesley Publishing Company.

Ministère du Commerce de L'Industrie et de la Privatisation. 1994. *Situation des Industries de Transformation*. Rabat: Dèlegation de Commerce et de l'Industrie de la Wilaya de Fes.

Nash, June. 1981. "Ethnographic Aspects of the World Capitalist System." *Annual Review of Anthropology* 10: 393–424.

Nash, June, and Maria P. Fernandez-Kelly, eds. 1983. *Women, Men and the International Division of Labor*. Albany: State University of New York Press.

Ong, Aibwa. 1987. *Spirits of Resistance and Capitalist Discipline: Factory Women in Malaysia*. Albany: State University of New York Press.

Ong, Aibwa. 1991. "The Gender and Labor Politics of Postmodernity." *Annual Review of Anthropology* 20: 279–309.

Peristiany, J. G. 1966. *Honor and Shame: The Values of Mediterranean Society*. Chicago: University of Chicago Press.

Rothstein, Francis A., and Michael L. Blim, eds. 1992. *Anthropology and the Global Factory: Studies of the New Industrialization in the Late Twentieth Century*. New York: Bergen and Garvey.

Sabbah, Fatna. 1984. *Woman in the Muslim Unconscious*. New York: Oxford Pergamon Press.

Salaff, Janet. 1981. *Working Daughters of Hong Kong: Filial Piety or Power in the Family?* New York: Cambridge University Press.

Wallman, Sandra, ed. 1979. *The Social Anthropology of Work*. London: Academic Press.

Warren, Kay B., and Susan C. Bourque. 1989. "Women, Technology and Development Ideologies: Frameworks and Findings." In *Gender and Anthropology*. Ed. S. Morgen, 382–411. Washington, DC: American Anthropological Association.

White, Jenny B. 1994. *Money Makes Us Relatives: Women's Labor in Urban Turkey*. Austin: University of Texas Press.

Chapter 13

Marriage, modernity, and migration

Changing dynamics of intimacy in a Mexican transnational community

Jennifer S. Hirsch

Adapted and revised by the author from Jennifer S. Hirsch, *A Courtship After Marriage: Sexuality and Love in Mexican Transnational Families* (Berkeley: University of California Press, 2003).

As I knit and listened to the local gossip in the tiny yarn store, and as I climbed the dusty hills to visit women in the sections of town without light or running water, I heard again and again from the younger women in Degollado, "Ya no somos tan dejadas como las de antes." We are not so easily pushed around as our mothers were. For their part, the older women told me, "Oh, in our day, men used to kidnap their brides – but now the brides kidnap the grooms!" Men, too, echoed these comments about historical change in gender regimes. The study on which this chapter draws began as an exploration of how gender and sexuality differ in two locations of a transnational Mexican community: the sending community in Western Mexico and the US-based community in Atlanta, GA – and of the implications of those differences in gender and sexuality for reproductive health practices. During the course of the fieldwork, however, it became clear that while there were some notable differences in the social construction of gender between the two locations, a marked transformation in gender and sexuality had taken place in the sending community over the past generation. I decided, then, that my question should not be just how gender changes with migration but, more properly, how the migration-related changes could be understood in the context of much broader historical changes taking place in the sending community. I saw two trajectories of change in this transnational community – generational and migration-related – and I discuss here the impact of both on ideals for marriage and intimacy.

This chapter draws on the work conducted for my doctoral dissertation, which subsequently served as the basis for *A Courtship After Marriage* (Hirsch 2003) as well as a number of other publications (Cornwall 1992; Hirsch and Nathanson 1998, 2001; Hirsch 2000, 2002, 2004, 2008; Hirsch, Higgins, et al. 2002). Here, however, I pull out threads from elements of that work to speak specifically to the questions raised in this section of the book about the emergence, reformulation, and lived experience of the public/domestic dichotomy – both as an approach to the analysis of social phenomena and as a cultural construct that shapes people's understandings of their lives and their communities.

DOI: 10.4324/9781003398349-15

This dual lens on the dichotomy bears underlining; as much as the assumed opposition between public and domestic underlies social science analyses of gendered social reproduction, and thus serves as one of our own sometimes-unquestioned native theories, it is also a feature of the cultural landscape through which our informants navigate. Indeed, in Mexico, as elsewhere in Latin American and Mediterranean societies (Da Matta 1987; Cole 1991; Gutierrez 1991; Lancaster 1992; Schneider and Schneider 1996; Collier 1997; Rebhun 1999; Carrillo 2002), the distinction between *la calle* (the street) and *la casa* (literally, the home, but more generally the domestic sphere) is a foundational principle of the gendered organization of space. This distinction predates the spread of wage labor and the separation of the productive and reproductive domains (Gonzalez 1974; Da Matta 1987; Gutierrez 1991; Parker 1991) but has been layered with new meanings, as homes have increasingly become sites for class-specific forms of gendered consumption (Collier 1997; Hirsch 2003: see especially the discussion of domestic altars). In the analysis that follows, I use that distinction between *calle* and *casa* as a lens through which to consider how marital ideals and practices are changing over time and across large distances, as well as reflecting on what those changes suggest about the power of that division between domestic and public space to shape and constrain the lives of individuals in these communities. I propose here that space itself is constitutive of gender, and that rather than analyzing particular spaces (the street, the house) for their gendered properties, the overall social organization of space and access to mobility through those spaces is crucial for understanding the social organization of gender in any society.

Research methods

The research was carried out in urban Atlanta and rural and semirural Western Mexico, with women all hailing from that same region of Mexico. The sampling consisted of a three-stage process: first, find a group of Mexicans in Atlanta who were all from the same place; second, select from among them 13 women to be life history informants; and third, match these women to women in the sending community. After several months of preliminary interviewing, I selected a group of women in Atlanta who were from Degollado, a town with a population of around 15,000 in Western Mexico, and El Fuerte, a small agricultural community outside of Degollado. In Atlanta, some informants lived in Chamblee, while others lived in trailer parks on the outskirts of the city. Migration from Western Mexico to the United States has deep historical roots; many of the women had grandfathers who worked on the railroads and fathers who worked in the lettuce fields in the United States. As others have discussed (Rouse 1991; Basch et al. 1994; Goldring 1996a, 1996b), towns that are intensely tied into migrant circuits form transnational communities, characterized by social ties and identity construction across national borders, as well as by frequent back-and-forth movement of people and gifts and a lightning-fast flow of information. Distinct locations of these transnational communities present an opportunity to explore the relative force of cultural and social influences on ideology and behavior, since first-generation migrants in the United States are quite similar culturally to their kin in Mexico but live in very different social settings.

Once I selected the sending location, I chose 13 women in Atlanta – purposely seeking out diversity in age, social class, fertility, migration history, and legal status – and then matched them to their sisters or sisters-in-law in Mexico. All the women in Atlanta were first-generation migrants, and they all came north as adults. These 13 pairs of women between the ages of 15 and 50 served as the core of my sample, although over the course of the fieldwork, I spoke with many more people. With each of these 26 key informants, I conducted six life history interviews on the following: (1) childhood and family life; (2) social networks and migration stories; (3) gender and social reproduction; (4) menstruation, reproduction, and fertility management; (5) health, reproductive health, sexually transmitted diseases, and infertility; and (6) courtship and sexuality. I also formally interviewed eight of the life history informants' mothers, who ranged in age from 45 to 70, and nine of their husbands and experimented with participatory methods such as body-mapping[1] and life history drawing. Overall, I spent 15 months in this community, seven months in the Mexican field-site, and eight months doing fieldwork in Atlanta. Throughout the chapter, references to "younger women" mean the younger of the life history informants; "older women" refers to those life history informants over age 40 and to their mothers.

Generational differences in marital ideals

In Mexico and among the Mexican community in Atlanta, younger women and men talked about generational differences both in the emotional texture of their relationships and in more concrete aspects of marriage. The older women emphasized *respeto* as the key axis along which to evaluate a marriage, while younger women and some of their husbands spoke more about *confianza*, about emotional closeness and sharing one's problems with a spouse. Older women wished for hardworking husbands who would not drink too much, while younger women spoke of courtship as a time of looking both for a man who would respect them and for someone who would be their companion, their friend. Their mothers never would have considered leaving a man who was a good provider but a poor communicator; in contrast, several of the younger women entertained the idea.

In marriages of *confianza*, which I also refer to as companionate marriages,[2] men and women say that they make decisions together – in response to the question "Quien manda en su casa?" they each, separately, told me that they both do, or that neither one does. Second, women and men said that sharing *el mando*, the power, means spending time together; this contrasts strongly with the idea that men belong in the street and women in the house. Third, people talk about how the gendered division of labor is eroding, noting a trend toward "helping," *ayudando*, with the other person's job. Behind closed doors, some men sweep and cook meals, and most women "help" their husbands support the family. The significant change is not in the gendered division of labor but in its meaning; lifting a broom or heating one's own dinner – once a source of shame for a man, or a comment on his wife's inadequacy – has become of source of pride, even if something men actually do only rarely. Together, these four qualities (an emphasis on *confianza*, intimacy, in addition to respect, more room for explicit disagreement, a growing heterosociality, and increased "helping") combine to form a new marital ideal.

Within these marriages of *confianza*, marital sexuality has been transformed from a way of producing social ties primarily through reproduction to a way to produce conjugal ties directly – in other words, sex makes a couple feel like a family, not just because it leads to babies, but also because it creates feelings of closeness which, in and of themselves, strengthen the marriage. For the older women, the marital bargain entailed mutual respect and an exchange of a woman's best efforts at housekeeping for her husband's economic support. For the younger women, in contrast, the exchange included the somewhat less-tangible sharing of pleasure and sentiment. The sexual relationship, they told me, creates and reinforces the *confianza*, the intimacy, on which the marriage is based. The way these younger women thought about sex is illustrated by the following conversation which I had with Victoria, a woman then in her mid-30s, in the spring of 1996.

J: "And what do you see as the role of the sexual relationship in marriage?"

V: "Yes, it's very important, it's half [of marriage]."

J: "And what's the other half?"

V: "The other half is getting along well, but sex is one of the most important things. For me personally, I think that the intimacy I have with [my husband] was worth a lot, to carry us through the big problems we have had."

J: "To strengthen the relationship?"

V: "Yes, it was the thing that really helped the most. Perhaps it wasn't so much that we cared for each other, that we loved each other, not even the kids, as it was the sexual relationship that we have."

J: "And why do you think it was so important? How did that work?"

V: "I don't know, because we enjoy it. I see that both of us enjoy it a lot. I sometimes ask myself, Does everyone enjoy it so much? I ask myself that because I really do enjoy it."

Younger women may not necessarily enjoy sex more than women of their mother's generation did. The difference, rather, is in the importance they give to the shared sexual experience between husband and wife. For their mothers, the marital bond was reinforced by the fulfillment of productive and reproductive activities. If a woman also happened to have the luck to marry a man who cared that she enjoyed sex – or who would allow her to refuse sex, rather than telling her, "Eres mi mujer y por eso me case contigo" (you are my wife and that's why I married you) – then that was icing on the cake, but if he forced her or did not care about her pleasure, that was hardly reason to leave an otherwise perfectly good mate. The younger women, in contrast, felt that a mutually satisfying sexual relationship forms the foundation for a good and happy marriage.

This intimacy-oriented thinking about sexuality was apparent both in the United States and the Mexico field sites. When I asked a woman in her early 30s in one of the Mexican field sites about the role of sex in marriage, she responded:

Well, it's what keeps us going, no? If you feel good in terms of intimacy, you will feel good in [the rest of] your life . . . because when you come, I think that when you end up happy, you get up in the morning happy, you have energy for things – I think it's what helps keep us going.

She describes sex as creating a direct emotional and physical connection between the couple.

Women's word choices reflect the shift to a paradigm of mutual desire. Many of the older women – including those who seem to have shared a pleasurable intimacy with their partners – employ the word *usar*, to use, to describe vaginal intercourse (e.g., they might say "Cuando el me usa" [when he "uses" me] to describe sexual relations). *Usar* is an instrumental word that describes the utilization of an inanimate object – one might use it to talk about an iron, or a plow. Younger women choose quite different words to describe intercourse: they talk about making love (*hacer el amor*) or being together (*estar juntos*) or having relations (*tener relaciones*). There were also generational differences in terms of other aspects of the sexual relationship, such as initiating or refusing sexual intercourse and engaging in sexual activities other than intercourse (such as oral sex).

This discourse, which uses gender and sexuality as measures of modernity, has a clear spatial component. Linda Ann Rebhun describes how, in Northeast Brazil, "each city generates its own figurative temporal wheel, forming the proudly modern center of a circle that grows more old-fashioned the further out you travel from it" (Rebhun 1999: 2). This modernity was evaluated at least in part in relation to gendered notions of progress (Wardlow and Hirsch 2006), with spaces becoming inherently more traditional the more distant they were from those urban centers. The young men I knew in Degollado went to great pains, in general, to represent themselves as engaged in marriages organized around a goal of emotional intimacy (although this frequently bore little relation to the actual gendered balance of power) (Hirsch 2007); these gendered performances were driven at least in part by their desire to show themselves as being just as modern as men whose labor migration provided better access to the material trappings of successful modern masculinity. The rise of the companionate ideal has as much to do with changes in Mexican society as it does with media- and migration-disseminated influences of Mexico's northern neighbor,[3] but the United States is perceived as inherently more egalitarian and less sexually constrained than Mexico. (As discussed later, the widely shared belief that "en el norte la mujer manda," that in the United States, women are the ones who give orders, is significantly complicated by an examination of the heterogeneity of migrant women's [and men's] lives.)

One of my favorite examples of this imagined sexual/moral geography was the time I was told by an informant – someone with whom I spent a great deal of time and who I generally experienced as liking and respecting me – that "in the US, women go through men like Kleenex." I found the comment more funny than offensive but could read into the contrast; she was drawing an important distinction between my world and her own, in which "going through men like Kleenex" would be a practice that would significantly diminish one's social value. Moreover, given that it was said in a conversational and not apparently aggressive context, I could only assume that she did not intend to offend, and therefore assumed that I would agree that women in my country behaved in a way that, were they to live in Mexico, would render them seriously damaged goods on the marriage market. The radiating spokes of the wheel indicate a continuum between an imagined tradition-bound sexual order and a liberated-by-modernity landscape of boundless sexual opportunity. In addition to potentially becoming more modern as one moves away from town and towards urban center, there are increasing opportunities, and declining social risks, associated with a variety of forms of sexual behavior that do not conform to norms of respectability. This is as true for men as it is for women, although it manifests in different ways. For young women crossing the border north, as they increasingly do, one's honor is best protected by arriving to live in a household that includes (or, ideally, traveling with) an older man who is a relative, someone whose social presence can serve as a sort of extension of the domestic moral umbrella under which an unmarried women ought to otherwise live. For men, the gendered sexual geography presents both reputational risks (it is common to hear of married or partnered men caught on videotape by friends and relatives smooching with a girlfriend) and opportunities for new partnerships and practices, far from the moral center of gravity of home (Bronfman and Minello 1995).

Three examples illustrate the importance of seeing the spatial component, including but not limited to the distinction between the public and private, of this gender order. First, regardless of the extent to which couples practice joint decision-making about priorities large and small in the privacy of their own homes, women are scrupulously careful not to contradict their husbands in public; the public challenge of a man's authority by his wife carries a very different meaning than it would at home. Second, gendered differences in men's and women's physical mobility – their *access* to space – also mark inequalities in power. Almost without exception, men are less likely to provide explanation or advance notice for trips beyond the town's limits, and the notion of a man seeking "permission" for a journey is laughable for the way in which it so clearly indicates his emasculation. (There are other, nonspatial manifestations of inequalities in access to power, most notably in terms of even younger men's dominion over their wives' bodies [exemplified in some cases by violence, and in other cases in a gentler but no less-controlling way by the shared assumption that women's husbands have the right to decide how short their skirts can be, or how revealingly tight their clothes can be].)

Third, a range of public spaces serves as a stage for the enactment of consumption-oriented modern intimacy and gendered embodiment. The diversity of these spaces helps us see the ways in which gender, social class, and *mestizo* ethnicity are mutually constitutive, but they are useful beyond that for how they show gender as social rather than as a characteristic of individuals. The activities in these spaces, and the sentiments and subjectivities that result from participating in these activities, are not inherent to the actors but rather a phenomenon that occurs at the intersection of the actors' access to resources that allow them to be in those spaces, the actors' socially structured desires to go to those spaces, and the broader social and economic factors that make those spaces exist at all.

Access to cars presents one example of how social class and gender intersect in the organization of space. The number of cars has increased precipitously in Degollado in the 15 years since I first began conducting fieldwork there. Older men and women still remembered a time when children could play unsupervised in the main street, but I had to rent a garage space for the car I brought with me in 2004, and the two main streets have been restricted to one-way traffic in response to the growing number of head-on accidents on those two busy streets. These cars, however, are, by and large, the property either of men and women with well-paying professional jobs or of the relatives of men and women working in the United States. Possession of a car enables access to Guadalajara's malls and movie theaters or to excursions to Michoacan to see the monarch butterfly nests and to experience what seems to them the exotic indigenous culture of Zinacantan and the other crafts villages surrounding Lake Patzcuaro. Closer by, the exclusive sport and tennis club in La Piedad or the newly opened "Fun Factory" (featuring a zip line, a climbing wall, a parachute drop, and a giant bouncy castle) provides other options through which families can demonstrate both their commitment to a companionate marriage heavy on the family togetherness and their success as middle-class consumers.

Those who travel on foot or by bus have different options, thrilling in their own way. On Sundays, the central plaza by the town's main church fills with couples and families attending one of the many Masses, and a main focus of being in the plaza is demonstrating consumption – particularly showing off new clothes (*estrenando*)[4] and buying ice cream, churros (fried dough filled with caramel sauce), bacon-covered hot dogs, and trinkets (balloons, plastic toys, whirligigs, giant bubble wands) for one's children. At least one water park is located immediately by the side of the main highway outside of town, and thus deliberately accessible to those reliant on public transportation, and the Sunday market is held within the town itself. Both the plaza and the water parks provide a context for gendered display of bodies as well as a space to enact companionate intimacy and a commitment to spending time as a family, which is so key to this new family ideal.

These spaces, however, are not just settings in which people can act out new gendered ways of being – they actually *shape* those subjectivities. The water parks, for example, demand that young women transgress the ideals their own mothers would have held about modesty. Two generations ago, marriageable-aged women in this region hid their bodies under rebozos to keep them from being seen and visually consumed by men (as one informant, whose own children are now of courting age, told me, her mother insisted that "santo que no es visto, no es adorado" [a saint who is not seen cannot be worshipped]). The water parks feature picnic areas and water attractions (slides, wading pools, waterfalls), organized with a layout that necessitates traversing fairly large spaces between picnic areas and those attractions. The wearing of street clothes, or even shorts and T-shirts, into the water is expressly forbidden, and thus participation requires a good deal of physical display. Men seemed to luxuriate in the opportunity to walk around in bathing trunks; women frequently chose to wear shorts and T-shirts over their bathing suits, although the clinging, sopping-wet clothes were more a gesture of acknowledgment of the ideal of modesty rather than a demonstration of modesty itself. The unmarried young men and women and nuclear and extended families for whom a Sunday at a water park is such a treat use this particular terrain to experience a modern gendered subjectivity.

I found even my own practices of bodily display transformed over the course of my fieldwork. The Sunday-morning market, moved recently to the edge of town so as not to disrupt traffic on the main street, provides a space for families to stroll and shop and for young people to gather and flirt. Rather than the beautiful folk art I had so enjoyed buying during my tourist travels in Mexico, this market features almost entirely inexpensive, frequently Chinese-produced consumer goods: apparel, housewares, linens, kitchen items, CDs, and plastic toys. And so I experienced my early visits to this market as somewhat disappointing. As Wardlow describes regarding her own experience perusing the shelves of the local store in rural Papua New Guinea, after several months, my own consumer desires had recalibrated to reflect local tastes, and I found myself lusting after (and actually excitedly receiving as a birthday gift) a purple- and pink-flowered angora cardigan with enormous purple plastic buttons. In response to critical remarks from women with whom I spent time in Degollado about my pants and skirts being too baggy, I acquired several other treasures from the *tianguis*, among them formfitting, low-rise, boot-cut black stretch pants; a scoop-necked pink shirt so tight I had to buy a new bra to wear under it; red plastic high heels; and a bias-cut printed acrylic skirt which was far tighter than anything I would wear in a professional or social context in the United States. I remember in particular how my friend Stela and I delightedly drew upon these items to plan an outfit I could wear to pick my husband up at the airport for one of his visits. I left all these clothes behind in Mexico as gifts for various friends; as I packed, my mind moving already back to the aesthetic of my "real" life as a middle-class feminist university professor, I knew that those clothes, which had elicited such complementary remarks about the success of my own gendered physicality and my improving taste in fashion, would never be worn at home.

Fourth, as I describe at great length elsewhere (Hirsch 2006; Hirsch, Wardlow, et al. 2009), this same intersection of gender, sexuality, space, and social class is manifest in the spaces that facilitate men's access to extramarital relations. Rather than being spaces for the performance of a sexuality harnessed to the strengthening of nuclear family bonds, these homosocial spaces – cantinas, strip clubs, pole dancing bars, and local red-light districts – are crucibles for the forging of men's emotional ties with one another. Just as those who go to the Fun Factory would not be caught dead shopping in the *tianguis*, men who frequent the luxury pole dancing venues in Guadalajara would not set foot in the dingy bars that populate the red-light district in the neighboring town, and the consumption of expensive tequila and fair-skinned women in the former setting, and cheap booze and dark-skinned women in the latter, provides opportunities for men to experience the intertwining of gender, sexuality, and social class in a most intimate way. These spaces are hardly the only contexts in which non-marital sex occurs, but their existence is a key context for the public production of classed and raced masculinities in Mexico.

Both within and outside the home, the spatial configuration of everyday life serves not just as a window into how women and men are constrained by gender but also as a means to mark how those constraints are changing. During my initial fieldwork in the region, from 1995 to 1996, I observed how increasing neolocality, combined with growing access to migration-related wealth, was creating opportunities for newlywed couples to begin their married lives in houses that featured separate bedrooms for parents and children, electricity, and indoor plumbing and that notably did not feature the watchful ears of a mother-in-law – circumstances propitious to the development of that companionate intimacy which was becoming such a focal indicator of marital success. Outside, however, the gendered organization of space seemed marked as much by continuity as by change. Adolescent girls with families wealthy enough to support postsecondary education were mostly limited to studying technical careers in nearby La Piedad because it was unthinkable for a nice girl to leave her father's home and reside somewhere else before marriage. I was told in no uncertain terms never to get in a car alone with a man, even on an innocent errand, because doing so would mark me as sexually available. Women rarely left town alone, instead frequently taking with them a child as a sort of moral shelter – proof that they were not going to meet a lover. And of course, women themselves rarely drove. In fact, the only woman I knew who drove was the other American woman in town, a working-class Polish American woman who had married a man from Degollado and whose gender nonconformity was marked by the way she was known: as "la Jenys, la que maneja y fuma" (that Jenny, the one who smokes and drinks).

Ten years after that, I found changes in women's physical mobility just this side of shocking. In addition to the well-documented feminization of migration (Cerrutti and Massey 2001), women were much more mobile locally: many women, married and not, knew how to drive, and some had cars of their own; adolescent girls in cropped tops were frequently seen zooming up and down the main street on loud four-wheeled all-terrain vehicles; young women began spending newfound leisure time at the indoor soccer rink, whose popular and very aggressive local team drew large crowds for important matches; and at least on one occasion, they gathered in large crowds at one of the local *terrazas* (relatively posh local cafés on the main square, serving alcoholic and nonalcoholic beverages) to drink and cheer for the Guadalajara *Chivas*, playing the rival Mexico City *Americas*, when the game was broadcast on the café's flat-screen television. It was only a decade earlier that, during one of my husband's visits to Degollado, I'd told him there was nowhere we could go for tacos and beers because nice women did not drink in public.

While it was not unknown for the women who had been the younger generation in my first research, those born in the 1960s and 1970s, to have had premarital relations, the secret was jealously guarded, and a girl ran a great risk in doing so because her marital prospects were irreparably damaged if, despite promises to the contrary, that first sexual partner refused to marry her. Printed T-shirts on sale in the Sunday marketplace, such as those that read "My boyfriend is out of town"; "Wanted: cute boys for personal hands-on services. Must be tall and good-looking. Respond only if you are HOT!"; "Powerful brave sexy cool"; "Sweet lover" underlined the intersection between women's increased mobility and a newly assertive female sexuality. What was different was not so much the implied behaviors but the public suggestion of them. Perhaps the most striking contrast to the generally recognized expectation in the mid-1990s that nice girls would be at home behind locked doors every night by ten was the moment I heard from my research assistant, Brenda, about the pole dancing contest that took place in the makeshift disco during the town's pork producer's festival; in that temporary disco, which also included blasts of foam spray which wet the whole assembled crowd and rendered already skintight clothing even more clingy and revealing, a sheet was hung, with a backlit pole behind it, and local girls competed to see who could do the sexiest faux striptease. The pace of change seemed ever-accelerating; during a brief return visit in 2006, I saw lesbian and gay couples publicly dancing together at a new, and even more ostentatiously decorated, disco that had been built in a former agricultural building on the edge of town.

The gendered spatial effects of migration

Women's own cross-border mobility presents an additional element of these geographies of gender and sexuality. Although women in both the Mexican and Atlanta communities shared the emerging companionate ideal, the privacy, legal protections against domestic violence, and economic opportunities enabled some of the women I knew in Atlanta in the 1990s to push their husbands further toward the companionate model. While women in communities on both sides of the border may share these companionate dreams, Mexicans say that *en el norte, la mujer manda* (in the United States, women give the orders); what they mean when they say this is that women have the social and economic resources to live without a husband, and thus the power to press for a marriage that is not just companionate but a bit more egalitarian.

Before comparing spatial aspects of gender and sexuality in the Atlanta-based migrant communities to those in the Mexican sending community, several caveats are in order. First, these gendered terrains should be thought of as constraining or enabling action among men as well as women; indeed, as Rouse suggested two decades ago (1991), Mexican migrant men's relative emasculation is most clearly seen – and in some ways produced – by the social organization of space. Second, rather than begin with the underlying assumption that women are moving to communities in which their lives will be less constrained by gender, I started with the notion that the comparison should be made not with sending locations frozen in time but rather with communities (as described earlier) situated in complex and fluid historical processes; moreover, just as the shift to a more companionate ideal is both enabling and constraining, so, too, will the gendered outcomes of migration include both new opportunities and new limitations. Moreover, there is not one story to tell about gender and migration but rather many; I found that rudimentary knowledge of English, having one's own kin nearby (as opposed to a husband's family), documentation of legal residence that includes the right to work, work experience, and possession of a car were just some of the factors that led to a great deal of heterogeneity in the experiences of migrant women (Hirsch 2003: see especially Chapter 6). Rather than reprise the study's broader findings about gender and migration, I focus here particularly on the ways in which the move from a Mexican provincial town to a semirural city in the American south reconfigures the division between public and private, and so the gendered social organization of marriage.

A central feature of small-town life is constant vigilance of one's movements, dress, and social interactions. It was not so much that appearances were more important than actual practice; rather, maintaining one's reputation through conforming to gendered expectations for appearance was itself a crucial element of practice. I found this true for my own behavior as well, as I was instructed by an informant not to do good things that might look like bad things (*no hagas cosas buenas que parecen cosas malas*) after she had observed me responding to a man's (what seemed to me) innocuous greeting of "buenos días." Politeness dictated that women who make eye contact when passing each other on the street exchange greetings, but apparently, doing so with an unknown man was, in and of itself, an act of moral turpitude. The plaza was a shared stage for the demonstration of respectable sexuality, and front doors with glass windows (to enable parental observation) served as critical locations for the negotiation of intimacy among dating couples.

The gendered organization of space in Atlanta

Life was laid out quite differently in the outlying suburbs of Atlanta where the Mexican women I knew settled. Domestic spaces were still locations for the development and preservation of companionate intimacy and modern practices of kinship, but they also became safe spaces for the performance of a newly experienced ethnic identity as Mexicans. I rarely entered a home that did not display some representation of the eagle and the snake – in addition, of course, to the icon of the Virgin of Guadalupe found in so many Mexican homes (and cars) on both sides of the border. Calendars produced by businesses back home were proudly displayed, as was other evidence of affiliation with one's hometown community.

At the same time, however, Mexican men, women, and children experienced the inviolability of the distinction between public and private as weaker than in Mexico. A recurrent element of the discourse about women being more powerful in the United States than in Mexico was mention of the protections against domestic violence offered by being able to call 911. (People also talked about this in relation to state intervention against child abuse, noting that American [and Mexican immigrant] children were less respectful because they knew that they could call the police if a parent became violent.) Regardless of the extent to which women (or children) did actually call for police protection – and regardless of the extent to which that police protection would actually have been provided – the existence of this shared notion about the state's right to intervene in domestic power dynamics presented a marked contrast with experiences of the domestic sphere on the other side of the border.[5]

In addition to some changes in what separates public and domestic spaces, the public spaces themselves are radically different than those in Mexico – sites not for the preservation of a moral community but rather for the emergence of the consuming individual.

Trailer parks and apartment complexes did, to be sure, feature shared spaces, but the size of the city meant that there were many more places people could go, and a much lower probability of observation by a fellow townsperson. As one married woman told me, remarking upon the difference, it would be easy to have an affair in Atlanta, and no one would ever know. The Catholic church no longer looms, physically or morally, with quite the same power that it did in Mexico (Hirsch 2008); Atlanta offers many other options for entertainment on Sundays, and neither priests nor other congregants have as much information about women's sexual or reproductive practices as they do in Mexico. In Degollado, the plaza is a free space, open to all, whereas access to Atlanta's recreational spaces such as the mall or the zoo depended both on disposable income and on legal status – some were much more able than others to afford both the risk and the expense of a day of leisure organized around commercialized forms of consumption. In addition to the greater options for commercially oriented leisure spaces found in Atlanta by comparison with Mexico, the social encounters that took place in workspaces – spaces that were more private than the street or the mall yet more public than the domestic sphere – presented new possibilities for both men and women, both in terms of potential partners and through exposure to new ideas about gender and sexuality.

Public spaces in Atlanta were also locations for the expression of the economic and legal inequality that is such a core element of the Mexican immigrant experience. In Atlanta's public spaces, the specter of the state which haunts the domestic context went considerably beyond just being a specter; indeed, early in the project, my ability to get to engage with the community was severely hampered by the understandable distrust engendered by the "*redadas*," immigrant raids in public spaces and workplaces, which were taking place at that time. At one point, the police set up a barricade across Buford Highway, the main thoroughfare in a neighborhood with one of the densest concentrations of Mexican immigrants, to stop drivers and demand papers. In part in response to 9/11 but also at least potentially as a reaction to the growing Mexican immigrant communities, regulations slowly came into place across the Southeastern states that made it impossible for immigrants to secure a driver's license and insure a vehicle. Particularly in cities such as Atlanta, which lack of adequate public transportation infrastructure, being unable to secure a license or insurance severely hampered mobility and served as a constant reminder of one's unequal status before the law. The acrid debates about the existence of spaces for day laborers to congregate was a particularly gendered example of these spatial manifestations of inequality; the spatial organization of immigrant women's work, although not exclusively in the domestic sphere, made them much less visible as targets for the xenophobia expressed by those who so vociferously opposed the presence of these migrants in their communities.

Conclusion

All these transformations in the public and domestic space, whether with time or migration, provide concrete examples of what it means to talk about gender as changing; thinking about the political and economic forces that shape those spaces also provides some insight into the factors that produce those changes. In rural Mexico, although young women are increasingly challenging the gendered nature of public space, men's freedom in that space – whether to play dominos by the main square, to urinate in public, to drink themselves senseless, or simply to lounge in the sun with their *compadres* – goes unquestioned. In Atlanta, the distinction between private and domestic space continues to exist, but both are reconfigured. Domestic space becomes a safe haven in a context of legal insecurity, a space where both men and women feel somewhat safer from the ever-present fear of Immigration and Customs Enforcement (ICE, the reconfigured, post-9/11 version of the INS) – and yet the possibility of government intrusion, so frequently remarked upon by the idea that women or children could call 911 and demonstrated by ICE raids that separate undocumented parents from their citizen children, is ever present, rendering the security of the domestic space an uncertain proposition at best. No matter how thickly adorned a home or apartment may be with Mexican flags, printed calendars from grocery stores and building supply companies back in Degollado, and icons of the Virgin of San Juan de Los Lagos and Guadalupe, the legal insecurity faced by undocumented men and women means that many never rest easy. For men, the idea that home presents a shelter from the dangers of the streets represents a powerful demonstration of how migration can curtail men's access to privileges they enjoyed in Mexico. For women, in contrast, the anonymity offered by urban environments – true not just for those who migrate to cities in the United States but also for women who travel to large cities in Mexico – presents opportunities to experiment with practices – sexual, social, and sartorial – which would have marked them quickly as fallen women back home. For us as scholars, the fluidity of this gendered patterning of space is a powerful reminder that gender is a property of societies, a phenomenon not entirely captured by a focus on ideologies of masculinity or femininity, as well as a window into tracing out the social and economic forces that are constantly recreating the gendered terrain through which people navigate.

Discussion questions

1. What are some of the generational differences in terms of spouse preference among the women in the community discussed in this chapter?
2. How did the different generations use language differently to express their relationships with their husbands?
3. What role does space play in the husband–wife relationship in terms of power inequalities and gendered performance?
4. How did women's spatial mobility change over time?

Notes

1 *Body-mapping* is a participatory research technique (Cornwall 1992) in which women are provided with an outline of the body and asked to draw comments on it, discussing the social meanings and embodied experience of various body parts.
2 There is a vast literature on companionate marriage, exploring it in relation to the emergence of "affective individualism": Bott 1957 (1971); Thadani 1978; Stone 1979; Skolnik 1991; Gillis et al. 1992. Scholars have also looked at how it varies globally (Inhorn 1996; Rebhun 1999; Hirschman and Minh 2002; Hirsch 2003; Hirsch and Wardlow 2006; Padilla et al. 2007). Briefly, I use the term here to denote relations in which mutual emotional satisfaction is the most salient indicator of the quality of a marriage.
3 The vast social, economic, and demographic changes that have taken place in the rural community in which the fieldwork was carried out, which include increased access to formal education, changes in the physical structures of housing, rising neolocal residence, declining fertility, later age at first marriage, and increased access to electricity and media, are described in great detail in

Courtship. Also worth noting conceptually here, and illustrated ethnographically in *Courtship*, is the intertwining of structure and agency exemplified by the dissemination and embrace of the companionate ideal.

4 *Estrenar*, which literally means to show off something new, was a word I learned early in my fieldwork with this community. Showing off new clothes was a much-prized activity, as indicated (at least to me) that there was a particular word for it, the equivalent of which I have not been able to find in English.

5 This contrast is likely to have waned in the years that have elapsed since that initial fieldwork took place. During the 2004 fieldwork, I noticed a widely disseminated media campaign against domestic violence, and I also heard of instances in which women in Degollado did receive police protection in response to reports of violence.

References

Basch, Linda, Nina Glick Schiller, and Cristina Szanton Blanc, eds. 1994. *Nations Unbound: Transnational Projects, Postcolonial Predicaments, and Deterritorialized Nation-States*. Langhorne: Gordon and Breach.

Bott, Elizabeth. 1957 [1971]. *Family and Social Network: Roles, Norms and External Relationships in Ordinary Urban Families*. New York: The Free Press.

Bronfman, Mario, and Nelson Minello. 1995. "Hábitos sexuales de los migrantes temporales Mexicanos a Los Estados Unidos de América: Prácticas de riesgo para la infección por VIH." In *Sida en Mexico: Migración, Adolescencia, y Genero*, ed. Mario Bronfman, 1–89. Mexico City, Mexico: Información Profesional Especializada.

Carrillo, Héctor. 2002. *The Night Is Young: Sexuality in Mexico in the Time of AIDS*. Chicago: University of Chicago Press.

Cerrutti, Marcela, and Douglas S. Massey. 2001. "On the Auspices of Female Migration from Mexico to the United States." *Demography* 38(2): 187–200.

Cole, Sally C. 1991. *Women of the Praia: Work and Lives in a Portuguese Coastal Community*. Princeton, NJ: Princeton University Press.

Collier, Jane Fishburne. 1997. *From Duty to Desire: Remaking Families in a Spanish Village*. Princeton, NJ: Princeton University Press.

Cornwall, Andrea. 1992. "Body Mapping in Health RRA/PRA." *PRA Notes* 16: 69–76. London: International Institute for Environment and Development.

Da Matta, Roberto. 1987. *A Casa e a Rua*. Rio de Janeiro: Editora Guanabara.

Gillis, John R., Louise A. Tilly, and David Levine. 1992. *The European Experience of Declining Fertility, 1850–1970: The Quiet Revolution*. Cambridge, MA: Blackwell.

Goldring, Luin. 1996a. "Blurring Borders: Constructing Transnational Community in the Process of U.S.- Mexico Migration." *Research in Community Sociology* 6: 69–104.

Goldring, Luin. 1996b. "Gendered Memory: Constructions of Rurality among Mexican Transnational Migrants." In *Creating the Countryside: The Politics of Rural and Environmental Discourse*. Eds. M. DuPuis and P. Vandergeest, 303–329. Philadelphia, PA: Temple University Press.

Gonzalez, Luis. 1974. *San Jose de Gracia: A Village in Transition*. Austin: University of Texas Press.

Gutierrez, Ramón A. 1991. *When Jesus Came, the Corn Mothers Went Away; Marriage, Sexuality and Power in New Mexico, 1500–1846*. Stanford: Stanford University Press.

Hirsch, Jennifer S. 2000. "En El Norte La Mujer Manda: Gender, Generation and Geography in a Mexican Translational Community." In *Immigration Research for a New Century*. Eds. N. Foner, R. Rumbaut and S. Gold, 369–389. New York: Russell Sage.

Hirsch, Jennifer S. 2002. "'Que, pues, con el pinche NAFTA?': Gender, Power, and Migration between Western Mexico and Atlanta." *Urban Anthropology* 31(3–4): 351–387.

Hirsch, Jennifer S. 2003. *A Courtship after Marriage: Sexuality and Love in Mexican Transnational Families*. Berkeley: University of California Press.

Hirsch, Jennifer S. 2004. "'Un Noviazgo Despues de Ser Casados': Companionate Marriage, Sexual Intimacy and Fertility Regulation in Modern Mexico." In *Qualitative Demography: Categories and Contexts in Population Studies*. Eds. S. Szreter, A. Dharmalingam and H. Sholkamy, 249–275. Oxford, Oxford University Press.

Hirsch, Jennifer S. 2006. "Que gusto Estar de Vuelta en Mi Tierra: Gender, Sexuality and Authenticity in las fiestas de la virgin de Guadelupe." In *Panel on Latin American Migration, Gender and Sexuality, Latin American Studies Association*. San Juan: Puerto Rico. Unpublished paper.

Hirsch, Jennifer S. 2007. "'Love Makes a Family': Globalization, Companionate Marriage, and the Modernization of Gender Inequality." In *Love and Globalization: Transformations of Intimacy in the Contemporary World*. eds. M. Padilla, J. S. Hirsch, R. Sember, M. Munoz-Laboy and R. Parker, 93–106. Nashville: Vanderbilt University Press.

Hirsch, Jennifer S. 2008. "Catholics Using Contraceptives: Religion, Family Planning, and Interpretive Agency in Rural Mexico." *Studies in Family Planning* 39(2): 93–104.

Hirsch, Jennifer S., Jennifer Higgins, Margaret E. Bentley, and Constance A. Nathanson. 2002. "The Social Constructions of Sexuality: Marital Infidelity and Sexually Transmitted Disease – HIV Risk in a Mexican Migrant Community." *American Journal of Public Health* 92(8): 1227–1237.

Hirsch, Jennifer S., and Constance A. Nathanson. 1998. "Demografia Informal: cómo utilizar las redes sociales para construir una muestra etnografica sistematica de mujeres mexicanas en smbos lados de la frontera." *Estudios Demograficso y de Desarolio Urbano, Mexico, D.F; El Colegio de Mexico* 12(1 & 2): 177–199.

Hirsch, Jennifer S., and Constance A. Nathanson. 2001. "Some Traditional Methods Are More Modern Than Others: Rhythm, Withdrawal, and the Changing Meanings of Gender and Sexual Intimacy in the Mexican Companionate Marriage." *Culture, Health & Sexuality* 3(4): 413–428.

Hirsch, Jennifer S., and Holly Wardlow, eds. 2006. *Modern Loves: The Anthropology of Romantic Love and Companionate Marriage*. Ann Arbor: University of Michigan Press.

Hirsch, Jennifer S., Holly Wardlow, Daniel Jordan Smith, Harriet M. Phinney, Shanti Parikh, and Constance A. Nathanson. 2009. *The Secret: Love, Marriage and HIV*. Nashville: Vanderbilt University Press.

Hirschman, Charles, and Nguyen Huu Minh. 2002. "Tradition and Change in Vietnamese Family Structure in the Red River Delta." *Journal of Marriage and Family* 64: 1063–1079.

Inhorn, Marcia C. 1996. *Infertility and Patriarchy: The Cultural Politics of Gender and Family Life in Egypt*. Philadelphia, PA: University of Pennsylvania Press.

Lancaster, Roger N. 1992. *Life Is Hard: Machismo, Danger, and the Intimacy of Power in Nicaragua*. Berkeley: University of California Press.

Padilla, Mark, Jennifer S. Hirsch, Miguel Munoz-Laboy, Robert E. Sember, and Richard G. Parker, eds. 2007. *Love and Globalization: Transformations of Intimacy in the Contemporary World*. Nashville: Vanderbilt University Press.

Parker, Richard G. 1991. *Bodies, Pleasures, and Passions: Sexual Culture in Contemporary Brazil*. Boston: Beacon.

Rebhun, Linda-Anne. 1999. *The Heart Is Unknown Country: Love in the Changing Economy of Northeast Brazil*. Stanford, CA: Stanford University Press.

Rouse, Roger. 1991. "Mexican Migration and the Social Space of Postmodernism." *Diaspora* 1(1): 8–23.

Schneider, Jane C., and Peter T. Schneider. 1996. *Festival of the Poor: Fertility Decline and the Ideology of Class in Sicily, 1860–1980*. Tucson: University of Arizona Press.

Skolnik, Arlene. 1991. *Embattled Paradise: The American Family in an Age of Uncertainty*. New York: Basic Books.

Stone, Lawrence. 1979. *The Family, Sex and Marriage in England 1500–1800*. New York: Harper and Row.

Thadani, Veena N. 1978. "'The Logic of Sentiment': The Family and Social Change." *Population and Development Review* 4(3): 457–499.

Wardlow, Holly, and Jennifer S. Hirsch. 2006. "Introduction." In *Modern Loves: The Anthropology of Romantic Courtship and Companionate Marriage*. Eds. J. S. Hirsch and H. Wardlow, 1–31. Ann Arbor: University of Michigan Press.

Chapter 14

Beyond romantic partnerships

Sese, gender egalitarianism, and kinship diversity in Mosuo society

Chun-Yi Sum, Tami Blumenfield, and Siobhán M. Cully

Original material prepared for this edition.

Mosuo 摩梭 (Na 纳) people in mountainous Southwest China are well-known to anthropologists and gender scholars.[1] They adhere to reproductive norms, which, while variable, center on a practice called *sese* (literally, "walking back and forth") that underscores flexibility in reproductive unions. The *sese* romantic partnerships normatively do not involve cohabitation. Rather, both men and women remain residents of their natal households. Men visit their romantic partner at night, in what outsiders have dubbed "visiting relationship" or "walking marriage" (Ch. *zouhun* 走婚). In the morning, they return or "walk back" to their natal households, to which they contribute the majority of their labor and economic resources. A man's primary authority is not over his own but his sisters' children.

Classically, these relationships are supposed to be relatively open, non-contractual, and non-committal. But men and women involved in a *sese* relationship are generally expected to be monogamous even as they do not live together. Children produced as a result of these unions are part of their mother's lineage (i.e., descent is traced matrilineally) and cared for by senior members of the matrilineal household, including their mother, maternal uncles, aunts, and relatives. A household's name and property are passed along the matrilineal bloodline via women's children. Individuals' primary allegiances are not to their reproductive partners but to their natal, matrilineal households – that is, the people who raised them.

Much has been made of how unusual this "non-marital" reproductive union is, with some scholars claiming that Mosuo are unique among human societies for lacking marriage, and others emphasizing the unusual role of men as authority figures for their sisters' children. More holistic accounts of Mosuo society recognize both the significance of their unique norms and institutions, but also the commonalities that link Mosuo to the rest of humanity. Here, we introduce Mosuo society as one that champions matrilineal cohesion and continuity. Its emphasis on female autonomy and gender egalitarianism ultimately drives the range of apparent reproductive unions, from *sese* to marriage. With this emphasis, we aim to deconstruct monolithic sociocultural norms and to depict them for what they are: central tendencies with significant variability built in to accommodate variable individual and household circumstances. We illustrate these points by

DOI: 10.4324/9781003398349-16

introducing three families with whom we grew close during our years of fieldwork in Southwest China. We hope that readers come away with a sense of how family-centered and gender-egalitarian matrilineal values support the longevity of *sese* as a resilient, if not exclusive, reproductive practice in Mosuo society.

Box 14.1 Matrilineal society and gender egalitarianism

Scholars have long emphasized the relationship between matrilineal cultures and relative gender egalitarianism. According to social scientists, matrilineal kinship tends to revolve around forms of subsistence like horticulture, where much of the household is involved in tending gardens and men do not have disproportionate roles in household production. Warfare and fishing – activities that often require men to be absent for long periods of time – are also associated with matrilineal kinship as women work together to run households in the absence of men.

Regardless of the underlying causes, matrilineal and matrilocal ("female-biased") forms of kinship have increasingly been shown to support relatively gender-egalitarian ethos, more similar behaviors between women and men, and sometimes even "reversals" in gendered behavior (we do not love this term, as it implies that there is a standard that is reversed whereas the standard is a range of options taken up by both women and men, depending on circumstances). Our own work has shown that certain health indicators are better in women in contexts of matriliny than in patriliny (Reynolds et al. 2020), supported by more friendships in women (Mattison et al. 2021) and perhaps more control over household decision-making (Reynolds et al. 2020). We have also shown that matrilineal women exhibit only slight preferences for daughters in their fertility behavior, whereas patrilineal women exhibit strong preferences for sons (Mattison et al. 2016). These results are consistent with numerous other studies showing that economic behavior involving risk and wealth redistribution are very different in matrilineal contexts than in patrilineal ones (Mattison et al. 2023). Such results are important for identifying how gender norms underlie differences in economic behavior, health, and well-being while undermining views that posit universal differences between women and men based on simplistic concepts of underlying "biology."

In the section that follows, we give a brief overview of how *sese* has historically transformed among Mosuo people, as people have adapted to varied environmental and sociopolitical circumstances. Then, we show through portraits of three Mosuo families how the persistence of Mosuo cultural values has continued to support women's empowerment even though family composition and relationship arrangements have become increasingly diversified in contemporary Mosuo society. We end with an analysis of various sociocultural factors that give rise to relative gender egalitarianism in Mosuo communities and a discussion of what their example can teach us about kinship diversity.

Changing eras, changing relationships

This chapter draws primarily on information collected in Yongning, in China's Yunnan Province, which is home to about one-third of all 40,000 Mosuo people.[2] Mosuo settlement in the Yongning basin can be traced back to more than 1,300 years ago (Mattison et al. 2021). The Yongning basin provides defensible land for animal husbandry and subsistence agriculture. Adjacent Lugu Lake provides fish and other resources as well. Even though the Mosuo economy has long been relatively self-sufficient, men would historically embark on months-long mercantile voyages with mule and horse caravans. They would travel hundreds of miles to as far as Tibet and India to trade tea, salt, opium, and livestock. Many young men also became Gelugpa or Sakya Buddhist monks, studying for years and often conducting ceremonies away from home. Protracted male absences were associated with women acting as primary caretakers of children and dependents, with support from the extended family (Wang and Luo 1991). From an evolutionary perspective, male absence would also have lowered men's paternity certainty, making them less interested in taking active roles in their children's lives (Mattison 2011).

While *sese* relationships have been common among Mosuo people for generations, they have always coexisted with a variety of reproductive practices, including cohabitation and marriage. Decisions about whether to practice *sese* were informed not only by household and individual circumstances but also by state policy and socioeconomic changes. For example, after the Chinese Communist Party obtained full control of Yongning in 1956, governmental policies resulted in much more common marriage. This is because matrilineal descent and inheritance were deemed a primitive form of family arrangement, following Marxist and unilineal evolutionist understandings of human family structures (Engels 1972 [1884]). Mosuo practices of partnership without formal marriage and people's ability to easily change partners or end relationships came under attack. Marriage reforms were imposed in full intensity during the Great Proletariat Cultural Revolution (1966–1976), which involved mass struggle against "backward" customs and morality. In 1974 and 1975, couples were forced to leave their own families and establish new households together. Sentries were posted in villages to prevent people from moving about at night, and work points were withheld from couples who had not married (Cai 2001: 388–395).[3] Various forms of political coercion left many Mosuo people little choice but to marry and cohabitate.

Box 14.2   Long-lasting impact of Communist marriage reforms

Even though Mosuo practice of *sese* revived almost immediately after the Cultural Revolution, Communist renunciation of unofficial romantic union and duolocal residence as "backward" had drastically and irreversibly changed Mosuo ways of life. Our interlocutor, Yangjin Zhuoma,[4] said:

> In the 1950s and 1960s, relationships really were more casual. "Today, with this one [partner]; tomorrow, with that other one." . . . The horse caravans would stay briefly and then depart, sometimes never to pass through again. Sometimes

it really was not clear who the father was. But then the marriage campaign happened, and suddenly people were forced to live together.

The period of state-mandated cohabitation lasted only a brief time in the early 1970s, but many Mosuo people chose to maintain the system even after they could return home rather than undergo more upheaval. For example, Yangjin Zhuoma's mother, born in the 1940s, moved to her husband's village during the Cultural Revolution and never left.

> Like everyone else, my parents were forced to get married during the marriage campaign. When it ended, many people went back to their former homes, but my mother was from a faraway mountain village, so she just stayed with my father in his lakeside village. His mother lived with them as well.

Normally, there would have been others in their household, but they all lived elsewhere. Yangjin Zhuoma explained:

> My father had an older brother, a younger brother, and a younger sister. At that time, his older brother was away, serving in the army. His younger brother was also away, studying. His younger sister still lived in the village but had also been forced to marry.

Yangjin Zhuoma's father and mother stayed together for four decades, until his death in 2015. The couple had six children, some of whom practiced *sese*, while others opted for marriage and cohabitation. All maintained strong connections to their ancestral home, where their mother still resided into the 2020s. The story of this family is featured in Household Portrait 3.

As the intense drama of the Cultural Revolution passed and people were no longer forced to live with their partners, many Mosuo people resumed forming *sese* relationships. They could once again find someone they were attracted to, begin a relationship, and become a parent, while continuing to live with their natal families and enjoying collective child-rearing support. Most young people forming relationships during the 1980s and 1990s, a period characterized by marketization reforms, economic growth, and increase in individual autonomy, practiced *sese*.[5] In certain situations, though, the couple would live together (1) if they lived in a city and worked in a setting where formal marriage was expected and unregistered relationships were not technically allowed; (2) if their partner was from another ethnic group or from outside Yongning, in a place where everyone was expected to marry; or (3) if they needed to accommodate unique family circumstances. For example, if a household lacked women or lacked men, the family might encourage a person to find a partner willing to leave their family and join this other household. After all, household survival depended on both men and women.

The norms of *sese* became disrupted again during the contemporary era, for very different reasons. As transportation and communication infrastructure began to improve during the early 2000s, many Mosuo people left their villages for school and work. Visitors also began to arrive in overwhelming numbers, as domestic tourism developed around scenic Lugu Lake. The region witnessed new levels of affluence for many, which helped fund tuition payments but also introduced unprecedented social changes (Mattison 2010; Walsh 2005). People who worked outside their village often found partners for whom marriage was the only viable option. Increased exposure to and interaction with people from other cultural backgrounds led many Mosuo people to prefer an arrangement where they could live with their partner.

By the mid-2010s, shifting state policies related to cultural autonomy also affected partnership and residence decisions. Yongning, as part of an autonomous county, had, for decades, benefited from a certain degree of freedom for practices like alternative partnership forms. (Elsewhere in China, the marriage law had long required officially sanctioned marriage prior to childbirth.) But local autonomy became less relevant as people moved into urban spaces with different policies, and as computerization of systems dissolved administrative flexibility. Marriage certificates were needed for an increasing number of transactions and situations, including real estate purchases and childbirth. In an era when women were strongly encouraged to give birth to their babies in hospitals, not at home, hospitals' demands for "permission-to-birth" certificates (Ch. *zhunsheng zheng* 准生证) that could only be issued upon presentation of a marriage certificate created a significant obstacle for those in unregistered *sese* relationships. These regulations have made marriage all but compulsory for many people, especially those living in cities.

What we see in contemporary Mosuo families, then, is a diverse set of relationship arrangements that partially reflect the political, economic, and societal contexts of the eras during which they formed. Changing patterns of romantic union and reproductive practices are products of both sociopolitical circumstances and the long-standing ability for individuals to make decisions befitting their own desires and situations.

Three Mosuo families

The portraits of three Mosuo families that follow demonstrate how kinship and family arrangements in Mosuo villages today are characterized by diversity and flexibility. They also show how matrilineal households and family-centered values establish a cultural foundation for women's empowerment. Even though people make different decisions – regarding whether to get married or maintain a *sese* relationship, and whether to reside in big matrilineal families or move out to form new households – the centrality of household and a strong sense of commitment to care for the young and the old remain core to Mosuo people's understanding about family and individual responsibilities.

Sona's family: two forms of sese under one roof

Sona was a dear sister to us. She was independent, entrepreneurial, and empowered; she was also kind, loving, and fiercely protective of her family and friends. She was a proud Mosuo woman who exemplifies how Mosuo culture makes it possible for women to simultaneously manage responsibilities associated with being a mother, a daughter, a sister, and a friend, as well as an entrepreneur and a breadwinner for the family. The following portrayal of Sona shows how a matrilineal family structure empowers women to be entrepreneurs: shared childcare responsibility among household members means that a woman can rely on her siblings to take care of her children while she works outside of the household. Retaining residence with her natal family means that she remains protected and provisioned by her kinspeople, which frees her from economic and emotional dependence on a spouse.

As opposed to classic modernization theorists who sometimes see family connections as constraining to individual autonomy (e.g., Goode 1963), Sona embraced her propensity for freedom not in spite of but because of the centrality of family in her life.

The youngest of three sisters, Sona resided in a Mosuo village with her parents; eldest sister, Duma; daughter; and three nieces and nephews. Her eldest sister, Duma, ran the household. She was the primary caretaker of their parents and children and took responsibility for many farming tasks, while Sona worked to support the family financially. In her free time, Sona loved to take her daughter for walks and spend time with friends. Sona did not have any male siblings, nor did she feel the need for one: the absence of a male breadwinner was not a hindrance for building a prosperous household. She had support from her father and male cousins, with whom she had grown up.

When we last saw Sona in 2018, she was in her mid-30s. She worked in the tourism industry, taking busloads of tourists around Lugu Lake and telling Mosuo stories along the way. Her outgoing personality and sense of humor made her a popular tour guide. During the couple of times that we were on tour with Sona, we, too, were mesmerized by her passion and pride in sharing Mosuo culture with curious tourists. But Sona confided to us that she did not always enjoy her job. The pay was not high, and the work was stressful and seasonal. When demand for tour guides at the Lugu Lake skyrocketed during tourist seasons, she found herself exhausted from having to jump from tour group to tour group without breaks in between, sometimes with very short notice. Most importantly, Sona's job often required her to stay overnight at the hotels where tour groups stayed. She was reluctant to be away from her family, especially from her 4-year-old daughter and 7-year-old niece.

Sona tried supplementing her income by exploring other business ventures, such as opening a small tea stall in the town center. If the business brought in enough revenue, she hoped to cut back on the number of tours she had to take and eventually became a full-time entrepreneur herself. But business at the tea stall struggled because there were not enough local customers. Sona sometimes felt guilty for not being able to spend enough time with her daughter and niece whenever she got busy. She would buy them candies or small toys when she returned home from a longer tour and enjoyed their excitement on receiving gifts.

Sona was no longer in a romantic relationship with the father of her daughter as of 2021. Before their relationship ended, the couple had practiced a revised version of *sese*, as this partner lived in a neighboring province approximately four hours away by car. The distance made it impossible for this man to "walk back and forth" every night. Rather, Sona's partner would come visit every few weeks and stay with the family for a few days. He would play with his biological daughter sometimes, but he did not formally take on responsibility for her care even when he was around to provide it. He respected that he was not his daughter's official guardian and did not try to assume that role. Sona was grateful for how supportive and protective her family was when the couple eventually decided to part ways. It was never a question which side Sona's parents would take in a conflict. As it is normal for Mosuo women to raise children with the support of their maternal family members, a woman who decides not to engage further with the person who fathers her child is not ostracized. Sona never had to worry about her daughter while away from home for work, as she knew that her parents and eldest sister, Duma, would take very good care of her.

Duma, three years older than Sona, was a very hardworking woman. In addition to cooking, cleaning, and taking care of children at home, Duma also maintained the few plots of rice paddy fields that the family owned. Duma rose early every morning to prepare breakfast for everyone. Other duties followed, such as handwashing clothes and dishes, watering and harvesting vegetables in their small garden, feeding pigs and chickens, and preparing lunch and dinner. Sona's comment that "this family could not operate without Eldest Sister (Ch. *Da Jie* 大姐)" was no exaggeration. Duma rarely had time off; she would only allow herself to indulge in a few card games with neighbors on special occasions, such as the Spring Festival (usually in January or February).

Duma was usually too tired to join the rest of the family for television time in the evenings. After cleaning up and washing dinner dishes, she would often retreat to her chamber with her *sese* partner, a man from a neighboring village who fathered Duma's 7-year-old daughter. Sona referred to this man as her brother-in-law (elder sister's husband, Ch. *Jiefu* 姐夫), even though the couple never officially registered a marriage. Brother-in-Law was always polite and friendly. He would dine with the family sometimes if he showed up before dinnertime, but he tried not to impose too often. He respected that he would always remain a guest in this household, even though he had, for years, visited almost every day. This *sese* arrangement worked for the couple, as it allowed both of them to care and provide for their own natal family, to which they felt a true sense of belonging.

In addition to her 7-year-old daughter, Duma had a son, to whom she gave birth when she was 26. The boy's father no longer visited, as his *sese* relationship with Duma had ended long before Duma met her current partner. Duma's son lived with the family and attended primary school in the village.

The other teenage boy who also assumed membership in this household was the only child of Sona's second sister, who worked at a tourist outpost on the other side of Lugu Lake and lived approximately an hour's drive from the village. This sister was legally divorced from her son's biological father, as the couple had opted for an official marriage rather than maintaining a *sese* relationship. Since her divorce, she had found another partner and maintained a long-term relationship with him. This sister came to the village to visit only a few times a year, but Sona's family insisted that she be counted as a household member in a household survey we conducted. Their ideal family was one where all siblings and children hailed from the same matrilineal bloodline. It was obvious that maintaining a large matrilineal household was core to this family's imagination about happiness and prosperity.

Both Duma and Sona shared the authority and responsibility to take care of not only their biological but also their sisters' children. Both boys, fathered by men who were no longer in the picture, called Duma *Emi-zhi* ("older mother") and Sona *Emi-ji* ("younger mother"). Sona would bear souvenirs from her work trips only to the younger girls, not because she played favorites, but because the teenage boys were becoming too cool for the family. The boys often locked themselves in their rooms, as rebellious teenagers would, to avoid their guardians' nagging. Sona would sometimes scold the boys for their rebellious behaviors, but she, too, understood that she could only wait for the adolescent angst to ride itself out. In spite of Sona's own carefree and free-spirited nature, the role she played was not just a fun aunt but a coparent of these boys, even though neither of them was her biological child.

Sona, like everybody in her household, deeply respected her parents. She talked often of trying to ease her mother's worry for her or of providing her parents with proper material comfort, as they deserved to be pampered in their old age. Sona's mother, in her early 60s in 2018, came from a *sipi* (hereditary nobility) family in a neighboring village. Her privileged upbringing was obvious in the fact that she had attended two years of school and spoke some Mandarin Chinese – a rarity among women in her generation. She told us that she quit school after two years because her family needed her labor for earning work points during the Cultural Revolution. It was probably not a coincidence that her schooling ended around the time when Maoist collectivization was in full force – a time during which every man and woman was mobilized to contribute to crop and steel production for the Chinese Communist state. It was also a time when many traditional elites saw their wealth "collectivized" and privilege stripped in many parts of China.

After Sona's parents got married – as many Mosuo couples were forced to do so in the Chinese Communist government's attempt to end their "backward" practice of "walking marriage" during the 1970s – Sona's mother left her natal village to move into her husband's ancestral house. She lived there with her husband's mother, her husband's siblings, and their children until the family became too big to fit under one roof. Her husband's siblings moved away, one to a new house in the same village and others to cities and townships close by. Although some of Sona's paternal uncles had moved away from the village, this ancestral household (Ch. *laojia* 老家) remained prominent in their imagination of home, lineage, and origin. For example, one of Sona's uncles brought his 13-year-old granddaughter back to the village to conduct her rite-of-passage ceremony over the Spring Festival in 2017. Even though the girl had not grown up in this village, she understood the importance of recognizing where she and her ancestors hailed from. As villagers celebrated her rite of adulthood through dancing and feasting, she was reminded of the significance of ancestral house in the identity of every Mosuo woman and man, even among those who lived elsewhere.

Sona's mother and father took care of Sona's paternal grandmother in this ancestral house until she passed in the early 2000s. When we visited in 2018, the photo of Sona's grandmother, placed on the right side of the hearth, was impossible to miss. Food was placed in front of the portrait as offering every evening before dinner, inculcating in children the proper Mosuo etiquette of letting the great-grandmother eat before anyone else could. This late grandmother, whom Sona's mother described as a strong and remarkable woman, was still watching over this family in spirit. After she passed, Sona's father and mother jointly inherited this household. Duma would probably become the next head of household in line. The humble work of cooking, cleaning, and caregiving she did, cementing the family together and keeping the household running, was well recognized by everybody.

Sona was a cheerful and spirited woman. Her laughter was contagious, and she was always generous with her friends. She did not need to live with a romantic partner to be happy. Sona and Duma were great examples showing how women could flourish when they enjoyed the loving support of their families in a matrilineal society where women were respected as autonomous individuals, empowered to pursue responsibilities in breadwinning, caregiving, and/or managing the household, depending on what they were skilled at and what their family needed.

Lamu, Archei, and his mother: a smaller household led by two generations of strong women

Compared with Sona's family, Lamu and Archei's family was a lot smaller, with only five people. It also assumed a patrilocal structure, as Lamu moved into Archei's household after the couple got married. Archei's mother ("Grandmother"), 69 years old in 2018, was the matriarch presiding over household affairs. While Lamu and Archei did not live in a big matrilineal family, the way family decisions were made was strongly influenced by matrilineal norms. As we show in what follows, everybody in the household worked to take care of each other, and the well-being of family members was always prioritized when important decisions were made.

Lamu, 45 years old when we met her in 2018, lived with her husband, Archei; their two children (both in their early 20s at that time); and Archei's mother. Lamu was a hardworking and resourceful woman. She was witty, talkative, and helpful to her neighbors. In addition to taking care of the family's rice fields and vegetable garden, Lamu sometimes worked in the kitchen in nearby hostels. Lamu was proud of her reputation as one of the best cooks in her village. She used her talent to turn mundane vegetables into flavorful delicacies, cooking not only for tourists but also for neighbors during communal events.

Archei was a mason who picked up day-labor work in villages close by. He worked hard to make money to support their daughter's education at a teacher's college. This daughter, who inherited her mother's cheerfulness, generosity, and culinary skills, wanted to become a teacher at the primary school in their village. This aspiration was very much influenced by her grandmother's wish for her to stay close to home, she said. When the young woman was home for summer break, she sometimes worked alongside Lamu in lakeside hostels to earn money toward her tuition.

The couple's son was one year younger than their daughter. He failed to earn high enough grades to get into high school. Rather than exploring alternative pathways to continue his education, he decided to quit school and join his father in day-labor work. For a short period of time, he even moved by himself to a southern Chinese city to work as a factory worker and a security guard. This young man tried his best to earn and save money, most of which he gave to his sister when she returned home for school holiday. He thought that his sister, being a full-time student, needed the money more than he did. Lamu's daughter said that she felt very moved when her brother insisted that she take his hard-earned money. The young man's generosity showed that the siblings cared deeply about each other. They truly considered taking care of household well-being and providing for each other their responsibility.

Lamu, like many women who live with in-laws in other parts of the world, maintained a delicate relationship with her mother-in-law. Archei's mother was mostly healthy, though she often complained about having back and knee pain. Despite being close to 70 in age, Grandmother insisted on participating in household tasks, feeding pigs every day, and taking oxen out for grazing. Lamu confided that it was sometimes not easy to live with her mother-in-law, as they disagreed at times about household and resource management. For example, Grandmother insisted on slaughtering the biggest pigs for festive consumption, without taking into consideration whether the small family would be able to consume the meat before it would spoil or whether they had enough room to store the preserved meat properly. Lamu would much rather have sold those fat pigs for additional income. Lamu also wished Grandmother had more friends with whom she could spend time, instead of relying on Lamu for companionship.

Lamu recalled that her decision to get married and move in with Archei was straightforward. She did not have other choices, because Archei had no living sibling. (His only brother did not survive his first four months.) Having separated from her natal household when Archei was still a young boy, Grandmother had only her son to lean on. The two lived together by themselves until Lamu moved in. Lamu understood that committing to a relationship with Archei would come with the responsibility of caring for his mother. Lamu agreed to do so because her own natal family did not need her as much: she came from a much larger family of seven siblings, and the household was getting too crowded anyway. The married couple lived only a few kilometers away from Lamu's natal household, and she visited every few weeks.

In spite of the occasional complaints, Lamu had a lot of respect for her mother-in-law. Lamu recognized that Grandmother had worked very hard her entire life. And she admired Grandmother for her bold determination to establish her own household for the welfare of Archei, which Lamu recognized as "not at all easy." She was grateful for the sacrifice Grandmother had made to raise Archei into a fine, responsible man.

When Archei was still young, Grandmother left her natal household to start a new family, because she wanted to provide for her boy's future as best as she could: food and resources were extremely scarce when Archei was born, during the Cultural Revolution. Grandmother was worried that resources in her big family, with many children to feed, were spread too thin. Even though establishing her own household was not easy for a young mother and her toddler son, the young Grandmother decided that she could provide for her boy better if she established her own household.

Initially, young Grandmother had invited Archei's father to join them in starting a nuclear family, but the man bailed for fear of the responsibility and hardship involved. His decision to stay with his own matrilineal family was the beginning of the end of their romantic relationship. He eventually stopped visiting altogether. Grandmother was not deterred. As a healthy and hardworking young woman, she knew that she did not need a husband to raise her own son. Also, Grandmother continued to draw on support from her extended family. Household separation did not mean that Grandmother was completely severed from her natal family – Archei continued to play with his cousins, and the two families visited each other often. The extended family still played a part in Archei's upbringing, even though they no longer resided under the same roof.

Lamu and her mother-in-law – both incredibly strong-willed and capable women – made decisions about marriage, location of residence, and household separation based on practical considerations about their dependents' welfare. Their family-centered values were passed along to their children, who similarly made important decisions about their study and work plans with family members' well-being in mind. Lamu would one day become the head of this family, even though she was not a direct descendent of Grandmother, who established their household. Recognizing the contribution that Lamu had provided and would continue to provide for this family, no one would dispute her legitimacy in taking over this role. Until then, the couple would work as hard as they could to ensure that Grandmother would live a comfortable, dignified life in her old age. Lamu's family was not rich, but she felt content and grateful for her children and her happy marital relationship with Archei.

Yangjin Zhuoma's family: six siblings and six ways of organizing households around a matrilineal core

The family of Yangjin Zhuoma was, as another Mosuo man from the same village put it, a "traditional matrilineal family" comprised of four generations of maternal kin residing at least part of the year in the same lakeside village – 22 people in all. It exemplifies the commingling of different forms of residence, partnership, and affiliation in contemporary Mosuo families. Yangjin Zhuoma took pride in being part of a big family, which demonstrated household harmony and prosperity. At the same time, the fact that she and some of her siblings decided to establish smaller nuclear households with their spouses and biological children, either as secondary or primary residence, showed that the Mosuo household composition adapted as circumstances changed.

Yangjin Zhuoma, born in the early 1980s, was a self-motivated, entrepreneurial woman. She often seized opportunities: When two of us started conducting fieldwork in the region in the 2000s, Yangjin Zhuoma took interest in practicing speaking English with us. When we returned in the 2010s, she had a side business selling clothing items and wanted to fit us with the elaborate garments. (How exactly should an anthropologist handle a sales pitch from a good friend? There is no clear answer in the how-to-conduct-field-research training manuals!) Her resourcefulness proved to be helpful in her day job in the local government. As a government employee, she regularly helped host visiting delegations of government officials, researchers, and journalists who wanted to learn more about the Mosuo people. She jokingly laughed away their sensationalist ideas about how easy it would be to attract a Mosuo lover while still managing to entertain them. We always enjoyed talking to Yangjin Zhuoma and hearing her stories.

Yangjin Zhuoma met her husband, a person from the Naxi ethnic group in rural Lijiang, while working in a government bureau. They married formally in 2008, holding a wedding and obtaining a marriage certificate. As government employees, Yangjin Zhuoma and her husband had to follow marriage regulations and forfeit the exemptions that other Mosuo could claim. "I didn't dare do otherwise!" she exclaimed, probably for fear of putting their jobs and careers in jeopardy. Since 2018, Yangjin Zhuoma resided with her two sons in the city of Lijiang, not only because schools were better in the city but also because she had begun to build a new business there selling lingerie and shapewear. Her husband visited two or three times a month, as he worked in the vicinity of the lakeside village where Yongjin Zhuoma's natal family lived. She noted quickly, "But as soon as the school breaks begin, we go back home to spend time with my mother." As much as Yangjin Zhuoma wanted to live in her natal village, she needed to live where she and her children could access the best career and educational opportunities.

Yangjin Zhuoma was the youngest of six siblings – five sisters and one brother. Her two eldest sisters lived in their ancestral home in the lakeside village, along with their elderly mother, their children, and grandchildren. The eldest daughter, born in the late 1960s, was in a *sese* relationship with another member of the same village and had no children. The second daughter, born in the early 1970s, met her partner, a Han man, when tourism to their village was just getting started. They formed a *sese* relationship. After their son was born, the man moved into his partner's household, helping the family as they hosted tourists and built structures to accommodate them. This couple never obtained a marriage certificate. To outsiders, their relationship seemed like that of a married couple, but they referred to it as a *sese* relationship. Their adult son had established a nuclear household with his wife in the same village, along with their two young children. The geographic proximity allowed the children to visit their grandparents and great-grandmother often.

Yangjin Zhuoma's only brother was born in the mid-1970s. This third sibling set up a separate household with his wife, where they raised two daughters together. Their relationship, in fact, began as a *sese* partnership, which the couple only later converted to a legally registered marriage. When this brother and his family went to his wife's village to pay their respects to her ancestral hearth (Ch. *Jing guozhuang* 敬锅庄, essentially asking her family to bless and formalize the relationship), the woman's family consented to a *sese* partnership but refused to let her leave home. As the only daughter in her generation, she was needed to keep the household thriving, and her children would, in turn, be the future of the family. For his part, he was the only son and could not be spared either. A *sese* arrangement allowed both parties to continue their relationship while fulfilling their duties to their natal household as filial daughter and son.

Around 2003, as tourism in the lakeside village kicked into high gear, Yangjin Zhuoma's brother wanted his partner to join him there.[6] Her family reluctantly consented. With only farming incomes, many families struggled to afford school fees and pay for other expenses, and they decided she might as well go and take advantage of the opportunity to earn some income. But Yangjin Zhuoma's mother did not agree to the young woman joining her household. "I already have five daughters," she said. What could possibly be the role of another woman in the household? Besides, it had already been agreed that theirs would be a *sese* relationship, not one where the couple lived together. So the young couple built a new house at the edge of the village, where they lived with their two daughters.

The three younger siblings – including Yangjin Zhuoma and her two elder sisters – came of age in the early 2000s, when tourism had begun to transform their village. All eventually set up households in the city so they could send their children to school there, but they still considered the village where their mother and sisters lived their true home. One of these women was in a *sese* relationship with a man from the same village. They had one daughter and one son before he passed away unexpectedly, when the little boy was just 1 year old. While in many families the death of a parent is a devastating loss economically as well as emotionally, these children had never lived with their father. They remained well cared for by their mother and her matrilineal family as they grew up. The absence of their father was a sad reality, but it did not irrevocably alter their lives.

The sister who was the closest to Yangjin Zhuoma in age was born in the late 1970s. During the days of intense tourism, in the early 2000s, she met a Han tourist from northern China and fell in love with him. They soon began living together, sometimes in the lakeside village, and sometimes elsewhere. But they never married. "Why would I marry?" this sister told a visiting filmmaker with a grin, when her daughter was a toddler. "A marriage license would be like a pair of handcuffs!"[7] The couple managed to obtain a cohabitation certificate (Ch. *Tongjuzheng* 同居证), which allowed them to give birth in a hospital, by pulling in favors from close connections with ties to government bureaus. Those without these connections would have had a hard time obtaining this authorization and would have found marrying a much more practical option. Birthing at home, long the preferred norm in Mosuo households and in other parts of rural China, had gradually been supplanted by hospital birthing.

All six adult siblings in this family – the older sisters in *sese* relationships and the married younger siblings who have built or bought separate homes – considered themselves part of a core household in a lakeside village, even if they may live in different places. Each of them made decisions about romantic unions and residence to ensure that they could take the best advantage of educational resources and professional opportunities in the region while ensuring that they were located geographically close enough to visit their ancestral village and matrilineal relatives. They continued to identify themselves as one big matrilineal family, even as they lived in different places.

Discussion and analysis

The three examples discussed earlier illustrate the variety and complexity of contemporary Mosuo families. These portraits demonstrate how political and economic changes influenced families, and how individuals made decisions regarding whether to get formally married or to establish new households. *Sese* arrangements afforded individuals freedom to live in their natal households and hence made moral and logical sense to many Mosuo. Others opted for marriage and co-residence with their partners, in order to avoid state sanctions (as with Sona's and Yangjin Zhuoma's parents), to care for dependents (Lamu and Archei), or out of professional necessity (Yangjin Zhuoma), among other reasons. Even though many Mosuo still expressed preferences for living in large multigenerational matrilineal households, some chose to establish their own households because of their desire to better provide for their children (Lamu's mother-in-law) or to pursue a more comfortable life in the city (Yangjin Zhuoma and her sisters). Like people in other parts of the world, Mosuo individuals might also move out because of conflict or disagreement with family members, or when their households became too crowded (Harrell 2001; Shih 2009). Reality is complicated, and people make decisions that suit the times and their own circumstances, then adapt them as needed.

Despite the varying size and shape of contemporary families, the cultural ideal of putting family first remained important to many Mosuo people. Mosuo boys and girls were taught to be kind, caring, and family-oriented from a young age. The willingness and ability to contribute to their family, whether through domestic labor, financial provisioning, or emotional support, were core to Mosuo understanding of moral personhood. Even for those who had relocated and established roots elsewhere, they were often reminded of home by making frequent or occasional trips back to their ancestral village. The household name they bore and the portraits of ancestors displayed on domestic altars were also everyday reminders of people's embeddedness in webs of connections with their matrilineal relatives and ancestors.

Even among Mosuo women who opted to officially register a marriage or move in with their husband's family, many did not, in practice, make a complete shift of their sense of belonging from her family of origin to her male partner's family. People usually maintained significant flexibility in residence and continued strong affiliations for their mother and maternal relatives, demonstrating a very strong matrifocal element in their everyday experience. After all, this is a society with an entire genre of songs about mothers (Yang 2023), where marriage does not weaken allegiance to one's mother and maternal kin. For example, we know of a few Mosuo women who did not move in immediately with their husband's family, even months after they got married. At least two married women we know returned to their natal home after giving birth, living there for months as their maternal relatives helped care for their newborn. In Mosuo communities, married couples' maintaining separate residence was not a sign of marital problem but rather a normalized, practical adaptation to varying familial situations.

Mosuo women's close ties with their natal family contrast with long-standing patrilineal customs among Han Chinese, the ethnic majority in contemporary China. The Han Chinese idiom that married daughters are like "water spilled out" (Ch. *po chuqu de shui* 泼出去的水) – that is, a vanished and unusable resource – encapsulates the traditional idea that a married daughter ceases to be part of her natal family. In traditional Han society, women's transient membership in her natal household engenders pressure to produce male heirs, lest a lineage cease to exist.[8] On the contrary, many Mosuo women never "marry out" in the real sense of the term. Men and women remain loyal to their natal household, no matter whether they live together in a single structure or in a number of places covering a wide geographic area. According to a community leader, many Mosuo people found it "painful" to have to separate from one's mother geographically for an extended period of time. There is a strong sense of commitment to take care of all biological kin, male or female, with particular attention to the elderly and the young, who are more dependent on kin provisioning. The idea of severing ties with one's daughter only because she "marries out" is culturally incompatible with Mosuo worldviews.

When viewed through the Mosuo household-centric lens, the function of *sese* in supporting the maintenance and continual development of multigenerational matrilineal households becomes obvious. *Sese* makes sense not because it allows for freedom in having multiple romantic partners but because it enables all maternal siblings to stay with their mother and maternal relatives, to whom their allegiance belongs. It also supports women's empowerment and relative gender egalitarianism in Mosuo society. A woman's physical proximity to her natal family allows her to draw on support from long-established kin and social networks when conflicts with male partner arise. Domestic violence against women is less likely than in other, more patriarchal contexts, as a woman has built-in protection from her own maternal kin. Romantically involved couples enjoy each other's companionship without having to worry about mundane aspects of everyday life. Conflicts about childcare and in-laws are minimized when couples do not share responsibility for them. When a romantic relationship does not work out, the absence of stigma against divorcees and "fatherless" households minimizes the costs associated with separation, empowering women to take risks and make bold decisions. Women are less likely to be stuck in bad situations when they can rely on their matrilineal family for support.

But *sese* as a singular practice does not explain the relative autonomy and respect that Mosuo women enjoy. Women are protected from patriarchal influence thanks to myriad sociocultural characteristics associated with matrilineal inheritance and a household-centric society. Overall, a culture that values domestic labor enhances women's status in both their household and community. Expectations to contribute to a large multigenerational family support and encourage both women and men to engage in economic production, in ways that best fit their abilities and aptitudes. Shared caretaking of children among maternal siblings and their elders creates opportunities for mothers to work full-time, sometimes away from home. And women's ownership of property and their role in managing domestic finances empower them to control resources, opening up pathways to becoming independent and self-reliant if they so desire. An overemphasis on *sese* distracts observers from many other admirable cultural ideas and matrilineal institutions that support the prospering of women in Mosuo communities as autonomous individuals, entitled to rights, responsibilities, and dignity that their male counterparts also enjoy.

Our discussion highlights the importance of foregrounding emic perspectives for capturing the range and diversity of kin and family arrangements, as well as the urgency and challenges involved in authentically representing diverse human experiences. A true appreciation for gender and family diversity requires not just the curiosity to learn about singularly unfamiliar (and oft-exoticized) gender practices but, more importantly, the critical knowledge and discerning insight to situate these practices in an appropriate social context and holistic cultural cosmology indispensable to supporting the flourishing of gender diversity. There is much we can learn from Mosuo culture, and these lessons promise to be rewarding for those who are humble enough to listen and curious enough to look beyond the superficial.

Discussion questions

1. How can understanding the diversity of Mosuo sexual and family/kin relationships open up new possibilities for relationships elsewhere?
2. In thinking about how important political and historical shifts shaped the possibilities for Mosuo people's romantic relationships, identify an important political or historical shift that influenced how society views sexual and romantic relationships in your own society. Which populations tend to be most influenced by political shifts?
3. In thinking broadly about kin and the household, how does Mosuo society help us rethink gender roles and the gendering of domestic and public space more generally?

Supplementary material

Recommended video

"Exploring the Kingdom of Women in China | TODAY":
This *Today Show* piece features NBC anchor Kate Snow as she visits Mosuo communities to learn more about what life is like for women and men living in their region of southwest China.
www.youtube.com/watch?app=desktop&v=AxCOrw2_2ww
Runtime: 10:52
June 3, 2019.

Notes

1 Non-alphabetic characters used in this chapter are Chinese. Transliterations using Mandarin pinyin, the lingua franca in China, are marked with "Ch." Other non-English words, including "*sese*," are romanized expressions in Naru, the Mosuo language.
2 This chapter focuses on the matrilineal Mosuo communities in and around Yongning. Mosuo people living in neighboring Labai Township follow a patrilineal system that includes cohabitative marriage. See, for example, Latami (2009) and Shih (2009).
3 Under the planned socialist economy, beginning in the 1950s, work points were needed for all basic necessities, including grain and other food rations. Without work points, feeding one's family would become extremely difficult.
4 Most family and individual names used in this chapter are pseudonyms.
5 Cai Hua presents several examples of *sese* relationships on the edge of the Yongning plain during this era, encountered during his fieldwork in 1988 (2001: 404–406).
6 Tourism provided the impetus for many families to splinter into separate households. Revenues from collectively managed tourist activities, like communal boat-rowing and nightly singing and dancing performances, were distributed evenly to each participating household. If a household of 22 people separated into two separate homes, they could immediately double their income. This proved an attractive incentive for many, with dramatic impacts on households and relationship decisions.
7 To protect anonymity, we refrain from providing further details from this film.
8 Preference for sons in rural China, while still prevalent, has become less pronounced in the twenty-first century (Shi 2017).

References

Dashi, Latami. 2009. *Chengxiang zhijian de cunluo 城乡之间的村落* [The Village between City and Countryside: Cultural life history of the Mosuo People in the Langqu Area of Ninglang Yi Autonomous County]. Kunming: Yunnan Minzu Chubanshe.

Engels, Frederick. 1972 [1884]. *The Origin of the Family, Private Property, and the State*. New York: Pathfinder Press.

Goode, William J. 1963. *World Revolution and Family Patterns*. New York: The Free Press.

Harrell, Stevan. 2001. *Ways of Being Ethnic in Southwest China*. Seattle: University of Washington Press.

Hua, Cai. 2001. *A Society without Fathers or Husbands: The Na of China*. London: Zone Books.

Mattison, Siobhán M. 2010. "Economic Impacts of Tourism and Erosion of the Visiting System Among the Mosuo of Lugu Lake." *The Asia Pacific Journal of Anthropology* 11(2): 159–176.

Mattison, Siobhán M. 2011. "Evolutionary Contributions to Solving the 'Matrilineal Puzzle': A Test of Holden, Sear, and Mace's Model." *Human Nature* 22: 64–88. https://doi.org/10.1007/s12110-011-9107-7.

Mattison, Siobhán M., Bret Beheim, Bridget Chak, and Peter Buston. 2016. "Offspring Sex Preferences among Patrilineal and Matrilineal Mosuo in Southwest China Revealed by Differences in Parity Progression." *Royal Society Open Science* 3(9): 160526.

Mattison, Siobhán M., Neil G. MacLaren, Adam Z. Reynolds, Ruizhe Liu, Gabrielle D. Baca, Peter M. Mattison, Meng Zhang, Chun-Yi Sum, Mary K. Shenk, Tami Blumenfield, Christopher von Rueden, and Katherine Wander. 2021. "Gender Differences in Social Networks based on Prevailing Kinship Norms in the Mosuo of China." *Social Sciences* 10(7): 253. https://doi.org/10.3390/socsci10070253.

Mattison, Siobhán M., Peter M. Mattison, Bret A. Beheim, Ruizhe Liu, Tami Blumenfield, Chun-Yi Sum, Mary K. Shenk, Edmond Seabright, and Sarah Alami. 2023. "Gender Disparities in Material and Educational Resources Differ by Kinship System." *Philosophical Transactions of the Royal Society B: Biological Sciences* 378: 1883. https://doi.org/10.1098/rstb.2022.0299.

Mattison, Siobhán M., Chun-Yi Sum, Adam Z. Reynolds, Gabrielle D. Baca, Tami Blumenfield, Sara Niedbalski, Ruizhe Liu, Meng Zhang, Lige Liu, Lin Wei, Mingjie Su, Hui Li, Mary K. Shenk, and Katherine Wander. 2021. "Using Evolutionary Theory to Hypothesize a Transition from Patriliny to Matriliny and Back Again among the Ethnic Mosuo of Southwest China." *Matrix: A Journal for Matricultural Studies* 2(1): 90–117.

Reynolds, Adam Z., Katherine Wander, Chun-Yi Sum, Mingjie Su, Melissa Emery Thompson, Paul L. Hooper, Hui Li, Mary K. Shenk, Kathrine E. Starkweather, Tami Blumenfield, and Siobhán M. Mattison. 2020. "Matriliny Reverses Gender Disparities in Inflammation and Hypertension among the Mosuo of China." *Proceedings of the National Academy of Sciences*. https://doi.org/10.1073/pnas.2014403117.

Shi, Lihong. 2017. *Choosing Daughters: Family Change in Rural China*. Stanford, CA: Stanford University Press.

Shih, Chuan-kang. 2009. *Quest for Harmony: The Moso Traditions of Sexual Union and Family Life*. Stanford, CA: Stanford University Press.

Walsh, Eileen Rose. 2005. "From Nü Guo to Nü'er Guo: Negotiating Desire in the Land of the Mosuo." *Modern China* 31(4): 448–486. https://doi.org/10.1177/0097700405279243.

Wang, Dexiang 王德祥, and Renqui Luo 罗仁贵. 1991. "Zouhun zhi zhi mi 走婚制 之谜 [On the Enigma of Walking Marriage]." *Minzu Tuanjie* 民族团结 7.

Yang Lifen 杨丽芬 (Nianzhe Xiaoma). 2023. "Mosuo Songs and Dances: From the Villages to the University Campus." trans. Tami Blumenfield. *Matrix: A Journal for Matricultural Studies* 3(1): 218–234.

Chapter 15

What to do with unmarried daughters? Modern solutions to a traditional dilemma in a polyandrous Tibetan society

Geoff Childs, Melvyn C. Goldstein, and Puchung Wangdui

Reproduced from Geoff Childs, Melvyn C. Goldstein, and Puchung Wangdui, "What to Do with Unmarried Daughters? Modern Solutions to a Traditional Dilemma in a Polyandrous Tibetan Society," *Journal of Cross-Cultural Gerontology* 26.1 (2011), pp. 1–22.

Similar to other societies that lack formal social security systems, the elderly in rural Tibet[1] depend on adult children to care for them in old age. Any changes in the ties that bind adult children to their parents can therefore affect the health and welfare of the elderly. Tibet is currently undergoing major social and economic transformations, which are affecting domestic relationships, gender ideologies, and gender roles. In the last decade, China has dedicated enormous resources toward improving the standard of living in Tibet. Policies aimed at achieving modernization are increasing opportunities for secular education, non-farm employment, and rural-to-urban migration (Goldstein et al. 2008, 2010). According to the seminal theory on aging and modernization (Cowgill 1974; Cowgill and Holmes 1972), the very forces of modernization that are now transforming Tibet can negatively impact the elderly by producing intergenerational competition, residential segregation, social distance, and an inversion of status.[2] The social, economic, and spatial mobility of children engendered by modernization is seen as a threat to the ability of families to provide care for aging members.

In this chapter, we use data collected in three Tibetan villages to demonstrate ways that externally resident daughters can positively impact the lives of their aging parents. Deciding which children to keep as caretakers, and which to send out of the household, has always been an important decision for parents. In traditional Tibetan societies, daughters who moved out through arranged marriages were considered a net loss to the household, as epitomized by the proverb "The hen eats at home and lays its eggs outside" (Pemba 1996: 81). Fraternal polyandry, a type of marriage in which two or more brothers share a wife, complicated matters by generating a surplus of potential brides. Simply put, there were more women than households into which they could marry. Retaining an unmarried daughter within the household was considered problematic due to potential conflicts that could erupt between her and her brothers' in-marrying bride, yet options for removing her from the household were limited and often left her vulnerable and impoverished.

DOI: 10.4324/9781003398349-17

Nowadays, however, social and economic changes associated with modernization are creating new opportunities for parents to send daughters out in ways whereby they can gain financial independence and continue to provide support for their parents in old age.

To explore the evolving nature of relationships between parents and externally resident daughters, we deploy the concept of social capital. *Social capital* refers to connections within and between social networks that facilitate action and promote cooperation between individuals. It is rooted in interpersonal relations that involve reciprocity over the life course and functions as a resource that people can draw upon to solve problems or achieve objectives (Bourdieu 2001; Coleman 1988; Putnam 2000). Research in social gerontology has focused on filial norms as a dimension of social capital. Silverstein et al. (2006) argue that the resources parents invest in their children from birth to adulthood generate a reserve of social capital, and hypothesize that the social capital imbued in the relationship with adult children may lie dormant for many years but can be activated during a time of need, such as a health crisis. The key is to determine when certain members of a latent kinship matrix (the sum of family members who vary from potential to actual providers of support) become active in providing support for the elderly, and why.

In this chapter, we view some externally resident daughters of Tibet's rural households – namely, beneficiaries of parental investments that facilitated financial independence and urban residence – as a novel form of social capital from which the elderly can solicit social support. *Social support* refers to various types of assistance a person can receive from others and, herein, is divided into three categories: emotional support, caretaking assistance, and financial assistance. A fundamental point of this chapter is that, compared with daughters who were sent as brides to other rural households, daughters who move out of their households through education or employment represent an important form of social capital because they possess a unique combination of income, urban residence, and greater freedom to assist aging parents. This combination enhances their ability to positively impact the lives of elderly parents by providing (1) leverage against coresident children who do not treat them well, (2) temporary places of refuge from ill-treatment at home, (3) caretaking services and financial support when they require hospitalization, and (4) financial resources which they can use whenever they want, for example, to pursue age-appropriate activities like pilgrimage.

Data presented in this chapter come from surveys and interviews conducted in three Tibetan villages between 2006 and 2009. The three villages, while not representing all of Tibet, were selected to meet a research design comparing a continuum of villages from relatively wealthy to relatively poor in a study of the impacts that modernization has on rural families. Sogang, the least affected by development, is in the upper part of a tributary river valley. Norgyong, the intermediate site, is situated below Sogang on the main river and is located immediately beside the rapidly growing town of Panam. Betsag, the third site, is located 10 kilometers from Shigatse, Tibet's second largest city, and represents a wealthy farming village that is heavily affected by modernization. Despite economic differences, the three villages are geographically close and are part of the same Tibetan sub-ethnic cultural and linguistic zone.

Moving children out of the household

From the 1960s until the early 1980s, rural Tibet was organized into collectives. When that system was dismantled, the commune's land was divided equally, and the household resumed its role as the primary unit of landholding and farm production. This occurred in the context of an economic paradigm shift in China, from an emphasis on common property and wealth equality during the Cultural Revolution to an emphasis on individual initiative in Deng Xiaoping's market economy with socialist characteristics.

People in our fieldwork area responded by renewing the traditional corporate family system and reviving one of the most salient strategies for advancing a family's economic interests – the practice of fraternal polyandry. This type of marriage creates a kind of stem family that is the functional equivalent of primogeniture in the sense that, with only one wife per generation, only one set of offspring (heirs) was produced, thereby facilitating family land being passed along intact to the next generation. Also, fraternal polyandry concentrated male labor within the family, enabling it to pursue a broad range of economic activities. For example, one brother could herd the sheep in a mountain pasture, a second could manage the farm, and a third could concentrate on trading (Goldstein 1987). Consequently, after decollectivization, there was a major revival of fraternal polyandrous marriages throughout our study area (Goldstein et al. 2002, 2003; Jiao 2001).[3]

Filial piety is a deeply held value in Tibetan society: children are expected to express gratitude to their parents and provide care for them in old age. The question is, Who is best suited to care for aging parents? Because the Tibetan marriage system is patrilocal, a bride moves to her husband's home at marriage. A daughter who marries out is in no position to provide support for her own parents, and in fact, a married woman who diverts resources to her natal household breaches a protocol that can compromise her status with in-laws. One household in our research area split apart after the daughter-in-law was accused of secretly sending butter and other items to her parents. The ensuing arguments prompted the family to build a wall through the center of their house; the elderly parents now live on one side of the wall, while their son, daughter-in-law, and grandchildren live on the other side.

The majority of the elderly in our study live in a family with adult sons and a daughter-in-law. They are the ones ideally tasked with providing care for elderly household members. Yet despite the cultural norms of patrilocal marriage and coresidence with sons, we found a widespread sentiment among the elderly that their own daughters are the people best suited to be primary caretakers, as elegantly expressed in a proverb one man recited when discussing the topic of elderly care: "On the morning of birth, [one prefers to have] a son. On the morning of death, [one prefers to have] a daughter." He explained:

It means we are happy when a son is born, but when we die, we are happy to have a daughter present. Parents try to keep sons in the home, but the sons have to work outside, so they cannot provide nursing care. When parents become invalids or are dying, then daughters are important because they can care for the elderly. Parents are happier if a daughter is nearby during their dying days.

Typically, old folks phrase their preference in terms of receiving "food from the hands of [their] own daughter." For example, one woman said:

Our family decided to keep two sons at home and get a bride for them. That is the custom of the area. We sent our daughters out. Now I regret that decision. If I chose to keep a daughter and get her an in-marrying husband, then I would get food from the hands of my own daughter and life would be easier right now.

Although sending daughters out as brides to other families remains the norm, the widespread practice of fraternal polyandry leaves many women unable to marry. In fact, a salient feature of fraternal polyandry is that it produces an abundance of unmarried females – 27 percent of women aged 25 to 39 in our fieldwork villages. What to do with them becomes a major issue.

Given the preference for having one's own daughter as the primary caregiver in old age, an obvious answer for parents would be to keep one or more unmarried daughters at home. However, many feel strongly that this should not happen, because the overriding goal is to maintain the family and its land intact across generations by having brothers jointly take one wife. Tibetans consider allowing an unmarried daughter to remain in the household after her brother(s)' bride has arrived almost as detrimental as allowing two brothers to each have their own wife under the same roof – the two women are likely to have conflicts over authority and control. Moving unmarried daughters out of the family, therefore, is considered an important strategy for safeguarding the integrity of the family.

What happens with a woman who is unable to marry into another rural household? Traditionally, parents could ordain her as a nun or help her build a small house in the village where she would live separately. Unmarried daughters living separately could not only contribute labor to their natal households but also often provided caretaking services as well as places of refuge for parents when relationships within the main household broke down. As for nuns, the combined forces of a gender ideology that devalues female celibacy and the underfunding of convents (Havnevik 1989; Klein 1995) meant that they were often expected to help care for aging parents and contribute to the welfare of their natal households (Gutschow 2004). A Tibetan proverb encapsulates the value of a nun to her parents: "If you want to be a servant, make your son a monk. If you want a servant, make your daughter a nun" (Lopez 1998: 211).

Today, many women still leave their natal households through arranged marriage or are split into independent residences once their brothers bring home a bride. The monastic option, on the other hand, is limited. During the 1980s, Sogang's residents petitioned the government to re-establish a local nunnery that had been destroyed during China's Cultural Revolution. The government granted permission but – similar to Tibetan areas throughout China – imposed a strict limit on the number of residents. The eight designated slots for Sogang's nunnery were filled immediately. Since then, no other woman has been able to gain admission.

Meanwhile, new options have emerged for sending a daughter outside the natal household in ways that allow her to achieve financial independence. These include establishing a small business in a city or town, finding her a low-level salaried job, or investing in her education in the hope that she attains a higher-level salaried position. However, we found that the strategies vary by village. Close to half of the women born to households in Betsag and Norgyong currently reside in a city or town, indicating an urban-oriented strategy. In contrast, almost three out of four women who left Sogang did so through the traditional means of arranged marriage.

Norgyong's residents are taking advantage of new economic opportunities in Panam, a rapidly growing town situated a short walking distance from the village.

Many parents raise capital to establish a small business for a daughter, such as a small restaurant or shop. We asked one of them to describe the process of splitting out from her natal household. She received monetary assistance from two brothers and recalled:

I was the eldest child of my parents. I helped raise my siblings and manage the household. All of my brothers' kids call me "*ani*" [aunt]. We have good relations. I stayed in the home for 13 years with the nama [bride]. After she had more kids, her power increased. She started to complain that I was not doing well. Our relationship became bad. We argued. I said to her, "In this village, the custom is that sons stay in the household and daughters move out. So if you take good care of my parents, I will split out." The nama and I did not have open arguments, but our relationship caused unhappy feelings within the family.

The restaurant/shop strategy gives a woman not only the chance to achieve economic independence but also to marry a partner of her choice and establish a neolocal household. Importantly, town-dwelling women are not beholden to in-laws and therefore remain in a position to assist their elderly parents. One elderly man in Norgyong helped his daughter establish a business in Panam with this purpose in mind. He said:

I planned and took action to keep my daughter near. At the time, my wife was already old and really needed a caretaker. We kept our daughter at home to do that. Then she fell in love with an electrician. They married, so we opened a restaurant for her [in Panam]. Last year, her husband got a job offer in Shigatse. It's in a bigger city and a higher salary. He wanted my daughter to move with him to Shigatse. I said to him, "Please don't go. I really need my daughter. After I die, you can take her as far away as you want. But while I'm alive, please stay nearby." Shigatse is not far away, but I still wanted her in the town. Therefore, he didn't change jobs.

Although some parents in Betsag have tried to help a daughter open a shop in the village or Shigatse, their preferred strategy is to invest in her education so she can secure employment with a regular salary. Our survey data reveals a connection between education and mobility. Women who have moved out of a Betsag household have attained an average of 7.4 years of education – nearly 5 years more than women of similar age living in a village household. They even have an average of 3.3 more years of education than their male siblings who still reside within natal households.

These days, many parents in Betsag devalue the traditional option of sending a daughter as a bride to another household. One elderly woman explained:

Parents are more likely to send girls to school in the hope that they get a life through education. For one, you can't keep daughters in the home; you must send them out as brides, which is costly [the household must provide her with sets of clothing, grain, and gifts for her marital household]. Secondly, if you send a daughter as a bride to another household, then she must serve people of another family. Most parents don't want their daughters living under such circumstances. They try to make a better life for them. Education is the best way, so parents try to send their daughters to school.

When we asked another elderly person in Betsag whether parents hope to gain benefits from an educated daughter, she responded:

> Yes, that is one reason to send daughters to school. Elders here are getting money from children who get jobs. Some parents are getting money, while others are hoping to receive it in the future.

In summary, parents in the three villages are using different strategies to move daughters out of the household. Sogang, the relatively poor and remote village, exhibits the most traditional pattern: most daughters continue to move out through arranged marriages. Meanwhile, many parents in Norgyong are taking advantage of opportunities provided by the burgeoning town of Panam to establish commercial enterprises for daughters. The fact that they are not beholden to in-laws in a marital household leaves these women in a position to provide continuing assistance to their parents. Finally, parents in the wealthier village of Betsag are using education as an opportunity to provide daughters with the means to attain financial independence. Similar to daughters in Norgyong, many of these women live neolocally and are not constrained by the obligations of living in a husband's natal household with elderly in-laws and are thereby free to assist their own aging parents.

Support from externally resident daughters

The way a daughter is moved out of her household affects the potential social support she can provide for aging parents. Although there is much variation in the support that individuals can give, in general, we find that daughters who were sent as brides to other rural households have the least potential to assist elderly parents because they are beholden to their marital families, whereas daughters who are educated and have secured salaried employment can provide the most support.

Emotional support

Parents sometimes seek solace from an externally resident daughter after receiving bad treatment from household members. For example, Kyipa[4] complains that the nama of her household serves her black tea rather than butter tea and locks food away, both of which are serious affronts in this village. When the situation becomes intolerable – a frequent occurrence – Kyipa makes the short walk to her daughter's restaurant in Panam. Often, she stays all day and only returns in the evening, after eating dinner. Kyipa's daughter thereby mitigates the situation, but beyond food and emotional support, there is not much she can do to improve her mother's plight.

In contrast, Butri has two educated daughters who now live in cities. Often, Butri is treated disrespectfully at home by her son and daughter-in-law. When we asked how she felt about this, she responded, "Even if I can't get kindness from my son, I still have my daughters in Shigatse and Lhasa. I can receive much love from them." She then told us, "My son and daughter-in-law listen to my daughters because they are more powerful. My daughters come home to scold them about once a year." More important, Butri's daughters exert leverage by threatening to cut off financial aid to the household if their mother is not treated kindly.

Nursing care

Sending a daughter to another family as a bride practically guarantees the loss of her support as a caretaker. Externally resident daughters who can potentially provide assistance include those who live independently or in urban, neolocal households. For example, Dorje from Norgyong intentionally kept his only daughter nearby by opening a restaurant for her in Panam. He explained:

> If I get sick, I can stay with my daughter. At the end of life, when I'm about to die, I'll have them send me home, and my daughter can stay a short time to provide nursing care with my son. I always openly say to my daughter that because of the [bad] family relationships, I'll face difficulties at the end of life. My daughter says, "There is no need to worry. I'm nearby. When you are sick, I won't let you stay with others who argue with you. I will take care of you." . . . Everybody in my household has to farm. If they were busy, I'd be home alone. I don't want that. If I am with my daughter, she can stay home all day. It is a better choice.

The improved transportation system in Tibet reduces the importance of close proximity as a precondition for children to provide nursing care. When we asked Migmar who would care for him if he becomes incapacitated, he responded:

> It should mainly be done by my daughter-in-law. She is in a position to serve food and provide nursing care. But of course, if I'm incapacitated, then my family will ask my daughter to help. It would be difficult for my other daughters to provide care because they married out. But my youngest daughter is in Lhasa. She doesn't have a regular job. Her husband also doesn't have a secure job. For both of them, it is easy to ask for a 15-day leave, so she could come here to care for me.

We then asked whether it is better to receive care from one's own daughter or a daughter-in-law. He said, "Of course from your own daughter, if possible. There is more trust with her. We two love each other very much – that is the reason."

Financial assistance for health care

Externally resident children often provide money to help parents access health care. For example, Purbu, an elderly man in Betsag, depends more on his government-employed daughter than any other family member when he is ill. When we inquired why he depends so heavily on this particular child, he responded, "Tsamchö has an office job. The others are farmers, so even if they wanted to help, they couldn't." Purbu credits Tsamchö's assistance with saving his live during a recent illness. He explained:

> Last summer, I had a serious illness. My son told me to go to the county clinic. I said, "We don't have the money, so we'd have to borrow it. How would we repay it?" I refused to go. Tsamchö came later to see me, and we discussed the situation. She asked if I was getting better, and I replied that I wasn't. She asked, "Should we go to the hospital in Shigatse?" I replied, "That is not possible. I understand it is very costly, and the household doesn't have the money to cover the expense." She said, "We should go to the doctor immediately. I'll pay." She then took me to the hospital. . . . I stayed

for one month in the hospital. I worried about not having money for the hospital. My grandchildren are in school, which is very expensive. . . . If Tsamchö had not paid my hospital expenses, I may have died. Our household doesn't have much money for health care.

Although the healthcare and insurance systems in rural Tibet are rapidly improving, the cost of health care remains a serious concern for many elderly people who fear the financial burdens they may impose on their families due to illness. In general, we find that the elderly who have externally resident children with reliable salaries feel more confident that they can obtain healthcare services when needed.

Pocket money, pilgrimage, and non-kin social networks

Going on pilgrimage and visiting temples are important age-appropriate activities that have both spiritual and social benefits. Similarly, having one's own pocket money for buying sweets and other treats for themselves and their grandchildren is also an important component of a satisfying old age.

From a religious perspective, pilgrimage allows a person to positively influence future lives by cleaning negative karma accrued over a lifetime. During the pilgrimage, the elderly accomplish this goal through prayer, ritual actions like prostration and circumambulation, making offerings of butter and cash to deities, and giving alms to beggars.

The ability to go on a pilgrimage is contingent on access to cash. In the rural Tibetan corporate household, all income generated by family members should be handed over to the household head. Typically, when a man reaches his mid-60s, he relinquishes the household head position to a son, including control of the household's cash, after which he is expected to withdraw from economic activities and concentrate on endeavors such as prayers and pilgrimages to monasteries that prepare one for death and rebirth. Thus, most elderly people who have given up the role of household head depend on others to provide spending money. Some coresident sons who are the head of the household readily give cash to parents. Others are more reluctant to do so, necessitating that the elderly obtain money from sources outside the household, namely, their externally resident sons and daughters. In Betsag, the richer village, where educating "excess" daughters so that they can live and work in the city is common, our research revealed that more than half of the elderly who received funds from outside the household got money from a daughter.

Pilgrimage and temple visits are some of the most important social activities for the elderly in rural Tibet; they are typically undertaken with a group consisting of friends and neighbors. The elderly commented that socializing during pilgrimage gives them pleasure, makes them more relaxed, and helps them forget about anxieties at home. Between visiting temples, making offerings, and performing circumambulations, they gather in parks or restaurants to share food and drink. One man explained:

We do a large circumambulation [around the temple complex], then sit together and eat and drink, then go do another large circumambulation, then sit together again and eat and drink. If we have more chang [fermented barley beverage] or are having a good time, then we sit together longer after lunch and forget to do the third circumambulation in the afternoon.

Three circumambulations of a sacred site are considered the most auspicious performance of a pilgrimage ritual. Admitting that he sometimes neglects the third circumambulation therefore highlights the relative importance of the social dimension of pilgrimage.

To further highlight the social and emotional benefits of pilgrimage, consider the situation of those elderly whose lack of cash hinders their ability to participate in group activities. For example, one elderly woman told us:

> My whole life has been difficult. I've been poor, so I don't have a friendship group. If you have such a group, then you must gather together and buy food [while visiting a monastery]. I don't have money for the expenses. Women say, "You should join us when we go there," or "Come sit and join us." I say I will, but usually I don't.

Another impoverished woman stated:

> Even though I could hitch a ride and therefore not have to pay [for transportation], it would still be embarrassing because, after visiting the temples, the elderly like to have food in a restaurant. If I went together with others, I would have no money to pay for it. If I remained alone, without a partner, that would be shameful. So I tell my adoptive daughter, "Nowadays it is better for me to stay in the village, drink tea, and do circumambulations." It is better for me.

The importance of group pilgrimage activities should not be underestimated, given the consistent finding that there exists a positive relationship between engagement with non-kin social networks and well-being.[5] For example, Litwin (2001) finds that the morale of the elderly is highest among those who engage in social networks that extend beyond close kin, while Giles and colleagues (2005) find that discretionary relationships (those one can choose) have a more positive effect on morale in old age and longevity than relationships over which the individual exerts little choice (i.e., one's own children).

Although our data do not allow us to test for relationships between engagement with non-kin social networks and health or well-being, at the very least, we can observe that (1) pilgrimage is an important undertaking in the lives of these Buddhist villagers; (2) pilgrimage provides solace for those approaching the end of life, because it allows people to feel as if they are proactively preparing for future lives; (3) the elderly derive pleasure from social activities with non-kin peers during pilgrimage; (4) those who cannot go on pilgrimage due to financial constraints feel sad or embarrassed about their inability to participate in non-kin social networks; and (5) externally residing children, sons and daughters, provided the elderly a highly valued resource – cash – and daughters, especially those from Betsag who are educated and earn steady incomes, have become important facilitators of their elderly parents' pilgrimage activities.

Conclusions

As Bourdieu (2001) points out, children living outside of a household remain connected to parents through durable kinship relationships that normatively entail exchanges at various levels. In rural Tibet, the practice of fraternal polyandry produces a large cohort of women who never marry and have difficult lives eking out a livelihood mainly by working for others. In recent years, parents in the richest two villages have sought to improve the situation of their unmarried daughters by investing in their education or business opportunities and, at the same time, thereby enhancing their own old-age security and quality of life. In these villages, the nature of expectations and exchanges differed depending on the circumstances under which a daughter left the household. Simply put, the social capital vested in a daughter who was sent to another rural household as a bride pales in comparison with that of a daughter who was moved out through education or by establishing a small business. Daughters living in neolocal households who have financial independence can, and often do, provide considerable social support for their elderly parents. Tangible benefits range from caretaking during a time of illness to gifts of cash that allow the elderly to engage in pilgrimage activities and interact more intensively with non-kin networks. Contrary to many predictions associated with aging and modernization theory, the effect of rapid socioeconomic changes on the well-being of the elderly are not invariably negative. Rather than being silent victims of changes, the elderly in rural Tibet are taking proactive measures that actually increase the capacity for externally resident daughters to provide them with various forms of support. Parents are thereby creating novel forms of social capital that they can draw upon to improve the quality of their lives in culturally relevant ways and to help sustain them during a health crisis or a breakdown of relationships within the household.

An important shift is underway in the composition of social support networks in rural Tibet. Most elderly still reside with a son (or multiple sons) and a daughter-in-law. Nevertheless, they are increasing their reliance for support on those nonresident daughters who have attained a degree of independence. Such women have more power, influence, and financial means to positively impact the lives of their parents compared with women who were sent as brides to other rural households. Based on the common sentiment that it is best to receive care from one's own daughter, externally resident daughters' increasing capacity to provide support is seen by many elderly in rural Tibet as a positive social development.

Discussion questions

1. How has Tibetan family life adapted according to societal shifts that occurred in the transition between the Mao and Deng eras in Chinese governance?
2. Despite the prevalence of son preference and the tradition of coresidence with sons, why did the elderly parents express preference for their own daughters as their primary caretakers?
3. What are the traditional options for unmarried women to live separately from their natal households?
4. In what ways do externally resident children provide support for their parents?

Notes

1 In this chapter, *Tibet* refers exclusively to China's Tibet Autonomous Region.
2 Cowgill and Holmes's theoretical framework, arguing that the status and material well-being of the elderly decline with the advent of modernization, engendered a lively debate due to conflicting research findings. Since the 1970s, a body of research has been produced by gerontologists, historians, anthropologists, and other social scientists who both support and contradict this theory. For examples, see Aboderin (2004), Albert and Cattell (1994), Bengtson et al. (1995), Goldstein and Beall (1981), Rhoads (1984), and Sokolovsky (1997).

3 Not all households practice polyandry. Those that do not include (1) households with only one son, (2) households lacking male heirs so that a daughter and her husband coreside with her parents, (3) households where parents send sons out in marriage and keep a daughter home instead, and (4) households consisting of infertile couples or spinsters who live alone or with an adopted child.
4 All personal names used in this chapter are pseudonyms.
5 Research across the globe shows that strong social networks have a positive correlation with longevity (Giles et al. 2005; Hanson et al. 1989; Penninx et al. 1997; Sugisawa et al. 1994), health among the elderly (House et al. 1988; Seeman 1996), functional abilities (Michael et al. 1999), morale (Litwin 2001; Wilson et al. 1994), ability to resist the onset of dementia (Fratiglioni et al. 2000), and access to health services (Logan and Spitze 1994).

References

Aboderin, Isabella. 2004. "Modernisation and Ageing Theory Revisited: Current Explanations of Recent Developing World and Historical Western Shifts in Material Family Support for Older People." *Ageing & Society* 24: 29–50.

Albert, Steven Mark, and Maria G. Cattell. 1994. *Old Age in Global Perspective: Cross-Cultural and Cross-National Views*. New York: G.K. Hall & Co.

Bengtson, Vern L., Klaus Warner Schaie, and Linda Burton. eds. 1995. *Adult Intergenerational Relations: Effects of Societal Change*. New York: Springer.

Bourdieu, Pierre. 2001 [1983]. "The Forms of Capital." In *The Sociology of Economic Life*, eds. M. Granovetter and R. Swedberg, 96–111. Boulder, CO: Westview Press.

Coleman, James S. 1988. "Social Capital in the Creation of Human Capital." *The American Journal of Sociology* 94(suppl.): S95–S120.

Cowgill, Donald O. 1974. "Aging and Modernization: A Revision of the Theory." In *Late Life*, ed. J. F. Gubrium, 123–145. Springfield, IL: Thomas.

Cowgill, Donald O., and Lowell D. Holmes. 1972. *Aging and Modernization*. New York: Appleton-Century Crofts.

Fratiglioni, Laura, Hui-Xin Wang, Kjerstin Ericsson, Margaret Maytan, and Bengt Winblad. 2000. "Influence of Social Network on Occurrence of Dementia: A Community-Based Longitudinal Study." *The Lancet* 355: 1315–1319.

Giles, Lynn C, Gary F. V. Glonek, Mary A. Luszcz, and Gary R. Andrews. 2005. "Effect of Social Networks on 10 Year Survival in Very Old Australians: The Australian Longitudinal Study of Aging." *Journal of Epidemiological Community Health* 59: 574–579.

Goldstein, Melvyn C. 1987. "When Brothers Share a Wife." *Natural History* 96(3): 109–112.

Goldstein, Melvyn C., and Cynthia M. Beall. 1981. "Modernization and Aging in the Third and Fourth World: Views from the Rural Hinterland in Nepal." *Human Organization* 40(1): 48–55.

Goldstein, Melvyn C., Geoff Childs, and Puchung Wangdui. 2008. "'Going for Income': A Longitudinal Analysis of Change in Farming Tibet, 1997–98 to 2006–07." *Asian Survey* 48(3): 514–534.

Goldstein, Melvyn C., Geoff Childs, and Puchung Wangdui. 2010. "Beijing's 'People First' Development Initiative for the Tibet Autonomous Region's Rural Sector – A Case Study from the Shigatse Area." *The China Journal* 63: 58–75.

Goldstein, Melvyn C., Ben Jiao, Cynthia M. Beall, and Phuntsog Tsering. 2002. "Fertility and Family Planning in Rural Tibet." *The China Journal* 47: 19–39.

Goldstein, Melvyn C., Ben Jiao, Cynthia M. Beall, and Phuntsog Tsering. 2003. "Development and Change in Rural Tibet: Problems and Adaptations." *Asian Survey* 43(5): 758–779.

Gutschow, Kim. 2004. *Being a Buddhist Nun: The Struggle for Enlightenment in the Himalayas*. Cambridge, MA: Harvard University Press.

Hanson, Bertil S., Sven-Olof Isacsson, Lars Janzon, and Sven-Eric Lindell. 1989. "Social Network and Social Support Influence Mortality in Older Men." *American Journal of Epidemiology* 128: 370–380.

Havnevik, Hanna 1989. *Tibetan Buddhist Nuns*. Oslo: Norwegian University Press.

House, James S., Karl R. Landis, and Debra Umberson. 1988. "Social Relationships and Health." *Science* 241: 540–545.

Jiao, Ben. 2001. "Socio-Economic and Cultural Factors Underlying the Contemporary Revival of Fraternal Polyandry in Tibet." Unpublished Ph.D. diss., Department of Anthropology, Case Western Reserve University.

Klein, Anne C. 1995. *Meeting the Great Bliss Queen*. Boston: Beacon Press.

Litwin, Howard 2001. "Social Network Type and Morale in Old Age." *The Gerontologist* 41(4): 516–524.

Logan, John R., and Glenna Spitze. 1994. "Informal Support and the Use of Formal Services by Older Americans." *Journal of Gerontology: Social Sciences* 49: S25–S34.

Lopez, Donald S. Jr. 1998. *Prisoners of Shangri-La: Tibetan Buddhism and the West*. Chicago: University of Chicago Press.

Michael, Yvonne L., Graham A. Colditz, Eugenie Coakley, and Ichiro Kawachi. 1999. "Health Behaviors, Social Networks, and Healthy Aging: Cross-Sectional Evidence from the Nurse's Health Study." *Quality of Life Research* 8: 711–722.

Pemba, Lhamo. 1996. *Tibetan Proverbs*. Dharamsala: Library of Tibetan Works and Archives.

Penninx, Brenda W. J. H., Theo van Tilburg, Didi M. W. Kriegsman, Dorly J. H. Feed, A. Joan P. Boeke, Jacques Th. M. van Eijk. 1997. "Effects of Social Support and Personal Coping Resources on Mortality in Older Age: The Longitudinal Aging Study Amsterdam." *American Journal of Epidemiology* 146: 510–519.

Putnam, Robert D. 2000. *Bowling Alone: The Collapse and Revival of American Community*. New York: Simon and Schuster.

Rhoads, Ellen C. 1984. "Reevaluation of the Aging and Modernization Theory." *The Gerontologist* 24(3): 243–250.

Seeman, Teresa E. 1996. "Social Ties and Health: The Benefits of Social Integration." *Annals of Epidemiology* 6(5): 442–451.

Silverstein, Merril, Daphna Gans, and Frances M. Yang. 2006. "Intergenerational Support to Aging Parents: The Role of Norms and Needs." *Journal of Family Issues* 27(8): 1068–1084.

Sokolovsky, Jay. 1997. "Aging, Family, and Community Development in a Mexican Peasant Village." In *The Cultural Context of Aging*, ed. Jay Sokolovsky, 191–217. Westport, CT: Bergin and Garvey.

Sugisawa, Hidehiro, Jersey Liang, and Xian Liu. 1994. "Social Networks, Social Support and Mortality among Older People in Japan." *Journal of Gerontology* 49: 3–13.

Wilson, Jane G., Robert J. Calsyn, and Jacob L. Orlofsky. 1994. "Impact of Sibling Relationships on Social Support and Morale in the Elderly." *Journal of Gerontological Social Work* 22: 157–170.

Chapter 16

Little princesses and tiny barons

Gender, microfinance, and parental priorities in urban Ecuador

Megan Bond Hinrichsen

Original material prepared for the 7th edition.

Microfinance, the provision of small, often collateral-free loans and other financial services to people for whom traditional banking services are unattainable, has emerged as a popular and promising tool for poverty alleviation worldwide. The foundational assumption of microfinance is that one of the most significant obstacles individuals in poverty must overcome is the lack of access to funding for economically productive activities. Given the opportunity, individuals use their small loans to invest in income-generating projects that should ultimately improve their financial situation. Hossain (2002) defines *microfinance* by its stated goal to reduce poverty in poor countries but also emphasizes its ability to raise the status of women within their societies. Mark Malloch Brown, an administrator of the United Nations Development Programme (UNDP), suggests that "microfinance is much more than simply an income-generation tool. By directly empowering poor people, particularly women, it has become one of the key driving mechanisms towards meeting the Millennium Development Goals" (2005: 2). The promises of microfinance do not end at the goal of increasing economic resilience and decreasing material poverty. Microfinance is promoted as a powerful instrument for social and cultural change: empowering women, promoting gender equity, improving household well-being, supporting greater investment in children's health, nutrition, education, and more.

Many households in the world, in industrial and developing nations alike, exist in a precarious state where a single shock could cause significant economic stress. Microfinance is meant to provide opportunities for self-employment in a productive microentrepreneurial enterprise that can protect the poor from economic shocks and help them escape poverty by promoting increased economic stability and predictability in their lives. This chapter examines these issues in the context of the most socially and economically marginalized areas of Quito, Ecuador, where thousands of adults and children work as informal self-employed microentrepreneurs to make a day-to-day living for their often-insecure households. Many live in situations of precarity, in which one unexpected event could erase any progress they have made toward living a life free of poverty. In these circumstances, investigating potential methods of poverty alleviation is essential. Mindful of microfinance's global focus on women and the strong social assertions it involves, this chapter explores whether women's participation in microfinance holds the potential

DOI: 10.4324/9781003398349-18

to improve a household's quality of life more so than when men are the loan recipients. The chapter examines shifting gender roles and expectations, gendered patterns of work and income generation, the destinations of income from informal microenterprises, and the hopes and dreams expressed by men and women working to overcome poverty in the south of Quito. Are women more likely to put their earnings toward household necessities and their children's well-being? Do women's goals center on their children while men's goals are less focused on them? Who supports these children, affectionately called *imdas princesitas* (beautiful little princesses) and *baroncitos* (tiny barons)?

Gender and work in Quito

I conducted interviews with 100 women and 20 men working in the informal sector of Quito, Ecuador, mostly as ambulant street vendors. Altogether, they parent 339 children. The majority live well below the national poverty line and engage in their informal microenterprises as a necessity for their household's survival. Low levels of education and opportunity and intergenerational patterns of poverty and child labor preclude other options for generating an income that is substantial enough to offer sustainable support for a household. Cultural norms defining the appropriate roles for men and women in the household and society have many implications for these microentrepreneurs. Male authority as the household head is the ideal expressed by the majority of informants, but the material conditions of the lives of most households in this study require women to work to help support their household. Although women's roles must be considered in relation to locally produced ideals of gender and specific social and environmental conditions, men are also shaped by these factors. Men's lives are shaped by cultural norms of gender that affect their decisions and actions. Their perspectives are also important because they contribute to an understanding of women's work–family conflicts and household dynamics in general. Despite a cultural ideal of a male breadwinner, entire families must sometimes work together to maintain household survival (Safa 1995; Pitkin and Bedoya 1997). Therefore, women's work becomes more visible as men's work becomes less stable in Ecuador. While the entry into the work of an informal sector vendor has few barriers for men or women because it requires very little capital or experience, it is one of the very few options that the population of Quito's marginal neighborhoods has to generate necessary resources. When women engage in this work, however, it often carries with it a difficult and burdensome balance act. Their waking hours are characterized by continually making concessions between multiple spheres of activity that all have to be dealt with simultaneously.

In contrast to expectations for men, the demand for increased income coming from the work of women must be merged with cultural norms of gender that give women the primary, and sometimes sole, responsibility for domestic tasks. Tasks like caring for family members, procuring and preparing food, washing clothing and general cleaning, shopping for products to sell, and selling their products for long hours each day fall onto the shoulders of hardworking women. Despite their capability to generate an income, women continue to be identified as and to identify themselves with the roles and tasks associated with motherhood and the domestic life (Safa 1995). Most of the women interviewed consider themselves mothers first and foremost, combining their identity as an income-earner with their other responsibilities. Women gain symbolic power from their roles as wives and mothers through their representation of the values idealized as the foundation of Andean family and society (Bourque and Warren 1981). The enactment of their feminine roles gives women certain realms of power while also subordinating them to men by increasing their reliance on men's economic contributions (Rojas 2002). Therefore, women lose opportunities to generate their own resources for economic independence when they take on the responsibilities of a wife and mother (Parson 2013). The traditional role of women as the primary caretakers of children fosters their need to combine their domestic and labor market activities and has great implications for their choice of occupation. Being self-employed offers a seemingly flexible work arrangement that is compatible with their reproductive tasks. In theory, microentrepreneurship gives women a better chance to create a balance between their work and family activities.

For the past several decades, feminist scholars and others in the field of gender and development have focused on the contributions of unpaid domestic labor toward economic and human development. In her work in Nicaragua, Cupples (2005) describes the increasing burden of work for women, emphasizing that they are doing a "double shift of paid and domestic work" (314). Studies of this "double shift" or "double day" phenomenon have called attention to the undervalued and unpaid labor performed by women worldwide (Anker 1982; Mueller 1983; Doyal 1995; Radcliffe and Westwood 1996). Still, much of this research centers on women who are involved in wage work. Even in developing countries, focus on women's work has been on their paid labor, from the maquiladoras of Mexico to the rose plantations of Colombia (Cravey 1998; Friedemann-Sánchez 2012). The situation of my research participants who work in the informal sector contrasts with the typical idea of a shift. In the informal sector, shifts and separate work and family time do not exist. In informal work, boundaries between work/family and public/private are unusually blurred. Referring to a shift does not capture the fluidity of the women's multiple roles and obligations. Women working in the informal sector are acutely aware of the various responsibilities that are required of them. Microfinance, while adding some perceived legitimacy and support to women's microenterprises, does not resolve these work–family conflicts. A woman's need to work to both earn an income and repay microloans with high interest rates can intensify the burden of work, particularly when it is accompanied by the expectation to fulfill every other responsibility of being a wife and mother. Women, in this situation, often become their family's "providers of last resort" (Ehlers 2000: xxxv). If men cannot or will not contribute enough to the household budget to ensure that basic needs will be met, women are resigned to making ends meet in whatever way they can.

Male authority and the household head

Despite any rise in visible status that comes from the investments that women make in commercial opportunities, their contributions to family expenses, and their many essential responsibilities in the household, male members of the family tend to exercise the most concrete levels of authority. I do not intend to apply here the simplistic stereotypes about *machismo* and male authority or *marianismo* and female submissiveness. However, there is strong evidence that men in the context of this study are privileged in ways that women are not. From having higher levels of education, larger incomes from more lucrative jobs or more time to dedicate to work, greater opportunities for salaried employment such as construction work, and fewer burdens of housework and care work (none are single fathers), the men in this sample are given advantages that most women are simply not entitled to receive. Given their privilege and authority, men are expected to be the heads of household. The expectation is also that they are good providers for their family's needs. While the role of provider is undermined by local economic conditions and women contribute earnings that are crucial for household survival, men continue to have the title as a household head in a majority of households.

In other studies, the privileges of being the household head include, but are not limited to, controlling access to financial resources, asserting the utmost authority in family decision-making processes, being the primary disciplinarian of children, having the freedom and impunity to pursue extramarital affairs or nights out for drinking and socializing, or even an excuse to abuse their partners and children (McKee 1989; Miles 2000). In her study of adolescent girls in urban Ecuador, Ann Miles (2000) found that the concept of *machismo* oversimplifies the situation of men's privileges and greater authority but concedes that men do have privileges over women. Men exercise more authority in the home in Quito as well. A sole male household head leads more than half of the 120 households in my research population. A woman heads around 18 percent of households without a male presence in the household, whether it be by a single mother on her own or a single mother living with a female family member. Around 19 percent of the households report that the responsibility of the household head is a completely shared responsibility between partners or that those different household head responsibilities are delegated between the partners.

In a study of urban street vendors in Lima, Peru, Bunster and Chaney (1989) observe that 21 of the 22 women they interviewed expressed that men should be the household head. The one other informant said that the man and the woman should work together. Even in households where men were not present, women would defer to them for decisions even if the man did not contribute toward supporting the child. They believed that men should have the command simply because they are the man (Bunster and Chaney 1989). A majority of women in Quito maintain this viewpoint. One example is Patricia,[1] a 35-year-old mother of three who knits items she sells in Quito's markets. Patricia has a man she refers to as the "father of her children" who does not live with her but who she still declares as household head.

A few men, even when they are not earning, oppose their wives working outside the home. Dilbert is one example of this position. A fruit seller who suffered a severe injury, Dilbert did not want his wife to take over his income-earning activity when he got hurt, preferring that she remain in the home, caring for their four young sons and doing the necessary domestic tasks. Elsewhere in Ecuador, research has documented that men are sometimes apprehensive about their wives entering the workforce, yet once the women start generating an income, their economic contribution to their households is appreciated and respected. An ideal pattern of relationships between women and men has been expressed by Pribilsky's (2004) research in Ecuador: women and children are meant to obey their husbands and fathers and treat them with *respeto* (respect), allowing them to *mandar* (rule) their household. In turn, women should show their respect to their husbands by raising their children. Only a few women in the study, but many of the men, expressed their negative sentiments about women having to work to support their households. As Pribilsky (2004) states, a man may *mandar* so long as he is supporting his family in the proper way. Unlike Dilbert, most men who are unable to work or meet all household expenses with their income see value in the economic contributions of women and make practical decisions to place family survival over a need to fulfill the provider role or assert male dominance. No matter how rigid they may seem, cultural norms are flexible. They can and do change over time in response to changes in people's lives. In some households, the material conditions can effect a change in the perception of men's and women's roles and can transform individual attitudes away from accepted societal norms.

Men and women working together and bringing in similar flows of cash redefine gender roles in their own households based on their own particular set of circumstances. There are similarities among the households with female heads living with male partners and households that report being dual-headed. More than half of the individuals in these dual-headed households are involved in the same occupation, as ambulant vendors. These households also have lower-than-average household incomes. Despite their lower incomes, these households tend toward more equality in decision-making and authority because male partners or other members contributing to household resources are not involved in higher-status or significantly more profitable work. As a result, the households have a more egalitarian distribution of power and more flexible gender roles.

While Latin American norms favor the ideals of a male breadwinner (*sostén de la familia*), the situations of individual families and households have rendered a less-rigid expectation for the role of the man as the sole provider in most cases. Safa (1995) challenges what she terms the "myth of the male breadwinner," the assumption that men are "the principal economic providers for the household and that women are at best supplementary wage earners" (169). In Safa's research in the Caribbean, shifts in the job market from agriculture to export-led industry increased demand for women in low-skill and low-paid factory work. As women's employment became more attractive, men's employment diminished. This transformation has resulted in a rising trend of women in the role of the primary household income-generator. This shift can be seen, to a much lesser extent, in Quito. Regardless of whether they are in industrial jobs, such as the rose export industry (Korovkin 2003), or informal microenterprises, Ecuadorian women of lower socioeconomic status are often active participants in the financial management of the home. The case of Maria and her family illustrates some of these characteristics.

Maria

Maria, 48, is a microentrepreneur who is actively engaged in the hard work of generating an income and supporting all members of her household. She is the mother of six children, ranging in age from her youngest son, Dylan, age 5, to her eldest daughter, Norma, 24. Norma is the single mother of a young son, Carlos, 7, who also lives with them. Maria, her husband, and the children are ambulant vendors selling vegetables in the Mayorista market, the main wholesale market in Quito. Formal vendors sell wholesale products in rented stalls directly from trucks transporting goods from where they are produced or imported. Maria's family, and dozens of other informal vendors like them, purchases goods from the formal vendors to resell in the same market in smaller quantities, with negligible profit margins. If she needs to shop for vegetables to sell, she and her husband must get up before dawn and purchase her stock at the Mayorista night market, when the best prices and selection are offered at around three in the morning. This occurs on a regular basis, as most bulk purchases are prohibitively expensive and proper storage for avoiding spoilage is difficult in a home without a refrigerator.

Overall, nearly half of the women interviewed are in business jointly with their husbands or partners. They share work responsibilities and decision-making power but must contend with other responsibilities that their husbands do not share. Maria and her husband do the same work drawing from household resources but operate separately. Maria takes care of her children as she works and has other obligations to fulfill during her day. Beyond working for 12 hours almost every day, Maria also has to ensure that she can acquire enough stock to sell the next day while still purchasing food for the family. Upon returning home, she must prepare a meal for the household. She works selling vegetables daily from 6:00 a.m. to 6:00 p.m. for 13 consecutive days. On the 14th day of her work cycle, Maria takes the entire day to wash the laundry of her nine-person household by hand. Her husband is able to work more consistently and without the distraction of child-rearing or domestic tasks and earns about double Maria's daily income.

Despite the long hours of work, the money taken in by Maria's family does not cover all their basic necessities. Although Maria's husband tends to bring in more money, their average weekly earnings are only approximately 60 dollars, which is far below a living wage in Quito. Maria's children and grandchild also work "out of necessity" to generate as much income from vegetable sales as possible. Maria also began working at a young age, saying:

> My parents taught me to work. I could only study until the second grade because my parents could not help me economically. I am the mother of six children, and I struggle [luchar] daily with my husband to dress them, provide them with shoes, feed them, and give them what they need.

She feels shame for being unable to give her children basic essentials, saying, "It's what we, as parents, should be capable of providing for them." Although they work cooperatively and are united by their goals to support their family, Maria refers to her husband as the head of their household. He is still able to earn a greater proportion of their income while doing the same productive work without the additional responsibilities expected of Maria. Maria mentions her constant feelings of exhaustion, stress, discomfort, and soreness. She struggles with fatigue and stomach problems due to hunger. While Maria, like many women, struggles with the burdens of work, life, and poverty, she does not often complain. She gives the impression that she is resigned to this burden and must carry on and move forward (seguir adelante), accepting that her extra work and exhaustion are just part of earning the money needed to survive.

Questioning male and female agendas

Research in developing countries across the world has shown that women are more likely to use their earnings to support their children's needs, particularly nutrition and education (Dwyer and Bruce 1988; Khandker 2003). Ehlers (2000) finds that men in Guatemala drink, gamble, give away, and spend money on themselves in the conspicuous consumption of televisions, motorcycles, and more. Regardless of bad habits that may consume portions of their incomes, male microentrepreneurs in this Guatemalan example normally reinvest their profits in their businesses, while most women use what money is left at the end of the day to purchase food for the household. Women rarely have money to spend on themselves or to better capitalize their small businesses (Ehlers 2000). Business profits are used to fuel household needs directly instead of being used as an investment toward growth. Ehlers (2000) goes on to write that the man is able to expand his business as time progresses. Women like Maria need to use their profits for much more than reinvestment and experience little to no change in their businesses in the future. Men's activities, therefore, are sustained by the small, but consistent, efforts of their wives that provide for the expenses that men do not or cannot meet. Women are less likely to take full advantage of the opportunities in the marketplace by reinvesting their earnings into the expansion on their microenterprise. "[Men] are entrepreneurial, their wives are definitely not," claims Ehlers (2000: xxxvii). This statement does not imply that women do not have the talent, interest, or capacity to be entrepreneurial, but rather that they do not have time, capital, or freedom from other obligations substantial enough to be more dedicated to their small businesses. This section explores further the different consumption and investment agendas in urban households involved in microenterprises in Quito. Is there a difference between men and women's investments? Do men focus more on themselves and their businesses rather than investing their resources in products and services that would likely benefit the household as a whole?

Among the 120 informants that participated in the research discussed here, there were several answers given to the open-ended question regarding the primary investment of profits. Overall responses from the most common to the least common are food, housing, children's educations, business reinvestment, household necessities, children's needs, paying down debt, healthcare expenses, investing in a partner's business, clothing, household utilities, and savings. These results are based on the individual's self-described precedence given to certain needs. It does not reflect where they actually spend their profits on a daily, or even a regular, basis. A *Pilsener* beer purchased on the way home by a man or ice cream purchased by a woman from a neighboring vendor might represent actual objects acquired on some days but do not necessarily depict what the informant thinks is the most important investment they typically make with their daily revenue. In fact, the primary destinations of earnings are few and are remarkably alike for both men and women. Money goes toward housing, food, educational expenses for children, and "household necessities" (*gastos del hogar*).

These responses reveal the precarious nature of informal sector self-employment. Profits are put toward the things necessary for survival and those that might allow the household members to *seguir adelante* (move ahead) in the future. They are very basic investments, but essential for life. Conventional thinking in the development world, supported by decades of research in various settings, indicates that mothers exhibit a higher level of concern for their children than their fathers. However, according to the reports of the informants in this study, it is the women who allude to the importance of reinvesting in their business most often. Although these responses do not definitely show how the informants and their household members actually spent their earnings, they reflect the perceptions, ideas, and priorities of the informant. Their point of view regarding their contributions to their household, their goals, and their struggles are central to this research and the everyday lives of the informants. Their answers also put the things that the informant sees as important on display.

Women in this study tend to share decision-making power when it comes to household purchases, but women who are working outside of the home in small microenterprises have greater levels of participation in other household decisions. Three out of four men who report sharing responsibility for managing the profits of their own enterprises with their female partners have partners who work outside the home. Men with partners who do not work outside the home are less likely to include their partners in financial decisions beyond the act of making important purchases. Working outside the home has allowed the "challenges women are posing to the habitus of the marital contract [including] having physical mobility, living free of domestic violence, and managing their own money" (Friedemann-Sánchez 2012: 39). Women in Latin America are socialized to put their maternal feelings above their own interests and needs, and to put the rest of the family's needs above all else (Hondagneu-Sotelo and Avila 1997). Observing the reinvestment priorities expressed by the informants reveals the economic self-interest, or lack thereof, among microentrepreneurs. Mayra's case illustrates some of these characteristics.

Mayra

Mayra, 39, works selling vegetables as an ambulant vendor, an occupation she began to meet her family's needs. She held a minimum-wage formal job before she had her first child 16 years ago. She concedes that she does not have an adequate income from her current work selling vegetables, but she believes this kind of work is all that she could manage while taking care of her children. She explains her decision to enter the informal sector, saying, "I could no longer work for someone else and went on my own." Mayra and many other women mention the value of flexibility in their vending activities. Mayra states that not being tied to a strict schedule or under the eye of a supervisor during a workday holds some advantages, but she did not choose to become a vendor for any reasons beyond needing to generate an income while balancing her child-rearing and domestic obligations. Mayra continues to care for her youngest child, 4-year-old Diana, as she works. In addition to the flexibility needed to care for their children, research participants are aware that their lack of education, training, and skills precludes other employment options. Women like Mayra operate their microenterprises not only out of economic necessity but also as a way to diversify their household's income and complement their husband's or partner's earnings.

Mayra's husband earns his living driving a taxi as a member of a cooperative. Both of their occupations share the kind of uncertainty and instability that makes envisioning and carrying out plans difficult. Their income is highly variable, and financially managing their household causes them a great deal of stress. Mayra gives the vast majority of her earnings to her husband to manage. Her microloan, officially intended for her to purchase vegetables to sell, was mostly used to pay down the debt her husband incurred when he purchased his vehicle. Mayra's husband is the head of the household and controls most of their financial decisions. On the surface, Mayra's act of relinquishing the majority of her microloan and profits to her husband suggests that she lacks decision-making power in her household. Yet Mayra attests that the decision to give her husband additional control over their finances was her own. Mayra is not forced to hand over her income because she is less empowered than other women; she chooses to invest her profits in his vehicle because she and her husband work together to maintain their household and care for their children. She began her microenterprise 16 years ago so that she could care for her child while generating an income. Using the fact that Mayra gives her income to her husband alone in order to determine household power dynamics obscures the collective action she and her husband are taking to make their living. Mayra does not present herself as an individual but as a member of a united social and family unit whose members support one another in their different roles and obligations.

Male and female agendas and aspirations: are they so different?

According to the narrative of microfinance, and often substantiated by research, children are supposedly the prime beneficiaries of the benefits of microloans given to women (Armendáriz and Morduch 2005; Duflo and Banerjee 2011). However, according to the 120 households in this study, men are just as likely as women to speak about providing for their children's needs. Men and women both demonstrate a commitment to their children in material terms. Daniela is the "*motor de vida*" for her father, Andres. Literally, *motor de vida* means the "engine of life," which expresses that Daniela is the motivation for all that Andres does in his work and life. Many men show great devotion to their *baroncitos* and *ibicOts princesitas*. The majority of the men involved in this research showed dedication and enthusiasm for their children of both sexes, which is a significant departure from the *macho* expectation.

Men and women alike focus on their children when discussing their future aspirations. Their stated goals and dreams reveal their personalities, priorities, and motivations. The most common goal, professed in the exact same words by three out of four informants, is to improve their family's "quality of life." Speaking even more broadly, every informant expressed a dream that involved the improvement of the quality of life or well-being (*bienestar*) for themselves or their families. Many focus on providing an education for their children, a future-oriented goal centered on improving the lives of their children. Many want to *ieguir adelante* (move forward), a goal that encompasses many possibilities toward attaining a better standard of living. Seven informants specifically dream of returning to school themselves in order to complete their own primary or secondary school educations. One woman reports that she wants to attain peace, a life free from constant worry. Another woman discusses her desire for "personal development." When asked what she meant by this goal, she reports that she wants to improve herself in any way possible, from getting an education to growing her business, being a better wife and mother, and more.

Some informants want not only to improve the quality of life for their immediate families and young children but also to provide for their children as they continue to grow older. Some work toward their goal of supporting their own parents in old age. Others wish to spend more time with their children, explaining that their lives are currently too busy to enjoy the time that they have with their children while they are still young. Working to realize each of these dreams would contribute to the greater sense of security and stability that every person interviewed hopes to achieve.

More than half reveal their goal to expand their business. Some discuss wanting their business to become more formalized, to have more customers, to expand their range of products, to sell their products on a national level, and to own their own formal business location, such as a factory, store, restaurant, or kiosk. One woman indicates that she wants to create a network of sellers and "support other women" in their businesses. One man wants to "beat the competition," and another woman has the goal of hiring others for her business. Over a third of the informants specifically mention that they would like to increase their incomes. All these goals, from increasing income to expanding microenterprises, support the most frequently stated dream of improving their family's quality of life. Another prevalent dream is to see their children become professionals. This goal entails their children having an education and being able to pursue a job in the formal labor market with a regular salary. These are the types of jobs that the informants continually indicate as the jobs that are beyond their reach. "I want them to do something easy," says one woman. Asked what kind of jobs she categorizes as "easy," she described office work with set hours and a steady paycheck. The goal to have professional children is pervasive, so much so that many informants even use the same words to describe this dream:

> I want my children to be professionals so that in the future they will be valuable to society. It is because I could not continue with my education because of my parent's living situation at the time.
>
> – Hector, 42, furniture maker

> I want them to study and be professional so they do not need to suffer.
>
> – Cecilia, 28, sells fruit and washes laundry

> I want my children to be professional and not be like me.
>
> – Maria de Jesus, 38, sells fruit

Another prominent dream is to own a house. From using their microloans to invest in their house to saving piles of bricks and tiles for future construction, having one's own house is a central goal that many Ecuadorians work toward. Among those who presently own a home, some would like to continue making improvements. Despite the pronounced importance of material conditions in the lives of the informants, few dreams center on acquiring more possessions. One would like to own her own land, and four dream of owning a car. Five women wish to be more comfortable. They explain "comfort" as wanting for less and having what they need in addition to physical comforts.

Some aspirations extend beyond these important tangible goals of better and more comfortable material conditions, strengthening their businesses, and providing opportunities for their children, toward something less tangible. For example, four women dream of being an inspiration to others. One woman adds greater specificity to her dream, saying that she wants to "show that hard work can improve your life." Another woman would like to "help her children improve Ecuador." From big goals to small, everyday considerations, dreams are the *motor de vida* (motivation) for many informants to continue working hard, sacrificing, and suffering. Moore (2011) describes this anticipation for a different future as the "alterity of the future," where hopes and dreams are able to take shape (21). Having dreams for the future for themselves, and mostly for their children, is grounded in the conditions of the present. The way that the informants envision their future goals and their attempts to bring them to fruition based on their current abilities reflect their present and their daily struggles. Although the conflicts and challenges of life in the present loom large and can dominate their thoughts, their dreams also appear and make their lives more purposeful and meaningful. Instead of a daily battle, their dreams provide motivation to continually go out and try to make a living. Jessica, a 20-year-old cosmetics seller, articulated this best:

> To achieve my goals, I should work steadily with discipline, commitment, and love. Only then will I be able to fulfill my dream of strengthening my business and giving my children a good education and improving the quality of life for all my family.

Nancy, a 52-year-old with multiple small ventures, and one of the oldest of the inform-ants, still exhibits her hopes and dreams, saying:

> I know to achieve my expected results, I must work with perseverance and dedication so I can work toward fulfilling my dream to own a well-known shop that generates higher returns so that I can give my family a better quality of life and well-being.

Everyday hardships become imbued with meaning and a greater purpose when there are goals and dreams worth fighting for.

Conclusion

In observing and speaking with the informants about their lives, responsibilities, and hopes and dreams, it becomes clear that most parents have goals and priorities that center on their children and families. In this Ecuadorian context, women's participa-tion in microfinance does not have the clear potential to elevate family quality of life or well-being more so than when a loan is given to a man. Women, however, do have greater responsibilities than men when it comes to caring for their families. Therefore, even though men and women may invest their profits toward the same resources and have similar goals in life, women have a much greater influence on the well-being of their families. They do most of the care work, cooking, cleaning, and are often responsible for earning and managing an income. They do the shopping and carry out most necessary tasks. Women are almost always the ones who use household resources to benefit their families directly. Yet men and women both express similar goals for their microenter-prises and households, and both genders report investing their resources on products and services that would likely benefit the household.

In the south of Quito, men who take on the role of partner and father also have an important role in their families. This role is partially their portrayal of the culturally accepted role of the male provider, but they do not express the "callous," self-centered, or idealized hypermasculine patterns of the stereotype of *machismo* in their priorities, goals, or dreams (Karnani 2007: 36). The most common goal for women is to improve their families' quality of life. The most common goal for men is also to improve their families' quality of life, but men were more likely to phrase their goal as to "give [their] family a better quality of life." This subtle difference in phrasing suggests men's more powerful position relative to women and their ideal role of provider with the ability to "give" this better life to household members but does not diminish the expression of the desire to support his family. Evidence from interviews and observation shows that men and women are powerfully united in their investment priorities: microloans are mostly invested in the microenterprises that support their households, and their profits go to fulfill basic necessities and promote everyday survival.

Men are clearly privileged in ways that women are not. They are afforded opportuni-ties and options that women do not have. Women are more likely to be excluded and left on the margins when it comes to issues related to finances, access to loans, time to dedicate to income-generating work, and other components of establishing and running a successful, sustainable microenterprise. Women are more likely to be constrained by social norms and other structural barriers as well, which partially justifies a microfinance institution's focus on lending to women. While women are seen as the natural clients of microfinance, the concept of men receiving microloans comes entangled with negative associations. The acceptance of the assumption that men will spend their microloans and microenterprise profits on alcohol, gambling, cigarettes, or other personal purchases that are often portrayed as selfish is unnecessarily harmful and discriminatory. Even worse, some men are cast as aggressors, abusers, and child abandoners who are not seen as needing or being worthy of microfinance. Using the words and experiences of men and women in Quito's informal sector, this chapter demonstrated that fathers and mothers both matter in the lives of their children and in the maintenance of households. Their goals, investments, and dreams are just as likely to center on their children as the goals, investments, and dreams of the women. Most men simply do not fall into the stereotype of the *machista* who behaves badly.

Presumptions that a man will concentrate more on himself and his own needs rather than on those of his family are not helpful in efforts to attain a central goal of socially oriented microfinance institutions, that is, to mitigate the effects of poverty. Although men have advantages in Ecuadorian society, the men in this study are still of lower socio-economic status. The Grameen Bank, one of the world's most influential microfinance institutions, declares that "[conventional banks focus on men, Grameen gives high priority to women" (2011 qtd. in Cao 2012: 985). This statement does not recognize that men in the context of this study also live on the margins of society, struggle to maintain a livelihood for their families, and have the same desire to improve the lives and well-being of their children that is unjustly defined as something only women possess. The biases of dominant gender ideologies place undue limits on what both men and women can or want to attain for their families and, especially, for their children's lives and futures.

Discussion questions

1. What sort of privileges do men in the study enjoy that women do not?
2. How do traditional gender roles and the division/distribution of labor change in response to the economic needs of the household?
3. Why, according to the study, are men more likely than women to reinvest their earnings into their microenterprise?
4. How do men's and women's goals for their microenterprises differ? How are they similar?

Note

1 All names are pseudonyms.

References

Anker, Richard. 1982. "Demographic Change and the Role of Women: A Research Programme in Developing Countries." In *Women's Roles and Population Trends in the Third World*, eds. Richard Anker, Mayra Buvinić, and Nadia H. Youssef, 29–54. London: Croom Helm.

Armendáriz de Aghion, Beatriz, and Johnathan Morduch. 2005. *The Economics of Microfinance*. Cambridge, MA: The MIT Press.

Bourque, Susan C., and Kay B. Warren. 1981. *Women of the Andes: Patriarchy and Social Change in Two Peruvian Towns*. Ann Arbor: University of Michigan Press.

Brown, Mark Malloch. 2005. "Why a Year?" In *International Year of Microcredit 2005: Building Inclusive Financial Sectors to Achieve the Millennium Development Goals*. New York: United Nations.

Bunster, Ximena, and Elsa M. Chaney. 1989. *Sellers and Servants: Working Women in Lima, Peru.* Granby, MA: Bergin and Garvey Publishers, Inc.

Cao, Lan. 2012. "Rethinking Microfinance." *University of Pennsylvania Journal of International Law* 33(4): 971–996.

Cravey, Altha J. 1998. *Women and Work in Mexico's Maquiladoras.* Lanham, MD: Rowman and Littlefield.

Cupples, Julie. 2005. "Love and Money in an Age of Neoliberalism: Gender, Work and Single Motherhood in Post-Revolutionary Nicaragua." *Environment and Planning* 37(2): 305–322.

Doyal, Lesley. 1995. *What Makes Women Sick: Gender and the Political Economy of Health.* New Brunswick, NJ: Rutgers University Press.

Duflo, Esther, and Abhijit Banerjee. 2011. *Poor Economics: A Radical Rethinking of the Way to Fight Global Poverty.* Philadelphia: Public Affairs.

Dwyer, Daisy, and Judith Bruce, eds. 1988. *A Home Divided: Women and Income in the Third World.* Palo Alto, CA: Stanford University Press.

Ehlers, Tracy. 2000. *Silent Looms: Women and Production in a Guatemalan Town.* Austin: University of Texas Press.

Friedemann-Sánchez, Greta. 2012. "Paid Agro-Industrial Work and Unpaid Caregiving: The Gendered Dialectics between Structure and Agency in Colombia." *Anthropology of Work Review* 23(2): 34–46.

Hondagneu-Sotelo, Pierrette, and Ernestine Avila. 1997. "I'm Here But I'm There: The Meanings of Latina Transnational Motherhood." *Gender and Society* 11(5): 548–571.

Hossain, Farhad. 2002. "Small Loans, Big Claims." *Foreign Policy* 2: 79–81.

Karnani, Aneel. 2007. "Microfinance Misses Its Mark." In *Stanford Social Innovation Review*, Summer.

Khandker, Shahidur. 2003. *Microfinance and Poverty: Evidence Using Panel Data from Bangladesh.* Washington, DC: World Bank.

Korovkin, Tanya. 2003. "Cut-Flower Exports, Female Labor, and Community Participation in Highland Ecuador." *Latin American Perspectives* 30(4): 18–42.

McKee, Katherin. 1989. "Microlevel Strategies for Supporting Livelihoods, Employment, and Income Generation of Poor Women in the Third World: The Challenge of Significance." *World Development* 17: 993–1006.

Miles, Ann. 2000. "Poor Adolescent Girls and Social Transformation in Cuenca, Ecuador." *Ethos* 28(1): 54–74.

Moore, Henrietta L. 2011. *Still Life: Hopes, Desires, and Satisfactions.* Cambridge: Polity Press.

Mueller, Eva. 1983. "Measuring Women's Poverty in Developing Countries." In *Women and Poverty in the Third World*, eds. Mayra Buvinić, Margaret A. Lycette, and William Paul McGreevey, 272–285. Baltimore: The Johns Hopkins University Press.

Parson, Nia C. 2013. *Traumatic States: Gendered Violence, Suffering, and Care in Chile.* Nashville: Vanderbilt University Press.

Pitkin, Kathryn, and Ritha Bedoya. 1997. "Women's Multiple Roles in Economic Crisis: Constraints and Adaptation." *Latin American Perspectives* 24(4): 34–49.

Pribilsky, Jason. 2004. "'Aprendemos a Convivir': Conjugal Relations, Co-Parenting, and Family Life among Ecuadorian Transnational Migrants in New York and the Ecuadorian Andes." *Global Networks* 4(3): 313–334.

Radcliffe, Sarah A., and Sallie Westwood. 1996. *Remaking the Nation: Identity and Politics in Latin America.* London: Routledge.

Rojas, Ximena. 2002. "Las mujeres chilenas, pilares de la familia." In *Más derechos, económicos, sociales y culturales: menos desigualdades de las mujeres en Chile.* Santiago de Chile: Corporación de Desarrollo de la Mujer La Morada.

Safa, Helen I. 1995. *The Myth of the Male Breadwinner: Women and Industrialization in the Caribbean.* Boulder, CO: Westview Press.

Chapter 17

Surrogate motherhood

Rethinking biological models, kinship, and family

Heléna Ragoné

Original to a previous edition of this text. Courtesy of Heléna Ragoné.

In the wake of publicity created by the Baby M case,[1] it seems unlikely that anyone in the United States could have remained unfamiliar with surrogate motherhood or could have failed to form an opinion. The Baby M case raised, and ultimately left unanswered, many questions about what constitutes motherhood, fatherhood, family, reproduction, and kinship. When I began my field research in 1987, surrogate mother programs and directors had already become the subject of considerable media attention, a great deal of it sensationalized and negative in character. Much of what has been written about surrogate motherhood, has, however, been largely speculative or polemic in nature. Opinions have ranged from the view that surrogate motherhood is symptomatic of the dissolution of the American family[2] and the sanctity of motherhood to charges that it reduces or assigns women to a breeder class structurally akin to prostitution (Dworkin 1978), or that it constitutes a form of commercial baby-selling (Annas 1988; Neuhaus 1988).

Data for this chapter derive from nine years of ongoing ethnographic research. Twenty-eight formal interviews with traditional surrogates and 26 with gestational surrogates were conducted, as well as 26 interviews with individual members of couples (i.e., individuals who had enlisted the services of traditional as well as gestational surrogates) and 5 interviews with ovum donors. Aside from these formal interviews, I also engaged in countless conversations with surrogates, observing them as they interacted with their families, testified before legislative committees, worked in surrogate programs, and socialized at program gatherings with directors and others. The opportunity to observe the daily workings of the surrogate mother programs provided me with invaluable data on the day-to-day operations of such programs. I attended the staff meetings of one such program on a regular basis and observed the consultations in which prospective couples and surrogates were interviewed singly by such members of the staff as the director, a psychologist, a medical coordinator, or the administrative coordinator.

In addition to these formal interviews, I conducted thousands of hours of participant observation and was able to observe numerous consultations between program staff, intending couples, and prospective surrogate mothers. I have attempted, whenever possible, to select individuals from the various phases of the traditional and gestational surrogacy process: those individuals who have not yet been matched, those who are newly

DOI: 10.4324/9781003398349-19

matched and are attempting "to get pregnant," those who have confirmed pregnancies, and those who have recently given birth, as well as those for whom several years have elapsed since the birth of their child. My decision to interview individuals in all stages of the process has been motivated by my wish to assess what, if any, shifts individuals might experience as they go through the process.

Historically, there have been three profound shifts in the Western conceptualization of the categories of conception, reproduction, and parenthood. The first occurred in response to the separation of intercourse from reproduction through birth control methods (Snowden et al. 1983), a precedent that may have paved the way for surrogate motherhood in the 1980s (Andrews 1984: xiii). A second shift occurred in response to the emergence of assisted reproductive technologies (ARTs) and to the subsequent fragmentation of the unity of reproduction, when it became possible for pregnancy to occur without necessarily having been "preceded by sexual intercourse" (Snowden et al. 1983: 5). The third shift occurred in response to further advances in reproductive medicine, which called into question the "organic unity of fetus and mother" (Martin 1987: 20). It was not, however, until the emergence of reproductive medicine that the fragmentation of motherhood became a reality; with that historical change, what was once the "single figure of the mother is dispersed among several potential figures, as the functions of maternal procreation – aspects of her physical parenthood – become dispersed" (Strathern 1991: 32).

Traditional surrogacy

There are two types of surrogate mother programs: "open" programs, in which surrogate and couple select one another and interact throughout the insemination and the pregnancy, and "closed" programs, in which couples select their surrogates from biographical and medical information and a photograph of the surrogate is provided to them by programs. After the child is born in a "closed" program, the couple and surrogate meet only to finalize the stepparent adoption. Due to advances in reproductive medicine and to consumer demand, there are now also two types of surrogacy: traditional surrogacy, in which the surrogate contributes an ovum to the creation of the child, and gestational or in vitro fertilization (IVF) surrogacy, in which the surrogate gestates the couple's embryos.

Studies of the surrogate population tend to focus, at times exclusively, on surrogates' stated motivations for becoming surrogate mothers (Parker 1983). Their stated reasons include the desire to help an infertile couple start a family, financial remuneration, and a love of pregnancy (Parker 1983: 140). Soon after I began my own research, I observed a remarkable degree of consistency or uniformity in surrogates' responses to questions about their initial motivations for becoming surrogates. It was as if they had all been given a script in which they espoused many of the motivations earlier catalogued by Parker: motivations that also, as I will show, reflect culturally accepted ideas about reproduction, motherhood, and family.

I also began to uncover several areas of conflict between professed motivations and actual experiences, discovering, for example, that although surrogates claim to experience "easy pregnancies" and "problem-free labor," it was not unusual for surrogates to have experienced miscarriages, ectopic pregnancies, and related difficulties. For example, Jeannie, age 36, divorced with one child, described the ectopic pregnancy she experienced while she was a traditional surrogate in this manner: "I almost bled to death: I literally almost died for my couple." Nevertheless, she was again inseminated a second time for the same couple. As this and other cases demonstrate, even when their experiences are at odds with their stated motivations, surrogates tend not to acknowledge inconsistencies between their initially stated motivations and their subsequent experiences. This reformulation of motivations can be seen in the following instance. Fran, age 27, divorced with one child, described the difficulty of her delivery in this way:

> I had a rough delivery, a C-section, and my lung collapsed because I had the flu, but it was worth every minute of it. If I were to die from childbirth, that's the best way to die. You died for a cause, a good one.

As both these examples illustrate, some surrogates readily embrace the idea of meaningful suffering, heroism, or sacrifice, and although their stated motivations are of some interest, they do not adequately account for the range of shifting motivations uncovered in my research.

One of the motivations most frequently assumed to be primary by the casual observer is remuneration, and I took considerable pains in trying to evaluate the influence of monetary rewards on surrogates. In all programs, surrogates receive between $10,000 and $15,000 (for three to four months of insemination and nine months of pregnancy, on average), a fee that has changed only nominally since the early 1980s. As one program psychologist explained, the amount paid to surrogates is intentionally held at an artificially low rate so as to screen out women who might be motivated by monetary gain alone. One of the questions I sought to explore was whether surrogates were denying the significance of remuneration in order to cast their actions in the more culturally acceptable light of pure altruism, or whether they were motivated, at least in part, by remuneration and in part by other factors, with the importance of remuneration decreasing as the pregnancy progressed, the version of events put forth by both program staff and surrogates.

The opinion popular among both scholars and the general population, that surrogates are motivated primarily by financial gain, has tended to result in oversimplified analyses of surrogate motivations. More typical of surrogate explanations for the connection between the initial decision to become a surrogate and the remuneration received are comments such as those expressed by Fran. "[Surrogacy] sounded so interesting and fun. The money wasn't enough to be pregnant for nine months." Andrea, age 29, who was married with three children, said, "I'm not doing it for the money. Take the money: that wouldn't stop me. It wouldn't stop the majority." Sarah, age 27, who attended two years of college and was married with two children, explained her feelings about remuneration in the following way:

> What's $10,000 bucks? You can't even buy a car. If it was just for the money, you will want the baby. Money wasn't important. I possibly would have done it for expenses, especially for the people I did it for. My father would have given me the money not to do it.

The issue of remuneration proved to be of particular interest in that, although surrogates do accept monetary compensation for their reproductive work, its role is a multifaceted one. The surrogate pregnancy, unlike a traditional pregnancy, is viewed by the surrogate and her family as work; as such, it is informed by the belief that work is something that occurs only within the context of a paid occupation (Ferree 1984: 72). It is interesting to note that surrogates rarely spend the money they earn on themselves. The majority of surrogates I interviewed spent their earnings on home improvement, gifts for their husbands, a family vacation, or simply to pay off "family debts."

One of the primary reasons that most surrogates do not spend the money they earn on themselves alone appears to stem from the fact that the money serves as a buffer against and/or reward to their own families, particularly to their husbands, who must make a number of compromises as a result of the surrogate arrangement. One of these compromises is obligatory abstention from sexual intercourse with their wives from the time insemination takes place until a pregnancy has been confirmed (a period that lasts, on average, from three to four months in length but that may be extended for as long as one year).

The devaluation of the amount of the surrogate payment by the surrogates themselves as insufficient to compensate for "nine months of pregnancy" serves several important purposes. First, this view is representative of the cultural belief that children are "priceless" (Zelizer 1985); in this sense, surrogates are merely reiterating a widely held cultural belief when they devalue the amount of remuneration they receive. For example, when the largest and one of the most well-established surrogate mother programs changed the wording of its advertising copy from "Help an Infertile Couple" to "Give the Gift of Life," the vastly increased volume of response revealed that the program had discovered a successful formula with which to reach the surrogate population. With surrogacy, the gift is conceptualized as a child, a formulation that is widely used in Euro-American culture – in, for example, blood donation (Titmuss 1971) and organ donation (Fox and Swazey 1992).

The gift formulation holds particular appeal for surrogates because it reinforces the idea that having a child for someone is an act for which one cannot be compensated. As I have already mentioned, the gift-of-life narrative is further enhanced by some surrogates to include the near-sacrifice of their own lives in childbirth (Ragoné 1996, 1999). Fran, whose dismissal of the importance of payment I have already quoted, also offered another, even more revealing account of her decision to become a surrogate mother: "I wanted to do the ultimate thing for somebody, to give them the ultimate gift. Nobody can beat that, nobody can do anything nicer for them." Stella, age 38, married with two children, noted that the commissioning couples "consider [the baby] a gift, and [she] consider[s] it a gift." Carolyn, age 33, married with two children, discussed her feelings about remuneration and having a surrogate child in these terms: "It's a gift of love. I have always been a really giving person, and it's the ultimate way to give. I've always had babies so easily. It's the ultimate gift of love." For Euro-Americans, it is "gift relations" rather than economic exchanges that characterize the family (Carrier 1990: 2). Thus, when surrogates minimize or dismiss the importance of money, they are, on the one hand, reiterating cultural beliefs about the pricelessness of children and, on the other hand, suggesting that the exchange of a child for money is not a relationship of reciprocity but of kinship.

Once a surrogate enters a program, she also begins to recognize just how important having a child is to the commissioning couple. She sees with renewed clarity that no matter how much material success the couple has, their lives are emotionally impoverished because of their inability to have a child. In this way, the surrogate's fertility serves as a leveling device for perceived, if unacknowledged, economic differences, and many surrogates begin to see themselves as altruistic or heroic figures who can rectify the imbalance in a couple's life. The surrogate's sense of place and her social network are greatly enlarged as she receives telephone calls from the program, rushes to keep doctor's appointments, meets with prospective couples (she may even be flown to other cities to meet couples), and later on attends (in the open programs) monthly or semimonthly surrogate support group meetings. In some programs, she may attend individual therapy sessions. She is often taken out socially by her couple; she may receive gifts from them for herself and her children, be telephoned regularly by them, or receive cards and letters from them; and she attends holiday parties and other social events hosted by the program. Her sense of importance is also enhanced when she tells others about her new and unusual work. Once a surrogate meets, selects, and is selected by her couple and begins insemination – another rite of passage that confers additional status upon her – the couple becomes central to her life, adding an important, steady source of social interaction and stimulation.

The entire surrogate experience serves to alter the balance of power in the surrogate's personal life, giving her entrée to a more public role and creating new and exciting demands upon her time. From the moment she places a telephone call to a surrogate mother program to the moment she delivers a child, the balance of power in a surrogate's personal life is altered radically. Her time can no longer be devoted exclusively to the care and nurture of her own family, because she has entered into a legal and social contract to perform an important and economically rewarded task: helping an infertile couple begin a family of their own. Unlike other types of employment, this activity cannot be regarded as unfeminine, selfish, or nonnurturant.

In this sense, we can see how surrogacy assists surrogates in their efforts to transcend the limitations of their domestic roles by highlighting "their differences from men . . . [b]y accepting and elaborating upon the symbols and expectations associated with their cultural definition" (Rosaldo 1974: 37), such as motherhood. The gravity of the task provides the surrogate with an opportunity to do more than care for her family alone, and surrogates often report feeling that they are undertaking a task laden with importance, a project that fills them with a sense of pride and self-worth. Sally, age 33, married with two children and a full-time homemaker, discussed how surrogacy provided her with a feeling of unique accomplishment: "Not everyone can do it. It's like the steelworkers who walk on beams ten floors up; not everyone can do it, not everyone can be a surrogate."

Gestational surrogates

From 1987 to 1993, over 95 percent of all surrogacy arrangements were traditional. As of 1994, a profound shift occurred, with 50 percent of all surrogacy arrangements gestational, and as of 1999, that percentage continues to increase at the largest surrogate mother program (which is also the largest ovum donation program). With the advent of gestational surrogacy, however, reproduction is separated not only from sexual intercourse and motherhood but also from pregnancy as well. In addition, gestational surrogacy creates three discernible categories of motherhood where there was previously only one: (1) the biological mother, the woman who contributes the ovum (traditionally assumed to be the "real mother"); (2) the gestational mother, the woman who gestates the embryos but who bears no genetic relationship to the child; and (3) the social mother, the woman who raises or nurtures the child.

The growing prevalence of gestational surrogacy is, in part, guided by recent legal precedents in which a surrogate who does not contribute an ovum toward the creation of a child has a significantly reduced possibility of being awarded custody in the event that she reneges on her contract and attempts to retain custody of the child. However, although legal factors have certainly contributed to the meteoric rise in the rates of gestational surrogacy, it should be remembered that, for couples, the ability to create a child genetically related to both parents is the primary reason that gestational surrogacy continues to grow in popularity.

But not all gestational surrogate arrangements involve the couple's embryos; numerous cases involve the combination of donor ova and the intending father's semen. Why, then, do couples pursue gestational surrogacy when traditional surrogacy provides them with the same degree of biogenetic linkage to the child, has a higher likelihood of being successful, and costs less? Several reasons are cited by the staff of the largest surrogate mother program. The primary reason is that many more women are willing to donate ova than are willing to serve as surrogate mothers. This surrogate program is now also the largest ovum donation program in the United States, with over 300 screened donors on file. The second reason, as previously mentioned, is that the US courts would, in theory, be less likely to award custody to a gestational surrogate than to a traditional surrogate who contributed her own ovum to the creation of the child.[3] But perhaps most importantly, when commissioning couples choose donor ova/gestational surrogacy, they sever the surrogate's genetic link to and/or claim to the child. By contrast, with traditional surrogacy, the adoptive mother must emphasize the importance of nurturance and social parenthood, while the surrogate mother de-emphasizes her biogenetic tie to the child.

An additional reason, and one of critical importance, is that couples from certain racial, ethnic, and religious groups (e.g., Japanese, Taiwanese, and Jewish) could find women who were willing to donate their ova but were rarely able to locate women who were willing to serve in the capacity of surrogate. Thus, couples from particular ethnic/racial/religious groups who are seeking donors from those groups often pursue ovum donation/gestational surrogacy.[4]

The gestational surrogate's articulated ideas about relatedness (or, more accurately, the presumed lack thereof) also produce a shift in emphasis away from potentially problematic aspects of gestational surrogacy, such as race and ethnicity. Unlike traditional surrogate arrangements, in which the majority of couples and surrogates are Euro-American, it is not unusual for gestational surrogates and commissioning couples to come from diverse racial, ethnic, religious, and cultural backgrounds. In fact, approximately 30 percent of all gestational surrogate arrangements at the largest program now involve surrogates and couples matched from different racial, ethnic, and cultural backgrounds. I have, over the last four years, interviewed a Mexican American gestational surrogate who was carrying a child for a Japanese couple; an African American gestational surrogate who had unsuccessfully attempted several embryo transfers for both a Japanese couple and a Euro-American couple; a Euro-American gestational surrogate who had delivered twins for a Japanese couple; and a Taiwanese couple looking for an Asian American ovum donor and gestational surrogate.

When I questioned Carole, an African American gestational surrogate (who, at 29, was single, with one child, and had yet to sustain a gestational pregnancy) about the issue of racial difference (between herself and her couple), she stated: "I had friends who had a problem because [they thought] I should help Blacks. And I told them, 'Don't look at the color issue. If a White person offered to help you, you wouldn't turn them down.'" However, the following statement by Carole reveals that the issue of racial difference is further nuanced as a positive factor, one that actually facilitates the surrogate/child separation process: "My mom is happy the couple is not Black, because she was worried I would want to keep [the baby]. The first couple I was going to go with was Black. I don't want to raise another kid."

When I questioned Linda, a 30-year-old Mexican American woman pregnant with a child for a couple from Japan, about this issue, her reasoning illustrated how beliefs concerning racial difference can be used by surrogates (and couples) to resolve any conflicting feelings about the child being related to a surrogate by virtue of having been carried in her body:

> No, I haven't [thought of the child as mine], because she's not mine, she never has been. For one thing, she is totally Japanese. It's a little hard for me. In a way, she will always be my Japanese girl; but she is theirs.

In this quote, we can see how Linda recapitulates one of the initial motivations cited by gestational surrogates, the desire to bear a child for an infertile couple while highlighting the lack of physical and racial resemblance, or biogenetic tie.

> If I was to have a child, it would only be from my husband and me. With AI [traditional surrogacy], the baby would be a part of me. I don't know if I could let a part of me. . . . AI was never for me; I never considered it.

Carole and Linda are aware, of course, as are other gestational surrogates, that they do not share a genetic tie with the children they produce as gestational surrogates. But concerns such as Carole's about raising an African American couple's child reveal how racial resemblance raises certain questions about relatedness, even when there is no genetic tie.[5] Although she knows that the child is not genetically hers, certain boundaries become blurred for her when an African American couple is involved, whereas with a Euro-American couple, the distinction between genetic/nongenetic or self/other is clear. Cultural conceptions, such as this, about the connection between race and genetics deserve further exploration.

Not surprisingly, the shift from traditional to gestational surrogacy has attracted a different population of women. Overall, women who elect to become gestational surrogates tend to articulate the belief that traditional surrogacy, even though less medically complicated,[6] is not an acceptable option for them because they are uncomfortable with the prospect of contributing their own ovum to the creation of a child. They also cannot readily accept the idea that a child who is genetically related to them would be raised by someone else. In other words, they explicitly articulate the opinion that, in traditional surrogacy (where the surrogate contributes an ovum), the surrogate is the mother of the child, whereas in gestational surrogacy (where she does not contribute an ovum), she is not. They are nonetheless interested in participating in gestational surrogacy because it provides them with access to the world of surrogacy.[7] This often includes, interestingly enough, women who have been voluntarily sterilized (tubal ligations). For example, Barbara, age 30, married with three children, a Mormon and a two-time gestational surrogate (now planning a third pregnancy), stated: "The baby is never mine. I am providing a needed environment for it to be born and go back to mom and dad. It's the easy kind of babysitting."

Oddly enough, the beliefs of IVF surrogates run contrary to current legal opinion, as expressed in the findings of both Britain's Warnock Report and the Australian Waller Commission's report that "when a child is born to a woman following the donation of another's egg the woman giving birth should, for all purposes, be regarded in law as the mother of that child" (Shalev 1989: 117). It should be noted that the opinion expressed in both the Warnock Report and the Waller Commission contradicts the views expressed not only by IVF surrogates but also by commissioning couples who choose gestational surrogacy precisely because it eliminates the issue of genetic relatedness for them. It also contradicts Euro-American kinship ideology, specifically the continued emphasis on the importance of biogenetic relatedness.[8] However, this effort to expand our definition of biological relatedness, which has until recently depended on a genetic component, runs contrary to the Euro-American emphasis on biogenetic relatedness, in which genetic parents are legally and socially considered the "real" parents. This fragmentation or dispersal of parenthood, a by-product of reproductive technologies, has resulted in what Marilyn Strathern has describes as the "claims of one kind of biological mother against other kinds of biological and nonbiological mothers" (1992: 32) and fathers.

How, then, to account for the gestational surrogate's motivations? Should a gestational surrogate's maternal rights be "modeled on the law of paternity, where proof of genetic parentage establishes . . . parentage, or . . . on the nine month experience of pregnancy as establishing the preponderant interest of . . . parentage" (Hull 1990: 152)? It is of fundamental importance to gestational surrogates to circumvent the biogenetic tie to the child, and they do so in spite of the greatly increased degree of physical discomfort and medical risk they face in IVF procedures (as compared to risks associated with traditional surrogacy, which are the same as those faced in traditional pregnancy).[9] Any effort, legal or ethical, to argue that pregnancy is a determining factor in parenthood not only fails to consider Euro-American kinship ideology but, perhaps most importantly, also neglects to consider the position of the gestational surrogate and commissioning couple.

The medical procedures commonly encountered by gestational surrogates (the self-administration of hormonal medications) can cause considerable discomfort. In the following example, Barbara discussed her experience:

> After a while, you dread having to do it; I had lumps from all those injections. Two times a day and twice a week, three injections a day. If you don't do it, the pregnancy would be lost. . . . You are just [as] concerned with the pregnancy as if it's your own, sometimes more.

Vicky, age 33, Euro-American, married with three children, who had given birth three weeks earlier, explained how she was able to sustain her motivation and commitment throughout the difficult medical procedures:

> It was hard, but it needed to be done for the baby's sake. All the shots [were] on a daily basis. I didn't mind it at all, but it had to be at a certain time. It was like a curfew. Sure it was painful, but it does go away.

The sentiments expressed by Barbara and Vicky are similar to those expressed by traditional surrogates who have experienced difficult, sometimes life-threatening pregnancies and deliveries. Both cast these experiences in terms of meaningful or heroic suffering

(Ragoné 1996). The vastly increased physical discomfort and scheduling difficulties are, however, a price that gestational surrogates are willing to endure in order to circumvent what they regard as the problematic biogenetic tie. Barbara expressed a belief shared by many gestational surrogates about their pregnancies when she stated:

> I separate AI [artificial insemination] and IVF completely, almost to the point I don't agree with AI. I feel like that person is entering into an agreement to produce a child to give to someone else. I feel it is her baby she is giving away.

In a similar fashion, Lee, age 31, married with two children, Euro-American, who was waiting for an embryo transfer, discussed the differences between traditional (AI) and gestational surrogacy. "Yes, it's [the fetus] inside my body, but as far as I am concerned, I don't have any biological tie. The other way [AI], I would feel that there is some part of me out there."

This view of surrogacy differs in several important ways from the one expressed by traditional surrogates, who advance the idea that the term "parent" should be applied only to individuals who actually choose to become engaged in the process of raising a child, regardless of the degree of relatedness. They achieve this perspective in part by separating motherhood into two components: biological motherhood and social motherhood. Only social motherhood is viewed by traditional surrogates as "real" motherhood; in other words, nurturance is held to be of greater importance than biological relatedness. In this respect, it is the gestational surrogate, not the traditional surrogate, who tends to subscribe to a decidedly more traditional rendering of relatedness.

It was perhaps impossible to predict with any degree of certainty that advances in reproductive medicine, coupled with an increase in consumer demand, would produce such a profound shift in the rates of traditional (AI) and gestational surrogacy. Assistive reproductive technologies (e.g., surrogate motherhood, ovum donation, and sperm donation) have called into question what was once understood to be the "natural" basis of parenthood. As we have seen, traditional surrogates underplay their own biological contribution in order to bring to the fore the importance of the social, nurturant role played by the adoptive mother. In this way, motherhood is reinterpreted as primarily an important social role in order to sidestep problematic aspects of the surrogate's biogenetic relationship to the child and the adoptive mother's lack of a biogenetic link. For traditional surrogates, nurture takes precedence and ascendancy over nature; motherhood is understood as a social construct rather than a biological phenomenon. Gestational surrogates, however, interestingly remain committed to the genetic model of parenthood,[10] reasoning that "real" parenthood is, in fact, genetic.

Many of the early theories about the future of surrogacy focused, at times exclusively, upon its potential for exploitation, but they failed to take into consideration the fact that both fertility and infertility must be contextualized: both are embedded in a series of personal, social, historical, and cultural processes and practices. Within surrogates' statements, assessments, and questions is testimony to the plasticity and resilience of family, which, in spite of these seemingly odd changes, persists.

Acknowledgments

I owe a very special thank-you to Dr. Sydel Silverman of the Wenner Gren Foundation for Anthropological Research for her support. An additional thank-you is also owed to the University of Massachusetts–Boston for their ongoing support in the form of faculty development grants. I am especially indebted to the women and men who have shared their experiences with me over the last ten years; their belief in and commitment to this research have made it an engaging and rewarding experience. I would also like to extend very special and heartfelt thanks to the directors, psychologists, and surrogate program staff who have, over the years, generously given of their time and their expertise.

Discussion questions

1. According to the author, what are the three shifts that challenge the Western conceptualization of conception, reproduction, and parenthood?
2. What are the three categories of motherhood that are created by gestational surrogacy?
3. How does race play a role in concerns about relatedness in gestational surrogacy?
4. How do views of nature/nurture differ between traditional surrogacy and gestational surrogacy?

Notes

1 A couple, Elizabeth and William Stern, contracted with a surrogate, Mary Beth Whitehead, to bear a child for them because Elizabeth Stern suffered from multiple sclerosis, a condition that can be exacerbated by pregnancy. Once the child was born, however, Whitehead refused to relinquish the child to the Sterns, and in 1987, William Stern, the biological father, filed a suit against Whitehead in an effort to enforce the terms of the surrogate contract. The decision of the lower court to award custody to the biological father and to permit his wife to adopt the child was overturned by the New Jersey Supreme Court, which then awarded custody to William Stern, prohibiting Elizabeth Stern from adopting the child, while granting visitation rights to Mary Beth Whitehead. These decisions mirrored public opinion about surrogacy (Hull 1990: 154).
2 See Rapp (1978: 279) and Gordon (1988: 3) for a historical analysis of the idea of the demise of the American family.
3 In June 1993, the California Supreme Court upheld the decisions of both the lower court and the court of appeals with respect to gestational surrogacy contracts. In *Anna Johnson v. Mark and Crispina Calvert*, Case #SO 23721, a case involving an African American gestational surrogate, a Filipina American mother, and a Euro-American father, the gestational surrogate and commissioning couple both filed custody suits. Under California law, both of the women could, however, claim maternal rights: Johnson, by virtue of being the woman who gave birth to the child, and Calvert, who donated ovum, because she is the child's genetic mother. In rendering their decision, however, the court circumvented the issue of relatedness, instead emphasized the "intent" of the parties as the ultimate and decisive factor in any determination of parenthood. The court concluded that if the genetic and birth mother are not one and the same person, then "she who intended to procreate the child – that is, she who intended to bring about the birth of a child that she intended to raise on her own – is the natural mother under California law."
4 Why women from certain cultural groups are willing to donate ova but not serve as surrogates is a subject of considerable interest. Since gestational surrogates reason that they (unlike traditional surrogates and ovum donors) do not part with any genetic material, they are able to deny that the child(ren) they produce are related to them. Given the parameters of Euro-American kinship ideology, additional research will be required to ascertain why ovum donors do not perceive their donation of genetic material as problematic.
5 During the course of the interview, I specifically asked her what her feelings and ideas were about having a child for a couple from another racial background (I also asked this question of all the surrogates who were matched with couples from different racial backgrounds).

6 Gestational surrogates often complain about the discomfort they experience as a result of having to self-inject two or three times per day for as long as three to four months of the pregnancy. They report that progesterone is especially painful, since it is oil-based and has a tendency to pool and lump under the skin. Even though the largest of the surrogate programs claims to inform gestational surrogates about the need to self-administer shots, several gestational surrogates reported that they had not anticipated either the frequency or the discomfort of the injections.

7 I have discussed elsewhere in great detail the system of rewards that makes surrogate motherhood attractive to this group of women (Ragoné 1994, 1996, 1998, 1999, 2000).

8 While there are, in fact, observable differences in family patterns within the United States, most notably among poor and working-poor African Americans, whose alternative models of mothering/parenting may stem from "West African cultural values" as well as "functional adaptations to race and gender oppression" (Collins 1988: 119; Stack 1974), we should not lose sight of the fact that such perceived differences in family patterns do not necessarily weaken Euro-American kinship ideology. They continue to privilege the biogenetic model of family.

9 Aside from studies of the increased rates of multiple births, there are few longitudinal studies on the effects of infertility treatments. Research does, however, suggest that infertility patients have an increased risk of ovarian cancer (Jensen et al. 1987). The question remains: Although an infertile woman knowingly accepts the risks associated with infertility treatments, do surrogacy and ovum donation programs provide their populations with adequate information about the possibility of long-term risk?

10 Once a gestational surrogate has begun to develop a relationship with her couple and has experienced several unsuccessful embryo transfers, she may begin to reformulate or revise her initial beliefs concerning relatedness and family. An unsuccessful gestational surrogate may, for example, opt to become what is referred to in surrogate mother programs as a "cross-over," someone who chose initially to participate in gestational surrogacy but then decided to become a traditional surrogate.

References

Andrews, Lori. 1984. *New Conceptions: A Consumer's Guide to the Newest Infertility Treatments*. New York: Ballantine.

Annas, George. 1988. "Fairy Tales Surrogate Mothers Tell." In *Surrogate Motherhood: Politics and Privacy*, ed. Larry Gostin, 43–55. Bloomington: Indiana University Press.

Carrier, James. 1990. "Gifts in a World of Commodities: The Ideology of the Perfect Gift in American Society." *Social Analysis* 29: 19–37.

Collins, Patricia Hill. 1988. *Black Feminist Thought: Knowledge, Consciousness and the Politics of Empowerment*. New York: Routledge.

Dworkin, Andrea. 1978. *Right-Wing Women*. New York: Perigee Books.

Ferree, Myra. 1984. "Sacrifice, Satisfaction and Social Change: Employment and the Family." In *My Troubles Are Going to Have Trouble with Me*, eds. Karen Sacks and Dorothy Remy, 61–79. New Brunswick, NJ: Rutgers University Press.

Fox, Renee, and Judith Swazey. 1992. *Spare Parts: Organ Replacement in American Society*. New York and Oxford: Oxford University Press.

Gordon, Linda. 1988. *Heroes of Their Own Lives*. New York: Viking.

Hull, Richard. 1990. "Gestational Surrogacy and Surrogate Motherhood." In *Ethical Issues in the New Reproductive Technologies*, ed. Richard Hull, 150–155. Belmont, CA: Wadsworth Publishers.

Jensen, P., B. Riis, P. Rodbro, V. Stram, and C. Christiansen. 1987. "Climacteric Symptoms after Oral and Percutaneous Hormone Replacement Therapy." *Matvritas* 9: 207–215.

Martin, Emily. 1987. *The Woman in the Body: A Cultural Analysis of Reproduction*. Boston: Beacon Press.

Neuhaus, Robert. 1988. "Renting Women, Buying Babies and Class Struggles." *Society* 25(3): 8–10.

Parker, Phillip. 1983. "Motivation of Surrogate Mothers: Initial Findings." *American Journal of Psychiatry* 140: 117–119.

Ragoné, Heléna. 1994. *Surrogate Motherhood: Conception in the Heart*. Boulder, CO and Oxford: Westview Press/Basic Books.

Ragoné, Heléna. 1996. "Chasing the Blood Tie: Surrogate Mothers, Adoptive Mothers and Fathers." *American Ethnologist* 23(2): 352–365.

Ragoné, Heléna. 1998. "Incontestable Motivations." In *Reproducing Reproduction: Kinship, Power, and Technological Innovation*, eds. Sarah Franklin and Heléna Ragoné, 118–131. Philadelphia: University of Pennsylvania Press.

Ragoné, Heléna. 1999. "The Gift of Life: Surrogate Motherhood, Gamete Donations and Constructions of Altruism." In *Transformative Mothering: On Giving and Getting, in a Consumer Culture*, ed. Linda Layne, 132–176. New York: New York University Press.

Ragoné, Heléna. 2000. "Of Likeness and Difference: How Race Is being Transfigured by Gestational Surrogacy." In *Ideologies and Technologies of Motherhood: Race, Class, Sexuality and Nationalism*, eds. Heléna Ragoné and France Winddance Twine, 56–75. New York and London: Routledge.

Rapp, Rayna. 1978. "Family and Class in Contemporary America: Notes toward an Understanding of Ideology." *Science and Technology* 42(3): 278–300.

Rosaldo, Michelle. 1974. "Woman, Culture and Society: A Theoretical Overview." In *Woman, Culture and Society*, eds. M. Rosaldo and L. Lamphere, 17–43. Stanford, CA: Stanford University Press.

Shalev, Carmel. 1989. *Birth Power: The Case for Surrogacy*. New Haven, CT: Yale University Press.

Snowden, Robert, Geoffrey Duncan Mitchell, and E. M. Snowden. 1983. *Artificial Reproduction: A Social Investigation*. London: Allen and Unwin.

Stack, Carol. 1974. *All Our Kin*. New York: HarperCollins.

Strathern, Marilyn. 1991. "The Pursuit of Certainty: Investigating Kinship in the Late Twentieth Century." *Distinguished Lecture*, Society of the Anthropology of Europe.

Strathern, Marilyn. 1992. *Reproducing the Future: Anthropology, Kinship and the New Reproductive Technologies*. Manchester, UK: Manchester University Press.

Titmuss, Richard. 1971. *The Gift Relationship: From Human Blood to Social Policy*. New York: Pantheon Books.

Zelizer, Viviana. 1985. *Pricing the Priceless Child*. New York: Basic Books.

Part 3

Gendered space and knowledge

If one accepts that space is produced by social relationships (see Lefebvre 1991) or that knowledge is always shaped by one's position in society (see Harding 1986), then it is also true that both space and knowledge can be and, indeed, *are* gendered. That is, physical space can be imbued with socially acceptable gender roles the same way bodies can be. In the United States, for example, public restrooms are so deeply intertwined with gender that some people invest incredible energy lobbying politicians and writing legislation in an attempt to reinforce and maintain the socially constructed system by which only one gender may collectively use one restroom to express their natural bodily functions.

Knowledge, too, is gendered according to what people with particular bodies are expected to know or do. Some kinds of domestic labor, care labor, and emotional labor, for example, we commonly understand to be feminine (even if they should not be). As a result, the knowledge of how to practice and perform these kinds of labor may not be taught to young boys, and so the cycle repeats itself into the next generation. Critically, it is common that one may see this as a deficit in a gendered divide: men are unable to know or do certain tasks (pejoratively known as "women's business"); therefore, women are burdened with taking up these roles, which are often thankless and unpaid (Federici 1975). On the other hand, in Senegal, Powis and Bunkley (2023) found that *affaire u jiggeen* (Wolof: "women's business") can be a domain of knowledge that women keep to themselves in the interest of preserving their autonomy from men. "Pregnancy is like the kitchen," one woman told Powis while conducting research on expectant fatherhood. "Keep men out of them both." (Notice, too, the spatial reference to the kitchen as a marker of gendered knowledge.)

In this section, we present a selection of works in which anthropologists have grappled with these relationships of gender, space, knowledge, and labor. To start, J. M. Adovasio, Olga Soffer, and Jake Page present a scenario representing the division of labor in a European village 26,000 years ago. Based on recent scholarship, they observe that it is now evident that female humans

> have been the chief engine in the unprecedentedly high level of human sociability, were the inventors of the most useful of tools (called the String Revolution), have shared equally in the provision of food for human societies, almost certainly drove the human invention of language, and were the ones who created agriculture.

They assess the meanings attributed to a famous female-bodied figurine, which came to be known as the "Vestonice Venus." In contrast to the conventional views, Adovasio,

DOI: 10.4324/9781003398349-20

Soffer, and Page note that it is most likely that this figurine was carved by a woman, probably the "priestess" who used it. They then turn to the important but overlooked "Fiber Revolution" or "String Revolution," referring to the gendered development of fiber arts (weaving, basketry, cordage). The String Revolution, they contend, is a technological breakthrough with profound effects on human destiny. Ethnographic accounts of fiber arts among contemporary band societies indicate that making things such as baskets, clothing, sandals, or other fiber items is not the exclusive prerogative of either sex; in such societies, both men and women know the production techniques. Further, weaving is practiced primarily by women in the tribal world today. Thus, they present their "default" position: most ceramics, weaving, and basketry was made by women in the time frame of the Vestonice Venus, 26,000 years ago. Hence, they conclude that the concept of gender, and some division of labor, was already in place at that time.

Toyin Falola's chapter describes Yoruba women who, through their predominance in market activities, have become part of the political landscape in various ways. Further, their control of market space also gives them control over market rituals and, hence, a role in religious life. Indeed, within the Yoruba pantheon, a female goddess, Yemonja, is central. The involvement of Yoruba women in trade, both regional and long-distance, dates to the precolonial period and has endured into the present. Trading activities allow women to build wealth and enjoy a high social status. Further, the marketplace has its own guild structure and everything that accompanies that structure, in terms of the power to set rules and regulations, as well as interface with, and occasionally challenge, the state. Falola illustrates these important connections between economic, social, and political power through a series of case studies of market women of the precolonial and contemporary period.

In a new chapter for this edition, Ashley Thuthao Keng Dam explores the complicated relationship between gender, knowledge, expertise, and identity in Cambodia. In particular, their chapter looks at the uses and interventions of Traditional Khmer Medicine (TKM) in reproductive and perinatal health. In Dam's research, pregnant people of Siem Reap, Cambodia, are surrounded by extensive social support networks which contribute care or advise on best care practices, which include TKM knowledge. Expertise in TKM, unlike pregnancy, is not bound by gender norms – in fact, men are expected to know all about plant medicine for perinatal health. Women's use of TKM puts social limitations on what they can and cannot do in terms of domestic labor, for example, which redirects those expectations onto men.

Louise Lamphere reviews the formulation of the domestic–public model and discusses the subsequent critiques of its validity and applicability. In this model, men are aligned with the public sphere, which confers powers, recognition, and prestige, as well as economic capital, whereas women are aligned with the domestic sphere, posited as largely a result of the demands of reproduction on women. As Lamphere observes, it has become increasingly clear that the domestic–public opposition is the heir to nineteenth-century social theory: rooted in a dichotomy contrasting home and woman with a public world of man and reflecting an understanding of political rights based on sex. The domestic–public dichotomy emerged from the Industrial Revolution and the separation of home and workplace. Conceptualizing social life as dichotomized into domestic and public domains does not make sense in societies in which management of production occurs within the household and in which household production itself involves the management of the "public" economy (Leacock 1978: 253). The domestic–public theory structured gender research for many years in early days in the field. As researchers learned more about global variation in gendered space, they challenged this theory.

Drawing on life histories from three generational cohorts in Uganda, Shanti Parikh's chapter chronicles the transformation of men's extramarital liaisons from private, family concerns to matters of public critique that blur the boundaries of the domestic and public. This transformation has been occasioned by shifts in the economy, gender equality campaigns, and the proliferation of discourses that have made sexuality a primary concern of public health and public morality regulation and surveillance. In particular contexts, it is strategic for women to "go public" with decidedly private matters in order to gain sympathy from neighbors, shame their husbands, and importantly, present themselves as modern rational actors who protect themselves from the risk of HIV infection. This chapter brings new insight into the ongoing debates about the usefulness of the public/private model by highlighting how public health and other interventions have worked to transform male infidelity from an intimate issue relevant to spouses and families into a matter of broader public concern, with paradoxical implications.

Anubha Sood's chapter discusses the relationship between spirit possession and healing at a temple site in Rajasthan, India. In Hindi, the word used for spirit affliction is *sankat*, which means distress, danger, or misfortune. Sood observes that women predominate among visitors to the temple and that they participate in the rituals in order to reconfigure the social and psychological ruptures in their gendered lives. These women come to the temple town, sometimes from great distances, and they stay for long periods of time; or they are constantly traveling back and forth, all with the goal of participating in a therapeutic process that will provide them with some resolution to what is troubling them. Sood illustrates this therapeutic process, focused on possession-trance, or *peshi*, through a case study of one woman, Meetu, who came to the temple with her family. Meetu was rebelling against her parents' wishes for her to marry. At one point during her therapeutic process, she was possessed by five or six spirits with different names. Eventually, all the malevolent spirits left her body and she began to reconcile with her family. Sood suggests that in her possession states, Meetu was able to challenge the hierarchical structures of her community and family and literally behave like a man, that is, to assume a role of power and freedom. Her family, in the end, promised to find her a husband from a family that would accord her a life different from that of her mother's generation.

Lastly, in her new chapter for this edition, Daphne Weber's chapter examines contemporary consequences of historical reshaping of gendered space and knowledge of Theravada Buddhism in Thailand. What was once considered a privilege for only men, because of the end of the lineage of female monks over 1,000 years ago, the ordination of women as Buddhist monks (called "bhikkhuni") has recommenced in the 1990s – and not without significant political and religious opposition, sometimes violent. In her chapter, Weber demonstrates how Thai women, frustrated by their precarious status and roles in society and looking for a kind of emotional regulatory practice, seek the counsel of ordained women. Through stories of trauma and tribulation, bhikkhuni create ritual spaces of vulnerability, empathy, and connection that invite Thai women to process their suffering and eventually find empowerment and self-worth.

References

Federici, Silvia. 1975. *Wages against Housework*. London: Falling Wall Press.

Harding, Sandra. 1986. *The Science Question in Feminism*. Ithaca: Cornell University Press.

Leacock, Eleanor. 1978. "Women's Status in Egalitarian Society: Implications for Social Evolution." *Current Anthropology* 19(2): 247–275.

Lefebvre, Henri. 1991. *The Production of Space*. Oxford, UK: Blackwell Publishing.

Powis, Richard, and Emma N. Bunkley. 2023. "Handbooks and Health Interpreters: How Men Are Assets for Their Pregnant Partners in Senegal." *Social Science & Medicine* 116074.

Chapter 18

The fashioning of women

J. M. Adovasio, Olga Soffer, and Jake Page

Reproduced from J. M. Adovasio, Olga Soffer, and Jake Page, "The Fashioning of Women," in J. M. Adovasio, Olga Soffer, and Jake Page, *The Invisible Sex: Uncovering the True Roles of Women in Prehistory* (Abingdon: Routledge, 2007), pp. 169–193.

In which we visit a pleasant encampment full of Brooks Brothers–style weaving and other womanly creations, the first fireworks, mammoth non-hunts, and people who could be your neighbors.

THE PLACE: A camp on the gentle, grassy slope of a hill in today's Pavlov Hills, from which three limestone outcrops rise above the broad south Moravian plain in the eastern region of today's Czech Republic. The view to the north, south, and east stretches for miles over grassland and forest: a broad valley that served people and wildlife as a highway from the flatlands of the mighty Danube into northern Europe. The Pavlov Hills lie along the right bank of a river that flows into the Morava River, a major tributary to the Danube. To the north, a month's march away, lies the great wall of glacial ice. Equally far to the southwest, ice blankets the great mountains known today as the Alps. The village is not far above a swampy area fed by the river that courses through the plains, its moisture supporting a variety of deciduous trees – alder, ash, birch, groves of willows, the occasional oak, and beyond, in drier soils, the conifers, pines, spruce, and others. Off in the distance, a few clusters of reindeer and small herds of horses head south. Beyond, a group of female mammoths and their young plod northward.

THE TIME: 26,000 years ago. The summer has ended, and the nightly temperatures in these early autumn weeks reach near freezing. It will get colder as the winter comes on, but for now the days are relatively warm once the sun rises above the hills.

THE VILLAGE: This is where several groups of people have come together to spend the long fall, winter, and early spring, just as they and their ancestors have done since longer than anyone can remember or compute. The camp is about 200 yards upslope from the river, at a place where natural mineral licks attract nutrient-starved animals in the spring months, especially mammoth females and their young. There the weaker ones die, leaving their bones for the people to use. Over the eons, people have made

DOI: 10.4324/9781003398349-21

use of their bones and tusks as raw materials to build dwellings and make tools and other objects. Now they have erected five tent-like structures over depressions in the ground they have cleaned out, throwing away last year's broken flint and bone and broken tools and other household trash. Walls and roofs of skins sewed together are held up by wooden poles, their edges held down against the force of the cold winds with rocks. In the largest of these structures, sitting in the middle of the camp, five hearths have been delineated with circles of rocks. The others contain single hearths. Upslope from the camp, about 80 yards sits another structure, with limestone slabs holding down walls of hide on three sides. Inside this structure are layers of ashes and ceramic fragments.

On this particular morning, just as the eastern sky is beginning to lighten, a woman emerges from one of the tents and nods to the sleepy youth who is tending the fire in the middle of the camp that burns through the night as a warning to predators. She walks slowly and painfully up the slope to this small structure. Taking sticks of wood from a pile she ordered her young grandchildren to make yesterday, she builds a fire. The flames lick hungrily at the pine sticks, reaching into the cold air. Not pausing to warm herself, she piles more sticks, larger ones, on the flames, and then retreats down the slope to her dwelling. Moments later, she re-emerges, carrying a tightly woven basket filled with water and a cloth carrying bag filled with dusty brown soil. By now the fire has rendered the fuel into glowing hot coals. She nods approvingly, then sits down beside the kiln with a grunt about her complaining knee joints. Making clay by mixing the fine dusty soil with water, she fashions a tiny bear's head and body. She sets that aside, fashions legs, and presses them into the body. She intones some words and throws the bear into the fire. In minutes, the bear explodes with a sharp *Crack!* and a cascade of sparks and pieces of the bear rattle off the walls of the kiln. Thus does the old woman's day begin, rendering their world as safe as she can for the rest of the people.

By now people are stepping outside their dwellings into the cold, scratching, yawning, looking up at the sky for signs of the weather for this day. Young children begin darting here and there, yelping and shouting, parents hissing at them to be quiet. Two women, each suckling a new baby, stand together, talking. Some of the group's men stand in a circle, chewing on narrow strips of rabbit jerky, glancing out to the horse herds moving across the plains far away, making plans. From up the hillside at the kiln, the sharp pops of the old woman's fireworks are reassuring sounds. As the sun rises over the hills, casting long shadows that reach down the slope, activity in the camp begins to pick up. Innumerable chores need doing. Several men are soon engaged in replacing the tiny old blades affixed to the ivory foreshafts of their wooden spears with newly knapped flint blades, renewing the lethally sharp array. These weapons are for hunting horses and the small red deer out on the plains, a task that could take several men an entire day and night and still result in failure.

Another man grinds a piece of gray slate into a pendant to replace the one that shattered the day before when he fell onto some rocks while running. An older man, his hands now gnarled and crooked, slowly opens up a long hunting net, unrolling it on the ground. He then inspects it from one end 40 feet to the other end, seeing that the knots are still all secure. Satisfied, he rolls it back up and places it on the ground near a lone tree that stands a few feet from the dwelling where he, with his family, sleeps.

Inside, his daughter boils a mush of various wild seeds in a tightly plaited basket with hardened clay inside. The thickening gruel bubbles, some of it slopping over the edge of the basket and falling into the hearth. The young woman has been feeding this to her 4-year old daughter for a week now, weaning her from the breast. Earlier, she and three other mothers sent their daughters off to collect the nettles that grow in the disturbed soil around the camp and are now ready to be processed. The girls and their mothers will set about soaking the nettles to remove the outer cover and free up the finer fibers inside. The fibers will then be twisted into string of various plies.

The old woman, the oldest person in camp, though she is still vigorous, will supervise the making of the string and will take the finest as warps and wefts for her own work on her loom. Last year, she taught the young girls five of the eight ways of twining, some for making baskets and floor mats, some for making the wall hangings that helped keep out the icy winds of winter, and yet others for the fine mysteries of creating loom-woven fabric to sew together into formfitting warm-weather clothes. The old woman, who is a bit scary for the girls because she is so powerful, has chosen one of the girls as a special student: she will learn to sew the seams of ceremonial shirts. She will show another girl the arts of the loom, and one day, perhaps this girl will become the old woman, the weaver who makes the finest fabric for clothing for whoever in her lifetime emerges as the leader.

As the day goes on, several of the men set out for the plains below, bristling with flint knives and spears of wood tipped with ivory and stone blades, sweating in the midday sun, their hide shirts hanging from their belts. They will be on the march most of the day, camping near a place on the river favored by horses and some of the local deer. Other men stay in camp, a few telling exaggerated tales of hunting to the boys, a few others digging up the loose dusty soil and carrying it up the hill in bags made of fiber to the old woman at the kiln. In the shade of one of the freestanding trees, three young women gossip and laugh as they grind the small tough seeds of certain prairie grasses. It is a good day for a feast to celebrate the coming together of these related families for the season.

By late afternoon, each family's net has been unrolled and carefully inspected and tied together to form two long nets, each some 80 feet across. Now the children, some of the women and men, and a few elders set out with the nets. The children carry sticks, which they brandish bravely as they run along behind the adults. Several of the adults carry clubs fashioned from fallen branches. Led by the oldest in the party, they pause after a half hour's walk on the slopes that are covered by underbrush. Carefully the oldsters unfurl the nets, unwinding them from the carrying poles, which are then used to anchor the nets to the ground. Several of the younger women, the men, and all the children silently circle upslope until they reach nearly to the top of the hill. There they form into a wide arc and, on a signal, begin the charge down the hill, shrieking wildly, whacking trees as they go by, setting up a terrifying din. Rabbits, foxes, and other small mammals emerge from the underbrush and dart back and forth, trending downhill to escape the mayhem coming their way. Within minutes, several dozen of these creatures have leaped into the nets to be quickly dispatched by people swinging their clubs. As the sun drops down to the western horizon, the people head back with more meat and fur than they will be able to use for days.

The camp bustles with activity as preparations for the feast get under way – skinning the animals, starting the hearth fires and the outdoor fire that will burn all night, and performing innumerable other chores. Meanwhile, the old woman who was first to greet the day has returned to the kiln up the slope with one of her youthful apprentices. She has kneaded into existence a few dozen small clay pellets, several animal figurines, and most elaborate, a figurine of a woman with broad hips and buttocks and pendulous breasts, faceless, footless, with lines etched into her back that suggest ample flesh, which bespeaks a prosperous woman. Carefully she places all these objects into her basket, except for the figurine, which she hands to the older of her two apprentices. The girl grins widely at the honor and holds the figurine carefully in her hand, and they set out for the camp below. As the feasting proceeds into the night, a few couples slip off into the dark, heading for courting camps a short walk away in a copse of trees. Others dance and chant, while the old woman throws an occasional pellet or animal figure into the fire as she sings a special song to herself in a high keening voice and the clay figurines explode. Toward the end of the festivities, she instructs the sleepy apprentice to throw the figurine of the woman into the flames. Most of the people in camp stop to watch as the girl flips the figurine into the fire, and they wait silently for a minute or so until a loud crack signifies the end of the ritual, of the feast, of the day.

With that, the people settle down for the night, eyelids drooping, stomachs full, ceremonies properly done to celebrate the successful hunt – a good day, indeed.

What is right about that picture

How much of this scenario is guesswork and how much is certain? What is the evidence that lies behind this view of a day spent at a site that would come to be known as Dolni Vestonice I? This site has been excavated and examined by numerous archaeologists over the last three-quarters of a century and, over this time, has yielded up several startling discoveries. Among the first such was the figurine of the woman that we saw tossed into the central fire of the camp at the end of the feast. She was subsequently discovered on July 13, 1925, during the Moravian Museum's excavation under the leadership of Karel Absolon. The workers found her in two unequal pieces less than a foot apart. The Vestonice Venus, as she came to be known, became famous as the earliest ceramic object ever found. A picture soon emerged – indeed, an actual illustration by Zdenek Burian – showing an elderly man with disheveled white hair, wearing a sleeveless shirt of some animal skin, with a necklace of teeth and other, no doubt, meaningful objects around his neck, carefully sculpting the figurine with a stick of animal bone. It is more likely that the figurine was carved by a woman, probably the "priestess" who used it.

At the time of its discovery, one member of the crew noted what appeared to be a fragmentary fingerprint left on the Venus's spine before firing. Recently, this fingerprint was analyzed microscopically to determine such features as the breadth of ridges, which correlate with the age of the originator of the print. It turns out that the person who held this figurine was between 7 and 15 years old and, almost surely, was not the maker of the figurine, since it is unlikely that a beginner or a child could have made it.

On the other hand, it was possible to call into question the actual ceramic skill of this "first" ceramicist. The site of the kiln upslope was first looked into by archaeologists in the 1950s. It yielded fragments of a total of 707 animal figurines and 14 human figurines, all fired clay. In addition, there were some 2,000 small pellets. This suggests two possibilities. One, the ceramicists were extremely incompetent. Two, they knew just what they were doing and had no interest in creating objects that would remain intact but instead were making objects that would, by design, harden in the flames and explode.

This can be achieved by, among other things, adjusting the wetness of the clay. The building of three walls of the kiln suggests that they knew full well that the figurines would explode, adding to the suggestion that a deliberate effort was going on – not only the first ceramic objects ever known, but also perhaps the first example of a kind of fireworks. Our description of this as embodying some sort of ritual is something of an imaginative leap, but it seems unlikely that such onerous activity would be done out of sheer frivolity at a time when survival was a full-time job.

The crucial role of the fiber arts

More important probably than the presumably ritual use of ceramics in Dolni Vestonice is the discovery that by 26,000 years ago, these Upper Paleolithic people of Eurasia were well along in what has been called the String Revolution, a technological breakthrough (better thought of as the Fiber Revolution) that had profound effects on human destiny – probably more profound effects than any advance in the technique of making spear points, knives, scrapers, and other tools out of stone. The term *String Revolution* was evidently the original idea of Elizabeth Wayland Barber of Occidental College in California. She wrote a lovely book, *Women's Work*, suggesting what a remarkable invention string was, whenever it first was used. String's invention, she wrote, "opened the door to an enormous array of new ways to labor and improve the odds of survival." Comparing it to the steam engine, she mentioned the need of string for weaving and said that, on a far more basic level,

> string can be used simply to tie things up – to catch, to hold, to carry. From these notions come snares and fishlines, tethers and leashes, carrying nets, handles, and packages, not to mention a way of binding objects together to form more complex tools.

Indeed, she thought, so powerful was string "in taming the world and to human will and ingenuity" that it may well have made it possible for humans to populate virtually every niche they could reach. So the fiber artifacts found in those old Moravian sites were far more important than their humble appearance would have suggested.

Three certainties exist about fiber artifacts. Compared with things made out of stone, bone, antler, shell, and even (in some cases) wood, fiber items are highly perishable. Because of this, there simply aren't as many fiber artifacts remaining in the ground as other kinds. And there are even fewer fiber artifacts in the archaeological record than have persisted in the ground, because practically all archaeologists have not been trained to see them in the ground, much less recover them (often an extremely delicate and technical task). There remain only a handful of archaeology departments in the United States and abroad where such training is available, particularly at the graduate level. The other certain thing about fiber artifacts is that, in dry caves and other places where they do not deteriorate and disappear, they have been found to outnumber stone artifacts by a factor of 20 to 1. In several other situations (places covered with water where aerobic bacteria cannot get to the artifacts, and in permafrost), fiber and wood artifacts have been found to account for 95 percent of all artifacts recovered. That amounts to a tremendous amount of information that archaeologists have missed in most parts of the world, including Late Pleistocene Eurasia.

A third certainty about fiber artifacts such as baskets is that, unlike stone or bone artifacts or even pottery, the method by which the artifact was made is apparent in the artifact itself. Modern stone-knappers who like to replicate old spear points, for example, can do so with considerable skill, and of course, they know the steps they took to get to the finished product. But the earlier steps made are not necessarily present in the point. By contrast, a practiced eye can perceive which of a finite number of logical steps the basket-maker took. Indeed, no weaver of baskets and fabrics and other items makes such things exactly as anyone else does, so one can actually glimpse a bit of the living individual craftswoman. At the same time, most basket-makers of prehistory operated within an identifiable cultural framework, just as one sees tribal distinctions in the baskets of, say, Apache women, as distinct from Paiute women. And within such a tribal tradition, one can also see what appears to be one generation, or even one basket-maker, who taught those who came along afterward.

If one takes modern ethnographic studies of hunter-gatherer societies as not wholly unrepresentative of Late Paleolithic societies, the work of most human beings – especially women – has been overlooked. One result was that this left room for the picture to emerge of Upper Paleolithic society and economics as dominated by the mighty hunters setting out to slaughter mammoths and other large animals – though mammoths especially caught the imagination of those reconstructing these ancient lifeways. There was some evidence for this, but only a smidgen. Most notably, archaeologists found stone points among huge mammoth bone assemblages in a few places in Eurasia (and also North America). It appeared to many that astonishingly efficient and daring hunters were taking on entire herds and killing them for food.

But there was a problem here of specialization. Paleontologists, whose interest lay in the realm of prehistoric zoology rather than in the affairs of humans and hominids, found numerous similar assemblages of mammoth bones in Eurasia (and smaller ones in Siberia and North America) that had no stone points. And even in those assemblages where stone points and other tools were found, butchering marks were few and far between. In other words, over thousands of years and in various places (such as mineral licks, as at Dolni Vestonice, where the remains of a hundred or so mammoths were found), proboscideans died and created boneyards from which the people made what use they could.

Ethnographic studies of modern people have turned up practically no instances of deliberate elephant hunting before the advent of the ivory trade in modern times. There is no evidence of Upper Paleolithic assemblages of enough hunters (maybe 40 or so) to take down a mammoth, much less the number needed to wipe out a herd. It is dangerous enough, in fact, to go after any animal the size of a horse or a bison if one is armed with a spear. Only the foolhardiest would attempt to kill an animal that stands 14 feet high and has a notoriously bad temper when annoyed. A statement that has been assigned to multiple originators suggests that it is more likely that every so often a Paleolithic hunter brought down an already-wounded mammoth (or one slowed down a bit in the mud of a swamp) and then talked about it for the rest of his life. The picture of Man the Mighty Hunter is now fading out of the annals of prehistory. By far, most of the animal remains found strewn about places like Dolni Vestonice consist of the bones of small mammals like hares and foxes.

The finds of perishable artifacts in Dolni Vestonice I and several other sites in Moravia have done much to blow the old picture of Upper Paleolithic life out of the water, and with it the dominant figure of the mighty male hunter, and replaced it with a picture something like the one with which this chapter began. The first of these finds was made in 1993, consisting of mysterious impressions in strange clay fragments in Dolni Vestonice I, which turned out to be the imprints of basketry and textiles made from wild plants. These were the earliest forms of the fiber arts known – indeed, some 10,000 years earlier than anything found before. Just what the fragments themselves were is not clear. They might have been pieces of flooring on which items of weaving or basketry had been impressed, and turned into hard evidence when the place burned down. In any event, they and subsequent finds in these sites showed that people here were already weaving and making basketry with at least eight different styles of twining, some of which remain common today. Some of the fabrics were as fine as a Brooks Brothers shirt. People had to have been weaving textiles on looms and making freestanding basketry for a very long time to have developed such ability and diversity and sophistication of technique.

Just exactly what those people were making from all this weaving, basketry, and cordage is impossible to say with certainty, but given the excellence of technique, there is reason to think that they were making baskets of various kinds, and possibly mats for sleeping and wall hangings, and clothing of various kinds, such as shawls, skirts, sashes, and shirts. They used whipping stitches like those used today to sew two pieces of fabric together, and that no doubt served the same end 26,000 years ago.

In addition to knots and other signs of weaving, numerous tools were turned up over the many times these sites were examined, which can now be seen as tools for weaving and other steps in the production of such materials. One puzzling artifact made

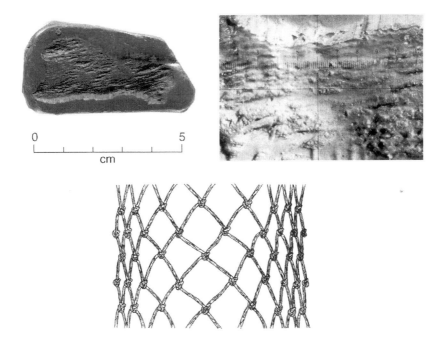

Figure 18.1 Fragment of netting at Zaraisk showing (clockwise from top left) positive impression of the cast, microphotograph of the netting structure, and schematic of the structure.

Source: Courtesy of O. Soffer, J. M. Adovasio, and Stephanie Snyder.

of mammoth ivory was shaped something like a boomerang, but without the curve. It makes perfect sense as a weaving batten (and, in fact, is nearly identical to the battens still in use today among Navajo weavers). Another tool, basically a rod with a doughnut-shaped end, has been fairly commonly found throughout the world, dating from later times, and has puzzled archaeologists, whose best idea for them is that they were used somehow to straighten spear and arrow shafts. But when they are thought about in the context of Moravian weaving, it seems that they would have been useful in the spinning of threads into string or yarn for weaving. Fairly large ivory needles were already known from such places, and the assumption was that they were used for sewing together skins and furs for clothing, but the proliferation of smaller needles found across Eurasia could not have been conveniently used for stitching such tough and unforgiving materials – except for the thinnest of leather. They are the right size, however, for stitching together pieces of woven fabric. Some of the ivory needles found are so fine that they would have permitted embroidery.

The very diversity of styles and workmanship that emerges from all these perishable artifacts and their associated tools, plus the fact that most of the stone used to make stone tools was not local, all suggests that these were people who assembled here for part of the year (perhaps a large part) and separated into smaller groups – probably near-nuclear family groups – at other times. It is reasonable to speculate that each such household might well have its (her) own favored techniques and brought them to the larger group, thus accounting for much of the remarkable diversity of products.

Group hunting

Four of the fragments examined had impressions of cordage tied into sheet bends or weaver's knots (along with what appear to be tools for measuring the spaces between knots), which strongly suggests that they were making nets for hunting relatively small mammals, as well as string bags. Earlier workers had noticed the abundance – indeed, prevalence – of bones of such small mammals as hares and foxes in Upper Paleolithic camps in eastern and central Europe but came up with fairly weak suggestions for the means of hunting them. Anyone who has watched these animals race and dart when threatened will find it implausible in the extreme to imagine people chasing them down in the open and clubbing them, or even throwing little spears at them, both of which have been offered as serious explanations (by male archaeologists, of course). The use of nets, on the other hand, as well as cordage snares, easily explains peoples' success. They could, obviously, have made nets of wider mesh and thicker cordage for hunting larger animals as well, but no evidence of this has been found. At the same time, the large bone needles that were assumed to be used for sewing skins together would have also been handy tools for making the nets.

What, then, are the social implications of all this? First of all, we know from such modern hunter-gatherer societies as the Pygmies of the Ituri Forest in Africa's Congo region that net hunting is a communal affair, involving women, children, and elderly people, as well as adult males. It engages essentially everyone in the group as beaters, clubbers, or net-holders and makes the acquisition of high-energy and high-protein food (meat) much less dangerous and more dependable. By adjusting the mesh, they could have caught even smaller forms of life – birds, even insects. This would ease the problems involved in feeding a relatively larger aggregation of people by providing a mass harvest in a short time – a surplus beyond their imme-diate need that, in turn, would make ceremonial feasts possible. Such behavior is noted ethnographically.

Making things out of fiber is not the sole prerogative of either sex in ethnographic accounts of small bands or larger tribal societies. More often than not, for example, men make sandals for themselves and their families, and it is also fairly clear that in such societies, both men and women *know how* to produce sandals and other items that use basketry techniques and materials. In many cases, men probably do make things like baskets that they need for their own purposes, but throughout the tribal world today, women make most basketry. But loom or frame weaving is a craft practiced almost exclusively by women in the tribal world, as is the gathering and processing of plant products for such weaving. This is the case in virtually all tribal societies where textiles and basketry are produced for domestic and commu-nal needs, and typically, it breaks down only when such perishable products enter the domain of market exchange. One rare exception to this among American Indian tribes is the Hopi of northeastern Arizona (an agricultural society), whose men do all the weaving – restricted to ceremonial wear, such as sashes and kilts and cos-tumery of brides made by their paternal uncles. Next door to the Hopi, as it were, Navajo women do all the weaving – almost entirely rugs – though the looms are often built by the husbands, and a weaver's son-in-law is expected to supply her with some of the weaving tools.

In addition, from cross-cultural studies throughout the world, the making of ceramic items, especially pottery, in many societies that we are familiar with is chiefly the province of women. There are, to be sure, innumerable variations that people have invented over time for all such matters, but even in the face of some scholarly quibbles, it is safe to assume what could be called the default position: that most of, if not all, the ceramics, weaving, basketry, and clothing was made by women in the years that Dolni Vestonice and the other Moravian sites were inhabited. And from that and other evidence – notably the Venus figures – it is safe to assume that the *idea* of gender, the separate category with its associated roles and identities, was now present. In other words, we see here the malleable social notion of gender, as opposed to (and in addition to) the clear biological function of sex. It is not clear from any particular archaeological evidence at these Moravian sites that the *idea* of man as opposed to male was prevalent. There is virtually no iconography that suggests oth-erwise, but Thurber's war of the sexes (read gender) would presumably soon begin. In any event, it is safe to say that some division of labor was in place, and with it probably a set of family relatives with whom one identified and by whom one identi-fied oneself on a permanent intergenerational basis, a group in which every segment – children, men, women, elders – stood to gain. The population explosion that took place in this period seems to bear this out. In other words, here is one of the most vivid examples yet discovered of what we can safely call thoroughly, recognizably, behaviorally modern humans.

Does this seem to be a great deal to read into these fragments of perishable items and ceramics, along with a few intact tools? In fact, it isn't, and new, closer looks at those enigmatic Venus figurines that are so fascinating a feature of this Upper Paleolithic Eurasian society tend to strengthen this hypothesis and round out our picture of life in those days.

Venuses

Some 200 Venus figurines and figurine fragments from across Europe are the most representational three-dimensional images made in the Gravettian period some 27,000 to 22,000 years ago, which, of course, includes the Moravian sites described earlier. Nothing is their equal before this period from anywhere in the world, and thousands of years go by before anything comparable appears again. As a result, they have claimed the attention of amateurs and professionals alike with almost the same continuing fascination certain scholars and most kids have for dinosaurs. The Venus of Willendorf is surely the best-known of all these sculptures. They remain in many ways enigmatic, mysterious, even confusing. They serve many purposes today, including as Rorschach emblems for some of today's hang-ups. They obviously mean "female," and they probably mean "woman," which suggests that they are not simply representations of the reproductive function of the female human, or gynecological and obstetrical "textbooks," as one scholar put it. At the same time, there is simply no denying that the sculptors of these figurines went to a great deal of trouble to show off the sexual and secondary sexual features of the female human, even to the point of leaving the rest of the figure – face, feet, arms, and so forth – either abstract or absent altogether. (There are exceptions to this, of course, but no exception in the entire matter is more obvious than the fact that there are only one or two examples of clearly male figurines from this region and period. There are many figurines that are androgynous, without visible sex.)

What escaped many observers, both male and female, for many years was that some of these figurines were partly clad. The Venus of Willendorf's head, for example, though faceless, did have hair, it seemed, braided and wrapped around her head. Others had little bits of decorations – body bands, bracelets, minor bits and pieces of material of some sort. But never mind – they were largely naked and had to represent fertility, menstruation, the godhead (as goddess), or (giggle) paleoporn.

Then, in 1998, coming off their discovery of the many fiber artifacts from Moravian sites, which many of their colleagues considered an important rearrangement of the picture of Upper Paleolithic society in Europe, Adovasio and Soffer turned their attention to these figures. To begin with, a close inspection of the braids of the Venus of Willendorf showed that her "hair" was, on the contrary, a woven hat, a radially hand-woven item of apparel that was probably begun from a knotted center in the manner of certain coiled baskets made today by Hopi, Apache, and other American Indian tribes, in which a flexible element is wrapped with stem stitches as the spiral grows. Seven circuits encircle the head, with two extra half-circuits over the nape of the neck. Indeed, so precise is the carving of all this stitchery that it is not unreasonable to think that, among the functions involved in this Upper Paleolithic masterpiece, it served as a blueprint or instruction manual showing weavers how to make such hats. Indeed, anyone who has done any sculpting in stone or wood can tell you that the fashioning of the body, while extremely closely realized, would have been easy compared with the astounding control and staying power needed to render the stitching (even a few splices) of this hat so true and precise. The carver had to have spent more time on just the hat than on the rest of the entire figurine.

Of all the scholars who have examined these figurines over the decades (and there must be hundreds), only one other, Elizabeth Barber, ever took notice of the fiber accoutrements some of them wore. One British scholar who studied the Venuses in his youth never noticed any clothing because, he recalled, he "never got past the breasts."

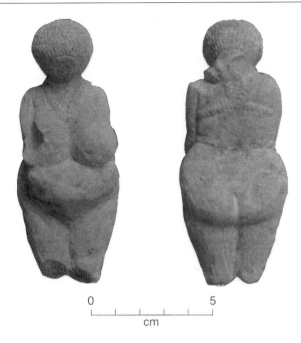

Figure 18.2 Front and back views of the female figurine in ivory from Kostenki I.

Source: Courtesy of O. Soffer.

Figure 18.3 Close-up of the coiling start of the basket hat depicted on the head of the Venus of Willendorf.

Source: S. Holland. Courtesy of O. Soffer.

Several other such figurines from central and eastern Europe wear similarly detailed radial or spiral woven hats as well as some begun by interlacing grids. Western European figurines tend to be more schematic, such as the Venus of Brassempouy, whose hair may be covered, in a more abstract rendering, by some sort of hairnet or snood. One thing that seems fairly common to all the partly clad figurines is that when they wear hats or

Figure 18.4 Left, right, and top views of the plaited start of the basket hat depicted on the marl head of the female figurine from Kostenki I.

Source: S. Holland. Courtesy of O. Soffer.

caps, the facial details are absent. This suggests a social importance to the headgear, rather than an individual statement of personal identity. In other words, these various forms of headgear may speak to a particular status or rank enjoyed by at least some women.

Other forms of clothing or cloth decorations found on Venuses of this Gravettian period include straps wrapped around the figure, often above the breasts, and sometimes held there with over-the-shoulder straps. Others wear belts, often low on their hips, sometimes connected to skirts of string. The Venus of Lespugue, for example – she of the truly overwhelming hips – wears a back skirt carved with a remarkable attention to detail. It consists of eleven cords attached to a base cord that serves as a belt. The cords are secured to the belt by looping both ends of a single-ply string over the belt and twisting the ends together with a final Z twist. On several of the cords, the carver made 30 and 40 separate incisions to show the individual twists, and she took great care to depict the progressive changes in angle of twist. At the bottom of the skirt, the angle of twist is much looser, clearly suggesting that the cords were unraveling or fraying at the hem.

What is to be made of all this? An important thing to note is that, except for one sexually ambiguous fragment that has a belt, such apparel appears only on figurines that are female. Clearly, the garments so carefully portrayed are not the normal daily wear of women in these times, since they lived in climates where such clothing would be utterly insufficient against the cold – except, of course, for the woven hats. In the few known burials of the time, people were interred fully clothed. The body bands, belts, string skirts, and so forth could have been for ritual purposes, or they could have been signs of status, perhaps worn over one's daily clothing – or not, in the case of ceremonial use. Indeed, they might have been imagined, as with the halos depicted on icons of saints. What they do suggest is that such apparel was a woman thing, not worn by males, and that it served to immortalize at some great effort the fact that such apparel set women (or at least certain women) apart in a social category of their own. Much of the woven

0   3
                              cm

Figure 18.5 The Venus of Brassempouy, carved from ivory.

Source: S. Holland. Courtesy of O. Soffer.

material from this period that was found imprinted on ceramic fragments is as finely done as anything done later in the Bronze and Iron Ages, and equal to much of the thin cotton and linen garments worn today. Given the amount of effort involved in weaving such cloth and also in carving a replica of it in stone, one can reasonably conclude that the pieces of apparel found on so many of the Gravettian Venuses were symbols of achievement, or prestige. And it is also fair to say that, for those who were weavers or ceramicists, the workaday world was more complex, the daily round of chores, tasks, and roles more intense. Who were they?

The precision with which the carvers of the Venuses represented woven items leads almost inevitably to the conclusion that they were created by the weavers themselves, or at least under the sharp-eyed tutelage of the weavers. That it was almost surely women who did most of this fine weaving and basketry is one matter to which the ethnographic record appears to be a reliable guide.

Discussion questions

1. According to the chapter, how has the gender of the researcher impacted the interpretation of the Venus figurines?
2. What does the author argue are the implications of the intricate clothing found on the Venus figurines?
3. What is unique about fiber items in archaeological finds?
4. What do modern people groups, such as Native American tribes or hunter-gatherer societies, suggest about prehistoric weaving?

Chapter 19

Gender, business, and space control

Yoruba market women and power

Toyin Falola

Reproduced from Bessie House-Midamna and Felix K. Ekechi (eds.), *African Market Women and Economic Power* (Westport, CT: Greenwood Press, 1995). Reformatted by the authors.

This chapter sets out to show a linkage between an economic activity (trade) and power as it relates to a segment of the population (women) and one subset (traders). Such a linkage is possible, as it is, indeed, between any two other aspects of the structure and institution of society. In this specific case, the assumption is that wealth translates into power. This is true, but there are limitations that must be borne in mind from the beginning. Wealth is only one criterion of power or, indeed, of upward mobility. There are ascriptive factors as well, like membership in ruling families, age, and sex, to mention but a few. In addition, in a male-dominated society, gender is built into the construction of power. No matter how wealthy a woman is, she cannot become an *oba* (king) or *balogun* (war commander) in most towns or wield the highest title in many lineages. Power and reward are, in general, distributed by a male hierarchy, concerned with articulating its own interest.

Nevertheless, as this chapter makes clear, women constitute part of the *political landscape* in a number of ways. Their predominance in market transactions, as sellers and buyers, enables the acquisition of control over an important sector of the economy. This control – of a space that is so central to production and exchange – provides considerable spinoff values and influence. One spinoff value is the ritual control of space in a society operating within a framework of a nonmechanical worldview that seeks spiritual balance with the universe. The marketplace is part of the *religious environment* that is integrated into the *religious pantheon*. Since women in Yorubaland control the market space, they also control the market rituals. Cases have been reported of powerful women heads of market who double as priestesses. One nineteenth-century example makes the linkage between such control and power so clear that is deserves to be quoted:

The Eni-Oja[1] is at the head of all the devil worshippers[2] in town. She also has charge of the King's market, and enjoys the perquisites accruing therefrom. She wears a gown like a man, on her arms the King leans on the day he goes to worship at the market, i.e., to propitiate the deity that presides over the markets. She has under her (1) the

DOI: 10.4324/9781003398349-22

Olosi who has joint responsibility with her for the market, and (2) the Aroja or market keeper, an officer whose duty it is to keep order, and arrange the management of the market, and who actually resides there.

(Johnson 1921: 66)

As we point out in what follows, the rituals cannot be ignored; they must be discussed as part of the makeup of the *political configurations*. Productivity and prosperity underline the concern for rituals by the power elite. Power is threatened without prosperity and productivity, and women become part of the means of maintaining both as well as, of course, of the spiritual balance. Thus, goddesses of wealth, productivity, and fertility must be seen as part of the process of explaining this intricate relationship between gender and power. Control of ritual power is crucial to the control of space and to the way interpersonal and intergroup relations are intricately constructed to distribute power and resources in a society.

The bulk of the financial transactions in the marketplace bring together people, goods, and money in a single setting. The very nature of the interaction in this space is useful in such ways as information exchange, social interactions, social control, influence building, and networking. Women are able to participate in all the privileges conferred by this space. It is because of the *relevance* of the market to the articulation of gender image and influence that I have chosen to underscore *space control* as part of the title of this chapter. In the more formalized power structure, women are marginalized and tend to operate within a clientele framework – serving as clients and agents to a male power elite – to tap opportunities. Gender and clientelism are also beyond the scope of this chapter, but it is important to point out that women flourish more within the framework of space control than anywhere else.

One dimension the specific concern of this project does not address is that of power acquisition through other means. For instance, there were several female leaders of substance in precolonial formations, including Queen Kambassa of Bonny and Queen Amina of Zaria. In both contemporary colonial and postcolonial settings, resistance to British rule and a new political process toward democracy have thrust a number of women leaders into the limelight. Studies of women have been more concerned with these high-profile political women – the queens of African history, for want of a more appropriate description[3] – than with market women, in order to demonstrate more glorified aspects of the political worth of women and their contributions – a justifiable reaction to male-dominated historical accounts. No one should dismiss this emergency rescue operation to construct the history of women of political substance, a part of creating a balance in historiography and of correcting a generation-old lapse in methodology. Nevertheless, an *archaeology* of the queens limits the range and possibility of social and political history.[4] As the case of market women demonstrates, the less-structured, informal sector produces its own "queens," its own mythology, and its own conception of order and values: it may be less dramatic, but it is more revealing of the dynamics of power interplay and social institutions.

The strength of this chapter lies in the elaboration of the linkage identified earlier. The data are limited to the domestic, informal arena of trade and politics from the precolonial period through the colonial to the present. One limitation is that the case studies used to illuminate general points are rather limited, a function of the state of gender historiography. Studies are few and far between, and their rationale is uncoordinated.[5] As I have pointed out elsewhere, the weakness in gender studies may result, among other factors, from the paucity of information in both oral and written sources on the contribution of women to the emergence and development of Yoruba kingdoms, the patrilineal nature of the Yoruba family, which emphasizes the supremacy of men over women, and the low position occupied by women in the policy- and decision-making machinery (Falola 1978).

Women and trade

Like members of most other societies, the Yoruba believe that everyone must work, irrespective of gender, as a means to avoid starvation and poverty, and to earn respect, fame, and prowess. While a number of activities associated with women are designed to help their husbands and raise their children, the society does not frown on women creating the opportunity to make money for themselves. Women spend money on household maintenance, social functions, and chieftaincy titles. In the process of achieving a variety of ambitions and fulfilling mutually related roles, women appear to have devoted more time to work than men, in a variety of activities ranging from the domestic to the high-profile ones of public administration and the priesthood of important cults.[6]

In precolonial formations, there was a sexual division of labor: men were farmers and craftsmen, and women engaged in food processing and trading.[7] In general, women's entry into many occupations was unrestricted, although they avoided the military and certain crafts. They were not excluded from the new occupations created during the colonial rule and beyond, even if they were marginalized by the very fact that a colonial society was male-dominated.[8] In the precolonial domestic economy, farming was the leading occupation, although Yoruba women were less involved in farming than, say, the Ijo and Igbo of eastern Nigeria, the Akan of Ghana, or the Tio of the Middle Congo.[9] Yoruba women contributed to harvesting, processing for final consumption and storage, livestock-keeping, and the selling of farm products.[10] Women of means were able to plow their profits into large-scale farming, as in the case of the nineteenth-century celebrity Efunsetan Aniwura of Ibadan, who had more than a thousand slaves on her farms (Johnson 1921: 393). Women were active in the manufacture of a variety of goods like oil, dye, ceramics, and textiles.

By far, the most important precolonial activity of women was trade, a professional occupation. The emphasis was on selling what they or their husbands produced from their farms, what they manufactured on their own, and the goods they bought from others for the purpose of reselling them. One of the earliest students of Yoruba markets, W. Hodder (1962: 110), was fascinated with the prominent role of women and dated this domination to the nineteenth century, "to the conditions of internal insecurity in which it was unsafe for men to move away from their farms, while women enjoyed relative immunity from attacks." That there was turbulence in the nineteenth century and women received better protection than men, there can be no doubt (Falola and Oguntomisin 1984). However, there is no strong evidence to associate the wars of the nineteenth century with women's dominance in trade. Earlier records reveal this domination as well (Marshall 1964: 73–78).

Two studies by Gloria Marshall (now Niara Sudarkasa) have established a close correlation among the roles of women as wives, mothers, and traders. There was the expectation that a man would assist his wife by providing some capital to start a small trade.

As the relationship between the husband and wife developed and the woman had borne a certain number of children, she increased her trading business, unhindered by occasional or regular separation from the husband, who could then take another wife. The woman could assist her husband with money; but more importantly, she had to take care of her children in the context of competition with the children of rival wives.

With the introduction of formal Western education, the need to sponsor children was used to further justify trading, especially in cases when the husband refused to pay for female children or had to limit the number of sons he could train (Belasco 1980; Sudarkasa 1973). Women also paid for the upkeep of their children and supplemented domestic expenses on food. The common pattern appears to be that a younger wife stayed closer to home to bear children and assist her husband with limited farmwork. When the children grew up, she had more time for herself, and the husband could fulfill the aspiration of taking another wife. Thus, Yoruba marriages matured in such a way that women were able to acquire their independence and men were able to divert their sexual exploits elsewhere.

The process of capital accumulation in the precolonial setting is best described by N. A. Fadipe, the first to write a sociology of his own people. A husband and network of relations furnished the necessary capital for a woman to start a trade:

> A percentage of the payment made as bride price by her husband was passed on to her before her marriage. A few days before marriage her own relatives made her, in addition to clothing and other articles of personal wear, presents of cash. . . . A few days after her marriage . . . she has an opportunity of receiving presents of money not only from the various households in her husband's compound, but also from some members of the neighborhood, and from principal members of her husband's kindred group. . . . Out of it she buys an animal (goat or sheep) or two and some fowls for rearing. If a wife was not brought in any trade, these animals and fowls would remain her principal investment. If she was skilled in some trade, part of it would be used for starting it.
>
> (Fadipe 1970: 156)

Here is perhaps the best description of the "sentiments of kinship and social solidarity" in creating mobility for a woman who had to start from scratch, sentiments devoid of "mercenary motives" or expectations of interest. A new wife benefited from more "sentiments" in the form of gifts and other support until the birth of her first child. Thanks also to Fadipe, the continuation of the practice of accumulation is reported for the colonial period as well:

> With regard to a woman who is not married in the customary sense of the word – i.e., who lives with a man as his wife without the consent of her parents – a more generous amount for trading purposes is usually granted. Women of this type are usually of the town-dwelling class, and are generally sophisticated Muslims or Christians. They usually have not learnt any craft. But when in their husband's house, they usually ask for and receive a sum of money with which to start trading in one line of goods or another – generally cheap articles of European manufacture. These women must get all they want for the purpose from their husbands, since they cannot rely upon the sources which are open to women married in the socially approved way.
>
> (Fadipe 1970: 156)

Starting in such small ways, the enterprising woman expanded by plowing capital back in, raising more capital, obtaining credit, and manipulating market opportunities.

In precolonial society, women traders could be found everywhere hawking cooked food. Many women held their trading activities in their homes, where they sold a variety of items, like foodstuffs, cosmetics, and tobacco. Such traders were patronized by those who could not attend the market. The practice of staying home for the purpose of trading was common among older women and new brides, who might not be permitted to begin full-time trading until they had spent a few years at home. There were women commissioned agents, obtaining supplies from craftsmen to sell.

Women traders were predominant in the village and town markets, the daily and periodic ones. Their activities were many, from preparations to actual selling and buying. Other trading activities took place outside the marketplace, with women hawking their wares, scouting around for goods from producers and farmers, intercepting other traders in order to buy cheap, and so on.[11] Women took part in the regional and long-distance trade, carrying their businesses to areas far away from home. Like men, they withstood the physical hardship of long journeys and the risks traveling involved, especially in periods of political instability. Those married to highly placed men like the *oba* and chiefs were also able to participate, either as independent operators or through proxies.[12]

Colonial and postcolonial rule has not diminished the role of women in trade. Throughout this century, the complex web of marketing that links villages with cities and one region with the rest of the country is dominated by women. Trade expanded considerably, thanks to the growth of cocoa, a major cash crop, improvements in transport systems, urbanization, and since the 1960s, substantial revenue from petroleum. Surveys on the division of labor conducted in the 1960s and 1970s show that higher percentages of women worked as traders – as in the case of Oje, a neighborhood in Ibadan, where 84 percent of the women were traders, and in Lagos, where women made up 70 percent of traders (Barnes 1986: 160; Lloyd 1967: 71; Marris 1961: 68). Certainly, older institutions of market and trade continued until the recent period, as the study by Hodder and Ukwu (1969) clearly demonstrates.[13]

Women and power: political systems and mythologies

One fact must be recognized: the Yoruba political systems create titles specific to women and recognize the need to incorporate successful women into the system. Opportunities are not many, compared to those offered men, and the distribution of principal functions and roles are no doubt male-dominated. Within the avenues created for women, however, and the opportunities open to them can be found all the successful cases of women who exploit and benefit from them. In the precolonial polities, women wielded political influence that varied in degree from one community to the other. Although the validity is yet to be ascertained, a few women are reputed to have reached the apex of authority as *oba*. Ile-Ife tradition mentioned, for instance, the reign of the tyrannical *Ooni* Luwo (Fabunmi 1969: 23–24), and there were similar cases in Akure and Ilesa.[14] There was no town without a woman chief of some kind, although the power attached to such offices varied. For instance, in Ondo, the *lobun* was a powerful woman chief, excluded from farming and secluded to her palace like the male *oba*. She took part in the selection of a new king, settled quarrels among the male chiefs, and officiated in the opening of new markets. In addition, she was also regarded as the priestess of *Aje*, the god of money.[15]

In Ilesa, another kingdom, the head of the women chiefs was the *arise*, supported by the *Risa Arise*, *Odofin Arise*, and *Yeye-Soloro*. Each ward had a female head as well (Falola 1976: 69). Other towns and villages had their *lyalode* as heads of women chiefs.[16] A few women chiefs constituted part of the membership of secret societies responsible for executive and judicial functions in a number of communities.[17]

As an integral part of the palace system, the oba's wives (*aya oba* or *olori*) occupied a strategic position that allowed them to hear and spread news and to influence major policies of state, especially in matters relating to their own lineages or communities. Many quarters in a town tried to be represented in the palace not only through the palace servants but also through marriage ties. There were marriage ties, too, with the neighboring states in order to use women to cement existing friendships or create new ones. Women were also employed to monitor and influence foreign policy decisions.[18] The *olori*, together with other palace officials, were assigned duties of much social and political significance.[19] Women of rank, royal wives, and princesses often formed organizations to protect their own interests, as in the case of Akure.[20]

Women and power: the ritual and market domains

Fertility, productivity, and wealth are some of the key elements associated with female power. Goddesses of wealth and productivity are many, dominated by female worshippers. Several goddesses were associated with market protection. The goddess of the river, *Yemonja*, derives her relevance from the power to give children and general prosperity. Some traditions call *Yemonja* the mother of all gods and the "mother earth," the fountain of life and productivity. For combining life with water, Yemonja personifies greatness, which perhaps explains the widespread nature of her worship.[21]

Many localized studies have revealed the centrality of the female goddess in the Yoruba pantheon (Drewal 1983). One recent example is on Ondo, where Jacob Olupona shows how the *Obitun* and the *Odun Aje* demonstrate the significance of women in the economy and politics (Olupona 1991). The *Odun Aje* in particular is more focused on wealth, as a celebration and worship of the goddess *Aje*, usually by the majority of adult females. According to Olupona, the *Aje* rituals bring out the dimensions of human reproduction and economy, symbolizing success in trade and prosperity. He provides the English version of an important lyric:

> Aje excreted on my head; Whoever Aje touches is made human.
> Aje slept on my head; Whoever Aje touches acts like a child.
> Aje elevates me like a king; I shall forever rejoice.
> Aje is happy, so am I.
> Aje is happy, so am I.
>
> (Olupona 1991: 156)

This lyric and others sing the gains of trade, gains attributable to this goddess.

By participating in various trading activities, women had the opportunity to become wealthy and could therefore enjoy the high sociopolitical status associated with people of wealth, such as collecting titles, building a following, and acquiring symbols of status like clothes and horses. The connection between the market and power is, however, much broader than the one-to-one relation of wealth and power.

Control and management of the marketplace yield power. The marketplace is an important aspect of local and national politics not only for its influence but also for its communication and social functions. It is the place where the bulk of community wealth circulates. To the political class, the market is a place to collect revenues (such as taxes, tolls, fees, dues, levies, and gifts), benefit from corruption (by way of stall allocation), and exercise power (by making laws to establish control or using physical coercion or violence). In all these facets, the target is the market women. In the modern era, political parties have extended the building of machine solidarity and opposition mechanisms to the marketplace, urging women to collaborate or resist. In periods of military rule, the marketplace is a venue of propaganda, used to announce and spread reforms, and the target is again the market women. Building a political constituency or a sphere of influence has always been one criterion to attain prominence, seek office, or wield and retain power. The incorporation of market women into such a sphere has been recognized since the 1930s by the early political parties, like the Nigerian Youth Movement, and virtually all subsequent political parties have adopted a similar strategy. In the process, power-seekers pursue the means to penetrate market women. In so many instances, competition for control of the marketplace by prominent women traders becomes part of the complications of local politics itself: one recent case study of the Mushin district in Lagos has explained very convincingly how the market, with its "large bloc of support," occupies a prominent part of power struggle and political factionalism (Barnes 1986).

Invisible to buyers and other visitors to the marketplace are the powerful associations and guilds that try to dominate the space in order to maximize economic gains, create order, and wade through the muddy terrain of politics. Traders dealing in a similar commodity organize into a guild. A guild has an executive that admits new members and discusses issues relating to pricing and market administration. In recent times, organizations of women traders control and discipline their members and oversee the recruitment to the marketplace. In major urban markets, the right to participate has to be negotiated cleverly, and it is difficult to bypass women's organizations. Expulsion from the market, enforcement of discipline, checks on the activities of illegal traders, improvement of market facilities – all are part of the activities and duties of market women associations. Because the unions are powerful, they are able to police the market, and they set up microadministrations respected and recognized by the state.

Presiding over the association is the *iyalode* or *iyaloja*, a woman of means and influence. An *iyalode* wields a lot of power derived from her individual capacity and charm, her personal resources, and the role of the association that she represents. She is the link between the market, market women, and the political authorities, both formal and informal. She implements the wish of the association with regard to all allocations and the admission of members, knows all the traders with stalls, and keeps an eye on a floating population of street traders and hawkers. She supervises the internal administration of the market, settles disputes, and interacts with external suppliers to ensure fairness.

The market political paraphernalia is more elaborate than the office of the *iyalode*. The *iyalode* herself has a long list of lieutenants, in some cases elected by the women's association, and in some others appointed by the town's traditional political authority. In Ibadan, for instance, there are such subordinate titles as *otun, osi, balogun, asipa, ekarun, abese, maye, are alasa*, and *ikolaba*. There are honorary titles, too, to reward successful and prominent women. As if to create a forest of titles, each guild runs a parallel order, headed by an *iya egbe* with subcommittees presided over by chairwomen known as the *alaga*. For those who could mobilize adequate capital to expand the scale of their operations, considerable scope exists to benefit socially and politically from their business acumen.

If the established political order, dominated by men, assumes that it can freely manipulate the marketplace and women traders through women's associations and leadership, it is wrong. These women also manipulate prominent men and political order, seeking the extension of their influence. The subject of female manipulation requires more treatment than is possible here, but its mechanisms can be highlighted briefly. Prominent male members are incorporated into market organizations through offices and honorary titles. Men are appointed as honorary consuls and to functional positions, such as secretary or treasurer. These appointments are no indication that women could not perform these tasks or manage their affairs, but they are clever ways of forging alliances with men. Incorporated male members and others are expected to deliver crucial linkages with power, authority, resources, and groups external to the market in ways defined or suggested by the women.

Coping with state power

What looms large in the discussion has been the role of the state. The state has always been interested in drawing women into its revenue network by collecting market levies, dues, and tolls from them. In trying to attain legitimacy and to govern, the state also makes use of the marketplace for propaganda and for building a constituency. In other words, the state understands the relevance of women. There was an argument in the 1950s that women did not understand the state and that market women were, in general, politically passive and are not "alive to demand their rights" (Mabogunje 1961: 16).

Akin Mabogunje, a geographer of international renown, responded to this position by saying that political response is a function of the interpretation of one's rights. He cited the Aba women's riot of the 1920s, which arose when women were asked to pay tax. As long as women's trade is not interfered with, Mabogunje contends, they are politically quiet. However, whenever there is an economic injustice, they tend to join in male-led protest against the state. He is ambivalent in his conclusion: while on the one hand there is the assumption of passivity, on the other hand, there is an acknowledgment of the market women's political role as objects of manipulation. Whenever politics have been studied as a *social phenomenon*, beyond the highbrow boardroom negotiations and cutthroat competitions, women have been seen to play an active role. This is made clear in the study by Cheryl Johnson-Odim (1978), to mention one important case study. Mabogunje (1961), too, underscores this point when he refers to the protest in the 1950s by women against the badly run Free Education Scheme of the Eastern region and a Yoruba *oba* who was using his power to control commerce to his advantage. In spite of his example of women's protest, Mabogunje still sees gender-based weakness: he concludes that women are more interested in deriving profits from their trade than participating in politics.

We cannot undermine women's understanding of politics as Mabogunje does, an error born of a limited conception of politics and trade. The marketplace itself is a *political space* dominated by women. We can move the discussion in yet another direction to show the limitation of Mabogunje's understanding and broaden the conception of women and politics. This direction is to see how women, by means that can be described only as political, confront the state.

Politics is about interest. To search for market women's role in the male-dominated arena is to abandon the substance in pursuit of a shadow. We must understand their interest: the pursuit of trade and the benefits arising therefrom. It is this interest that determines their political role, which explains why they fight the state over the allocation of market stalls, price control, regulation of street trading, and the location of new markets, to mention some important issues. These conflicts are many, as reading any of Nigeria's newspapers and magazines will reveal. Conflict is an expression of politics: it is public, challenging, and result-oriented.

There is also resistance; a common, almost daily, occurrence is to ignore the state and disregard laws that are considered stupid or injurious to their interests. For example, most price-control measures have failed simply because the market women refused to cooperate.[22] So also is commodity rationing in moments of scarcity (Falola 1992). Rather than succumb to pressure, market women are known to close down their shops, thus bringing economic activities to a halt. Resistance is politics, a most intense manifestation of a hostile social and political intercourse between the market women and the agents of the state. To repeat an important point: in seeking data to validate assumptions about market women and politics, let us look in the right place, which is the space they dominate and manipulate better than men.

Precolonial case studies

So far, I have exposed the contours of the linkage. Now I turn to a few cases to illustrate the theme, drawing from four experiences of women who used the marketplace to obtain power. There are two cases of *iyalode* of the nineteenth century who attained their positions because of their trading connections and wealth. In the turbulent history of the nineteenth century, women took part in the decision to go to war, financed military expeditions, saw to the efficient organizations of markets, and competed with their male counterparts.

The first case is that of Tinubu, the Egba woman who achieved fame because of her trade. She left her town of Owu and settled in Badagry, where she traded in salt and tobacco and acted as a middleman to Brazilian traders. The trade brought her immense wealth; Akitoye, the exiled king of Lagos, met her in Badagry in 1846 as one of the most influential citizens of the town. In 1851, Tinubu followed Akitoye to Lagos, where she decided to settle. The change did not affect her fortune, and she was able to increase the number of her slaves.[23] She became very influential in Lagos politics and participated actively in the attacks both on the Lagos government and on the foreign merchants, whom she saw as monopolists denying the indigenes their economic rights. By 1856, this lady, now known to her opponents as "the terror of Lagos,"[24] could no longer be tolerated. She was forcibly expelled from Lagos by Consul Campbell, who breathed a sigh of relief after her departure. The move was not without local protest against the British by hundreds of Tinubu's supporters. She resettled in Abeokuta, where, in a short while, she re-established herself as an astute politician and a patriot who supplied the town with weapons during warfare. Her contribution to trade and Egba politics fetched her the highest title of *iyalode* in 1864.

The second case is that of Efunsetan Aniwura of Ibadan, who, through trade and large-scale farming, was able to rise to the leading position of *iyalode*. Her wealth was such that she could afford to build a private army of personal guards. She was active in local trade and built an extensive network of regional trade, which included the profitable articles of salt, guns, and gunpowder.[25] Her success generated considerable resentment among the male chiefs. Such resentment took a turn for the worse in the 1870s, when the political head of the city-state, *Are Latosa*, instigated her brutal murder on May 1, 1874. The official reasons for this murder were all tied to her political influence and wealth: a male leader of the town accused her of political insubordination and arrogance (Johnson 1921: 391). Her death almost led to civil war, and the authorities had to use the face-saving device of executing the slaves who carried out the assignment.[26]

There were perhaps many more examples of rich and powerful women contemporaries of Tinubu and Efunsetan, although records of their careers did not survive. For instance, Aniwura's predecessor as *iyalode* is described as a rich woman who "lost her wealth" (Johnson 1921: 392). Another lady, Adu of Ijanna, a town under Ijaye, is also mentioned in the tradition as "a rich lady" of influence (Johnson 1921: 331).

Contemporary case studies

A few biographies and case studies are emerging, indicating a positive shift in the recent period. As was to be expected, the biographies have focused more on those active in political life (Adeniyi 1993; Johnson-Odim 1978). To keep our concern, we take two examples of traders. One prominent example in the colonial period is Alimotu Pelewura of Lagos, whose concern was to protest colonial policies that threatened the interest of Lagos market women.[27] Her leadership of a market association 8,000-strong lasted four decades and derived from a recognition by other traders of the need to unite for a common cause. An illiterate fish trader, Pelewura emerged as a stronger leader in 1923, in alliance with the newly formed Nigerian National Democratic Party, led by Herbert Macaulay, the "father of Nigerian nationalism." Pelewura became a member of the Ilu Committee, the traditional executive committee of the town. There was a row in the mid-1930s over the attempt by the government to relocate Eleko market, a decision that met with popular protest led by her. She also successfully opposed the move to ask women to pay tax in the 1930s and 1940s, and she vigorously protested the price-control measures introduced during the Second World War. She participated in party campaigns; on one occasion, at Abeokuta, she reminded the audience that there was nothing men could undertake without the support of women. She mobilized market women to accord a decent burial to Herbert Macaulay in March 1946, hosted receptions for party dignitaries, and was picked to be part of a team in 1947 to travel to London to protest the Richards Constitution, although illness prevented her from traveling. She became the *erelu* of Lagos in 1947, a traditional chieftaincy that conferred upon her the right to represent women's interests. When she died in 1951, a crowd estimated at 25,000 people attended her burial.

My final example is a living legend, Humoani Alade, the *iyalode* of Ibadan at the time of my research.[28] Born in the late nineteenth century, Humoani did not have the privilege of Western education but received apprenticeship as a trader in textiles. With little capital, she gradually built up her trade until she became wealthy and influential. She is the president of the Oyo State Market Traders' Association (*iyaloja*) and the *iyalode* of Ibadan. In a noncombative manner, she has contributed to a number of women's causes, ranging from market palaver to conflicts with the government. The general perception of her is that of a leader who wants peace, mediating between the government and market women. In the 1980s, she assisted the state government in seeking and building a new market and preventing a clash over street trading. She has also participated in party politics since the 1940s, identifying with the Obafemi Awolowo–led party of the Action Group (AG) and the Unity Party of Nigeria (UPN). She provided support for the AG and the UPN, mobilizing people to support the party and its programs. She never sought any party elective office, nor was she ever appointed to any political position in the government; but she is a moderating influence on the party and a mediator in intraparty rivalry. In addition, she is a member of the *Egbe Ilosiwaju Yoruba* (Yoruba Progressive Union), seeking the progress of the Yoruba people. She is a philanthropist. As the *iyalode*, she receives dignitaries to the town on behalf of women and attends the meeting of the Olubadan-in-council, where issues relating to the town are discussed. She is the link between the women and the traditional chieftaincy. Many of her contemporaries, including political rivals, are full of praise for her. In the words of Lam Adesina, a prominent educator:

> She has been a true leader of women and a lover of the less fortunate . . . Iyalode is a very successful trader. She is also a first-class manager of human beings. Since the old Western Region, Iyalode Alade has been leading the Market Women and Traders Association. The association likes her and respects her. She commands them and they obey her. She is able to do this because her leadership is acceptable and respected.
>
> (Layonu 1990: 32)

And to take a second testimony, this time from Archibong Nkana, a former commissioner of police in Oyo state:

> She is a dynamic traditional chief in Ibadan, Oyo State. She is diligent, patriotic and very honest. This respectable woman is ever willing to assist the police for the common good of the people. She has used her position as President of Oyo State Market Traders Association to foster peaceful co-existence and mutual understanding between the police and the market traders in the state. I also want to emphasize that this special mother was a serving catalyst to my glorious tenure as commissioner of police in Oyo State. I wish her well in life.
>
> (Layonu 1990: 35)

Conclusion

Yoruba women have plenty of scope and opportunity to trade, and they dominate the marketplace. Since the colonial period, complex factors of migration, urbanization, and Western influence have brought a number of changes to women's lives and roles, but without diminishing their domination of the marketplace. The linkage between the marketplace and power takes several forms. First, there is the power and influence that accrue to those who grow wealthy. Second, the control of the marketplace confers ritual and symbolic power. Third, domination of the marketplace and of business provides opportunities to relate and negotiate with the political authorities, traditional and modern.

The case studies have revealed women who were able to actualize power in traditional and modern settings. Some dominated national politics, and others influenced local politics. A number of other interpretations can be drawn from these case studies.

The women were able to mobilize capital to enlarge trading opportunities. They were enterprising, calculating, and shrewd. They faced considerable risk: Tinubu was expelled from Lagos, and Efunsetan was assassinated, to mention two examples. In general, they faced considerable resentment and antagonism from the male power elite. The women were independent, rejecting the stifling conditionalities of marriage, or at least overcoming the barriers that marriage and child-rearing posed. They demonstrated courage in breaking from traditions that constrained their activities and, in the case of Tinubu, of fighting powerful political authority and vested interest. Once they acquired economic power, they were astute and wise enough to add political power unto it. Economic power also changed the conduct of social relations: a rich woman would certainly reject undue subordination. In general, as many studies have pointed out, Yoruba women enjoyed economic independence and limited constraints on their movement, thus enabling not a few to exercise freedom and associate with a constituency of their own choice and creation.

In spending their wealth, they behaved in ways similar to those of the male chiefs, by acquiring followers, showing generosity to a large number of people, and obtaining titles for themselves and their supporters. They received *oriki*, great eulogies that captured their lives in grandiose ways and beautiful language. Part of the *oriki* of Efunsetan will suffice for our purpose, but it needs to be emphasized that *oriki* is not a peculiar trademark of this lady.[29]

> Efunsetan, Iyalode
> One who has horses and rides them not.
> The child who walks in a graceful fashion.
> Adekemi Ogunrin!
> The great hefty woman who adorns her legs with beads
> Whose possessions surpass those of the Aare
> Owner of several puny slaves in the farm.
> Owner of many giant slaves in the market.
> One who has bullets and gunpowder, Who has the gunpowder as well as guns, And
>   spends money like a conjurer, The Iyalode who instills fear into her equals.
> The rich never give their money to the poor; The Iyalode never gives her wrappers to
>   the lazy.[30]

Localized within its Yoruba setting and idioms, this is a brilliant rendition, made more powerful by the drumming and dancing that would accompany it. It encapsulates a message, with all the metaphors of greatness. The abundant slaves, the horses, the "graceful fashion," the guns, and gunpowder are all evidence of wealth and success. Power is adequately reflected in the references to slaves, the poor, access to weapons of violence, and warfare. There is rivalry too: "The Iyalode who instills fear into her equals." And there is the bold comparison with the male political head of this city-state, with the *iyafode*'s possessions surpassing that of the *Aare*. Grace resonates beautifully: the horses in the compound, the "great hefty" woman, "the child who walks in a graceful fashion." And here is a woman so rich in money that she spent like someone who was conjuring (i.e., minting) her own currency.

From this *oriki* and other evidence, we see how aspirations centered on the "good things of life": money, long life, power, children, and good health. In this focus on aspirations, there is no difference from how men defined what they wanted.

The case studies should not obscure the problems women faced. Access to large amounts of capital was always a problem, and men tended to have more opportunities. Not every woman grew wealthy or powerful from trade; indeed, for the majority, trade did not translate to wealth or power. Trade was competitive, losses were recorded, and some high-profit-yielding commodities like cocoa and cattle were in the hands of male dealers. Women experienced other constraints, such as domestic responsibility, which curtailed activities in the early years of marriage; many lost a lot of time to social and religious events and to illness (Fadipe 1970: 166). Since the colonial period, obstacles to mobility and ingrained prejudices have lingered. Contemporary concerns of women are focused on the penetration of the more formal, public sector through better access to school, jobs, and promotion[31]; current studies tend to ignore the informal sector, including the dynamic marketplace that has played such a significant role for so long.

Discussion questions

1. What did the sexual division of labor look like in precolonial times versus colonial times for women?
2. What are the forms of linkages between the marketplace and power?
3. What forms of resistance are employed by women to cope with the state?

Notes

1 This is the same as the *iyaloja* (head of market).
2 This is a reference to the god *Esu*, misunderstood by Christian writers of the nineteenth century who adopted his name for the biblical devil. Now variously interpreted, *Esu* can also be described as the god of order.
3 See, for instance, Awe (1992), Coker (1987), Johnson (1981), Mba (1982), and Sweetman (1984).
4 For the celebration and limitation of gender historiography in Africa (with little stress on the Yoruba, however), among others, see Hay (1988), Staudt (1988), Strobel (1982), and Wipper (1988).
5 Among others, see Harris (1940), Kaberry (1952), Ross (1939), Southall (1961), and Ward (1938).
6 See, for instance, Idowu (1962), Chapter 8, and Johnson (1921: 64–65).
7 Several works have described the sexual division of labor among the Yoruba. See, for instance, Beier (1955), Izzett (1961), and Sudarkasa (1973), Chapter 2.
8 See, for instance, UNESCO (1956).
9 A more intense role is described for women elsewhere, as in the case of the Ijo. See Leis (1964: 55).
10 For a gender-based discussion of farming, see Fadipe (1970), Chapter 5.
11 See, for instance, the remark by Dr. Irving, who traveled in Ibadan, Egba, and the Ijebu territories between December 1854 and January 1855, in *C. M. S. Intelligencer*, 1859, p. 259.
12 A number of nineteenth-century sources specifically mention encounters with these women. See, for instance, *C. M. S. Intelligencer*, January 1856, p. 20; and Lander and Lander (1833: 122).
13 See also William Bascom (1984), Chapter 3.
14 The thirteenth *deji* of Akure is said to be a woman who did not wear a crown. Nigerian National Archives, Ibadan (NAI), "Intelligence Report on Akure" compiled by N. A. C. Weir, 1934, p. 10. See also Falola (1976).
15 NAI, "Intelligence Report on Ondo," by A. F. Bridges, 1934/5, p. 10. There were other women chiefs to assist the *lobun*: these included the *lisa lobun*, who settles quarrels among the women, the *ogese lobun*, and *sara lobun*, both of whom were "remembrances" to the *lobun*. These offices were duplicated in the Ondo nonmetropolitan area, where the *oloja* (*baale* or village

head), together with his chiefs, appointed a *lobun*. In villages such as Ajua and Aiyesan, women chiefs were called *iyalode*, not *lobun*.

16 NAI, "Intelligence Report on Abeokuta," by John Blair, 1937, p. 48; NAI, "Intelligence Report on Ijebu Ife," by E. A. Hawkersworth, 1935, p. 9. For an overview of this institution, see Awe (1977).

17 For instance, in Ago, an Ijebu village, "female members, known as *Erelu*, were allowed in the society (i.e., Osugbo society). The *Erelu* were consulted in all matters that concerned the female community, though they did not sit with the other members in judicial matters." See "Intelligence Report on Ago," by A. F. Abell, 1934, p. iii. Women membership in secret societies was, however, uncommon.

18 One interesting and mythical example of this is that of Moremi of Ile-Ife. The Igbo people are said to have repeatedly attacked Ile-Ife, with success, until the beautiful Moremi married the king of Igbo, from whom she was able to learn the secrets of Igbo's military success. She returned to Ile-Ife and exposed the secrets. This enabled Ile-Ife to resist and defeat the Igbo.

19 For instance, Samuel Johnson (1921: 63) mentions eight women of "the highest rank," whose roles could not be dispensed within the Oyo palace (*Iya Kekere, Iya Oba, Iya Naso, Iya Monari, Iyalagbon, Orun Kumefun*, and *Are Orite*). On *Iyakekere*, Johnson writes: "She has the charge of the king's treasures. The royal insignia are in her keeping, and all the paraphernalia used on state occasions, she has the power of withholding them, and thus preventing the holding of any state reception to mark her displeasure with the king's head at the coronation." Other women holding important offices were mentioned besides those eight, and their roles within and outside the palace reveal the political influences they could wield on state matters (pp. 64–66).

20 In Akure, there was an Apate club, with a membership restricted to 50 people at a time. They were "not expected to carry loads on their heads." Other clubs included the *Ukoji*, comprising daughters of titled men, and *Esari*, daughters and granddaughters of all late obas (Weir, "Intelligence Report on Akure," p. 21).

21 On this goddess, among others, see Gleason (1971: 137) and Lucas (1948: 218–219).

22 See, for instance, Oyemakinde (1973).

23 Public Record Office (PRO), London, Foreign Office (EO) 84/950, Campbell to Clarendon, 11 Aug. 1854.

24 PRO, FO 84/920, Fraser to Malmesbury, 20 Feb. 1853.

25 For one interesting account of this lady, see Bolanle Awe, "Iyalode Efunsetan Aniwura (Owner of Gold)," in Awe (1992: 55–72).

26 For the political background to the crisis, see Falola (1984).

27 The account of Pelewura is based on the evidence of C. Johnson (1981).

28 This reconstruction is based on a pamphlet by T. A. Layonu (1990).

29 On this genre, see Barber (1991).

30 Translation by Awe (1992: 57).

31 See, for instance, Adeyemo (1991), Chapter 3, and Sola-Onifade (n.d.).

References

Abell, A. F. 1934. *Intelligence Report on Ago*. Ibadan: National Archives of Nigeria.

Adeniyi, Tola. 1993. *The Jewel: A Biography of Chief (Mrs.) H. I. D. Awolowo*. Ibadan: Gemni Press Ltd.

Adeyemo, O. A., ed. 1991. *Women in Development*. Ibadan: National Center for Economic Management and Administration.

Awe, Bolanle. 1977. "The Iyalode in the Traditional Political System." In *Sexual Stratification*, ed. Alice Schlegel. New York: Columbia University Press.

Awe, Bolanle. 1992. *Nigerian Women in Historical Perspective*. Lagos and Ibadan: Sankore and Bookcraft.

Barber, Karen. 1991. *I Could Speak Until Tomorrow: Oriki, Women, and the Past in a Yoruba Town*. Edinburgh: Edinburgh University Press.

Barnes, Sandra T. 1986. *Patrons and Power: Creating a Political Community in Metropolitan Lagos*. Manchester: Manchester University Press.

Bascom, William. 1984. *The Yoruba of Southwestern Nigeria*. Prospect Heights: Waveland Press [reprint].

Beier, H. U. 1955. "The Position of Yoruba Women." *Presence Africaine* 1(2): 39–46.

Belasco, Bernard I. 1980. *The Entrepreneur as Cultural Hero*. New York: Praeger.

Blair, John. 1937. *Intelligence Report on Abeokuta*. Ibadan: National Archives of Nigeria.

Coker, Folarin. 1987. *A Lady: A Biography of Lady Oyinkan Abayomi*. Ibadan: Evans Brothers.

Drewal, Henry John. 1983. *Gelede: Art and Female Power among the Yoruba*. Bloomington: Indiana University Press.

Fabunmi, Chief M. A. 1969. *Ife Shrines*. Ile-Ife: University of Ife Press.

Fadipe, Nathanie Akinremi. 1970. *The Sociology of the Yoruba*. Ibadan: Ibadan University Press.

Falola, Toyin. 1976. "A Descriptive Analysis of Ilesa Palace Organization." *The African Historian* 8: 69–79.

Falola, Toyin. 1978. "The Place of Women in the Yoruba Pre-Colonial Domestic Economy." In *Seminar Proceedings*. Ile-Ife: University of Ife Press.

Falola, Toyin. 1984. *The Political Economy of a Pre-Colonial African State, Ibadan, ca. 1830–1893*. Ile-Ife: University of Ife Press.

Falola, Toyin. 1992. "Salt Is Gold: The Management of Salt Scarcity in Nigeria during World War II." *Canadian Journal of African Studies* 26(3): 412–436.

Falola, Toyin, and Dare Oguntomisin. 1984. *The Military in 19th Century Yoruba Political Systems*. Ile-Ife: University of Ife Press.

Gleason, Judith Illsley. 1971. *Orisha: The Gods of Yorubaland*. New York: Atheneum.

Harris, Jack. 1940. "The Position of Women in a Nigerian Society." *Transactions of the New York Academy of Sciences* 2(5): 141–148.

Hawkersworth, E. A. 1935. *Intelligence Report on Ijebu Ife*. Ibadan: National Archives of Nigeria.

Hay, Margaret Jean. 1988. "Queens, Prostitutes, and Peasants: Historical Perspectives on African Women." *Canadian Journal of African Studies* 22(3): 431–447.

Hodder, B. W. 1962. "The Yoruba Market." In *Markets in Africa*, eds. Paul Bohannan and George Dalton. Evanston, IL: Northwestern University Press.

Hodder, B. W., and U. I. Ukwu. 1969. *Markets in West Africa*. Ibadan: Ibadan University Press.

Idowu, E. Bolayi. 1962. *Olodumare, God in Yoruba Belief*. London: Longman.

Izzett, A. 1961. "Family Life among the Yorubas in Lagos, Nigeria." In *Social Change in Modern Africa*, ed. Aidan Southall. London: International African Institute and Oxford University Press.

Johnson, Cheryl. 1981. "Madam Pelewura and the Lagos Market Women." *Tarikh* 7(1): 1–10.

Johnson, Samuel. 1921. *The History of the Yorubas*. Lagos: Church Missionary Society.

Johnson-Odim, Cheryl. 1978. *Nigerian Women and British Colonialism: The Yoruba Example with Selected Biographies*. Ph.D. diss., Northwestern University, Evanston, IL.

Kaberry, Phyllis Mary. 1952. *Women of the Grassfields*. London: Her Majesty's Stationery Office.

Lander, John, and Richard Lander. 1833. *Journal of an Expedition to Explore the Course and Termination of the Niger*, Vol. 1. New York: J. and J. Harper.

Layonu, Taslim Abiola. 1990. *Iyalode Hunmoani Alade (The Embodiment of Truth)*. Ibadan: Famlod Books.

Leis, Nancy Borric. 1964. *Economic Independence and Ijaw Woman: A Comparative Study of Two Communities in the Niger Delta*. Ph.D. diss., Northwestern University, Evanston, IL.

Lloyd, B. 1967. "Indigenous Ibadan." In *The City of Ibadan*, eds. Peter Cutt Lloyd, Akin L. Mobogunje, and B. Awe. Cambridge: Cambridge University Press.

Lucas, Jonathan Olumide. 1948. *The Religion of the Yorubas*. Lagos: C.M.S. Bookshop.

Mabogunje, Akin. 1961. "The Market-Woman." *Ibadan* 11(February): 16–17.

Marris, Peter. 1961. *Family and Social Change in an African City*. London: Routledge and Kegan Paul.

Marshall, Gloria. 1964. *Women, Trade and the Yoruba Family*. Ph.D. diss., Columbia University, New York.

Mba, Nina Emma. 1982. *Nigerian Women Mobilized: Women's Political Activity in Southern Nigeria, 1900–1965*. Berkeley: Institute of International Studies, University of California.

Olupona, Jacob Obafemi Kehinde. 1991. *Kingship, Religion, and Rituals in a Nigerian Community: A Phenomenological Study of Ondo Yoruba Festivals*. Stockholm: Almqvist & Wiksell International.

Oyemakinde, Wale. 1973. "The Pullen Marketing Scheme: Trial in Food Price Control, 1941–47." *Journal of the Historical Society of Nigeria* 4: 413–423.

Ross, S. Leith. 1939. *African Women*. London: Faber and Faber Ltd.

Sola-Onifade, Bosede. n.d. [1980s?]. *The Nigerian Woman*. Lagos: Julia Virgo Enterprises.

Southall, Aidan, ed. 1961. *Social Change in Modern Africa*. London: International African Institute and Oxford University Press.

Staudt, Kathleen. 1988. "Women Farmers in Africa: Research and Institutional Action, 1972–1987." *Canadian Journal of African Studies* 22(3): 567–582.

Strobel, Margaret. 1982. "African Women." *Signs: Journal of Women in Culture and Society* 8(1): 109–131.

Sudarkasa, Niara. 1973. *Where Women Work: A Study of Yoruba Women in the Marketplace and in the Home*. Ann Arbor: University of Michigan Press.

Sweetman, David. 1984. *Women Leaders in African History*. London: Heinemann.

UNESCO. 1956. "The Rise of the New Elite amongst the Women of Nigeria." *International Social Science Bulletin* 8(3): 481–488.

Ward, Edward. 1938. "The Yoruba Husband-Wife Code." In *Catholic University of America Anthropological Studies*, No. 6. Washington, DC: Catholic University of America.

Weir, N. A. C. 1934. *Intelligence Report on the Akure District of Ekiti Division*. Ibadan: National Archives of Nigeria.

Wipper, Audrey. 1988. "Reflections on the Past Sixteen Years, 1972–1988, and Future Challenges." *Canadian Journal of African Studies* 22(3): 409–421.

Chapter 20

Taming internal weather, together

Gendered knowledge flows during maternity under Khmer traditional and folk medicine systems

Ashley Thuthao Keng Dam

Original material prepared for this edition.

Introduction

"But how will you know if they have the knowledge on maternity or even remember?" *Bong* Sarom asks from behind the visor on his helmet; small particles of dust disperse around us as our motorbike cruises down a road in Angkor Park.[1] It is March, a transitional month between the seasons of dry and rainy – the heat is oppressive and sweat pools everywhere it can. The paradise of springtime Siem Reap, Cambodia, has begun its transformation into flaming inferno a lot sooner than I expected. "Bong Sarom, I think you are gravely underestimating the power of word of mouth and social relationships," I respond before pointing out a hidden village roadway. As we pulled up to the first house we spotted, a crowd of five children ran by, screaming and laughing. "I find it a bit surprising that you think that people do not just talk about their childbirth experiences. Don't you have any siblings with children?" I ask. Outside of the house sit two women of varying ages, both scrolling through their phones and drinking beverages while chattering away. "Yes, but my sisters never tell me anything about the childbirth stuff, because it's an issue for the women!" Bong Sarom retaliates as he parks his motorbike and leans it on its pop-out kickstand.

We are continuing our interviews with people living in the province on the plants they use as a part of Traditional Khmer Medicine (TKM) during maternity. Instead of focusing on the perspectives of traditional healers, we were interested in how everyone else was thinking about, relating to, and using the plants around them. Despite the associated intimacy and taboos around the topics, we had found ourselves in another enthusiastic group interview. A half an hour in, Bong Sarom is struggling to keep up with the plant names listed by the women. Collecting local Khmer names for plants is crucial to the study because, while current botanical records include many scientific names for different plant species, these have not been consistently systematically matched with what people call them, or know them as, colloquially. This has caused many issues in deciphering local knowledges around the use and importance of different plants in TKM and within greater Cambodian culture, a challenge several scholars from various disciplines continue to address (Chassagne et al. 2016, 2017; Walker 2017; Cui et al. 2020). Scribbling into

DOI: 10.4324/9781003398349-23

his journal, Bong Sarom comments, "I'm so shocked they are so knowledgeable, even after many years after giving birth!" Not flinching, I reply, "It's like my mother told me before coming to Cambodia: people never forget about these things." Behind us, another motorbike pulls up to the house, and its rider – the husband of one of the women we are interviewing – greets us both. After hearing his wife's explanation about our study in addition to our own explanations, the husband decides to join the interview. As his wife recants the plants she used during pregnancy, Bong Sarom says to the husband, "Did you also know about these plants for pregnancy, Bong?" to which the husband replies rapidly, "Oh, you do not know about *vohl meas* [វល្លិមាស, *Cassytha glabella R. Br.*], *Oun?*"[2]

The previous scene briefly sketches the tensions and dynamics of reproduction in Siem Reap Province, Cambodia, in regard to traditional ecological knowledge (TEK), ethnobotany, gender roles, and traditional, complementary, and alternative medicine (TCAM) practices. This chapter attempts to thoughtfully express captured nuances around these topics as they manifested during anthropological fieldwork in Siem Reap Province, Cambodia, from February 2020 to July 2020. Myself, along with my two research collaborators, Hang Chansophea and Reth Sarom, spoke with 40 people living in villages within the Siem Reap municipality district about their relationships with local plants for medicinal or food-related uses in circumstances of uncertainty, such as seasonality, maternity, and COVID-19. Given the widespread use of local flora in the TKM system for the protection, maintenance, and improvement of health, we sought to understand how plant usage and care practices change under stressful circumstances (Ros et al. 2018). These use patterns are important because as climate change impacts deteriorate natural resources and health crises become more common, it is necessary to design solutions which are cognizant of ongoing practices to promote effective adoption by targeted populations (Theilade and De Kok 2015).

Through semi-structured interviews (both one-on-one and in focus groups), foraging walks, and recipe collection, we captured how people living in northwestern Cambodia interacted with local plants in pursuit of health care and treatment during maternity under traditional, complementary, and alternative medicine (TCAM) systems such as TKM. It was in these interactions that we witnessed how roles and expectations relating to gender during maternity, herein defined as the periods of pregnancy, birth, and postpartum, deviated from past characterizations of maternity knowledge in Southeast Asia as exclusively known, used, and circulated by women (Dennis et al. 2007). We noticed that TKM maternity knowledge was not only "women's business" but a shared aspect and responsibility for all those involved in, whether directly or indirectly, supporting someone during maternity (Buggenhagen 2011). As a result, we noted specific conditions where gatekeeping around these knowledges based on gender, and the incentive of providing care at all costs, overruled these contextual gender roles, expectations, and obligations.

In this chapter, I discuss how different aspects of maternity care under the Traditional Khmer Medicine (TKM) system challenge past understandings and characterizations of traditional ecological knowledge (TEK) around human reproduction as exclusively known, used, and circulated by women. *TEK* refers to a "cumulative body of knowledge and beliefs, handed down through generations by cultural transmission, about the relation of living beings (including humans) with one another and their environment" (Berkes 1993). In essence, TKM embodies how generations of people living in what is known today as Siem Reap, Cambodia, managed their reproductive health with natural resources, such as local flora and fauna. This TEK, encapsulated in the TKM system, has been historically entrusted and proliferated by certain groups. Of these groups, some are considered authorities or experts and designated as TKM practitioners – other non-specialists who know, apply, and circulate this same TKM knowledge represent Khmer Folk Medicine (KFM) users.

In contrast, I argue that, presently, TKM maternity knowledge is widely known and disseminated across genders and age groups as KFM because of its perceived overarching importance in Khmer culture, links to social roles and obligations, as well as contributions to the shared investment of community health and wellness. I highlight how this communal approach to (and undertaking of) care is embodied by extensive social support networks (SSNs) which facilitate and uphold different norms and expectations around care under the TKM system. I attribute linking the possession and use of TKM maternity-related knowledge to the performance and practice of being "good parents" to demonstrate how the responsibilities encapsulated in having children are shared across genders as opposed to being solely the concern of women in their roles as mothers. Instead, these responsibilities are delegated to entire communities of care within a pregnant person's social support network; as the idiom goes, "it takes a village."

Furthermore, I argue that, to some extent, people reinforce their community citizenship and ties to a shared Khmer cultural identity through being familiar with plants and their applications under the TKM system. In this way, I demonstrate how the collective approach to care responsibilities during maternity under the TKM system allows for situational lapses in the partitioning of this TEK in accordance to gender. Such insights provide glimpses into how, within a TKM context, it is also true that "human reproduction is never an entirely personal affair," through its integration of expansive communities of care which transcend various roles and expectations relating to age, gender, or even species (Browner 1986: 710).

First, I will provide an overview of TCAM systems in Southeast Asia and within Cambodia to provide guiding definitions and concepts of TKM to frame the historical trends in this TEK, its holders, and pathways of sharing. Then, I follow up with details on the study's design to explain and justify my qualitative methodology and how they contribute towards answering the following question: How is maternity-related traditional ecological knowledge (TEK) under the Traditional Khmer Medicine (TKM) system learned, shared, and applied as Khmer Folk Medicine (KFM)? Afterwards, I provide an overview of the study's findings and analyze them to identify how gender shapes the safeguarding, sharing, and application of this TEK by TKM/KFM users. To finish, I explain the implications of these findings and how they contribute to a wider understanding of how gender roles and expectations within TCAM practices should be perceived as dynamic entities instead of stagnant and unmoving, considering their evolving applications and expanding user base.

Traditional, complementary, and alternative medicine

The term "traditional medicine" (TM) means different things to different people. Within academic study, TM is often linked to, or used interchangeably with, the terms "complementary medicine" and/or "alternative medicine" – each of which expresses a particular arrangement of historical importance, cultural elements, and relationships between different structures and authorities which are involved in healing. To account for these overlaps, international health governance structures like the World Health Organization (WHO) combine them in their policies and interventions, under the phrase "traditional, complementary, and alternative medicine," or TCAM, which has led to unified strategies in addressing associated problems among member states. TM, according to the WHO (2021), is defined as

> the sum total of knowledge, skill, and practices based on the theories, beliefs, and experiences indigenous to different cultures, whether explicable or not, used in the maintenance of health as well as in the prevention, diagnosis, improvement or treatment of physical and mental illness.

This is then differentiated from *complementary* and *alternative medicine*, which refer to "broad[er] set[s] of healthcare practices that are not a part of that country's own traditional or conventional medicine and are not fully integrated into the dominant healthcare system" (WHO 2021). While these definitions could certainly be improved, this chapter uses them as a baseline to demonstrate three points: (1) TM is a combination of knowledge, skills, and practices; (2) TM is culturally informed; and (3) TM addresses a wide range of health issues across many stages of care-seeking and healing.

TCAM systems play an important role for health care globally, but especially in lower- to middle-income countries (LMIC), because of their low costs and accessibility in remote areas (Chaudhury et al. 2001: 273). Given the high costs and access issues with biomedicine, both the use and importance of TCAM are experiencing a global revival. TCAM provides a flexible means of disease prevention, management of lifestyle-related chronic diseases, and ways for aging populations to meet their health needs (WHO 2019). TCAM systems aid in the pursuit of universal health coverage and contribute towards creating more culturally considerate essential health services, making their ongoing use, development, and improvement important (WHO 2019: 10). This has had numerous implications, including the revision and promotion of the WHO policy on TCAM, which emphasizes the importance of supportive national legislation, integration, and regulation across member states (WHO 2019). While not perfect by any means, the policy provides a blueprint for intersectoral collaborations towards achieving better health through realizing, utilizing, and improving upon available resources – all of which are crucial towards achieving Sustainable Development Goal 3: Good Health and Well-Being.

In comparison to biomedicine, TCAM systems take a more holistic approach to disease etiology, diagnosis, and treatment. While many TCAM systems may have attributes and features in common, they are inherently complex because they arise from specific cultural and ecological contexts (Pan et al. 2014: 1). Culture unsurprisingly shapes health, and as Napier et al. (2014) argue, culture is an important factor in promoting global health, and its systematic neglect is the "single largest barrier" towards attaining and maintaining health worldwide (Napier et al. 2014: 24–26). These cultural contextual specificities allow for different "explanatory models" (EM) of health, or the culturally determined process of "making sense of one's illness," to arise (Kleinman 1978: 88; Dinos et al. 2017: 106). At times, these EMs may clash with commonplace biomedical ones, which cause the TCAM related to them to be underestimated as a health resource entirely considering the privileging of biomedical knowledge over those of TCAM due

Table 20.1 Overview of humoral associations

Humor	Associated organ	Season	Atmospheric conditions
Blood	Heart	Spring	Hot/wet
Phlegm	Brain	Winter	Cold/wet
Yellow bile	Liver	Summer	Hot/dry
Black bile	Spleen	Autumn	Cold/dry

Note: While humoral theory is globally present among TCAM systems, this theory is often considered a central component of many TCAM systems in the Asia region (Foster 1979; Horden and Hsu 2013).

Source: (Lagay 2002; Horden and Hsu 2013).

to historical knowledge hierarchies based in colonialism, racism, sexism, and more (Abuduli et al. 2011: 1; Ijaz and Boon 2018; WHO 2019).

A common TCAM model of health is humoral theory, which attributes good health to a balancing of various humors, which include blood, black bile, yellow bile, and phlegm – each humor is associated with a particular bodily organ, season, and collection of atmospheric conditions (Lagay 2002; Horden and Hsu 2013). TCAM systems with humoral medicine components often prescribe changes in diet, consumption of humorally-imbued substances, physical exercise, and bathing to correct the humoral imbalances believed to cause poor health (Foster 1979: 19).

TCAM in Southeast Asia and Cambodia

Southeast Asia has an extensive history with traditional medicine. As noted in a WHO regional report, "[a]ll countries in the Southeast Asia region have a heritage of traditional systems of medicine" (Chaudhury et al. 2001). Southeast Asian TCAM systems are known for their strong community component, which joins together a range of skill sets and experiences in its implementation – application of humoral theory, dietary restrictions, and plant medicines are just some of the ways diagnosing and treating diseases are handled (Dennis et al. 2007). Many Southeast Asian TCAM practitioners also occupy multiple community roles, such as teachers, historians, priests, and magicians, which is perceived to aid in their healing practices (Ahmad 2002). While numerous countries have developed formal certification programs for their traditional healers, Cambodia included, there are still many TCAM practitioners who provide care without these qualifications (Chaudhury et al. 2001). While certification procedures ensure TCAM users with safer and more standardized care and treatment while providing TCAM practitioners with an expanded community network, practitioners without certifications are still consulted and provide communities with care (Lim et al. 2022). The gender division among TCAM practitioners vary per country, with some being dominated by men and others being more balanced among different genders (Junsongduang et al. 2020).

TCAM systems in Cambodia exist as a part of a medical pluralism, meaning, they coexist alongside other medical traditions and practices with differing epistemological positions and worldviews (Cant 2020: 31–33). This is due to a complex cultural past, with French colonizers introducing biomedicine to the country during their rule from 1867 to 1953 and the Khmer Rouge Regime dismantling that very infrastructure from

1975 to 1978 (Guillou 2004). Alongside biomedicine, there are many TCAMs present in Cambodia, such as Traditional Khmer Medicine (TKM), Traditional Vietnamese Medicine (TVM), Traditional Chinese Medicine (TCM), and Ayurvedic medicine (Ashwell and Walston 2008). Despite the findings of the most recent Cambodian Demographic Health Survey (2014), many studies have found that TKM use is still commonplace in Cambodia (NIS et al. 2015). "In the face of disease, 70 to 80 percent of Cambodians opt for traditional medical methods with approximately 40 to 50 percent using medicinal plants daily" (Chassagne et al. 2017; Walker 2017). Even with many options available, it appears that "Khmers [continue to] trust their own traditional medicine" (Hiegel 1981: 252; Van Esterik 1988).

The term "Traditional Khmer Medicine" has been broadly used to describe various TCAM systems by Khmer people living in Cambodia. While the exact origins of TKM are not known, evidence suggests that it was developed during 9 to 15 century AD and combines aspects of Ayurvedic medicine, Traditional Chinese Medicine, as well as Khmer beliefs, superstitions, and local ancient animism (Lim et al. 2022). TKM has three explanatory models of disease: supernaturalistic (magic and spirits), naturalistic (environment and food), and metaphysical (humoral theory) (Richman et al. 2010). As a result, illness is commonly perceived as "disturbance[s] of the physical, mental, emotional balances within the individual or his or her community . . . that is subjected to the influence[s] of a socio-cultural environment, nature, a spiritual world, the cosmos, or universe, and divine principles" (Ahmad 2002: 51.) Therefore, health is ultimately tied to an individual's interrelated surrounding contexts, which are inevitably reflected in processes of diagnosis and treatment.

TKM has two major diagnostic techniques: clinical, which involves examining the patient directly, and magical-religious techniques, which center divination and supernatural explanations (Chassagne et al. 2017). TKM has four primary forms of care which are delivered by communities of (in)formal medicinal personnel: spiritual offerings, derma-abrasive practices, humoral balancing, and herbal medicines (Richman et al. 2010). TKM remedies take numerous forms, and some are consumable while others are not. They are widely available as pre-prepared regimens for sale in marketplaces or individually crafted by TKM practitioners directly and, at times, are combined with biomedical treatments during use (Chassagne et al. 2017). TKM remedies may differ in composition due to regional variations in flora, fauna, and religious traditions (Richman et al. 2010).

TKM practitioners are referred to by many names in accordance with their specializations. Common distinctions include healers as *Kru Khmer* (meaning, "Khmer teachers"), spiritual mediums as *Kru Chol Ruup*, and Buddhist monks (WHO 2012). While some communities who partake in traditional healing have balanced involvement of men and women as healers, TKM's Kru Khmer and Buddhist monks are predominantly men and spiritual mediums; Khmer Chol Ruup are mostly women (Eisenbruch 1992: 284; Junsongduang et al. 2020). People also use TKM remedies without the consultation of *Kru Khmer* as "home remedies," which are highly variable in composition and quality for many reasons (Richman et al. 2010).

The use of TKM remedies without the consultation of a TKM specialist or practitioner is an example of Khmer Folk Medicine (KFM). The term "Khmer Folk Medicine" refers to the application of TKM knowledge, beliefs, and practices by non-specialists. Comparatively to TKM, KFM focuses on the application of superficial limited knowledge of

TKM by those who are not considered dedicated experts or specialists in TKM within their communities. While KFM operates under certain principles of TKM, its use, practice, and efficacy are comparatively unstable due to lack of specialized knowledge and expertise on the intermingling of different active ingredients or chemicals within remedies. TCAM in Cambodia straddles between TKM and KFM – where health care is sought through the advice of both specialists (as TKM) and/or non-specialist yet knowledgeable individuals (as KFM). Among TKM users, TKM practitioners who are men are considered more knowledgeable, even in cases where they do not have firsthand experience with a disease or symptoms. For instance, TKM practitioners who are men are perceived to have greater authority and knowledge on conditions which inflict mostly women, such as those caused by menstruation. While there are women TKM practitioners, many focus on being spiritual mediums and/or exclusively sell TKM remedies prepared by TKM practitioners who are men. Overall, we can attempt to characterize care-seeking in Cambodia as an ongoing process of negotiations and tinkering with multiple kinds of health resources, practitioners, and knowledge bases. Identifying and charting the movement of shaping factors, motivations, and priorities for each are important for understanding how people understand and engage with their (reproductive) health and how sociocultural elements like gender come into play.

Despite progress towards gender equality in recent decades, Cambodian women still possess lower social status and are expected to be household managers (Asia Development Bank 2011). Conversely, men are expected to be providers, whose domains extend predominantly away from the home and domestic tasks. Maternity, to some extent, disrupts these trends by necessitating collective attention and efforts towards the safeguarding and protection of different knowledges and multiple dimensions of health. Having and raising children is an incredibly communal experience in Cambodia. Household compositions are often multigenerational and are supplemented by support from surrounding members of one's immediate community – Khmer kinship is rather expansive and extends beyond blood ties (Ebihara 1977). The domestic and emotional work encompassed in raising children is often led by women (Walston 2005). Ensuring the best conditions for one's children is an assumed joint responsibility for parents, and within the TKM system, opportunities to be a "good parent" start as early as conception.

Due to a historical record of high maternal mortality and morbidity in-country as well as cultural beliefs, many Khmer women perceive maternity as a risky, life-threatening period (White 2004). While these fears and perceived dangers are not exclusive to Khmer and Cambodian contexts, several forms of TKM remedies have been developed specifically for health issues which arise across pregnancy, birth, postpartum, and breastfeeding. These TKM remedies are to be used as particular points of time in accordance with the stages of pregnancy, birth, postpartum, and breastfeeding – these remedies are tied to the perceived required humoral needs for the given stage (Sargent et al. 1983). During pregnancy, the body is believed to be humorally "hot," and therefore, the corrective remedy would provide a humoral "cooling" effect (ibid.). Contrastingly, during birth and postpartum, TKM characterizes these processes as "cold," thus necessitating remedies which "warm" the body humorally (ibid.). Because humoral imbalances are believed to cause health complications, having meticulous knowledge of TKM ethno-pharmacopeia and its plant remedies is necessary to ensure the health of a pregnant woman and their future child(ren). For this reason, such attention to the humoral ecologies and the methods to stabilize them, becomes inherently linked to ideas and performances of "good" parenting, gender roles, and to some extent, community citizenship.

TKM is an emic way of understanding health from a Khmer perspective, it is a system entrenched in cultural idiosyncrasies and insights. As medical anthropologist Arthur Kleinman (1978) explained, medical systems can be understood as cultural systems, and the two are governed by the same rules. To navigate and participate in a medical system is to be a part of some greater community and society. As a result, assumptions and expectations towards securing and maintaining sufficient humoral ecological balance in TKM are then made more complex through the communality of maternity. As more people become involved in the protection, maintenance, and improvement of a pregnant person's health during maternity, varying dimensions of decision-making and prioritization arise. These tensions generate hierarchical categorization of both knowledge and experience, all of which have historically been dominated by factors like age, gender, class, and beyond.

Guiding questions and research design

At the intersections of maternity, TCAM, and TEK of plants in Cambodia are a few questions: (1) How is maternity-related TEK under the TKM system learned? (2) How is TEK shared? (3) How does gender shape the safeguarding, sharing, and application of said knowledges? To investigate these questions, I traveled to Siem Reap Province, Cambodia, for fieldwork during February 2020 to July 2020. In a team composed of myself, Hang Chansophea, and Reth Sarom, we collected insights from 40 people living across 10 villages and 4 communes in the Siem Reap Municipality District. We interviewed 34 women aged 20 to 76 years old, and 6 men aged 25 to 71 years old.

Triangulating our differing yet complementary expertise in anthropology, conservation biology, and food studies, we conducted qualitative data collection. We primarily drew methodologies from anthropology, ethnobotany, and food studies. Relying on convenience sampling, we zoomed around on motorbikes around Angkor Archaeological Park (hereon "Angkor Park") to conduct semi-structured interviews. The interviews, which unfolded more so along the lines of storytelling listening sessions, were undertaken in Khmer, audio-recorded, transcribed, and then translated into English (Hart and Hart 2019: 268). Both Hang Chansophea and Reth Sarom acted as field translators to account for regional variations and slang terms; these bilingual recordings were then reviewed and thematically coded by myself with respect to research aims and objectives. Interviewees were a mixture of TKM practitioners and KFM users; this variance in target population was accounted for with differing questionnaires. In addition to standardized demographics, research briefing, and consent procedures, study participants were asked about their knowledge of TKM plant medicines, their eating and foraging habits, as well as their decision-making process when seeking and using healthcare resources. From these conversations, participants were encouraged to show us plants they know to be used as part of TKM. During these "walk in the woods" sessions, we collected plant samples by unearthing the entire plant. These plants were then pressed flat and dried, to create botanical voucher specimens for the National Herbarium of Cambodia. In addition to providing botanists with a preserved representation of a plant at a specific point of growth, we collected information about its local Khmer name, the season of growth, uses and preparations, as well as the location in which it was found. This information is valuable when trying to understand how different plant species in an area grow, disperse, and are used by the people living there – all crucial when researching ethnobotany. These research activities were supplemented with visual ethnography in the form of digital and film photographs to capture and further express the conditions of the fieldwork's undertaking. Collectively, these methodologies provided the basis for outlining the intersections between plants, food, and health among people living Siem Reap, Cambodia. This study received ethical clearance from the Research Ethics Committee of Università degli Studi di Scienze Gastronomiche in December 2019. The study was co-funded by Università degli Studi di Scienze Gastronomiche and the Center for Khmer Studies' Dissertation Senior Research Fellowship.

Knowledge sources

When walking towards the village, I could not help but look up in awe at the canopies overhead. Children ran around, giggling, ducking behind trees, and playing amongst one another. In the corner of my eye, I spotted a young boy, perhaps 2 years old, perched upon a fallen tree trunk, staring curiously at *Meeng* Sophea and I as we made our way on foot toward a cluster of houses on stilts.[3] Once we reached one of the houses, a crowd of women greeted us from their respective sewing machines, which buzzed in rhythmic unison. After exchanging pleasantries and conversation about where we were from, what we did for a living, and why we visited their village, we explained the premise of our study. As we described the plant component of our work, a few of them smirked in amusement. A woman whispered, "Well, I'm not sure if I can remember the names of them all." Despite these initial skepticisms, with some time, our casual conversations shifted into detailed stories about various local plants and their uses. Whenever someone forgot a plant name, another would chime in with an anecdote which would then effortlessly flourish into an epiphany of plant-centered memories. On occasion, the children of these women would come sit nearby or even directly on their laps during the interviews, listening attentively. Through these moments of inquiry, Meeng Sophea and I documented the acute TKM knowledge of these women while witnessing transfers of this knowledge to the next generation.

The working knowledge of surrounding local flora in Siem Reap among the sample was extensive. An intense awareness of local plants and their potential was palpable during the interview process, but it was expectedly varied. Anywhere from listing full local names, precise amounts used in remedies, and preparation methods to vague physical descriptions of the plants themselves or where they could be generally found. Overall, all study participants had some knowledge of TKM plant names, their medicinal qualities, as well as the methods of preparation required to use them.

Across the interviews, participants identified and referenced a total of 130 different plant species. Out of the 130 plant species identified, 67 have been matched with their accepted scientific names using botanical keys compiled by the National Herbarium of Cambodia and the School of Field Studies (SFS). Of these scientifically matched plant species, 39 plant families were represented. The remaining 63 were documented using only their local Khmer names written as romanizations. Around 112 of these 130 plant species are used as a part of maternity remedies alone or along with other ingredients: 30 plants are used during pregnancy (in the second and third trimesters), 52 plants are used during postpartum and breastfeeding (starting from day 1 after birth to up to 10 years after), 1 plant is used as an abortifacient, and 2 plants are used during all stages of maternity. The remaining species were said to be used "during maternity," but no specific stages were mentioned.

Several people credited their local TKM practitioner or family members for the knowledge they had on TKM maternity plants. Within families, grandparents and parents were commonly named as knowledge sources, with family members that are women being most common. Contrastingly TKM practitioners mentioned were mostly men, and in the event of the TKM practitioner being a woman, it was mentioned that she had "taken over" for her husband, usually following his retirement or death. Surprisingly, there was not a preference for insights from women over men when discussing maternity plants, remedies, or general advice. Often, the expertise and knowledge range of men was characterized as more extensive and trustworthy over those of women. "Mostly men are knowledgeable about medicinal plants in comparison to women." This delegation of specialized knowledge, as several study participants clarified, is linked to how being knowledgeable in TKM maternity plants is a vital component of men's expected roles and responsibilities as husbands providing for their wives – this will be elaborated on later. Furthermore, women remarked that although they were not aware of exact names of the plants they used, they were confident that the men in their lives (brothers, fathers, uncles, neighbors, etc.) knew them.

> I trust my older brother because I am an orphan. . . . [H]e told me this information about TKM maternity plants.
>
> (Rath, F, 37 years old)

It is important to note that while women did possess a large amount of TEK about TKM/KFM plants used during maternity, the resounding takeaway from interviews and conversations is that the men within their lives actively support them during their maternities, and this should not be overlooked. Such division of labor and responsibilities is not exclusive to TKM/KFM or Cambodia, but it has been drastically under-documented.

In cases where people sought or received advice from non-family members, participants generally described their sources for TKM knowledge as "people with experience" (PWE). This phrase was divided into two common streams: either specifically respected village elders (or, more generally, older people) or those who have experience in the using of the TKM plant in question for dealing with specific diseases, conditions, or health issues during maternity. Such "experience" includes people who have previously used the plants for their own health issues or have witnessed someone else use it strategically. These perspectives were prioritized when neither the pregnant women nor their families had any firsthand experiences or acute knowledge using TKM maternity remedies. During an interview with three generations of women in a family, the grandmother remarked that despite "habits of her generation" and the popularity of TKM maternity remedies at that time, she did not use them because her sister was a biomedical doctor and advised against it. As a result, the grandmother's daughter, who was interested in using TKM maternity remedies, was forced to rely on extra-familial knowledge sources for this information. After positive experiences with TKM maternity remedies, she then encouraged her own daughter (granddaughter) to use them, therefore generating new practices and affinities for them across the family. The granddaughter then collaged together the TKM knowledge her mother taught her, along with additional knowledge she accrued through extra-familial sources, thus demonstrating the creativity and flexibility involved in pursuing knowledge on TKM maternity care.

A study participant emphasized that while her husband was ultimately her source and supplier of TKM plants, the knowledge which he shared and the plants he brought for her were derived from village elders.

> There's so many different plants it was very confusing for my husband. Right now, he knows over 100 different kinds of plants, and he learned about them from the elder people in our village.
>
> (Kannary, F, 39 years old)

This tendency to value elders' wisdom within TKM knowledge and practices was also reflected in other study participants' responses:

> Yes, I followed everything they said to me. I'm younger, and I should listen to their good wisdom and experience.
>
> (Chenda, F, 41 years old)

> Advice on maternity is a good thing. . . . [W]e trust the elders 100 percent.
> (Sophal, F, and Vuthea, F, 59 and 72 years old)

> When we follow the advice of the elders, our deliveries will be easier. . . . I always follow the elders in the village.
>
> (Sreypich, F, 65 years old)

Even Meeng Sophea's comments on how her mother learned about TKM plants demonstrated similar sentiments: "Older or more experienced people told her some things." With regards to elders' knowledge across the study sample, gender continued to supersede age in TKM knowledge hierarchies.

This collaging of care-related knowledge and practices by TKM users demonstrates how TKM maternity knowledge does not only flow downwards from generation to generation but, rather, also ripples outwards into the minds and actions of a pregnant woman's social support network (SSN) and beyond, while traversing boundaries of age and gender. Inevitably, the pregnant woman's SSN becomes familiar with maternity TEK. However, it is important to note that while SSN members may be exposed to this knowledge, their ability to recall it correctly or at all is questionable. As Chanthea (40 years old) explained, because she has never been pregnant herself and is not considering it in the near future, she overlooks this information because it is not relevant to her.

Knowledge diffusion and safeguarding

Given that TKM maternity knowledge and its diffusion are not confined to the realms of the family, certain ages, or gender, it can be argued that it is communally constructed and maintained. People perpetually select, undertake, and share their TKM maternity care experiences with the input and involvement of many others. Khmer kinship structures are very wide-spanning – the well-being and care of a village member, especially during such a precarious and exciting time like maternity, is a concern of the community. The ability to hide or obscure pregnancy within village contexts is nearly impossible. "Pregnancy is very public. . . . [E]veryone in the village will know." Once a woman is known to be pregnant, both she and her family are often recipients of increased levels of attention, gifts, and advice from those around them. At times, this communality of maternity can be overwhelming for the pregnant woman and her spouse because of the multitude of sociocultural obligations, expectations, and dynamics at play.

Study participants emphasized that they consider their relationships towards different SSN members throughout their maternity care decision-making when assessing and applying the knowledge and advice received. SSNs are complex and dynamic communities – their compositions often change, and members' perspectives and inputs also shift in prioritization. Like a "therapy management group" (TMG) outlined by Janzen (1987), SSNs take an active role in providing lay insights on potential diagnoses and available treatment options. Similarly to Senegalese "entourages," SSNs provide spaces for sharing intergenerational obstetric knowledge and mutual shared support (Powis and Bunkley 2023). However, unlike entourages, there were no reported distinctions made between roles for women based on kinship ties (ibid.).

Depending on the context, some pieces of maternity advice may be more valuable or relevant than others, thus creating situations of categorization and hierarchy within pools of TKM knowledge. Subsequently, distinguishing factors around who or where the TKM knowledge has been derived from contribute toward these processes of categorization and evaluation. While generally women prioritize their immediate family members' advice over others in the SSNs, amount of experience with TKM overruled gender, meaning, grandfathers who were TKM practitioners had more authority than grandmothers and mothers. Expectedly, this makes considering options and making care choices in TKM maternities difficult for women as they maintain their own individual perspectives and values – this was even harder if it was their first pregnancy. Gender often guided balancing processes between personal and SSN considerations. Women's frustrations highlighted the challenging of their bodily autonomy and decision-making about their own health and how trapped they felt between expectations relating to gender and age dynamics in Khmer culture. As Annida and Thyda (37, F; 38, F) expressed, "We must do it anyways." Men instead focused on the reduction of their roles as protectors and advocates for their wives. For Mohasal (M, 29 years old), members of SSNs have pushed against what he believed was appropriate for his wife during her pregnancy. "Sometimes people who know that your wife is pregnant will be you gifts of different foods and say she can eat whatever she wants . . . but it's too much for her, you know?"

Study participants clarified that while having members of their SSNs who have first-hand experience with TKM increases their overall knowledge of it, knowledge depth and use were not determined by these SSN histories of use. Women were not fated to follow the footsteps of their SSNs – maternity care decision-making among study participants maintains levels of personalization throughout. Women customize their care for each "stage" of maternity (pregnancy, postpartum, and breastfeeding), oscillating between a spectrum of TKM-only, mixing TKM and biomedicine, and biomedicine-only. Despite this, people still felt the pressure to follow advice from elders and close friends, even when they felt that these SSN members were wrong or misinformed. Expressions of the tensions and frustrations with SSNs arose occasionally during interview conversations with younger, "less-experienced" study participants. They emphasized that while they understood that the communal concern and involvement in their maternity came from a place of love and care, that did not stop such interventions from being irritating and overwhelming. Annida and Thyda (37, F; 38, F) lamented, "The maternity advice is very boring and annoying for us."

SSNs during maternity provide ample logistical and material support at best, additional sociocultural pressures at worst. Possessing an extensive SSN encouraged the use of TKM maternity remedies, because there are more opportunities to gather, procure, and/or prepare plant medicines. Inevitably, SSNs become catalysts for continued use of TKM remedies – they act as safeguards of TEK. Generally, foraging, gathering, and preparing TKM plants are not gender-specific practices. However, during maternity, these responsibilities often fell upon men who were socially proximal to the pregnant or postpartum woman within their social support networks (SSNs). As Rattana (F, 42 years old) explained, "My husband tried to collect any type of medicine plants and dry them for me." There are several reasons for this labor shift, based on practicalities and TKM maternity beliefs. Plant gathering is physically demanding, so pregnant women are often told to avoid such activities to safeguard health. While this may be logical in a biomedical sense, this avoidance is made more important in a TKM context because of beliefs about malevolent spirits present within some plants and specific activities. Gathering plants while pregnant presents a two-fold risk at minimum within biomedical and TKM framings, thus prompting SSN members to take up the responsibilities. However, there is one caveat to this gendered shift in labor delegation: women with lower household income or poor/non-existent SSNs tended to forage and gather TKM maternity plants on their own. In these cases, study participants explained that the benefits of using TKM plant remedies during their maternity outweighed the risks involved in foraging, demonstrating the dynamism of such decision-making.

While SSNs play a large role in providing and sharing TKM maternity knowledge on plant remedies, they are not foolproof entities. The range of technical knowledge in plant identification, recipes, and preparation varies greatly depending on the SSN composition. In these cases, study participants explained that they relied on local TKM sellers' suggestions and guidance. TKM sellers often have pre-prepared regimens for several health conditions and issues, therefore simplifying the process of choosing suitable remedies. These so-called maternity mixes are often compiled into the compelling description of medicines for "women's troubles," despite also containing plants that are also used to address health issues outside of maternity. As a result, the plants within these mixes are unexpectedly imbued with gendered dimensions within their use and efficacy, therefore calling into question potential instances of disrupted healing due to bodily compatibilities tied to sex and gender.

Although there were several ways to experience maternity within the TKM systems, some approaches are positioned as better in their efficacy or cultural prestige. Naturally, this was often entangled with class – more socioeconomically advantaged people were able to access finer-quality TKM ingredients and resources to undertake specific practices. One example is *ang pleung* (roasting), where postpartum women lay atop controlled fires, in attempts to humorally warm their bodies after giving birth – women of higher socioeconomic standing were able to do this for as long as they wanted because their domestic responsibilities could be covered by their SSNs. By following the "appropriate" TKM plant remedies, people are able to improve their performances as ideal mothers and fathers, thus elevating their social standings.

Khmer maternities and paternities

When asked about why they use TKM, either alone or in tandem with biomedicine, several study participants made comments pertaining to their knowledge and use of TKM as tied to their "Khmerness." Therefore, TKM use during maternity can be characterized as heavily intertwined with notions of Khmer sociocultural identity. Using TKM during maternity requires different forms and levels of knowledge and participation, depending on gender. Being designated as a "good" Khmer mother and father demanded different abilities and competencies. Among the sample, which featured married heteronormative relationships, pregnant wives and their husbands performed their roles as "good" Khmer parents in complementary ways.

Some study participants argued that there is an inherent incompatibility between biomedicine and their biology. For some Khmer people, biomedicine "doesn't work for their bodies." Study participants alluded that they were unable to manage their health issues with biomedicine because their identity as Khmer people meant that their bodies required treatments based within TKM/KFM systems. This suggests an emic understanding of the body and its biology – Khmer bodies and biologies required methodologies found within Khmer culture. Through qualifying biomedicine as insufficient for healing Khmer bodies, study participants asserted their allegiance towards an amorphous, shared, concept of what it means to be Khmer – a means of worldbuilding and truth-making.

Women are expected to use and be enthusiastically interested in TKM remedies throughout maternity, especially within a context of growing biomedical penetration and influence in the Cambodian health scape. There are multiple reasons for this, but much of it has to do with TKM being the only means to combat specialized conditions, such as *Toas*, which denotes localized varieties of postpartum fatigue (White 2004). Those perceived as "good" Khmer mothers are aware of this gap in biomedicine's efficacy and prefer to be cautious. As one woman elucidated: "When it comes to treating different types of toas, you can only use TKM and not Western medicine, so then women will only use TKM." Therefore, women are perceived as performing Khmer maternity appropriately and bolstering their Khmerness by simply being aware and open to TKM use.

Women's use of TKM includes but is not limited to consuming remedies, practicing specific rituals during different stages of maternity, and avoiding certain foods and activities. As a result, women's roles, expectations, and responsibilities are transformed, if not completely reversed. Under the TKM system, many of their domestic tasks are either exceptionally limited or forbidden completely – cooking, washing clothes, and gathering wild foods are just a few. This unearths and reforms the dynamics of the household, redirecting often femininely coded practices towards men, which inevitably impact them in different ways.

Men are expected to be knowledgeable of the wide range of TKM maternity plants; this means being able to identify, procure, and prepare them accordingly throughout each maternity stage for their wives. Obtaining, using, and maintaining such TEK is vital towards performing their roles and responsibilities as husbands. Whether men foraged for TKM plants themselves or purchased them from marketplace sellers, securing health for their wives and future children is among their core concerns and responsibilities. Study participants explained that TKM plant knowledge, in general, is seemingly concentrated in men to begin with. Therefore, this expectation for men to be leaders in care and safeguarding of their wives' health and reputation as "good" Khmer mothers was inevitable to some. This association was made more salient as study participants remarked that although they were not aware of exact names of the plants they used, they were confident that the men in their lives knew.

> Mostly men are knowledgeable about medicinal plants in comparison to women. Men are more knowledgeable about TKM plants for maternity than the wives because that is a part of their role as a man. They learn about the plants and where to find them from the elders in the village.
>
> (Sivorn, F, 76 years old)

> After I gave birth, my husband went to go forage for TKM plants for me to use. There's so many different plants.
>
> (Kannary, F, 39 years old)

> Mostly the husbands take care of their wives during pregnancy. That's why husbands are so knowledgeable about TKM maternity plants.
>
> (Darinah, F, 65 years old)

As a result, men, in their roles as husbands supporting their wives through TKM-informed maternities, acquire additional competencies relating to plant TEK. Such TEK accruement, coupled with increased day-to-day domestic labor requirements and responsibilities, demonstrates how TKM maternities embody liminal instances where common gender roles, expectations, and relationalities shift, mutate, and occasionally fall away altogether. What remains are strains of evolving constellations of care, whose primary objectives seek to support and maintain connections between bodies, communities, and culture through times of biological and sociocultural duress.

Implications of research

While these are just some pieces of a larger mosaic of research, the implications of their insights are immense. Individually and in combination, we can better understand the links between global health, gender, TCAM, and Cambodian plant biodiversity simultaneously. This work demonstrates that local flora provides a valuable contribution to local (reproductive) health access, needs, and care needs. Given this one aspect of the entanglements of biodiversity, culture, and health, protecting biodiversity and its associated TEK is crucial in the mission to tackle global health issues and disparities. Performing contextually appropriate or correct forms of maternity and paternity is encapsulated in what kinds of reproductive care you are seeking, receiving, and ignoring. To be truly Khmer was to have a Khmer maternity, with a supportive husband with extensive TKM/KFM plant knowledge to ensure sufficiently performed Khmer paternity. While the boundaries of what it means to be a "good" Khmer parent is still yet to be fully defined and agreed upon, as participants have emphasized, utilizing TKM/KFM throughout maternity is at least one component.

The importance of plants you are using, how you prepare them, and how you access them reflect greater surrounding patterns of positionality within SSNs. Unsurprisingly, having knowledge of local medicinal plants, and how to use them, imbues the user with elevated social importance within respective SSNs. Having access to TEK about TKM/

KFM plants used during maternity provides the pregnant woman with higher perceived levels of care and potentially higher levels of health for both them and their future child(ren).

Being a "person with experience" in TKM and KFM transcends the previously dominating standards and expectations around the possession, safeguarding, and sharing of TEK about maternity. This TEK within TKM maternity is communally constructed and shared with all those willing to listen; it is not exclusively learned, safeguarded, or shared by women. What is illuminated is that "experiences" in maternity which people denoted as being important or useful in their decision-making processes during TKM maternity remedy selection, preparation, and consumption do not depreciate in relation to the knowledge/advice-giver's age or gender. Contrary to Walston (2005), who noted that Cambodian women found it difficult to jointly discuss sexual and reproductive health (SRH), this study found that men, no matter their position in the SSN, openly discussed topics about maternal health with women. This study also found that men have increased involvement in the maternity, either through material or emotional support as members of the SSN throughout various stages, which contrasts to Walston's (2005) past findings of men being absentee or generally disinterested.

As these insights from people living in villages in Siem Reap, Cambodia, have demonstrated, TKM is an ever-evolving system of care which marries together sociocultural and ecological diversity. It is a collaborative, flexible, and creative means of engaging and healing within one's surrounding environments. It is a mechanism of nourishing Khmer bodies while temporarily transcending some restrictions and obligations of localized gender norms, roles, and expectations.

Discussion questions

1. What does the author argue, and what evidence do they provide in support of their argument? Are you persuaded by their argument and their evidence? Why or why not?
2. What is "medical pluralism," and how does TKM fit in?
3. Discuss the relationship between maternity and gendered labor. Who is involved in the SSN, and what is the role of the SSN?
4. How does this chapter demonstrate the gendering of space and/or knowledge?

Notes

1 *Bong* is a Khmer kinship term to refer to someone older than you are respectfully.
2 *Oun* is a Khmer kinship term to refer to someone younger than you are.
3 *Meeng* is a Khmer kinship term to refer a woman who is younger than your mother, but older than you.

References

Abuduli, Maihebureti, and Syed Aljunid. 2011. "Guest Editorial Role of Traditional and Complementary Medicine in Universal." *Malaysian Journal of Public Health Medicine* 11(2): 1–5.

Ahmad, Shaharuddin. 2002. "Traditional Medicine in Southeast Asia with Special Reference to Malaysia and Indonesia." In *Geography, Culture and Education*, eds. Rod Gerber and Michael Williams, 51–64. Dordrecht: Springer Netherlands. https://doi.org/10.1007/978-94-017-1679-6_5.

Ashwell, David, and Naomi Walston. 2008. "An Overview of the Use and Trade of Plants and Animals in Traditional Medicine Systems in Cambodia." In *TRAFFIC Southeast Asia, Greater Mekong Programme*. Hanoi: Traffic Southeast Asia.

Asian Development Bank. 2011. "Cambodia: Country Gender Analysis." 1–28. www.adb.org/sites/default/files/institutional-document/33752/files/cambodia-country-gender-analysis.pdf.

Berkes, Fikret. 1993. "Traditional Ecological Knowledge in Perspective." In *Traditional Ecological Knowledge: Concepts and Cases*, 1–9. Ottawa: Canadian Museum of Nature.

Browner, Carole H. 1986. "The Politics of Reproduction in a Mexican Village." *Signs: Journal of Women in Culture and Society* 11(4): 710–724. https://doi.org/10.1086/494273.

Buggenhagen, Beth. 2011. "Are Births Just 'Women's Business'? Gift Exchange, Value, and Global Volatility in Muslim Senegal." *American Ethnologist* 38(4): 714–732.

Cant, Sarah. 2020. "Medical Pluralism, Mainstream Marginality or Subaltern Therapeutics? Globalisation and the Integration of 'Asian' Medicines and Biomedicine in the UK." *Society and Culture in South Asia* 6(1): 31–51. https://doi.org/10.1177/2393861719883064.

Chassagne, François, Eric Deharo, Hieng Punley, and Geneviève Bourdy. 2017. "Treatment and Management of Liver Diseases by Khmer Traditional Healers Practicing in Phnom Penh Area, Cambodia." *Journal of Ethnopharmacology* 202: 38–53. https://doi.org/10.1016/j.jep.2017.03.002.

Chassagne, François, Sovanmoly Hul, Eric Deharo, and Geneviève Bourdy. 2016. "Natural Remedies Used by Bunong People in Mondulkiri Province (Northeast Cambodia) with Special Reference to the Treatment of 11 Most Common Ailments." *Journal of Ethnopharmacology*. https://doi.org/10.1016/j.jep.2016.06.003.

Chaudhury, Ranjit Roy, and Uton Muchtar Rafei, eds. 2001. *Traditional Medicine in Asia.* World Health Organization: Regional Office for South-East Asia Regional Publications 39. New Delhi: World Health Organization.

Cui, Xinyun, Weijie Li, Jianhe Wei, Yaodong Qi, Rongtao Li, Yun Yang, Yuhua Shi, et al. 2020. "Assessing the Identity of Commercial Herbs from a Cambodian Market Using DNA Barcoding." *Frontiers in Pharmacology* 11(March): 1–10. https://doi.org/10.3389/fphar.2020.00244.

Dennis, Cindy-Lee, Kenneth Fung, Sophie Grigoriadis, Gail Erlick Robinson, Sarah Romans, and Lori Ross. 2007. "Traditional Postpartum Practices and Rituals: A Qualitative Systematic Review." *Women's Health* 3(4): 487–502. https://doi.org/10.2217/17455057.3.4.

Dinos, Sokratis, Micol Ascoli, John A. Owiti, and Kamaldeep Bhui. 2017. "Assessing Explanatory Models and Health Beliefs: An Essential But Overlooked Competency for Clinicians." *BJPsych Advances* 23(2): 106–114. https://doi.org/10.1192/apt.bp.114.013680.

Ebihara, May. 1977. "Residence Patterns in a Khmer Village." *Annals of the New York Academy of Sciences* 293(1): 51–68. https://ehrafworldcultures.yale.edu/document?id=am04-177.

Eisenbruch, Maurice. 1992. "The Ritual Space of Patients and Traditional Healers in Cambodia." *Bulletin de l'Ecole Française d'Extrême-Orient* 79(2): 283–316. https://doi.org/10.3406/befeo.1992.1882.

Foster, George M. 1979. "Humoral Traces in United States Folk Medicine." *Medical Anthropology Newsletter* 10(2): 17–20. https://doi.org/10.1525/maq.1979.10.2.02a00130.

Guillou, Anne Yvonne. 2004. "Medicine in Cambodia during the Pol Pot Regime (1975–1979): Foreign and Cambodian Influences." *East Asian Medicine under Communism: A Symposium*, July 2004, Graduate Center, City University of New York.

Hart, Kathy E., and Claudia Hart. 2019. "Listening to Story: Narratives Shared by Female Khmer Rouge Survivors." *Journal of Asian Research* 3(3): 264–278. https://doi.org/10.22158/jar.v3n3p264.

Hiegel, J.P. 1981. "The ICRC and Traditional Khmer Medicine." *International Review of the Red Cross* 224: 251–262. https://international-review.icrc.org/articles/icrc-and-traditional-khmer-medicine.

Horden, Peregrine, and Elisabeth Hsu. 2013. *The Body in Balance*. New York: Berghahn Books.

Ijaz, Nadine, and Heather Boon. 2018. "Statutory Regulation of Traditional Medicine Practitioners and Practices: The Need for Distinct Policy Making Guidelines." *Journal of Alternative and Complementary Medicine (New York, N.Y.)* 24(4): 307–313. https://doi.org/10.1089/acm.2017.0346.

Janzen, John M. 1987. "Therapy Management: Concept, Reality, Process." *Medical Anthropology Quarterly* 1(1): 68–84. https://doi.org/10.1525/maq.1987.1.1.02a00040.

Junsongduang, Auemporn, Wanpen Kasemwan, Sukanya Lumjoomjung, Wichuda Sabprachai, Wattana Tanming, and Henrik Balslev. 2020. "Ethnomedicinal Knowledge of Traditional Healers in Roi Et, Thailand." *Plants* 9(9): 1177. https://doi.org/10.3390/plants9091177.

Kleinman, Arthur. 1978. "Concepts and a Model for the Comparison of Medical Systems as Cultural Systems." *Social Science & Medicine. Part B: Medical Anthropology* 12(January): 85–93. https://doi.org/10.1016/0160-7987(78)90014-5.

Lagay, Faith. 2002. "The Legacy of Humoral Medicine." *AMA Journal of Ethics* 4(7). https://doi.org/10.1001/virtualmentor.2002.4.7.mhst1-0207.

Lim, Thona, Elizabeth Oneita Davis, Brian Crudge, Vichet Roth, and Jenny Anne Glikman. 2022. "Traditional Khmer Medicine and Its Role in Wildlife Use in Modern-Day Cambodia." *Journal of Ethnobiology and Ethnomedicine* 18(1): 61. https://doi.org/10.1186/s13002-022-00553-5.

Napier, A. David, Clyde Ancarno, Beverley Butler, Joseph Calabrese, Angel Chater, Helen Chatterjee, François Guesnet, et al. 2014. "Culture and Health." *The Lancet* 384(9954): 1607–1639. https://doi.org/10.1016/S0140-6736(14)61603-2.

National Institute of Statistics (NIS), Directorate General for Health, and ICF International. 2015. "Cambodia Demographic and Health Survey 2014." *National Institute of Statistics, Directorate General for Health, and ICF International.* www.nis.gov.kh.

Pan, Si Yuan, Gerhard Litscher, Si Hua Gao, Shu Feng Zhou, Zhi Ling Yu, Hou Qi Chen, Shuo Feng Zhang, Min Ke Tang, Jian Ning Sun, and Kam Ming Ko. 2014. "Historical Perspective of Traditional Indigenous Medical Practices: The Current Renaissance and Conservation of Herbal Resources." *Evidence-Based Complementary and Alternative Medicine.* https://doi.org/10.1155/2014/525340.

Powis, Richard, and Emma N. Bunkley. 2023. "Handbooks and Health Interpreters: How Men Are Assets for Their Pregnant Partners in Senegal." *Social Science & Medicine* 331(August): 116074. https://doi.org/10.1016/j.socscimed.2023.116074.

Richman, Mark J., Suhaila Nawabi, Lauren Patty, and Irwin Ziment. 2010. "Traditional Cambodian Medicine." *Journal of Complementary and Integrative Medicine* 7(1). https://doi.org/10.2202/1553-3840.1194.

Ros, Bandeth, Gillian Lê, Barbara McPake, and Suzanne Fustukian. 2018. "The Commercialization of Traditional Medicine in Modern Cambodia." *Health Policy and Planning* 33(1): 9–16. https://doi.org/10.1093/heapol/czx144.

Sargent, Carolyn, John Marcucci, and Ellen Elliston. 1983. "Tiger Bones, Fire and Wine: Maternity Care in a Kampuchean Refugee Community." *Medical Anthropology* 7(4): 67–79. https://doi.org/10.1080/01459740.1983.9987047.

Theilade, Ida, and Rogier De Kok. 2015. "Editorial – The Status of Botanical Exploration and Plant Conservation in Cambodia." *Phnom Penh Cambodian Journal of Natural History* 2015(2): 117–120.

Van Esterik, Penny. 1988. "To Strengthen and Refresh: Herbal Therapy in Southeast Asia." *Social Science & Medicine* 27(8): 751–759. https://doi.org/10.1016/0277-9536(88)90227-4.

Walker, Taylor J. 2017. "An Examination of Medicinal Ethnobotany and Biomedicine Use in Two Villages on the Phnom Kulen Plateau." http://digitalcommons.hollins.edu/researchawards/36.

Walston, Naomi. 2005. "Challenges and Opportunities for Male Involvement in Reproductive Health in Cambodia." *USAID.GOV.* USAID. https://pdf.usaid.gov/pdf_docs/PNADD199.pdf.

White, Patrice M. 2004. "Heat, Balance, Humors, and Ghosts: Postpartum in Cambodia." *Health Care for Women International* 25(2): 179–194. https://doi.org/10.1080/07399330490267477.

WHO and Ministry of Health, Cambodia. *Health Service Delivery Profile: Cambodia, 2012.* Phnom Penh, Cambodia: WHO and Ministry of Health Cambodia. www.wpro.who.int/health_services/service_delivery_profile_cambodia.pdf.

World Health Organization [WHO]. 2019. *WHO Global Report on Traditional and Complementary Medicine 2019.* World Health Organization. https://apps.who.int/iris/bitstream/handle/10665/312342/9789241515436-eng.pdf?ua=1.

World Health Organization [WHO]. 2021. "Traditional, Complementary and Integrative Medicine." *World Health Organization.* World Health Organization. www.who.int/health-topics/traditional-complementary-and-integrative-medicine#tab=tab_1.

Chapter 21

The domestic sphere of women and the public world of men

The strengths and limitations of an anthropological dichotomy

Louise Lamphere

Original to a previous edition of this text. Courtesy of Louise Lamphere.

Since 1974, there has been a burgeoning interest within anthropology in the study of women, sex roles, and gender. Anthropology has long been a discipline that contained important women (Elsie Clews Parsons, Ruth Benedict, and Margaret Mead, among the most famous) and a field in which women have been studied as well (e.g., Kaberry 1939, 1952; Landes 1938, 1947; Leith-Ross 1939; Paulme 1963; Underhill 1936). However, with the publication of *Woman, Culture, and Society* (Rosaldo and Lamphere 1974) and *Toward an Anthropology of Women* (Reiter 1975a), women scholars, many of whom were identified as feminists, began to critique the androcentric bias in anthropology to explore women's status in a wide variety of societies, and to provide explanatory models to understand women's position cross-culturally.

One of the most powerful and influential models was proposed by Michelle Rosaldo in her introductory essay to *Woman, Culture, and Society* (1974). Her argument began by asserting that although there is a great deal of cross-cultural variability in men's and women's roles, there is a pervasive, universal asymmetry between the sexes. "But what is perhaps most striking and surprising," Rosaldo writes, "is the fact that male, as opposed to female, activities are always recognized as predominantly important, and cultural systems give authority and value to the roles and activities of men" (Rosaldo 1974: 19).

One of the quotes we chose to appear at the beginning of the book, a passage from Margaret Mead's *Male and Female*, sums up what we saw in 1974 in all the ethnographies and studies we examined.

> In every known society, the male's need for achievement can be recognized. Men may cook, or weave, or dress dolls or hunt hummingbirds, but if such activities are appropriate occupations of men, then the whole society, men and women alike, votes them as important. When the same occupations are performed by women, they are regarded as less important.
>
> (Mead 1949: 125)

Not only were there differential evaluations of women's activities, but Rosaldo argues, "everywhere men have some authority over women, that [is] they have culturally legitimated right to her subordination and compliance" (1974: 21).

DOI: 10.4324/9781003398349-24

Having argued for a pervasive sexual asymmetry across cultures, not just in terms of cultural values, but also in terms of power and authority, Rosaldo accounted for this difference between men and women in terms of a dichotomy.[1] She argued that women are associated with a "domestic orientation," while men are primarily associated with extradomestic, political, and military spheres of activity. By "domestic" Rosaldo meant "those minimal institutions and modes of activity that are organized immediately around one or more mothers and their children." In contrast, the "public" referred to

activities, institutions, and forms of association that link, rank, organize, or subsume particular mother–child groups. Put quite simply, men have no single commitment as enduring, time-consuming, and emotionally compelling – as close to seeming necessary and natural – as the relation of a woman to her infant child; and so men are free to form those broader associations that we call "society," universalistic systems of order, meaning, and commitment that link particular mother–child groups.

(23)

Rosaldo, along with Sherry Ortner and Nancy Chodorow, who also wrote essays in *Woman, Culture, and Society*, insisted that the connection between women's role in reproduction (the fact that women everywhere lactate and give birth to children) and their domestic orientation is not a necessary one. In other words, biology is not destiny. Women's domestic orientation was structurally and culturally constructed, and "insofar as woman is universally defined in terms of a largely maternal and domestic role, we can account for her universal subordination" (Rosaldo 1974: 7).

Rosaldo writes:

Although I would be the last to call this a necessary arrangement or to deny that it is far too simple as an account of any particular empirical case, I suggest that the opposition between domestic and public orientations (an opposition that must, in part, derive from the nurturant capacities of women) provides the necessary framework for an examination of male and female roles in any society.

(Rosaldo 1974: 24)

For Rosaldo, then, women were involved in the "messiness" of daily life; they were always available for interruption by children. Men could be more distanced and may actually have had separate quarters (such as men's houses) away from women's activities. Men could thus "achieve" authority and create rank, hierarchy, and a political world away from women. The confinement of women to the domestic sphere and men's ability to create and dominate the political sphere thus accounted for men's ability to hold the greater share of power and authority in all known cultures and societies.

At the time Rosaldo wrote her overview, and in the introduction we both wrote, we were faced with building a framework where none existed. Despite the number of monographs on women, Margaret Mead's work (1949) and that of Simone de Beauvoir (1953) were the most provocative, and perhaps the only, theoretical works we knew.[2] The argument for universal sexual asymmetry followed in a long tradition in anthropology where scholars have sought to look for what is broadly "human" in all cultures. In addition to language, anthropologists have discussed the universality of the incest taboo, marriage, and the family. The notion that women might be universally subordinate to men thus made sense as a first attempt at theory-building in this newly revived "subfield" within anthropology.

Although Rosaldo argued for universal subordination, she was careful to make clear that women are not powerless. They exercise informal influence and power, often mitigating male authority or even rendering it trivial (Rosaldo 1974: 21). In addition, there are important variations in women's roles in different cultures, and variation was discussed in most of the rest of the articles in the collection. For example, Sanday and Sacks compared women's status in a number of different societies, while Leis examined the structural reasons that women's associations are strong in one Ijaw village in Nigeria yet absent in another. Finally, in my own article, I examined the differences in women's strategies within domestic groups in a number of societies, which related to the relative integration or separation of domestic and political spheres.

Since 1974, the hypothesis of universal subordination of women and the dichotomous relationship between women in the domestic sphere and men in the public sphere have been challenged and critiqued by a number of feminist anthropologists. As appealing as this dichotomy seemed in the abstract, it turned out to be difficult to apply when actually looking at examples of women's activities in different cultures. For example, in an important article written about the same time as Rosaldo's introduction, Rayna Reiter (now Rayna Rapp) described women's and men's distinct lives in a small French village in the south of France. "They inhabited different domains, one public, one private. While men fraternized with whomever they found to talk to in public places, women were much more enmeshed in their families and their kinship networks" (Reiter 1975b: 253). However, two categories of public space fell into women's domain: the church and three shops, including the local bakery. Men tended to avoid women's places, entering the bakery, for example, only when several men were together and joking, "Let's attack now" (Reiter 1975b: 257).

Reiter argues that men and women use public space in different ways and at different times.

> The men go early to the fields, and congregate on the square or in the cafes for a social hour after work. Sometimes they also fraternize in the evenings. These are the times when women are home cooking and invisible to public view. But when the men have abandoned the village for the fields, the women come out to do their marketing in a leisurely fashion. The village is then in female hands. In the afternoon, when the men return to work, the women form gossip groups on stoops and benches or inside houses depending on the weather.
>
> (Reiter 1975b: 258)

Despite the powerful imagery – women associated with the private or domestic domain and men with public space – the description also shows that the dichotomy is not neat. After all, women are in public a great deal; they have taken over, in some sense, the Church and the shops and even the public square in the middle of the day.

In Margery Wolf's description of women in a Taiwanese village based on data she collected in the late 1950s, she emphasizes that because researchers have focused on the dominance of patrilineal descent in the family, they have failed to see women's presence. "We have missed not only some of the system's subtleties but also its near-fatal weaknesses" (Wolf 1972: 37). Women have different interests than men and build uterine families – strong ties to their daughters, but primarily to their sons, who give their mothers loyalty and a place in the patrilineal extended family. Outside the family, in the community women formed neighborhood groups – around a store, at a platform where women washed their clothes in the canal, or under a huge old tree. In Peihotien, a village strung out between a river and a canal, there was no central plaza dominated by men, as in the South of France.

In Peihotien, Wolf did not describe a cultural geography where women were in a private sphere and men in the public one; rather, there was more of a functional separation – men and women had different activities and interests. They were often located in the same places but had a different relationship to the patrilineal extended family and the male-dominated community. Women's lack of power led them to different strategies, different tactics that often undermined male control of the household and even the community. As Sylvia Yanagisako (1987: 111) has pointed out, the notion of domestic–public entails both a spatial metaphor (of geographically separated or even nested spaces) and a functional metaphor (of functionally different activities or social roles) in the same conceptual dichotomy. Analysts often "mix" these different metaphors in any particular analysis sometimes using domestic–public spatially and at other times functionally.

Even in the Middle East, the association of women with a private domain (and a lack of power) and men with a public domain (and the center of politics) was too simple, as Cynthia Nelson pointed out in her article "Public and Private Politics: Women in the Middle Eastern World" (1974). Because they are born into one patrilineal group and marry into another, women are important structural links between social groups and often act as mediators. Because there are segregated social worlds, all-female institutions are important for enforcing social norms: women fill powerful ritual roles as sorceresses, healers, and mediums; women are important sources of information for their male kin; and women act as "information brokers," mediating social relations within both the family and the larger society.

From Rosaldo's point of view, these aspects of women's power are primarily "informal" and very different from the public, legitimate roles of men. Nevertheless, even though Nelson affirms the separation of male and female worlds (both spatially and functionally), what is "domestic" has public ramifications (the arrangement of a marriage, the transmission of highly charged political information), and the shadow of the family and kin group (the "domestic") is present in even the most "public" of situations. What at first seemed like a simple, straightforward dichotomy, in light of actual case material seems very "slippery" and complex.

Furthermore, in many cultures, particularly those with an indigenous band or tribal structure, a separation of "domestic" and "public" spheres makes no sense because household production was simultaneously public, economic, and political. Leacock pointed out the following after reviewing the literature on the Iroquois during the seventeenth and eighteenth centuries:

Iroquois matrons preserved, stored, and dispensed the corn, meat, fish, berries, squashes, and fats that were buried in special pits or kept in the long house. Brown (1970: 162) notes that women's control over the dispensation of the foods they produced, and meat as well, gave them de facto power to veto declarations of war and to intervene to bring about peace. . . . Women also guarded the "tribal public treasure" kept in the long house, the wampum quill and feather work, and furs. . . . The point to be stressed is that this was "household management" of an altogether different order from management of the nuclear or extended family in patriarchal societies. In the latter, women may cajole, manipulate, or browbeat men, but always behind the public facade; in the former case, "household management" was itself the management of the "public economy."

(Leacock 1978: 253)

Sudarkasa has made much the same point about women in West African societies, such as the Yoruba. She argues that many of the political and economic activities anthropologists discuss as public are actually embedded in households (Sudarkasa 1976, as quoted in Rapp 1979: 509). Furthermore, "in West Africa, the 'public domain' was not conceptualized as 'the world of men.' Rather, the public domain was one in which both sexes were recognized as having important roles to play" (Sudarkasa 1986: 99).

A more appropriate conception would be to recognize two domains, "one occupied by men and another by women, both of which were internally ordered in a hierarchical fashion and both of which provided 'personnel' for domestic and extradomestic (or public) activities" (Sudarkasa 1986: 94).

Furthermore, a careful examination of "domestic domain" indicates that the categories of "woman" and "mother" overlap in western society, but the meaning of motherhood may be vastly different in another society. Women may not be exclusively defined as mothers and child-rearers in terms of their status and cultural value (see Moore 1988: 20–29 for a discussion of this point).

In addition to the issue of whether the domestic–public dichotomy can provide an adequate *description* of men's and women's spatial and functional relationships in our own and other societies, the model has problems as an *explanation* of women's status. One of these problems is the inherent circularity of the model. A central point is to account for the nature of these domains, yet they are already assumed to exist widely and are treated as categories in terms of which women's activities (such as food preparing, cooking, childcare, washing) can be classified (as opposed to male hunting, warfare, political councils). Comaroff says that the model "can only affirm what has already been assumed – that is, that the distinction between the domestic and politico-jural is an intrinsic, if variable, fact of social existence" (Comaroff 1987: 59). When the model is used to explain women's positions in different societies in relation to these two orientations, the reasoning is equally circular. To put it in the words of Yanagisako and Collier:

> The claim that women become absorbed in domestic activities because of their role as mothers is tautological given the definition of "domestic" as "those minimal institutions and modes of activity that are organized immediately around one or more mothers and their children."
>
> (Yanagisako and Collier 1987: 19)

Finally, we have come to realize that the concepts of domestic and public were bound up in our own history and our own categories, grounded particularly in a Victorian heritage. Rosaldo, in a thoughtful re-evaluation of her model, came to argue this position herself.

The turn-of-the-century social theorists whose writings are the basis of most modern social thinking tended without exception to assume that women's place was in the home. In fact, the Victorian doctrine of separate male and female spheres was, I would suggest, quite central to their sociology. Some of these thinkers recognized that modern women suffered from their association with domestic life, but none questioned the pervasiveness (or necessity) of a split between the family and society.

(Rosaldo 1980: 401–402)

Rosaldo traced the historical roots of domestic–public from the nineteenth-century evolutionists through twentieth-century structural functionalists to her own work. Instead of two opposed spheres (different and apart), Rosaldo suggested an analysis of gender relationships, an examination of inequality and hierarchy as they are created particularly through marriage (Rosaldo 1980: 412–413).

The dichotomy has been usefully employed in several ways since 1974. First, several authors have shown us how it works in Western societies (e.g., France and the United States, where it arose historically and still has an important ideological function) (Collier et al. 1982; Reiter 1975b). In a related way, analysts have explored the meanings surrounding domestic activities of women, putting together a much more complex picture of women's relation to men in this sphere (Chai 1987; Murcott 1983, reprinted in this book). Second, anthropological analysis has helped us understand the historical development of domestic–public spheres in societies under colonialism. John Comaroff's analysis of the Tshidi chiefdom in South Africa during the early twentieth century is an excellent example of this approach (1987: 53–85). Finally, some analysts have used the cultural concepts of other societies to critique our own model of domestic–public orientations. Sylvia Yanagisako's essay on the clear separation of "inside–outside" domains (a spatial metaphor) and "work–family" activities (a functional dichotomy) in Japanese American culture demonstrates how the anthropological model of domestic–public mixes these metaphors, which has made analysis confusing and difficult (Yanagisako 1987).

Despite these useful attempts at examining women's lives through the lens of a domestic–public opposition, many of us would agree with Rayna Rapp's 1979 summary of the problems with this dichotomy.

We cannot write an accurate history of the West in relation to the Rest until we stop assuming that our experiences subsume everyone else's. Our public/private conflicts are not necessarily the same as those of other times and places. The specific oppression of women cannot be documented if our categories are so broad as to decontextualize what "womanness" means as we struggle to change that definition. A Tanzanian female farmer, a Mapuche woman leader, and an American working-class housewife do not live in the same domestic domain, nor will the social upheavals necessary to give them power over their lives be the same. We must simultaneously understand the differences and the similarities, but not by reducing them to one simple pattern.

(Rapp 1979: 511)

Thus, many of us have tired of the domestic–public dichotomy. We feel it is constraining, a "trap," while new approaches try to get away from dichotomous thinking. These approaches do one of several things. Often, they take history seriously, examining women's situation as it has evolved, often in a colonial context. Furthermore, they treat women as active agents and, following Collier (1974), as people who have interests, often divergent from men, and who act on them. Third, they often focus on gender relationships, rather than only on women. Finally, they do not treat all women as part of a single universal category of "woman." Rather, women are usually analyzed in terms of their social location. Age, class, race, ethnicity, and kinship are all likely to divide women, so newer analyses examine women's strategies and identities as they are differently shaped. Several examples will illustrate some of the different approaches taken in recent years.

Collier's examination of Comanche, Cheyenne, and Kiowa gender relationships (1988) illustrates the recent focus on gender and on the multiple positions that men and women hold in societies in which the domestic–public dichotomy seems inappropriate. This is because these "spheres" are integrated, and there is no firm line between domestic and public space (see Lamphere 1974; Leacock 1978).

The Comanche are an example of a bride service society in which, like many hunter-gatherer societies, men and women were relatively autonomous, the concept of femininity was not elaborated, and the greatest status differences were between unmarried and married men. Marriage established men as having something to achieve (e.g., a wife), leaving women without such a cultural goal. Young men, through providing meat for their in-laws (bride service), become equal adults, and older men, through egalitarian relations and generosity, become the repositories of wisdom and knowledge. Politics focused on the issue of sexuality and on male–male relationships, which often erupted in conflict and violence. Women celebrated their health and sexuality, and hence, the roles of "woman the gatherer" or even "woman the mother" did not emerge as cultural themes.

Among the Cheyenne, an equal bridewealth society, and among the Kiowa, an unequal bridewealth society, marriage relationships were structured in a much different way in the nineteenth century, so gender relationships had a much different content, politics were more hierarchical, and ideology played a different role. Collier's interest is not in the subordination of women in these three societies, because in all three there are several kinds of inequality: between men and women, between older women and girls, between unmarried men and married men, and between kin and affines. An interest in "spheres" and "domains" has been replaced by an emphasis on relationships and an analysis that focuses on the ways in which inequality gets reproduced through marriage transactions, claims on the labor of others, and giving and receiving of gifts. Dominance and subordination become a much more layered, contextualized phenomenon – more interesting than the simple assertion that women are universally subordinated. The processes through which women's inequality (and that of young men) is constructed are laid bare, rather than flatly asserted.

Mary Moran's study of civilized women (1990) explores the historical beginnings and present-day construction of the category "civilized," which does confine educated women among the Glebo of southeastern Liberia to a "domestic sphere." The dichotomy between "civilized" and "native" (or even tribal or country) is a result of missionization and has created a status hierarchy differentially applied to men and to women. Men, once educated and with a history of paid wage work, never lose their status as "civilized," while women, even though married to a "civilized man," may lose their status if they do not dress correctly, keep house in specific ways, and refrain from farming and marketing. Native women who market or have farms are more economically independent but occupy positions of lower prestige. Here we see not only the importance of historical data in examining how cultural categories evolve but also the ways in which both civilized and native women actively manage their status positions. Civilized women, through the practice of fosterage, recruit younger women to their households to carry out the more elaborate household routines in which they must engage and to train these fostered daughters to become civilized themselves.

The civilized–native dichotomy represents the juxtaposition of two systems. One is a parallel-sex system, in which native men and women are represented by their own leaders in two linked but relatively autonomous prestige hierarchies (as suggested by Sudarkasa 1986). The other is a single-sex system (based on a Western model), in which men in political positions represent both sexes and women have little access to prestige except through their husbands. Thus, this is a much more complex system than one based on a domestic–public dichotomy. There are dichotomous categories – civilized–native, male–female – but they do not fit neatly together. Moran (1990) speaks of categories as "gender-sensitive" and suggests that "the Glebo have inserted gender into the civilized/native dichotomy to the point that women's status is not only more tenuous and vulnerable than men's but also very difficult to maintain without male support." In some respects, civilized women trade dependency for prestige, but Moran provides a sympathetic picture of how both civilized and native women manage their lives.

Lila Abu-Lughod's study (1986) of Bedouin women's ritual poetry gives us further insights into the complexity of women who, in 1974, we would have simply thought of as "confined to a domestic sphere." Among the Bedouin, women's marriages are arranged, wives wear black veils and red belts (symbolizing their fertility), and women must behave within a code of behavior that emphasizes family honor and female modesty and shame. When they are confronted with loss, poor treatment, or neglect, the public discourse is one of hostility, bitterness, and anger. In the case of lost love, the discourse is of militant indifference and denial of concern. In contrast, Bedouin poetry, a highly prized and formally structured art, expresses sentiments of devastating sadness, self-pity, attachment, and deep feeling (Abu-Lughod 1986: 187). Although both men and women recite poetry for women, it may express conflicting feelings concerning an arranged marriage, a sense of loss over a divorce, or sentiments of betrayal when a husband marries a new wife. The poems are used to elicit sympathy and get help, but they also constitute a dissident and subversive discourse. Abu-Lughod sees ritual poetry as a corrective to

> an obsession with morality and an overzealous adherence to the ideology of honor. . . . Poetry reminds people of another way of being and encourages, as it reflects, another side of experience. . . . And maybe the vision [offered through poetry] is cherished because people see that the costs of this system, in the limits it places on human experiences, are just too high.
>
> (Abu-Lughod 1986: 259)

Bedouin women in this portrait are not simply victims of patriarchy confined to a domestic sphere; they are active individuals who use a highly valued cultural form to express their deepest sentiments, acknowledge an alternative set of values, and leave open the possibility of subverting the system in which they are embedded.

A large number of studies have been conducted in the United States that loosely focus on what used to be termed the domestic sphere and the public world of work. As in the Native American, African, and Middle Eastern cases cited previously, when one begins to examine a topic in detail, global notions like domestic–public seem too simple to deal with the complexities of women's lives. Clearly, work and home are distinctly separated spheres in the United States. Women who have been employed in the paid labor force have experienced the disjunction of spending eight or more hours of the day in a place of employment, where they are "female workers," and the rest of their time in the home, where they are daughters, wives, and/or mothers. With this come responsibilities for cooking, cleaning, and providing nurturance, care, and intimacy for other family members. Several recent studies have examined the contradictions women face when combining work and family, the impact of paid employment on family roles, and vice versa. I will refer to only three examples of this growing literature.

Patricia Zavella's research on Chicana cannery workers examines women's networks that link the workplace and the family (Zavella 1987). Calling these "work-related networks," Zavella describes groups of friends who saw each other outside work and who were members of a kin network employed in the same cannery. Women used work-related networks as sources of exchange for information, babysitters, and emotional support. Networks operated in more political ways as workers organized a women's caucus and filed a complaint with the Fair Employment Practices Commission. Women's cannery work was seasonal and had relatively little impact on power relations in the family or the household division of labor. On the other hand, work-related networks of friends or kin were an important "bridging mechanism," helping women deal with the contradictions and demands that came from two different spheres.

Karen Sacks's study of hospital workers at the Duke Medical Center examines the ways in which Black and White women brought family notions of work, adulthood, and responsibility to work with them and used these values to organize a walkout and subsequent union drive (1988). Sacks focuses on the activities of "center women" – leaders in the union drive. Unlike the men, who were often the public speakers at rallies and events, the center women organized support on an interpersonal, one-to-one basis. Rather than emphasizing the bridging aspect of women's networks, Sacks shows how the family is "brought to work" or, in the old terminology, how the "domestic" influences the "public."

In my own research, I have traced the changes in the relationship between women, work, and family historically through the study of immigrant women in a small industrial community, Central Falls, Rhode Island (Lamphere 1987). Using the twin notions of productive and reproductive labor, I examined the rise of the textile industry in Rhode Island and the recruitment of working daughters and, later, of working mothers to the textile industry and to the other light industries that have replaced it since World War II. Rather than seeing production and reproduction as a rigid dichotomy (like public and domestic), I have used these categories to study relationships and to examine the kinds of strategies that immigrant women and their families forged in confronting an industrial system where wage work was a necessity and where working-class families had no control over the means of production. Such an approach revealed a great deal of variability both between and within ethnic groups – the Irish, English, French Canadian, and Polish families who came to Central Falls between 1915 and 1984 and the more recent Colombian and Portuguese immigrants. Examination of strikes and walkouts in the 1920s and 1930s and my own experience as a sewer in an apparel plant in 1977 led me to emphasize the strategies of resistance the women workers used on the job, as well as the impact of women's paid labor on the family itself. When daughters were recruited as workers in textile mills, the internal division of labor within the household did not materially change, because wives and mothers continued to do much of the reproductive labor necessary to maintain the household. Fathers, teenage sons, and daughters worked for wages. In the current period, in contrast, as more wives have become full-time workers, immigrant men have begun to do some reproductive labor, particularly childcare. Immigrant couples often work different shifts and prefer to care for children themselves rather than trust babysitters from their own ethnic group. In my study, I argue that "the productive system as constituted in the workplaces has shaped the family more than issues of reproduction have shaped the workplace" (Lamphere 1987: 43).

More recently, Patricia Zavella, Felipe Gonzalez, and I have found that young working mothers in Sunbelt industries have moved much further than cannery women or New England industrial immigrant women in changing the nature of the household division of labor (Lamphere et al. 1993). These new committed female workers have been employed since high school and do not drop out of the labor force for long periods of time to have children. Thus, they and their husbands construct a family life around a two-job household. Although some couples have a "traditional" division of housework (women do the cooking and the majority of the cleaning, and husbands take out the garbage, do minor repairs, and fix the car), many husbands participate in "female chores" and do substantial amounts of childcare (often caring for children while the wife is at work). Here we see the impact of what we used to call the "public sphere" on the domestic one, but in our analysis, we have focused more on the varied ways that Anglos and Hispanics (including single mothers) have negotiated household and childcare arrangements, viewing husbands and wives as mediating contradictions. Subtle similarities and differences among and between working-class Anglo and Hispanic women have emerged from this analysis, making it clear that the impact of work in the public world is not a monolithic but variegated process.

In summary, the dichotomy between the public world of men and the domestic world of women was, in 1974, an important and useful starting point for thinking about women's roles in a cross-cultural perspective. As anthropologists have written more detailed and fine-grained studies of women's lives in a wide variety of other cultures and in our own society, we have gone beyond the use of dichotomies to produce analyses of the complex and layered structure of women's lives. We now treat women more historically, viewing them as social actors and examining the variability among women's situations within one culture and in their relationship to men.

Discussion questions

1. What is the *domestic–public dichotomy*, and how has it been used in anthropology to explain women's subordination to men?
2. What are some of the ethnographic examples offered by Lamphere to challenge the argument for women's universal subordination and the domestic–public dichotomy?
3. Why does Lamphere argue against treating "woman" as a universal category to which all women belong?
4. Despite arguing against the domestic–public dichotomy, why does the author maintain that this theory was an important starting point in the anthropological study of gender?

Notes

1 Rosaldo says that "the opposition does not *determine* cultural stereotypes or asymmetries in the evaluations of the sexism, but rather underlies them, to support a very general . . . identification of women with domestic life and of men with public life" (Rosaldo 1974: 21–22). Thus, I would argue, Rosaldo did not attempt to *explain* women's subordination through the dichotomy but saw it as an underlying structural framework in any society that supported subordination and that would have to be reorganized to change women's position.

2 It is interesting that we did not know of Elsie Clews Parson's extensive feminist writing during 1910 to 1916, much of which is reminiscent of the kind of position we took in *Woman, Culture, and Society*. In another article, I have noted the similarities between Shelly's prose and that of Parsons (see Lamphere 1989; Parsons 1913, 1914, 1915).

References

Abu-Lughod, Lila. 1986. *Veiled Sentiments: Honor and Poetry in a Bedouin Society*. Berkeley and Los Angeles: University of California Press.

Brown, Judith. 1970. "Economic Organization and the Position of Women among the Iroquois." *Ethnohistory* 17(3/4): 131–167.

Chai, Alice Yun. 1987. "Freed from the Elders But Locked into Labor: Korean Immigrant Women in Hawaii." *Women's Studies* 13: 223–234.

Collier, Jane. 1974. "Women in Politics." In *Woman, Culture, and Society*, eds. Michelle Z. Rosaldo and Louise Lamphere, 89–96. Stanford, CA: Stanford University Press.

Collier, Jane. 1988. *Marriage and Inequality in Classless Societies*. Stanford, CA: Stanford University Press.

Collier, Jane, Michelle Rosaldo, and Sylvia Yanagisako. 1982. "Is There a Family? New Anthropological Views." In *Rethinking the Family: Some Feminist Questions*, eds. Barrie Thorne and Marilyn Yalom, 25–40. New York and London: Longman.

Comaroff, John L. 1987. "Sui Genderis: Feminism, Kinship Theory, and Structural 'Domains'." In *Gender and Kinship: Essays Toward a Unified Analysis*, eds. Jane Fishburne Collier and Sylvia Junko Yanagisako, 53–86. Stanford, CA: Stanford University Press.

de Beauvoir, Simone. 1953. *The Second Sex*. New York: Alfred A. Knopf. Originally published in French in 1949.

Kaberry, Phyllis M. 1939. *Aboriginal Women, Sacred and Profane*. London: G. Routledge.

Kaberry, Phyllis M. 1952. *Women of the Grassfields*. London: H. M. Stationery Office.

Lamphere, Louise. 1974. "Strategies, Cooperation, and Conflict among Women in Domestic Groups." In *Woman, Culture, and Society*, eds. Michelle Z. Rosaldo and Louise Lamphere, 97–113. Stanford, CA: Stanford University Press.

Lamphere, Louise. 1987. *From Working Daughters to Working Mothers: Immigrant Women in a New England Industrial Community*. Ithaca, NY: Cornell University Press.

Lamphere, Louise. 1989. "Feminist Anthropology: The Legacy of Elsie Clews Parsons." *American Ethnologist* 16(3): 518–533.

Lamphere, Louise, Patricia Zavella, Felipe Gonzales, and Peter Evans. 1993. *Sunbelt Working Mothers: Reconciling Family and Factory*. Ithaca, NY: Cornell University Press.

Landes, Ruth. 1938. *The Ojibwa Woman, Part 1: Youth*. New York: Columbia University. Contributions to Anthropology, Vol. 31.

Landes, Ruth. 1947. *The City of Women: Negro Women Cult Leaders of Bahia, Brazil*. New York: Macmillan.

Leacock, Eleanor. 1978. "Women's Status in Egalitarian Society: Implications for Social Evolution." *Current Anthropology* 19(2): 247–275.

Leith-Ross, Sylvia. 1939. *African Women: Study of the Ibo of Nigeria*. London: Faber and Faber.

Mead, Margaret. 1949. *Male and Female*. New York: William Morrow and Co.

Moore, Henrietta L. 1988. *Feminism and Anthropology*. Minneapolis: University of Minnesota Press.

Moran, Mary H. 1990. *Civilized Women: Gender and Prestige in Southeastern Liberia*. Ithaca, NY: Cornell University Press.

Murcott, Anne. 1983. "'It's a Pleasure to Cook for Him': Food, Mealtimes and Gender in Some South Wales Households." In *The Public and the Private*, eds. Eva Gamarnikow, D. H. J. Morgan, June Purvis, and Daphne Taylorson, 78–90. London: Heinemann Educational Books.

Nelson, Cynthia. 1974. "Public and Private Politics: Women in the Middle East." *American Ethnologist* 1: 551–563.

Parsons, Elsie Clews. 1913. *The Old Fashioned Woman*. New York: G. P. Putnam's Sons.

Parsons, Elsie Clews. 1914. *Fear and Conventionality*. New York: G. P. Putnam's Sons.

Parsons, Elsie Clews. 1915. *Social Freedom: A Study of the Conflicts between Social Classifications and Personality*. New York: G. P. Putnam's Sons.

Paulme, Denise, ed. 1963. *Women of Tropical Africa*. Berkeley: University of California Press.

Rapp, Rayna. 1979. "Anthropology." *Signs* 4(3): 497–513.

Reiter, Rayna, ed. 1975a. *Toward an Anthropology of Women*. New York: Monthly Review Press.

Reiter, Rayna. 1975b. "Men and Women in the South of France: Public and Private Domains." In *Toward an Anthropology of Women*, ed. Rayna Reiter, 252–283. New York: Monthly Review Press.

Rosaldo, Michelle. 1974. "Woman, Culture and Society: A Theoretical Overview." In *Woman, Culture, and Society*, eds. Michelle Z. Rosaldo and Louise Lamphere, 17–43. Stanford, CA: Stanford University Press.

Rosaldo, Michelle Z. 1980. "The Uses and Abuses of Anthropology." *Signs* 5(3): 389–417.

Rosaldo, Michelle Z., and Louise Lamphere, eds. 1974. *Woman, Culture, and Society*. Stanford, CA: Stanford University Press.

Sacks, Karen. 1988. *Caring by the Hour: Women, Work, and Organizing at the Duke Medical Center*. Urbana and Chicago: University of Illinois Press.

Sudarkasa, Niara. 1976. "Female Employment and Family Organization in West Africa." In *New Research on Women and Sex Roles*, ed. Dorothy McGuigan. Ann Arbor, MI: Center for Continuing Education of Women.

Sudarkasa, Niara. 1986. "The Status of Women in Indigenous African Societies." *Feminist Studies* 12: 91–104.

Underhill, Ruth. 1936.escrybiography of a papago woman." *Supplement to American Anthropologist* 38(3), Part II. Millwood, NY: American Anthropological Association.

Wolf, Margery. 1972. *Women and the Family in Rural Taiwan*. Stanford, CA: Stanford University Press.

Yanagisako, Sylvia Junko. 1987. "Mixed Metaphors: Native and Anthropological Models of Gender and Kinship Domains." In *Gender and Kinship: Essays toward a Unified Analysis*, eds. Jane Fishburne Collier and Sylvia Junko Yanagisako, 86–119. Stanford, CA: Stanford University Press.

Yanagisako, Sylvia Junko, and Jane Fishburne Collier. 1987. "Toward a Unified Analysis of Gender and Kinship." In *Gender and Kinship: Essays toward a Unified Analysis*, eds. Jane Fishburne Collier and Sylvia Junko Yanagisako, 14–53. Stanford, CA: Stanford University Press.

Zavella, Patricia. 1987. *Women's Work and Chicano Families: Cannery Workers of the Santa Clara Valley*. Ithaca, NY: Cornell University Press.

Chapter 22

From "private" affairs to "public" scandals

The modern woman's challenge to husbands' infidelities in Uganda

Shanti Parikh

Original to a previous edition of this text. Courtesy of Shanti Parikh.

Introduction

Uganda is widely touted as *the* HIV success story. Once considered the epicenter of the global HIV epidemic, with an HIV prevalence rate of 19 percent in the early 1990s, the country experienced a remarkable decline, reporting a low of 5.4 percent in 2007 (UNAIDS 2008). During this period of decline, all age and sex groups reported a decrease in infection rate, except for women between the ages 30 and 39, an age group whose members are most likely married or had been married (Mbulaiteye et al. 2002). Other studies showed similar risk for married women. For instance, a study in southeast Uganda found that when both spouses were HIV negative, husbands were two times more likely than their wives to eventually bring HIV infection into marriage, suggesting that husbands' extramarital liaisons were the likely source of HIV infection (Carpenter et al. 1999). Ironically, for women around the world, the very liaison that is promoted by public health, religious, and other campaigns as the "safest" type of sex – marital sex – is precisely the one that presents women with the greatest risk for HIV infection (Hirsch et al. 2010; Newmann et al. 2004; O'Leary 2000; UNAIDS et al. 2004).

On the surface, the domestic–public model initially proposed by Michelle Rosaldo (1974, 1980, Lamphere this book) provides a compelling analytic framework for understanding married women's increased risk for HIV infection. Men's mobility in the public sphere and access to resources provide them opportunities for extramarital trysts, while wives' responsibilities, which tie them to the domestic sphere, impede their ability (and desire) to find out and to take action. Research I conducted in Uganda between 2004 and 2006 supports this general explanation. However, a closer examination of ethnographic and historical data indicates that overreliance on the domestic–public divide precludes an understanding of the historic fluidity of these categories and how women strategically blur the boundaries for their marital advantage.

In this chapter, I explore three major findings that build upon and complicate the domestic–public model. My first argument demonstrates how the domestic–public model can be used to understand structural factors that underlie married women's HIV risk. My second argument is historical. It highlights how sexuality and sexual meanings, like

DOI: 10.4324/9781003398349-25

all cultural forms, are neither static nor timeless relics but are dynamic and responsive to wider shifts and trends. I use life histories from three generational cohorts in Uganda to chronicle how the practices of polygyny (a man having more than one wife) and fairly indiscreet extramarital liaisons of men have been transformed gradually into informal secondary households and more secretive trysts, respectively. This transformation has been occasioned by shifts in the economy, gender equality campaigns, and the proliferation of discourses that have made sexuality a primary concern of public health and public morality regulation and surveillance. Hence, whereas in the past men's extramarital activities were primarily considered a private family matter, today they have become a matter of great public attention, critique, and gossip.

Finally, the third argument I make in this chapter concerns married women's varied responses to their husband's infidelities. While respectable middle-class women are expected to maintain the reputations of their marriages by not airing grievances publicly, in some cases, women strategically disrupt the boundaries between private (marital affairs and domestic sphere) and public (reputations of spouses and men's worlds) in an attempt to effect a desired outcome. While the private–public divide may enable men's extramarital trysts and underlie women's willful silence or unawareness, in some cases, it is strategic for women to "go public" with decidedly private matters in order to gain sympathy from neighbors, shame their husbands, and importantly, present themselves as modern rational actors who protect themselves. In the contemporary context in Uganda, the notion of "rational" is shaped by the highly visible messages about protecting oneself from sexual risk as espoused in public health campaigns, from gendered violations as promoted by the women's rights movement, and from moral decline as championed in religious teachings. Yet going public with their husband's affairs can also have unpleasant consequences. This chapter brings new insight to the ongoing debates about the usefulness of the public–private model by highlighting how public health and other interventions have worked to transform male infidelity and women's responses to what had been largely a private concern – among families and close social networks – into a matter of public concern with paradoxical implications.

Ethnographic setting and methods

This chapter is based on ethnographic research in the agrarian, eastern central town of Iganga and its network of outlying villages, a region in which I have conducted research since 1996. I draw upon data that my research assistants and I collected during a six-month period in 2004 and three months of follow-up visits in 2005 and 2006. The research was part of a five-country comparative study on married women's HIV risk and men's extramarital sexuality.[1] Data consist of marital and life histories of 74 men and women, key informant interviews (including mistresses, bar owners, health officials, and religious leaders), participant observation, and discourse analysis of media and popular representations of contemporary sexuality in Uganda.

Iganga town is the rapidly growing administrative and commercial center for the Iganga District (the population of the district was roughly 600,000 in 2004). The town sits along the Trans-Africa Highway, the major international road that runs from the coast of Kenya through Rwanda and into the Democratic Republic of the Congo. Iganga was once known as the "HIV corridor," with the interactions between long-distance truck drivers and commercial sex workers at the rest stops along the highway documented as being early transmitters of the virus, eventually spreading the infection to the general population. To residents in Iganga, however, this highway also represents their connection to the rest of East Africa and beyond.

The Basoga are Bantu-speaking and have exogamous and patrilocal marriages, that is, people must marry someone outside their clan, and the couple relocates to the man's residence after marriage (Radcliffe-Brown 1950). The exchange of bridewealth from the groom's family to the bride's solidifies the marriage and is considered an important sign of respect. It essentially transfers authority over a woman's productive and sexual labor from her father to her husband. Bridewealth, combined with the patrilocal residence pattern, has the effect of isolating a new bride from the protection of her natal family. This limits a wife's ability to negotiate within marriage, a point that is critical to this chapter.

Historically, residents of Iganga relied on subsistence agricultural and livestock activities as their primary source of income. To meet their needs in an increasingly monetized economy, today, households must supplement farming with other income-generating activities, such as small trading, shopkeeping, manual labor, driving bicycle or motorcycle taxis, repair work, selling cooked food, and working in service industries. Having a salaried position in a school, government office, bank, or a local branch of a development agency elevates a person's socioeconomic status, but such positions are few and more readily available to men, exacerbating gender inequalities. Life and marriage in Iganga is fraught with economic uncertainty, which has profound implications for marital happiness and men's extramarital behaviors. In addition to economic frustrations, this uncertainty is complicated by what I call high HIV anxiety, a by-product of Uganda's aggressive campaigns that have successfully made people aware of the possibility that they have HIV.

The domestic–public divide: a starting point for understanding men's extramarital opportunity structures

Despite many critiques and counterexamples, the domestic–public model provides a useful entryway into understanding gendered patterns of HIV risk. The model is compelling primarily because it moves away from a narrow focus on individuals' actions, a tendency of many conventional public health models, and instead redirects attention to the wider social and economic factors that shape and constrain options from which people may choose. In other words, instead of assuming that men and women act as independent health droids who make decisions devoid of any social context, the private/domestic framework draws attention to what my collaborators and I have called "opportunity structures" that facilitate or discourage men's extramarital sexuality (see Hirsch et al. 2010). Recognizing the role of opportunity structures in facilitating men's extramarital sex is not to excuse husbands' behaviors or wives' inaction but, rather, to situate both within a wider context of enabling and disenabling factors.

Findings from my research in Uganda readily support the idea that the private–public divide is both a product of and recreates the gender inequality that undergirds men's participation in extramarital sexuality and married women's increased risk for HIV. Men's migration and mobility and subsequent access to resources in the public sphere provide them opportunities for extramarital encounters away from the surveillance of "domestically" situated wives and relatives. Physically, labor-related migration with spousal separation, which is a common feature at some point in the lives of the men in Iganga, almost inevitably leads men into sexual liaisons with women who are not their longer-term partners. Unlike their wives or girlfriends who often remain behind where mutual social and kin networks can easily provide watchful eyes on behaviors, men's absence from these connections permits them to engage in extramarital activities without similar repercussions. Conversely, instead of tarnishing a man's reputation, we found that participating in sexual liaisons sometimes has the counter-effect of bolstering his reputation within the masculine prestige structure among his migrant peer and work groups. Not only may men's peer groups directly or indirectly encourage men's extramarital activities, but men in our study also mentioned feeling lonely and desiring companionship while away from wives and children (Campbell 1997). For instance, an army man I interviewed frequently was assigned to posts far from Iganga for up to a year at a time. He described how it was virtually assumed that he would get an "informal wife" to take care of his domestic needs at the army camp. He also explained that army men are seen as a valuable source of money and safety to the families and young women in the conflict-ridden and often economically depressed regions where they are assigned, and hence, there is a steady flow of sex-for-favors/money offers (also called transactional sex). Although possible, not participating in extramarital sexuality would seem odd to both his peers and the community.

Even men who were not participating in labor migration during the time of our study experienced greater physical mobility than their wives, which produced similar opportunity structures. As Iganga transforms from its landscape of daytime businesses into a lively nighttime outdoor bazaar, the sexual geography of the town becomes visible as men and unmarried women venture to and in between the variety of commercial drinking and eating places that pepper the landscape. Similar to distant migration destinations, the semi-anonymity of town and its social distance from overseeing wives and kin serve to facilitate men's sexual networking.

Some men expressed feeling pulled to Iganga's evening activities. Ironically, although husbands are considered the "rulers" of their households, many men revealed feeling out of place and limited in the domestic arena, especially in the evening, when many household chores are performed. While some men have adopted the idea of assisting with domestic chores and life, local gender convention still dictates otherwise. According to a middle-class office worker who often did assist with household chores, "If you go home, what is there for you? Your wife quarrels with you about this and that, wonders why you are not looking for money. Or she and children have their chores, so you sit alone. Nothing to do." This common sentiment essentially pulls men out of the home and into bars, pool halls, or other "public" places in which drinking and socializing with single women are central to male homosocial bonding. Masculine prestige structures dominant in many of these settings are based on sexual conquests, creating a favorable atmosphere for men's extramarital liaisons.

While married men are expected to build an expanding social world in order to increase their abilities to provide for the home, married women often experience a different reality because their duties draw them to the household. Women's domestic responsibilities tie them to the home, which results in a smaller social network and more limited access to resources, restricting their ability to find out about and to have an influence on their husbands' nondomestic activities. Recently, married women and women with young children have particularly limited mobility not only because of breastfeeding and child-raising but also because of the need to establish themselves as competent wives and mothers in new families and communities. Women's shrinking postmarital social networks leave them dependent on husbands and nearby in-laws and less able to discuss husbands' recreational activities or to negotiate HIV preventative practices. As women matured in their marriages, we found that their social worlds expanded as they began to involve themselves more with community activities, but the earlier years were particularly precarious.

Gendered inequality in access to resources, social networks, and mobility translates into husbands' having greater authority over their wives and leaving wives dependent on their husbands. For the wives, this means that they may have a difficult time raising concerns about their husbands' suspected infidelities and negotiating HIV preventative techniques. A main reason is the fear of possible consequences, such as withdrawal of a partner's support or affection, violence, counteraccusations, or even that the ideal of monogamy has failed. Furthermore, two goals of many marriages – to bear children and to maintain a "happy" public reputation – may work to further women's HIV risk. The desire to reproduce discourages condom use, and the desire to maintain the appearance of a happy marriage means that women may choose to willfully ignore husband's extramarital liaisons. Thus, a woman's inability or even hesitation to negotiate HIV preventative techniques with her husband (such as condom use or the timing or frequency of sex) is influenced by her own desire, by familial pressure, or by fear of negative reactions from partners.[2]

A historical view: the state, economy, and shifts in men's extramarital sexuality

While the domestic–public model allows us to understand marital dynamics within a specific context, it restricts our ability to understand how categories have changed over time. In this section, I use interviews with three generations of residents to examine how marital and extramarital relations were shaped by changes in the state, society, and the economy.

The British colonial era: profits, laws, and exacerbating gender inequalities

Beginning in the early 1900s, British colonial policies and ideologies interacted with the precolonial Basoga agrarian economy and patrilineal kinship system in ways that bolstered gender inequality in marriage and that provided structural incentives for men's concurrent liaisons.[3] Of particular interest to this project was the introduction of cash crops as a means of extracting wealth from the colony, which was the basis of colonial presence. Informed by prevailing British gender ideologies regarding property rights, colonial officials gave men greater control over economic resources, including land and cash crops, distancing women from new forms of capitalist wealth. The workloads of ordinary women increased as they became expected to work on both their households' subsistence gardens as well as their husbands' cash crop farms, controlling the profits from neither. Not only did this bolster husbands' control over wives, but profits from cash crops also provided men a greater incentive for polygyny. The more wives and children a man had translated into greater wealth in the form of crop production, social prestige, and subjects. Polygyny became a way for men to secure labor for cash farming.

Since the family unit became the basis for guaranteeing steady cash crop production, the colonial state had a vested interest in ensuring marital instability. In the 1940s and 1950s, British officials in Iganga became concerned about the increasing divorce rate and the negative effect it would have on farm production (Fallers 1969). In an effort to stabilize and regulate marriage, they collaborated with local male leaders to institute laws that gave husbands greater control over their "unruly" wives. One attempt to control women was greater enforcement of the 1904 Divorce Law, which required a full refund of bridewealth (by either the woman's father or new husband) upon the dissolution of a union. This had the intended effect of making divorce more difficult for women to initiate.

Another tool used to stabilize marriage was the Adultery Law, which, following British law, was defined differently for husbands and wives. For a married woman, *adultery* was having an affair or running off with another man. For a man, *adultery* was defined as sexual relations with a married woman, with the offense committed against the "owner" of the woman, such as her husband. Sexual relations with an unmarried woman were not considered adultery. In other words, while a man could divorce a wife if she had extramarital sex, his own extramarital sexuality was neither legally nor socially considered grounds for divorce. The law codified a gendered double standard for extramarital sex: a man could *safely* have an extramarital liaison without any legal ramification or wider social consequence as long as it was with a woman over whom another man did not claim rights, such as a prostitute, divorcée, widow, or orphan.

In my discussions with Iganga residents about their parents' marriages, the double standard regarding the definition, meanings, and consequences of adultery clearly emerges. When asked to reflect on their parents' marriages, many older participants recounted stories of their fathers' flagrant extramarital liaisons. For instance, Tapenensi,[4] an older woman in her late 60s, whose mother had come of age during the colonial period, explained that her mother had protested her husband's repeated bringing of other women into their bedroom by eventually refusing to sleep in her matrimonial bed. She chose, instead, to sleep on the floor of their bedroom. Tapenensi, as a result, was determined to never "surrender control over [her] bedroom as [her] mother did." After she had borne five children, her husband had brought a younger woman into the home as a second wife to bear more children. Remembering the fate of her mother, Tapenensi had remained steadfast about giving up neither her bedroom nor her senior position in the household. She describes how this had occurred twice, with both co-wives eventually leaving when Tapenensi's stubbornness and oversight became too much for them. After two failed attempts at polygyny, her husband did not bring another woman into the house, keeping his extramarital lovers outside the home and their marriage. Tapenensi's story shows how men's extramarital liaisons were not grounds for divorce, but also women's coping strategies.

In sum, colonial policies interacted with precolonial Basoga kinship and economic systems in ways that facilitated and encouraged men's multi-partnering. While the dependence of wives on their husbands was structurally bolstered through adultery and divorce laws, women did employ varying degrees of resistance, including divorce, silent protest, and managing domestic interactions.

The postcolonial era: the emergence of the middle class and the myth of monogamy

During the postcolonial era, a visible middle class emerged. Their public dominance further shaped notions of marriage and extramarital liaisons, working in some instances to transform polygyny into a form of informal secondary households or outside wives (see Karanja 1987; Mann 1994; Musisi 1991). The marital histories of three generations reveal a pattern in which the hegemonic notion of wealth in the form of wives and children gradually was challenged as capitalist desires and Christian ideologies were further absorbed into the local landscape. In Uganda's increasingly monetized economy, wives and children not only meant more labor for farming but also more household dependents to feed, clothe, educate, and the like. The notion of "wealth in people" as a motivator for a man to marry multiple wives was displaced – in ideology, if not in practice – by the ideal of marital monogamy, particularly among Uganda's emerging elite. In some cases, in order to manage multiple partnerships while not officially participating in polygyny, wealthy men took on informal "outside wives." This blurring of polygyny and extramarital sexuality is demonstrated in marital histories of Iganga's first postcolonial educated adult men, for whom professional mobility and success depended on depicting a certain type of marital image to European patrons and other elite Africans.

Take, for example, Joshua Waigona, who had been a top civil servant in Uganda's first postcolonial government. He had married Mary in 1965; he was 25, and she was 16. He described how monogamy and big church weddings were expected at that time within his social network. While he had had several lovers before marriage who were, according to him, "*ababulidho*" (common women), he had selected Mary as his wife because she was "a conservative, educated girl" from one of the female boarding schools in the area. He had thought that Mary would fit nicely into his peer network and would represent him well. He described how activities such as attending movies in the city, eating at fancy restaurants, and taking weekend trips were inaccessible to most Ugandans but had formed an important aspect of their middle-class identity. As John reflected on the prestige and the social worlds associated with Christian, monogamous marriage, he simultaneously talked about the various lovers he had maintained while away in England for training and in the Ugandan towns he had frequented for work, relationships indirectly and silently encouraged by his co-workers and supervisors.

In the late 1970s, Joshua, Mary, and their children relocated to the capital, Kampala, for his job promotion with a British bank. Joshua made frequent trips to Iganga for work and to visit his natal family. He had met and become "familiar with" the daughter of the owner of a popular pub. She got pregnant, and he eventually married her. The story has an interesting twist.

Ironically, it was his angry and disappointed wife who insisted that he take his pregnant lover as a second wife. Mary's reason: she wanted to keep a watchful eye on the younger woman's behavior and hoped to have greater control over the rumors about the affair and her marriage. Joshua initially opposed turning the extramarital liaison into formal polygyny, for fear that his reputation among European patrons and other African elites would be tarnished, but in the end, he gave in when the competing pressures from his wife, his mother, and the mother of his pregnant lover became too great. His second wife, however, never gained the full social status of a wife of a wealthy man. This was partly because Mary's clever planning and her position as an educated woman left no room for another wife in their social networks, and because their Christian community only recognized one formal wife. The second wife passed away in 1989, to which Mary commented, "My marriage was able to return to normal – the way it was supposed to be."

Joshua and Mary's case offers insight into how marital practices and men's management of multiple partnerships became important class markers and indexes of modernity during Uganda's recent history. Although the public appearance of marital monogamy was expected by their social networks, the wealth and mobility of many middle-class professional men gave them great access to a large pool of women – who, in turn, found them highly desirable.

Furthermore, while formal polygyny was frowned upon in elite circles, the maintenance of girlfriends was quietly accepted and facilitated by men's peer groups. Although Joshua formalized his marriage with his second wife, it was, and still is, more common for a long-term girlfriend relationship to turn merely into an "informal secondary" household, particularly after the birth of a child. Finally, Joshua and Mary's story also reveals the way in which a wife can participate in presenting a certain type of public appearance of her marriage in order to maintain her public reputation as well as to exert some influence over her husband's actions.

Modern marriage: the economy, love, and secrecy

Scholars have noted that over the last 50 years, around the world there has been a rise in companionate (or love) marriage occasioned by global influences, changes in the marketplace, and the increasing importance of individualism (Wardlow and Hirsch 2006). The same can be said of marriage in Iganga. In our study, both men and women described marriage today in terms of mutual investment in "developing the home." According to both wealthy and poor people in Iganga, this goal requires mutual economic and emotional commitment from husbands and wives to the marital project, the cornerstones of which are communication and cooperation.

As residents reflected on their parents' marriages, they were critical of their fathers' irresponsible use of income on women other than their own mothers (although this did not necessarily stop men from engaging in similar behaviors). Women commented on their mothers' passivity and seeming complacence regarding their fathers' philandering. As a result, when asked how they wanted their marriages to be different from those of their parents, most men and women said that they wanted fewer children and more equal participation in decision-making and income generation. The joint economic and social investments in developing a modern household were regularly contrasted to the past, in which husbands were seen as autocratic leaders who made decisions without input from or consent of their wives. Today, wives can and do express their anger to husbands who misuse household funds for their own pleasures, including inquiries about suspected extramarital liaisons.

Uganda's aggressive HIV-prevention campaigns have served to reinforce public ideals of monogamy and fidelity, particularly through the ABC (abstinence, be faithful, condom use) campaigns. Furthermore, Uganda's omnipresent public health campaigns have provided medical reasons and scientific support for avoiding certain types of sexual behaviors in favor of marital fidelity and partner reduction. Simultaneously, within the last couple of decades, the fast-growing Evangelical Pentecostal (or "born again") movement has had a tremendous impact on residents' ideas about the connections among marriage, monogamy, and capitalist consumption. Both men and women in our study thought that monogamy was economically and socially more desirable than polygyny. Although the ideal of monogamy was pervasive, actual practice was different. In a baseline study I conducted in a sample village in 1998, about a third of all household heads ($N = 423$ households) were in a polygynous union at that time (Parikh 2016).

Consumption patterns play an important role in defining a modern marriage. In reality, however, desired goods and lifestyles that mark a marriage as "modern" remain unobtainable or unsustainable for many residents in Iganga, leading to problematic outcomes. Many women in our study said that their husbands had promised greater economic success than what their current realities are. When a husband could not meet his premarital promises of wealth and luxuries, it frequently led to frustrations and disagreements within the marriage. In order to avoid conflict and questions about their failed economic pursuits, a strategy that men employed was to stay away from home, finding solace in mistresses who seldom required the same financial investment that wives and households did. Lovers frequently demanded some material reward, such as rent, money, gifts, or assistance with children, but to a much lesser degree, and did not ask questions otherwise.

Public discourses that have challenged gender inequalities within modern marriage have led to a different set of tensions within marriages. Women generally believe that the social campaigns surrounding gender reform and women's rights are positive; however, some husbands see it as threatening to their status. A man in his late 60s explains the effects of Uganda's gender equality campaigns on marriage:

Women [in the past] had good discipline. They were not behaving like today's young wives. There was a lot of respect given to the husband. If the man said, "I want to find such a thing done," that will be final, and by the time he came back, the thing will have been done. The wife would not have any complaint or anything to add. Marriage then was good, although there was a lot of wife beating.

Men repeatedly expressed the feeling that their masculine authority – once seen as both natural and a cultural given – was constantly under attack on multiple fronts, including development discourses, HIV-prevention messages, women's rights campaigns and legislation, and popular songs, plays, and radio shows. Thus, one could read men's extramarital liaisons as a "protest" against the new gender regime, in which men feel their power has diminished.

According to residents, another significant social factor has had tremendous impact on marriages and extramarital liaisons – the availability of young unmarried women who are no longer under the authority of their fathers. Locally, these young women are called *nakyewombekeire*, or literally "a young woman who lives on her own," which can also be understood to mean lacking steady employment. Residents view the growing supply of unmarried young women as the most immediate threat to the stability of marriages. Whereas feminist analysis portrays young and adolescent women as vulnerable victims of wealthier men's sexual advances, residents as well as the media often construct a narrative in which unmarried women are intentionally pursuing married men. Particularly depicted as "vulnerable" are wealthy men and men of social power. Within this "men-as-victims" trope, male infidelity is construed less the result of men searching for women and more as a function of too many single women chasing after the few men with money.

The anxiety surrounding young women's sexual agency has been heightened by people's awareness of the HIV epidemic and Uganda's sizable population of young people who have come of age as orphans. This pool has contributed to the growing number of young men who find themselves searching for income opportunities, suspended in menial work, or in between jobs, and subsequently delaying marriage. As younger men postpone marriage for economic reasons, relationships with older and wealthier married men provide young women with opportunities for economic support and social networks. When asked why men cheat, one man remarked, "There are just too many unmarried beautiful young women without money, and they simply tempt us [*light laughter*]."

In today's shifting moral economy, dominated by religious, public health, and popular culture discourses, a new demand for discretion has emerged – an image of discretion that privileges the appearance of sexually safe and monogamous couples. Managing social reputation requires conflicting actions from men: appearing to have sexual prowess and vitality remains an important aspect of masculine status within many male peer groups, but uncontained public knowledge of his sexual exploits can ruin a man's reputation in the wider community. Hence, a man's friends or co-workers might serve as accomplices or encouragers for his dalliances, but he may also go to great lengths to keep knowledge of his extramarital relations away from people in his home and his family's social networks. Having liaisons with women not in his wife's socioeconomic group is the socially safest type of affair from the perspective of not getting caught.

Modern wives: love, geographies of blame, and the other woman

While I was doing research for this project, the album *Spare Tyre* by the popular husband-and-wife duo Sam and Sophie Gombya was wildly popular. In the album's title song, Sophie warns and ridicules mistresses, or "spare tyres," who sleep with married men. The song asserts that official wives have the real power and that mistresses are simple fools who are just being (ab)used and discarded like spare tires.

The music video depicts a doting Sophie hugging and intimately touching her "husband" (played by an actor), speaking to and pointing her finger at the other woman, and looking directly at the camera to remind all "spare tyres" of their subordinate position. In response to what Sophie and other wives see as such women's unapologetic and boastful flaunting of their affairs with married men, the feisty singer reminds them:

> You have forgotten
> That you are called the *malaya* (prostitute).
> I am called the wife. . . .
> I know that you are there
> You are my helper
> You are a spare tyre
> I am his real wife. . . .
> When he comes and deceives you . . .

He loves you in hiding
I am the one in control
Better wake up . . .
You are like alcohol
Only used to take away his boredom

The video ends with a defiantly bold Sophie pulling the wig off the head of the other woman in front of a crowd of onlookers, symbolically and publicly baring the inauthenticity of her husband's lover.

The song easily resonates with women in Iganga rebelling against its history of philandering husbands. These acts of rebellion have been gaining further validation and moral support through a variety of public movements in Uganda that forcefully denounce the historical norms that have allowed men to have multiple partners without major consequences. Furthermore, sex scandals involving Uganda's political and social elite have been constantly featured in the country's lucrative social media.

The popularity of these moral discourses reflect a wider social anxiety that surrounds the contradictions inherent in conceptions of modern marriage and the persistent expectations, opportunity structures, and gender inequality that facilitate male infidelity. Christine Obbo (1987) observed that in the early 1980s, in Uganda, "high status women, while striving to make their homes as comfortable as possible for the husband, [would] turn a blind eye and deaf ear to his extramarital activities," in part to spare their reputations and maintain marital harmony. Conducted 20 years after Obbo's study, my research suggests that among women in Iganga, men's infidelity is becoming increasingly intolerable, even for middle-class women who might have more at stake in terms of public reputation. In fact, during our interviews with women in Iganga, most spoke easily about their husbands' misbehaving (most commonly womanizing or overdrinking) as the source of their marital discontent. Public outcries by women were not uncommon during the research period, and there were cases in which a wife or an assigned intermediary secretly followed an adulterous husband to "catch him red-handed" with his mistress.

Wives are presented with a paradox: while the search for prestige – the appearance of modern monogamous marriage – largely motivates women's silences around their husbands' infidelities, the desire for another kind of prestige – the status of being "rational" modern women who have the knowledge and desire to protect their bodies and rights – leads some wives to go public with their complaints about their husbands' infidelities. Feigning indifference or being willfully ignorant can prove detrimental to a woman's reputation, particularly in a context in which women's rights agencies, public health campaigns, and global discourses of modernity promote notions of personhood based on rational choice, individual agency, and self-efficacy. While the consequences of going public can, in some cases, be dire, if executed well, such displays can prove to be a productive and almost necessary reaction. In airing their grievances to the wider community, women can hope to prompt three effects: to shame her husband in hopes of securing greater community surveillance, to gain sympathy from her neighbors, and to present herself as a modern woman, which in rights and public health discourses is based on a model of rational choice, in which a woman has the will to protect her self-interest and well-being.

Yet rarely did wives' outcries or public acts of rebellion lead them to initiate a divorce. As in Sophie's song and in cases I saw in Iganga, a wife's anger is often not directed at the husband but at the other woman, who is often referred to by what has turned into the derogatory term *nakyewombekeire*. No longer publicly tied to fathers, brothers, or uncles, and not yet tied to husbands, *nakyewombekeire* have been set free to compete with each other and, importantly, with older or married women. The conflict between wives and mistresses is not simply about generational tensions; it also reveals class struggles among women. While an elite man might befriend a driver or subordinate and have him collaborate in his secrets, people in Iganga speak about relationships among women in different socioeconomic classes as being fraught with distrust and animosity. This vertical class animosity among women provides another opportunity structure that facilitates men's extramarital liaisons. For mistresses, relationships with the husbands of older women or women from a higher class can be read as a form of social revenge against the women who look down on them.

By breaking their silence and going public with knowledge of their husbands' infidelities, women rebel against the (not-so) secret contradictions that exist between what has come to be expected of modern monogamous marriage and the realities that wider forces converge to make that expectation seemingly impossible, or what one older man called the "sexual hypocrisy" of the modern world. But like the song "Spare Tyre," in local geographies of blame, the mistress (not the husband) is constructed as the provocateur of men's infidelity. Blaming the other woman for a husband's behaviors is not only a way of articulating awareness of wider opportunity structures that propel men into extramarital liaisons but also a way in which a wife can make her husband's infidelities a bit more tolerable, and a way for her to protect her own reputation as a modern rational woman when she forgives him and attempts to maintain her modern marriage.

Discussion questions

1. How is Rosaldo's public–domestic framework employed and challenged in understanding the HIV epidemic in Uganda?
2. How and why did men's extramarital activities go from private affairs to the public domain, where they are subject to critique and gossip?
3. Marriage entails the transfer of authority over a woman's productive and sexual labor from her father to her husband, thus cutting her ties with her natal family. How does this limit a wife's ability to protect herself from HIV transmission in Uganda?
4. How has Uganda's legal history codified a gendered double standard?

Notes

1 This project is part of a larger comparative study, "Love Marriage, and HIV: A Multi-Site Study of Gender and HIV Risk," funded by the National Institutes of Health (NIH) R01 41724–01A1. My four collaborators conducted the same research in different countries – Jennifer S. Hirsch (Mexico), Holly Wardlow (Papua New Guinea), Harriet Phinney (Vietnam), and Daniel Smith (Nigeria). Some of the ideas and concepts (particularly the notion of "opportunity structures" and the role of migration in facilitating extramarital sex) were developed jointly by our group (see Hirsch et al. 2010). I would like to thank my collaborators listed earlier and my research assistants in Uganda (Janet Kagoda, Isabirye Gerald, Moses Mwesigwa, John Daniel Ibembe, and Harriet Mugulusi) for the analytic insights they have provided.

2 For a fuller discussion of opportunity structures and sexual geography that facilitate men's extramarital sexuality, see Parikh (2007).
3 See Allman and Tashjian (2000) and Hunt (1991) for discussions of colonial influences on gender relations in Africa.
4 All names in this chapter are pseudonyms.

References

Allman, Jean, and Victoria B. Tashjian. 2000. *I Will Not Eat Stone: A Women's History of Colonial Asante, 1900–1925*. Portsmouth, NH: Heinemann.
Campbell, Catherine. 1997. "Migrancy, Masculine Identities and Aids: The Psychosocial Context of HIV Transmission on the South African Gold Mines." *Social Science and Medicine* 45(2): 273–281.
Carpenter, Lucy, Anatoli Kamali, Anthony Ruberantwari, Samuel Malamba, and James A. G. Whitworth. 1999. "Rates of HIV-1 Transmission within Marriage in Rural Uganda in Relation to the HIV Sero-Status of the Partners." *AIDS* 13: 1083–1089.
Fallers, Lloyd. 1969. *Law without Precedent: Legal Ideas in Action in the Courts of Colonial Busoga*. Chicago, IL: University of Chicago Press.
Hirsch, Jennifer S., Holly Wardlow, Daniel Jordan Smith, Harriet M. Phinney, Shanti Parikh, and Constance A. Nathanson. 2010. *The Secret: Love, Marriage, and HIV*. Nashville, TN: Vanderbilt University Press.
Hunt, Nancy Rose. 1991. "Noise over Camouflaged Polygamy, Colonial Morality Taxation, and a Woman-Naming Crisis in Belgian Africa." *Journal of African History* 32(3): 471–494.
Karanja, Wambui Wa. 1987. "'Outside Wives' and 'Inside Wives' in Nigeria: A Study of Changing Perceptions in Marriage." In *Transformations of African Marriage*, eds. David Parkin and David Nyamwaya, 247–261. Wolfeboro, NH: Manchester University Press.
Mann, Kristin. 1994. "The Historical Roots and Cultural Logic of Outside Marriage in Colonial Lagos." In *Nuptiality in Sub-Saharan Africa*, eds. Caroline Bledsoe and Gilles Pison, 167–193. Oxford: Clarendon Press.
Mbulaiteye, Samuel, C. Mahe, J. Whitworth, A. Ruberantwari, J. Nakiyingi, A. Ojwiya, and A. Kamali. 2002. "Declining HIV-1 Incidence and Associated Prevalence over 10 Years in a Rural Population in South-West Uganda: A Cohort Study." *The Lancet* 360: 41–46.
Musisi, Nakanyike. 1991. "Women, 'Elite Polygyny,' and Buganda State Formation." *Signs* 16(4): 757–786.
Newmann, S., P. Sarin, N. Kumarasamy, E. Amalraj, M. Rogers, P. Madhivanan, T. Flanigan, S. Cu-uvin, S. McGravey, K. Mayer, and S. Solomon. 2004. "Marriage, Monogamy and HIV: A Profile of HIV-Infected Women in South India." *International Journal of STD & AIDS* 11: 250–253.
Obbo, Christine. 1987. "The Old and the New in East African Elite Marriages." In *Transformations of African Marriage*, eds. David Parkin and David Nyamwaya. Wolfeboro, NH: Manchester University Press.
O'Leary, Ann. 2000. "Women at Risk for HIV from a Primary Partner: Balancing Risk and Intimacy." *Annual Review of Sex Research* 11: 191–234.
Parikh, Shanti. 2007. "The Political Economy of Marriage and HIV: The ABC Approach, 'Safe' Infidelity, and Managing Moral Risk in Uganda." *The American Journal of Public Health* 97: 1198–1208.
Parikh, Shanti. 2016. *Regulating Romance: Youth Sexual Culture, Moral Anxiety, and Love Letters in Uganda's Time of AIDS*. Nashville: Vanderbilt Press.
Radcliffe-Brown, Alfred R. 1950. "Introduction." In *African Systems of Kinship and Marriage*, eds. A. R. Radcliffe-Brown and Daryll Forde, 1–85. London: Oxford University Press.
Rosaldo, Michelle Z. 1974. "Theoretical Overview." In *Women, Culture, and Society*, eds. Michelle Z. Rosaldo and Louise Lamphere, 17–43. Stanford, CA: Stanford University Press.
Rosaldo, Michelle Z. 1980. "The Uses and Abuses of Anthropology." *Signs* 5(3): 389–417.

UNAIDS, UNFPA, and UNIFEM. 2004. *Women and HIV/AIDS: Confronting the Crisis*. Geneva: UNAIDS.

UNAIDS/WHO. 2008 Update. *Epidemiological Fact Sheets on HIV and AIDS [Uganda]*. Geneva: UNAIDS/WHO.

Wardlow, Holly, and Jennifer S. Hirsch. 2006. "Introduction." In *Modern Loves: The Anthropology of Romantic Courtship & Companionate Marriage*, eds. Jennifer S. Hirsch and Holly Wardlow, 1–31. Ann Arbor: University of Michigan Press.

Chapter 23

Possessing spirits and healing gods

Female suffering and agency in North India

Anubha Sood

Original material prepared for 7th edition.

Introduction

In the medically plural landscape of the Indian subcontinent, folk mental health traditions based in religious lifeways serve as popular venues of psychosocial care for the population (Basu 2014; Quack 2012; Ferrari 2011; Sebastia 2009).[1] A vast variety of such healing sites in the region, including Hindu and Buddhist temples devoted to a multitude of local deities, the pervasive Sufi *dargahs*,[2] and Christian churches, includes therapies involving causal attributions of supernatural afflictions and possession-trance practices that are overwhelmingly preferred over state-driven Western psychiatry.

Much social scientific research on religious healing in South Asia has shown that a number of facilitative dimensions make these practices especially attractive to the population (Naraindas et al. 2014; Sax 2009; Halliburton 2009; Jain and Jadhav 2008; Raguram et al. 2002). These dimensions include (1) the congruence between cultural belief systems and explanatory models of illness in these traditional systems, (2) the close involvement of the family and community in the healing process, (3) the absence of stigmatizing psychiatric labels, and (4) the greater aesthetic appeal of religious rituals in comparison to Western biomedical practices.

Explanations that move beyond these general understandings and focus specifically on gender highlight women's greater affiliation for possession-trance phenomena. Women's preponderance as the "possessed" is well-documented from cultures across the world as well as South Asia (Seligman 2014; Ranganathan 2015; Ram 2012; Ong 2010; Bourguignon 2004; Boddy 1994). Studies, reaching as far back as I. M. Lewis's (1971) work on the association between deprived social status and vulnerability to demonic attacks, and Erica Bourguignon's writings (1978) on women's affiliation for possession-trace states across diverse societies, claim that women's greater susceptibility to being possessed by malevolent spirits speaks of the mental and social suffering they bear in patriarchal settings. Spirit possession, according to this view, is a language of resilience, resistance, or rebellion for women, and traditional healing sites thus offer safe spaces for the culturally permissible expression of distress and self-assertion for women (Ong 2010; Bourguignon 2004).

DOI: 10.4324/9781003398349-26

Other scholars, most notably Janice Boddy (1988) in her work on the zår cult in Sudan, called attention to the nuances of the cultures in which women's possession takes expression, highlighting "women's and men's cosmological statuses, their culturally attributed abilities, vulnerabilities and constraints" to conceptualize the links between gender and possession-trance phenomena (Boddy 1994: 415). These arguments stress the cultural typification of female nature and roles in diverse societies, such as notions about women's weaker dispositions, emotionally excessive characters, and gendered learning regarding bodily comportment, as well as women's association with the "impure" biological processes of menstruation and childbirth, that make them vulnerable to spirit possession (Ram 2012; Boddy 2010; Kapferer 1997).

Finally, public health literature on South Asia emphasizes underdevelopment, and the related ignorance and stigma surrounding psychiatric illnesses, as the primary factor in explaining the popularity of traditional healing systems (Murthy 2015). Women's greater use of explanatory models involving spirit possession and healing-trance practices is cited as a marker of their low mental health literacy, the low priority accorded to their health needs in general, and their incapacity to access modern health care to make informed choices (Kermode et al. 2007; Patel et al. 2006; Fikree et al. 2004).

This chapter sits in conversation with these existing debates to look at women's engagement with possession-trance phenomena in a renewed light. Based on research in the Hindu temple of Bālaji in Rajasthan, a popular healing site in the North Indian region for those suffering from psychosocial problems that present as spirit afflictions, the chapter examines why women seek religious healing in overwhelming numbers. Drawing from the female healing-seekers' everyday lives and healing practices in the temple, I argue that women find healing in the Bālaji temple efficacious because, first and foremost, it lends them the power to reconfigure and negotiate their troubled gendered lifeworlds in agentic ways. I demonstrate how the idiom of spirit possession employed in the Bālaji temple, as both an expression of distress and as a mode of healing, is engaged as a deliberate "technique" of healing psychological and social ruptures.

The female healing-seekers in Bālaji spend weeks and months in the temple town to seek a resolution for their troubles. On returning home, they continue to travel to the site multiple times during the year, staying in Bālaji for extended periods upon each visit. The ethnographic research on which this chapter is based followed a set of these "long-term" female healing-seekers and their family members in the temple over a period of ten months and documented the minute therapeutic processes and trajectories of healing as they unfolded over space and time. The chapter begins by sketching a general picture of the Bālaji temple and town and the lives and community of the female healing-seekers there. Next, it discusses the healing practices in the temple and their therapeutic logic and effects. Finally, it illustrates how the treatment in the temple unfolds over time, by presenting the case study of a young woman whom I followed through her stay in Bālaji.

The Bālaji temple: a world of deities and spirits

The Bālaji temple is located 170 miles west of India's capital, Delhi, in the small town of Mehandipur, also known widely as the town of Bālaji, in the desert state of Rajasthan. Mehandipur is a valley nestled between the hills of the famous Aravali range in north-western India and rife with myths and otherworldly beings that give the temple its popularity as a powerful and magical healing place. The site is well-known across the

Hindi-speaking region as a site for curing spirit afflictions that manifest as behavioral, emotional, and/or relational difficulties – problems that may be classified as "characteristic of various psychiatric illnesses" (Pakaslahti 2009: 158). Healing in Bālaji takes place by practicing ritualized trance, and through a range of religious prescriptions for remedying spirit affliction, which are elaborated in temple booklets and manuals and shared among the community of healing-seekers through word of mouth.[3] The temple is frequented each day by hundreds of men and women in the quest for divine blessings and protection from misfortunes attributed to spiritual agencies. However, among those who come to the temple with the explicit purpose of seeking cures for malevolent spirit afflictions, women far outnumber men. The demographic profile of these female visitors to the temple is generally urban, middle-class, and educated (Dwyer 2003; Pakaslahti 1998).

In local parlance, the most common usage for spirit affliction is *sankat*, meaning distress/danger/misfortune in Hindi, and those who come to the temple to seek healing from spirit afflictions are known as the *sankat-wale*, meaning, "those afflicted with the spirit." These individuals, primarily women, are often accompanied by close relatives, also referred to as the *sankatwale* (anglicized: *sankatwalas*), for spirit affliction in Bālaji is conceived not just as an individual problem but as a relational and social one.

Generally speaking, spirit affliction is assigned as a reason for visiting Bālaji if the woman behaves in a socially inappropriate or destructive manner; suffers from disturbing thoughts and feelings, unexplainable fears, and anxieties; experiences vague bodily aches and pains, or physical symptoms that are unexplainable in medical terms; and/or faces serious strife in her relationships. In terms of psychiatric diagnoses, although they are difficult to ascertain, given the sheer distinctiveness of illness categories in the temple, the *sankatwalas* may be seen as presenting symptom complexes akin to psychosomatic, dissociative, affective, and sometimes, psychotic disorders. It is important to note that the kinds of distressing symptoms for which women seek healing in Bālaji are not considered exclusively "mental"; as the notion of *sankat* suggests, illness and suffering are regarded as a crisis that originates from conflicts in the social, relational, psychological, and spiritual dynamics of the woman's life. The resolution of such a crisis, too, requires extended commitment, for which the *sankatwalas* spend anywhere from two weeks to several months in the temple town.

The therapeutic process in Bālaji entails long periods of engagement, which translates into long periods of stay in the temple town or constant travel back and forth for the *sankatwalas*, and, in the process, facilitates the forging of strong "therapeutic communities." Like many religious healing sites in the Indian subcontinent, Bālaji may be conceived as a "microcosmic public space" where individuals, through participation in the rituals and everyday life of the place, develop new identities (Bellamy 2011: 21). The healing-seekers come to Bālaji from far-flung domiciles and coalesce around their shared identity as *sankatwalas* – a community of sufferers that undergo the same trials and tribulations of life and healing in Bālaji. In fact, identifying as a *sankatwala* in the temple serves as a mnemonic strategy of sorts; the afflicted women as well as their family members often introduce themselves using the term, mentioning who really has the *sankat* – the daughter, sister, mother or themselves, only as addendum. This "new" identity as a *sankatwala* not only sets the group of healing-seekers apart from the sea of pilgrims to Bālaji the year round, creating cohesiveness based on collective purpose, but also lends a sense of comfort in a scenario where the familiarity and safety of domestic social networks are no longer available.

The temple is devoted to the child-form (*bāl*) of the pan-Hindu simian god Hanuman (child = *ba'l*, hence the name *Ba'laji*), worshipped in the temple for his power to cure malevolent spirit possession. Hanuman is known among Hindus as *Sankat-mochan*, literally, "one who liberates from distress/danger." The god is depicted in Hindu texts and mythology as having the special powers to navigate the worlds of the divine and the demonic with equal ease (Lutgendorf 2007). Such powers make Hanuman the god of choice for those seeking redress from malevolent spirits as well as for protection by godly agencies.

Besides Bālaji, the "presiding" deity of the temple, two other gods, Bhairav and Prêtraj, are also worshipped in the temple for their influence over wayward spirits believed to trouble the human world. These two gods have more local roots and followings, in contrast to Hanuman's widespread popularity across Hindu India. The worship of Bhairav and Prêtraj is associated largely with occult Hindu traditions and is confined to certain regions/communities in India. In addition to the three primary deities, there are a number of spirits who are believed to reside in the temple and assist in the healing function. These spirits, according to the temple myth, were once harmful, like the ones that possess people visiting the temple. But they were eventually "corrected" and recruited by Bālaji to assist in protecting the *sankatwalas*. Above the temple, on the high cliffs, lies the abode of the spirits freed by the temple gods. Big stone steps lead up to the cliffs from further down at the rear of the temple complex. Tiny stacks of stone and small platforms, constructed with concrete and painted white, are strewn along these cliffs and offer a view of interest to otherwise bare hills. These strange-looking mounds are the *pitr-sthan* – literally, "place of the ancestors," which people construct to symbolically rest the souls of their passed-away kin, or the spirits that have been exorcised. Sometimes, the names of the ancestors are chiseled on the stones, and kin make offerings to them on these mounds, which are eaten later by the monkeys that populate the hills and the town.

Finally, the now-deceased first head priest of the temple, Ganesh Puriji, is also worshipped as a deity in Mehndipur for his extraordinary healing powers in his lifetime and beyond. The sacred space that holds his last remains, the *Samadhi*, is a major venue for prayer, exorcisms, and a number of healing rituals. On the hills (*dupatta*) surrounding the valley of Mehndipur, smaller temples dedicated to a number of other major Hindu gods and goddesses were established over the years and are now frequented by devotees coming to the Bālaji temple. Life in Mehndipur revolves around the pantheon of deities and spirit-beings that populate its landscape and envelop the lives of the *sankatwalas* on a day-to-day basis.

Healing in Bālaji: gender, religion, rhetoric, and practice

On an average day in Bālaji, the *sankatwalas* may be observed performing a range of temple-specific healing activities. Of these, possession-trance, or *peshi*, as it is called in the temple, is easily the most striking, but looking beyond its spectacle also reveals an array of other daily rituals and practices with which the *sankatwalas* engage. All healing practices in the temple tend to be largely self-directed and flexible in both form and meaning, tailored as compilations of disparate religious activities and possession-trance routines. The *sankatwalas*' healing practices in the temple constitute a "therapeutic self-process" (Lester 2005), engaging both bodily sensibilities and rhetorical practices over a sustained period of engagement to garner concrete healing effects. This section begins by describing some of the everyday routine practices as they are carried out over the *sankat-walas*' typical day in Bālaji and then goes on to describe the therapeutic practice of *peshi*.

Everyday routine practices

Most of the routine everyday healing practices of the *sankatwalas* mirror common Hindu worship rituals in form but are performed with the explicit intention to heal. Gunn (2008), in a review of anthropological research on the religious lives of Hindu women, talks of how the female body, according to the classical Hindu model, is considered ritually impure because of its association with biological processes such as menstruation and childbirth and hence excluded from full participation in religious life.[4] In the vast majority of South Asian, not just Hindu, religious healing sites, these rules of bodily purity and pollution and understandings of female sexuality become crucial for constructing local understandings of affliction and healing from spirit possession; in fact, in local conceptions at these healing sites, the impurity of women's bodies constitutes a key reason for their greater affliction by malevolent spirits (Ram 2012; Bellamy 2011; Skultans 1991).

For instance, in Bālaji, the female healing-seekers follow a number of prescriptions related to rules of female sexuality and purity, such as (1) not using any personal care and cosmetic products that may have a fragrant smell, since such products are believed to heighten the woman's "attractiveness" to malevolent spirits; (2) not adorning oneself with makeup and jewelry, for the same reasons as the preceding; and (3) strictly following menstrual prohibitions. The latter is among the strictest rules of bodily conduct in Bālaji. When menstruating, a woman's body is considered to be in its most "polluted" state and is therefore barred from entering the spaces of the temple.[5] As a result, women do not visit the temple at all at such times. Similar to Janice Boddy's (1988) description of zār possession among Hofriyati women in Sudan, in Bālaji, possession and healing are intimately tied to these feminine standards of conduct.

When the lens moves away from textual conceptualizations of gender to the practice of religion in everyday life, however, women's creative engagements with, and even shaping of, Hindu traditions become apparent (Pechilis 2013; Gunn 2008; Narayanan 1999). The practices of *bhog* (offerings) and *seva* (service) in the Bālaji temple serve as useful examples. Preparing the *bhog* or the offering for the gods and performing *seva* or service to the gods derive from a larger pool of generic Hindu worship rituals. As Eck (1998) observes, forging a relationship with god in Hindu worship often requires utilizing "the entire range of intimate and ordinary domestic acts," such as cooking, serving, washing, etc. – in other words, creating the perceived comforts of the human realm for the gods (p. 47).

In the Bālaji temple, preparing the *bhog* and performing *seva* are engaged not as worship rituals but as intentional healing practices. As healing practices, these rituals are specifically directed toward the inculcation of a direct and loving relationship between devotee and deity, which is considered essential for healing in the temple. For the *sankat-walas* who prepare the *bhog* and perform *seva*, the activities signify an intimate engagement with the deity. The *bhog* is prepared with meticulous detail; in a manner, as the women will often explain, similar to how one feeds a very special and important guest. As a cooked meal for the deity, the *bhog* involves various permutations of different kinds of sweets, breads, rice, and lentils, depending on the deity to whom it is served. It can also involve combinations of edible and non-edible things, like food along with other ritual objects such as lamps made by hand with kneaded flour or flowers threaded into garlands. Making the *bhog* can be a completely absorbing activity that takes a lot of the *sankatwalas'* time and effort.

Seva includes activities such as cleaning and arranging the ritual spaces of a deity's sanctum; sweeping and washing the spaces considered to be the "abode" of the deity, such as the courtyards of temples; and involving oneself in philanthropic acts that are carried out in the name of the deities. The women might perform a number of these activities as *seva* and alternate between them from time to time. For instance, a *sankatwala* might help with cooking in the communal kitchen of the temple for food that is distributed to poor people as an act of charity by the Temple Trust, or she may help with cleaning in the many temples. Whatever form these activities take, the essential point is that women engage in these rituals as specialists and as agents in directing the process of their healing based on their practice.

Peshi

A woman in *peshi* is one of the most arresting sights in Bālaji.[6] At any time of the day in the temple precincts, one may find many women swinging their heads in rapid circular motion in cue to some internal rhythm, their hair open and flying as they sway.[7] While such whirling of the head, called *jhumna* (swinging), is considered a classic expression of *peshi*, women engage in an array of other rhythmic and repetitive movements that are considered signs of *peshi* as well.[8] Women in *peshi* may be found somersaulting and rolling on the ground, running at high speed and hitting themselves against the walls, screaming, hurling angry words into space, and participating in a range of similarly strenuous and strident actions. These women can be characterized as being in a "trance" state, a "behavioral pattern in which a subject displays intense absorption in internal sensory stimuli with diminished peripheral awareness" (Luhrmann 2004: 106).[9]

Graham Dwyer's (2003) understanding of the ritual analyzes *peshi* primarily as a phenomenon that manipulates the individual's emotions. Dwyer (2003) views *peshi* as a method of *producing or activating* emotions that then may be engaged, reworked, and rearranged in the positive direction of healing. According to Dwyer, in the theatrical performance of *peshi* as an exorcism ritual in Bālaji, the emotions are correspondingly *experientially felt* by the *peshi* practitioner. Such an activation of emotional charge, according to Dwyer (2003), leads to a healing transformation for the individual, especially since local conceptions of *peshi* also avow its transformative power (as the *peshi practitioners* strongly believe as well). Dwyer (2003) believes that *peshi* is a more active "process in which patients de-identify with pathological states of being and re-identify or reconstruct the self in accordance with positive feelings and conceptions" (p. 112).

Antti Pakaslahti (1998) argues that *peshi* is an efficacious healing ritual in the temple because it is part of a holistic "family-centered treatment" wherein both the afflicted individual and her family members are actively engaged (p. 141). The therapeutic benefit of *peshi*, therefore, accrues not only to the *sankatwala* but also involves putting right her ruptured interpersonal world as a whole. For Pakaslahti, an episode of *peshi* is like a performance session, where the grievances and wrongs done within a family are resolved through the cultural idiom of spirit possession. The hostile emotions that the *sankatwala* expresses in *peshi* are attributed to her afflicted spirit and, in this manner, "acknowledged" by her family without evoking associated feelings of blame or victimization. Moreover, while the woman's status in the family may have been socially disvalued and peripheral earlier, *peshi* draws attention to her. Thus, *peshi*, according to Pakaslahti (1998), is a communication system for not only psychological but also interpersonal problems and even a form of "family therapy" (p. 162). Both these explanations, Dwyer's and Pakaslahti's, broadly align with Gananath Obeyesekere's (1981) understanding of "transformative symbol systems" as the cornerstone of religious healing, that is, the powerful idea that individuals may employ culturally derived symbol sets, in this case spirit possession, for the communication and resolution of inner and relational turmoil.

My research emphasizes the value of *peshi* for its "consciousness-changing potential" akin to a religious practice involving notions of penance and sacred pain (Sood 2016; Bellamy 2011). The most striking aspect of *peshi* is the involvement of the body in ways that are extremely physically discomforting and may, in fact, be considered forms of self-inflicted pain. For instance, the most common manifestation of *peshi* involves shaking the head vigorously from side to side, or moving it in fast, circular rhythm, often for an hour or more at a time. These actions constitute a difficult and painful feat, for no ordinary person, as the *sankatwalas* proclaim, can sustain such forceful movements of the head and neck even for a few moments. Apart from its role in triggering and sustaining dissociative states, pain can also, as a voluntary bodily practice, become *directly* therapeutic as a kind of powerful religious experience. Intentionally painful manipulations of the body could lead to self-transcendence or self-effacement.

Glucklich (2001) engages the notion of sacred pain to understand the transformative effects of self-inflicted pain – what he calls "healing pain" (p. 33). He refers to a long list of ways that pain has been employed throughout religious history, including many extreme forms of penance, mortifications, and a range of ascetic practices. It is interesting, in this regard, that so little attention has been paid to bodily pain in the study of possession phenomena, since it is so integral to religious healing systems across the world. Following Glucklich (2001), I argue that the bodily pain experienced by the *sankatwala* during *peshi* serves as a key healing modality in the temple. Furthermore, the healing effects of voluntary pain induced during *peshi* stem from the same kinds of mechanisms that Glucklich explicates for the self-transformative effects of sacred pain in religious contexts. In the therapeutic logic of the Bālaji temple, not only does the meaning of bodily pain gradually alter from negative sensations of hurt to empowering feelings of endurance and transformation, but the pain of suffering that brings the women to the temple may also transition into a "socially and spiritually integrative force" (Glucklich 2001: 34).

Thus, *peshi* can be conceived as a religious practice, much like many other South Asian religious practices that entail the voluntary discipline of the mind and body through causing pain to the body. In this sense, the intense employment of the body in *peshi* is fundamental to understanding how *peshi* heals, decidedly in a very agentic way, employed as a deliberate "technique" of healing by the female *sankatwalas*. The agentic dimension of healing is well illustrated by the story of Meetu, who came to the temple for healing from spirit affliction.

Meetu

Meetu first came to Bālaji at the age of 21 with her mother, father, and younger sister, Koyal, in early July 2009. She belongs to the small city in Uttar Pradesh, where she was going to university for a masters in sociology. She knew how to work with computers and volunteered as a part-time accountant in her uncle's shop. In our first meeting, she had told me that she wished to be a "working girl" (using the same term). As I interacted with her in Bālaji over the next few months, I saw that Meetu's aspirations for her life were in conflict with her family's plan to find a suitable match and get her married as soon as possible. I saw that Meetu was rebelling, that she refused to be the docile person that young girls in her social position (a low status within North Indian patriarchal arrangements) were expected to be. Her mother called her insolent; so had her extended family back home. But then they had figured that it wasn't really Meetu who rebelled at every opportunity and could turn dangerously angry at the bat of an eyelid. It was her *sankat* that made her behave that way.

One evening, I saw Meetu in the temple grounds, but she did not seem to recognize me. She had her *dupatta* tied around her waist and behaved like a rowdy young man. Her mannerisms were masculine, and as she saw me, she began flirting, claiming that she wished to marry me. Her father and sister told me her long-deceased brother was possessing her. He would have been a young man now if he had lived. The scene of Meetu's possession was at once distressing and amusing. Meetu kept running away, and her father would run behind her and hold her arms behind her back. She would then start struggling, kicking, and beating him if she was freed. She called out to other men in the crowd and used abusive language if they noticed or turned to look. Men who got interested and continued to look became the target of Meetu's ridicule. This continued for a while, until Meetu was forcefully taken to the guesthouse where the family was staying. The next day, when I met Meetu, Koyal, and their mother, they told me that Meetu had been possessed late into the night. She had eaten copious amounts of food and beaten up her father more. Meetu's mother said that Meetu would often beat her father:

> She is beating up her father and using filthy language [*gandi bhasha*] in front of him when she is possessed. The *sankat* is so troublesome [*kapti*]. It makes her so shameless [*besharam*].

As I observed Meetu through many such possession states, I found that she was intermittently possessed by five or six spirits that had different names and personalities – young men and women who were aggressive, flirtatious, fashionable, and flamboyant. They would possess Meetu at any time of the day for brief moments, but mostly in the evenings. If Meetu said something aggressive, behaved out of the bounds of social norms, showed "undue" self-pride, or threatened to do something that she wasn't supposed to do, her family would point to the presence of a malevolent spirit speaking through Meetu, instead of her own volitional self. For instance, Meetu often liked to dress in nicer clothes in the evenings and wear lipstick before venturing out. Meetu's mother and Koyal attributed this behavior to Meetu's *sankat* that distracted her from piety to God and pulled her towards frivolous deeds. Then, as we would walk out and toward the crowded venue of the evening prayers at the temple, Meetu would tease, push, and laugh at people. On other occasions, when Meetu would stubbornly demand to do certain things, like go out for a stroll late in the night, eat restaurant food, or spend time in the internet café around the corner, it was interpreted as a manifestation of her *sankat* by her family, rather than Meetu's own wishes. It was through such constant interactions and iterations that Meetu's family made her *sankat* "real" for themselves and for Meetu.

For Meetu herself, what gave the *sankat* a compelling sense of reality were the things that she did out of some strange compulsion, like beating up her father and jumping from the high terrace of her maternal grandparents' house, which she had attempted a few years ago. As Meetu narrated her life story to me over several weeks, it turned out that these behaviors were deeply related to her life circumstances. I learned that Meetu's present mother was not her real mother. Her real mother had been married to her father and had two daughters with him, Meetu being the older one. She was heavily pregnant with a third child, Meetu's brother, when she fell off the terrace of her parents' house and died. There was a suggestion in Meetu's story that Meetu's father had not treated her mother very well. Meetu was 2 years old when she lost her mother but claimed that she did not recall any of it. When the accident that took her mother's and unborn brother's life happened, the family decided that Meetu's father should marry Meetu's mother's younger sister. They came to this decision because the older sister had left two young children behind to be taken care of, and if the father married another woman who was not related to the children, this new mother might not treat the children like her own. Meetu's maternal aunt thus married Meetu's father and raised Meetu and four other children from Meetu's father.

Meetu told me that now that she reflected back on her childhood, she could see that she had always felt an "unseen presence (*ehsaas*) in her life." As a child, she had been afraid of sounds and sights that others did not perceive. Meetu's (step)mother agreed that Meetu had, indeed, been a frightened child. At age 5, Meetu was sent by her paternal grandmother off to a boarding school, *Kanya Gurukul*, or school for the Vedic (Hindu religious) education of young girls, for two years, a time that Meetu recalled with deep distress, a time when she learned to recite the Hanuman Chalisa, a devotional hymn for Hanuman (of whom Bālaji is the infant form), to quiet the sounds and sights that had become a part of her life. Since then, at many difficult turns in Meetu's life, she had turned to the devotion of Hanuman.

At the age of 14, Meetu officially "found out" that the woman she had considered her mother all along was not her real mother. This was a time of immense upheaval for Meetu, for even though she loved this woman dearly, she had doubts about her loving Meetu as much. Meetu began to judge all her stepmother's behaviors towards her in comparison with her younger siblings. She convinced herself that her mother loved her real children more than she loved Meetu. Meetu was also devastated to find out that her father had married again and so completely abandoned the memory of his first wife, Meetu's real mother. "All of this [the spirit affliction] is my fault [*galti*]," Meetu told me. Meetu believed that she had longed for her mother so much that her mother returned to possess her. Meetu started writing letters to her dead mother and leaving them in their local temple. She could not stop thinking about her.

In the years before coming to the temple, Meetu had begun to behave in an extremely destructive manner. This was also around the time that she turned 18 and her family began thinking about finding a marriage alliance for her. She began to behave badly and getting into fits of rage. In these "breakdown" moments, when Meetu lost control, she felt that a force greater than her was making her feel and act abnormally. She felt powerless against it.

These strange experiences became even more pronounced a year or so before coming to Bālaji, when Meetu fell from the roof of her house and broke her arm. Before falling, she had heard someone commanding her to jump! At this time, the family decided that Meetu might be possessed and sought an intervention for her in Bālaji. Now in the temple, as her possession was beginning to slowly reveal itself, Meetu could spend hours conjuring elaborate conversations between her dead brother and his selection of malevolent spirit friends when she was alone – hatching plans to make her family's life difficult. The spirit of her mother whispered jealous and bitter talk about the family; she made her vengeful toward them as well.

By December, however, about five months into Meetu's arrival in Bālaji, the dramatic possessions had ceased and the voices had become less frequent. As Meetu continued to participate in Bālaji's therapeutic process, which included getting up at five in the morning, preparing and making offerings to the deities at different times of the day, attending the devotional hymn singing in the mornings and evenings, and performing *seva* or service for the gods, she became more observant of the changes that these practices brought to her life. For one, Meetu was becoming more adept at experiencing *peshi*, the ritualized trance practiced in the temple. In the initial days in Bālaji, Meetu had slept through most of the communal *peshi* sessions, but with passing days, Meetu had become more proficient at it. Meetu interpreted her increasing adeptness at *peshi* as being a sign that her practice was becoming successively purgative. In late December, she told me that all her malevolent spirits had left her body, barring the spirit of her mother, but now her presence felt benevolent instead of afflictive. This spirit would eventually leave Bālaji with Meetu as the helper-spirit – in the temple's therapeutic logic, possessing spirits share an intimate relationship with the possessed and, if treated well, turn from being malevolent beings to protectors, until they are ready to move on and pass into the realm of the otherworldly.

Meetu also seemed to be mending her relationship with her family. After coming to Bālaji and staying with her for part of the time, her father had finally quit drinking alcohol. He had been a heavy drinker all his life and had not stopped despite the best efforts of family and friends, but coming to Bālaji and not drinking for the period that he lived there had helped him quit. The relations between her father and the maternal side of her family, which had been strained all her life, were now improving as well. This was immensely important to Meetu for the sake of her mother, as she told me, since it caused her mother so much pain that her husband did not let her associate much with her natal family. Meetu believed that it was with Bālaji's help that her family had been able to accomplish these positive changes.

But the most important shift seemed to be happening in Meetu's relationship with her mother. In how she expressed her feelings toward her present mother, Meetu vacillated between caring deeply for her and, at other times, disliking her. She felt gratitude for her, but anger too, emotions that she could not reconcile. "If anything, she has loved me more than my brother and sisters," Meetu told me in one interview.

> She has done more for me than was in her capacity. She fought with my *dadi* [grandmother] when she wanted to marry me off at age 18. She told her that her daughter [Meetu] would not be like her. She would study and be old enough to make her own "decisions" [in English] before getting married. My mother, she is a woman of "modern thinking" [in English]. She wanted to work outside the home too, but my father never let her. He has a suspicious attitude. My mother, however, lets me go out, hold a job, and wants me to further myself.

In the days and months that Meetu spent with her mother in Bālaji, she began to see it as a test of her mother's love for her. Meetu told me that the fact that her mother had left the comforts of her home and her own young children to follow Meetu to Bālaji and was caring so deeply for her meant that she loved Meetu. She acknowledged so in front of her mother. "Only one's own mother would suffer such hardship for her children. My mother really loves me [*chaahti hai*]." I could sense a positive shift in Meetu's feelings for her mother, which had a distinctly different emotional tone than how she felt during our earlier interactions.

Meetu's conflicting feelings for her mother also arose from the fact that she idolized her for being a strong woman but did not understand why she would become so "weak" (the term she used) as to sacrifice her education and marriage to a potentially younger, more eligible man to marry Meetu's father, simply at the request of the elders. Meetu told me how difficult her mother's life was in a joint family where she was expected to single-handedly care for everyone without expecting much appreciation in return

> My mother has always listened to the elders in the family and to her husband, despite the fact that she had to sacrifice so much. She wanted to have a job, but my father did not let her. He was always suspicious of her dealings outside the home, and my grandmother supported him. My mother suffers silently but stays strong for us [the children].

Meetu's narrative was sympathetic instead of being grudging and angry. She seemed to really feel for her mother and share in her struggles. I felt a sense of deep solidarity between the mother and the daughter then, a kind of healing.

I left Bālaji a few weeks after that but got a short e-mail from Meetu a few months later. Meetu was back at home and preparing for job interviews even as she simultaneously finished coursework for her masters. In subsequent phone conversations, Meetu told me that her family had begun to look for a suitable alliance for her marriage and Meetu was trying to shed a few pounds and look good in anticipation of meeting someone she liked. When I asked her if she was happy with how her life was unfolding, Meetu told me that her parents had assured her that they would not marry her into a family she did not like. They were trying to look for boys who did not have big joint family setups so she did not have to do housework all the time.

Conclusion

> In countries such as India, all institutions may be described as having a double articulation in tradition and modernity. These do not simply form stages in the successive development of society; neither do they lie side by side in perfect harmony. For example, a traditional institution such as the family is shaped today as much by concepts of purity and honor, by a vision of life in which the telos of individual lives is given by caste and gender, as by the codification of personal law, the attempts of the state to recruit the family as an ally in its progress on health and education and the electronic images received in the domestic space by the pervasive popularity of television.
>
> (Veena Das 1994: 52)

This observation by Das (1994) is deeply reflective of the lives of the women I met in the Bālaji temple. The *sankatwalas* were women experiencing some of the same conflicts of navigating the confusing boundaries between traditional lives and the visions of modernity seemingly in grasp, but never quite so, a conflict pervasive in the lives of countless women in contemporary India. In the accounts of young women like Meetu, a stable narrative of the female life cycle within traditional families in India comes forth, and so do the ruptures in which education and fleeting freedoms seem to provide brief escapes but often fail to carry through. Meetu's anxieties about her future, for instance, were informed by the life her mother had led before her, and her healing closely tied to how she interpreted her own life as materializing within the possibilities granted to her. Meetu had a postgraduate education and had grown up with the knowledge of the many possibilities her life could take besides marriage in a traditional family, and undertaking the domestic labor she had seen her mother perform all her life. Just like the women she encountered in television images, films, and modern institutions, and occasionally among her friends and community, Meetu, too, wished to break out of the social rules her family imposed on her. Meetu wanted to be a woman with a career. She wished to venture out of the domestic sphere to accomplish something that brought her recognition. She articulated her ambitions as such, in contrast to the life of her mother, who had also wished to seek a similar future (as Meetu narrated with consternation) but had instead become tied to the "thankless" life of toiling for her husband's family.

To the extent that possession as a pathological experience is "associated with situations in which individuals find it desirable to shift attention from ordinary self-awareness to expand the social possibilities of the self or to escape its psychological and emotional burdens" (Seligman 2010: 304), Meetu's *sankat* may be considered an expression of what she felt to be her stifled ambitions for a very different social existence than her circumstances allowed. Meetu's *sankat* seemed to be able to transgress the gendered boundaries that she may never have been able to. In Meetu's possession states, she could question the hierarchical structures her community and family setting created for her, move and behave in a world free of the constraints her femininity imposed on her, and even, quite literally, behave like a man, that is, take on a "role" that indicated relative power and freedom in her world.

The resolution of Meetu's distress, then, came from the renewed perspective she Developed of her stepmother's life, and in how she negotiated her own future vis-à-vis her family's plans for her. Staying in Bālaji may have provided Meetu the opportunity to come to terms with what she perceived as "grave injustices" committed by her father and his family on her biological mother and stepmother, and to recognize how she might be able to escape those injustices in her own life. Meetu had identified with her mother and stepmother's life's conditions too much, to the extent that she had actually become "afflicted" by the spirit of her dead mother. Eventually, however, and over a period of close engagement with her family in the therapeutic space of Bālaji, Meetu was able to reconcile herself to this history.

Most significant in Meetu's narrative was the manner in which she came to terms with her stepmother's inability to craft a life on her own terms, her "failure" to resist the pressures of the community and family to disregard her education and marry a man of their choosing. While this fact had troubled Meetu immensely and caused her to feel anger and resentment toward her stepmother for a long time, she seemed to be able to recognize her stepmother's efforts to advocate for a different life for her daughters as a kind of "redemption." Her stepmother's sacrifices to see Meetu heal and prosper brought this understanding for Meetu to the fore and led her to feel more positively towards her. While it is clear, in Meetu's narrative, how her conflictive gendered relations in her lifeworld were, to a large extent, the cause of her distress and pathological behaviors, it would seem that Bālaji seemed to offer her the space to engage with those conflicts and navigate her way through them in a constructive manner.

Meetu's *tarkatt*, just as the possession of many other women I met in Bālaji, offers multiple therapeutic functions and interpretations, which is significant for understanding the relationship of women to spirit possession phenomena more generally. Extant theories focused on either/or explanations of possession as resistance, rebellion, or power fail to recognize the multiplicity of meanings and uses possession experiences may have for the women who become afflicted by spirits.

While common scholarly understandings of women in religious healing systems have highlighted the social-communicative aspects of possession phenomena, emphasizing how women attempt to resist subjugated positions through engaging in possession cults, in this chapter, I suggest that possession may be regarded as a conscious practice that requires paying minute attention to multiple interacting psychological, familial, cultural, and religious facets to locate its agentive capacity. I approach women's actions within fields of power from the perspective of what Anthony Cohen (1994) has called "creative self-consciousness," that is, the view that women are conscious and reflexive actors in their lives. My attempt in this chapter has been to locate agency in the women's actions as a critical aspect of grasping the phenomenon of malevolent spirit possession and subsequent healing at the Bālaji temple.

Discussion questions

1. What are some of the existing explanations for the high rate of spirit possession among South Asian women?
2. Why is the female body considered to be ritually impure in Hinduism, and how does this impact religious beliefs and practices?
3. How did Meetu's experience at the temple help her deal with conflict and distress in her life?
4. Why does the author argue that spirit possession is a conscious and purposeful act that gives women greater agency in their lives?

Notes

1 Studies on the preferential use of mental health systems in medically plural societies such as India point to the complex patterning of treatment choices involving the use of multiple systems based on a diverse range of sociocultural and pragmatic considerations. Even as an array of traditional systems operating outside the official biomedical psychiatric system, including Ayurveda and Unani medicine, are utilized by the general Indian population, mystical-spiritual healing practices are believed to hold special expertise and competence in treating mental afflictions.
2 *Dargahs*, or the shrines of Sufi saints, have served as an age-old subculture of Islamic healing in South Asia (Bellamy 2011).
3 As Bellamy (2011) writes about healing in a popular Sufi *dargah* in central India, a large number of healing sites in the region do not involve the therapeutic dyad of healer and patient so common in religious therapies. Healing in these sites is, instead, conducted as a self-propelled and communal praxis among collectives of healing-seekers.
4 Narayanan (1999), speaking from a feminist position, considers these rules a "non-issue." According to Narayanan, these understandings of the female body are superseded by many more egalitarian local customs in Indian communities, pointing to a dissonance between scripture and

actual practice. The importance of these orthodox rules is still seen as holding a sway over Hindu women's lives, according to Narayanan (1999), because of the erroneous assumptions of the colonizers, and later Western research that equated Brahminical culture to "a," "generalized," Hindu culture.

5 Bellamy (2011) refers to menstrual prohibitions as the "South Asian gender trope par excellence," since they form an integral part of ritual practices across the region and have been widely cited in studies of religion and gender in South Asia (p. 98) (see also Gunn 2008).

6 In conveying the truly impressive nature of *peshi*, I draw upon the sentiments of the *peshi practitioners* themselves, who consider it a spectacle commanding special attention from every visitor to Bālāji. For these women, *peshi* illustrates the supernatural (*chamatkari*) healing powers of the temple. As many of them ask rhetorically, How else can one explain how their weak female bodies come to display such extraordinary strengths in *peshi*, if not for the magical powers of Bālāji?

7 Women can be observed to experience *peshi* in cue to congregational singing and rhythmic clapping as well, in addition to, occasionally, drums (*dholak*).

8 *Jhumna* is a common expression of possession across many South Asian cultures and connotes both negative possession by malevolent spirits and positive embodiment by a deity. The act typically involves rapid and rhythmic circular motion of the head while the rest of the body remains stationary in relation.

9 As Tanya Luhrmann (2011) notes, these trance states can closely resemble the phenomenon of dissociation as it is understood in clinical terms, generating experiences such as visualizations and hallucinations, or even "switching" behaviors recognized as dissociative identity disorder. Similar observations have been made by other scholars who study trance as religious experience and healing, notably Thomas Csordas's (1998) research on glossolalia and multisensory imagery among Charismatic Christian groups and, more recently, Seligman and Kirmayer's (2008) review of dissociative states and practices in a cross-cultural perspective.

References

Basu, Helene. 2014. "Listening to Disembodied Voices: Anthropological and Psychiatric Challenges." *Anthropology & Medicine* 21(3): 325–342.

Bellamy, Carla. 2011. *The Powerful Ephemeral Everyday Healing in an Ambiguously Islamic Place*. Berkeley: University of California Press.

Boddy, Janice. 1988. "Spirits and Selves in Northern Sudan: The Cultural Therapeutics of Possession and Trance." *American Ethnologist* 15(1): 4–27.

Boddy, Janice. 1994. "Spirit Possession Revisited: Beyond Instrumentality." *Annual Review of Anthropology* 23: 407–434.

Boddy, Janice. 2010. "The Work of Zar: Women and Spirit Possession in Northern Sudan." In *The Problem of Ritual Efficacy*, eds. William Sax, Johannes Quack, and Jan Weinhold, 113–130. London: Oxford University Press.

Bourguignon, Erika. 1978. "Spirit Possession and Altered States of Consciousness: The Evolution of an Inquiry." In *The Making of Psychological Anthropology*, ed. George D. Spindler, 479. Berkeley: University of California Press.

Bourguignon, Erika. 2004. "Suffering and Healing, Subordination and Power: Women and Possession Trance." *Ethos* 32(4): 557–574.

Cohen, Anthony P. 1994. *Self Consciousness: An Alternative Anthropology of Identity*. London: Routledge.

Csordas, Thomas J. 1998. *The Sacred Self: A Cultural Phenomenology of Charismatic Healing*. Berkeley: University of California Press.

Das, Veena. 1994. "Modernity and Biography: Women's Lives in Contemporary India." *Thesis Eleven* 39: 52–62.

Dwyer, Graham. 2003. *The Divine and the Demonic: Supernatural Affliction and Its Treatment in North India*. London: Routledge.

Eck, Diana L. 1998. *Darśan: Seeing the Divine Image in India*. New York: Columbia University Press.

Ferrari, Fabrizio M., ed. 2011. *Health and Religious Rituals in South Asia: Disease, Possession and Healing*. London and New York: Taylor & Francis.

Fikree, Fariyal F., and Omrana Pasha. 2004. "Role of Gender in Health Disparity: The South Asian Context." *British Medical Journal* 328(7443): 823–826.

Glucklich, Ariel. 2001. *Sacred Pain: Hurting the Body for the Sake of the Soul*. New York: Oxford University Press.

Gunn, Janet. 2008. "Women's Experiences of Hindu Traditions: A State of the Field Review." *Religion Compass* 2(1): 53–65.

Halliburton, Murphy. 2009. *Mudpacks and Prozac: Experiencing Ayurvedic, Biomedical, and Religious Healing*. Walnut Creek, CA: Left Coast Press.

Jain, Sumeet, and Sushrut Jadhav. 2008. "A Cultural Critique of Community Psychiatry in India." *International Journal of Health Services* 38(3): 561–584.

Kapferer, Bruce. 1997. *The Feast of the Sorcerer: Practices of Consciousness and Power*. Chicago: University of Chicago Press.

Kermode, Michelle, Helen Herrman, Rajanikant Arole, Joshua White, Ramaswamy Premkumar, and Vikram Patel. 2007. "Empowerment of Women and Mental Health Promotion: A Qualitative Study in Rural Maharashtra, India." *BMC Public Health* 7(1): 225.

Lester, Rebecca J. 2005. *Jesus in Our Wombs: Embodying Modernity in a Mexican Convent*, Vol. 5. Berkeley: University of California Press.

Lewis, Ioan M. 1971. *Ecstatic Religion: An Anthropological Study of Spirit Possession and Shamanism*. New York: Penguin.

Luhrmann, Tanya M. 2004. "Yearning for God: Trance as a Culturally Specific Practice and Its Implications for Understanding Dissociative Disorders." *Journal of Trauma & Dissociation* 5: 101–129.

Luhrmann, Tanya M. 2011. "Hallucinations and Sensory Overrides." *Annual Review of Anthropology* 40(1): 71–85.

Lutgendorf, Philip. 2007. *Hanuman's Tale: The Messages of a Divine Monkey*. New York: Oxford University Press.

Murthy, R. Srinivasa. 2015. "Mental Health Programs at Community Level in South Asian Countries: Progress, Problems and Prospects." In *Mental Health in South Asia: Ethics, Resources, Programs and Legislation*, eds. Jitendra Kumar Trivedi and Adarsh Tripathi, 155–190. Dordrecht, Netherlands: Springer.

Naraindas, Harish, Johannes Quack, and William S. Sax, eds. 2014. *Asymmetrical Conversations: Contestations, Circumventions and the Blurring of Therapeutic Boundaries*. Oxford: Berghahn Books.

Narayanan, Vasudha. 1999. "Brimming with Bhakti, Embodiments of Shakti: Devotees, Deities, Performers, Reformers, and Other Women of Power in the Hindu Tradition." In *Feminism and World Religions*, eds. Arvind Sharma and Katherine K. Young, 25–77. Albany: SUNY Press.

Obeyesekere, Gananath. 1981. *Medusa's Hair: An Essay on Personal Symbols and Religious Experience*. Chicago: University of Chicago Press.

Ong, Aihwa. 2010. *Spirits of Resistance and Capitalist Discipline: Factory Women in Malaysia*. Albany, NY: SUNY Press.

Pakaslahti, Antti. 1998. "Family-Centered Treatment of Mental Health Problems at the Bālaji Temple in Rajasthan." In *Changing Patterns of Family and Kinship in South Asia*, eds. A. Parpola and S. Tenhunen, 129–168. Helsinki: University of Helsinki.

Pakaslahti, Antti. 2009. "Health-Seeking Behavior for Psychiatric Disorders in North India." In *Psychiatrists and Traditional Healers: Unwitting Partnerships in Global Mental Health*, eds. M. Incayawar, R. Wintrob, and L. Bouchard, 149–166. Oxford: Wiley.

Patel, Vikram, Betty R. Kirkwood, Sulochana Pednekar, Bernadette Pereira, Preetam Barros, Janice Fernandes, Jane Datta, Reshma Pai, Helen Weiss, and David Mabey. 2006. "Gender Disadvantage and Reproductive Health Risk Factors for Common Mental Disorders in Women: A Community Survey in India." *Archives of General Psychiatry* 63(4): 404–413.

Pechilis, Karen. 2013. "Illuminating Women's Religious Authority through Ethnography." *Journal of Feminist Studies in Religion* 29(1): 93–101.

Quack, Johannes. 2012. "Ignorance and Utilization: Mental Health Care Outside the Purview of the Indian State." *Anthropology & Medicine* 19(3): 277–290.

Raguram, R., A. Venkateswaran, Jayashree Ramakrishna, and Mitchell G. Weiss. 2002. "Traditional Community Resources for Mental Health: A Report of Temple Healing from India." *BMJ* 325(7354): 38–40.

Ram, Kalpana. 2012. "How Is Afflictive Possession 'Learned'? Gender and Motility in South India." *Ethnos* 77(2): 203–226.

Ranganathan, Shubha. 2015. "Rethinking 'Efficacy': Ritual Healing and Trance in the Mahanubhav Shrines in India." *Culture, Medicine, and Psychiatry* 39(3): 361–379.

Sax, William S. 2009. *God of Justice: Ritual Healing and Social Justice in the Central Himalayas: Ritual Healing and Social Justice in the Central Himalayas*. New York: Oxford University Press.

Sebastia, Brigitte, ed. 2009. *Restoring Mental Health in India: Pluralistic Therapies and Concepts*. New Delhi: Oxford University Press.

Seligman, Rebecca. 2010. "The Unmaking and Making of Self: Embodied Suffering and Mind-Body Healing in Brazilian Candomblé." *Ethos* 38(3): 297–320.

Seligman, Rebecca. 2014. *Possessing Spirits and Healing Selves: Embodiment and Transformation in an Afro-Brazilian Religion*. London and New York: Palgrave Macmillan.

Seligman, Rebecca, and Laurence J. Kirmayer. 2008. "Dissociative Experience and Cultural Neuroscience: Narrative, Metaphor and Mechanism." *Culture, Medicine and Psychiatry* 32(1): 31–64.

Skultans, Vieda. 1991. "Women and Affliction in Maharashtra: A Hydraulic Model of Health and Illness." *Culture, Medicine and Psychiatry* 15(3): 321–359.

Sood, Anubha. 2016. "The Global Mental Health Movement and Its Impact on Traditional Healing in India: A Case Study of the Bālaji Temple in Rajasthan." *Transcultural Psychiatry* 53(6): 766–782.

Chapter 24

Empathetic Bhikkhuni

Navigating emotion and gender in Thailand

Daphne Weber

Original material prepared for this edition.

Introduction

"I can tell you everything," she said with a smile, adjusting her distinctly orange jivara. The *jivara* is one of three parts of a monk's robes, typically draped around the ascetic during cooler weather, or folded and resting on their shoulder during warmer weather. The night was cool compared to the intense April heat during the day. Though our temple was immediately off the highway in Nakhon Pathom, Thailand, the maintained natural foliage around us absorbed the sounds of cars and semis. She did not seem uncomfortable or anxious, as some other women had before I told them these interviews were anonymous and all names and identifying information would be changed. I immediately wrote down *Daow* (Thai: ดาว), the Thai word for *star* and the pseudonym I thought might depict her bright smile and confident composure for future readers.

There still stood the irony of her clothes, though. The orange monk's robes intended only for men over the past 1,000 years draped carefully around her female body despite obstacles against female ordination in her Theravada tradition. Women have been told that even touching a monk's robe would impurify it, accumulating poor merit that might even mean rebirth in a realm of Buddhist hell. Many women I spoke with were terrified to even be in close proximity alone with monks, especially since it might risk her reputation. Nearly every woman recalled gossip in her home village about a young girl presumed to have an affair with a monk since she spent so much time alone at the temple. Now, I sat in Thailand's first official temple of female monks who, despite the odds, claimed ordination as Theravada female monks.

Within the so-called "conservative"[1] sect of Theravada Buddhism, there are many people and corresponding institutions who do not recognize female monks. Most believe that there is no one to carry on the practice, since the lineage of female monks died nearly 1,000 years ago (De Silva 2004: 126; Mrozik 2009: 361; "Theravada Buddhism: A Chronology" 2013). Those who do not recognize ordained women as monks often cite the *Garudhammas*, or eight rules of respect within the female monk rules of conduct that state women must receive ordination from other ordained women (Horner 1952: 335; Thanissaro 2013: 1326). Therefore, without any living female monks to

DOI: 10.4324/9781003398349-27

conduct the ordination, no woman can receive ordination as a monk (see discussions of the *Garudhammas*, such as Analayo 2014; Seeger 2006: 169 for more information). In the past, women who have dressed and referred to themselves as Theravada monks have been forcibly disrobed, jailed, and even beaten (Kawanami 2007: 232–234; Koret 2012; Bonnet-Acosta 2014: 44). Despite these difficult conditions, some Theravada women have received ordination in the modern period. In the mid 1990s, a new academic interpretation of Buddhist lineage inspired women to restart the Theravada lineage of female monks. These scholars argued that though Korean bhikkhuni are now viewed as Mahayana Buddhists, they originally received their ordination materials and rituals from Theravada Buddhists. Therefore, the Korean Bhikkhuni lineage is an acceptable stand-in for ordination in addition to the Theravada male monks. However, Thailand has legally restricted any male monks from participating in any ordination of a woman, forcing all Thai women to seek ordination in Sri Lanka or India.

The cost of an international ordination is not the only barrier women face on their path to receive ordination. First, a woman must find a teacher willing to mentor her and teach her the *Vinaya*, or Monk's code of conduct, along with the required chants, history, and languages to pass her exam before ordination. Before 2013, there were only two verified teachers in Thailand women could study with located outside of Chiang Mai and Bangkok. If the woman lived too far away, she would have to raise funds to get to the temple and risk not seeing her family for long periods of time. Once someone joins the temple, they can only leave for extenuating circumstances, such as family deaths and serious medical appointments. Families are welcome to visit the woman at the temple, but traveling and taking time off from work is often too costly. Once a woman has gone through a ritual to express her determination (to herself, the community, and the spiritual world) to become a bhikkhuni, she starts a two-year probation period. During that period, she strictly observes the first eight *precepts*, or rules of conduct. These precepts prohibit the woman from killing, lying, cheating, stealing, taking intoxicants, taking meals after noon, beautifying the self (as in using makeup, deodorant, perfume, etc.), or indulging in entertainment (as in dancing, singing, listening to music, etc.), and sleeping on a high and luxurious bed. After those two years, she is eligible for full ordination, which, up until 2019, could only be done in Sri Lanka, as that was the only place Theravada male monks were willing to give ordination to women. As of 2022, candidates can receive ordination in India. However, fundraising for her airfare in addition to at least six other women who will serve as witnesses and mentors is quite expensive. Some women save money for years before even starting their journey into monkhood, because monks are not allowed to make or collect money. Finally, after her full ordination, she must live with her teacher for two additional years to continue her training and education. Most women who go through full ordination are doing it to "die in the robes" or become a monk for life. Those who disrobe after full ordination usually do it because of unforeseen circumstances. I personally only know of women who disrobed for health reasons, and even then, they were not forced to disrobe. Instead, they felt guilty for not being able to contribute as much physical labor to the temple and felt it best to seek full-time medical help. Since bhikkhuni are not socially recognized by the institution of Theravada Buddhism, they receive no financial assistance or tax breaks while ordained.

So why do women want to receive ordination as a bhikkhuni, especially when there are alternative ways for them to practice?

Many scholars and activists have attempted to answer this question, especially because a small following (approximately 300–400 women pursuing bhikkhuni ordination in Thailand) has drawn vast international attention toward gender in Theravada Buddhism, unsettling Buddhist gendered practice. Some researchers find this bhikkhuni and their determination to be a representation of a broader global push for women's equality and empowerment (Gross 1993; Satha-Anand 1999; Puntarigvivat 2001; Tomalin 2006, 2009; Lindberg-Falk 2007; Tsomo 2010; Gray 2015). Other investigators argue the Buddha wanted Buddhism to have a female order, balancing gender relations (Ito 1999; Satha-Anand 1999; Shizuka 2004; Mrozik 2009; Bodhi 2009; Koret 2012: 114; Analayo 2014: 17). Together, these two perspectives have provided us with useful explanatory frameworks that help us understand how doctrine supports the revitalization of bhikkhuni ordination and how formal religious recognition changes women's social positions. However, these frameworks are not typically used locally by the bhikkhuni or their supporters. While there are a few supporters who call for the equality of women religiously and economically and there are similarly supporters who claim Buddhism is more stable with female monks, most respect bhikkhuni for their knowledge of Buddhist texts and ability to follow the Vinaya. Still, bhikkhuni and the movement for recognition is relatively unknown to most Thais, who generally only know that women can become *Mae Chis*, or white-robed ascetics that normally perform duties around male temples, such as cooking and cleaning. While there are some prolific mae chi who host meditation retreats and teach *Pali*, the ancient language of Buddhism (Brown 2001; Cook 2010: 164; Collins and McDaniel 2010; Seeger 2006), both academics and local Thais comment on the ambiguity of the mae chi's positions and the likelihood of exploitation. In order to figure out why Buddhist women would rather become bhikkhuni, despite all the deterrents, we must look to their personal reasons for ordination.

Based on ethnographic fieldwork I have collected since 2018 in Nakhon Pathom, Thailand, I argue that some Thai women are receiving ordination as bhikkhuni because it helps them openly grieve their gender roles. While living at the temple for as little as six weeks and as long as seven months at a time, I collected life histories of the bhikkhuni and their supporters while carrying out a daily routine alongside them. Even the most mundane tasks, like sweeping leaves, were related to emotional regulation, as we were told to sweep inside *while* we sweep our inside selves. This temple is a place where women come to reflect on their life experiences, often sharing the frustration they felt in their gender roles. Once they found solace through the community of like-minded women, some were ready to re-enter the world with a new perspective on *why* their life has been the way it has. The women who leave are ready to redefine themselves and their roles according to the tools they learned at the temple. Those who stay, however, are prepared to counsel others with similar stories and frustrations to their own past gender roles. While most people expect the ultimate lesson from the temple to be detachment and ultimate equanimity leading to Nirvana, bhikkhunis and supporters in Nakhon Pathom are instead given an environment to express their anxiety, frustrations, and sorrows about their traditional gender roles, especially as it relates to filial piety. While equanimity and gender roles will be discussed later in this chapter, I first want to center the women's own voices through a scene that demonstrates the pervasive feeling of frustration some Thai women have with their lifestyles.

The good feelings ceremony

The Good Feelings Ceremony (Thai: แบ่งปันความรู้สึกดีๆ) takes place once a week in the Medicine Buddha Vihara. This building is located at the back of the lot of land, far away from the noise of the interstate that would distract from the "good vibrations" we exclusively harbor here. The stairway leading up to the Medicine Buddha Vihara is lined with *yak noi*, or little giants, who are placed strategically to protect the vihara. Finally, the vast wooden doors open, and the giant lapis lazuli Medicine Buddha greets visitors.

The immense statue is intimidating, not only because of his size, but also because of his central location in the vihara. Placed on the center of the back wall, he demands attention as soon as one walks through the vihara doors. Sitting on a lotus throne raising the statue approximately four and a half feet above the ground, the Medicine Buddha measures just under eleven feet tall and nine feet wide. In a seating arrangement hierarchically organized, together we prostrate-chant his incantation 108 times, asking for his help in healing our mental and spiritual illness. After receiving a blessing from the abbess, we form a circle with no attribution to status. The orange-robed women pass around fruit baskets and tell others to take the food "as medicine," so as not to break the eighth rule of not taking food after noon.[2]

Many women tend to share how impacted they are by the Dhamma talk earlier in the day. Dhamma talks serve as sermons, and on that particular day, the abbess spoke about the emphasis and value Thai families place on male children and how female children are sometimes neglected. During her conclusion, the abbess assured the women that they are important and they do have a place at the monastery. At least four women shared how this personally touched them, but one woman stood out from the rest. While sharing with the group, she frequently stopped to collect herself, taking a breath to separate the words that were particularly hard for her. Tears welled in her eyes as she told us that she never felt like her parents loved her. She compared this to her parents' affections toward her brother, taking another breath and letting a tear fall. As I listened, I looked around the room and noticed the myriad faces nodding in agreement. Others bowed their head, refraining from the eye contact I saw with past sharers. Some had tears in their eyes, and a select few let tears fall, quickly wiping them away.

The ceremony is unusual in that it calls attention to emotions and affective states. As will be discussed in the following section, sharing feelings is often discouraged in Southeast Asian cultures, as it could arouse similar feelings in others, diverting their Buddhist path to Nirvana. The contagious effect of emotion *seemed* clear in this ritual; one person shared her story and started crying, resulting in lower energy and more tears from others. Similarly, pleasant feelings shared during the ceremony were met with pleasant arousal. However, there are moments where pleasant feelings are juxtaposed with painful feelings once felt in lay life. The ceremony isn't meant to induce emotional equanimity; instead, the ceremony is a means to generate *henjai* or compassion within the community. Once the woman finds an empathetic community, she is more likely to have an opportunity for reflexivity, perhaps giving her the daily tools to *try* and cultivate equanimity. So what is *equanimity*?

Equanimity and emotional expression in Thai Buddhism

Most psychological anthropologists agree that a person learns emotional expression based on what is culturally acceptable and appropriate (Levy 1973; Hochschild 1979;

Rosaldo 1984; Obeyesekere 1990; Briggs 1998; Lutz 1998; Abu-Lughod 2016), even if some defend the likelihood of cross-cultural emotional states (Keyes 1985: 154; Shweder 1985: 207; Mageo 2011: 389). Thus, I can feel angry, someone in Thailand can feel angry, and someone in Siberia can feel angry, and we are all designating a basic state of emotionality. I can also feel hot, designating a sensational state or physicality. Though basic states of emotion can show the potential for the universality of feeling, understanding how emotion is both expressed *and* received shows much more about cultural values of communication. For example, abandonment likely implies different contexts in different cultures. This difference stems from the way cultures distinctively relate abandonment to their own knowledge of what it means to be abandoned in their own culture, which is also known as a cultural model. Mageo (2013: 389) convincingly provides an example of Dylan, an undergraduate student in the United States, who feels abandoned. But upon further investigation into her life history and dream, Mageo argues that Dylan feels abandoned <u>not</u> because her parents and sister left her alone in college hundreds of miles away. Instead, Dylan feels abandoned by her peers because they are progressing in their achievements faster than her. Dylan feels abandonment in relation to the US achievement cultural model, where socioeconomic progression is highly valued.

We can similarly examine why Southeast Asian displays of grief, sadness, and overall discontent are unusual. While it is important to note there is no direct translation of the word "emotion" in Buddhist doctrine, there is an explanation of the three affective states people experience: pleasure, pain, and equanimity. In order to reach Nibbana or have a better rebirth, Buddhists strive to cultivate neutral affective states. Though one might understand why pain is not a valued feeling, pleasure might be more complex. Attachment to pleasure ultimately leads to dissatisfaction when the pleasure is gone and a craving for more pleasure emerges. Therefore, both pleasure and pain lead to volatile affective states. *Equanimity*, or neutral feeling, is the safest state and one that, when practiced correctly, helps achieve Nibbana. We can therefore conclude that emotional expression, whether positive or negative, negates the Buddhist cultural model of equanimity.

Equanimity does not mean that Buddhists do not experience those feelings, however. Many scholars have different interpretations of what displays of equanimity represent in Thailand. Keyes (1985) argues that these subdued displays are an internal suppression of emotion, where the person still feels anger but does not communicate or express the anger (160). In contrast, Obeyesekere (1985) finds these displays evidence of the "work of culture," where discontent is transformed and communicated as socially acceptable and recognized meanings and symbols (147). In this case, a sufferer might demonstrate equanimity towards their problems as a kind of karmic acceptance; they might believe they did something bad in a past life, and therefore, the struggles they face today are a consequence of that action. Contextualizing their problems in terms of karma is a culturally acceptable way of gaining sympathy and understanding in Buddhist cultures.

Others argue for evidence of emotional training through embodiment (Cassaniti 2017: 57; Aulino 2019: 28, 78). Under these circumstances, the sufferer still struggles with feelings of grief, and anger cultivates equanimity through ongoing practices of calmness and acceptance. Cassaniti (2017) shows how letting go of attachments cultivates calmness, otherwise known as *jai yen*, and leads to overall well-being. Alternatively, those who cling to attachments have trouble developing *jai yen*, even if they value the practice, and suffer, often in silence. This withdrawal relates to the broader "don't ask, don't tell" Thai emotionality according to Aulino (2019). Aulino found that sharing adverse emotions put everyone, not just the sharer, at risk of presenting similarly unwholesome emotions. People still share turbulent emotions, but the listener holds an obligation to reframe the experience in equanimous terms. Aulino presents Mam as an example of someone who talked a friend out of murder: The friend called her husband, who unwittingly answered the call while having sex with another woman. Enraged, the friend listened for 40 minutes before hanging up and calling Mam. Though Mam acknowledged the deplorability of the husband's actions, she was sure *not* to arouse further negative emotion in the friend, since that would have negative karmic effects (Aulino 2019: 72). Thai doctors similarly conceal grim prognoses from patients, instead sharing the diagnosis with family. Stonington (2020) explains that concealing the diagnosis preserves the patient's *kamlang jai*, or heart–mind energy, which maintains morale and vitality. The degree of deception is variable, but Stonington shows how patients who already know their diagnosis maintain a naive performance to equally maintain familial kamlang jai.

Despite Buddhist teaching's emphasis on neutrality, doctrine explicitly calls for the development of an additional two "illimitable" attitudes: compassion (*karuna*) and loving-kindness (*metta*). Those with karuna and metta cannot bear the suffering of others and seek to remove instances of suffering. Karuna is temporal; it only occurs in the moment of commiserating with a suffering being. While compassion involves empathy for the sufferer, sadness or sorrow never accompany empathy since these associations are considered unwholesome and antithetical to karuna (Bodhi 2012: 137n20). Metta, on the other hand, arises from non-hatred, transcending temporality and becoming a virtue (ibid., 124). Most importantly, the practitioner must realize metta first for themselves before sharing loving-kindness with a dear friend, a neutral person, and an enemy, in that specific order (ibid., 292–293). The eminent fifth-century Buddhist philosopher Bhikkhu Buddhaghosa shows this importance through the following example:

> Suppose [a monk] is sitting in a place with a dear [friend], a neutral [individual], and a hostile person . . . then bandits come to him and say, "Venerable sir, give us [the monk]," and on being asked why, they answer, "So that we may kill him and use the blood of his throat as an offering;" then if that bhikkhu thinks, "Let them take this [person], or this one," he has not broken down the barriers [of attachment and loving-kindness]. *And also if he thinks, "Let them take me but not these three," he has not broken down the barriers either. Why? Because he seeks the harm of him[self] whom [the bandit] wishes to be taken and seeks the welfare of the other [people] only.*
> (Bhikkhu Buddhaghosa 2010: 302, emphasis added)

In other words, if a bandit comes and demands the blood of a monk, the monk offering another person, be it a friend, a neutral stranger, or an enemy, is unreasonable and without metta. However, offering himself is another action without metta because the monk volunteers harm to himself. This example also demonstrates the difficulty in attaining true equanimity, the only acceptable answer to this sacrifice. Regardless, anyone who wishes to practice with metta and karuna must first realize it for themselves before sharing it with others. Women at the temple would often demonstrate this concept with a less dramatic example: If your cup is not full, how can you offer water to someone else? You will only be able to give them a little, ultimately hurting yourself and leaving the other person in need. This view brings us back to the intersubjectivity of emotion, especially within Thai Buddhism. Without self-realization, others are at risk of arousing unwholesome states in others.

I agree with Winichakul (1997) that the capacity to know and respond to the unstated needs of others is not just a marker of Thai-ness; I also find this ability to be a mediating technique of *karuna* and, subsequently, *metta*. Karuna's temporal nature focuses on the present source of suffering. The listener cannot bear the distress of another and thus offers alternative forms of expression – cooking, caring, hosting parties, or perhaps even ignoring the sufferer – so as not to arouse their emotions further. In Buddhist terms, this helps the sufferer trend back toward equanimity. However, this mediation also helps the listener *maintain* equanimity. The omission of aroused states negates the possibility for spreading arousal. Thus, karuna repudiates the contagious effect of emotion in Buddhism.

However, for the past thousand years, Thai women have not had a doctrinally official religious authority who could offer karuna and metta that *understood* and *empathized* with a female sufferer as another female sufferer. According to the aforementioned scholars, women struggling with their gender roles either (1) repressed the frustration; (2) believed that it was their karma from a past life to be born female, thus divinely cursed with the burden of being a woman; or (3) practiced and implemented ideas of non-attachment through reminders that nothing is permanent according to Buddhist doctrine, meaning, this struggle will also pass and it is better to observe the frustration rather than act on it. Daow's life story and reason for ordination, which we will soon visit, show how some Thai bhikkhuni are actually staging a new intervention of equanimity, especially as it relates to gender roles. Bhikkhuni in Nakhon Pathom are serving as a mediator between arousal and equanimity. Their previous social positions as laywomen give them knowledge of gender roles and dissatisfaction therein, allowing them to empathize with other women. However, their religious authority gives them Buddhist tools to bring sufferers to equanimous levels of emotion, negating the emotional contagion. This delicate balance is portrayed during the aforementioned weekly Good Feelings Ceremony. Now, we can see the actual process of mitigation through Daow's life story.

Daow: a shining star in the face of frustration

Daow, the charismatic woman who opened this chapter and introduced us to the controversy over ordination, was previously ordained as a bhikkhuni for nearly a decade. Daow's experiences are representative of the many reasons women come to the temple: an abusive relationship, a feeling of hopelessness, and a lack of social outlets. She worked at the front desk as a receptionist and regularly counselled visitors and callers, showing the role of emotional expression and regulation central to bhikkhuni social practice. Though Daow disrobed many years ago for health reasons, I chose her as a case study primarily for her degree of anonymity. This bhikkhuni temple is internationally famous, and many foreigners visit the temple year-round. Though I am not presumptuous enough to assume this chapter will somehow make its way back to Thailand, using a case study of a woman still residing at the temple risks exposing her (somewhat) fragile and precarious identity as a bhikkhuni in Thai society. Though practicing as a bhikkhuni is constitutionally protected as a religious freedom, the social restriction of women's roles in Buddhism sometimes puts the women at risk of harassment. Once, while I was touring temples in Bangkok with a group of around 20 bhikkhuni, a male tour guide abruptly confronted us, verbally shaming the bhikkhuni for "wearing the robes" and pretending to be monks. However, Daow's distance from the temple assures her a degree of protection, for reasons that will become clear during her case study. Daow's life demonstrates the personal reasons someone seeks help from the temple while also showing an intervention on gender roles through outward displays of emotion.

> *At first, Luang Mae didn't want to accept my application because I was sick. . .* [But] Luang Mae saw my personality. Even if I was sick, I'd work a lot, and I'm talkative and well-spoken. I smile a lot too.

As her little sister, Noi, walked up to the concrete awning, Daow immediately stopped speaking. Sharply and concisely, she lifted her hand in Noi's direction, physically shooing her away while telling her she cannot eavesdrop and learn about her background. At 43 years old, Daow had already experienced a lifetime of suffering, from which she wanted to shelter her sister. Noi shrugged away, upset she could not sit in on interviews as she sometimes did. Periodically, the teenager would show back up, lurking around the dimly lit table. Though it was late in the night and less than an hour before curfew, Daow was constantly aware of Noi's presence. I would hesitate to continue asking questions, as would my research assistant, Raven. We learned to follow Daow's cues; as my fervent typing turned into cautious pecking, Raven would look at Daow, me, then Noi, waiting for a signal. Initially, Daow made smooth transitions between speaking about her past and stopping to gently snap at Noi. Later in her interview, she did not make such transitions. Instead, she continued with conversation, seeming to find those details less critical for her little sister to hear. When Noi first showed up, Daow had been talking about something that may have been especially upsetting to Noi, as it may have been a time Daow felt her actions did not align with her perception of Buddhist values: when she was encouraged to have an abortion.

At that time, Daow was not married. Her boyfriend's family did not accept her and encouraged the abortion. She was relieved to find out the pregnancy was too far along, but had to move in with the boyfriend's family. Working tirelessly through her pregnancy to support the family, she found it necessary to "endur[e] the suffering just to be accepted by them." She eventually had her baby prematurely, leading to months of incubation in the hospital. After the baby's release, Daow continued to face a hostile home environment with a condescending and belittling mother-in-law. "I am a good person. Why did I have to go through bad things?" she asked while recalling her loss of faith in Buddhism. At her breaking point, Daow stopped praying and had thought of killing her boyfriend's family. Instead, at the age of 27, Daow took poison in a suicide attempt.

After her suicide attempt, Daow struggled to find anyone to talk to about her problems. Though she was close to her father, she saw how her suicide attempt hurt him and felt she had to pretend to be happy to give him *kamlang jai*. The act was draining on her mental and emotional health, and her body seemed to be deteriorating as well. After a few years, she went to the doctor and received a diagnosis of systemic lupus erythematosus (SLE) in addition to diabetes.[3] SLE is an autoimmune disorder where the immune system attacks its own tissue, often confining the affected to a bed, immobilized on days of severe inflammation. At that time, there weren't many treatment options for Daow, and she felt there wasn't much prospect left in her life with a medical death sentence at only 33 years old. I asked Daow how she felt about such a grave diagnosis, and she said, "Happy. I wanted to die. I felt bored. This [diagnosis] was my way out [of life]."

But as she recovered, Daow started to think about other women in a similar position. She realized she could be a confidant for women who suffered like her. She told me:

> I thought about a woman who would go to the temple a lot. Why does she do that? Because of dukkha [she is suffering]. But for me, as a woman, when I suffered, I couldn't just go talk to a male monk. I was ordained so I could be there to listen to women who don't know who to talk to. Some people come to the temple and talk with me. I wanted to do that so they could share feelings, and I want to encourage them to fight [persevere] like me. I can encourage them to carry on like I did.

At 38 eight years old, she was advised by her father to ordain as a bhikkhuni. At first, her husband did not accept the decision. He consistently called the temple, harassing her and telling her she needed to come home to care for his family, specifically his parents. Her children were grown, however, and she had the support of the other bhikkhuni to resist the guilt. Finally, Venerable Dhammananda asked for the husband to come to the temple. Venerable and the husband met, and though we are not sure how the meeting went, the calls lessened, and those that came through, she felt empowered to block.

However, the guilt of leaving her own parents seeped into her daily thoughts. She decided to meet her father and apologize.

> I was really mad [about my husband's accusations of leaving my family]. I prostrated my father and said, "Father, in this life, I have given you everything I can. I could not care for you because I [was forced] to care for [my husband's] family." He hugged me, crying, and said, "It's okay, child. You doing this [becoming a bhikkhuni] is want I wanted for you."

Before ordination, Daow's husband expected her to care for him and his family, calling it a "debt" for taking her and the baby in all those years ago. He kept her from her family, intentionally restricting the social outlets she had. When she went to the temple, she felt male monks could not understand what she, as a woman, was enduring from her husband. She also felt the male monks could not understand the guilt she felt leaving her family behind, because socially, that is what Thai men do when they ordain. In her generation, young boys were sent to the temple for ordination in order to receive an education, often staying there through high school and sometimes college. Daow was frustrated that the male monks could not understand the weight she felt leaving her father, in particular, and the impact it had on her daily life.

Her father's forgiveness and acceptance fueled Daow to help other women struggling with abuse, suicide, and familial problems. Daow often received calls to temple from women contemplating suicide. She told me of a 23-year-old who called from a different province. The young woman found the temple on the internet and called, crying hysterically. "She called and cried and cried. I said, 'Yom, calm down, Yom. . . . What is it that you need? . . . Would you like to come see me at the temple?'" Daow's referral to the young woman as *Yom* (โยม) was indicative of her authority and position: only monastics used this term to refer to laypeople. In that moment, Daow was not only comforting the young woman and inviting her into the safety of the monastery but also establishing her legitimacy as a monk.[4] Further, inviting the woman to the temple while she experienced this crisis validated the monastery as a place of refuge. As the conversation continued, Daow found out the source of her suffering: "Her mother passed away, and another woman came in, taking everything. Her father had his own business, and the stepmother took it over with her relatives. The stepmother even made the father suspicious and distrusting of the young woman." The young woman wasn't very good at school but felt like she could not go home. She took pills for the stress, and she took pills to sleep. She took too many pills, in fact, and Daow knew driving was dangerous in her state. Daow convinced her to go to a hotel and stay on the phone. "She [doesn't feel like she is] very good at anything, so she doubted her self-worth." For two hours, Daow spoke with the young woman and calmed her down. She was able to de-escalate the situation and empower the caller to realize her value and abilities. The young woman mirrored the problems with which Daow once struggled: thoughts of suicide, no one to empathize with her, and no safe place to go. In her quest to help those who "suffer like [her]," Daow sees her decision to ordain as a selfless act; she did it so she could help others and be a confidant for them.

Daow told us that her proudest moment was when her parents *wai*-ed her as a monk. Before Daow's generation, wai-ing a woman as a monk would have been sacrilegious. In that moment, however, Daow received affirmation from her family as the primary merit-maker and person responsible for her family's good rebirth. Receiving ordination as a monk is *the* best way to make merit for yourself and your family. Thai men are expected to ordain as a monk for at least three months to pay back the "milk-debt" of their mother's birthing and raising them. Because of this relationship, an old Thai saying (and belief) is that women must "cling on to the saffron robes of their sons in order to ascend to heaven" (as cited in Yavaprabhas 2018: 24), as there is no better way for women to make merit. Now, in this moment, Daow wore the sacred saffron robes that would fly her father to heaven.

Unfortunately, Daow had no idea that time was coming so soon. Her father was very sick and confined to the bed. When Daow heard he was too sick to chase away the fire ants and was subsequently covered in bites, she decided to visit him.

> I stayed with him for three days. I fed him, carried him, repositioned him, and prayed with him. . . I told him I would come back after the holiday. I returned to the temple and my sister said he was doing very well.

But the next morning, Daow's father was unconscious and having problems breathing. He was taken to the ER, but the family did not want to bother Daow during the important Buddhist holiday. Later in the day, she found out and asked permission to go to the hospital. "Venerable Dhammananda told me not to cry, because we are monks and people look up to us. If I were to cry, everyone would cry." In this moment, Daow's equanimity was just as important socially as it was emotionally. Arousing others as a monk is demeritous and would look especially bad, since the bhikkhuni are not yet recognized by Theravada Buddhists as monks. Daow had to keep her practice according to her precepts so others would gain faith in bhikkhuni's practice, even though she was losing the person who meant the most to her.

> I told him, "Father, if you're tired, then get some rest. You have done so much, and we can take care of ourselves now. You don't have anything else to worry about." I wanted to cry, so I left the room. . . . I held my tears [till the next day, when he passed away]. I went to Venerable Dhammananda and cried. . . . I didn't cry at all at his funeral. I composed myself [as a monk].

Reflecting on this, Daow told us the most impactful advice from the whole interview:

Daow: Like I said, being a monk, not everyone has reached Nirvana. We practice to get there quicker, but how far can we make it? It's not like ordaining makes you stronger; it gives us the knowledge of people's conditions so we can become *hen-jai* [*considerate*] to others and give *henjai* [compassion] to others. These days, Raven, I look at my [dead] father's picture and I still cry. It's like six years of being ordained, and it didn't take me anywhere [closer to Nibbana]. It's almost like I got nothing from it. [My father's death] is like dust in my eyes that I can't get out.

Raven: Daow, you've taught many people and attained so much! But the thing is . . . it's normal, Daow. You can't just attain everything at once; maybe it's a step-by-step process.

Daow: This is what I learned, the truth about reality. [Daow pauses for a deep breath.] *It's not about reaching heaven through a sudden realization. It's about learning about life, step-by-step.*

Sometimes, Buddhist stories depict enlightenment and subsequent ascendence to heaven as a sudden realization. An ongoing popular anime series, *Saint Young Men*, depicts Jesus and Buddha as roommates going through everyday life. The series often depicts Buddha attaining enlightenment multiple times a day through a sudden realization. This image permeates many Western audiences, too, who believe monks are holy, untouchable, equanimous beings on a quest to end their rebirths for good. While I have met monks studying and meditating for this realization, Daow shows us what is much more common: people ordaining for the family's well-being in their current and future lives. Because of current gender roles, it is hard for some people (like Daow's husband) to understand how a wife, mother, or daughter's ordination could help their family.

Female ordination, as shown through Daow's life story, has the potential to change Thai gender roles in terms of who can provide a good afterlife for their family. Traditionally, without an order of female monks, only men have been able to send their families merit for a potentially better rebirth. Women, on the other hand, were expected to nourish the family physically, emotionally, and mentally. Thai women have also been the regarded as the upholders of morality in the family (Keyes 1984: 229; Cassaniti 2017: 106) but, before the possibility of ordination, were not seen as an authority on the topic. Therefore, the introduction of Thai bhikkhuni has the potential to change gender roles, even if by only creating a safe space to express emotional frustration *with* traditional gender roles. To understand this concept, however, we need to recognize Daow's stakes, both personally and religiously. Though I presented the events of Daow's life in chronological order, I analyze her narrative in reverse. In part, this is because she uses her current position to justify the events that led her to this point. Additionally, I chose this technique to show how Daow reflects on her own experiences to inform and counsel others through a mutual vulnerability via empathy, then equanimity.

At the conclusion of her interview, Daow told us ordination is not about reaching a higher standard but understanding the "truth of reality." This engagement alleviated some of the mysticism surrounding bhikkhuni and showed a vulnerability on Daow's behalf. Though the Theravada lineage of bhikkhuni died a while ago, there were never official bhikkhuni in Thailand. People may be unsure of how to interact with female monks: Should they be as formal as they have been taught with male monks? Or is there a degree of informality that is socially acceptable because of the familiarity and cherishing of women as mothers? For example, when Daow told us she still cries about her father's death, she showed us a lowered metaphorical barrier between superiors and inferiors. Daow did not tell us this is a Buddhist lesson on the impermanence of life or that being a bhikkhuni resolves the emotions surrounding impermanence; instead, she shared with us that learning how to be an empathetic person showed her the truth of reality and the truth of life. Though she knows this concept and teaches it through Buddhist sermons, she acknowledges the difficulty of the lesson, and that knowledge alone does not lead to enlightenment.

Similarly, the environment Daow created while counselling a layperson on the phone validated the bhikkhuni role as representative of a compassionate and considerate community. She affirmed her authority as a bhikkhuni through her usage of *yom* and offered her own place of refuge to the caller. This environment extended into our interviews as well. A set time (such as Catholic confession) or designated space is not necessary for bhikkhuni to engage the population in an empathetic (hen jai) space. Daow was able to affirm the self-worth of the caller and able to soothe Raven's concerns about impermanence with her narrative. More importantly, Daow uses the bhikkhuni role to situate herself as a religious mentor actively relieving the suffering of others caused by expectations of social roles and, more specifically, gender roles.

Gender roles also extend to limitations within one's society. Thai cultural models strongly regulate how women interact with male monks. Daow expressed this concern when she said, "But for me, as a woman, when I suffered, I couldn't just go talk to a male monk." But this time, she had a solution: "I was ordained so I could be there to listen to some women who don't know who to talk to." Again, Daow creates a shared empathetic space where women can appropriately confide in another woman. Previously, she lacked this space. She told us, "[My mentor] was a man. I was a woman. When I had a problem, who could I talk to? Who would listen?" This inability to find a place and/or person to alleviate the suffering led to her suicide attempt.

Conclusion

There were only two times the vibrant, very outspoken woman I call Daow fell silent and placed her hands gently on her lap instead of gesticulating her story while she spoke. The first time was when she told us about her potential abortion; the second was when she told us about her suicide attempt. The attempt to end her life is the experience that almost took her away from this world but will forever ground her within it. The intensity of emotion she felt parallels the intensity with which she shares this experience to engage the listener. Daow recalls her feelings surrounding that event with such power that the emotions infiltrate all involved. Usually, when she tells this story, she intentionally evokes emotion in the listener to spark a connection. The listener shares a conflict they feel alone in confronting, but Daow offers a common experience to invite her into a shared space. However, the only way Daow could have gained this authority so quickly was through a community that supports her and her personal journey.

The Good Feelings Ceremony in front of the Medicine Buddha creates a safe environment for women to reflect of their emotions and experiences while trying to bring back a traditional role in a radical way. In front of the Medicine Buddha, the bhikkhuni chant incantations asking for healing and protection but understand they must also attain these things through their own actions. The Medicine Buddha is, therefore, simply a symbolic presence of power and safety and a tipping point for the real work being done. The genuine power is found in the connections formed during the Good Feelings Ceremony, where mutual vulnerability and empathy create connections between resilient women. The way that bhikkhuni ritual practices incorporate everyday lived subjectivities from women's lay lives initiates a sort of intervention, first with themselves at the temple, then outside the temple. With bhikkhuni, women can openly grieve their gender roles with a religious authority who has already successfully transgressed societal expectations and gender roles.

Glossary

Bhikkhu – A male who has received ordination as a monk, wears the saffron orange robes, and follows 227 precepts. Often used as a title similar to Venerable, Father, or Sir.

Bhikkhuni – A female who has received ordination as a monk, wears the saffron orange robes, and follows 311 precepts. Often used as a title similar to Venerable, Mother, or Ma'am.

Garudhammas – Eight rules of respect within the Vinaya. Rule 6 states that women must receive ordination from other, previously ordained women.

Kamlang Jai – Encouraging someone to go on, often translated as heart–mind energy.

Lay Person – A Buddhist who typically follows between two and five precepts.

Nirvana – Buddhist heaven, also referred to as *Nibbana*.

Precepts – Rules of conduct. The first five are not to kill, lie, cheat (within the rules of your relationship), steal, or take drugs. An average person who strictly follows all five rules is typically thought to be a very good Buddhist and *very* pious.

Renunciate – A person who gives up their worldly possessions, either temporarily or forever, typically wears white robes or clothes and follows at least eight precepts.

Vihara – Sacred building.

Wai – Palms pressed flat together as a sign of greeting, respect, and acknowledgment. Thai society has three different placements of a wai according to status. Placement on the chest is for younger, lower-status people, or equal-status people. Placement on the lips is for elders or higher-status people. Placement on the forehead is exclusively for monks.

Discussion questions

1. What does the author argue, and what evidence do they provide in support of their argument? Are you persuaded by their argument and their evidence? Why or why not?
2. Why do women want to receive ordination as bhikkhuni?
3. Instead of "emotion," the author explains that there are three affective states that people experience. What are they, and how does the author describe them?
4. How does this chapter demonstrate the gendering of space and/or knowledge?

Notes

1 *Theravada* is often described as the "Doctrine of the Elders," in which elders preserve the Buddhist tradition and have undergone very little change since its founding (Gombrich 1988: 3, 22).
2 It is important to note that most women did not accept the fruit, and if they did, they gave it to me after the ceremony – as medicine.
3 Though the *Vinaya* prohibits people from receiving ordination if they have severe health problems, the abbess welcomed Daow into the community after advocation from another bhikkhuni on Daow's behalf. Daow had the appropriate skills to fulfill the temple's need for a cook, and she relied on her strong work ethic and personality to advance herself within the community.
4 Notice at this point that I do not distinguish between male or female monk. Instead, I simply refer to the legitimacy of a monk, regardless of gender, as a thought exercise as to why many assume a term carries masculine or feminine characteristics.

References

Abu-Lughod, Lila. 2016. *Veiled Sentiments: Honor and Poetry in a Bedouin Society*. Berkeley, CA: University of California Press.

Analayo, Bhikkhu. 2014. "On the Bhikkhuni Ordination Controversy." *Sri Lanka International Journal of Buddhist Studies* 3: 1–22.

Aulino, Felicity. 2019. *Rituals of Care: Karmic Politics in an Aging Thailand*. Ithaca, NY: Cornell University Press.

Bodhi, Bhikkhu. 2009. *The Revival of Bhikkhuni Ordination in the Theravada Tradition*. Penang: Inward Path Publisher.

Bodhi, Bhikkhu, ed. 2012. *Abhidhammattha Sangaha: A Comprehensive Manual of Abhidhamma*. Onalaska, WA: BPS Pariyatti Editions.

Bonnet-Acosta, Cristina. 2014. "Brave Daughters of the Buddha: The Feminism of the Burmese Buddhist Nuns." In *Eminent Buddhist Women*, ed. Tsomo, 35–54. Albany, New York: SUNY Press.

Briggs, Jean L. 1998. *Inuit Morality Play: The Emotional Education of a Three-Year-Old*. New Haven, CT: Yale University Press.

Brown, Sid. 2001. *Journey of One Buddhist Nun: Even against the Wind*. Albany, NY: SUNY Press.

Buddhaghosa, Bhadantācariya. 2010. *The Path of Purification*. Onalaska, WA: Buddhist Publication Society.

Cassaniti, J. 2017. *Living Buddhism: Mind, Self, and Emotion in a Thai Community*. Ithaca, NY: Cornell University Press.

Collins, Steven, and McDaniel Justin. 2010. "Buddhist 'Nuns' (Mae Chi) and the Teaching of Pali in Contemporary Thailand." *Modern Asian Studies* 44: 1373–1408.

Cook, Joanna. 2010. *Meditation in Modern Buddhism: Renunciation and Change in Thai Monastic Life*. Cambridge: Cambridge University Press.

De Silva, Ranjani. 2004. "Reclaiming the Robe: Reviving the Bhikkhuni Order in Sri Lanka." In *Buddhist Women and Social Justice: Ideals, Challenges, and Achievements*, ed. Karma Lekshe Tsomo, 119–136. Albany, New York: SUNY Press.

Gombrich, Richard. 1988. *Theravada Buddhism: A Social History from Ancient Benares to Modern Colombo*. Abingdon, UK: Routledge.

Gray, Dennis D. 2015. "'Rebel' Female Buddhist Monks Challenge Thailand Status Quo." *Asian Reporter*. https://ntserver1.wsulibs.wsu.edu:3080/docview/1720413377?accountid=14902.

Gross, Rita. 1993. *Buddhism after Patriarchy: A Feminist History, Analysis, and Reconstruction of Buddhism*. Albany, NY: State University of New York Press.

Hochschild, Arlie Russell. 1979. "Emotion Work, Feeling Rules, and Social Structure." *American Journal of Sociology* 85(3): 551–575.

Horner, Isaline B. 1952. *The Book of the Discipline Vinaya-Pitaka (Cullavagga)*, vol. 5. Bristol: Burleigh Press.

Ito, Tomomi. 1999. "Questions of Ordination Legitimacy for Newly Ordained Theravada Bhikkhuni in Thailand." *Journal of Southeast Asian Studies*: 55–76.

Kawanami, Hiroko. 2007. "The Bhikkhunī Ordination Debate: Global Aspirations, Local Concerns, with Special Emphasis on the Views of the Monastic Community in Burma." *Buddhist Studies Review* 24: 226–244.

Keyes, Charles F. 1984. "Mother or Mistress but Never a Monk: Buddhist Notions of Female Gender in Rural Thailand." *American Ethnological Society* 11(2): 223–241.

Keyes, Charles F. 1985. "The Interpretive Basis of Depression." In *Culture and Depression: Studies in the Anthropology and Cross-Cultural Psychiatry of Affect and Disorder*, eds. Arthur Kleinman and Byron Good, 153–174. Berkeley: University of California Press.

Koret, Peter. 2012. *The Man Who Accused the King of Killing a Fish: The Biography of Narin Phasit of Siam (1874–1950)*. Chiang Mai, Thailand: Silkworm Books.

Levy, Robert I. 1973. *Tahitians: Mind and Experience in the Society Islands*. Chicago, IL: University of Chicago Press.

Lindberg Falk, Monica. 2007. *Making Fields of Merit: Buddhist Female Ascetics and Gendered Orders in Thailand*. Seattle, WA: University of Washington Press.

Lutz, Catherine A. 1998. *Unnatural Emotions: Everyday Sentiments on a Micronesian Atoll and Their Challenge to Western Theory*. Chicago: University of Chicago Press.

Mageo, Jeannette. 2011. "Empathy and 'As-If' Attachment in Samoa." In *The Anthropology of Empathy: Experiencing the Lives of Others in Pacific Societies*, eds. Doug Hollan and Jason Throop, 69–93. Oxford: Berghahn Books.

Mageo, Jeannette. 2013. "Dreaming and its Discontents: US Cultural Models in the Theater of Dreams." *Ethos* 41(4): 387–410.

Mrozik, Susanne. 2009. "A Robed Revolution: The Contemporary Buddhist Nun's (Bhikṣuṇī) Movement." *Religion Compass* 3(3): 360–378.

Obeyesekere, Gananath. 1985. "Depression, Buddhism, and the Work of Culture in Sri Lanka." In *Culture and Depression: Studies in the Anthropology and Cross-Cultural Psychiatry of Affect and Disorder*, eds. Arthur Kleinman and Byron Good, 134–152. Berkeley: University of California Press.

Obeyesekere, Gananath. 1990. *The Work of Culture: Symbolic Transformation in Psychoanalysis and Anthropology*, Vol. 1982. Chicago: University of Chicago Press.

Puntarigvivat, Tavivat. 2001. "A Thai Buddhist Perspective." In *What Men Owe to Women: Men's Voices from World Religions*. eds. J. Raines and Daniel C. Maguire, 211–237. Albany: State University of New York Press.

Rosaldo, Michelle Z. 1984. "Toward an Anthropology of Self and Feeling." *Culture Theory: Essays on Mind, Self, and Emotion*: 143–157.

Satha-Anand, Suwanna. 1999. "Truth over Convention: Feminist Interpretations of Buddhism." In *Religious Fundamentalisms and the Human Rights of Women*, ed. Courtney Howland, 281–291. New York: St. Martin's Press.

Seeger, Martin. 2006. "The Bhikkhunī Ordination Controversy in Thailand." *Journal of the International Association of Buddhist Studies* 29(1): 155–183.

Shizuka, Sasaki. 2004. "A Problem in the Re-Establishment of the Bhikkhuni Sangha in Modern Theravada Buddhism." *The Eastern Buddhist* 36(1 & 2): 184–191.

Shweder, Richard A. 1985. "Menstrual Pollution, Soul Loss, and the Comparative Study of Emotions." In *Culture and Depression: Studies in the Anthropology and Cross-Cultural Psychiatry of Affect and Disorder*, eds. Arthur Kleinman and Byron Good, 182–215. Berkeley: University of California Press.

Stonington, Scott. 2020. *The Spirit Ambulance: Choreographing the End of Life in Thailand*. Berkeley, CA: University of California Press.

Thanissaro, Bhikkhu. 2013. *The Buddhist Monastic Code I & II*, 3rd ed., ed. Geoffrey DeGraff. Access to Insight (BCBS Edition).

"Theravada Buddhism: A Chronology." *Access to Insight (BCBS Edition)*, November 30. www.accesstoinsight.org/history.html.

Tomalin, Emma. 2006. "The Thai Bhikkhuni Movement and Women's Empowerment." *Gender and Development* 14(3): 385–397.

Tomalin, Emma. 2009. "Buddhist Feminist Transnational Networks, Female Ordination and Women's Empowerment." *Oxford Development Studies* 37(2): 81–100.

Tsomo, Karma Lekshe. 2010. "Gender Equity and Human Rights." In *Dignity and Discipline: Reviving Full Ordination for Buddhist Nuns*, eds. Thea Mohr and Jampa Tsedroen, 281–289. Boston, MA: Wisdom Publications.

Tsomo, Karma Lekshe. 2014. *Eminent Buddhist Women*. Albany, NY: SUNY Press.

Winichakul, Thongchai. 1997. *Siam Mapped: A History of the Geo-Body of a Nation*. University of Hawaii Press.

Yavaprabhas, Kakanang. 2018. "The Values of Ordination: the Bhikkhuni, Gender, and Thai Society." PhD diss., UCL, University College London.

Part 4

Gender and the state

In this section, we present a collection of chapters which help us think about relationships between gender and the state. In particular, we will look at how the state expresses an interest in what gender is and what it is capable of through legislation, regulation, market reforms, and other policy. On the other hand, what interests us and the authors of these chapters is how people adapt or push back – resist and refuse – the constraints of the state. These constraints, unsurprising to many, are more acutely felt by women, LGBTQIA+ folks, BIPOC, and the working class, which betrays the white cis-hetero-masculinity of the state.

First, in a classic chapter, Nancy Scheper-Hughes examines the inevitability of maternal–infant attachment among mothers in the shantytowns of northeast Brazil. In an environment of poverty, chronic hunger, and economic exploitation, Scheper-Hughes finds that mothers adopt a strategy of delayed attachment and neglect of weaker children thought unlikely to survive. Such attitudes of resignation and fatalism toward the death of children are documented in historical studies of other cultures as well; for example, Ransel's account of child abandonment in Russia relates the passive attitude toward childhood death to child death rates in the 50 percent range (1988: 273; see also Boswell 1988). Parental attitudes are reflected in an entire category of lullabies with the motif of wishing death on babies; women sang these lullabies to infants who were sick, weak, or crippled (Ransel 1988: 273). Thus, mother love seems less a "natural and universal maternal script" than a luxury reserved for the strongest and healthiest children. In the context of frequent infant death, maternal attachment means grief, and mother love emerges as culturally and socially constructed rather than as an innate emotion. In a new addition to this edition, we include an update about the Alto from Nancy Scheper-Hughes in which she describes decreases in infant death as overall conditions have improved over the last 35 years.

State interests in shaping reproductive strategies are nowhere more evident than in the case of Romania during the Ceausescu regime, as Gail Kligman documents in her powerful analysis of official pronatalist policies and citizens' everyday lived experiences. Romanian policy, from the mid-1960s, was one of extreme pronatalism, aimed at supporting a demographic trajectory that would build a strong socialist labor force. In this "political demography," the state engaged in coercive measures to underscore the significance of family and population growth. As Kligman observes, the bodies of Romanian women became instruments used in the service of the state. According to state rhetoric, women occupied a position of singular value, as mothers (and thus as reproducers of the workforce) and as workers themselves. Mothers who gave birth to and raised many children

DOI: 10.4324/9781003398349-28

were honored as socialist heroes. Yet in reality, officially obligatory childbearing in the absence of social supports (job security, childcare, maternity leaves) and in the context of a deteriorating economy generated overwhelming burdens for women and families and resulted in skyrocketing rates of abortion and led to a crisis of overwhelmed orphanages with appalling conditions.

The state can also take an interest in the gendered bodies of women. The vexing issue of acceptable dress for Muslim women in France offers such an example. John R. Bowen's chapter traces the historical trajectory of French public anxieties and state intervention in the realm of Muslim women's clothing, from the colonial period to the present. He notes that from 1989 through 2011, a recurring justification for state regulation of Muslim women's bodies has been their putative lack of autonomy. Insofar as Muslim girls and women claim to "choose" to wear a headscarf or a "veil," they are assumed to be victims of Islamist ideology and male oppression. Given the important state values of Republicanism and secularism and long-standing government efforts to negate "cultural difference," those who choose to wear a face veil represent a threat to core constructs of French citizenship and identity. Wearing a headscarf in France today, Bowen argues, involves negotiations, anticipations, and weighing of benefits and costs. It is not simply an "obligation" or a "choice" but a subtle dance among convictions and constraints. Many young French Muslim women have made clothing choices precisely to negotiate space for their autonomy but confront widespread assumptions that head and face coverings violate the most minimal conditions of civic life. The headscarf comes to represent a profound affront to human rights upheld by the state, and far-right governments throughout Europe, in particular, continue to use banning the hijab or the niqab in public as a key part of their platform. The fact that an incredibly small percentage of women wear the niqab, for instance, in countries like the Netherlands demonstrates that these policies seeking to control women's choices are, at their root, tied to Islamophobia.

New to this edition, Rine Vieth's chapter explores how LGBTQIA+ asylum-seekers in the UK must navigate and negotiate a system designed to be skeptical of their claims. Their examination of the circuitous process reveals that asylum-seekers, in general, are at a strict disadvantage due to language barriers and confusing rules and routes by which claims can be made. Frustratingly, LGBTQIA+ asylum-seekers have additional, often humiliating barriers by which they are compelled to divulge personal experiences, entertain stereotypes, and relive traumas in order to "prove" the dire circumstances of their need. Moreover, the state's policies are often refracted through individual "decision-makers," some of whom are not required to have any legal training and whose decisions are entirely at their own discretion. Drawing on the work of Jasbir Puar (2018), Vieth introduces a framework of "homonationalist futurities" to think through how a state's process of legal recognition of LGBTQIA+ folks could have a variety of consequences on the future of asylum-seeking in particular and nation-building in general.

Yet another perspective on the role of the state in promoting particular gender roles, and especially concepts of motherhood, is offered by Üstek and Alyanak's discussion not only of how the Turkish state attempts to control how family and private life are represented in the media (in this case, popular drama series) but also how these regulations are challenged by the transnational reach of some exported Turkish productions. These authors describe the tug-of-war between the Turkish state and its regulatory apparatus on the one hand and popular desires for more sensual and sensational plots that also reframe Turkish womanhood, in particular by displaying women who demonstrate strength and modernity alongside traditional gender roles, on the other. The result is a "unique blend" of alternative narratives. The widespread popularity of these shows outside Turkey should also make us question the effects of exporting particular forms of acceptable gender roles to new settings. For instance, Adrienne often watches Turkish shows dubbed in Swahili while staying with friends in Tanzania. How might Turkish gender roles portrayed in these shows be influencing, combining, reinforcing, or conflicting with gender ideologies in places where these shows enjoy a large audience outside Turkey?

Caroline S. Archambault's chapter explores the association between pastoralism, patriarchy, and early marriage for girls among Maasai pastoralists in Kenya. The Maasai are facing challenges derived from land tenure reform, state neglect and political marginality, population growth, and climactic instability. While early marriage is often viewed as a relic of tradition and a product of "malicious" patriarchy, Archambault argues that it can instead be viewed as a contemporary adaptation to livelihood insecurity. Her focus, therefore, is on the structural factors that help explain early marriage and turn attention away from more effective policies to help the Maasai sustain their way of life. "Under circumstances in which families struggled to provide for their children, marrying out a daughter to a good family," Archambault writes, "would better secure the daughter's future and would relieve some of the pressure of providing for the remaining members of the family." Marrying daughters early may be less a decision rooted in custom, tradition, and patriarchy than one rooted in insecurity and concern. While the state emphasizes education as an alternative, and while the Maasai have internalized it as a "key to life," there are obstacles, including joblessness, that lead parents to explore alternatives. What is perhaps most intriguing about Archambault's argument, particularly in relation to issues of gender inequality, is the emphasis on collective rights. She writes:

> When put into context, the collective right of arranging marriages appears to be an expression of individual rights to integrity and security. Father and daughter can be understood as sharing fundamental goals (security of well-being) while disagreeing on the means through which to achieve them.

Sharon Hicks-Bartlett offers a portrait of poor African American families in the United States who are experiencing urban poverty. Her research population resides in a small Black suburb outside a major Midwestern city, but they, too, call on family-based, helping networks to minimize risk and fulfill immediate needs. Hicks-Bartlett describes the emotionally draining and labor-intensive work of parenting in a neighborhood marred by police corruption and violence. The necessity of hypervigilance means that women often call on kin to help them with their children so that they can work. Adult children also put aside self-interest to assist one parent in the care of the other. In the context of state-defunded public programs and facilities, it is the kinship networks that become the lifelines of the urban poor. It is kin who provide transportation, housing, food, and employment leads, in addition to childcare service. But given the extent of poverty and hardship, the kin networks are often stressed and overwhelmed.

Also new to this edition, Andrea Bolivar's chapter is a moving narration of queer kin-making in the context of the trans Latinx sex-working community of Chicago. There, and elsewhere, trans women who provide advice and guidance to those who are in transition act as "trans mothers." As Bolivar writes, "their role and impact is much greater," and in this chapter, she sheds new light on the strengths of spiritual kinship, mentorship, and motherhood in trans and queer kinship. Bolivar's thorough intersectional analysis challenges the centering of White transnormative experiences in the fight against transphobic laws and policies. With ethnographic richness, Bolivar demonstrates how trans mothering and queer kinship are necessary bulwarks against the White-cis-heteropatriarchy of the state and the mounting onslaught of anti-trans legislation in the United States in particular.

Finally, Nolan Kline's new contribution to this edition examines the social movement of the LGTBQ+ community in the wake of the 2016 Pulse nightclub shooting in Orlando, Florida. Recognizing the need for a social and political transformation that squarely focused on people at the intersection of identifying as a person of color and LGBTQ+, new organizations emerged to provide leadership opportunities to the most minoritized queer communities and those most impacted by the Pulse shooting. Kline demonstrates that this was achieved by three major strategies: harnessing the financial power of philanthropy that was directed specifically at LGBTQ+ people of color; supporting leadership of social support organizations focused on trans women of color, Latinx individuals, and Black same-gender loving men; and advancing undocumented LGBTQ+ (undocuqueer) social and political mobilization. Kline argues that the social movement that emerged after Pulse combated long-standing social divisions based on race, sex, gender, sexual orientation, immigration statuses, and other notions of difference.

References

Boswell, John. 1988. *The Kindness of Strangers: The Abandonment of Children in Western Europe from Late Antiquity to the Renaissance*. New York: Pantheon Books.

Puar, Jasbir K. 2018. *Terrorist Assemblages: Homonationalism in Queer Times*. Durham, NC: Duke University Press.

Ransel, David L. 1988. *Mothers of Misery: Child Abandonment in Russia*. Princeton, NJ: Princeton University Press.

Chapter 25

Lifeboat ethics

Mother love and child death in Northeast Brazil

Nancy Scheper-Hughes

Reproduced from *Natural History* 98.10 (1989), pp. 8–16. © Nancy Scheper-Hughes.

"Why do the church bells ring so often?" I asked Nailza de Arruda soon after I moved into a corner of her tiny mud-walled hut near the top of the shantytown called the Alto do Cruzeiro (Crucifix Hill).[1] I was then a Peace Corps volunteer and a community development/health worker. It was the dry and blazing hot summer of 1965, the months following the military coup in Brazil, and save for the rusty, clanging bells of N. S. das Dores Church, an eerie quiet had settled over the market town that I call Bom Jesus da Mata. Beneath the quiet, however, there was chaos and panic. "It's nothing," replied Nailza, "just another little angel gone to heaven."

Nailza had sent more than her share of little angels to heaven, and sometimes at night, I could hear her engaged in a muffled but passionate discourse with one of them, 2-year-old Joana. Joana's photograph, taken as she lay propped up in her tiny cardboard coffin, her eyes open, hung on a wall next to one of Nailza and Zé Antonio taken on the day they eloped.

Nailza could barely remember the other infants and babies who came and went in close succession. Most had died unnamed and were hastily baptized in their coffins. Few lived more than a month or two. Only Joana, properly baptized in church at the close of her first year and placed under the protection of a powerful saint, Joan of Arc, had been expected to live. And Nailza had dangerously allowed herself to love the little girl.

In addressing the dead child, Nailza's voice would range from tearful imploring to angry recrimination: "Why did you leave me? Was your patron saint so greedy that she could not allow me one child on this earth?" Zé Antonio advised me to ignore Nailza's odd behavior, which he understood as a kind of madness that, like the birth and death of children, came and went. Indeed, the premature birth of a stillborn son some months later "cured" Nailza of her "inappropriate" grief, and the day came when she removed Joana's photo and carefully packed it away.

More than 15 years elapsed before I returned to the Alto do Cruzeiro, and it was anthropology that provided the vehicle of my return. Since 1982, I have returned several times in order to pursue a problem that first attracted my attention in the 1960s. My involvement with the people of the Alto do Cruzeiro now spans a quarter of a century and three generations of parenting in a community where mothers and daughters are often simultaneously pregnant.

The Alto do Cruzeiro is one of three shantytowns surrounding the large market town of Bom Jesus in the sugar plantation zone of Pernambuco in Northeast Brazil, one of the many zones of neglect that have emerged in the shadow of the now-tarnished economic miracle of Brazil. For the women and children of the Alto do Cruzeiro, the only miracle is that some of them have managed to stay alive at all.

The Northeast is a region of vast proportions (approximately twice the size of Texas) and of equally vast social and developmental problems. The nine states that make up the region are the poorest in the country and are representative of the Third World within a dynamic and rapidly industrializing nation. Despite waves of migrations from the interior to the teeming shantytowns of coastal cities, the majority of people still live in rural areas on farms and ranches, sugar plantations, and mills.

Life expectancy in the Northeast is only 40 years, largely because of the appallingly high rate of infant and child mortality. Approximately one million children in Brazil under the age of 5 die each year. The children of the Northeast, especially those born in shantytowns on the periphery of urban life, are at a very high risk of death. In these areas, children are born without the traditional protection of breastfeeding, subsistence gardens, stable marriages, and multiple adult caretakers that exists in the interior. In the hillside shantytowns that spring up around cities or, in this case, interior market towns, marriages are brittle, single parenting is the norm, and women are frequently forced into the shadow economy of domestic work in the homes of the rich or into unprotected and oftentimes "scab" wage labor on the surrounding sugar plantations, where they clear land for planting and weed for a pittance, sometimes less than a dollar a day. The women of the Alto may not bring their babies with them into the homes of the wealthy, where the often-sick infants are considered sources of contamination, and they cannot carry the little ones to the riverbanks where they wash clothes, because the river is heavily infested with schistosomes and other deadly parasites. Nor can they carry their young children to the plantations, which are often several miles away. At wages of a dollar a day, the women of the Alto cannot hire babysitters. Older children who are not in school will sometimes serve as somewhat-indifferent caretakers. But any child not in school is also expected to find wage work. In most cases, babies are simply left at home alone, the door securely fastened. And so many also die alone and unattended.

Bom Jesus da Mata, centrally located in the plantation zone of Pernambuco, is within commuting distance of several sugar plantations and mills. Consequently, Bom Jesus has been a magnet for rural workers forced off their small subsistence plots by large landowners wanting to use every available piece of land for sugar cultivation. Initially, the rural migrants to Bom Jesus were squatters who were given tacit approval by the mayor to put up temporary straw huts on each of the three hills overlooking the town. The Alto do Cruzeiro is the oldest, the largest, and the poorest of the shantytowns. Over the past three decades, many of the original migrants have become permanent residents, and the primitive and temporary straw huts have been replaced by small homes (usually of two rooms) made of wattle and daub, sometimes covered with plaster. The more affluent residents use bricks and tiles. In most Alto homes, dangerous kerosene lamps have been replaced by light bulbs. The once-tattered rural garb, often fashioned from used sugar sacking, has likewise been replaced by store-bought clothes, often castoffs from a wealthy *patrão* (boss). The trappings are modern, but the hunger, sickness, and death that they conceal are traditional, deeply rooted in a history of feudalism, exploitation, and institutionalized dependency.

My research agenda never wavered. The questions I addressed first crystallized during a veritable "die-off" of Alto babies during a severe drought in 1965. The food and water shortages and the political and economic chaos occasioned by the military coup were reflected in the handwritten entries of births and deaths in the dusty, yellowed pages of the ledger books kept at the public registry office in Bom Jesus. More than 350 babies died in the Alto during 1965 alone – this from a shantytown population of little more than 5,000. But that wasn't what surprised me. There were reasons enough for the deaths in the miserable conditions of shantytown life. What puzzled me was the seeming indifference of Alto women to the death of their infants, and their willingness to attribute to their own tiny offspring an aversion to life that made their death seem wholly natural, indeed all but anticipated.

Although I found that it was possible, and hardly difficult, to rescue infants and toddlers from death by diarrhea and dehydration with a simple sugar, salt, and water solution (even bottled Coca-Cola worked fine), it was more difficult to enlist a mother herself in the rescue of a child she perceived as ill-fated for life or better off dead, or to convince her to take back into her threatened and besieged home a baby she had already come to think of as an angel rather than as a son or daughter.

I learned that the high expectancy of death, and the ability to face child death with stoicism and equanimity, produced patterns of nurturing that differentiated between those infants thought of as thrivers and survivors and those thought of as born already "wanting to die." The survivors were nurtured, while stigmatized, doomed infants were left to die, as mothers say, *a mingua*, "of neglect." Mothers stepped back and allowed nature to take its course. This pattern, which I call mortal selective neglect, is called passive infanticide by anthropologist Marvin Harris. The Alto situation, although culturally specific in the form that it takes, is not unique to Third World shantytown communities and may have its correlates in our own impoverished urban communities in some cases of "failure to thrive" infants.

I use as an example the story of Zezinho, the 13-month-old toddler of one of my neighbors, Lourdes. I became involved with Zezinho when I was called in to help Lourdes in the delivery of another child, this one a fair and robust little tyke with a lusty cry. I noted that while Lourdes showed great interest in the newborn, she totally ignored Zezinho, who, wasted and severely malnourished, was curled up in a fetal position on a piece of urine- and feces-soaked cardboard placed under his mother's hammock. Eyes open and vacant, mouth slack, the little boy seemed doomed.

When I carried Zezinho up to the community day-care center at the top of the hill, the Alto women who took turns caring for one another's children (in order to free themselves for part-time work in the cane fields or washing clothes) laughed at my efforts to save Zé, agreeing with Lourdes that here was a baby without a ghost of a chance. Leave him alone, they cautioned. It makes no sense to fight with death. But I did do battle with Zé, and after several weeks of force-feeding (malnourished babies lose their interest in food), Zé began to succumb to my ministrations. He acquired some flesh across his taut chest bones, learned to sit up, and even tried to smile. When he seemed well enough, I returned him to Lourdes in her miserable scrap-material lean-to, but not without guilt about what I had done. I wondered whether returning Zé was at all fair to Lourdes and to his little brother. But I was busy and washed my hands of the matter. And Lourdes did seem more interested in Zé now that he was looking more human.

When I returned in 1982, there was Lourdes among the women who formed my sample of Alto mothers – still struggling to put together some semblance of life for a now-grown Zé and her five other surviving children. Much was made of my reunion with Zé in 1982, and everyone enjoyed retelling the story of Zé's rescue and of how his mother had given him up for dead. Zé would laugh the loudest when told how I had had to force-feed him like a fiesta turkey. There was no hint of guilt on the part of Lourdes and no resentment on the part of Zé. In fact, when questioned in private as to who was the best friend he ever had in life, Zé took a long drag on his cigarette and answered without a trace of irony, "Why, my mother, of course!" "But of course," I replied.

Part of learning how to mother in the Alto do Cruzeiro is learning when to let go of a child who shows that it "wants" to die or that it has no "knack" or no "taste" for life. Another part is learning when it is safe to let oneself love a child. Frequent child death remains a powerful shaper of maternal thinking and practice. In the absence of firm expectations that a child will survive, mother love, as we conceptualize it (whether in popular terms or in the psychobiological notion of maternal bonding), is attenuated and delayed, with consequences for infant survival. In an environment already precarious to young life, the emotional detachment of mothers toward some of their babies contributes even further to the spiral of high mortality–high fertility in a kind of macabre lockstep dance to death.

The average woman of the Alto experiences 9.5 pregnancies, 3.5 child deaths, and 1.5 stillbirths. Seventy percent of all child deaths in the Alto occur in the first six months of life, and 82 percent by the end of the first year. Of all deaths in the community each year, about 45 percent are of children under the age of 5.

Women of the Alto distinguish between child deaths understood as natural (caused by diarrhea and communicable diseases) and those resulting from sorcery, the evil eye, or other magical or supernatural afflictions. They also recognize a large category of infant deaths as fated and inevitable. These hopeless cases are classified by mothers under the folk terminology "child sickness" or "child attack." Women say that there are at least 14 different types of hopeless child sickness, but most can be subsumed under two categories – chronic and acute. The chronic cases refer to infants who are born small and wasted. They are deathly pale, mothers say, as well as weak and passive. They demonstrate no vital force, no liveliness. They do not suck vigorously; they hardly cry. Such babies can be this way at birth, or they can be born sound but soon show no resistance, no "fight" against the common crises of infancy: diarrhea, respiratory infections, tropical fevers.

The acute cases are those doomed infants who die suddenly and violently. They are taken by stealth overnight, often following convulsions that bring on head banging, shaking, grimacing, and shrieking. Women say it is horrible to look at such a baby. If the infant begins to foam at the mouth or gnash its teeth or go rigid with its eyes turned back inside its head, there is absolutely no hope. The infant is "put aside" – left alone – often on the floor in a back room, and allowed to die. These symptoms (which accompany high fevers, dehydration, third-stage malnutrition, and encephalitis) are equated by Alto women with madness, epilepsy, and worst of all, rabies, which is greatly feared and highly stigmatized.

Most of the infants presented to me as suffering from chronic child sickness were tiny, wasted famine victims, while those labeled as victims of acute child attack seemed to be infants suffering from the deliriums of high fever or the convulsions that can accompany electrolyte imbalance in dehydrated babies.

Local midwives and traditional healers, praying women, as they are called, advise Alto women on when to allow a baby to die. One midwife explained:

If I can see that a baby was born unfortuitously, I tell the mother that she need not wash the infant or give it a cleansing tea. I tell her just to dust the infant with baby powder and wait for it to die.

Allowing nature to take its course is not seen as sinful by these often very devout Catholic women; rather, it is understood as cooperating with God's plan.

Often, I have been asked how consciously women of the Alto behave in this regard. I would have to say that consciousness is always shifting between allowed and disallowed levels of awareness. For example, I was awakened early one morning in 1987 by two neighborhood children who had been sent to fetch me to a hastily organized wake for a 2-month-old infant whose mother I had unsuccessfully urged to breastfeed. The infant was being sustained on sugar water, which the mother referred to as *soro* (serum), using a medical term for the infant's starvation regime in light of his chronic diarrhea. I had cautioned the mother that an infant could not live on *soro* forever.

The two girls urged me to console the young mother by telling her that it was "too bad" that her infant was so weak that Jesus had to take him. They were coaching me in proper Alto etiquette. I agreed, of course, but asked, "And what do you think?" Xoxa, the 11-year-old, looked down at her dusty flip-flops and blurted out, "Oh, Dona Nanci, that baby never got enough to eat, but you must never say that!" And so the death of hungry babies remains one of the best-kept secrets of life in Bom Jesus da Mata.

Most victims are waked quickly and with a minimum of ceremony. No tears are shed, and the neighborhood children form a tiny procession, carrying the baby to the town graveyard, where it will join a multitude of others. Although a few fresh flowers may be scattered over the tiny grave, no stone or wooden cross will mark the place, and the same spot will be reused within a few months' time. The mother will never visit the grave, which soon becomes an anonymous one.

What, then, can be said of these women? What emotions, what sentiments motivate them? How are they able to do what, in fact, must be done? What does *mother love* mean in this inhospitable context? Are grief, mourning, and melancholia present, although deeply repressed? If so, where shall we look for them? And if not, how are we to understand the moral visions and moral sensibilities that guide their actions?

I have been criticized more than once for presenting an unflattering portrait of poor Brazilian women, women who are, after all, themselves the victims of severe social and institutional neglect. I have described these women as allowing some of their children to die, as if this were an unnatural and inhuman act rather than, as I would assert, the way any one of us might act, reasonably and rationally, under similarly desperate conditions. Perhaps I have not emphasized enough the real pathogens in this environment of high risk: poverty, deprivation, sexism, chronic hunger, and economic exploitation. If mother love is, as many psychologists and some feminists believe, a seemingly natural and universal maternal script, what does it mean to women for whom scarcity, loss, sickness, and deprivation have made that love frantic and robbed them of their grief, seeming to turn their hearts to stone?

Throughout much of human history – as in a great deal of the impoverished Third World today – women have had to give birth and to nurture children under ecological conditions and social arrangements hostile to child survival, as well as to their own well-being. Under circumstances of high childhood mortality, patterns of selective neglect and passive infanticide may be seen as active survival strategies.

They also seem to be fairly common practices historically and across cultures. In societies characterized by high childhood mortality and by a correspondingly high (replacement) fertility, cultural practices of infant care and childcare tend to be organized primarily around survival goals. But what this means is a pragmatic recognition that not all of one's children can be expected to live. The nervousness about child survival in areas of northeast Brazil, northern India, or Bangladesh, where a 30 percent or 40 percent mortality rate in the first years of life is common, can lead to forms of delayed attachment and a casual or benign neglect that serves to weed out the worst bets so as to enhance the life chances of healthier siblings, including those yet to be born. Practices similar to those that I am describing have been recorded for parts of Africa, India, and Central America.

Life in the Alto do Cruzeiro resembles nothing so much as a battlefield or an emergency room in an overcrowded inner-city public hospital. Consequently, morality is guided by a kind of "lifeboat ethics," the morality of triage. The seemingly studied indifference toward the suffering of some of their infants, conveyed in such sayings as "Little critters have no feelings," is understandable in light of these women's obligation to carry on with their reproductive and nurturing lives.

In their slowness to anthropomorphize and personalize their infants, everything is mobilized so as to prevent maternal overattachment and, therefore, grief at death. The bereaved mother is told not to cry, that her tears will dampen the wings of her little angel so that she cannot fly up to her heavenly home. Grief at the death of an angel is not only inappropriate but also a symptom of madness and of a profound lack of faith.

Infant death becomes routine in an environment in which death is anticipated and bets are hedged. While the routinization of death in the context of shantytown life is not hard to understand, and quite possible to empathize with, its routinization in the formal institutions of public life in Bom Jesus is not as easy to accept uncritically. Here, the social production of indifference takes on a different, even a malevolent cast.

In a society where triplicates of every form are required for the most banal events (registering a car, for example), the registration of infant and child death is informal, incomplete, and rapid. It requires no documentation, takes less than five minutes, and demands no witnesses other than office clerks. No questions are asked concerning the circumstances of the death, and the cause of death is left blank, unquestioned, and unexamined. A neighbor, grandmother, older sibling, or common-law husband may register the death. Since most infants die at home, there is no question of a medical record.

From the registry office, the parent proceeds to the town hall, where the mayor will give him or her a voucher for a free baby coffin. The full-time municipal coffin-maker cannot tell you exactly how many baby coffins are dispatched each week. It varies, he says, with the seasons. There are more needed during the drought months and during the big festivals of Carnaval and Christmas and São Joao's Day because people are too busy, he supposes, to take their babies to the clinic. Record-keeping is sloppy.

Similarly, there is a failure on the part of city-employed doctors working at two free clinics to recognize the malnutrition of babies who are weighed, measured, and immunized without comment and as if they were not, in fact, anemic, stunted, fussy, and irritated starvation babies. At best, the mothers are told to pick up free vitamins or a health "tonic" at the municipal chambers. At worst, clinic personnel will give tranquilizers and sleeping pills to quiet the hungry cries of "sick-to-death" Alto babies.

The church, too, contributes to the routinization of, and indifference toward, child death. Traditionally, the local Catholic church taught patience and resignation to domestic tragedies that were said to reveal the imponderable workings of God's will. If an infant died suddenly, it was because a particular saint had claimed the child. The infant would be an angel in the service of his or her heavenly patron. It would be wrong, a sign of a lack of faith, to weep for a child with such good fortune. The infant funeral was, in the past, an event celebrated with joy. Today, however, under the new regime of "liberation theology," the bells of N. S. das Dores parish church no longer peal for the death of Alto babies, and no priest accompanies the procession of angels to the cemetery, where their bodies are disposed of casually and without ceremony. Children bury children in Bom Jesus da Mata. In this most Catholic of communities, the coffin is handed to the disabled and irritable municipal gravedigger, who often chides the children for one reason or another. It may be that the coffin is larger than expected and the gravedigger can find no appropriate space. The children do not wait for the gravedigger to complete his task. No prayers are recited and no sign of the cross made as the tiny coffin goes into its shallow grave.

When I asked the local priest, Padre Marcos, about the lack of church ceremony surrounding infant and childhood death today in Bom Jesus, he replied:

> In the old days, child death was richly celebrated. But those were the baroque customs of a conservative church that wallowed in death and misery. The new church is a church of hope and joy. We no longer celebrate the death of child angels. We try to tell mothers that Jesus doesn't want all the dead babies they send him.

Similarly, the new church has changed its baptismal customs, now often refusing to baptize dying babies brought to the back door of a church or rectory. The mothers are scolded by the church attendants and told to go home and take care of their sick babies. Baptism, they are told, is for the living; it is not to be confused with the sacrament of extreme unction, which is the anointing of the dying. And so it appears to the women of the Alto that even the church has turned away from them, denying the traditional comfort of folk Catholicism.

The contemporary Catholic Church is caught in the clutches of a double bind. The new theology of liberation imagines a kingdom of God on earth based on justice and equality, a world without hunger, sickness, or childhood mortality. At the same time, the church has not changed its official position on sexuality and reproduction, including its sanctions against birth control, abortion, and sterilization. The padre of Bom Jesus da Mata recognizes this contradiction intuitively, although he shies away from discussions on the topic, saying that he prefers to leave questions of family planning to the discretion and the "good consciences" of his impoverished parishioners. But this, of course, sidesteps the extent to which those good consciences have been shaped by traditional church teachings in Bom Jesus, especially by his recent predecessors. Hence, we can begin to see that the seeming indifference of Alto mothers toward the death of some of their infants is but a pale reflection of the official indifference of church and state to the plight of poor women and children.

Nonetheless, the women of Bom Jesus are survivors. One woman, Biu, told me her life history, returning again and again to the themes of child death, her first husband's suicide, abandonment by her father and later by her second husband, and all the other losses and disappointments she had suffered in her long 45 years. She concluded with great force, reflecting on the days of Carnaval '88, which were fast approaching:

> No, Dona Nanci, I won't cry, and I won't waste my life thinking about it from morning to night. . . . Can I argue with God for the state that I'm in? No! And so I'll dance and I'll jump and I'll play Carnaval! And yes, I'll laugh and people will wonder at a pobre like me who can have such a good time.

And no one did blame Biu for dancing in the streets during the four days of Carnaval – not even on Ash Wednesday, the day following Carnaval '88, when we all assembled hurriedly to assist in the burial of Mercea, Biu's beloved *casula*, her last-born daughter, who had died at home of pneumonia during the festivities. The rest of the family barely had time to change out of their costumes. Severino, the child's uncle and godfather, sprinkled holy water over the little angel while he prayed: "Mercea, I don't know whether you were called, taken, or thrown out of this world. But look down at us from your heavenly home with tenderness, with pity, and with mercy." So be it.

Discussion questions

1. Alto mothers have no means to support their children, nutritionally, medically, or emotionally. Under these structural circumstances, can we look at these women's actions as survival strategies? Why or why not?
2. How does Scheper-Hughes's research of Alto women challenge the notion of a natural and maternal "mother love"?
3. In Alto do Cruzeiro, why is a mother's bereavement over the death of her infant considered a symptom of madness and a lack of faith?
4. In this chapter, what parallel is drawn regarding the seeming indifference of Alto mothers toward their infants' death and the official indifference of the church and state to the plight of poor women and children?

No more angel babies on the Alto do Cruzeiro

A dispatch from Brazil's revolution in child survival

By Nancy Scheper-Hughes

It was almost 50 years ago that I first walked to the top of the Alto do Cruzeiro (the Hill of the Crucifix) in Timbaúba, a sugar-belt town in the state of Pernambuco, in Northeast Brazil. I was looking for the small mud hut, nestled in a cliff, where I was to live. It was December 1964, nine months after the coup that toppled the left-leaning president João Goulart. Church bells were ringing, and I asked the woman who was to host me as a

Peace Corps volunteer why they seemed to ring at all hours of the day. "Oh, it's nothing," she told me. "Just another little angel gone to heaven."

That day marked the beginning of my life's work. Since then, I have experienced something between an obsession, a trauma, and a romance with the shantytown. Residents of the newly occupied hillside were refugees from the military junta's violent attacks on the peasant league movement that had tried to enforce existing laws protecting the local sugarcane cutters. The settlers had thrown together huts made of straw, mud, and sticks or, lacking that, lean-tos made of tin, cardboard, and scrap materials. They had thrown together families in the same makeshift fashion, taking whatever was at hand and making do. In the absence of husbands, weekend play fathers did nicely as long as they brought home the current baby's powdered milk, if not the bacon. Households were temporary; in such poverty, women were the only stable force, and babies and fathers were circulated among them. A man who could not provide support would be banished to take up residence with another, even more desperate woman; excess infants and babies were often rescued by older women, who took them in as informal foster children.

Premature death was an everyday occurrence in a shantytown lacking water, electricity, and sanitation and beset with food scarcity, epidemics, and police violence. My assignment was to immunize children, educate midwives, attend births, treat infections, bind up festering wounds, and visit mothers and newborns at home to monitor their health and refer them as needed to the district health post or to the emergency room of the private hospital – owned by the mayor's brother – where charity cases were sometimes attended, depending on the state of local patron–client relations.

I spent several months making the rounds between the miserable huts on the Alto with a public health medical kit strapped on my shoulder. Its contents were pathetic: a bar of soap, scissors, antiseptics, aspirin, bandages, a glass syringe, some ampoules of vaccine, several needles, and a pumice stone to sharpen the needles, which were used over and over for immunizations. Children ran away when they saw me coming, and well they might have.

But what haunted me then, in addition to my own incompetence, was something I did not have the skill or maturity to understand: Why did the women of the Alto not grieve over the deaths of their babies? I tucked that question away. But as Winnicott, the British child psychoanalyst, liked to say, "Nothing is ever forgotten."

Sixteen years elapsed before I was able to return to the Alto do Cruzeiro, this time as a medical anthropologist. It was in 1982 – during the period known as the abertura, or opening, the beginning of the end of the military dictatorship – that I made the first of the four trips that formed the basis for my 1992 book, *Death without Weeping: The Violence of Everyday Life in Brazil*. My goal was to study women's lives, specifically mother love and child death under conditions so dire that the Uruguayan writer Eduardo Galeano once described the region as a concentration camp for 30 million people. It was not a gross exaggeration. Decades of nutritional studies of sugarcane cutters and their families in Pernambuco showed hard evidence of slow starvation and stunting. These nutritional dwarfs were surviving on a daily caloric intake similar to that of the inmates of the Buchenwald concentration camp. Life on the Alto resembled prison camp culture, with a moral ethic based on triage and survival.

If mother love is the cultural expression of what many attachment theorists believe to be a bio-evolutionary script, what could this script mean to women living in these conditions? In my sample of three generations of mothers in the sugar plantation zone of Pernambuco, the average woman had 9.5 pregnancies, 8 live births, and 3.5 infant deaths. Such high rates of births and deaths are typical of societies that have not undergone what population experts call the demographic transition, associated with economic development, in which, first, death rates and, later, birth rates drop as parents begin to trust that more of their infants will survive. On the contrary, the high expectation of loss and the normalization of infant death was a powerful conditioner of the degree of maternal attachments. Mothers and infants could also be rivals for scarce resources. Alto mothers renounced breastfeeding as impossible, as sapping far too much strength from their own "wrecked" bodies.

Scarcity made mother love a fragile emotion, postponed until the newborn displayed a will to live – a taste (gusto) and a knack (jeito) for life. A high expectancy of death prepared mothers to "let go" of and to hasten the death of babies that were failing to thrive, by reducing the already-insufficient food, water, and care. The "angel babies" of the Alto were neither of this earth nor yet fully spirits. In appearance, they were ghostlike: pale and wispy-haired, their arms and legs stripped of flesh, their bellies grossly distended, their eyes blank and staring, their faces wizened, a cross between startled primate and wise old sorcerer.

The experience of too much loss, too much death, led to a kind of patient resignation that some clinical psychologists might label "emotional numbing" or the symptoms of a "masked depression." But the mothers' resignation was neither pathological nor abnormal. Moreover, it was a moral code. Not only had a continual exposure to trauma obliterated rage and protest; it also minimized attachment so as to diminish sorrow.

Infant death was so commonplace that I recall a birthday party for a 4-year-old in which the birthday cake, decorated with candles, was placed on the kitchen table next to the tiny blue cardboard coffin of the child's 9-month-old sibling, who had died during the night. Next to the coffin, a single vigil candle was lit. Despite the tragedy, the child's mother wanted to go ahead with the party. "Parabéns para você," we sang, clapping our hands. "Congratulations to you!" the Brazilian birthday song goes. And on the Alto it had special resonance: "Congratulations, you, survivor, you – you lived to see another year!"

When Alto mothers cried, they cried for themselves, for those left behind to continue the struggle. But they cried the hardest for their children who had almost died but who surprised everyone by surviving against the odds. Wiping a stray tear from her eye, an Alto mother would speak with deep emotion of the child who, given up for dead, suddenly beat death back, displaying a fierce desire for life. These tough and stubborn children were loved above all others.

Staying alive in the shantytown demanded a kind of egoism that often pits individuals against each other and rewards those who take advantage of those weaker than themselves. People admired toughness and strength; they took pride in babies or adults who were cunning and foxy. The toddler that was wild and fierce was preferred to the quiet and obedient child. Men and women with seductive charm, who could manipulate those around them, were better off than those who were kind. Poverty does not ennoble people, and I came to appreciate what it took to stay alive.

Theirs were moral choices that no person should be forced to make. But the result was that infants were viewed as limitless. There was a kind of magical replaceability about them, similar to what one might find on a battlefield. As one soldier falls, another takes his place. This kind of detached maternal thinking allowed the die-offs of shantytown babies – in some years, as many as 40 percent of all the infants born on the Alto died – to pass without shock or profound grief. A woman who had lost half her babies told me:

> Who could bear it, Nancí, if we are mistaken in believing that God takes our infants to save us from pain? If that is not true, then God is a cannibal. And if our little angels are not in heaven, flying around the throne of Our Lady, then where are they, and who is to blame for their deaths?

If mothers allowed themselves to be attached to each newborn, how could they ever live through their babies' short lives and deaths and still have the stamina to get pregnant and give birth again and again? It wasn't that Alto mothers did not experience mother love at all – they did, and with great intensity. But mother love emerged as their children developed strength and vitality. The apex of mother love was not the image of Mary and her infant son but a mature Mary grieving the death of her young adult son. The Pietà, not the young mother at the crèche, was the symbol of motherhood and mother love on the Alto.

In *Death without Weeping* I first told of a clandestine extermination group that had begun to operate in Timbaúba in the 1980s. The rise of these vigilantes seemed paradoxical, insofar as it coincided with the end of the 20-year military dictatorship. What was the relationship between democracy and death squads? No one knew who was behind the extrajudicial limpeza ("street cleaning," as their supporters called it) that was targeting "dirty" street children and poor young Black men from the shantytowns. But by 2000, the public was well aware of the group and the identity of its leader, Abdoral Gonçalves Queiroz. Known as the "Guardian Angels," they were responsible for killing more than 100 victims. In 2001, I was invited, along with my husband, to return to Timbaúba to help a newly appointed and tough-minded judge and state prosecutor to identify those victims whose relatives had not come forward. In the interim, the death squad group had infiltrated the town council, the mayor's office, and the justice system. But 11 of them, including their semiliterate gangster boss, Queiroz, had been arrested and were going on trial.

The death squad was a residue of the old military regime. For 20 years, the military police had kept the social classes segregated, with "dangerous" street youths and unemployed rural men confined to the hillside slums or in detention. When the old policing structures loosened following the democratic transition, the shantytowns ruptured and poor people, especially unemployed young men and street children, flooded downtown streets and public squares, once the preserve of gente fina (the cultivated people). Their new visibility betrayed the illusion of Brazilian modernity and evoked contradictory emotions of fear, aversion, pity, and anger.

Excluded and reviled, unemployed Black youths and loose street kids of Timbaúba were prime targets of Queiroz and his gang. Depending on one's social class and politics, the band could be seen as hired serial killers or as justiceiros (outlaw heroes) who were protecting the community. Prominent figures – well-known businessmen and local politicians – applauded the work of the death squad, whom they also called "Police 2," and some of these leading citizens were active in the extrajudicial "courts" that were deciding who in Timbaúba should be the next to die.

During the 2001 death squad field research expedition, I played cat-and-mouse with Dona Amantina, the dour manager of the cartorio civil, the official registry office. I was trying to assemble a body count of suspicious homicides that could possibly be linked to the death squad, focusing on the violent deaths of street kids and young Black men. Since members of the death squad were still at large, I did not want to make public what I was doing. At first, I implied that I was back to count infant and child deaths, as I had so many years before. Finally, I admitted that I was looking into youth homicides. The manager nodded her head. "Yes, it's sad. But," she asked with a shy smile, "haven't you noticed the changes in infant and child deaths?" Once I began to scan the record books, I was wearing a smile too.

Brazil's national central statistics bureau, the Instituto Brasileiro de Geografia e Estatística (IBGE), began reporting data for the municipality of Timbaúba in the late 1970s. In 1977, for example, IBGE reported 761 live births in the municipality and 311 deaths of infants (up to 1 year of age) for that same year, yielding an infant mortality rate of 409 per 1,000. A year later, the IBGE data recorded 896 live births and 320 infant deaths, an infant mortality rate of 357 per 1,000. If reliable, those official data indicated that between 36 and 41 percent of all infants in Timbaúba died in the first 12 months of life.

During the 1980s, when I was doing the research for *Death without Weeping*, the then mayor of Timbaúba, the late Jacques Ferreira Lima, disputed those figures. "Impossible!" he fumed. "This município is growing, not declining." He sent me to the local private hospital built by, and named for, his father, João Ferreira Lima, to compare the IBGE statistics with the hospital's records on births and deaths. There, the head nurse gave me access to her records, but the official death certificates only concerned stillbirths and perinatal deaths. In the end, I found that the best source of data was the ledger books of the cartorio civil, where births and infant and child deaths were recorded by hand. Many births were not recorded until after a child had died, in order to register a death and receive a free coffin from the mayor's office. The statistics were as grim as those of the IBGE.

In 2001, a single afternoon going over infant and toddler death certificates in the same office was enough to document that something radical had since taken place – a revolution in child survival that had begun in the 1990s. The records now showed a completed birth rate of 3.2 children per woman, and a mortality rate of 35 per 1,000 births. Subsequent field trips in 2006 and 2007 showed even further reductions. The 2009 data from the IBGE recorded a rate of 25.2 child deaths per 1,000 births for Timbaúba.

Though working on other topics in my Brazilian field trips in 2001, 2006, and 2007, I took the time to interview several young women attending a pregnancy class at a newly constructed, government-run clinic. The women I spoke with – some first-time mothers, others expecting a second or third child – were confident in their ability to give birth to a healthy baby. No one I spoke to expected to have, except by accident, more than two children. A pair – that was the goal. Today, young women of the Alto can expect to give birth to three or fewer infants and to see all of them live at least into adolescence. The old stance of maternal watchful waiting accompanied by deselection of infants viewed as having no "talent" for life had been replaced by a maternal ethos of "holding on" to every infant, each seen as likely to survive. As I had noted in the past as well, there was a preference for girl babies. Boys, women feared, could disappoint their mothers – they could kill or be killed as adolescents and young men. The Alto was still a dangerous place, and gangs, drug dealers, and the death squads were still in operation. But women in the state-run clinic spoke of having control over their reproductive lives in ways that I could not have imagined.

By 2001, Timbaúba had experienced the demographic transition. Both infant deaths and births had declined so precipitously that it looked like a reproductive workers' strike. The numbers – though incomplete – were startling. Rather than the more than 200 annual infant and child mortalities of the early 1980s, by the late 1990s, there were fewer than 50 childhood deaths recorded per year. And the causes of death were specific. In the past, the causes had been stated in vague terms: "undetermined," "heart stopped, respiration stopped," "malnutrition," or the mythopoetic diagnosis of "acute infantile suffering."

On my latest return, just this June, the reproductive revolution was complete. The little two-room huts jumbled together on the back roads of the Alto were still poor, but as I visited the homes of dozens of Alto residents, sometimes accompanied by a local community health agent, sometimes dropping in for a chat unannounced, or summoned by the adult child of a former key informant of mine, I saw infants and toddlers who were plump and jolly, and mothers who were relaxed and breastfeeding toddlers as old as 3 years. Their babies assumed a high status in the family hierarchy, as precious little beings whose beauty and health brought honor and substance – as well as subsistence – to the household.

Manufactured cribs with pristine sheets and fluffy blankets, disposal diapers, and plastic rattles were much in evidence. Powdered milk, the number one baby killer in the past, was almost a banned substance. In contrast, no one, literally, breastfed during my early years of research on the Alto. It was breast milk that was banned, banned by the owners of the sugar plantations and by the bourgeois patroas (mistresses of the house), for whom the women of the Alto washed clothes and cleaned and cooked and served meals. Today, those jobs no longer exist. The sugar mills and sugar estates have closed down, and the landowning class has long since moved, leaving behind a population of working-class poor, a thin middle class (with washing machines rather than maids), and a displaced rural labor force that is largely sustained by the largesse of New Deal–style federal assistance.

Direct cash transfers are made to poor and unemployed families, and grants (bolsas, or "purses") are given to women, mothers, babies, schoolchildren, and youth. The grants come with conditions. The bolsa familiar (family grant), a small cash payment to each mother and up to five of her young children, requires the mother to immunize her babies, attend to their medical needs, follow medical directions, keep the children in school, monitor their homework, help them prepare for exams, and purchase schoolbooks, pens and pencils, and school clothes. Of the 30 Alto women between the ages of 17 and 40 my research associate, Jennifer S. Hughes, and I interviewed in June, the women averaged 3.3 pregnancies – higher than the national average, but the real comparison here is with their own mothers, who (based on the 13 of the 30 who could describe their mothers' reproductive histories) averaged 13.6 pregnancies and, among them, counted 61 infant deaths. Jennifer is my daughter and a professor of colonial and postcolonial Latin American history at the University of California, Riverside. I like to think that her awesome archival skills were honed more than 20 years ago when I enlisted her, then a teenager, to help me count the deaths of Alto babies in the civil registry office. She agreed to help me on this most recent field trip, and it was our first professional collaboration.

Jennifer, for example, looked up Luciene, the firstborn daughter of Antonieta, one of my earliest key informants and my neighbor when I lived on the Alto do Cruzeiro. Now in her 40s, Luciene had only one pregnancy and one living child. Her mother had given birth to 15 babies, 10 of whom survived. Daughter and mother now live next door to each other, and they spoke openly and emotionally about the "old days," "the hungry times," "the violent years," in comparison to the present. "Today we are rich," Antonieta declared, "really rich," by which she meant her modernized home on the Alto Terezinha, their new color television set, washing machine, and all the food and delicacies they could want.

Four of the 30 women we interviewed had lost an infant, and one had lost a 2-year-old, who drowned playing with a large basin of water. Those deaths were seen as tragic and painful memories. The mothers did not describe the deaths in a monotone or dismiss them as inevitable or an act of mercy that relieved their suffering; rather, they recalled with deep sadness the date, the time, and the cause of their babies' deaths and remembered them by name, saying that Gloria would be 10 today or that Marcos would be 8 years old today had she or he lived.

What has happened in Timbaúba over the past decades is part of a national trend in Brazil. Over the past decade alone, Brazil's fertility rate has decreased from 2.36 to 1.9 children per family – a number that is below the replacement rate and lower than that of the United States. Unlike in China or India, this reproductive revolution occurred without state coercion. It was a voluntary transition, and a rapid one.

A footnote in *Death without Weeping* records the most common requests that people made of me in the 1960s and again in the 1980s: Could I possibly help them obtain false teeth? A pair of eyeglasses? A better antibiotic for a sick older child? But most often I was asked – begged – by women to arrange a clandestine sterilization. In Northeast Brazil, sterilization was always preferable to oral contraceptives, IUDs, and condoms. Reproductive freedom meant having the children you wanted and then "closing down the factory." "A fábrica é fechada!" a woman would boastfully explain, patting her abdomen. Until recently, this was the privilege of the upper middle classes and the wealthy. Today, tubal ligations are openly discussed and arranged. One woman I interviewed, a devout Catholic, gushed that God was good, so good that he had given her a third son, her treasure trove, and at the same time had allowed her the liberty and freedom of a tubal ligation. "Praise to God!" she said. "Amen," I said.

In Brazil, the reproductive revolution is linked to democracy and the coming into political power of President Fernando Henrique Cardoso (1995–2002), aided by his formidable wife, the anthropologist and women's advocate Ruth Cardoso. It was continued by Luiz Inácio Lula da Silva, universally called "Lula," and, since 2011, by his successor, Dilma Rousseff. President Lula's Zero Hunger campaign, though much criticized in the popular media as a kind of political publicity stunt, in fact has supplied basic foodstuffs to the most vulnerable households.

Today, food is abundant on the Alto. Schoolchildren are fed nutritious lunches, fortified with a protein mixture that is prepared as tasty milk shakes. There are food pantries and state and municipal milk distribution programs that are run by women with an extra room in their home. The monthly stipends to poor and single mothers to reward them for keeping their children in school has turned elementary school pupils into valuable household "workers," and literacy has increased for both the children and their mothers, who study at home alongside their children.

When I first went to the Alto in 1964 as a Peace Corps volunteer, it was in the role of a visitadora, a public health community worker. The military dictatorship was suspicious of the program, which mixed health education and immunizations with advocating for water, street lights, and pit latrines as universal entitlements – owed even to those who had "occupied public land" (like the people of the Alto, who had been dispossessed by modernizing sugar plantations and mills). The visitadora program, Brazil's version of Chinese "barefoot doctors," was targeted by the military government as subversive, and the program ended by 1966 in Pernambuco. Many years later, President Cardoso fortified the national healthcare system with a similar program of local "community health agents" who live and work in their micro-communities, visiting at-risk households, identifying crises, diagnosing common symptoms, and intervening to rescue vulnerable infants and toddlers from premature death. In Timbaúba, there are some 120 community health agents, male and female, working in poor micro-communities throughout the municipality, including dispersed rural communities. On the Alto do Cruzeiro, 12 health agents each live and work in a defined area, each responsible for the health and well-being of some 150 families comprising 500 to 600 individuals. The basic requirement for a health worker is to have completed ensino fundamental, the equivalent of primary and middle school. Then, he or she must prepare for a public concurso, a competition based on a rigorous exam.

The community health agent's wage is small, a little more than the Brazilian minimum wage, but still less than US $700 a month for a 40-hour workweek, most of it on foot up and down the hillside "slum," responding to a plethora of medical needs, from diaper rash to an emergency home birth. The agent records all births, deaths, illnesses, and other health problems in the micro-community; refers the sick to health posts, emergency rooms, and hospitals; monitors pregnancies and the health of newborns, the disabled, and the elderly. He or she identifies and reports communicable diseases and acts as a public health and environmental educator. The agent participates in public meetings to shape health policies. Above all, the community health agent is the primary intermediary between poor people and the national healthcare system.

I am convinced that the incredible decline in premature deaths and useless suffering that I witnessed on the Alto is primarily the result of these largely unheralded medical heroes, who rescue mothers and their children in a large town with few doctors and no resident surgeons, pediatricians, and worst of all, obstetricians. A pregnant woman of the Alto suffers today from one of the worst dilemmas and anxieties a person in her condition can face: no certain location to give birth. The only solution at present is to refer women in labor to distant obstetric and maternity wards in public hospitals in Recife, the state capital, a 67-mile drive away. The result can be fatal: at least one woman in the past year was prevented (by holding her legs together) from delivering her baby in an ambulance, and both mother and child died following their arrival at the designated hospital in Recife. For this reason, Alto women and their health agents often choose prearranged cesarian sections well in advance of due dates, even though they know that C-sections are generally not in the best interest of mothers or infants.

Then, beyond the human factor, environmental factors figure in the decline in infant mortality in the shantytowns of Timbaúba and other municipalities in Northeast Brazil. The most significant of these is the result of a simple, basic municipal public health program: the installation of water pipes that today reach nearly all homes with sufficient clean water. It is amazing to observe the transformative potential of material conditions: water = life!

Finally, what about the role of the Catholic Church? The anomaly is that, in a nation where the Catholic Church predominates in the public sphere and abortion is still illegal except in the case of rape or to save a mother's life, family size has dropped so sharply over the last two decades. What is going on? For one thing, Brazilian Catholics are independent, much like Catholics in the United States, going their own way when it comes to women's health and reproductive culture. Others have simply left Catholicism and joined evangelical churches, some of which proclaim their openness to the reproductive rights of women and men. Today, only 60 percent of Brazilians identify as Roman Catholic. In our small sample of 30 women of the Alto, religion – whether Catholic, Protestant, Spiritist, or Afro-Brazilian – did not figure large in their reproductive lives.

The Brazilian Catholic Church is deeply divided. In 2009, the Archbishop of Recife announced the Vatican's excommunication of the doctors and family of a 9-year-old girl who had had an abortion. She had been raped by her stepfather (thus, the abortion was legal), and she was carrying twins – her tiny stature and narrow hips putting her life in jeopardy. After comparing abortion to the Holocaust, Archbishop José Cardoso Sobrinho told the media that the Vatican rejects believers who pick and choose their moral issues. The result was an immediate decline in church attendance throughout the diocese.

While the Brazilian Catholic hierarchy is decidedly conservative, the rural populace, their local clerics, and liberation theologians such as the activist ex-priest Leonardo Boff are open in their interpretations of Catholic spirituality and corporeality. The Jesus that my Catholic friends on the Alto embrace is a sensitive and sentient Son of God, a man of sorrows, to be sure, but also a man of compassion, keenly attuned to simple human needs. The teachings of liberation theology, while condemned by Pope John Paul II, helped dislodge a baroque folk Catholicism in rural Northeast Brazil that envisioned God and the saints as authorizing and blessing the deaths of angel babies.

Padre Orlando, a young priest when I first met him in 1987, distanced himself from the quaint custom of blessing the bodies of dead infants as they were carried to the municipal graveyard in processions led by children. He also invited me and my Brazilian research assistant to give an orientation on family planning to poor Catholic women in the parish hall. When I asked what form of contraception I could teach, he replied, "I'm a celibate priest. How should I know? Teach it all, everything you know." When I reminded him that only the very unpredictable rhythm method was approved by the Vatican, he replied, "Just teach it all, everything you know, and then say, but the Pope only approves the not-so-safe rhythm method."

The people of the Alto do Cruzeiro still face many problems. Drugs, gangs, and death squads have left their ugly mark. Homicides have returned with a vengeance, but they are diffuse and chaotic, the impulsive murders one comes to expect among poor young men – the unemployed, petty thieves, and small-time drug dealers – and between rival gangs. One sees adolescents and young men of the shantytowns, who survived that dangerous first year of life, cut down by bullets and knives at the age of 15 or 17 by local gangs, strongmen, bandidos, and local police in almost equal measure. The old diseases also raise their heads from time to time: schistosomiasis, Chagas disease, tuberculosis, and even cholera.

But the bottom line is that women on the Alto today do not lose their infants. Children go to school rather than to the cane fields, and social cooperatives have taken the place of shadow economies. When mothers are sick or pregnant or a child is ill, they can go to the well-appointed health clinic supported by both state and national funds. There is a safety net, and it is wide, deep, and strong.

Just as we were leaving in mid-June, angry, insurgent crowds were forming in Recife, fed up with political corruption, cronyism, and the extravagant public expenditures in preparation for the 2014 World Cup in Brazil – when the need was for public housing and hospitals. Those taking to the streets were mostly young, urban, working-class, and new middle-class Brazilians. The rural poor were generally not among them. The people of the Alto do Cruzeiro (and, I imagine, in many other communities like it) are strong supporters of the government led by the PT (Partido dos Trabalhadores, or Workers' Party). Under the PT, the government has ended hunger in Pernambuco and has opened family clinics and municipal schools that treat them and their children with respect for the first time in their lives.

The protesters in the streets are among the 40 million Brazilians who were added to the middle class between 2004 and 2010, under the government of President Lula, and whose rising expectations are combustible. When the healthy, literate children of the Alto do Cruzeiro grow up, they may yet join future protests demanding more accountability from their elected officials.

Note

1 For a reflection on the changes that have occurred in Alto do Cruzeiro since the research was first conducted, please see the end of the chapter for an update from 2013.

Chapter 26

Political demography

The banning of abortion in Ceausescu's Romania

Gail Kligman

In Nicolae Ceausescu's Romania, the "marriage" between demographic concerns and nationalist politics turned women's bodies into instruments to be used in the service of the state. The paternalist state exercised its authority partially through the elaboration of a discourse and related set of practices centered on "the family." In that "traditional" Romanian family structure is patriarchal, the state's rhetoric about the family resonated with familiar cultural patterns (see Kligman 1988); the dependency relations created through patriarchal family organization were elevated to the level of the socialist state's "legitimate" rule over its citizens. In this chapter, I explore the relationship between official rhetoric, policy, and everyday practice through an analysis of the politics of reproduction during Ceausescu's reign. Analysis of the politics of reproduction (or *political demography* in regime parlance) serves partially as a focused case study of the relations between the state and its citizens. These policies brought the state directly into its citizens' bodies and their intimate relations. As such, the pronatalist policies may be viewed as indicative of the character of the polity, of how the state conceived of and represented itself. Analysis of the complex relationship between the official discourse about reproduction, the policies that translated this official rhetoric into state practices, and citizens' lived experiences of these policies in Ceausescu's Romania enables us to understand the means by which the regime was perpetuated and by which compliance and complicity were systemically structured. At the same time, analysis of this complex relationship underscores the increasing separation between the official rhetoric of the regime and the average citizen's experience; this growing disjunction ultimately contributed to the regime's downfall.

The former socialist states, driven by command economies, were actively engaged in social engineering. In theory, societal transformation incorporated all levels of life, and the population had to be mobilized accordingly. The "building of socialism"

DOI: 10.4324/9781003398349-30

was predicated on a productionist mentality, the underlying rationale of which was the contribution of each citizen "according to his abilities." In recognition of one of women's "abilities" – childbearing – the socialist state intended to help women enter the economy by providing various forms of social assistance: guaranteed maternity leaves, job security, childcare facilities. These entitlements functioned as positive incentives and were progressive in intention, if not in realization. Although gender equity was ideologically extolled in all the formerly existing socialist states, the progressive legislation regarding women's rights as workers often came into conflict with their obligations as reproducers of the labor force – that is, with their roles as mothers. The resultant relation between state policy and demographic factors bore directly on issues of changing gender relations and underscored the often-contradictory interests of the state and its citizens, especially women. Romanian policy was an "extreme case of the generalized pronatalism" (Teitelbaum and Winter 1985: 100) that, from the mid-1960s, typified the region. Pronatalist policies, aimed at securing an adequate workforce to build socialism, formed part of the modernization strategies of these states.

Following a brief summary of key ideological tenets that contributed to the shaping and implementation of the Ceausescu regime's pronatalist policies, I present an overview of the development of these political-demographic policies, concentrating on their full elaboration in the 1980s. I comment on the human dramas born of the pronatalist policies: illegal abortion, child abandonment, infant AIDS among abandoned "surplus" babies, and international adoption. I next discuss the politics of reproduction in post-Ceausescu Romania. Between 1989 and 1992, two phases of policy formulation related to reproduction may be distinguished. These phases reflect the gradual formation of effective institutional procedures meant to recognize and protect the rights of individuals in society. They are indicative of the fundamental changes taking place in Romania, however traumatically.

The pronatalist policies

Under Ceausescu's rule, the Romanian state increasingly intruded into its citizens' intimate lives to ensure "normal demographic growth" of the labor force and the "triumph of socialism" (Resolution of the Executive Political Committee of the Central Committee of the Romanian Communist Party, March 1984). The Constitution and the Family Code laid the groundwork for active political-educational campaigns as well as for the implementation of positive incentives, augmented over the years by an increasing number of coercive measures (see, for example, Trebici 1988). The Constitution of the Socialist Republic of Romania (SRR) granted all citizens the right to work, as well as equal pay for equal work. Measures for protection and safety at work and special measures for the protection of women's and youth's work were also established by law.

The state assumed legal responsibility for the family as a way to underscore the family's significance in the development of the "new socialist person." The family's primary contributions to the building of socialism were in the realms of reproduction of the population (and, by implication, of the workforce) and of education, with respect to the "spiritual reproduction of society" and the social integration of youth into society (see Liciu

1975: 10). Marriage into which partners entered on the basis of "free consent" was the legal foundation of the family. Law 4/1953, Article 1, of the Family Code read:

> In the SRR, the state shall protect marriage and the family; it shall support the development and strengthening of the family through economic and social measures. The state shall defend the interests of mother and child and shall display a special care for the upbringing and education of the young generation.

In the state-controlled public sphere, women, like minorities, were represented in positions of authority. An operative quota system paid lip service to the participation of women and minorities (Hungarians, Germans, Gypsies, Jews) in leadership roles. Access to power was stratified. A few women entered the ranks of the Central Committee, such as Elena Ceausescu and Lina Ciobanu, who – as workers – respectively represented chemistry and the textile industry; most women, however, generally filled positions in cultural or educational institutions or in light industry – that is, positions deemed suitable for women. Women in the labor force tended to occupy lower-status, more poorly paid job niches. Moreover, the early emphasis on heavy industrialization as a modernizing strategy often led to the feminization of agriculture. Agricultural labor was more attractive to women because of flexible work schedules. They could both work and tend to families; they were not tied strictly to the clock of industrial production.

Women's participation in the national economy and society as workers and mothers created the classic double and triple burdens: working in the state sphere, doing housework, and raising children. (These burdens increased over the decades as the double burdens of the 1960s and 1970s became triple burdens in the 1980s, when childbearing became officially obligatory.) Occupational "advances" were not coupled with the production of time-saving household devices or with any emphasis on changing gender roles within the family.

The initial pronatalist measures were instituted in 1966. The birth rate in Romania had fallen to 14.3 per 1,000 from a 1960 rate of 19.1 per 1,000 (*Anuarul statistic al Romaniei* 1990: 67). This decline was attributed, in part, to the liberal law that had legalized abortion and made it readily accessible. To remedy this situation, Law 770/1966 was introduced. This law prohibited abortions except if the pregnancy endangered the life of the woman and no other means could be taken to save it, a hereditary disease was involved, the pregnancy was the result of rape, the woman was 45 years of age or over, or she had delivered and reared four children. The imposition of this law caught Romanians by surprise; in 1967, the birth rate dramatically shot up to 27.4. (There were 527,764 live births in 1967 compared with 273,678 in 1966; *Anuarul statistic al Romaniei* 1990: 66.) The antiabortion law was accompanied by a series of progressive measures meant to encourage women to bear children, including financial allowances for families and child-support benefits (Decree 410/1985),[1] maternity leaves and work protection (Decision 880/1965, Articles 13–17; maternity leaves were usually 52 days prior to delivery and 60 days thereafter, these being interchangeable), protection for working women and children (the Work Code, especially section VII), access to medical attention throughout all phases of pregnancy and to medical care for mother and child (Law 3/1978; Decree 246/1958), and access to childcare facilities (Decree 65/1982). Similar incentives existed throughout Eastern Europe, although their particulars varied. Romania followed the spirit of this progressive legislation but had the least adequate provisions. Ultimately, as shall be seen, Ceausescu added coercive measures unparalleled elsewhere.

As in other spheres of production, mothers who bore many children were honored as "heroes of socialist labor," for which they were awarded decorations and minor privileges. To this end, State Council Decree 190/1977, Article 13, announced that:

- Women who delivered and reared ten or more children were awarded the title of "Heroine Mother."
- Women who had delivered and reared nine children received the first-class "Order of Maternal Glory"; those with eight children, the second-class "Order of Maternal Glory"; those with seven, the third-class award in this category.
- Women who had delivered and reared six children were awarded the first-class "Medal of Maternity"; those with five, the second-class "Medal of Maternity."

The stipulations of this decree must be read carefully. A woman who bore ten children did not automatically qualify for the honor of Heroine Mother. She also had to have reared them. Given the high incidence of infant mortality, especially in rural areas, this honor was difficult to achieve. Wording is also significant in the 1966 abortion law, which states that women must have given birth to "four children and have them in her care." Children acquired through second marriages or adoption did not qualify women for medals or abortions.

The pronatalist policies introduced by Ceausescu in the 1960s were a mild version of what was later to become a draconian policy, and in the 1970s, the minimum age for abortion was lowered to 40 (Article 2, Instructions 27/1974). In these earlier years, Ceausescu emphasized the role of women in politics, the economy, and society. In 1971, he began promoting his wife, Elena. To legitimize this first step in the creation of "dynastic socialism,"[2] a political-educational campaign glorifying women in the labor force as workers and as mothers of future workers was inaugurated. Ceausescu opposed gender discrimination:

If we speak about the creation of conditions of full equality between the sexes, this means that we must treat all people not as men and women, but in their qualities as Party members, as citizens, for which they are exclusively judged according to their work contributions.

(Address to the Plenary Session of the Central Committee of the Romanian Communist Party 1973)

He also began stressing that

an obligation of national interest is the protection and consolidation of the family, the development of a corresponding consciousness about the growth of an increased number of children, and the formation of healthy and robust generations profoundly devoted to the cause of socialism; in this realm women have a distinguished role and a noble mission.

(Decisions of the Plenary Session of the Central Committee of the Romanian Communist Party 1973)

Ceausescu superficially recognized the stress created for women by their roles as mothers and workers. In 1978, he urged that particular attention be paid to the solving of these problems through the construction of childcare facilities, the production and distribution of household appliances, and the sale of semi-prepared foods, so that women could use their time efficiently in their many pursuits. However, these exhortations were not fulfilled, and women experienced an inverse relationship between Ceausescu's official statements about their lives and the demands of their everyday reality.

Propaganda notwithstanding, by 1983, the birth rate had again declined to the 1966 level, although there had long been no pro-choice law to which this decline could be attributed, as was the case in 1966. Romanians had managed as best as they could in an environment in which contraceptives were unavailable through legal means[3]; pregnancies were avoided through illegal abortions, abstinence, and coitus interruptus. The decline in the birth rate coincided with a steady deterioration in the material conditions of everyday life. In the interest of national self-determination, Ceausescu had decided that Romania's outstanding foreign debts would be repaid – at enormous cost to the quality of life. Production was targeted for export. By 1984, winters were endured with little heat or electricity; food staples were rationed.

The Orwellian reproductive politics that inspired Margaret Atwood's novel *The Handmaid's Tale* and a Romanian national tragedy were unveiled on International Women's Day, March 8, 1984: Ceausescu saluted women's importance to the nation by again exhorting them to bear four or more children in order to fulfill the national goal of increasing the population from 22.6 to 25 million by 1990. As was inevitably the case, the popular response could be gauged by jokes. One noted that people were willing to agree to the four-child plan as long as it was applied consistently with state production policy: keep one child and export the other three. This joke also referred to the unpublicized state trade in babies for hard currency. Also in 1984, Ana Blandiana, a revered poet (and now a fêted member of the Civic Alliance social movement), wrote a poem, "Children's Crusade," criticizing such brutal policies as the legal obligation of women to bear four (later five) children:

> An entire population
> as yet unborn
> but condemned to birth
> lined up in rows, before birth
> fetus beside fetus
> An entire population
> which doesn't see, doesn't hear, doesn't understand
> but develops
> through the convulsed bodies of women
> through the blood of mothers
> Unasked.
>
> *Amfiteatru*

Blandiana's poignant words presaged the death sentence unwanted children were later to face as a consequence of the AIDS-infected transfusions given routinely to children in orphanages. Statistics on this situation were deliberately suppressed. Nonetheless, pronatalist propaganda flourished. Demographers, doctors, and women's and youth organizations were solicited to participate in the propaganda campaign. Sex education was stepped up, including premarital health counseling and checkups, lectures, and films at work locales. Competitions about "health knowledge" were promoted in magazines such as *Sanatatea*. Ideological bombast was cemented by threats of punishment which ensured widespread complicity. The women's magazine *Femeia*, found in all the cultural centers across the country, soon ceased being a typical magazine for women. By the 1980s, articles about household concerns were limited, while those about women in the workforce had increased. The ads for clothing and household items characteristic of the 1960s had been replaced by pictures of the ruling couple, his speeches, and "patriotic" poems or stories from the national cultural festival, *Cintarea Romaniei*, the Singing of Romania. A new section on children, "the supreme joy, supreme responsibility," was introduced in 1987, in the interest again of increasing the birth rate. Motherhood – regardless of marital status – was the message.

Morality tales about good and bad mothers abounded. A young single mother wanting to give her child up for adoption was chastised in the response to her letter of inquiry (of the "Dear Abby" sort). What kind of young woman was she? She had a job, was healthy, with her whole future ahead of her. She herself had been left motherless at the age of 13. The thrust of the argument was that a

> single mother is not to be condemned; a mother will always be respected. Perhaps for a while you won't be able to offer your child the maximum, but be certain that no one in this world can offer what you can [mother love].
>
> (*Femeia* 12, 1988: 13)

Educators and activists received all manner of booklets about the relationship between health and demography, about marital harmony, care of infants and children, and the consequences of abortion. For example, one publication of the Health Ministry's Institute of Hygiene and Public Health included topics such as the methods and contents of health education in relation to the problems of demography; protection of mothers, children, and youth (including the topic of reproduction and problems related to it: fecundity, pregnancy, birth); elementary notions of infant care and childcare; and venereal diseases. A normal, regulated sexual life, with "normal relations of 3–4 weekly," was recommended.

The virtues of motherhood were extolled: "motherhood is itself the meaning of women's lives" was a ubiquitous formula. Articles in the state paper *Scinteia* instructed the population about the patriotic virtues of large families and the noble mission of mothers. For example, the headline for March 9, 1984, read: "Goals of extraordinary significance for the nation's future are contained in Comrade N. Ceausescu's address: Families with many children – a law of life and of human fulfillment, a noble patriotic duty." This theme was reiterated incessantly for the rest of the decade. A series of articles titled "A House with Many Children" (January to April 1986) highlighted individual families and whole villages as "heroes of socialist labor." Other headlines read: "Demographic growth – an exalted responsibility of the entire society" (April 3, 1984); "For the eternity of families, for the vigor of our people" (March 16, 1984); "The joy of being a mother" (June 4, 1987). Images of the happy maternal–child relation abounded.

Women were differentially affected by the pronatalist policies. Urban women with higher education managed to acquire black market contraceptives or to arrange for illegal abortions performed by medical personnel. Others, such as factory workers, bore the costs, material and bodily, of these policies. It is assumed that rural women were less radically affected because of the influences of religion and local habits. Although these assumptions may generally be true, there was considerable regional variation. Many rural women participated in the seasonal migrant labor force and, as a consequence, were introduced to different practices. Some of them married outside their own region and had abortions that they might not have had in their natal villages. In an unsuccessful bid, the regime attempted to get rural women to sign contracts to produce four children in the same way that peasants signed contracts with the state to meet production quotas. "Women as cows" were castigated by village women, who questioned what would happen if they were unable to have a third or fourth child. Would they be sent to prison? What if a child died? Would they be required to produce another? The "what-ifs" were recounted with outrage. These same women, and their families, often expressed a desire to have more children, although they were unable to support those they already had.

Also, and again undocumented by hard data, responses to these policies were differentiated by ethnicity as well as class. Physicians repeatedly pointed out that Hungarian Romanians, for example, had greater access to black market contraceptives through their kin or ethnic networks. (Hungary was a source for contraceptives.) Moreover, many medical practitioners mentioned that Hungarian Romanians drew upon a different cultural and educational heritage, the relation between educational level and family planning being relevant. In 1983–1984, as the pronatalist campaign intensified, and in keeping with the ideological line, a Hungarian Romanian radio station offered a program on stimulating fertility. The editors of this show and of other Hungarian radio programs were informed that there was no need for them to offer this information. Although the pronatalist policies were formally applicable to all, there seems to have been an unstated preference to increase the birth rate of Romanians, but not "hyphenated" Romanians, such as Hungarians.[4]

Demographers also quietly called attention to the need to bring under control the birth rates of the Gypsy population. "Their exaggerated reproduction is determined especially by their lifestyle, the degree of their social and cultural backwardness."[5] The Gypsy natality rate created concern among Romanians, who pointed out derogatorily that Gypsies "multiply like rabbits," like people in the developing world, while the "European" birth rate – such as that of Romanians and Hungarian Romanians – mirrored West European trends (zero or declining population growth; this concern has been heightened throughout Europe). It is believed that most Gypsy women, in accordance with cultural beliefs, do not practice abortion, although this is not considered true for assimilated, urban middle-class Gypsies. It seems that, at the end of the 1970s, Gypsy women, regardless of their age or the number of children in their care, could get abortions in Arad, a city in Transylvania; whether this was a local initiative or a general policy remains unverified. In any event, the politics of reproduction in Romania had hidden dimensions to it: stringent measures could be more leniently applied in the case of ethnic "others."

When it became obvious in 1983 that the birth rate was not increasing despite the pronatalist policies already in effect, the regime resorted to a more determined strategy: coercion. On December 26, 1985, a stringent antiabortion law was passed. The age at which women became eligible for legal abortions was again raised to the 1966 limit of 45; the number of children "delivered and under her care" was increased to five. Also, on this day, another pronatalist measure (originally signed into law in 1977) was modified, increasing the monthly "contributions of childless persons" – that is, all persons over the age of 25, regardless of sex or marital status, who were childless. The sums subtracted from monthly wages varied, depending on the sector of the state economy in which one worked, those in agriculture being taxed somewhat less. To avoid this monthly fee, some quit their jobs in state enterprises to work as migrant laborers – a little-discussed adaptive strategy. One way or another, reproductive and abortion statistics had become political tools to discipline the population and were used accordingly.

The altered antiabortion law, and the "instructions" regarding its application, included provisions to punish both physicians and women. In an attempt to secure the obedience of the medical profession, medical practitioners were held responsible for rectifying the birth rate crisis, in part associated with alarming abortion and infant mortality statistics (discussed later). Health practitioners were assumed to assist in illegal abortions for personal gain. They became subject to imprisonment for any infraction of the abortion law, including failure to notify the prosecutor's office. Such notification alerted that office to cases for which doctors could be held responsible. Of course, prosecutors also had wives, sisters, and daughters who might need abortions, and so not all acted in strict accordance with the law. Others were paid off by concerned, and profit-interested, physicians. Given the penal sanctions for doctors, abortion costs were from 2,000 to 10,000 lei (then approximately $160 to $830, with basic salaries ranging between 1,500 and 2,400 lei per month).

Medical personnel were disciplined by various means, depending on their relations with legal authorities, co-workers, and immediate superiors, as well as the nature of the legal infraction. Publications such as *Muncitorul Sanitar* (*The Health Worker*) regularly printed moralizing articles about professional responsibility. (These were similar in form to the articles in women's magazines about good and bad mothers, discussed earlier. Official rhetoric was disseminated homologously in all realms.) Such articles reported cases that had come before a Disciplinary Board for Health Personnel, which existed in each administrative region of the country. These boards functioned as public, institutionalized confessionals through which medical practitioners were disciplined.

From time to time, there were show trials of doctors, midwives, and backroom-abortion practitioners. In one case, several women were convicted of having performed illegal abortions or of having been involved in arranging them. The abortionist received 500 lei plus a package of coffee and dried soup for her efforts. Her sentence was lessened, however, because of her lack of prior convictions as well as her "sincerity" (cooperation with the police). Generally, those who informed on others were not sent to prison. Their sentences often made it possible for them to remain at work on carefully scrutinized probation. Those who did not cooperate, however, received prison sentences. If they were women, they frequently left children motherless at home – hardly the "ideal conditions" for their upbringing that the Romanian state claimed to have created.

The intrusion of the state into the intimacy of the body was inescapable. In 1986, Ceausescu introduced a campaign – unique in the history of Romanian medicine – to analyze the health of the population, particularly that of women between the ages of 16 and 45, the years when most women are fertile. These exams, regardless of officially professed intentions, subjected women of childbearing age to state control of their reproductive lives. Women working in or attending state institutions were given at least annual, and in some places, trimesterly, gynecological exams to verify that their reproductive health was satisfactory.[6] If, in such a routine exam, a woman was discovered to be pregnant, the development of her pregnancy could then be closely followed, lest there be any untoward mishap. Women who had already had abortions (legal or not) were carefully watched for "preventive reasons" and, in some cases, were confined to a hospital. For women living in rural areas, local medical personnel were expected to follow up with home visits (a practice resented by all involved).

Much was written in the official press about these exams, and the language of these stories was telling. According to them, the intent of obtaining medical histories about women of childbearing age was to have "in evidence . . . all of the elements that might negatively influence the normal evolution of a pregnancy." While pre- and postnatal care may be commendable under normal circumstances, in the context of a coercive pronatalist policy, such prenatal care served to police the body, with doctors put in the position of aiding and abetting the interests of the state. Women were not always aware that they were deliberately being checked to see whether they were pregnant; annual exams were considered routine, another obligation. One doctor confided that among her staff, some took pleasure in "finding" a pregnant woman. Others, who were more compassionate, did not.

Despite the consequences for nonconformity with the law, many doctors – of all ranks in the party hierarchy (most doctors being party members) – became adept at manipulating both the official rhetoric and statistics. Strikingly, most people I queried offered praise for the attempts doctors made to assist women and families during these harsh years. Many doctors tried to "hide" a woman's pregnancy if she indicated that she, or she and her husband, did not want the child. As one doctor remarked: "If a woman adamantly was against having a child, there was nothing you could do about it. She would risk dying rather than bear the child. So we tried to help." Various ailments such as measles, recurrent fevers, hepatitis, tuberculosis, syphilis, malignant tumors, and diabetes qualified a woman for a legal abortion. Doctors took advantage of this rule as much as possible. Similarly, taking certain medications that are counter-indicated during pregnancy (chemotherapy, antimalarial drugs, anticonvulsants) could be used as the excuse for an abortion. Given the dearth of medications available in Romania, this excuse was not easily manufactured. Nonetheless, whenever possible, most doctors seem to have done what they could to accommodate a woman's "choice."

According to a document stamped *secret de serviciu* that circulated internally in the health ministry in 1988, the number of abortions increased between 1979 and 1988, with the exception of a decline in 1948–1985 (Roznatovschi 1989). A similar drop in abortion rates occurred following the original 1966 antiabortion law. Citizens needed time to learn to adapt to the intensified pronatalist campaign. The increase in abortions coincided with the previously mentioned deterioration in the conditions of everyday life. Families were unable to feed the children they had yet were required by law to have more.

In many cases, unwanted children were abandoned to the care of the paternalist state that had demanded them. That "care," best described as systematic neglect, resulted in institutionalization of the innocent, the rise of infant AIDS, and international trafficking in babies and children through adoption. Abandoning a child was the consequence of despair combined with dependence on the state for the basics of life. Centralized production and distribution limited what families had to eat. (The rise of the second economy paralleled that of illegal abortions; these were the means through which people managed their everyday lives.) These material and psychological conditions make it possible to understand why parents gave up their children. Traditionally, peasant families unable to support another child would ask a relative to raise one; others were adopted by child-less couples. During the Ceausescu years, some mothers left their infants in the hospital; others left them at orphanages or in other places where they were likely to be found. (I have not heard of infanticide as a common practice, although punitive statutes exist in the legal code – for example, Article 177.) Some parents relied upon state institutions as a temporary residence for children; they then attempted to retrieve them later when they were able to support them at home. This "pawnshop" strategy often succeeded; in other cases, parents were unable to locate the children they had given up. Only after the fall of the regime did they – and the rest of the world – learn why: institutionalized children often died of neglect or were put up for adoption.

Women who did not comply with the pronatalist law resorted to illegal abortions. Those privileged with connections and the means could bribe medical practitioners. Those without sought the assistance of less-qualified abortionists or used the varied remedies that abortion lore and popular practice offered them. When the state punished physicians who, for humanistic or economic reasons, performed illegal abortions, the increase in maternal deaths or deformities due to nonmedically performed abortions was assured. Between 1965 and 1989, 9,452 women died because of complications arising from illegal abortions. As Mezei notes:

> The liberation of abortion in January 1990 proves yet again the positive dependent relation between delegalization of abortion and the rise of maternal mortality rates. If, following the chronology of events, 1989 represents the year with the most elevated maternal mortality figures [545] . . . for 1990, 181 cases of maternal deaths due to illegal abortions were registered, [numbers] that had not been seen since 1968.
>
> (1991: 4)

Among those who died were women who already had three or four children but who were unable to deal with yet another cold, hungry child. Thus, the population of orphaned or abandoned children necessarily increased.[7] So great were the traumas associated with the pronatalist policies that months after the legalization of abortion, the Ministry of Health still received files of mothers who had died as a result of illegal abortions; some of these were mothers of five children who would have been eligible for legal abortions even during the Ceausescu regime.

The heartbreaking and chilling irony of Ceausescu's pronatalist policies was that illegal abortion became the predominant contraceptive method. According to Ministry of Health statistics, the greatest number of abortions – 60.1 percent – were "incomplete abortions" recorded upon the arrival of a woman at the hospital for emergency treatment.[8] The decision to abort (made by the woman alone or with her husband's consent) was a rational decision based on the real conditions of daily life. Insensitive to the realities of the lives of most Romanian citizens, the regime clung to its ideological visions of everyday productive – and reproductive – life. A stringent pronatalist policy was enforced through a series of coercive legal measures even as data on the rise of infant AIDS were suppressed and as the recording of births was delayed so that infant mortality rates would not appear too large. The consequences of legislating reproduction without regard for the material conditions of daily life meant that many women, unable to fulfill their "patriotic duties" and "noble mission" in life, gave up their lives – and, frequently, those of their children – in the service of the state.

Post-Ceausescu abortion and international adoption

The "revolution" of December 1989 liberated most women's bodies from the grip of the centralized state. The day after the execution of Ceausescu, abortion became fully legal in Romania. Legalization simultaneously kept abortion the preferred method of fertility control, other means being generally unavailable.[9] Urban and rural women alike expressed gratitude for the legalization of abortion. The fear of becoming pregnant had dramatically colored the sexual lives of women (especially), married or not. This fear compounded the basic culture of fear that had pervaded everyday life. The right to abortion granted women in Romania basic, if minimal, control over their lives again. Abortion, in this context, was understood as a fundamental aspect of the right to self-determination being articulated by republics and nationalities demanding their independence, as well as by ethnic groups clamoring for recognition and respect. Abortion was assumed to be an essential ingredient of democratic practice.

As a consequence of legalization, by the summer of 1990, the principal hospitals in Bucharest were each reporting 70 to 100 abortions daily. This rate seemed potentially problematic for women's health and future demographic trends. However, health officials and physicians (personal communications) pointed out that the legalization of abortion had quickly alleviated one of the problems from the past; they also suggested that there were more urgent concerns than these, given that the country was in total disorder. In addition to finding ways to finance the development and distribution of contraceptives, the country desperately needed funds for AIDS research, treatment, and education.

By summer 1991, the skyrocketing number of abortions made attention to this issue imperative. The ratio of abortions to live births was reported at 3 to 1. (At the same time, the marked decrease in maternal mortality recorded for 1990 continued. The birth rate also declined.)[10] Doctors at one of the largest maternity wards in Bucharest stated that they had performed as many as three abortions for the same woman during the course of the year. In response, the government began to address the need for family planning and sex education. Several nongovernmental associations (NGOs) established soon after 1989 had already become active, although with limited means. NGOs hoped to maintain their politically independent identities. However, in the heightened political atmosphere in Romania, doing so has not been easy. One of the primary tasks for health workers is to educate the population. Because television remains essentially state-controlled and the majority of newspapers have political agendas, access to, and use of, the mass media for education is fraught with problems that have subordinated health issues to political struggles. NGO workers have expressed concern that governmental institutions will co-opt their efforts. At present, both governmental and nongovernmental organizations depend on international assistance, financial and instructional. As many of the doctors with whom I spoke noted, it is difficult for them to train specialists in family planning when they themselves are not trained. Obviously, in view of the former policies, physicians and others lacked access to such training.

Furthermore, years of propaganda against the use of contraceptives must be combated. Thus far, the Ministry of Education – unlike the Ministry of Health – has not been overly receptive to governmental or nongovernmental proposals to introduce health and sex education into the high school curriculum. There has been more interest at the university level. The state-controlled media have also been reticent to engage in discussion of these issues, which are vital to the nation's health.

A similar mentality exists toward AIDS: ignore or downplay its importance. Some Romanian physicians insisted that AIDS was not a real problem in their country, claiming that the epidemic among children who received transfusions was contained within that population. By 1992, 1,557 cases of AIDS had been recorded. AIDS is likely to be on the rise because of poor hygiene in hospitals, increased drug traffic and usage, and increased prostitution without "safe sex" practices. Married women with children often become prostitutes with the full consent of their husbands so that they can obtain hard currency and increase household cash flow. One doctor interviewed who was concerned about the state of public health in Romania pointed out: "Here, people do not have respect for their own bodies." He attributed much of this attitude to the destructive effects of the former regime.

Without a concerted campaign to educate the population (including medical practitioners) about reproductive health, some physicians fear that women's health, in particular, will continue to be at risk. Most of the women factory workers I interviewed informally in 1990 mentioned often that their husbands would object to the use of contraceptives even if they were more readily available. In addition, although condoms are obtainable from tobacco shops, in general, birth control devices and pills have to be obtained from pharmacies, hospital clinics, and some private medical practitioners. As several young gynecologists remarked, "people associate hospitals with illness. They will not come to the hospital to get contraceptives. It's impractical!" (This attitude also points to the problems of the medicalization of family planning. See Hord et al. 1991: 237–238.) Thus, for the immediate future, abortion will remain the primary method. Women of all ages wait in endless lines for abortions performed in factory-like conditions.

In an attempt to discourage women from having abortions, the hospital price was raised from 30 to 500 lei (500 lei was equivalent to about $2.50 in the summer of 1991). Obstetrician-gynecologists expressed concern that raising the price would encourage poor women to seek cheaper abortions done by nonmedically qualified persons, thereby repeating the problems of the past. Well-to-do women were already going to doctors in private practice, where prices are significantly higher, in exchange for privacy, personal attention, and more sterile conditions. At the same time, these physicians emphasized that the current situation has to be changed; raising the price of an abortion, increasing contraceptive availability, and introducing a multifaceted educational campaign were all considered necessary. Unfortunately, it is easier to adjust prices upward than to introduce family planning and sex education or to assure the production and distribution of contraceptives. Thus, women's health, especially among the poor and less educated, remains particularly vulnerable.

The vulnerability of women and children also emerged in another context that is only partially the direct result of Ceausescu's pronatalist policies: the international adoption of Romanian children.[11] During the later years of the regime, Ceausescu authorized limited foreign adoption of Romanian babies for hard currency. This little-publicized practice was a facet of the "commerce in human flesh" that usually enabled Jews and Germans to be "bought" out of Romania. (Hungarians wanting to immigrate to Hungary were not so fortunate, the *forint* not having been convertible to hard currency.) Children began to figure among Romania's export goods, in direct contradiction to the stated ideological goals of the pronatalist policies.

When the regime fell and the plight of Romania's orphans surfaced, international humanitarian groups moved in to help. Many institutions and individuals contributed greatly to alleviating the pain of these children.[12] As it became known that not all the children incarcerated in orphanages were "irrecoverable" or were the victims of the infant AIDS epidemic, foreigners journeyed to Romania with hopes of adopting children.

As word spread in the international community of persons wanting to adopt, Romania became an adoption hot-spot. In early 1990, to deal with the growing number of adoptions, the Romanian government formed the National Adoption Commission. Among its tasks was coordination of data about available institutionalized children. However, lack of an adequate staff or a computerized information system led to bureaucratic inefficiency. Inadvertently, rather than facilitate the adoption process, creation of the commission encouraged expansion of the private market in adoptions, or "baby trading."

Gradually, as different channels for adoption developed, the emotional rhetoric about the humanitarian rescue of children from abysmal conditions in the orphanages lost its force. In its stead, a more generalized rhetoric emerged about saving children from the difficult living conditions in Romania and giving them the opportunity for a better life in the West. By July 1991, most children no longer came from the orphanages but were acquired through private connections, a fact usually overlooked in the numerous media accounts about the baby trade in Romania. According to US consular representatives, most of these children were Gypsies, or Roma. Though they are notably dark-skinned by Romanian standards, Westerners do not generally consider them markedly different in appearance.[13] Given that prejudice against the Gypsies in Romania is unlikely to be eliminated in the near future, adoption was thought to provide a humanitarian road out for some of these children, whose chances for productive lives would otherwise be slim. Many Romanians viewed the exodus of adopted Gypsy children as a legitimate means to rid the country of them at the expense of foreigners; there are others who resented the squandering of Western altruism and resources on Gypsies.

For Westerners, opting for the private adoption process was faster than going through official bureaucratic procedures; it was also more expensive, arbitrary, and led to coercion and corruption. The victims of this process were not only, as is often implied in Western media coverage, foreign adoptive parents but also poor or single (or both) Romanian mothers, many of whom were Gypsies. Some poor women considered their bearing of children to be little more than the means of production that yielded a valuable commodity. In these cases, private adoptions contributed to the exploitation of women's reproductive labor. Husbands, brothers, and parents found compensation for their "public shame" in the money so readily obtained. With it, they purchased refrigerators, video recorders, and the like, or finished building or furnishing their homes. Given the sharp rise in prices in Romania, increasing unemployment, and depressed wages, it is not difficult to explain why people were tempted to sell their own children, as well as those of other people. Dealing in babies is also a lucrative business for intermediaries, bureaucrats, and lawyers, who may be bribed to falsify papers and speed up the process.

Hence, for all the legitimate adoptions, there were many that were not legitimate. Coercion of Romanian mothers happened in various ways. By law, a mother had 15 days in which to change her mind about consenting to the adoption of her child. When a mother had a change of heart (or conscience), her decision was not necessarily accepted graciously by the adoptive parents or their negotiators, regardless of the law. One Romanian woman was told by the translator that she would be responsible for the costs accrued during the stay of the American adoptive parents (personal communication from an official investigator of this case). No Romanian could conceivably have covered such expenses. Whether the Americans knew of the translator's methods is not known. That the translator had much to lose if the adoption fell through *is* known, as is the fact that the American woman intended to appeal to her congressman. Most adoptive parents in such situations chose not to know about possible coercion, even though they may have intuited that something was amiss. Because of the language barrier, lack of knowledge was easy to rationalize. To have allowed themselves to know meant that they would have had to deal with their own emotional pain at the loss of a child with whom they might already have bonded. It was (and is) easier to believe, whatever the temporary experience, that adoption was simply for the good of the child, who would thereby escape from the hardships of Romania.

Since the fall of the Ceausescu regime, the Romanian government has embraced measures that suggest at least a minimal recognition of the fundamental significance of respecting citizens' rights. To be sure, these measures have been noticeably inadequate, particularly in the realm of ethnic rights. Nonetheless, in the midst of traumatic change, there has been some movement to redress certain of the dehumanizing policies of the past. Hence, the legalization of abortion in 1990 may be considered a necessary response to a dramatic situation fostered by the stringent political-demographic policies. At the same time, the legalization of abortion was not a policy decision made with socioeconomic and demographic aims, or long-term trends, in mind. The formation of the National Adoption Commission was similarly a practical response to circumstances – in this case, to the growing number of foreign adoptive parents. While the institutionalization of adoption procedures at that time may have been well-intentioned, it was not carefully planned, and it inadvertently contributed to the expansion of the private adoption market. Indeed, the systemic and societal confusion generated by the fall of the Ceausescu regime did not initially lead to effective policy formulation in the realm of family-related issues. This first phase of policy formulation was, in actuality, characterized by the lack of effective policy formulation and implementation.

On July 16, 1991, President Ion Iliescu signed a new adoption law meant to stop the Romanian baby trade; adoption would henceforth be done through institutional channels, thereby removing the private profit motives of all involved.[14] Among the law's provisions is the necessary institutionalization of orphaned children. This provision is meant to prevent the sale of children and to determine the legal status of children as orphans. (Children must be orphaned or abandoned; if they are under the care of a parent, then they are not legally adoptable.) Children must reside in an orphanage for six months, during which time the natal parents may change their minds or, if possible, adoptive parents may be found among Romanian citizens.[15] Only after that are foreigners legally able to adopt Romanian children.

The adoption law should be applauded for its attempt to apply the rule of law operative elsewhere in Europe. The politics of reproduction in Romania are now different from the situation in the Ceausescu period. Under Ceausescu's rule, the masses were forced to reproduce in the service of the state. Women's reproductive lives and human rights were blatantly exploited. Today, as Romania struggles with the "transition" and as Romanian society becomes more clearly class-differentiated, those who were most vulnerable – poor and single women – have often been forced to reproduce in the service of market demands. The adoption law has helped diminish one source of abuse suffered by those women coerced into giving up their children.[16]

Moreover, this law was an important step toward the recognition and protection of citizens' rights, especially those of women and children. The political-demographic policies of the Ceausescu regime contributed significantly to the social atomization and dehumanization that remain a tragic legacy. Women's bodies were glorified as the machines that produced the future workers of the state. Celebrated in public political rhetoric, women were overwhelmed by the exigencies of daily life. Their identities as workers and mothers were ideologically dictated, but the conditions of everyday life did not make such identities attractive. The institutionalized violence of the state against its citizens resulted in the denial of women's rights in particular. The state's violence against its citizens was bolstered by a web of interdependent practices that engaged most people in the prescribed practices of the state: doctors were expected to perform gynecological exams; adults without children were taxed; those who had had an abortion were manipulated into becoming police informants. Men's and women's sexual relations were intimately affected, at great psychological cost to the population. Fertility control was proclaimed to be the right of the state, not of women or families. The loss of life (for women and children) due to illegal abortions was evidence of societal despair and increasing dehumanization. The abandonment of children to the "care" of the paternalist state's orphanages was yet another indicator of the extremely deteriorated conditions that made the upbringing of children next to impossible for most citizens of Romania.

By 1991, life in Romania had gradually acquired more routine; the government began to function somewhat more smoothly. The Ministries of Health, Labor, and Education – which were important for the concerns addressed here: reproduction, health, and welfare – each turned to the details of restructuring; what may be viewed as the second phase of policymaking began. Foreign agencies and individuals continued to offer needed and welcome assistance, particularly with respect to scientific exchange about AIDS (testing, research, education) and problems related to the orphanages. Diverse specialists came to train Romanians to care for the handicapped and to teach Romanian health professionals about family planning. All these efforts, combined with the passage of the adoption law, have pointed to a recognition that the state must participate responsibly in the protection of its citizens' rights and well-being. To what extent it shall do so remains to be seen.

Implications for reproductive policy

Romania's experience in the realm of reproductive health can guide policymakers, health administrators, and reproductive health professionals throughout the world.

> At a time when reproductive rights are increasingly threatened by conservative forces throughout central and eastern Europe and other parts of the world, the tragic elements of Romania's reproductive health experience under Ceausescu and the country's struggle to reverse that grim legacy can serve as a guide for health care professionals everywhere.
>
> (Hord et al. 1991: 238–239)

Restrictive reproductive legislation is on the agenda throughout Eastern Europe, with the notable – and understandable – exception of Romania. Similar legislation is being considered and contested in the United States, as well as elsewhere. Here, I wish to stress that the Romanian case must not be categorized as specific to the evils of the Ceausescu regime or of Communism. This study enables us to focus on the social implications and human costs of restrictive reproductive legislation and policies, especially as they affect the lives of women and children.

The effects of banning abortion transcend political or religious interests. When abortion is criminalized, women resort to illegal abortions; that is a comparative as well as historical fact. Banning abortions does not stop women from having them; it simply makes abortion "invisible." Prohibiting abortion – as has always been the case – forces abortion underground and makes it the privilege of the wealthy, while further disenfranchising poor women, who generally bear the brunt of such policies. For poor women, illegal abortions are typically done by unqualified practitioners – the woman herself, back-room abortionists – and result in increased maternal deaths as well as maternal and fetal physical deformities. In Romania, the masses were poor. The tragic consequences have been detailed earlier.

Again, these consequences are specific neither to Communism nor to Ceausescuism. Indeed, these consequences suggest that the Romanian case must be borne in mind by those who would ban abortion in the United States. If, as James Madison understood, a test of democracy lies in its treatment of society's most vulnerable members, among whom are women and children, then democracy in the late twentieth-century United States (and elsewhere) may fail.

Discussion questions

1. In what ways did Romanian policies turn women's bodies into instruments to be used in the service of the state?
2. What measures did the state take to make childbearing officially obligatory?
3. What sorts of regulations allowed Gypsy women to access abortion? Why?
4. How was adoption against the state's pronatalist policies?

Notes

This chapter is drawn from a final grant report (Kligman 1992c) submitted to the National Council for Soviet and East European Studies, which supported the final phase of a field research project. Additional funding was granted by the American Council of Learned Societies, the International Research and Exchanges Board, and the Rockefeller Foundation. Kligman (1992a) is based on the final section of the grant report and this chapter; Kligman (1992b) is an almost-complete version of the grant report. Because of space constraints, notes have been kept to a minimum. For references and commentary, refer to the aforementioned works.

1 These allowances were adjusted according to income level, number of children, and place of residence (urban or rural). They were lower in rural areas, the rationale being that rural families were able to provide some of their food from their personal plots, although these same citizens were required to provide "barter" to receive their ration cards for staples. Rural payments were erratic. As was typical, this system functioned well only in theory.
2 Ceausescu's consolidation of power involved securing key loyalties through the appointment of extended family members. Thus, his version of Communist rule was variously described as *socialism in one family* or *dynastic socialism*. See, for example, Tismaneanu (1986). That so many members of the extended family were in key positions was captured in the play on the

acronym for the Romanian Communist Party: PCR. Popularly, this also meant Petrescu (Elena Ceausescu's natal family), Ceausescu, and Rudele ("relatives"). Other plays on *PCR* underscore the importance of personal relations and influence in this regime.

3 Contraceptives were not forbidden by law; however, they were unavailable and thus could be obtained only through illegal, black market connections. Abortion was illegal. The distinction is worth noting.

4 According to a study prepared by the Ministry of Health in 1986, the number of live births varied by nationality. For Romanian women, the median was 1.93 children; for Hungarians, 1.73; for Germans, 1.6; and for others, 2.56. The lower German birth rate is probably due to the older population of Germans; as conditions worsened under Ceausescu, many younger Germans with relatives abroad immigrated.

5 Mesaros (1990: 29). Dr. E. Mesaros was a member of the National Commission on Demography until 1985, when he resigned. The cited article was dated October 3, 1974. The distinction between a social and a national problem was meant partially to signal the class distinctions operative in reproductive behavior. The Gypsy birth rate was considered troublesome because of their low levels of education and presumed high degree of participation in delinquent behavior.

6 The Western press did exaggerate the extent and frequency of these exams. I could not obtain any verification from women that they had been subjected to the much-heralded monthly exams. The exams were ordered; how they were done is quite another matter. The Western press had little justification for sensationalism.

7 For 1989, the number of children left orphaned because of illegal abortions was reported to be 1,193; between 1981 and 1989, 8,004 children were orphaned as a consequence of illegal abortions. See Mezei (1991: 8).

8 These numbers do not include women who died from complications prior to arrival at a hospital. In 1989, at one of Bucharest's largest maternity clinics, 3,129 women were hospitalized for complications associated with illegally performed abortions. Of these, 26.6 percent needed intensive treatment for raging infections, 3.9 percent had hysterectomies, and 1.1 percent died (see Mezei 1991). The second highest number of abortions were among women who had five or more children and had at least five in their care (22.8 percent), followed by those with legal medical reasons (16.6 percent) and those who were of legal age (0.5 percent 45 years or older). See Roznatovschi (1989).

9 While international contributions of contraceptives began to pour into Romania in response to this tragic situation, problems associated with distribution and lack of contraceptive education meant that perceptions and behavior did not change significantly, even though Romanians were tired of "natural" methods and their uncertainty.

10 The maternal mortality figures for 1990 were 83 deaths per 100,000 live births, with maternal deaths from abortion decreasing to 69 percent of 249 maternal cases as compared with 87 percent of 588 maternal deaths attributable to abortions in 1989. Reported in Hord et al. (1991: 234).

11 It is beyond the scope of this chapter to discuss fully the adoption of Romanian children or the situation of children in Romanian orphanages. Refer to my grant report (Kligman 1992c) as well as to Kligman (1992b) for fuller discussions and references.

12 By the summer of 1992, almost all orphanages had a foreign agency (governmental or nongovernmental) working collaboratively with them.

13 Anti-Roma sentiment is widespread in Europe and, since 1989, has led to violence. Romania was the first of several countries with which Germany concluded agreements to deport illegal immigrants, among whom are many Roma.

14 Some Romanians accused the government of wanting to rob ordinary people of one of the few means by which they could make money so that the government might profit instead. Some foreigners criticized the government for preventing them from taking Romanian children to a better life. In an update to a guide written by a woman who had adopted two Romanian children, the author summarized the consequences of the new law. (See Delvecchio 1991.) Her letter closed with: "God Bless You in your efforts to rescue a little one." The new adoption law modified Law No. 11 signed in 1990. Another law, No. 47/1933, specifies the terms by which a court may declare a child legally abandoned. The adoption of Romanian children has been a prickly issue between the United States and Romania and has been manipulated on both sides.

15 Infertility has reportedly been on the rise in Romania as a consequence of pollution, malnutrition, and deteriorated conditions. The preferential treatment accorded Romanian citizens

in adopting Romanian orphans is meant to eliminate the demographic problems posed by a declining birth rate as well as the problems that may accompany intercultural adoptions as the children grow older.

16 Virtually no public attention is given to the physical abuse of women. Here, the government and its agencies, including research institutes that might well address such issues, are sorely negligent.

References

Anuarul Statistic al Romaniei. 1990. Bucharest: Comisia Nationala Pentru Statistica.

Decisions of the Plenary Session of the Central Committee of the Romanian Communist Party, July 18–19, 1973, with Attention to the Growth of the Role of Women in the Economic, Political, and Social Life of the Country. 1973. Bucharest: Editura Política.

Delvecchio, A.-M. 1991. *How to Adopt from Romania: A Comprehensive Step-by-Step Guide.* Sebastopol, CA: Hearthstone Publishers.

Hord, Charlotte, Henry P. David, France Donnayi, and Merrill Wolf. 1991. "Reproductive Health in Romania: Reversing the Ceausescu Legacy." *Studies in Family Planning* 22(4): 231–240.

Kligman, Gail. 1988. *The Wedding of the Dead: Ritual, Poetics, and Popular Culture in Transylvania.* Berkeley: University of California Press.

Kligman, Gail. 1992a. "Abortion and International Adoption in Post-Ceausescu Romania." *Feminist Studies* 18(2): 405–420.

Kligman, Gail. 1992b. "The Politics of Reproduction in Ceausescu's Romania: A Case Study in Political Culture." *East European Politics and Society* 6(3): 364–418.

Kligman, Gail. 1992c. *When Abortion Is Banned: The Politics of Reproduction in Ceausescu's Romania.* Washington, DC: National Council for Soviet and East European Studies.

Liciu, Valentina T. 1975. *Pregatirea pedagogica a adolescentiilor pentru viata de familie: Cu privire speciala asupra educatiei afectivitatii si sexualitatii.* Bucharest: Editura didactica si Pedagogica.

Mesaros, Emil. 1990. "Consideratii asupra politicii demografice a Romaniei." *Alternative 90* 1(4): 29.

Mezei, S. 1991. "Une analyse démo-sociologique des conséquences de la politique démographique roumaine." Unpublished manuscript.

Roznatovschi, L. 1989. *Aspecte ale intreruperilor de sarcina in R. S. Romania 1988.* Bucharest: Centrul de Calcul si Statistica Sanitara, Ministerul Sanatatii.

Teitelbaum, Michael S., and Jay M. Winter. 1985. *The Fear of Population Decline.* New York: Academic Press.

Tismăneanu, Vladimir. 1986. "Byzantine Rites, Stalinist Follies: The Twilight of Dynastic Socialism in Romania." *Orbis* 30(1): 65–91.

Trebici, Vladimir. 1988. "Demografie intre stiinta si actiune sociala." *Viitorul Social* 81(1): 69–78.

Chapter 27

Women's autonomy, Islam, and the French State

John R. Bowen

Original to a previous edition of this text. Courtesy of John R. Bowen.

In a nation where some think that *assimilation* means looking the same, the appearance in the late 1980s of an increasing number of women wearing Islamic scarves troubled many French public figures. The overblown reaction in the French media comparing the presence of three girls in scarves to the Munich capitulations of the 1930s started off two decades of hyperbole and anxiety. Feminists took the lead, recalling their historic struggle with the Catholic Church for control of their reproductive rights. But they faced a dilemma: feminism in France, as elsewhere, had championed a woman's right to choose how to treat her own body, so what could be said to Muslim women who claimed to choose to wear Islamic headscarves (*foulard* or *hijâb*) or, later, a veil covering all but the eyes (*niqab* or, in France, *burqa*)? Feminists and others seeking to limit these choices of dress had to discount the very possibility of choice, by claiming that radical Islam undermined women's autonomy and thus made choice meaningless. I consider here the uses made of the scarves by Muslim women and changing critical responses to these practices in public and legal arenas.[1]

Veiling and the republic

Although French theories and anxieties about Islamic headscarves date back to colonial days, they took on added force in the late 1980s, when fears about international political Islam combined with the greater domestic visibility of Islam to produce new cries of alarm. Objections to public wearing of Islamic scarves were based on multiple claims: some expressed concern that boys would place pressure on girls to don scarves; others argued that the scarves had become signs of political Islam; still others claimed that the scarf stood for the oppression of women. The debate centered on the presence of such scarves in schools and produced a 2004 law banning conspicuous signs of religious affiliation from public schools (Bowen 2007). No longer were scarves (*foulards*) at issue but rather the inexact term "the veil" (*le voile*).

"The veil" evokes memories of colonial rule, when women's dress became salient signs of affiliation to indigenous or to Western modes of life. In metropolitan France, however, for the first half of the twentieth century, Islam was largely present in the form of North

DOI: 10.4324/9781003398349-31

African male workers cycling between their birthplaces and France to work in factories. But during the postwar recovery period, the Algerian War, and especially after the 1970s, Algerians and other Muslims from northern and western Africa increasingly settled in France with their wives and children. Labor migration as such ended and was replaced by immigration based on family reunification, which usually meant that a man or woman came to join her or his lawfully resident spouse in France. The presence of Islam now included settled women and men.

By the 1980s, the sons and daughters of those resident Muslim families began to come of age and to search for their identities. Many found it difficult to find acceptance as French, despite their status as French-born citizens. Prejudice against Muslims and against people of color, coupled with bitter memories of the recent conflict, made their acceptance difficult, and the economic downturn of the 1970s exacerbated tensions. But the new generation did not find themselves at ease "back home" either: they were French in some way and not Algerian or Senegalese.

For some of these young Muslims, their search led them to study Islam as a formal religion rather than to inherit it as a tradition. They began to attend lectures by charismatic young preachers, read books that taught them "true Islam," and frequented mosques. They were joined by new immigrants from Muslim countries, and some members of the new generation of younger Muslims, French- and foreign-born, began to "look Muslim." Some younger women wore scarves that were pulled tightly over their heads, concealing their hair and ears. This contrasted with their mothers' scarves, worn more loosely and casually. They might wear a simple scarf or a combination of two head coverings, one covering the forehead, and the other the top of the head and the shoulders, or a more unified garment including head covering, blouse, and skirt. The many elements that make up markedly Islamic dress – head coverings, blouses and tunics, skirts and trousers, and perhaps gloves – tended to be reduced by critical French observers to the matter of how, and how much of, the head was covered, as an index of radicalism. Did the particular scarf cover the ears, leave the roots of the hair exposed or not, come down over the forehead? For many non-Muslims in France, these differences in degree of covering came to signify differences in the degree of religiosity or of moral difference being signaled by a Muslim woman.

Then, in September 1989, three girls showed up for the first day at their middle school wearing Islamic dress. At another moment, the girls' appearance would likely have passed unnoticed. Girls had been showing up at school with scarves for years and either attended the school with their scarves or agreed to remove them during class. But now, international "political Islam" appeared on magazine covers in the form of Iranian women in Islamic dress, adding a new dimension to scarves in French schools. The conjuncture of domestic and foreign threats made scarf-wearing into a national "affaire." After initial negotiations, the local dispute became a national incident, on which everyone eventually had to take a position. The mass media jumped on the incident. The Right was relatively silent on the issue, but the Left was sharply split. Antiracism groups associated with the Socialist Party emphasized the Revolution's legacy of equality and *laïcité* (secularity) and resisted allowing religion into the schools.

Why wear headscarves?

When two sociologists, Françoise Gaspard and Farhad Khosrokhavar (1995), set out to interview girls and young women who wore headscarves, they found two major motives.

Some wore a headscarf as a way to satisfy their parents and ease their transition across the line of puberty and into late adolescence. Many of these girls adopted it during middle school years but then abandoned it during high school. They were not necessarily regular practitioners of their religion. But other, usually older girls began to wear a headscarf as part of a conscious effort to create a new identity as they entered or left high school. For them, wearing a scarf was part of two simultaneous processes: defining themselves in Islamic terms and entering the world of postsecondary education and work. These women tended to be educated and successful, and to regularly pray, fast, and observe dietary rules.

Subsequent studies, most carried out toward the end of the 1990s, confirmed Gaspard and Khosrokhavar's findings that young women chose to adopt Islamic dress, including a headscarf, as part of efforts to negotiate a sphere of social freedom and authority and to construct an identity as a Muslim, and that the relative weight of these two reasons depended on her age and social situation. Many of the women also drew explicit contrasts between, on the one hand, their own efforts to become better Muslims through study and regular prayer and, on the other, the ways in which their parents merely followed tradition, by, for example, fasting and sacrificing but rarely praying. Some distinguished between two ways of wearing a headscarf: "as in the old country" (letting some hair show), and wearing it in an Islamic manner (covering the hair). In other words, donning the scarves was part of a quest for autonomy.

When, in 2004, I interviewed three young women of Algerian Kabyle background living in Paris, I found that they had thought long and hard about how to meet their sense of their faith requirements and how to present themselves to the outside world (Bowen 2007: 72–81). One had begun wearing a hijâb (the term she used) at 15 and had kept it ever since. Highly educated in Algeria and in France, she was a cosmopolitan intellectual and cultural actor, working for various foreign cultural services over the years while she completed a thesis on US history.

A second had not been brought up to obey religious commandments and had learned about Islam during her high-school years by reading books suggested to her by friends. She began to wear a small hair band with her friends "so that people would get used to it" before eventually putting on a scarf when "one day [she] decided to become a woman, not a boy." She began by responding to God's call to her while adapting herself to her society.

> [A]nd I succeed at this, for, when I am at work I wear the scarf not like I have it now [tightly covering her head] but on top, swirled around, like the Africans; that seems to work. I began wearing it as an intern, and it worked. This shows that there are still people who are very tolerant. They knew me before and after the scarf, and their attitude did not change. They saw that my work did not change, even got better.

The third young woman did not wear a headscarf. She observed Ramadan and avoided pork but no longer performed the prayer, insisting that her dress and her religious practices were entirely a matter of personal choice.

These three women have fashioned their public behavior both by their personal religious trajectories and by their sensibilities as to how others do and will see them. Each describes a long history of reflecting on religion and on her ability to adequately carry out religious obligations. And each also makes decisions about dress and behavior that take into account others' reactions. They reject the idea that headscarves are "religious signs," because they see the decision to wear hijâb as the result of a personal commitment rather than an intention to signal something to others. But they also acknowledge that making that decision does and should take into account the responses of others and the importance of schooling, work, and family; they see the effects that such a decision has (on attractiveness as a potential spouse, for example) as part of the entire picture. Wearing a headscarf in France today involves negotiations, anticipations, and weighing of benefits and costs. It is not simply an "obligation" or a "choice" but a subtle dance among convictions and constraints.

Charging sexual oppression

But this autonomy has been dismissed by many who have supported laws restricting women's clothing. Some claim that the headscarf has the objective meaning of oppression. On the Stasi Commission, advocates of a law were able to frame the question in those terms; Bernard Stasi himself declared that "the voile is objectively a sign of women's alienation" (*Ouest France* October 31, 2003). Proponents of a law made at least three distinct claims: schoolgirls were pressured by men and boys to wear the voile; the voile intrinsically attacked the dignity and the equal status of women; and because it did so, it encouraged violence against women living in the poor suburbs. These claims strengthened the antiscarf movement in two major ways. First, they strongly appealed to French principles and emotions concerning the equality and dignity of women. Who could defend oppression of women? Second, they shifted the debate from the constitutionally sensitive area of religious freedom and onto the legally safer ground of protecting rights and dignity. But what precisely was the argument? Teachers and principals testifying to the Stasi Commission mentioned the voile unfavorably, but the practices that they most strongly denounced were anti-Semitic remarks, proselytizing, praying in school, arguing over history lessons, and general incivility. What was the scarf's role in encouraging these practices? Did wearing a scarf contribute to anti-Semitism? How was that the case?

The most successful answer went as follows. The voile stands for the oppression of women and also acts as a direct mechanism for their oppression in France. Boys terrorize girls, and the voile normalizes this state of affairs. Girls who refuse to wear the voile are told they should wear it and thus are oppressed even within the school. Foreign Islamists are manipulating girls, making them think they need to wear the voile. Do away with the voile and you would do these girls a big favor. At last, a clear, causal argument! And in the end, it won the day.

With few exceptions, feminists who were active during the 1970s in the *Mouvement de la libération des femmes* (MLF, Women's Liberation Movement) opposed wearing the voile. Their opposition was clear early on, when, during the first "affaire" of 1989, most major feminist leaders and organizations denounced the scarves. The leading feminist politician at that time, Yvette Roudy of the Socialist Party, claimed that "the foulard is the sign of subservience, whether consensual or imposed, in fundamentalist Muslim society. . . . To accept wearing the voile is tantamount to saying 'yes' to women's inequality in French Muslim society." The Family Planning Movement (*le Mouvement pour le planning familial*, one of the MLF's pillars) agreed: "Women wearing the voile are a sign of sexist discrimination incompatible with a secularist and egalitarian education" (*Le Monde* October 25, 1989).

Two long-standing feminists intervened in the 2003 debates over the law, in an article whose title proclaims their position: "Laïcistes because feminists" (*Le Monde* May 30, 2003). Although the term *laïciste* is usually employed to refer negatively to people carried away by their enthusiasm for *laïcité* (secularity), the two authors here embrace it in order to attack the wearing of the voile. They begin by acknowledging that women or girls who wear the "Islamic veil" do so in the name of their freedom to practice their religion. However, they add:

> [W]earing the voile is not only a sign of belonging to a religion. It symbolizes the place of women in Islam as Islamism understands it. That place is in the shadow, downgraded, and submitting to men. The fact that some women demand it does not change its meaning. We know that dominated people are the most fervent supporters of their domination.

They argue that laïcité presupposes a "neutral public space, free of any religious belief, where citizens develop under the same treatment, sharing common rights and duties, and a common good, all of which places them beyond discriminating differences." They call, in the end, for prohibiting the voile "in all places of teaching and of life together (*vie commune*) (school, university, business, government offices), and if attacks on women continue, forbidding the voile in the street."

Their article confronts two critical questions that arise once the debate has been reframed around women's rights rather than around the laïcité of the schoolroom: How broad should be the scope of a headscarf ban? And should one place any weight on the testimony of the girls in scarves themselves? The two questions are related. If the issue is keeping the schools free from outside pressures in order to allow pupils to learn in an atmosphere free of ideological pressures, then it makes sense to limit the ban on the scarves to the school grounds, or perhaps, as was the case in a number of schools, to the classroom. In class, all identities other than that of pupil in France are to be suppressed; in the rest of life, they may flourish, and freedom of religion requires that expressions of faith be permitted. Even if schoolgirls choose to wear the scarves, they still prevent the classroom from functioning as it should.

Now, however, the claim is that the voile is the symbol and instrument of broad, global forces that oppose French values and that, in particular, oppress women. It no longer matters where the voile appears; it is equally noxious and dangerous in any public place – and why only in public places? It should be abolished everywhere that French people try to develop a life together, a *vie commune*. Such is Vigerie and Zelensky's argument, and their sentiments were shared by others. It was about this time, in May 2003, that one began to see banks, doctors' offices, and municipal offices refusing entry to women in headscarves, as well as cases where an ordinary person would ask a woman in a scarf to "leave this public place" on a bus or subway. The ambiguity of the French "public," which means sometimes "having to do with the state" and sometimes "out in public view," was at work here, generating or reinforcing a variety of norms about what such women should or should not do. For Zelensky and Vigerie, and, I suspect, for many French feminists, the relevant meaning of *public* is that of *la vie commune*, a notion which includes the workplace as well as the government office.

In this broader view of the problem, how to treat the girls' own views becomes more difficult. In the narrower argument concerning the school, one that starts from the legal and perhaps the philosophical requirements of laïcité, the claim that scarf-wearing girls have freely chosen their garments need not be refuted, because good pedagogy requires a scarf-less classroom, whatever the pupils might think. In the broader argument that starts from the voile's socially corrosive force, however, statements by girls and women that they chose to wear headscarves must be addressed. What if they do not find the voile corrosive or oppressive at all?

Television strategies

If giving voice to young women in headscarves might lead viewers to see things from their point of view, one can perhaps better understand why French television viewers seldom had to trouble themselves over such a possibility. During the critical period for shaping public opinion, from approximately April 2003 through February 2004, one seldom heard young Muslim women in headscarves setting out their positions on French television. An exception was the Lévy sisters, Alma and Lila, expelled from their *lycée* in the fall of 2003, who appeared as foils for those who would defend the Republic.

The sisters appeared on February 19, 2004, on *Campus, le magazine de l'écrit*, a book-oriented talk show moderated by Guillaume Durand and shown regularly on France 2. Three of the evening's guests were the "moderate" Muslim author Malik Chebel, the strongly anti-Islamist author Martin Gozlane, and the very media-friendly Carmen bin Ladin, the ex-wife of Osama's brother.

That evening, moderator Duran let the sisters begin by explaining their decision to wear the voile; they state that the decision came from studying religious books, and not from any outside pressure.

Lila:	We read the verse and then decided to wear the voile; but the four main scholars of Islam agree that it is required. . . . When we started to wear the voile, I knew no one who wore it, I did not know how it was considered.
Moderator:	Do you plan to keep it for your life?
Lila:	Yes.
Moderator:	Why? Good Lord! . . . and why "good lord?'
Alma:	Because it is our freedom of conscience, and I agree that what happens in the projects with girls who choose not to wear the foulard is terrible, but the solution is not to deny us our right to choose, but to guarantee everyone their rights.

Carmen bin Ladin picked up the questioning: "You consider that when women wear skirts men automatically think of sex and that you wear the voile to keep men from having impure thoughts, so you are in a state of submission." Bin Ladin then describes her life in Saudi Arabia as a life of submission to men: "it is in the very nature of the voile." She then turns to Alma and Lila and questions them: "You are very young and do not understand what the voile means for you as women. You are not like the others even though you say you are. Do you do sports?"

Alma:	Yes, my best grades were in sports.
BL:	Do you take off the voile for sports?
Alma:	No.

BL: And you wear shorts?
Alma: No one wears shorts, boys or girls.
BL: My daughter wears team uniforms when she plays sports.
Alma: No one wears shorts.
Bin Ladin, trying another tack: Now women who come to Europe and refuse to be treated by a male doctor, that's the problem!

The Lévys' efforts to focus on their real motives and choices in the specific French context are parried at each instance by claims about the voile's objectively sexist and Islamist meaning, best seen through the struggle of "sisters" in Muslim-majority countries, and the doubtless naiveté of the girls, objects of manipulation. Gozlan:

> Every time there is an advance for women, Islamists react against it, as in Egypt in the 1920s, when feminists took off their voiles – yes it happened that way, Mesdemoiselles, and now in France les "beurettes" are showing signs of a wonderful integration, and so you see reaction, a new visibility of radical Islam, they bring out the voile. You say "[it is] your choice" but it is your choice in the context of a huge apparatus that encompasses you.

The most striking aspect of this and many other programs that appeared during this period, roughly late 2003 to early 2004, is the asymmetry of roles played by guests. Of course, hosts and commentators are expected to provoke and pose questions. But the guests, all of them invited on grounds that they had recently published books, were not all positioned in the same way. The journalist Sylvain Attal appeared as an expert, who informed us about anti-Semitism through his book and on the program. The authors Malik Chebel, Martine Gozlan, and Carmen bin Laden were asked about their books, but much less than they were asked to comment on (or simply intervened on their own to comment on) the persons and acts of the Lévy sisters. Alma and Lila, and secondarily their book, were the main object of discussion. Their claims, their choices, and their headscarves were the real text for the evening. They were only allowed to speak as examples of the problem, the real understanding of which was provided by the "experts." They do not have real autonomy; they have been duped into thinking they do, but their garments show otherwise.

Raising the ante against autonomy

By 2008, some officials had moved from condemning scarves in public spaces to condemning certain putative values shared by some Muslims, sometimes signaled by their choice of dress. Major roles were played by two of France's highest tribunals: the State Council, which rules on decisions from administrative bodies, and the Constitutional Council, which is asked to give opinions about the constitutionality of proposed or enacted laws. These decisions pushed further forward the argument that not all Muslim women can be presumed to be in a position to make their own decisions concerning their bodies, and that the decisions they have made are *ipso facto* signals of their unsuitability as autonomous citizens.

In June 2008, for example, the French State Council refused to grant French nationality to a woman from Morocco on the grounds that her religious practices had led her to hold values that ran counter to the equality of men and women and caused her to suffer from insufficient assimilation to become a French citizen: she had an "assimilation defect" (*défaut d'assimilation*) (Conseil d'État 2008). The woman had married a French convert to Islam who had requested that she wear a full-face covering (called a *burqa* by the court). She was reported to stay at home and to have insufficient knowledge of the right to vote and the basics of laïcité. She had met the formal conditions for citizenship, having waited the required period of time after marriage before requesting naturalization. However, at the government's request, the Council ruled that her failure to accept the values of women's equality made her unfit for French citizenship. They were careful not to make the couple's religion the explicit grounds for rejecting her request, in order to avoid a subsequent finding of unconstitutionality.

This decision had quick results. In July 2008, a housing authority in Vénissieux, a suburb of Lyon with a large Muslim population, refused to allow a family to occupy the apartment officially allotted to them because the wife wore a burqa. The letter of refusal repeated the words of the State Council's decision: "Madame wears the burqa, which characterizes a radical religious practice that is incompatible with the essential values of the French community and with the principle of the equality of the sexes" (*Le Monde* 2009).

Just over a year later, France was debating whether to ban the wearing of a face veil in public. Called the burqa in France but generally known as the niqab, the face veil generally leaves the eyes uncovered, sufficiently so that women have been allowed to drive while wearing the garment. In October 2010, Parliament passed such a law, notwithstanding an opinion by the State Council that such a law would unduly restrict religious freedom (Conseil d'État 2010). Because of uncertainty about whether the law would stand an eventual challenge, Parliament asked the Constitutional Council to rule on whether it was in accord with the Constitution. In upholding the law, the Council cited two principles. They argued, first, that covering the face "misrecognizes the minimal requirements of living in society" and, second, that those women who decide to wear a face veil "find themselves placed in a situation of exclusion and inferiority clearly incompatible with the constitutional principles of freedom and equality" (Conseil Constitutionnel 2010). Burqa-wearing violates minimal conditions for civic life, and it objectively reduces the autonomy of the wearer, regardless of her knowledge, capacities, or intentions, argued the Council.

These ideas have strong appeal for many in France. The decision evokes the idea that normal citizens are civil; they interact in the "shared life" of civic France. As Dominique Schnapper put it in a public forum in July 2010, giving a justification for banning burqas, "France is the country where everyone says 'bonjour'" (presentation, Université d'été d'Irrisarry, July 6, 2010). Implicitly, one cannot really greet one another from behind a veil. Here we have essentially the same claim about communication made by British minister Jack Straw a few years earlier, but whereas Straw made it on personal grounds – he would not speak with someone whose face was covered – Schnapper made it on grounds of a theory of civic life.

This argument draws on scares about "communalism" most commonly heard in the 2001–2003 period, scares that draw from the fundamental French ambivalence concerning intermediate groups. Communalism (*communautarisme*) is used in French to evoke a sense that a group defined in ethnic or religious terms has closed itself off to others in the society; "intermediate groups" include guilds, unions, and ethnic associations.

Similar concerns were evinced then about refusals to shake hands: France is the country where one says *bonjour* and then shakes hands. Issues intersect here: a distaste for "communalism," an embrace of "mixité," which tends to mean in particular mixing of men and women, and gender equality. This set of concerns appears time and again in French public discussions. In the unusually hot summer of 2003, a debate erupted over the existence of women-only hours at some municipal swimming pools in several French cities. In southern Lille, one of the four municipal pools had offered such hours for two years when reporters finally stumbled on the practice in June 2003. The mayor, Martine Aubry, who later became Socialist Party leader, had authorized the special hours upon request from a number of women of North African background. In other parts of France, Jewish associations had successfully petitioned to have sex-segregated hours at municipal pools, with no media attention. But in 2003, the existence of the "Arab" women-only hours shocked certain commentators. The president of the association Europe and Laïcité, Etienne Pion, considered the arguments for women-only hours – modesty, ease with babies – to be but "alibis to force the acceptance of communalist principles" (Bowen 2007: 109–110).

A more striking instance where modesty is declared to take the back seat to mixité comes from the well-known 2002 book *The Lost Territories of the Republic* (Brenner 2002: 194–195). One (female) lycée teacher describes how she and others felt challenged on a deeper level by Islamic attire.

The striking fact here is that girls and boys cover themselves with a kind of violence that makes one ill at ease. It seems that prior to the religious meaning of head coverings is the notion that the head ought to be covered because the body itself presents a problem. That is what one finds again and again, in pupils' refusal to attend swimming class, in their challenges to mixité, in the problems they raise on account of modesty [*pudeur*]. We even had to refuse their demand for separate toilets for girls and boys, so as to avoid an anti-Republican politics, even though the poor treatment suffered by girls justified it for their sexual protection.

In this striking account, the field of combat is no longer the school but the girls' attitudes toward their own bodies. A measure that might strike an outsider as normal (building separate toilets) and that, in this school, would have protected girls from aggressions by boys was considered to send the wrong message about Republican norms. Providing separate toilets would have meant accepting, even promoting, shame about one's body. It is this shame that lies behind wearing a headscarf and refusing to play sports with boys. It must be fought even at the cost of the girls' well-being. Gender mixing fights bad Islamic values and affirms both sociability and gender equality.

Conclusion

From 1989 through 2011, a recurring justification for state regulation of Muslim women's bodies has been their putative lack of autonomy. In the classroom, boys tell girls how to dress; the solution is to forbid girls to wear Islamic scarves. Lest they accept archaic Islamic ideas about sexuality, they should not be permitted to absent themselves from swim classes, or, when grown, from swimming in mixed company. Claims of modesty conceal oppression by Muslim men. Those who choose to wear a face veil show their inability or unwillingness to function as French citizens – so objectively contrary to French

Republican values is that garment. Women who protest, those who say "It's my choice," are presumed to be dupes of Islamist ideology.

And yet many young French Muslim women have made clothing choices precisely to negotiate space for their autonomy. For some, this has involved adopting Islamic dress as a way of convincing their parents that they can be trusted to succeed in French schools and careers. For others, it has been a way to make clear to the wider world who they are and how they choose to live their lives. Many younger women are trying out various ways of being in the French social world as religiously practicing people. Some of those ways involve clothing; others involve ways of speaking, shaking hands (or not) with men, carving out women's space, or finding Muslim space in cultural associations or mosque events. Much as Catholics and Jews have found ways of preserving religiosity in Republican France through the path of associational life – private schools, clubs, religious events – Muslims are only beginning to develop their social forms of a religious life. The challenge is perhaps greater for Muslim women, who must overcome presumptions of submission and oppression. For men and women, however, the issue remains the classic one of creating ways to, if one so chooses, fashion oneself as deeply Republican and deeply religious.

Discussion questions

1. What sociocultural factors led to French Islamic women veiling in the 1970s, and what sociopolitical factors led to the headscarf ban in 2010?
2. What sorts of clothing choices have young French Muslim women made to negotiate space for their autonomy?
3. In what manner did French activists who were against veiling use French culture as a reason to deny women the choice to veil?
4. How would you resolve the conflicts related to the issues raised by this author?

Note

1 In this chapter, I draw on analyses already set out in Bowen (2007, 2011); see these works for the fuller arguments.

References

Bowen, John R. 2007. *Why the French Don't Like Headscarves: Islam, the State, and Public Space*. Princeton: Princeton University Press.

Bowen, John R. 2011. "How the French State Justifies Controlling Muslim Bodies: From Harm-Based to Values-Based Reasoning." *Social Research*, Summer 78(2): 1–24.

Brenner, Emmanuel, ed. 2002. *Les territoires perdus de la République: Antisémitisme, racisme et sexisme en milieu scolaire*. Paris: Mille et une nuits.

Conseil Constitutionnel. 2010. *Décision no, 2010–613 DC*, October, par. 4. www.conseil-constitutionnel.fr/conseil-constitutionnel/francais/les-decisions/accespar-date/decisions-dep-uis-1959/2010/2010-613-dc/decision-n-2010-613-dc-du-07-octobre-2010.49711.html.

Conseil d'État. 2008. *Mabchour*, req. n. 286798, juin 27.

Conseil d'État. 2010. *Étude relative aux possibilités juridiques d'interdiction du port du voile intégral*, mars 25.

Gaspard, Françoise, and Farhad Khosrokhavar. 1995. *Le foulard et la République*. Paris: La Découverte.

Chapter 28

Gender, sexuality, and asylum assessment

Rine Vieth

Original material prepared for this edition.

Introduction

On a warm spring day, I met Alan – someone deeply involved in supporting LGBTQ+ asylum-seekers – over coffee in an urban Northern English café. Someone I knew in migrant support suggested I reach out to Alan due to his long-standing dedication to and significant role in supporting LGBTQ+ asylum-seekers. Over the past decade, Alan helped start support groups, facilitated efforts for LGBTQ+ Christian asylum-seekers who were isolated in their parishes, liaised with local LGBTQ+ NGOs, and was otherwise a nexus of knowledge and support for LGBTQ+ asylum-seekers in his city. After brief introductions and securing a large latté for each of us, we began our conversation by chatting about his role showing up to appeal hearings for asylum-seekers he supported in his volunteer work. After a few minutes of talking about the more institutional work he did, Alan was quiet for a moment before explaining how he saw his role accompanying asylum-seekers in appealing initial rejections of their applications:

> The asylum-seeker knows I'm there to support them, and I will have probably had spent some time with them before we go into court, saying, "You will be okay." They value the fact that I observe the case, and that I will tell them the truth about what I think afterwards. So it's a kind of hand-holding, an accompanying.

This chapter comes out of conversations with people like Alan and the asylum-seekers he supported, as well as my own experiences observing asylum tribunals. In this chapter, I will delve into how LGBTQ+ asylum-seekers in the UK are required by the state to evidence their claims within particular parameters, and how state expectations shape asylum claims. My interest in gender and sexuality in asylum claims is focused here on the broader questions of how gender and sexuality are evidenced, the role of this process in nation-building, and the impacts of these processes on asylum-seekers themselves.

Every year, thousands of people claim asylum in the UK, with recent upticks resulting from humanitarian crises in Ukraine, and some increases post-2020 caused by borders re-opening after closures caused by COVID-19. While recent crises and significant changes

DOI: 10.4324/9781003398349-32

Table 28.1 Number of asylum claims on the basis of sexuality, by top total counts since 2015

	Applications	2015	2016	2017	2018	2019	2020	2021	2022	Total
	Total	1,768	2,212	1,936	1,502	1,800	1,341	707	1,334	12,600
1	Pakistan	509	621	551	324	301	182	109	278	2,875
2	Bangladesh	149	299	305	148	125	66	58	149	1,299
3	Nigeria	154	222	184	90	165	111	97	119	1,142
4	Uganda	201	130	63	95	71	76	7	32	675
5	Iran	100	136	59	75	92	81	72	35	650
6	Albania	61	53	55	50	74	65	24	65	447
7	Iraq	18	46	59	60	98	65	58	30	434
8	Other	33	56	52	43	57	62	26	76	405
9	Malaysia	19	21	53	139	94	29	7	37	399
10	Ghana	41	66	56	43	59	33	25	34	357
10	Cameroon	63	76	77	51	29	18	11	32	357

Source: Data from UK Home Office (2023a).

to legislation make an "average" amount difficult to concretely claim, at the end of June 2023, most recent data on asylum claims awaiting an initial determination number over 130,000 (UK Home Office 2023b). While the landscape of asylum-seekers' countries of origin are somewhat clear, a significant issue when considering particular types of asylum claims is data – and this issue is magnified in claims on the basis of gender and/or sexuality, where not only can outing oneself or engaging with a potentially hostile interviewer be an issue but also the UK's lack of data collection for specific claims. For claims on the basis of sexuality, which can additionally include transgender asylum-seekers who claim on the basis of sexuality, the statistics are less straightforward; initial errors in the first dataset have slowly been replaced over time.

The data for this chapter comes out of my doctoral fieldwork, which took place between 2017 and 2018 – with online, legal, and archival research that extended before and after that yearlong period – and was largely based at Manchester Piccadilly Tribunal, located in Manchester, England. I attended over 100 public tribunal hearings within His Majesty's Courts and Tribunals Service (HMCTS), and as there was no recorded transcript, my shorthand notes form the archive on which I draw here. In addition, I conducted over two dozen interviews with individuals who supported asylum-seekers, as well as spent months as a participant-observer at a church, known for its social justice work, with a number of asylum-seekers. For anonymity, names that are used in the chapter have been changed, as well as some identifying information. Finally, building on existing work that focuses on specifically LGBTQ+ asylum-seekers' lives (e.g., Bachmann and Singer 2016; Dustin 2018), this chapter aimed more at systemic understandings that build upon state bureaucrats and supporters' work and, to that end, includes more voices of supporters and state officials than asylum-seekers.

I begin this chapter by explaining the dynamic process of the localization of human rights law and norms, which subsequently leads to an overview of the process for claiming asylum. Understanding these two components is vital, I argue, for noticing how gender and sexuality are embedded in the entire process of seeking asylum: "localization" of human rights is not just how the transnational becomes embedded in the local but also how the local – in this case, the UK Home Office and the First-Tier Tribunals within His Majesty's Courts and Tribunal Service (HMCTS) – views the migrant other. I then go on to explain how the knowledge infrastructures of the UK asylum system create and reinforce a particular "scaffolding" that is more receptive to some expressions of gender and not others. Subsequently, I point out that the affective states generated through documents and processes within the asylum system are embedded in particular understandings of what I call "homonationalist futurities," which come into being through the skepticism of the Home Office. Drawing on interviews with interlocutors, I further point out how the experiences of the asylum process can itself be heavily gendered, and I explore experiences and understandings of how gender plays a role in tribunal hearing rooms, for those who appeal their initial asylum determinations. Much of the focus in this chapter is on understandings of gender and sexuality of cisgender lesbian, gay, or bisexual asylum-seekers, but I will go on to discuss the difficulties facing transgender asylum-seekers in navigating existing administrative processes.

As a final note in this introduction, I want to be clear that at no point am I assessing the gender or sexuality of asylum-seekers themselves. It can be too easy for a researcher to call asylum-seekers' identities into question, thus replicating the same dynamics of surveillance, evidencing, and more that we may seek to critique. To that end, the position I take is one of refusal: my interest is not in assessing whether or not an asylum-seeker is "genuine" in their gender and/or sexuality, and I instead attend to the processes through which these assessments take place. My endeavor is not to reinscribe the violent bureaucracies of state governance; instead, I seek to elaborate on the processes through which gender and sexuality are understood, rendered legible, and at times forced to be hidden within the context of asylum-seeking.

Contextualizing gender and sexuality

Asylum-systems are convoluted – frequently looping back for appeals, sometimes restarting with fresh claims, and with ever-present uncertainty. In this section, I will give a brief overview of the UK asylum-seeking process and an introduction to the knowledge infrastructures within the system. To start the process of seeking asylum, individuals submit a claim from inside the UK. The UK state – through case law and Home Office guidance – emphasizes the importance of claiming at the first possible instance, such as upon reaching the customs desk at a UK airport or other port of entry (UK Home Office 2022). Not claiming as soon as possible can be seen as detrimental to an asylum-seeker's claim, even if the asylum-seeker simply did not know that they should be claiming as quickly as possible due to information about claiming being largely visible in ports of entry in English only. A lack of knowledge of how one might be assessed is again an issue – someone who becomes an asylum-seeker may delay claiming out of fear or lack of knowledge about the process. Asylum-seekers' interviews, evidence, and claims are received within a particular cultural context, which shapes the possibilities and constraints on what is considered "proof" for a "genuine" asylum claim. For claimants in the UK, British LGBTQ+ subcultures might vary dramatically from their home countries. Therefore, cultural contexts shape not only how asylum-seekers experience their sexuality in the UK but also how the Home Office and HMCTS understand, assess, and evaluate LGBTQ+ claims.

After an initial application, the asylum-seeker is later – perhaps weeks or months – called to the Home Office's offices in Croydon, South London. This is generally the only instance during which an asylum-seeker will meet the person handling their file. During this visit to South London – or, as during the first years of the COVID-19 pandemic, over videolink – decision-makers interview asylum-seekers. An interpreter, provided by the UK state, who attempts to help asylum-seekers realize their rights to represent themselves, generally accompanies the asylum-seeker. Interpreters also translate cultural contexts, body language, and more intangible aspects of language. At this point, it is generally one person who determines the initial outcome: a government employee known as a "decision-maker" (Thomas 2011). Decision-makers may consider a case to be "genuine" and grant humanitarian protection or reject the claim outright on a variety of bases. As some scholars have noted, if a case seems to be clear-cut and if an asylum-seeker is forthcoming with the details, a decision-maker may consider the speed and ease of the decision as evidence that an asylum-seeker is genuine (Jubany 2017: 180).

As an effort to standardize the process for assessing an asylum-seeker's claim itself – as well as to establish the bases of assessing credibility – the Home Office created Country Policy Information Notes (CPINs) and Asylum Policy Information (APIs). These form an archive of documents that Home Office employees use during initial assessments, judges refer to in determining asylum appeals, and a variety of UK state employees rely upon to establish whether or not a state bureaucrat can consider a country safe for a claimant to be deported back to. Country information documents establish not just a particular narrative of what the asylum-seeker's cultural context is – flattening nuance and cultural experience to only a few dozen pages – but are constructed by an underfunded department, which only relies on English-language, freely available information. Further, staff producing these reports are not specialists or researchers with any particular credentials (Bolt 2018).

If an asylum-seeker's initial claim is assessed and subsequently rejected, the claimant can appeal the initial decision and then go in front of a tribunal judge, along with a Home Office presenting officer (HOPO), a government employee who represents the state at a tribunal hearing. At tribunal, asylum-seekers must convince a judge that their case is worthwhile – or, at the very least, that the Home Office's case is flawed. Tribunals were created to be more informal spaces, in contrast to the formalities of a court of law. However, these tribunals are shaped by both the argumentative nature of the juridical spaces and simultaneous lack of access to certain rights, such as legal representation, found within courts of law but not tribunals (Drewry 2009; Jacobs 2011). As one example of these contradictions, while the HOPO acts as a lawyer for the Home Office, they are not required to have any legal training (Campbell 2019), and none I spoke to during my fieldwork were legally qualified.

The power for determining claims rests on individuals making assessments, as well as individuals representing the Home Secretary and judges at tribunal hearings. Shifting centralized state power to individuals is an aspect of modern governance; this bureaucratic move allows for the state to avoid certain kinds of accountability (Gill 2009). In addition, while individual discretion forms a significant part of a migrant's experience with an immigration regime, I here attend not just to the decision made but to what Satzewich (2015) calls the "social constitution of discretion," the local and global contexts that shape individual state employees' decisions. As an example, I frequently overheard HOPOs lamenting their cases, at times implicating me into these complaints when it was just the HOPO and I sitting in an empty hearing room. After one particular morning's hearing had concluded and the other parties had departed, I sat with Rachel, the HOPO that day, who had a tight, blond bob and glasses. Rachel frequently chatted to me in short breaks between cases, and on that day, while reorganizing her files, Rachel sighed and again turned to me. "I'm tougher on the gay ones," she said, alluding to the earlier case that included a gay male Iranian asylum-seeker. "My brother's gay, you see. So I have a problem when people claim to be gay. They're just faking it." Unsure how to respond, I asked her why she might think anyone would be "faking it." While we knew each other by sight, she did not know I was queer and transgender, and I decided to not out myself in that moment. She went on to point to the numerous cases she heard as evidence to support her claim of gay claimants who were not "genuine," as well as her understanding of what being gay should "look" or "seem" like. Her decisions – including whether or not to pursue a case – were based not only upon UK government information but also on her personal experience, which made its way into her approach at tribunal hearings.

Homonationalist futurities

Asylum claims invoke a speculative future, as at the heart of an asylum claim is a singular question: If returned, would someone be at serious risk? Further, while not the only framing of long gaps between administrative interactions, the experience of asylum is one of waiting (Tuckett 2018); LGBT asylum-seekers in the UK are pushed – for the sake of the acceptance of their claims – to at least briefly embrace an imagined future brought about through a lens that posits the UK as an enforcer of human rights, even if that may not be the case. Asylum-seekers and their supporters, then, are invested in an *afterwards* – one of more safety, more possibility after fleeing their countries of origin and after receiving status. However, at the same time, there is friction between what asylum-seekers might want for their futures, what these future possibilities can be within the context of the British state.

To elucidate some of the power dynamics and political processes at play, I use homonationalism as a way to frame this conversation about future possibility. Asylum claims on the basis of sexuality *do* something to the UK state as well as the claimants in the context of contemporary liberal democracy that ostensibly claims to abide by human rights. Here, I turn to Jasbir Puar's elaboration of homonationalism, a way of understanding the simultaneous deployment of human rights rhetoric to LGBT people on one hand and the weaponization of human rights (such as through the US invasion of Iraq) on the other:

> National recognition and inclusion, here signaled as the annexation of homosexual jargon, is contingent upon the segregation and disqualification of racial and sexual others from the national imaginary. At work in this dynamic is a form of sexual exceptionalism – the emergence of national homosexuality, what I term "homonationalism" – that corresponds with the coming out of the exceptionalism of American empire.
>
> (Puar 2018: 2)

Homonationalism can be understood as a practice of regulating and withholding rights alongside recognition. Homonationalism prominently comes to the fore when nation-states commodify, legalize, and otherwise seek to integrate LGBT people through legal recognition (McNeal and Brennan 2021: 163). This process includes the enactment of international human rights obligations around the right to live free from persecution on the basis of gender and sexuality – therefore making the recognition of LGBT asylum-seekers part of the nation-building project.

LGBT asylum-seekers are therefore caught in a bind: asylum-seekers who fall into British notions of what an LGBT person should comport themselves or know about have the possibility of receiving status, but those who conform more towards cultural contexts not encompassed by UK state understandings lose their possibilities for future asylum (Lopes Heimer 2020: 191). These expectations might include being out at work, participating in LGBTQ+ nightlife events, familiarity with particular iconography (e.g., rainbow flag, pink triangle), and more; however, these flattened expectations can quickly shift into stereotypes that miss out on the lived experiences of LGTBQ+ life in the UK that is shaped by geography (McKearney 2021), age, gender, family's cultural background, and ethnicity (McKeown et al. 2010). Further, in some cases, these state understandings take the form of cisgender, heterosexual government employees making mistaken assumptions about what it means to be LGBTQ+ in the UK. During the examination stage of one hearing I observed, a cisgender, heterosexual HOPO – someone who represents the Home Office at tribunal hearings and is generally charged with defending an initial determination – argued that an asylum-seeker could not be "genuinely" gay because the asylum-seeker, a heterosexual and cisgender young man, did not have something that he assumed a gay person would have:

Brian (HOPO):	Do you go to the gay community's pubs and clubs?
Jawad (asylum-seeker):	Previously, yes. But now, no.
Brian (HOPO):	So you have nothing in the way of photographs or membership cards for gay pubs and clubs?
Jawad (asylum-seeker):	I have been [to gay bars], but they didn't have membership cards, and I didn't see a reason at the time for photos.

Manchester – where this took place, and where Jawad lived – has a vibrant LGBTQ+ scene, which in the downtown area is centered on the bars and clubs that pack Canal Street. I had been to a few of these places, as had friends, and none of us had ever heard of any kind of "membership card" that was offered, beyond a "VIP" discount card.[1] Further, attending a gay bar or not is not evidence that someone is gay; these bars are open to all and attract a diverse clientele that includes cisgender and/or heterosexual attendees.

Homonationalism embedded in the process of asylum shapes the future possibilities of asylum-seekers. In the preceding case, it is the balancing between the broader UK advocacy for sexual minorities as part of British liberal, democratic values and – building upon both border logics and legal ontologies that extend from the past to the present (Han and O'Mahoney 2014) – withholding status from minority ethnic,[2] migrant LGBTQ+ people. This balancing comes in part in the form of evaluating the sexualities of asylum-seekers, granting status if the expression of sexuality or gender is found legible in the right ways (Hertoghs and Schinkel 2018: 712). At the same time as this enforced restriction, some LGBT asylum-seekers do describe feelings of safety, belonging, and independence when they reach the UK (Singer 2021: 244). Yet because of the processes and pressures of asylum-seeking, LGBT asylum-seekers are pushed towards considering the UK a "queer haven" where they can live in a "homonationalist" future (Raboin 2017: 19), the past broken from the future through the rupture of claiming asylum.

Claiming status in Europe may therefore necessitate "playing along" with particular understandings of gender and sexuality. Therefore, for LGBT asylum-seekers to be legible to the UK state, they must fit themselves into a homonationalist understanding of what it means to act, look, and be LGBT. This includes narratives of "coming out," which are seen both as requirements of "credible" LGBT narratives, even though participating in events to mark a "coming out" – like a Pride parade, or even just a family event – might be impossible, given the asylum-seeker's race, class, or country context (Lopes Heimer 2020: 191). As Raboin writes:

> [T]he cruel optimism of LGBT asylum is to consider happiness as a neoliberal prom-ise, where being able to build a safe, open life in the UK is linked to a wider set of discourses about what it means to be a happy and successful LGBT worker and citizen in the UK.
>
> (Raboin 2017: 128)

In the case of Brian and Jawad, Brian used the evidence of a lack of "membership cards" during his submissions, at the end of the tribunal hearing. However, Brian's attempts to determine that Jawad was not gay resulted in a judicial interjection:

Brian (HOPO):   The Secretary of State has not evidenced that the appellant [Jawad] was not genuinely gay, and he has not evidenced a gay lifestyle –

Eileen (Judge):   But he has. Turn to the witness statement for the last witness he heard, paragraph 5, the reference to the LGBT fellowship.

In this case, the judge had little patience for the HOPO's assertion – she rolled her eyes visibly and interrupted him – and directed his attention to a witness who led an LGBT faith group for those new to the Church of England, and who had just given evidence.

Proving gender and sexuality

To return to the issue raised at the beginning of this chapter – how precisely claims for asylum are assessed in the UK system – the questions of evidence and narrative around these two kinds of asylum claims are rooted in an asylum-seeker's "credibility." For the state offices engaged with assessing asylum claims, credibility is an attempt to ascertain a "true essence" of an asylum-seeker's sexuality or gender (Calogero 2017). In the case of LGBTQ claims, this often depends on whether an asylum-seeker is able to prove their sexuality. The UK asylum system is not about to take in any and all who may be at risk of persecution, so the state instead requires asylum-seekers to "prove" their claim. In this section, I elaborate on how asylum-seekers are required to "prove" themselves, in order to receive access to state protection.

The UK is, of course, not the only state that assesses asylum-seekers on the basis of external evidence, nor are claims of belief or conversion singular in their require-ments to provide particular evidence of persecution. Translation of international law to national law, rules, and policy is part of the process of implementing international law. As McGuirk (2018) notes in her work on NGOs supporting LGBT applications in the United States, asylum-seekers claiming on the basis of sexuality may feel pressure to out themselves for the sake of their asylum application – balancing the desire to not be "out" and a concern for safety with the need for status – and the rhetoric of proving oneself inside a particular discourse of homosexuality can be the way to successfully receive status. Hertoghs and Schinkel consider how asylum-seekers in the Netherlands engage an "infrastructure of selfhood" to argue for a consideration of the "account" of sexuality demanded by the state (2018). Asylum processes force individuals to describe their private lives in a public fora and potentially face risks if returned – not just as a failed asylum-seeker, who might draw state attention anyways through the deportation process, but there are particular risks for those like a failed LGBTQ+ asylum-seeker who would be returned to a place with anti-LGBTQ+ sentiment or legislation. However, these risks and post-deportation harm remain seriously understudied, in large part because of the difficulties in following up and monitoring outcomes with so-called "failed asylum-seekers" (Alpes et al. 2017).

While states require claims of sexuality and belief as a way to determine internal states, other kinds of asylum applications use external evidence – frequently found on the body – to substantiate claims of harm made in the past. This is most notably the case for claims of asylum on the basis of torture, where doubt is embedded in evaluations of past harm. To provide a standardized way of assessing bodily harm caused by torture, the UN established the Istanbul Protocol in 1999. The Istanbul Protocol outlines guidance for rendering narrative out of physiological marks of harm. In response, some scholars have noted how medical assessments highlight the range of uncertainties available to medical experts assessing torture (Kelly 2012). Others have called attention to how medical assessments at all stages of asylum-seeking – including of those at risk for self-harm – continue to both fail and contradict the duty of care the Home Office has towards even detained asylum-seekers (Bhatia and Burnett 2019).

While cases like claims on the basis of gender or sexuality do not have these kinds of guides that discern external evidence of sexuality, asylum-seekers, their supporters, and their legal support (if they have any) must supply evidence in order to prove their credibility as "genuine." What this "evidence" is, and how it is considered, encompasses a range of information, from oral testimony to documents, to physical artifacts brought to an asylum interview or tribunal hearing. At an initial claim, an asylum-seeker might be asked to provide additional details about their sexuality, or particular details about their religious beliefs and practices. However, these details have included requests from the Home Office to provide photographic evidence of homosexual sex (Hall 2013), or extremely graphic questions about sexual activities, including details about ejaculation and condom use (Taylor and Townsend 2014).

This approach has received pushback not just from asylum-seekers and legal professionals but also from individuals doing community support work. In an interview with two community leaders, Daniel and Phil, we commiserated about how the Home Office and HMCTS failed to properly understand or evaluate LGBT asylum-seekers. Daniel, Phil, and I had been speaking about faith-based cases, but in noting how many claims on the basis of gender or sexuality we had observed, we began to speak about the similarities. For example, Home Office decision-makers have asked newly converted Christian asylum-seekers detailed questions about the Bible. While knowing particular details about the Bible is not the benchmark for determining who is and who is not a Christian, Home Office employees have been known to get these details wrong themselves, while still assessing asylum-seekers' answers against this "Bible test" framework (e.g., Ainsworth 2016; Sherwood 2016; Schaverien 2019). "It's because it's intangible. . . . [I]t is similar to some of the stuff around LGBT issues, and some of the issues and some of the work that I've done in supporting LGBT Christians for asylum-seekers, not from Muslim countries, but from sub-Saharan African, very conservative Christian countries like Uganda," the older man, Daniel, said, with a shake of his head. "And again, at one point the Home Office [employees] were first expecting people to produce videos of themselves indulging in sex,[3] and [sex] with somebody does not prove that they genuinely were gay. And, you know, how far do you get with stuff?"

All three of us shook our heads in acknowledgment of what asylum-seekers were subjected to; while we knew that some things had improved, asylum-seekers still faced difficulty in overcoming not only state doubt but also the impacts of continued intrusions into all aspects of their private lives. Daniel went on to discuss how he had previously appeared as a witness at a tribunal hearing for a gay man from Uganda, attending to testify not just that the man was indeed gay but also that he had seen the asylum-seeker at a meeting for LGBT Christians and that the man was also a Christian convert. As our conversation went on, both Daniel and Phil seemed aware of how the training of, and documentary evidence provided to, Home Office decision-makers impacted the quality of decisions made. "A lot of them are just out of university, don't have a lot of life experience, and they live in nice places and don't have much understanding of what goes on over there," lamented Phil, gesturing to a lack of training to government bureaucrats on life outside the UK, particularly outside of Europe. "So they've got all this stuff to process, and after those eight weeks [of initial orientation training], they get specific training. [For] LGBT claims, they get a day's worth of training." While some has changed in terms of Home Office training since our conversation in 2018, there remain serious issues in the lack of institutional support and ongoing education for Home Office employees (UK Comptroller and Auditor General 2020).

Skepticism here should be understood as something that is both individual – such as that of a decision-maker or tribunal judge – or can be something embedded within the asylum system itself. The impact of systemic skepticism within the Home Office – as well as in the British public – around asylum-seekers' claims subsequently finds its way to the street-level bureaucrats making individual determinations on asylum applications. Discretion is a necessary component of modern governance, as it allows for the application of law in a way that can allow some flexibility in the face of binary legal logics and individual actors representing and making decisions on behalf of the state. However, as the decisions of state employees are constrained by binary decisions – such as determining whether an asylum-seeker is credible or not, or whether someone will receive humanitarian status or they will not – discretion can still lead to situations of unjust assessment. Even with attempts at standardization, skepticism remains a serious issue, particularly in the face of the asymmetrical power relations between an asylum-seeker and a state bureaucrat; the state bureaucrat is the one who can determine what is and is not a "fact" or can be considered "evidence" (Dahlvik 2017: 373–374). As a result, asylum-seekers must therefore comport themselves and evidence their claims in such a way that a decision-maker or a judge believes their gender or sexuality to be what it is.

Localizing international and transnational human rights regimes

Asylum claims offer a unique perspective into the way international human rights frameworks practically work: asylum claims are submitted through processes initiated through international human rights regimes but largely implemented at the state – and sometimes local – level. Bureaucratic processes like asylum-seeking can therefore be understood to be a process of localizing human rights, of translating rights-based frameworks from one context to another. As Raboin emphasizes, LGBT asylum claims are important objects of study in part because these kinds of claims offer a way to locate transnational human rights discourse as embedded in a host country's context, thus allowing LGBT asylum claims to speak to the maintenance of the idea of the nation (2017: 2). Merry calls attention to the importance of women's rights as not just human rights discourse but also in terms of how they are leveraged in development contexts (Merry 2006: 39). Drawing upon this approach, in this section I highlight how human rights travel from the international to the local, and from the state-enforced to the individually supported. These human rights processes, I argue, are inflected with the homonationalist futurities I described earlier.

The processes of localization I allude to are, more explicitly, the enactment of obligations in the Refugee Convention, which includes rights to live free from certain kinds of persecution, as well as the right to seek safety elsewhere (UN General Assembly 1951). For UK asylum-seekers, this also includes the European Convention on Human Rights, as well as the UK Human Rights Act. Localization can be understood as a process of implementing and institutionalizing international legislation into national and local laws and policy (De Feyter 2006). The formal implementation of localization is therefore largely conducted by nation-states and can further involve discussions of how to implement particular human rights norms within a specific cultural context, such as regional or national approaches to human rights localization that include attention to Islamic legal practices (An-Naim 2021). In the UK, the implementation of international law happens not just through the broader process of asylum-seeking but also through guidance for Home Office decision-makers, the composition and critiques of which I discussed in the first section of this chapter. In these guidance documents, decision-makers are given brief descriptions of international instruments, like the 1951 Refugee Convention, the UN High Commissioner for Refugees (UNHCR) Guidelines on International Protection, and the Yogyakarta principles, as well as EU and European Court of Justice (ECJ) case law (UK Home Office 2016: 7–10).

It is not just nation-states who take on the rhetoric of human rights but also community groups, NGOs, and other groups or institutions. For example, groups like legal aid organizations that provide support to asylum-seekers attempt to enact international obligations around safety from persecution, and large NGOs link their local fights to transnational fights for safety from persecution in awareness campaigns and workshops for those supporting asylum-seekers. Attention to how gender and sexuality are understood by the UK state offers a better understanding of how the genders and sexualities of asylum-seekers are received by the state – which claims are seen by the Home Office or HMCTS as legitimate, and which experiences are simply not apprehended by the state (Urquiza-Haas 2017: 8). While nearly all the NGOs I engaged with did not provide specific legal services – and therefore did not "screen" for "genuine" LGBT asylum-seekers – non-state legal aid organizations can and do reinforce state understandings of what it means to be a "good" or "genuine" LGBT liberal subject, in part on the basis of whether a case is ascertained by the NGO to be "winnable" (McGuirk 2018). Human rights are therefore implemented on the ground through not just states but also non-state "translators" who render international human rights from text on a page into a particular lived, socio-historical context (Merry 2006).

However, sometimes this work of local groups includes pushing back against how states, transnational human rights NGOs, and international organizations seek to realize particular rights. During my fieldwork, I met numerous people who were part of local groups and national networks who spoke out against gestures towards human rights on a major scale – particularly campaigns that used images of asylum-seekers that many called "trauma porn" for the graphic images of suffering used to fundraise for NGOs or make political points. People like Alan, described in the introduction to this chapter, affirmed to me the importance of interpersonal relationships over this kind of campaigning; Alan himself explained to me that those around him worked hard to raise funds for events, nights out, and other ways to build community and friendship between asylum-seekers and Mancunians. This perspective aligns with the critiques of some scholars around the deployment of human rights rhetoric in ways that continue the marginalization of particular populations, such as critiques of Britain simultaneously deploying the rhetoric of human rights in the interest of a liberal political agenda while additionally restricting refugee status and support (Sales 2002).

Different genders, different categorizations

Thus far, I have generally focused on cisgender asylum-seekers who may be lesbian, gay, bisexual, queer, or otherwise not heterosexual. Here, I present an interesting legal conundrum in the framing of asylum-seeking claims made on the basis of gender: How can the asylum legal system consider the claims of transgender claimants? Should claims be considered singularly on the basis of being transgender – what Florence Ashley calls "transitude" (Ashley 2022) – or on the basis of persecution of a current gender? Within the UK asylum system, how might transgender claimants cases fall under claims on the basis of sexuality? In this section, I do not offer solutions to these questions but instead highlight how claiming status involves relying on certain bases for claims over others – as asylum-seekers' struggles can frequently fall under multiple categories, claiming can be strategic, and it is frequently complicated. Further, the framing I offer here shows that state conceptions of transgender identities are fractured, enacted through patchwork policies framed through the lens of cisgender ontologies.

As noted, the Home Office has guidance both targeted at countries and particular topics, including transgender asylum-seekers as a broad category. Guidance on claims based on sexuality make it clear that the Home Office does not group claims on the basis of being transgender as necessarily in the same category as claims on the basis of sexuality, contending that transgender people can be heterosexual, as well as lesbian, gay, or bisexual (UK Home Office 2016: 8). These topical policies are updated based on cyclical review, but the transgender category has not been updated since 2011. Sadly, given the Conservative government's anti-gender policies and contemporary anti-gender activism (Davies and MacRae 2023), delaying a review may be a positive for transgender asylum-seekers. In the meantime, the Home Office, HMCTS, barristers, and asylum-seekers themselves rely upon country information and guidance on sexual minorities. Therefore, it is trans asylum-seekers' categorization as "not heterosexual" that allows the framing of particular claims.

Toward the end of an interview with a group that provides free or low-cost legal support to asylum-seekers, we spoke about how asylum claims based on internal beliefs and identities – such as religion, political beliefs, gender, and sexuality – relied, at times, on strategic claims. These legal professionals additionally noted another point in how asylum claims are processed – that is, that they, at that time, had engaged with very few transgender cases, and that they had not seen a case based on gender, rather than being transgender. While I was discussing cases I had observed involving religious conversion to Christianity – the topic of my doctoral thesis – Layla and Mark began to talk about the implications of "genuine"-ness of gender. Neither doubted the "genuine" nature of transgender experiences, but instead they raised the point that transgender cases are generally classified as issues of sexuality, rather than of gender, and also pointed out that "gender-based persecution" can frequently exclude transgender people.

Layla: If I was born a male, and I came here [to the UK], and then I said I was a female, I would be at risk of persecution if I was returned to the country that I came from. . . . I wonder how the Home Office would treat them.

Mark: I think that it would depend on the kind of country. There are arguments for certain countries.

Layla: Have they been tested out?

Mark: No. Although, the Home Office guidance does cover Home Office cases.

Layla: But what would that be under? That's "gender" . . .

Mark: No, that would be under the label under *sexuality*, and in the guidance they'd have a bit of gender.

Layla: It blows your mind, as soon as you start thinking about it.

Mark: I think I came across a case, I'm not sure what happened. It's one of the referrals. Oh, that's right. South Africa.

Layla: So I looked at that, and that was when the person was absolutely adamant, they were convinced that our advice was wrong because it was so clearly obvious [to them] that because they were transgender, that would be their reason for seeking asylum – and so I remember being intrigued about that.

As they point out here, there is a difference between making a claim as a transgender asylum-seeker, making a claim as a transgender woman on the basis of a country being unsafe for all women, including cisgender women, and making a claim on the basis of sexuality. The two went on to discuss the case of an asylum-seeker who was referred to their office. The person, from South Africa, was transgender.[4] Mark, in particular, emphasized how Home Office country guidance and specific guidance on sexuality would be most helpful for the claimant. One reason that this kind of argument – that of transfeminine asylum-seekers claiming on the basis of discrimination against women, not just *transgender* women – might not be used is that it could open the UK to take in more applicants. Through case law, this reasoning could, for example, lead to precedent that might suddenly support half a particular country's population asylum applications with minimal evidentiary requirements, an outcome at odds with the Home Office's attempts to restrict borders. Regardless of possibilities for new precedents and shifts in asylum case law and policymaking, for Layla and Mark's client, the legal logicking did not matter: like with many asylum-seekers I heard about from legal professionals, this particular claimant's outcome was unknown. Given the state of overwork for those providing free or low-cost legal aid to asylum-seekers, there are always too many people to help and not enough helpers, so this claimant was swiftly lost in the system.

Living 'discreetly': get back in the closet?

One significant complication that comes up in UK LGBT claims is the issue of an asylum-seeker's ability to "live discreetly" (Wessels 2021). One might assume that a claim on the basis of gender or sexuality would involve an assessment of risk on return – again, the basis for asylum claims – as to whether or not someone can live openly in their gender or sexuality. However, in the UK, that is not the case. Within the UK asylum system, an asylum-seeker can be asked if they can live in a surreptitious manner – though I will go on to discuss some restrictions on this – or if they can be relocated within their country of origin to another area. Legal requests for LGBT asylum-seekers to live "discreetly" have been implemented in other common-law systems like Canada and Australia, though even when these policies are finally struck down, the normative assumptions and biases remain – frequently repackaged as "disbelief" in an asylum-seeker's narrative account (Millbank 2009). The pressure to "live discreetly" is a provision of liberal tolerance for marginalized individuals, and such pressure – particularly enshrined in state policy – is not new in the UK. The response of the UK state to the existence of homosexuality has been a push toward discretion, including for UK citizens, as far back as the 1957 Wolfenden Report, which emphasized a person's right to privacy as the reason for decriminalizing homosexuality (Millbank 2005). The pressure for migrants to live discreetly is therefore not something new within the contemporary asylum system but is rather an embedded aspect of state policy.

In the UK, the 2010 case of *HJ Iran* instituted restrictions on the imposition of "living discreetly," arguing that there is no way to parse the line between a condition enforced by the UK for an asylum-seeker to live discreetly upon being deported to their country of origin, and a Home Office or HMCTS determination that the asylum-seeker would be discreet if returned: mandating an LGBTQ+ asylum-seeker go back in the closet and assuming they would both curtail the rights of the asylum-seeker (*HJ Iran*, 53). In several of the tribunal hearings I attended, I noted frequent references to *HJ Iran* in closing submissions, given orally by the HOPO and barrister for the case. As one example, I observed a barrister invoked *HJ Iran* not in detail but as a now taken-for-granted aspect of asylum assessment that could be used as a bulwark against the HOPO's claims the asylum-seeker could simply be less "overtly" gay. "HJ Iran applies on return, as he cannot be quiet about his sexuality," the barrister said in final submissions. In this asylum hearing, I noted how the barrister emphasized the inapplicability of discretion. Living discreetly, the barrister claimed, was simply not an option. Rather than try to reason through a claim of why living a closeted life was not possible in this scenario, the barrister refuted it wholeheartedly.

In addition to the impact of *HJ Iran*, many LGBTQ asylum-seekers' claims rely on a claim to a breach of ECHR Article 8, privacy and family life (Millbank 2005). For asylum-seekers claiming in the UK after October 2000, when the UK Human Rights Act required adoption of the European Convention for Human Rights (ECHR), the consideration of one's Article 8 rights – the right to privacy and family life – provided additional grounds on which one could claim humanitarian status. Put together, these two components mean that asylum-seekers in the UK have been assessed not just as to whether they might be at risk if returned but also that they cannot hide their sexuality and/or religious beliefs in their country of origin. Therefore, asylum-seekers are required to simultaneously have a "coming out" narrative that establishes that their country of origin is likely to notice or persecute them and also entertain the possibility of "discreet" living.

Discretion around one's gender or sexuality is not applied to cisgender and hetero-sexual claimants, though it does appear in cases I observed involving claimants applying on the basis of religion, as I observed when judges asked Christian converts if they would be able to practice discreetly to avoid state detection. This push for asylum-seekers to be "discreet" should therefore be understood as a systemic issue, and one at the heart of a particular tension between international obligations and domestic policy. In short, liberal democracies are caught in the tensions between recognizing international human rights obligations and restricting state borders. Therefore, the UK created a way to reject LGBT claimants: the language of "discretion" (Raboin 2017: 72–73). Discretion allows the Home Office to reject LGBT asylum-seekers not just through not receiving their experiences of gender or sexuality but also because the Home Office or HMCTS could ask an asylum-seeker about the possibility to return and live "discreetly," which LGBT asylum-seekers subsequently have to prove is not possible (Dustin 2018: 110).

This push to go "back into the closet" is not universal, however. In several hearings I observed, judges made clear that the asylum-seeker in question could not be expected to suppress their sexuality or gender expression. To return to the case I described earlier, involving Jawad, during submissions, Jawad's representative emphasized this fact:

Maura (Barrister):   And of course, he can't be quiet about his sexuality, and he can't be expected to be quiet about it if forced to return to Iran.

Eileen (Judge):   Yes, of course – this is well-established.

In Jawad's case, he was lucky on a few counts. First, his representative was well-prepared and had relevant photographic evidence, witness testimony, and other ways of establishing his sexuality. Second, there was a judge who was known to have little patience for questionable HOPO behavior, and she made it clear in her words and physical comportment to all in the hearing room that she disagreed with the HOPO's attempt to claim a psychiatric assessment would be needed for a gay asylum-seeker. Jawad's appeal has a good ending – he won his appeal and received status to remain in the UK.

Conclusion

State conceptions of "genuine" gender or sexuality impact not just those seeking safety from persecution in another country but those already within that other country's borders. Attention to categories of law can help unsettle these particular assumptions. Issues with the UK Home Office's support of asylum-seekers are amplified when it comes to LGBT asylum-seekers, who find themselves caught in between expectations of how they may understand their gender or sexuality and how the UK state categorizes them (McIndoe 2018; Singer 2021: 257–258). In this chapter, I have emphasized how state conceptions of gender and sexuality – which are subsequently embedded in documentation, bureaucrats' dispositions, and affective experiences of governance and recognition – form an important aspect of the asylum process for LGBT asylum-seekers.

I want to end here with another refusal that echoes my initial refusal to assess asylum-seekers. Given the issues I have outlined here – as well as additional hurdles for LGBT asylum-seekers to overcome (Brewer 2020; Gruffydd-Jones 2020; Henley

2020; Knan and Hakuba 2020) – I do not offer policy changes to make LGBT asylum assessments "better": any policy outcome to change the kinds of evidence required by the state will subsequently turn into another hurdle for asylum-seekers to overcome. Instead, I urge attention to the processes and practices of assessment, with a critical eye on the assemblages of gender and sexuality that the UK state uses to measure asylum-seekers against.

Notes

1 An archived example of this is here: https://web.archive.org/web/20180723204700/www.canal-st.co.uk/vip-card.
2 The usual term in the UK is *Black, Asian, and minority ethnic* (BAME), which is used to refer to people who are not White. While the term is usually used for people who have some kind of status in the UK, I am using the term here to reiterate how asylum-seekers are indeed very much *within* the UK.
3 This only ceased as the result of a 2014 determination in a Dutch case to the Court of Justice of the European Union, *A, B, C v. Staatssecretaris van Veiligheid en Justitie*, which sought to delineate further what assessment measures for LGBTQ+ asylum-seekers could be understood to be rights violations.
4 The only information I was given about this individual was "transgender," so I am not sure if the person was transmasculine, transfeminine, non-binary, or another identity. I raise this to note that not just anti-transgender hate but transmisogyny in particular is increasingly making countries dangerous for transfeminine people. Future research on the experiences of different transgender people would be helpful in better understanding the contours of how the UK asylum system understands gender and transgender genders particularly.

References

Ainsworth, Michael. 2016. "'What Colour Is the Bible?': Asylum-Seekers and Immigration Officers | Law & Religion UK." *Law & Religion UK* (blog), August 15. http://www.lawandreligionuk.com/2016/08/15/what-colour-is-the-bible-asylum-seekers-and-immigration-officers/.

Alpes, Jill, Charles Blondel, Nausicaa Preiss, and Meritxell Sayos Monras. 2017. "Post-Deportation Risks for Failed Asylum Seekers." *Forced Migration Review* (54). https://ora.ox.ac.uk/objects/uuid:4aee3270-ff85-46ac-9fb0-b45bc992d742.

An-Naim, Abdullahi Ahmed. 2021. *Decolonizing Human Rights*. Cambridge: Cambridge University Press.

Ashley, Florence. 2022. *Banning Transgender Conversion Practices: A Legal and Policy Analysis*. Law and Society Series. Vancouver, BC: UBC Press.

Bachmann, Chaka L., and Sarah Singer. 2016. "No Safe Refuge: Experiences of LGBT Asylum Seekers in Detention." UK Lesbian & Gay Immigration Group and Stonewall UK.

Bhatia, Monish, and J. Burnett. 2019. "Torture and the UK's 'War on Asylum': Medical Power and the Culture of Disbelief." In *Tortura e Migrazioni (Torture and Migration)*, eds Fabio Perocco, 161–180. Venice: Edizioni Ca' Foscari. https://edizionicafoscari.unive.it/en/edizioni/libri/978-88-6969-359-5/tortura-e-migrazioni/.

Brewer, Kirstie. 2020. "How Do I Convince the Home Office I'm a Lesbian?" *BBC News*, February 26, sec. Stories. www.bbc.com/news/stories-51636642.

Calogero, Giametta. 2017. *The Sexual Politics of Asylum: Sexual Orientation and Gender Identity in the UK Asylum System*. Routledge Advances in Critical Diversities. New York and London: Routledge.

Campbell, John R. 2019. "The World of Home Office Presenting Officers." In *Asylum Determination in Europe: Ethnographic Perspectives*, eds. Nick Gill and Anthony Good, 91–108. Palgrave Socio-Legal Studies. Cham, Switzerland: Palgrave Macmillan.

Dahlvik, Julia. 2017. "Asylum as Construction Work: Theorizing Administrative Practices." *Migration Studies* 5(3): 369–388. https://doi.org/10.1093/migration/mnx043.

Davies, Huw C., and Sheena E. MacRae. 2023. "An Anatomy of the British War on Woke." *Race & Class* May: 03063968231164905. https://doi.org/10.1177/03063968231164905.

De Feyter, Koen. 2006. "Localizing Human Rights." *Discussion paper*, Antwerp, Belgium. https://repository.uantwerpen.be/docman/irua/ab5f01/a7de0e20.pdf.

Drewry, Gavin. 2009. "The Judicialisation of 'Administrative' Tribunals in the UK: From Hewart to Leggatt." *Transylvanian Review of Administrative Sciences* 5(28): 45–64.

Dustin, Moira. 2018. "Many Rivers to Cross: The Recognition of LGBTQI Asylum in the UK." *International Journal of Refugee Law* 30(1): 104–127. https://doi.org/10.1093/ijrl/eey018.

Gill, Nick. 2009 "Presentational State Power: Temporal and Spatial Influences over Asylum Sector Decisionmakers." *Transactions of the Institute of British Geographers* 34(2): 215–233. https://doi.org/10.1111/j.1475-5661.2009.00337.x.

Gruffydd-Jones, Eleanor. 2020. "LGBT Asylum Process Criticised by Applicants and MP." *BBC News*, March 1, sec. Wales politics. www.bbc.com/news/uk-wales-politics-51677425.

Hall, John. 2013. "'Inhuman and Degrading': Gay Asylum Seekers Feel They Must Go to Extreme Lengths to Prove Their Sexuality, Including Filming Themselves Having Sex." *The Independent*, February 4, sec. *Home News*. http://www.independent.co.uk/news/uk/home-news/inhuman-and-degrading-gay-asylum-seekers-feel-they-must-go-to-extreme-lengths-to-prove-their-8480470.html.

Han, Enze, and Joseph O'Mahoney. 2014. "British Colonialism and the Criminalization of Homosexuality." *Cambridge Review of International Affairs* 27(2): 268–288. https://doi.org/10.1080/09557571.2013.867298.

Henley, Jon. 2020. "LGBT Asylum Seekers' Claims Routinely Rejected in Europe and UK." *The Guardian*, July 9, sec. UK news. www.theguardian.com/uk-news/2020/jul/09/lgbt-asylum-seekers-routinely-see-claims-rejected-in-europe-and-uk.

Hertoghs, Maja, and Willem Schinkel. 2018. "The State's Sexual Desires: The Performance of Sexuality in the Dutch Asylum Procedure." *Theory and Society: Renewal and Critique in Social Theory* 47(6): 691–716. https://doi.org/10.1007/s11186-018-9330-x.

"HJ (Iran) (FC) (Appellant) v Secretary of State for the Home Department (Respondent) and One Other Action and HT (Cameroon) (FC) (Appellant) v Secretary of State for the Home Department (Respondent) and One Other Action." 2010.

Independent Chief Inspector of Borders and Immigration. 2018. *An Inspection of the Home Office's Production and Use of Country of Origin Information: April–August 2017*. https://assets.publishing.service.gov.uk/media/5a82b3c040f0b6230269c40e/An_inspection_of_the_production_and_use_of_Country_of_Origin_Information.pdf

Jacobs, Edward. 2011. *Tribunal Practice and Procedure*, 2nd ed. London: Legal Action Group.

Jubany, Olga. 2017. *Screening Asylum in a Culture of Disbelief: Truths, Denials and Skeptical Borders*. Cham: Palgrave MacMillan. https://doi.org/10.1007/978-3-319-40748-7.

Kelly, Tobias. 2012. "Sympathy and Suspicion: Torture, Asylum, and Humanity." *JRAI Journal of the Royal Anthropological Institute* 18(4): 753–768.

Knan, Shaan, and Susanne Hakuba. 2020. "Rainbow Pilgrims: The Rites and Passages of LGBTQI Migrants in Britain." *Oral History* 48(1): 97–116. www.jstor.org/stable/48568052.

Lopes Heimer, Rosa dos Ventos. 2020. "Homonationalist/Orientalist Negotiations: The UK Approach to Queer Asylum Claims." *Sexuality & Culture* 24(1): 174–196. https://doi.org/10.1007/s12119-019-09633-3.

McGuirk, Siobhán. 2018. "(In)Credible Subjects: NGOs, Attorneys, and Permissible LGBT Asylum Seeker Identities." *PoLAR: Political and Legal Anthropology Review* 41(S1): 4–18. https://doi.org/10.1111/plar.12250.

McIndoe, Gary. 2018. "Opinion: This Is What LGBTQI+ People Have to Go through to Gain Asylum in the UK." *The Independent*, July 29, sec. Voices. www.independent.co.uk/voices/lgbt-rights-gay-lesbian-bisexual-transgender-asylum-uk-a8468456.html.

McKearney, Aidan. 2021. "Sexual Citizenship: Rhetoric or Reality for Rural Gay Men in Ireland and England?" *Citizenship Studies* 25(5): 678–693. https://doi.org/10.1080/13621025.2021.1952930.

McKeown, Eamonn, Simon Nelson, Jane Anderson, Nicola Low, and Jonathan Elford. 2010. "Disclosure, Discrimination and Desire: Experiences of Black and South Asian Gay Men in Britain." *Culture, Health & Sexuality* 12(7): 843–856. https://doi.org/10.1080/13691058.2010.499963.

McNeal, Keith E., and Sarah French Brennan. 2021. "Between Homonationalism and Islamopho-bia: Comparing Queer Caribbean and Muslim Asylum Seeking in/to the Netherlands." In *Queer Migration and Asylum in Europe*, ed. Richard C. M. Mole, 162–183. UCL Press. https://doi.org/10.2307/j.ctv17ppc7d.15.

Merry, Sally Engle. 2006. "Transnational Human Rights and Local Activism: Mapping the Mid-dle." *American Anthropologist* 108(1): 38–51. https://doi.org/10.1525/aa.2006.108.1.38.

Millbank, Jenni. 2005. "A Preoccupation with Perversion: The British Response to Refugee Claims on the Basis of Sexual Orientation, 1989–2003." *Social & Legal Studies* 14(1): 115–138. https://doi.org/10.1177/0964663905049528.

Millbank, Jenni. 2009. "From Discretion to Disbelief: Recent Trends in Refugee Determinations on the Basis of Sexual Orientation in Australia and the United Kingdom." *The International Journal of Human Rights* 13(2–3): 391–414. https://doi.org/10.1080/13642980902758218.

Puar, Jasbir K. 2018. *Terrorist Assemblages: Homonationalism in Queer Times*. Durham, NC: Duke University Press.

Raboin, Thibaut. 2017. *Discourses on LGBT Asylum in the UK: Constructing a Queer Haven*. Manchester: Manchester University Press. https://doi.org/10.7228/manchester/9780719099632.001.0001.

Sales, Rosemary. 2002. "The Deserving and the Undeserving? Refugees, Asylum Seekers and Welfare in Britain." *Critical Social Policy* 22(3): 456–478. https://doi.org/10.1177/0261018302022200305.

Satzewich, Vic. 2015. *Points of Entry: How Canada's Immigration Officers Decide Who Gets in*. Vancouver, BC: UBC Press

Schaverien, Anna. 2019. "Rejecting Asylum Claim, U.K. Quotes Bible to Say Christianity Is Not 'Peaceful.'" *The New York Times*, March 21, sec. World. https://www.nytimes.com/2019/03/21/world/europe/britain-asylum-seeker-christianity.html.

Sherwood, Harriet. 2016. "Refugees Seeking Asylum on Religious Grounds Quizzed on 'Bible Trivia.'" *The Guardian*, June 7, sec. UK News. https://www.theguardian.com/uk-news/2016/jun/07/refugees-asylum-religious-grounds-quizzed-on-bible-trivia.

Singer, Sarah. 2021. "'How Much of a Lesbian Are You?': Experiences of LGBT Asylum Seekers in Immigration Detention in the UK." In *Queer Migration and Asylum in Europe*, ed. Richard C. M. Mole, 238–260. London: UCL Press. https://doi.org/10.2307/j.ctv17ppc7d.18.

Taylor, Diane, and Mark Townsend. 2014. "Gay Asylum Seekers Face 'Humiliation'." *The Observer*, February 8, sec. UK news. www.theguardian.com/uk-news/2014/feb/08/gay-asylum-seekers-humiliation-home-office.

Thomas, Robert. 2011. *Administrative Justice and Asylum Appeals: A Study of Tribunal Adjudica-tion*. Oxford and Portland, OR: Hart Publishing.

Tuckett, Anna. 2018. *Rules, Paper, Status: Migrants and Precarious Bureaucracy in Contemporary Italy*. First. Stanford, CA: Stanford University Press.

UK Comptroller and Auditor General. 2020. "Immigration Enforcement." *HC 110*. National Audit Office.

UK Home Office. 2016. "Sexual Orientation in Asylum Claims." Asylum Policy Instruction.

UK Home Office. 2022. "Assessing Credibility and Refugee Status in Asylum Claims Lodged on or after 28 June 2022." *GOV.UK*. https://assets.publishing.service.gov.uk/government/uploads/system/uploads/attachment_data/file/1083449/Asylum_interview.pdf.

UK Home Office. 2023a. "Asylum Claims on the Basis of Sexual Orientation, Year Ending June 2023." *Excel Spreadsheet. GOV.UK*. https://assets.publishing.service.gov.uk/government/uploads/system/uploads/attachment_data/file/1178027/asylum-sexual-orientation-jun-2023-ta-bles.ods.

UK Home Office. 2023b. "How Many People Do We Grant Protection To?" *GOV.UK*, August 24. www.gov.uk/government/statistics/immigration-system-statistics-year-ending-june-2023/how-many-people-do-we-grant-protection-to.

UN General Assembly. 1951. *Convention Relating to the Status of Refugees*. www.ohchr.org/en/instruments-mechanisms/instruments/convention-relating-status-refugees.

Urquiza-Haas, Nayeli. 2017. "Mistranslating Vulnerability: A Defense for Hearing." *Tilburg Law Review* 22(1–2): 5–30. https://doi.org/10.1163/22112596-02201002.

Wessels, Janna. 2021. *The Concealment Controversy: Sexual Orientation, Discretion Reasoning and the Scope of Refugee Protection*. Cambridge: Cambridge University Press.

Chapter 29

The "unique blend"

Reframing womanhood through Turkish drama series

Funda Üstek and Oğuz Alyanak

Original material prepared for the 7th edition.

In January 2016, the Turkish Council of Ministers released its 2016 program, outlining the duties allocated to each of the 21 ministries under its jurisdiction. Among the 519 measures proposed, one that was listed under the "Family and Woman" subheading concerned the regulation of the Turkish media and suggested the need "to diminish the negative effects of visual, auditory and social media on family" so as to "accommodate productions such as news, entertainment, films, etc. . . . to be suitable with our traditional family values."[1] Four ministries – amongst them the Ministry of Family and Social Policy – and one state institution, the Radio and Television Supreme Council (RTÜK), were put in charge of implementing this measure.[2]

Despite the measures, the goal of regulating gender roles, and redefining family structure and the role of women therein, is not an easy task, particularly at a time when these representations can no longer be contained within the boundaries of the nation-state. The last couple of years have witnessed an upsurge in the number of productions and exports of Turkish series. Today, Turkey is the world's second largest TV series exporter (Hurriyet Daily News 2014). Gender roles and family ideals portrayed in Turkish series are no longer consumed only by Turkish households but also by Turkish and non-Turkish households in the Middle East, Europe, and Latin America. As the series attain a transnational distribution, they transmit values about the Turkish family and convey messages to wider audiences. Politicians, in return, feel a greater need to tighten the grip on producers and to take measures to regulate mediatized representations of family and private life *a la turca*.

Neither the official attempts to regulate the production and circulation of popular media nor the focus on women within the broader context of family is new in the Turkish context. What is new, rather, is the name of the political elite in charge of these measures and its success in pursuing its political agenda. Since 2002, a self-declared conservative-democratic party, the Justice and Development Party (the AKP hereafter), has monopolized Turkish politics. The AKP, which represents the most contemporary and dominant face of Turkey's Islamic movement, envisions the construction of a society that takes Islam as its guiding principle in public and private domains. To that end, its members make repeated calls for raising a devout youth in Turkey – a responsibility

DOI: 10.4324/9781003398349-33

that they assign to state institutions (such as schools, mosques, the media), as well as the family (Hürriyet 2012). More recently, the need for a return to the roots – that is, "the traditional family and its traditional values" – has been one of the central components of the AKP's political discourse.

But what are these representations? In what ways do they comply with traditional family structure and idealized gender roles, and in what other ways do they contradict them? Through an examination of a select sample of internationally exported Turkish drama series since 2000, this chapter seeks answers to these questions.[3] The series were all initially presented to the Turkish audience and marketed abroad only after their acclaimed success in Turkey. Thus, the drama series open a window for us to examine the boundaries of gender roles in Turkish society, as well as the common themes through which discussions on womanhood are framed. Our analysis shows that the series, which are stuck in a tug-of-war between the Turkish state and its regulatory apparatus, and a popular demand for more sensational as well as sensual plots, display women who can incorporate strong, modern ideals while abiding by traditional gender roles. The women characters of the drama series represent what we call a "unique blend"; they are both rebellious for pushing the boundaries of traditional gender roles, and also conformist for not deviating radically from them.

We begin this chapter with a brief overview of the political context that shapes the trajectory of discussions on gender and family in Turkey, where we revisit some of the key policies pertaining to this subject. We retain our focus on Turkish women, whose positions in society are shaped by patriarchal gender roles, irrespective of secular or Islamist actors shaping the gender discourse. We then move to a discussion of what mediatized accounts, such as drama series, can tell us about the representations of womanhood and motherhood and ask in what ways these representations may serve or come in conflict with traditional gender values. Here, we are more interested in the politics behind the production of what gets broadcasted than its interpretation and consumption by local audiences.[4] In the final section, we share an analysis of Turkish drama series and present the "unique blend" concept. This concept helps us explain the ways alternative narratives are blended with traditional ones and how this enables Turkish series to make room for changes in gender roles without radically altering the dominant gender discourse.

"The woman question": girl, woman, or mother?

"The woman question" has always been topical in the Turkish context. While the answer has come in many forms, depending on the ideological currents shaping a given period, what remained central to discussions on women in Turkey was woman's position in society as wife and mother. The modern women of the late Ottoman Empire, the self-sacrificing mothers of the Independence War, the Western, *mondaine* women of the newly established secularist Republic, the sisters ("*bacı*") of the socialist 1960s and 1970s, or the oppressed Muslim girls of the post-1980s were all defined first and foremost through their duties at home as faithful wives and caring mothers. Women's biological capacity to bear the future generations of the nation, coupled with their moral capacity to represent the integrity and continuity of the family – "the building block" of the Turkish nation – has remained primary in nationalist and moralist discourses.

Today, the idea of a sovereign Turkish nation-state continues to rely on a gendered familial citizenship model, where "the ideal citizen is inscribed as a sovereign husband

and his dependent wife/mother rather than an individual, with the result that position within a familial discourse provides the person with status within the polity" (Sirman 2005: 148). As women are evaluated in relation to their familial status in their encounters with the outside world, status emerges as an important category that helps classify women. This categorization is also underpinned by the Turkish language, where a married woman would be referred to as woman (*kadın*) and an unmarried woman as girl (*kız*), regardless of age (with implicit references to the virginity of the latter).

Islam also plays an important role in this categorization process. In her ethnography on gender in rural Anatolia, Delaney shows how the connection of womanhood to procreation and fertility is seen as natural and legitimized through references to the Qur'an. Women, according to Delaney,

> are imagined as "soil", which can be either barren or fertile. They receive the seed-child and, if fertile, provide the generalized medium of nurture that helps to make it grow. Villagers used to cite the Qur'an in order to legitimate their views.
>
> (1995: 183)

Hence, procreation is part of the repertoire of speaking about women. Womanhood can hardly be described without referencing the ultimate duty of motherhood. As Özbay argues;

> [I]n Turkey, woman and mother can be used as synonymous categories. In such a cultural structure, for a woman to have no children is greatly demeaning. A childless woman was either not able to find a husband [*evde kalmış*, lit. left at home] or infertile [*kısır*]. Both words are used to degrade a woman.
>
> (1992: 5)

Despite the seeming rigidity of these categories, the cases of "unmarried women," "married childless women," and "single mothers" do exist. These cases, which blur the boundaries of the categories of "mother" and "wife," might be completely rejected at first sight as impossible, immoral, non-Turkish, or un-Islamic. They may be considered as radically deviating from traditional family values and gender roles. Those who blur the lines may be seen and treated as whores,[5] as opposed to mothers, who are conceived as "almost totally devoid of sexuality" (Saktanber 1995: 155). The dichotomy of single and unmarried, married with children, may hold in discourse, yet in practice, it fails to explain the reality on the ground. Alyanak and Üstek (2011) show that, within the context of single mothers and "illegitimate" children, as much as these categories are treated discursively as non-existing, they are part of reality. As these authors argue, this reality may not be discussed in political circles. It may not be problematized in public circles for fear of transgression, or even subversion. Yet even the existence of separate legal processes for registering illegitimate children reveal that they are not only imagined scenarios.

The "making" of Turkish woman

A closer look at what gets to be debated, and under what circumstances, in the political field might provide us with a better sense of the repertoires that make some categories of womanhood more acceptable than others. Most scholars trace the beginnings of the women's movement in Turkey to the early days of the Tanzimat era (1839–1876), as this period represents the opening up of the Ottoman Empire to Western modernization in all aspects of life, including influences on law, but also family structure. In this respect, measures such as the Land Law, which provided equal rights of inheritance to daughters and sons, abolition of slavery and concubinage, opening of state schools and Teachers' Training Colleges for girls, and the founding of women's organizations, including the first Woman's Labor Organization, are posed as some of the key developments (Dursteler 2008: 376). Subsequently, the first Family Code (from 1917) (though short-lived) gave important rights to women for divorce, annulment of marriage, and protection against forced marriages and hence played a crucial role in the enactment of women as citizens.

According to Kandiyoti (1989), whose work traces women's movements from the Tanzimat up until the founding of the new (Turkish) Republic in 1923, the early feminists attempted to carve themselves a space in a field dominated by patriarchy and Islam. In a widely circulated publication of late nineteenth/early twentieth century, *The Ladies' Gazette*, a woman's role was defined by a much-celebrated female activist of the time, Fatma Aliye Hanım, through three principles: "being a good mother, a good wife, and a good Muslim" (Kandiyoti 1989: 132). Challenging woman's status in society outright and attempting to overturn it would be an impossible endeavor, but by conforming to the established order, the early feminists were able to make their demands compatible with patriarchy and Islam and able to normalize aspects of women's public visibility, albeit in small steps. The attempts for women to gain ground and prestige by working within the system, rather than against it, is a strategy that Kandiyoti called "bargaining with patriarchy" (Kandiyoti 1988a). This strategy continues to play a crucial role in the imagining of women's status in a society that is still defined by patriarchal and Islamic values.

Following the founding of the Turkish Republic in 1923, the questions posed during the Tanzimat on the status of women in society came once again to the fore. This time, being "modern" was not seen as paradoxical for women, though being "Western" was. The fear of women becoming "over-Westernized" and *mondaine* was evident. For instance, the first beauty contest was held in 1929, leading to the crowning of Keriman Halis as Miss World in 1932 (Shissler 2005). Beauty contests opened up new spaces for women to participate in public life and tested the limits to their public visibility. Although Keriman Halis's success was much celebrated, some newspapers reported that upon her return, Miss Halis's family wanted to marry her off immediately, now that "the whole world 'knew her'" (Libal 2014: 51).

The secular Republic's institutions were profoundly influenced by the Western imaginary. The adoption of (a modified version of) the Swiss Civil Code and Italian Penal Code, the Latin Alphabet, the International Gregorian Time and Calendar System, and the introduction of surnames and the workweek marked important institutional changes. The modernization of women's status in society was seen as an almost-natural outcome of the Westernization of the Turkish institutions and organizational infrastructure, and necessary reforms were made wherever needed in this regard. Unification of the education system, for instance, would involve co-education, and Turkish women would be given the right to vote; or the adoption of the Western attire would also be expanded to women (though veiling was never publicly banned like *fez*). But there was a significant difference between the modernization of women's public status and the gender values pertaining to their existence in public and private life. In the context of modernization of gender values, a link with a distant Turkish past was made, and "Western values" were never imported like the legal and organizational systems. Instead, it was ascertained that gender values did not need to be taken from elsewhere (including the West), because they were already an inherent part of Turkish culture. This meant that women's rights already existed among Turks prior to their conversion to Islam but had been forgotten. Accordingly, the dominant discourses on women's honor and chastity would still be counted as among the norms that would not change even if women would be modernized, and links with the mythic Turkish past were drawn when necessary (Sirman 1989: 12). As White duly argues, "the young Republic need not look to the West, with its dangerous notions of romance and individualism, for a model of feminism and egalitarianism, but could look to its own semi-mythic past in pre-Islamic Turkic Central Asia" (2003: 147).

The blending of mythic Turkish gender values and the modern public status of women could only be possible if Islam was kept out of public affairs. Accordingly, the Office of the Caliphate and Shari'a Courts were abolished, and *laïcité* was incorporated into the constitution. The ideal Republican woman was portrayed as "pure, honorable and unreachable, serving the higher cause of modernization. In that manner . . . as self-sacrificing, sacred creatures whose integration into public sphere as teachers, nurses, and professionals does not threaten morality or order" (Müftüler-Baç 1999: 307). Women's integration to the public sphere was supported and celebrated, but as Mustafa Kemal Atatürk famously noted, "the primary responsibility of women is motherhood" (Taşkıran 56; 62–63, cited in Delaney 1995). In this regard, motherhood became one of the important ways in which Turkish women could both modernize and adhere to the Turkish gender roles at the same time as "the correct femininity" was "to be the merciful and virtuous mother of the nation" (Sirman 2005: 163).

Although motherhood was much celebrated, it was only supported when it was the outcome of marriage. Single women, moreover, were still seen "as a threat to the social order" (Müftüler-Baç 1999: 307). Islam and the early Republican discourse on women were, in many ways, similar, as they both put forth asexual stereotypes in order to deal with women's potentially threatening status. In both discourses, marriage was considered a responsibility. As White notes, "choosing not to marry was an egocentric act, amoral and irresponsible. . . . Motherhood was a patriotic duty. Love and passion in the early Republic were to be subordinated to love of nation" (2003: 154). Single mothers, childless wives, and children born outside of wedlock were seen as social anomalies and played a central role in the social imaginary about how things could go wrong if women did not properly follow their ascribed gender roles and traditional gender norms.

Another important turning point in the women's movements in Turkey was the post-1980 coup d'état period, whereby a significant effort to put Islam back into the governance of social and political and family life took place. This period also marked the emergence of an Islamist elite, who were on the lookout for their own "unique blend" of modernity and gender roles. Kadıoğlu notes that the new Islamic elite "voice(d) grievance regarding the double burden placed on modern Kemalist women who successfully managed the home and a career" (1994: 647). The early Republican ideals of intellectual modern women who also served as the breeders of the nation were just too difficult to achieve. Like the Kemalist elite who envisioned a pre-Islamic feminist ideal which they deemed authentic to Turkish culture, the Islamist elite sought an ideal femininity in a mythical Islamic golden age (*asr-ı saadet*), one in which women would be treated with dignity, and also had assigned duties and roles in family life, without necessarily aspiring to be literal "equals" of men. In this regard, Islam provided new opportunities for political mobilization, especially for conservative women, whose access to the public sphere was limited by Turkey's secular principles (especially with respect to veiling), and a new patriarchal moral order grounded in an Islamic worldview (White 2002; Ayata and Tütüncü 2008).

In this period, Kemalist ideals about women as modern mothers of the future nations became seasoned with a touch of Islam. This time, women's role as reproductive and nurturing agents were described as natural and God-given. Islamic notions such as *fıtrat* (disposition), *nesil* (generation), and *ümmet* (religious community) started to define the woman's status in public and private life. Family, already conceptualized as the central piece for the perpetuation of the Turkish nation, became the container of an Islamic moral order (Sirman 1989: 26). Women, who were already perceived as a threat to the social order and whose visibility had to be contained, now carried "the danger of *fitna*, ability to create chaos through sexual attraction" (Müftüler-Baç 1999: 306). This dichotomization of women into wife and mother (thus good) and single or child-less wife (thus dangerous) categories found much support in public policy as well. The right-wing parties of the post-1980 period normalized the practice of virginity tests as a vital means of upholding "our practices, customs, and traditions [*örf, adet ve gelenek*]" and a "proper and effective means of ensuring good upbringing [*terbiye*] in girls [*when*] sustaining the 'value judgments' of the society were at stake" (Parla 2001: 61). Also, in this period, rape would be decriminalized if the rapist would agree to marry his victim (Ilkkaracan 2007).

Until the mid-2000s, the political scene in Turkey witnessed a tug-of-war between secular-minded Kemalist politicians and their conservative-minded Islamic counterparts. Women were always at the center of their political debates. The question to allow or not allow the veil in public offices and universities, for instance, became a matter of heated debate (Göle 2002; Çınar 2005).[6] Following the European Union's opening of the accession negotiation talks with Turkey in 2005, the subsequent AKP governments passed a string of legislations. Some of them became key developments for gender equality, whereas others signaled significant setbacks. For instance, a new Civil Code in 2001 enabled women to take equal share of property in cases of divorce (Dedeoğlu 2012: 276), and a new Labor Code in 2003 abandoned the prohibition of women from night shifts (Kılıç 2008: 497). However, simultaneously, there have been attempts to reinstitute an Islamic social order, akin to the pre-Republican period. The first was the adultery debate of 2004, where the AKP attempted to re-criminalize adultery, which was decriminalized in 1998. While the attempt was not successful, it was an important reminder that progressive legislation did not always come from progressive worldviews (Ayata and Tütüncü 2008; Çıtak and Tur 2008: 463). The second was the discussion over an amendment to the constitution to implement gender quotas the very same year, which was rejected by AKP politicians, including the then–prime minister, now president, Recep Tayyip Erdoğan, who argued that women should not be treated as tradable goods on which one could impose a quota (Ayata and Tütüncü 2013: 375–378; Çıtak and Tur 2008: 457). More recently came the cohabitation debates of 2012 and 2013, when then–Prime Minister Erdoğan vocalized his dislike for couples outside of wedlock living (cohabitating) in the same house (Üstek and Alyanak 2013). In Turkey, where most single individuals are dependent on their family and most women are dependent on men (fathers, brothers, or husbands) for survival (Özar and Yakut-Cakar 2013), living alone or cohabitating is considered a transgression of established order.

Moreover, legislation does not necessarily mean implementation. For example, the Regulation on Working Conditions of Pregnant and Nursing Women made it obligatory for businesses to provide nursery rooms and preschool facilities if they employed more than 50 women (Dedeoğlu 2012: 282). But the law was not strictly enforced, and the lack of interest from some businesses in employing women so as to avoid the costs of nurseries was often overlooked (Dedeoğlu 2012: 282). In a similar vein, an amendment to the Law on Municipalities in 2005 enforced the opening of women's shelters for all municipalities with a population size of more than 50,000 (Coşar and Yeğenoğlu 2011: 562). This population size is significantly lower than the one recommended by the EU (7,500), yet the number of women's shelters is still worryingly low, with 86 shelters for a female population of over 38 million women.[7] In a way, this obvious gap between legislation and implementation signals that the projection of the image of an emancipated woman is more important than their actual emancipation (Muftuler-Bac 1999: 304).

In the post-2000 period, Turkey also witnessed a neoliberal transformation of social services which see the family (women in particular) as the carriers and breeders of the state, and thus pushes for replacing welfare services with incentives for women to stay at home and engage in care activities (Yılmaz 2015). Legislation which (1) provides women the possibility to claim financial income in return for caring for their sick, disabled children, or relatives; (2) reduces the necessary amount of time spent at full-time work for pensions for women who give birth to more than three children (Coşar and Yeğenoğlu 2011: 557, 568; Yazıcı 2012: 110, 115); or (3) provides monetary incentives for couples to marry before the age of 28 under the rubric of "Dowry Transfer" (*Çeyiz Yardımı*) are just a few examples of such incentives.

Earlier in this chapter, we mentioned the difficulty of categorizing women in the early Republican period. This difficulty, as demonstrated, persists to date, with obvious favoring of married women and mothers over their single or childless counterparts. Be it secular or Islamic, the policies that shape Turkish women's public visibility and rights and roles are defined almost always through their inscribed patriarchal gender roles. In the next section, we will elaborate more on how this "unique blend" is taken up and performed in Turkish media.

Mediatization of gender roles and regulation of mediatized discourse

Although televised broadcasting in Turkey dates back to 1968, it was not until 1990 that satellite broadcasting was introduced and airwaves were made available for the use of private entrepreneurs (Öncü 2006: 228). The introduction of private channels and broadcasting brought new representations of family life and gender into the public sphere. Some of these representations would radically challenge traditional gender roles, such as the women characters who were "dominated objects of sexual pleasure," instead of the "devoted mother" and "faithful wife" characters of the single-channel TRT era (Saktanber 1995: 154). There was, however, always an unspoken limit to how much sexuality could be shown on TV, and certain productions, in particular foreign ones, could only be broadcast after being censored (Saktanber 1995: 158). Despite the abundant use of censorship, which continues to the present, private media tested the boundaries of "acceptable" gender roles, often by providing alternative narratives to the mainstream patriarchal gender discourse in an attempt to please the heterogeneous audiences of Turkish society (Öncü 1995: 228). Soon, the types of women characters on Turkish TV started to multiply, although they were not all welcomed by diverse sectors of Turkish society to the same degree.

One example is the *femme fatale* characters, which were common in Turkish cinema. When Turkish movies were screened on TV, these characters also entered people's homes. The main difference after commercialization was their number, frequency, and level of exposure. This led to concerns over the transformation of Turkish cultural identity with too much Western influence from American, as well as European, productions, and their Turkish adaptations triggered a long-ingrained fear of Turkish women becoming "too Westernized" (Sahin and Aksoy 1993; Aksoy and Robins 1997). In response, a new law was passed in 1994 to establish the Radio and Television Supreme Council (RTÜK), a media-watch institution, to punish and criminalize those representations that did not comply with the national and spiritual values of the society and public morality.[8] These broad ideals were particularized by stressing that RTÜK would essentially oversee the protection of the family and ensure that women would not be oppressed or exploited. Children were also noted as within the RTÜK's target group, as they would prevent programs that might hinder children's mental and moral development. Men were not listed in RTÜK's target group.

RTÜK's founding principles can be read in two related ways. The first is that the targeting of women and children signifies that they are psychologically vulnerable and can easily derail from the "right" public morality ideals. By ensuring that they are not presented with "wrong" representations on TV, RTÜK essentially protects their moral and psychological well-being and serves as a reminder of the right path in life. Following this logic, the Turkish state infantilizes women and children, who need moral and spiritual guidance. This also envisions a higher moral capability for men, as their moral and psychological well-being is not considered to be "threatened" like that of women and children.

The second way of reading RTÜK's mission stems from the aforementioned age-old fear of Turkish women becoming too Westernized. As television became an indispensable part of everyday life, more channels started competing for this lucrative market through seeking higher ratings. This led to the gradual pushing of the boundaries of the dominant discourse on the right order of gender roles in society. The equation of women to family, as presented earlier, left little room for discussing the anomaly categories. Although such cases became topics of inquiry in the Turkish cinema between 1940 and 1980, women who challenged their ascribed gender roles and values were often depicted as immoral characters who would never be able to find true love and happiness. Regardless of class and social status, women's representation was limited to the axis of their vulnerability in the outside world/public life and their being saved by falling in love and marrying their love (Künüçen 2001: 57). Nonetheless, this end was only achievable for those women who did not attempt to challenge the gender discourse. For example, having a child born outside of marriage was acceptable only if the woman bearing the child chose to "cover up" by marrying someone, through which she would be able to hide the fact that she became pregnant out of wedlock. The man she married could well be the father of the child, but also acceptable was a man arranged for her by her family or one they forced her into marrying. Single motherhood was tolerated if women were deserted by their husbands or their husbands died. Not marrying would be acceptable if women needed to commit their lives to the care of sick or frail family members. Since Turkish cinema was still heavily regulated by the Turkish state, the new TV channels would need a similar type of screening so as to ensure that the women characters would not become too Westernized or face the tragic fates their counterparts faced in Turkish cinema.

RTÜK is endowed with punitive measures to ensure these gender roles and values. These measures come in the form of monetary fines, banning of certain shows altogether, or imposing "blackout" days. Showing a sexual scene too explicitly, a passionate kiss, or swearing could all potentially be considered sufficient for facing such measures. For instance, in 2009, a private TV broadcaster's (Kanal D) popular TV series *Aşk-ı Memnu* (Forbidden Love) was fined 250–500 thousand Turkish lira (162,500–325,000 USD). The fine was justified under the following rationale by the AKP-leaning board members of RTÜK: "Sex scenes are far too long. The male character's half naked body, and the female character's naked shoulders are shown for minutes. These scenes are unacceptable in a family series" (Milliyet 2009). In 2010, in another series, *Kılıç Günü* (Sword Day), shown on ATV, the depiction of a sexual scene between two men caused significant uproar in RTÜK, and the series was fined 250–500 thousand Turkish lira (162,500–325,000 USD). The head of RTÜK, Davut Dursun, argued that the fine was a way to defend against the normalization of homosexual relationships, which, he added, was damaging and contradictory to the national and spiritual values of the public and Turkish family structure (Hürriyet 2010). In another famous case, in 2012, the then–prime minister of Turkey, Erdoğan, slammed the producers of *Muhteşem Yüzyıl* (Magnificent Century) for misrepresenting Turkey's past and the lives of Turkish ancestors (Batuman 2014). The series, which became Turkey's most exported TV series, was based on the life of the Ottoman sultan Süleyman the Magnificent. The sequel to the series in 2016, this time based on the life of Kösem Sultan (one of the most influential woman figures in the Ottoman harem and later wife of Ottoman Sultan Ahmet I) was fined in 2016 for putting on display a fratricide scene set in the Imperial Palace. The practice, the RTÜK argued, displayed elements that would hinder a child's trust in his family, thereby harming his physical, mental, and moral development, and hence contrary to Turkish family values and principles (Yılmaz 2016).

Today, in addition to the state and its regulatory apparatus, non-government organizations, too, take an active stance in preserving gender ideals on TV and on other media platforms. One recent example is IKADDER (Foundation for Women and Women's Institutions in Istanbul). The NGO recently completed a project called "My Family-P: Family Oriented Media Observation and Evaluation Project," whose mission was to raise public awareness about mediatized misrepresentations of the Turkish family and to transform each TV viewer into a media watchdog.[9] Supported by the Ministry of Family and Social Policies and funded by the Ministry of the Interior, the project provides detailed information on the steps a conscientious citizen could take to vocalize his/her individual reaction, and to reach out other regulatory agencies, such as RTÜK.[10]

Amidst these restrictive measures, in recent years, the Turkish TV series industry has achieved an insurmountable boom. In 2015 alone, Turkish exports of drama series exceeded 250 million USD, bringing Turkish dramas into the living rooms of families in more than 70 countries worldwide. These series build on stories that take place in Turkey or are based on Turkish history (such as the Ottoman Empire). In doing so, they present to the audience not just a storyline but also characters whose very identity shapes that storyline. Gender here is an evident one, as nearly all drama series are based on a love story – often complicated by cultural differences pertaining to class or religiosity.

The storylines juxtapose different families with different worldviews and discuss how these differences might be interpreted in diverse ways by family members, each of which takes a different stance based on his/her social role. The attempt is to give a moral lesson – one that usually involves the effects of cultural change on traditional values and family structure (Işık 2013: 568). The audience gets introduced to different lives through snapshots of different gender roles, which are often provided in a binary fashion, such as modern versus traditional, secular versus religious, immoral versus moral, rich versus poor, wrong versus right. The plot "opens up new discursive spaces and maps out new constituencies where the actors, representative of competing definitions, come to clash. In this process, some are augmented while others are muffled" (Öncü 2006). It is within this ongoing struggle over definitions and categories, images and portrayals, that we find women's identity to be "made" and "remade" (Abu-Lughod 1998). Similar to representations of womanhood in novels and magazines of the late nineteenth and early twentieth century (Kandiyoti 1988b), drama series bring our attention to competing repertoires of social, cultural, and public narratives (Sirman 2000).

For the purposes of our analysis, the drama series are important because they offer snapshots of different categories of women: as single or married, or mother and childless. The clash and the concomitant remaking is a political one (Çetin 2014) in that it brings into question the legitimacy of the tradition and makes the fight over defending this tradition visible. And in making these categories, the anomalies come to be discussed on-screen: What happens to women who give birth outside of wedlock? What happens to women if their husbands die or desert them? What happens if they get raped? What happens if married women do not have children? One common theme cross-cutting the anomalies is that they are all female characters; unmarried men, childless men, or single fathers do not constitute problematic characters, except when their fatherhood qualities are put to test.

In light of these discussions, the following pages present an analysis of recent Turkish series which reach wide audiences on a transnational scale. Our analysis shows that these series present us with uniquely blended women narratives, that is, women who are capable of embodying both strong and self-empowering ideals as well as traditional gender roles. This unique blend, we argue, proves to be a palatable hybrid that caters to women within and beyond Turkey.

The "unique blend": strong and modern woman, but always a (potential) wife and mother

The "woman question" remains one of the major puzzles of modern Turkish history. What is rather curious is that the attempts to answer it – whether they are pursued by secular or Islamic actors – lead to a similar conclusion. That is, Turkish women's public visibility and rights are defined through dominant patriarchal gender roles, or what has come to be known in recent discussions as "traditional family values."

One of the reasons that popular TV dramas appeal to wide audiences seems to be that they challenge these traditions by providing alternative narratives to approach the woman question. The female characters offer alternative representations that describe, often in vivid detail, possible scenarios if routes other than marriage and legitimate (as opposed to out-of-wedlock) children are to be taken. Through the alternative paths they take, they question women's traditional roles as mothers and wives. However, one should also be reminded that these deviations are often juxtaposed with their traditional counterparts. Sometimes a friend, other times a mother-in-law, is brought into the picture to challenge the lead female character's actions and to evaluate her judgments so as to push the leading character to revisit her decisions. In this manner, they provide a litmus test for the lead character to reach a balance. Usually, we see that the lead character, upon further evaluation, comes to a conclusion that blends deviating aspirations with traditional gender roles. Hence, the audience follows a fluctuating life trajectory that takes the leading female character from one extreme to another until she reaches a middle ground, in some cases one that is more progressive than the one she has begun with, in other cases less. And in cases where such a middle ground is not attainable, the series often ends with the leading female character either taking her own life or being the victim of (or killed as a result of) an unfortunate event.

The drama series that we examine show that nearly all of them have at least one female character that derails from the ascribed gender values and/or norms. In *Aşk-ı Memnu* (*Forbidden Love*), an adaptation of a classic turn-of-the-twentieth-century novel, the lead female character enters an adulterous relationship with her husband's nephew; in *Binbir Gece* (*1001 Nights*), the modern-day *Arabian Nights*, the lead female character accepts money in return for a one-night stand; in *Aşk ve Ceza* (*Love and Punishment*), which has been exported to and broadcast in over 40 countries, the lead female character gives birth to a child from a one-night stand with a stranger, which she engages in when she gets drunk after a breakup; in *Iffet* (*Chastity*), a remake of a famous 1980s drama, the lead female character gets raped by her lover and seeks revenge; and in *Bir Istanbul Masalı* (*An Istanbul Fairytale*), a modern-day Romeo-and-Juliet, the lead female character enters a relationship with two brothers, one after another.

In case the lead female character is not challenging the dominant gender values and/ or norms, a supporting female character may be given the role of taking the unorthodox path. In *Fatmagül'ün Suçu Ne?* (*What's Fatmagul's Fault?*), the audience finds out that the supporting female character, who is married to the brother of Fatmagül (the lead female), fooled him into marriage when she was actually pregnant with someone else's child. In *Gümüş* (*Silver/Nour*), a much-celebrated series, especially in the Arab world, the lead actor's sister returns from the United States only to reveal that during the time her parents (and everyone else) thought she was studying, she actually gave birth to an illegitimate child. These examples can be further enumerated, but one important theme emerges: women do not always fit into the ascribed categories of marriage and legitimate children.

The drama series not only show anecdotal cases of women who do not follow ascribed gender roles but also situate them in a world in which they attempt to justify their actions or try to situate themselves in a society shaped by patriarchal gender norms and values. The audience witnesses women characters "bargaining with patriarchy" as a survival strategy, especially when they come to the realization that attempting to radically change the society they are in is not an easily achievable endeavor. For instance, in *Binbir Gece*, the lead female character engages in a one-night stand in exchange for money, but the audience knows that she does so to save her son, who needs to go through an expensive operation and treatment for leukemia. The norm that motherhood comes first and mothers would sacrifice anything – including their bodies – for their children is repeated throughout the series to justify that though not entirely a "pure" action, there cannot be any limit to a woman's sacrifice for her children. The audience is also informed numerous times that the lead character accepts this offer only after exhausting each and every other possibility for raising money for her son's treatment.

In another series, *Gümüş*, the sister later reveals that the father of her illegitimate daughter is actually her brother's best friend, and they get married shortly after this announcement. This way, her grandfather, who initially refrains from talking to her and listening to "her side of the story," forgives her and embraces his granddaughter, and the family goes back to their lives as if nothing has ever happened. In *Iffet*, the lead female character marries another man to take revenge on her lover, who rapes her, but eventually realizes that she is still in love with her (rapist) lover and returns to him. In making this decision, she follows her best friend's advice to start a family and forget the past. In this scenario, her friend is presented as an ideal wife in a happy marriage, who knows the secrets to making a marriage work. Finally, in *Bir Istanbul Masalı*, the lead character dates both brothers but engages in a sexual relationship with one of them and does so only after marrying him.

For women who do not learn from their mistakes or try to push the boundaries of what is acceptable "too little too much," some sort of "punishment," or at least a series of misfortunes, awaits. When the lead female character in *Aşk-ı Memnu* does not want to settle for just an affair but actually would like to run away from her marriage, she finds out that she is actually alone in this desire. Her lover not only refuses to accept their affair publicly but also plans to marry his uncle's daughter. At the turn of events, she cannot find any way out and kills herself. In *Eve Düşen Yıldırım* (*Lightning That Struck Our Home*), the lead female seduces two brothers, although unintentionally. When she finally realizes the misfortunes that happened to the family as a result of her entering their lives, she also finds resolution in suicide. In *Adını Feriha Koydum* (*I Named Her Feriha* [*Merry*]), one supporting actress who cheats on her husband faces a series of misfortunes throughout the series. First, her husband finds out about it and has a heart attack and dies. Then, her lover leaves her. Finally, her children despise her. The impossibility of happiness for women characters who push the boundaries of what is acceptable too much is an important theme that cuts across all the TV series examined here. They also present the limits to the Westernization of women and test their morality *vis-à-vis* Western values, as children outside of marriage, premarital sex, and adultery remain taboos for women.

An element common to these series is that a woman's fight against challenges posed by a patriarchal society is seen as an empowering act. Women who face misfortunate do not see it as an act of fate. Nor do they simply accept the outcomes. Instead, they fight against the obstacles and carve a new path for themselves. *Fatmagül'ün Suçu Ne?*, the two-season, 80-episode series, tells the story of a young village girl, Fatmagül, who is subjected to gang rape by children of powerful and rich families. Consequently, Fatmagül is forced to marry one of her rapists (who later turns out to have not raped her but "merely" watched the act) so as to save her family's honor. Rather than caving in to the powerful family's attempts to cover up the rape and drop the case, Fatmagül chooses to pursue the legal battle against her rapists. The whole trial process, and the fight she puts up for her dignity and rights, makes her a stronger woman who not only wins the case but also becomes an example for others who are afraid of coming out with their experiences of sexual violence.

As another example, in *Bitmeyen Şarkı* (Unending Song), the lead character gets raped at a young age and gives birth to an illegitimate child. Unable to take care of the child, since her family denounces her, she puts the baby up for adoption. As her family no longer supports her, she takes whatever job she can find to support herself. Eventually, she becomes a singer in nightclubs. Years later, as she is running away from mafia leaders who are the owners of the nightclub where she works, she runs into a rich gentleman, who saves her life and falls in love with her. He also helps her get back on her feet and leave her nightclub job. Quickly this sweet love story turns into an empowering journey for the lead character, as she finds out that her child has been adopted by her lover's brother's family. She tries to claim his custody as well as gain his trust and love as his biological mother.

In *Gümüş*, the audience watches the struggles of the female character, who gets married to a rich Istanbulite playboy as a result of an arranged marriage. In this case, the audience witnesses her using the arranged marriage to her advantage, through which she transforms herself from a housewife into a modern businesswoman who establishes her own designer clothing line and is able to provide for her child. Eventually, she decides to leave her husband to lead a life on her own (after her husband's ex-lover returns and she finds out that he has a child with her). A similar story is told in *Yol Arkadaşım* (*My Travel Buddy*), where the female character leaves her husband, who cheats on her, and decides to build a life from scratch with her daughter. Eventually, she becomes a successful business entrepreneur.

The female characters' journey to emancipation plays a key role in the success of some of these TV series, as they show that women living without men is a possible reality, no matter how difficult the path may be. They also reveal that the misfortunes that might happen to women, such as adultery, abortion, forceful marriage, and rape, are not only an act of fate they need to accept but could also be considered as life lessons. However, there is a limit to optimism and rebellion. As discussed earlier in this section, only women who continue to conform to patriarchal gender norms and roles at some level, or at least do not radically alter the gender discourse, reach that happy ending. For instance, in *Yol Arkadaşım*, the lead character falls back in love with a lover from the distant past, but she does not immediately get involved with him (because she has a daughter), and certainly not before her divorce is finalized. In *Bitmeyen Şarkı*, though the lead character works in a nightclub, the audience is shown that she has never engaged in a romantic or sexual relationship with anyone since the birth of her child, and certainly not for money, even when she is extremely poor. The story is similar with that of the main character in *Iffet*, who, despite marrying another man for revenge, asks for time from her new husband before they engage in a sexual relationship, which the new husband abides by. The husband is portrayed as a considerate man who believes that Iffet will eventually fall in love with him, and is ready to wait for her until then. Throughout the time (possibly years) they remain married, they never sleep together, which helps Iffet conform to the meaning of her name (chastity), which, as discussed in the earlier sections, is a value expected of women in Turkey. Hence, Iffet's strategizing (i.e., marrying another man for revenge) is contextualized within acceptable moral boundaries. And in *Fatmagül'ün Suçu Ne?*, Fatmagül ends up keeping her marriage to a man who was present during her gang rape once she is sure that he did not rape her but was only present at that time. At the final scene of the show, Fatmagül is shown as pregnant and happy in her marriage.

In these examples, we see an important trend that cuts across all the Turkish TV series that have been successfully exported since the 2000s. This trend reveals recurring images of women who can blend strong and even rebellious characteristics with those that conform to traditional gender norms. We consider these ideals "palatable" because, rather than challenging the dominant gender norms radically, they bargain with them. Women not only sit and accept their fate but also continuously strive to challenge their position in society, albeit in small steps. They negotiate new possibilities and futures for themselves even when they face significant challenges from their own families and the larger society. In a way, the strong women role models portrayed in these series present a hope for the audiences struggling with patriarchy within their own contexts. The series present not only likely scenarios when unorthodox routes are taken, such as premarital sex and/or illegitimate children, but also ways of dealing with such circumstances if they happen, or ways to prevent them from happening. We call this the "unique blend" that the Turkish series offer to both Turkish and international audiences.

Conclusion

This chapter provided an overview and analysis of the "woman question" in Turkey, as it is portrayed in a select sample of exported Turkish TV series since 2000s. The Turkish drama series industry has achieved an incredible boom in recent years. Similar to the importance of novels and magazines in understanding the cultural, social, and public narratives of societies, the drama series present important lenses through which we can approach the "woman question" in the Turkish society today. We argued that the woman question entails an inquiry over categories of womanhood, and this is also evident in the categories shown and affirmed on the series, with extreme dichotomization of married women and mothers versus "single women" or "married but childless women" categories. Amidst this dichotomization, however, our analysis revealed that although the women characters are stuck in a tug-of-war between these extremes, the characters that can incorporate both strong, modern ideals and traditional gender roles dominated popular TV series. We called this the "unique blend," as the women characters who were both rebellious against the injustices they faced and at the same time able to or willing to yield to traditional gender role ideals achieved a "happy ending" in the series. What these series mean for the audiences should be the topic for another discussion, but we believe that the series, at the very least, present hope and potential strategies for the audiences who are carrying out their own struggle with dominant patriarchal ideologies.

Discussion questions

1. How would you construct an analysis of American drama series or soap operas in comparison with the analysis presented here of Turkish dramas?
2. What is the "ideal citizen" according to Turkey's gendered familial citizenship model as described in the chapter?
3. How are women who do not comply with the ideal categorization as wife/mother or virgin/girl viewed?
4. What is meant by the phrase "bargaining with patriarchy"?
5. How have women's roles and position in Turkish society changed over time?

Notes

1 All translations from Turkish by the authors.
2 The other Ministries in charge of the implementation of this measure are Culture and Tourism, Youth and Sports, National Education.

3 In selecting our sample, we relied on a database that we built using various online platforms, including beyazperde.com, sinematurk.com, and Turkish Wikipedia pages for TV series. The database includes all TV series produced between 2000 and 2015. In total, we have identified 277 series, of which 55 have been exported. There is no public data that indicates how many countries each series has been exported to, or the average sales value of them. The lack of transparency in this regard might have resulted in our undercounting some of the series. We tried to overcome this problem by scanning newspaper and online news about TV series exports.

4 For consumption of mediatized representations, see Abu-Lughod (1997), Miller (1995), and Mayer (2003).

5 This dichotomy is reminiscent of the madonna/whore dichotomy used in Western literature (Müftüler-Baç 1999: 310).

6 The question was gradually resolved by allowing headscarves in universities starting in 2008, and state institutions starting in 2013.

7 The Turkstat News Release can be found at www.tuik.gov.tr/PreHaberBultenleri.do?id=18616, accessed March 6, 2016.

8 Prior to Law No 3984, Law No. 2954, also known as the Turkish Radio and Television Law, was in effect. Ratified in 1983, Law No. 2954 indicated that one of the main principles of broadcasting was to observe the requirements of public (general/*genel*) morality, national traditions, and spiritual/moral (*manevi*) values. The law founding RTÜK was replaced in 2011 by Law No. 6112, which expands the duties of RTÜK.

9 IKADDER is one of approximately 100 institutions that form TÜRAP, the Turkey Family Platform (which carries the slogan "For Family"). Founded in 1992, the platform aims to "bring together NGOs around Turkey who share an ideal of a strong, natural family that is in charge of upbringing healthy generations" and to undertake projects that enhance the status of the family: http://turkiyeaileplatformu.com/.

10 This involves a six-step process, explained in the My Family-P brochure: (1) For the future of our family and children, watch TV broadcasts. (2) Fill out the online survey to help us spot negative broadcasts. (3) Submit your petition via e-mail or telephone to four institutions (RTÜK, TV channels, producers, sponsors). (4) Form a group of seven members and submit your petition to your group representative. (5) Your representative will write a report and contact us. (6) IKADDER will compile a report and submit it to various institutions (Ministry of Family and Social Planning and RTÜK; other NGOs; media and public; other TV channels and media; producers and sponsors). The brochure also includes sample petitions to guide individuals with the writing process. www.ailemizprojesi.org/wp-content/uploads/2013/04/ailemiz_p_rehberi.pdf.

References

Abu-Lughod, Lila. 1997. "The Interpretation of Culture(s) after Television." *Representations* 59: 109–134.

Abu-Lughod, Lila. 1998. *Remaking Women: Feminism and Modernity in the Middle East: Feminism and Modernity in the Middle East*. Princeton, NJ: Princeton University Press.

Aksoy, Asu, and Kevin Robins. 1997. "Peripheral Vision: Cultural Industries and Cultural Identities in Turkey." *Environment and Planning A* 29(11): 1937–1952.

Alyanak, Oğuz, and Funda Üstek. 2011. "Evlilik Dışı Çocuklar ve Annelik" [Children Out of Wedlock and Motherhood]. *bianet*. http://bianet.org/biamag/toplum/134433-evlilik-disi-cocuklar-ve-annelik, last accessed March 9, 2016.

Ayata, Ayşe Güneş, and Fatma Tütüncü. 2008. "Critical Acts Without a Critical Mass: The Substantive Representation of Women in the Turkish Parliament." *Parliamentary Affairs* 61(3): 461–475.

Ayata, Ayşe Güneş, and Fatma Tütüncü. 2013. "Party Politics of the AKP (2002–2007) and the Predicaments of Women at the Intersection of the Westernist, Islamist and Feminist Discourses in Turkey 1." *British Journal of Middle Eastern Studies* 35(3): 363–384.

Batuman, Elif. 2014. "Ottomania." *New Yorker*. www.newyorker.com/magazine/2014/02/17/ottomania, last accessed March 9, 2016.

Çetin, Kumru Befrin Emre. 2014. "The 'Politicization' of Turkish Television Dramas." *International Journal of Communication* 8: 2462–2483.

Çınar, Alev. 2005. *Modernity, Islam, and Secularism in Turkey: Bodies, Places, and Time.* Minneapolis: University of Minnesota Press.

Çıtak, Zana, and Özlem Tur. 2008. "Women between Tradition and Change: The Justice and Development Party Experience in Turkey." *Middle Eastern Studies* 44(3): 455–469.

Coşar, Simten, and Metin Yeğenoğlu. 2011. "New Grounds for Patriarchy in Turkey? Gender Policy in the Age of AKP." *South European Society and Politics* 16(4): 555–573.

Dedeoğlu, Saniye. 2012. "Equality, Protection or Discrimination: Gender Equality Policies in Turkey." *Social Politics: International Studies in Gender, State & Society* 19(2): 269–290.

Delaney, Carol. 1995. "Father State, Motherland, and the Birth of Modern Turkey." In *Naturalizing Power: Essays in Feminist Cultural Analysis*, eds. Sylvia J. Yanagisako and Carol L. Delaney, 177–199. Washington, DC: American Anthropological Association.

Dursteler, Eric. 2008. "Ottomans." In *The Oxford Encyclopedia of Women in World History*, ed. B. G. Smith. Oxford: Oxford University Press.

Göle, Nilüler. 2002. "Islam in Public: New Visibilities and New Imaginaries." *Public Culture* 14(1): 173–190.

Hürriyet Daily News. 2010. "RTÜK'te 'Gay Sahne' çatlağı" [The Gay Scene Crack in RTÜK], December 22. www.hurriyet.com.tr/rtukte-gay-sahne-catlagi-16578585, last accessed March 9, 2016.

Hürriyet Daily News. 2012. "Dindar Gençlik Yetiştireceğiz" [We'll Raise a Devout Youth], February 2. www.hurriyet.com.tr/dindar-genclik-yetistirecegiz-19825231, last accessed March 31, 2016.

Hurriyet Daily News. 2014. "Turkey World's Second Highest TV Series Exporter after US," October 26. www.hurriyetdailynews.com/turkey-worlds-second-highest-tv-series-exporter-after-us.aspx?pageID=238&nID=73478&NewsCatID=345, last accessed March 31, 2016.

Ilkkaracan, Pinar. 2007. "Reforming the Penal Code in Turkey: The Campaign for the Reform of the Turkish Penal Code from a Gender Perspective." In *Citizen Engagement and National Policy Change Project.* Brighton: Institute of Development Studies. www.kadinininsanhaklari.org/static/yayin/wwhr/reformingPenalCode.pdf, last accessed March 9, 2016.

Işık, Nuran Erol. 2013. "Parables as Indicators of Popular Wisdom: The Making of Piety Culture in Turkish Television Dramas." *European Journal of Cultural Studies* 16(5): 565–581.

Kadıoğlu, Ayşe. 1994. "Women's Subordination in Turkey: Is Islam Really the Villain?" *The Middle East Journal* 48(4): 645–660.

Kandiyoti, Deniz. 1988a. "Bargaining with Patriarchy." *Gender & Society* 2(3): 274–290.

Kandiyoti, Deniz. 1988b. "Slave Girls, Temptresses, and Comrades: Images of Women in the Turkish Novel." *Gender Issues* 8(1): 35–50.

Kandiyoti, Deniz. 1989. "Women and the Turkish State: Political Actors of Symbolic Pawns?" In *Women-Nation-State*, eds. N. Yuval-Davis, F. Anthias, and J. Campling, 126–149. London: Palgrave McMillan.

Kelly, Liz, and Lorna Dubois. 2008. "Combating Violence against Women: Minimum Standards for Support Services." *EG-VAW-CONF (2007) Study Rev.* Strasbourg: Directorate General of Human Rights and Legal Affairs, Council of Europe. www.coe.int/t/dg2/equality/domesticviolencecampaign/Source/EG-VAW-CONF(2007)Study%20rev.en.pdf.

Kılıç, Azer. 2008. "The Gender Dimension of Social Policy Reform in Turkey: Towards Equal Citizenship?" *Social Policy & Administration* 42(5): 487–503.

Künüçen, Hidayet Hale. 2001. "Türk Sinemasında Kadının Sunumu Üzerine" [On Presentation of Women in Turkish Cinema]. *Kurgu Dergisi* 18: 51–64.

Libal, Kathryn. 2014. "From Face Veil to Cloche Hat: The Backward Ottoman versus New Turkish Woman in Urban Public Discourse." In *Anti-Veiling Campaigns in the Muslim World: Gender, Modernism and the Politics of Dress*, ed. Stephanie Cronin, 39–59. London and New York: Routledge.

Mayer, Vicki. 2003. "Living Telenovelas/Telenovelizing Life: Mexican American Girls' Identities and Transnational Telenovelas." *Journal of Communication* 53(3): 479–495.

Miller, Daniel. 1995. "The Young and the Restless and Mass Consumption in Trinidad." In *To Be Continued . . .: Soap Operas around the World*, ed. Robert C. Allen, 213–232. London and New York: Routledge.

Milliyet. 2009. "RTÜK: Çok Ateşli Sevïştiler" [They Made Love Too Passionately], June 29. www.milliyet.com.tr/o-sahneye-ceza-geliyor/gundem/gundemdetay/29.06.2009/1111886/default.htm, last accessed March 9, 2016.

Müftüler-Baç, Meltem. 1999. "Turkish Women's Predicament." *Women's Studies International Forum* 22(3): 303–315.

Öncü, Ayşe. 1995. "Packaging Islam: Cultural Politics on the Landscape of Turkish Commercial Television." *Public Culture* 8: 51–71.

Öncü, Ayşe. 2006. "Becoming Secular Muslims: Yaşar Nuri Öztürk as a Super-Subject on Turkish Television." In *Religion, Media and the Public Sphere*, eds. Birgit Meyer and Annelies Moors, 227–240. Indiana: Indiana University Press.

Özar, Şemsa, and Burcu Yakut-Cakar. 2013. "Unfolding the Invisibility of Women without Men in the Case of Turkey." *Gendering Social Policy and Welfare State in Turkey* 41, Part 1(November): 24–34.

Özbay, Ferhunde. 1992. "Kadının Statüsü ve Doğurganlık" [Status of Women and Fertility]. In *Türkiye'de Kadın Olgusu* [The Concept of Woman in Turkey], ed. Necla Arat, 147–165. Istanbul: Say Yayınları.

Parla, Ayşe. 2001. "The 'Honor' of the State: Virginity Examinations in Turkey." *Feminist Studies* 21(1): 65–88.

Sahin, Haluk, and Asu Aksoy. 1993. "Global Media and Cultural Identity in Turkey." *Journal of Communication* 43(2): 31–41.

Saktanber, Ayşe. 1995. "Women in the Media in Turkey: The Free, Available Woman or the Good Wife and Selfless Mother?" In *Women in Modern Turkish Society*, ed. Sirin Tekeli, 153–170. London: Zed Books.

Shissler, A. Holly. 2005. "Beauty Is Nothing to be Ashamed of: Beauty Contests as Tools of Women's Liberation in Early Republican Turkey." *Comparative Studies of South Asia, Africa and the Middle East* 24(1): 107–122.

Sirman, Nükhet. 1989. "Feminism in Turkey: A Short History." *New Perspectives on Turkey* 3: 1–34.

Sirman, Nükhet. 2000. "Writing the Usual Love Story: The Fashioning of Conjugal and National Subjects in Turkey." In *Gender, Agency and Change: Anthropological Perspectives*, ed. V. Goddard, 250–272. London: Routledge.

Sirman, Nükhet. 2005. "The Making of Familial Citizenship in Turkey." In *Citizenship in a Global World: European Questions and Turkish Experiences*, eds. E. Fuat Keyman and Ahmet Icduygu, 147–172. Oxford and New York: Routledge.

Üstek, Funda, and Oguz Alyanak. 2013. "Extreme Measures: Invoking Moral Order in Turkey." *Open Democracy*. www.opendemocracy.net/arab-awakening/funda-ustek-oguz-alyanak/extreme-measures-invoking-moral-order-in-turkey, last accessed March 9, 2016.

White, Jenny B. 2002. *Islamist Mobilization in Turkey: A Study in Vernacular Politics*. Seattle, WA: University of Washington Press.

White, Jenny B. 2003. "State Feminism, Modernization, and the Turkish Republican Woman." *National Women's Studies Association Journal* 15(3): 145–159.

Yazıcı, Berna. 2012. "The Return to the Family: Welfare, State, and Politics of the Family in Turkey." *Anthropological Quarterly* 85(1): 103.

Yılmaz, Önder. 2016. "Aileye Olan Güveni Sarsıyor" [Affects Trust for Family]. *Milliyet*. www.milliyet.com.tr/-aileye-olan-guveni-sarsiyor-gundem-2183488/, last accessed March 9, 2016.

Yılmaz, Zafer. 2015. "'Strengthening the Family' Policies in Turkey: Managing the Social Question and Armoring Conservative-Neoliberal Populism." *Turkish Studies* 16(3): 371–390.

Chapter 30

Ethnographic empathy and the social context of rights

"Rescuing" Maasai girls from early marriage

Caroline S. Archambault

Reproduced by permission of the American Anthropological Association from *American Anthropologist*, Volume 113, Issue 4, Pages 632–643, December 2011. Not for sale or further reproduction.

Esther was the first of five young women in line to talk to me. We sat on the steps of the boardinghouse of a Maasai school on the edge of town in southern Kenya. Esther is tall, is thin, and even at the young age of 17, has an air of confidence about her. Without much prompting on my part, she dove into her story – one she has clearly told many times before.

> My father wanted to give me away. I went to my sister in Kiserian, and she sent me to school. My mzee [father] came to remove me from school. I got help from my brother and a teacher. They brought me to the District Officer. He wrote me a letter to bring to the head teacher. I came here and started in class 2. Now I am in class 5.
>
> (interview, June 24, 2007)

Esther is one of several young Maasai girls in Kenya who have been "rescued" from early marriage, taking up residence in centers specifically created to shelter, feed, and educate them. The centers, first pioneered almost two decades ago, are largely funded by international donors. They have gained considerable momentum following Kenya's Free Primary Education initiative in 2002 and the growing popularity of a rights-based approach to development. The centers are part of a wider network of initiatives and organizations that support the second and third Millennium Development Goals: gender equality, female empowerment, and the rights of all children to an education. Maasai practices of early marriage and the associated practice of female circumcision, in particular, have come under fire internationally, as they constitute some of the most obvious examples of gender-based violence and infringements on the rights of the child.

Several years prior to this meeting with Esther, as part of my doctoral fieldwork on Maasai education, I volunteered at a Maasai boarding school known for pioneering the rescue center service. I was encouraged by the administration to interview several of the 22 "rescued girls" that took refuge in this center. As they explained, getting their stories out to the public was an important strategy in finding sponsors to support the girls' continued studies. In 2007, I returned to follow up on these interviews and met Esther for the first time. Esther's story shared a distinct narrative structure with the stories told to me by the other girls. A typical narrative begins with a father's or uncle's marriage plans for her, is followed by a brief explanation of her narrow escape, and concludes with the girl happily in pursuit of an education. This storyline is usually framed by a set of prevailing binaries that distinguish violators from victims, patriarchy from female empowerment, tradition from modernity, and collective culture from individual rights. I came to recognize this as the narrative form commonly used to depict early marriage in the international media, in development circles within Kenya, and even locally in Enkop, Esther's home. Although such a framework may be effective in mobilizing public support, it essentializes and renders static notions of "victimhood," "tradition," "culture," and "rights"; it obscures the real structural underlying factors that give rise to the practice of early marriage among the Maasai; and it deflects attention from important policy interventions that could more effectively address the issue. Because Esther had run away from Enkop, the community where I have been working for more than seven years, the profound limitations of these conventional narratives were apparent to me. Interviews with her friends, family members, and other members of the community, as well as regular periods of fieldwork on a variety of topics, brought out the complexity of the issue of early marriage and the importance of ethnographic contextualization for effectively addressing this problem.[1,2,3]

As my interview with Esther's father illustrated, the fathers, who are commonly viewed as responsible for these incidences of early marriage, are often not the caricature of the traditional, conservative, pastoral patriarch. Esther's father proclaims himself to be "a very good man of education" (interview, November 3, 2007). Formal education, he hopes, will offer his children alternatives to the exclusive practice of pastoralism in a region where rapid land fragmentation and dispossession, continued neglect by the state, increased climactic instability, and heightened population pressure have all compromised the viability of a pastoral livelihood for Maasai youth. Though he has three wives and 26 children, his educational record is rather exceptional compared to that of the average family in Enkop. Despite never attending school himself and raising his children in a time when it was uncommon to send many children to school, Esther's father has served for years as the chairman of the primary school management committee. He has managed to send all but 8 of his 26 children to school. Esther's mother, who never attended school herself, has had three of her seven children (two boys and one girl) pursue secondary studies – a remarkable feat by Enkop standards. Esther, the fifth-born child and fourth-born daughter, together with her eldest sister, were the two children in her family who were not sent to school. "[Esther] was not a schoolgirl," her father explained.

> She was a girl of the home. . . . We tried to educate all our children, but it depended on our cows and goats and poverty. . . . I have had children in six different schools, so I am a very good man for education. The problem is [too few] animals.
> (interview, November 3, 2007)

Esther's father decided it best to secure her future as a pastoralist by marrying her to a good family and husband at the age of 14.

Esther resisted her status as a "girl of the home." Shortly before her marriage, she secretly enrolled herself in school under the pretense of visiting her sister. When news reached her parents, her mother was sent to retrieve her, and the wedding plans were expedited. The night of her wedding, when friends and family of the bride and groom were in attendance and the festivities had started, Esther ran away to the center with the help of her brother and a local teacher. The wedding had to be cancelled, and initial bridewealth payments returned to the groom and his family. Following her escape, domestic conflict ensued: Esther's father suspected his wife and son of colluding with his daughter and forced them to temporarily leave their home. On visiting the center to retrieve Esther, Esther's father was told by the headmistress that she was now "a school-child." "Esther will be your child," he replied. "You will give her a husband, and she will never set foot in my house again. I don't count her as a child in my family" (interview, June 1, 2007). Esther was disowned.

Years have passed, and because Esther has been successful in her studies, her father has now accepted her back as his daughter. He recognizes and appreciates her as a "girl of school" and hopes that education will provide her with a secure livelihood and a good husband.

There are significant limitations to the conventional view of Esther's story as a simple tension between culture-patriarchy-tradition and a girl's right to an education. In this chapter, I offer novel research findings by ethnographically contextualizing the underlying factors giving rise to practices of early marriage among the Maasai in Enkop. The investigation provides a unique perspective on contemporary predicaments that the practice of pastoralism encounters in the face of land-tenure reform, political marginality and state neglect, climactic instability, and population growth. It demonstrates the insecurities and challenges associated with formal education. Through the intimate portrayal of Esther's case against this backdrop of societal change, early marriage is situated not as a relic of tradition and malicious patriarchy but, rather, as a contemporary adaptation to livelihood insecurity. This case study illustrates how prevailing concepts of "tradition," "culture," "victimhood," and "collective rights" in human rights theory obscure important structural factors that give rise to early marriage and deflect attention from effective policy initiatives. This chapter responds to recent calls for a critical anthropology of human rights, one that not only pursues an ethnography of human rights practice but also uses its findings to reflect back on basic theoretical and practical dimensions of the human rights project (Goodale 2006, 2009a, 2009b).

The transnational version: human rights talk on early marriage

Kenya has signed and ratified all major international human rights treaties that carry provisions to protect young girls from early marriage. Protections against early marriage have also been nationally legislated through the 2002 passage of the Children Act (Cap 586, Laws of Kenya). Article 2 of the Children Act entitles all children to free, basic, and compulsory education. Article 14 stipulates that "no person shall subject a child to female circumcision, early marriage or other cultural rites, customs, or traditional practices that are likely to negatively affect the child's life, health, social welfare, dignity, or physical or psychological development" (Government of Kenya 2001).

Since passing this legislation, Kenya has experienced a flood of activity by international, national, governmental, and nongovernmental organizations that are campaigning against and monitoring gender-based infringements on the rights of the child. The term *early marriage* is powerfully constituted, as it simultaneously signifies an inappropriate age to marry (also captured in the term *child marriage*) as well as an inappropriate time to marry, implying that one ought to be doing something else during this period of childhood (mainly, pursuing an education). Thus, even if not explicitly addressing early marriage, these organizations often take issue with many practices associated with or implicated in what has come to be defined as early marriage, including child marriage, female circumcision, girl-child education, reproductive rights, and arranged marriage or betrothal (Shell-Duncan and Olungah 2009). This conceptual overlap makes early marriage a powerful infringement of child rights, one that has become a prevalent concern among many organizations addressing Maasai development, most centrally the recent network of rescue centers.

Rescue centers and rights activists have played a key role in perpetuating a particular narrative of the early marriage issue that circulates both transnationally and locally. An article from the news brief section of the UN Population Fund website (2005) describing a rescue center in Kenyan Maasailand serves as a typical illustration of this popular early marriage narrative:

> Silvia Selula looks dazed and lost. A faint wrinkle creases her otherwise cherubic face. Occasionally a furtive smile appears at the corner of her mouth. Her face says a lot about what she has endured, especially in the last few weeks, and about her optimism about the future. Silvia is the latest addition to the Tasaru Ntomonok Girls Rescue Centre in Narok, Kenya. Most of those who listen to her mumble her story shake their heads and wonder how the fate that almost befell Silvia could be tolerated in Kenya today. Silvia is nine years old. A few weeks ago, her father married her off to a 40-year-old man. She had no say in the arrangement. Neither did her mother, who reluctantly acquiesced. It is, after all, still a man's world on the rolling plains of the Southern Rift Valley, the home of the Maasai.

The writer continues on to explain how the events of Silvia's marriage were progressing as Maasai "custom" and "tradition" would dictate, with Silvia being "frog-marched" to her fate as a fourth wife. The rescue center proceeds to "free" Silvia from the common fate of "child marriage" and "the harmful practice of female genital mutilation/cutting (FGM)" that is inflicted on so many young Maasai girls. Readers are assured that the center has "reconciled" girls with their families and that education of these girls will help put an end to "gender-based violence" by promoting "gender equality" and, ultimately, empowering women.

This prevailing narrative form is characterized by the use of a storyline structure and the framing of issues through morally unambiguous and emotionally charged dichotomies – rhetorical techniques that Emery Roe (1994) and others (Gasper and Apthorpe 1996; Stirrat 2000) argue serve only to simplify complexity and render social life manageable and more amenable to policy action. The storyline limits the issue to a problem between traditional patriarchs and progressive daughters. Esther, Silvia, and other young women are cast into the role of innocent victims fighting against the evil intentions of fathers or uncles whose actions are propelled by the force of "deeply rooted" and "patriarchal" "traditions" and "customs" in which wives and daughters "acquiesce" and "have no say." "After all it is still a man's world," concludes the UNPF article. The simple story, with its simple characters, becomes more than a fight between a girl and her father. It is a battle waged against patriarchy in the name of women's rights, against tradition in the name of modernity and progress. There is, thus, no doubt about who should win. Action is imminent, inaction morally reproachable. Such narrative frames effectively obscure and render irrelevant the larger and more complicated context giving rise to early marriage.

Anthropologists have been on the forefront of criticizing representational frameworks within human rights discourse (Wilson 1997). "Legalistic" accounts of human rights violations are said to strip events of their social meanings and subjectivities and conceal the ambiguities and contingencies that are at the heart of acts of injustice. This goes against the very goal of ethnographic investigations of human rights practices, which aim to restore subjectivity and contextualize rights violations by exploring their local interpretations and "vernacularizations" (Goodale 2007; Merry 2006a, 2006b).

Local versions: proliferation of rights-based discourses in Enkop

Enkop, the predominantly Maasai community and central site of this study, stretches over 200,000 acres in the southern district of Kajiado. It is home to approximately 10,500 residents. Low altitudes, variable and little rainfall, and poor soils produce a semiarid climate with little agricultural potential. Consequently, traditional livestock husbandry is the primary economic activity in Enkop. Cattle, goats, sheep, and even a few camels are raised through a form of transhumant husbandry: during the wet season, animals are grazed within the vicinity of a permanent homestead, and during the dry periods, they are moved to distant pastures. There is little infrastructure in Enkop. Residents have access to water through scattered boreholes, seasonal streams, and hand-dug wells. There is no electricity and no paved roads. The closest paved road is 35 kilometers away from a small town center, which is comprised of a number of shops, an administrative office for the local chief, a health clinic, a primary school, a newly built secondary school, and a weekly livestock and goods market.

Rights discourses flow to Enkop residents through three main channels. Most notably, schooling provides a platform through which national perspectives are disseminated locally. Survey data on schooling I carried out in Enkop show a dramatic and relatively recent increase in school participation within the community, with gender parity in the youngest cohorts. According to the 2005 survey, two-thirds (66 percent) of children ages 6–15 years old had attended formal schooling for one year or more, compared with less than half (47 percent) of the age group above them (ages 16–25 years old). Among adults ages 46 and above, only 16 percent had ever attended school. With regard to female participation rates, the changes are even starker, with gender parity being reached in the youngest ages. In the cohort of children ages 6–10 at the time of the survey, the percentage of girls having attended one or more year of formal schooling was even higher than that of boys (64 percent of girls compared to 60 percent of boys). Among women ages 46 years and above, only 9 percent had ever attended one or more years of schooling (Archambault 2007). The rise in primary education participation in Enkop is linked to the perceived decreasing viability of pastoralism as a livelihood strategy for future generations, which I will further discuss later. Schoolchildren read about human rights in their textbooks and hear rights proclamations from their teachers and school visitors. On special occasions (sports days or celebrations), they disseminate these messages through song and dance to their guests, parents, and fellow peers. Churches act as a second prominent channel with, according to the 2005 survey, approximately half of the adult population self-identifying as Christian (Archambault 2007). Early marriage is an issue raised during church sermons, prayer meetings, and other social religious gatherings. The church leadership quite actively promotes education of the girl-child, the sanctity of love marriages, and free choice of life partners and condemns polygyny as well as both early and out-of-wedlock pregnancy. The third prominent channel is the growing local presence of the numerous NGOs servicing the Enkop community, whose agendas focus on women's and children's rights. These organizations hold local meetings, visit churches and schools, and sometimes distribute posters or other reading materials to educate the public on the rights of the girl-child and to issue warnings against the practice of early marriage.

How influential are the (trans)national discourses on the ways in which people in Enkop think about early marriage? Sally Engle Merry (2006a) provides a classificatory continuum for situating the degree of similarity between transnational rights discourses and local variations, distinguishing between replication, hybridization, and subversion. Although Esther's case seemed to elicit reflections that spanned the spectrum, all those interviewed seemed to retain the prevailing structural binaries found in popular narratives. They identified Esther as a victim and her father as a violator. They invoked early marriage as a traditional custom that was incongruous with modern times. They spoke of tension between individual rights and culture and collective practices. Some interviewees replicated the emotional charge of these binaries by angrily condemning Esther's father for his patriarchal and malicious intentions to violate and oppress his daughter's rights to an education. One young female respondent went as far as to accuse Esther's father of marrying off Esther as a way to punish his least favorite wife (Esther's mother). "He's a bad man," she insisted. "He does not like when girls go to school . . . and he does not love Mama Esther" (interview, August 11, 2010). Some directed their blame, more generally, on Maasai men's greed for livestock, as reflected in the words of a young pastor: "Most of the people give out their girls to be married just . . . to get cows. They are greedy" (interview, August 13, 2010). Such sentiments reflect the transnational narrative constructions depicted in the UNPF article or the slogan "Don't sell your daughters for a cow" that adorns the walls of NGOs in Kajiado and Nairobi.

Most people interviewed, however, seemed to embrace a hybrid variation by retaining the binary structures while infusing them with local meaning, which significantly softened their antagonism. A less-aggressive perspective seemed to arise not only from an intimate understanding of the people involved (and their intentions) but also from an experience and interpretation of "tradition" and "culture" as something that, while perhaps outdated, was nonetheless largely dignified. "He is not a bad man. He has just taken a wrong decision," expressed an elderly mama (interview, August 13, 2010). "The guy is an innocent guy. It is the culture," said an educated young man (interview, August 11, 2010). Much of the empathy shared in the case of Esther's father was not only because of his outstanding record of educating his children and commitment to education but also to the fact that Esther had not originally been enrolled in school. "She was a girl of the home," her father and others insisted. The educated young man explains:

> It was the traditional agreement. So that is what you follow. . . . I don't blame him. He had two [uneducated] girls and . . . they got married. . . . That is the criteria of the father. . . . It is not wrong. That is how it is for our culture.
>
> (interview, August 11, 2010)

The common distinction made by many interviewed between the marital rights of "local" or uneducated girls versus those of schooled girls could be considered subversive to the transnational discourse. Educated girls, several insisted, are given the right to decide on the timing of their marriage and choose their own partners, whereas the marital decisions for "girls of the home" are determined by their parents. The way in which Esther escaped her marriage was raised on several occasions and elicited some sympathy for her father. Several people I interviewed felt that Esther should not have waited until the day of her wedding to assert her rights. They believe she should have talked to her father or called a meeting with the local chiefs before the groom and his family arrived. Especially the men interviewed seemed to empathize with how shameful the turn of events must have been for Esther's father, and how disappointing and disruptive for the groom and his family.

Remarkably, no interviewee explicitly or fundamentally rejected the use of the dichotomous conceptual framework described earlier to explain practices of early marriage. Even if the meanings were softened and sympathies with the parties involved were expressed, Esther's father was seen to be at fault and early marriage rendered as a cultural practice of the past. From the perspective of those interviewed, there seemed to be only one way to secure the well-being and future of daughters in Enkop: through education. Only one age-mate of Esther's father came close to breaking out of the confines of this frame by suggesting that the path of early marriage could be a modern possibility and the result of love felt for a daughter: "He had other girls whom he sent to school and others to be married," suggested the man. "He loves a lot his children. And he is not a bad person. He chose a very good person [for her to marry]" (interview, August 18, 2010).

"Another" version: predicaments of the patriarch

"Had I know she would have been this good of a student, I would have chosen her all along," Esther's father explained (interview, November 3, 2007). Admittedly, I first dismissed his statement as a simple justification. However, the more I learned about Esther's situation and situated it within the larger context of social change in Enkop, the more significant it became. Assuming that fathers love and want the best for their daughters – which I strongly believe holds true for most fathers in Enkop – I have come to appreciate the difficulties parents face in choosing the "best" path to secure the future well-being of their daughters.

Most parents in Enkop today question the viability of pastoralism as an exclusive livelihood strategy for all their children. There is a pervasive sentiment throughout the region that pastoralism is becoming much more difficult because of the combined forces of land and resource fragmentation and dispossession, which have been accelerated by recent land-tenure reforms, increased climactic instability, continued state neglect, and increasing population pressure. Over the past few decades, per capita livestock holdings in Kajiado district have fallen well below subsistence survival levels (Anderson and Broch-Due 1999; Talle 1988). Residents of Enkop periodically suffer dramatic droughts that threaten to decimate their herds. The drought of 2000 killed an estimated 80 percent of cattle and 70 percent of small stock. Estimates of livestock losses from the most recent drought (2008–2009) are still undetermined, but many people believe that droughts have become more frequent and more severe. In the nineteenth century, pastoralists faced great environmental calamities, outbreaks of disease, and severe drought, but many managed to recuperate their losses over time. Today, however, environmental adversity is compounded with a long history of political marginalization by the colonial and post-colonial states, which has resulted in an increase in economic marginalization (Anderson and Broch-Due 1999). Investments in the pastoral sector have been neglected by a long-standing view that pastoralism is an unproductive, inefficient, environmentally destructive, and archaic mode of production (Waller 1999). With little understanding of pastoral ecology and indigenous systems of resource management, many of the development initiatives aimed at "rationalizing" animal husbandry disrupted the livelihood and rendered pastoralism more precarious. The state has also long been implicated in pastoral land dispossession, through colonial treatises of relocation, the allocation of pastoral lands for national parks and reserves or for other commercial interests, and the continued encouragement to privatize communally held grazing lands (Galaty 1992; Lesorogol 2008; Mwangi 2008). Although privatization has been pursued by many Maasai as a way to prevent further dispossession of their rangelands because of encroachments by the state and neighboring groups, it has made them vulnerable to territorial losses through land sales or exclusion from private property. Despite the fact that privatization is not yet complete in Enkop, many complain that it has already intensified the difficulties of pastoralism by considerably restricting livestock mobility. According to the 2008–2009 land-tenure survey, 59 percent of men and 71 percent of women interviewed in Enkop reported that the subdivision of land made pastoralism more difficult, while only 10 percent of men and 2 percent of women reported that privatization made pastoralism easier.

Given these growing constraints on pastoralism, residents of Enkop must turn to their social networks for protection of and access to resources – arguably more than ever before. Maasai lineage, clanship, age-set, and marriage systems provide an institutional foundation for these networks. In this light, and at the risk of sounding reductionist, the continued (or even heightened) importance of "customary" marriage in connecting families to pastoral resources now under individual title and providing strong links of mutual support and reciprocity must be noted.

Although recognizing the diversity of marriage practices among the Maasai (Bledsoe and Pison 1994; Coast 2006; Hodgson 1996; Talle 1988; Mitzlaff 1988), still there exists a strong set of cultural norms that define the "customary" system of Maasai marriage. This system is exogamous, in that both men and women should take their spouses from clans other than their paternal and maternal clans. Typically, customary marriages are arranged by the parents of both bride and groom when both girls and even boys are young and uncircumcised. They are often arranged through lengthy processes of negotiations and are characterized by a "protracted" form of marriage payment (Hakansson 1989). Compared to other East African patrilineal groups, Maasai pay a small initial bridewealth payment of a few animals, beer, blankets, and more recently, cash, with the understanding and expectation that transactions of livestock and other forms of support will continue through the course of the marriage. This form of marriage is understood and valued as an alliance of families. Although parents look at the individual qualities of potential brides and grooms for their children, much consideration is given to the wider qualities and characteristics of the families that are being united. Marriage is understood as creating powerful linkages to new resources and obligations of mutual social and economic support. There is probably no greater gift, as viewed by the Maasai, than having been given a daughter. Affines share a special bond. Daughters do not disappear from their natal homes into their new families but remain central nodes of sociality and security between these families. "The relationship will be very strong [between affines]. They will help each other throughout," explains an elder man. "They have a very strong relationship because of the girl that was given to that family," he continues (interview, August 18, 2010). An educated young mother who is a third wife to her husband adds: "[The two families] are now becoming like sisters and brothers" (interview, August 8, 2010).

Given increasing pressure on pastoral practices and the role that customary marriage plays in providing extended family support, it is perhaps less surprising to note that, in contrast to the general trends in Kenya and elsewhere in East and sub-Saharan Africa (Mensch et al. 2006), age at first marriage among the Maasai seems to be actually decreasing rather than increasing. In the not-so-distant past, explains one young man, "the girls waited until they knew how to milk a cow and to carry a container of water and carry firewood and also to know how to feed the small kids" (interview, August 11, 2010). An elder mother adds: "Men took a very long time [to marry]. They even grew beards. They stayed for a long time before they were circumcised. Not like now" (interview, August 13, 2010). Survey data from Enkop supports the common assertion that the age of marriage for both girls and boys has been decreasing over time because the age of female circumcision, which is commonly performed immediately prior to marriage, shows a steady decrease. Women ages 60–69 years old at the time of the survey were circumcised on average at 19.7 years old, whereas women ages 20–29 were circumcised at 16.6 years old.

Ernestina Coast (2001, 2006) finds a similar trend in several other Maasai communities in Kenya and Tanzania. She attributes this change to "modernizing" influences, as young men step out of the livelihood and out of the control of their fathers. They no longer have to wait to amass livestock wealth or wait for the ritual sanctions to be married. In Enkop, several explanations circulate. Similar to Coast, many point to the attrition of cultural practices, whereby young boys and girls forego or expedite rites of passage and are circumcised at increasingly younger ages. An educated young man, himself circumcised at the age of 15 because of the social pressure of other circumcised boys at his school, reflects: "I think it is the community culture which is changing slowly. They circumcise both boys and girls at a very young age . . . and then girls are let out for marriage" (interview, August 14, 2010). Education is identified as a powerful force in expediting adulthood, as students want to attain adulthood before reaching the final grades of primary school. Many also attribute the decreasing age of marriage to increases in early pregnancy, discussed in more detail later.

Finally, people claim that early marriage is a product of insecurity and poverty, exacerbated by the heightened challenges to pastoral livelihoods. "Sometimes the children are so many at home that you cannot educate them, you cannot provide food for them, so the only alternative is to marry them," explains an elderly mother (interview, August 13, 2010). Several residents explained that under circumstances in which families struggled to provide for their children, marrying out a daughter to a good family would better secure the daughter's future and would relieve some of the pressure of providing for the remaining members of the family. As one elder explains: "You cannot just give your daughter to be married by anyone. You must choose for someone who you know will care for your daughter. And they do that by marrying their daughters to see that they have a good future" (interview, August 18, 2010). Logos on T-shirts chastise fathers for selling their daughters for cows. Although their blame may be arguably misdirected, the link between early marriage and poverty is probably quite salient, as marriage remains one of the important mechanisms through which families can draw on support and security and ensure that daughters are well protected in good homes.

As elsewhere in Maasailand, people in Enkop have responded to the insecurities of pastoralism by finding ways to diversify their sources of income (Hodgson 2001; Homewood et al. 2009; Thompson and Homewood 2003). The options for diversification and small-enterprise development are limited in Enkop by the lack of electricity, poor infrastructure, low levels of education among the adult population, and a difficult climate for agricultural endeavors. For this reason, pastoralism and the marketing of livestock is still one of the most important sources of income and security for families in the region. However, for the younger generation, parents are investing in formal schooling in the hopes that this will provide their children with the skills and opportunities to enhance opportunities for livelihood diversification. "Education is the key to life" is a common saying today in Enkop. Schooling and the employment that it promises are seen as new options by which Maasai families protect themselves against the vulnerabilities of pastoralism (Archambault 2007).

Schooling is by no means, however, the panacea that many (especially young) enthusiasts in Enkop suggest. Parents, mothers especially, have taken on increased herding and domestic responsibilities to compensate for the loss of their children's labor while they attend school. Schools in Enkop are few and dispersed over a wide area. According to my 2005 survey, on average, children live 57 minutes' walk away from the nearest primary school, with many children having to walk for upward of two hours through wild shrub land to reach school. Consequently, parents wait for children to be "big" enough to make it to school, sit through the day and learn productively, and return home safely. The practice of sending children to live with family or friends living closer to schools is common in Enkop and demonstrates the level of dedication both children and parents have toward schooling (Archambault 2010).

As a consequence of difficulties in accessing school, Maasai children – girls especially – often begin their education at a relatively late age. Consequently, girls often reach reproductive age while still in primary school. The school environment affords considerably more exposure and unsupervised interaction between boys and girls, and according to many, this has resulted in a surge of early pregnancies. In Kenya, not just in Maasailand, pregnant girls are discouraged from remaining in school because they are often perceived as a bad influence on their peers. Among the Maasai, an early and unexpected pregnancy will commonly trigger circumcision, followed by marriage. "It is a taboo for a Maasai girl to be pregnant when she's not circumcised," an elder man explains. "Fifty years ago, there were no girls who just got pregnant [so young]. . . . But nowadays it is very common. They circumcise quickly . . . so that she is not pregnant when she is a girl," he continues (interview, August 18, 2010). Over the years, I have witnessed more and more cases where young school-going mothers leave their newborns in the care of their family and return to their studies after giving birth. Whether pregnancy should preclude further education and mark a young girl's transition to customary family life is contested in Enkop. In fact, the two other cases of "rescued girls" in Enkop that I have heard about concerned situations of school pregnancies. The risk of early pregnancy weighs heavily on the minds of parents as a real risk of formal schooling.

Parents are also concerned that their children will not be able to translate their education into livelihood security. Formal-sector salaried jobs in Kenya seem to demand increasingly higher levels of education, and the Kenyan school system is highly competitive, with positions in secondary school available for only just over half (55 percent) of primary graduates (Nyerere 2009). Young women in Enkop who manage to avoid pregnancy or other situations resulting in their dropping out nevertheless have to obtain high-enough marks on the national primary leaving exam to secure a spot in the competitive secondary system. Low-quality educational provision in Enkop – because of large class sizes, understaffing, lack of learning resources, and a nonconducive study environment, among other factors – make this a real challenge, especially for girls. Those who manage to obtain high-enough marks often find the secondary school fees and associated costs prohibitive. According to the 2005 survey data, a little over one-quarter (28 percent) of girls between the ages of 26 and 35 who attended primary school entered secondary school, with only 10 percent pursuing some form of tertiary education (Archambault 2007).

With high levels of dropping out inevitable in the current competitive system, there is great pressure to offer good-quality basic and primary education. Yet parents in Enkop complain that even primary school graduates have substandard levels of literacy and numeracy and observe that secondary school graduates often come home jobless but unwilling to herd livestock, a job they associate with the uneducated. Inadequate access to vocational and technical training, pedagogical approaches focused on rote learning and the acquisition of exam-based knowledge, and a biased curriculum that presents pastoralism as an archaic mode of production are all aspects of the current school system that render even primary graduates, in the opinion of many parents and in the words of a primary school teacher, as "half-baked cakes." Furthermore, schoolchildren often want to arrange their own marriages, leading many parents to fear the implications this will have on their security and well-being. They question whether such alliances will provide a strong protection for their children and whether they themselves will be in the position to mediate marital disputes if they are not responsible for having formed the union.

So although sending girls to school is the path that most parents in Enkop are choosing to secure the future well-being of their daughters (recall that in the 2005 survey, the percentage of girls with at least one year of schooling was higher than that of boys), the risks of dropping out and uncertainties related to whether or not formal education will lead to livelihood security make it less of an obvious choice than the human rights discourse suggests. In this light, choosing early marriage may be understood as a decision taken by parents who have lost confidence in the education system or in the economy or who do not trust their daughters' future to the hands of the state. So contrary to popular belief, early marriage may be more effectively understood as a modern adaptation – a decision made not out of a "deeply rooted custom" and "patriarchy" but, rather, out of love, concern, and insecurity.

Implications of an ethnographic version

The ethnographic version I have provided earlier, which breathes social life into Esther's story and situates her father's decision in a wider context of profound socioeconomic and ecological change, threatens to dismantle the prevailing dichotomies that are often used to frame the issue of early marriage among the Maasai. Such an approach debunks the powerful dualism of victim and violator that is pervasive in (trans)national and local accounts of early marriage. In light of the circumstances in which Esther's father's decision was made and his intentions, he shifts from a symbol of patriarchal oppression to a concerned father. No longer simply a violator of his daughter's rights to an education, he can be understood as a victim himself of economic, ecological, and political forces beyond his control that render the path that would attain security for Esther (and other young women like her) more uncertain. Other anthropologists engaging in human rights issues have, similarly, found the lens of victim versus violator limiting in its neglect of the range of subjectivities and historically situated positions people embody (Ross 2003; Wilson 1997; Wilson and Mitchell 2003). The binary framework also deflects attention from human rights abuses that are not perpetrated by individuals but, rather, by economic, political, or social forces at large.

An ethnographic perspective on Esther's case challenges the tradition–modernity dichotomy. Early marriage is historicized and situated not as a relic of an age-old tradition among conservative pastoralists but, to the contrary, as a modern phenomenon: a shift downward in the age of marriage in response to cultural change and increasing poverty and marginalization. Anthropologists have heavily scrutinized the culture–tradition concept, moving away from a static and bounded interpretation only to find its essentialized forms clung to by informants and fueled by "rights talk" (Cowan 2006; Cowan et al. 2001; Eriksen 2001; Merry 2006b; Preis 1996). Esther's uneducated father, an exclusive pastoralist and polygynist who is simultaneously an educational leader and advocate, sits precariously on both sides of the tradition–modern binary. And Esther, who rejected her status as a "traditional" girl of the home in favor of the status of a "modern" schoolgirl (even at a late age), illustrates the agency people possess to move themselves in and out of such symbolic categories. Her case serves as a warning to human rights theorists and practitioners to avoid essentialized, nonpoliticized, and nonagentive notions of culture and tradition in human rights theory.

Further, this ethnographic approach challenges the perceived irreconcilable conflict between individual and collective rights (Berting et al. 1990). It reveals a redundancy, argued by Jack Donnelly (1990), wherein the rights of individuals acting as members of social groups become disaggregated into separate forms of entitlements:

> There is no necessary logical incompatibility between the idea of human rights and peoples' rights (or other group rights) – so long as we see peoples' rights as the rights of individuals acting as members of a collective group, and not rights of the group against the individual.
>
> (Donnelly 1990: 48)

When put into context, the "collective right" of arranging marriages appears to be an expression of individual rights to integrity and security. Father and daughter can be understood as sharing similar fundamental goals (security of well-being) while disagreeing on the means through which to achieve them. The reverse also holds true in Enkop. What gets classified as an individual right, in this case the right to education, is also perceived locally as a collective right and a responsibility. Many people in Enkop think about formal education as a means of empowering the community at large. "The pen is the spear of today" is a common saying meant to instill in the young a commitment to defend and protect their community with the knowledge, networks, and resources afforded by education. So although the binary frame obscures the conceptual overlap of individual and collective rights, it also ignores the plurality of collectivities of which individuals are a part. For example, Esther's father is part of a collectivity of elders who continue to practice pastoralism and who perceive it as an enduring and important form of security for some. Esther is a part of a growing collectivity of young women who are striving to attain security and status through schooling. Different collectivities may very well perceive different pathways by which to achieve shared goals or rights.

In this light, Esther's case also speaks to another powerful dichotomy structuring children's rights discourse: how to reconcile the will of parents with the will of (underage) children. Interestingly, this issue was never raised in local discussions about the practice of early marriage. Several people made mention that Esther had a very strong will to go to school, as she had enrolled herself very late and was willing to start at a grade typically well below her age. This showed great determination and promise that she would do well in school. However, those who reprimanded Esther's father's decision to marry her did so not because they believed parents should listen to the will of their children but, rather, because they strongly believed that education was the right path to a better future for young girls. For every young girl or boy who pleads to their parents to be sent to school, there is likely one who pleads against being sent or who wishes to discontinue. Children drop out from school for many reasons, but some do so, to the great disapproval of their parents, because they simply lose interest or would rather be doing something else with their time. Maasai parents strongly hold on to the responsibility and the authority to make decisions for their children. There is a strong belief that the young lack the hindsight or experience necessary to make informed decisions about their future. This belief is held not just about young children. Age-based seniority is central to Maasai social organization and sociocultural life. Throughout one's life, one always remains under the authority and decision-making power of a group of elders who are perceived as parents of a generation. Although parental authority is highly valued and institutionalized in Maasai society, it is important to note that young people find ways to exercise their will. Esther is an obvious reminder of such agency.

Although the discursive binaries distort a proper understanding of the practice of early marriage, the situation of early marriage nevertheless reveals a real injustice in gender inequality. It is unjust that the "modern" path of a good education followed by job opportunities and free partner choice is so insecure for both young girls and boys – but especially for young girls. In the current context in Enkop, young boys can have an earlier start at schooling because they are believed to better withstand the difficulties and risks associated with long travel to and from school. Unlike girls, boys do not bear the responsibilities of out-of-wedlock parenthood and consequent withdrawal from school if their sexual relations result in an early pregnancy. According to many, boys have less-demanding responsibilities in the home after school and thus have more time to study. They generally have higher test scores than girls in Enkop and are encouraged by better job prospects. The discourses present this injustice and inequality as a product of a state of mind (of culture, tradition, and patriarchy), and thus policy measures focus on the punishment of fathers and the need to educate men on the rights of the girl-child. When Enkop residents were asked how to solve the problem of early marriage, the reply of a young pastor was indicative of most opinions:

> The only way they can solve this problem is to discipline these people who force their children to be married early [and take] them out from school . . . so that it is an example for other people. . . . They will have that fear: "I will not do it because the government does not like it."
>
> (interview, August 13, 2010)

Without dismissing such approaches, which may be necessary in the short term for safeguarding young girls' opportunities to pursue formal education, Esther's situation reveals how the focus on culture and patriarchy obscures important underlying forces that perpetuate such inequalities. Dorothy Hodgson (1999) wrote of patriarchy among the Maasai as a "consequence of history" rather than a situation inherent to the culture and temperament of pastoralists. She situates the gradual political and economic disempowerment of women in relation to men as a product of colonial and postcolonial interventions in political life and the commoditization and monetization of the pastoral economy. Similarly, there are real historical and structural factors underlying the practice and injustice of early marriage that deserve serious policy attention and hold the promise of being more effective in the long term.

Esther's case identifies the root cause of early marriage as economic insecurity and lack of confidence in the ability of the educational system to provide for the well-being of Maasai children. In this light, policy initiatives aimed at eliminating the practice of early marriage should focus on securing better livelihoods for Maasai by addressing the challenges that impinge on arid land livelihoods and, in particular, on extensive animal husbandry. More economic security would allow parents to hire labor for domestic and herding needs, allowing children to attend school and focus on their education. Parents could then afford education and could nondiscriminately send their children to primary school and support them through the high costs of secondary education and onward. Greater economic security would reduce the pressure on the institution of marriage as a means of enhanced security and preclude the need to marry daughters into more supportive homes. To enhance economic security among families in Enkop, the government should recognize the continued centrality and economic importance of pastoralism – not only to the Maasai and other communities inhabiting the semiarid and arid lands of Kenya but also to the country as a whole. Investments should be made in improved infrastructure (e.g., transport and communication technology) that would allow pastoralists greater mobility and access to markets. Pastoralists need much more assistance preparing for, coping with, and recovering from dramatic income shocks brought about by drought. Arguably most pressingly, careful attention needs to be paid to the ongoing process of land privatization, which in Enkop and many other localities is rife with corruption in terms of the allocation of parcels, undermining effective forms of land use and further marginalizing the poor.

Alongside investments aimed at improving pastoralism and raising economic security, numerous educational improvements would render the path of schooling for young girls more secure. Investments in building and staffing more schools would decrease the average distance to and from school, thus allowing young girls to start school at competitive ages. This, in itself, would contribute to reducing the risk of early pregnancy, which should also be a focus of policy attention. Early pregnancy prevention and management efforts (in the form of, for example, educational awareness programs and support for childcare) should focus not only on young women but also young men, ensuring that girls are not alone, as they often are, in shouldering the responsibilities and implications of an early pregnancy. Furthermore, numerous educational interventions could help address the poor quality of primary education in Enkop. More schools and more teachers would reduce class sizes, which are currently reaching over 100 pupils per class in the early grades of some primary schools in Enkop. With smaller class sizes, teachers could give each student more instruction and attention. They would be able to spend more time grading and giving feedback and could more easily employ child-centered pedagogical approaches for classroom learning. Primary schools in Enkop are also very underresourced. Teachers in Enkop complain that their students perform poorly on the national placement exams for secondary school because they do not have the resources to purchase practice exams or to give students their own textbooks for home study. Addressing school access, early pregnancy, and educational quality could all productively contribute to reducing the practice of early marriage by securing the path to higher education for young women.

If livelihood and educational insecurity for the people of Enkop could be better addressed, fathers could then make the choice to keep their daughters in school, not in "fear of the government," but in confidence that the decision is a good investment in their daughters' and their families' futures.

Conclusion

In this chapter, I have examined the limitations of (trans)national and local discourses in understanding and addressing the practice of early marriage among the Maasai. These discourses depict early marriage as a violation of a girl's right to education by fathers who are motivated by tradition, culture, patriarchy, and greed. From this perspective, solutions to early marriage target fathers and focus on enforcing the law through fines and jail time.

Through an ethnographic exploration of Esther's particular case, this chapter has contextualized the practice of early marriage and situated it as a recent phenomenon brought about by cultural change and growing poverty and marginalization. Land and resource fragmentation and dispossession, increasing climactic instability, continued state neglect, and rising population pressure have weakened the viability of pastoralism as an exclusive livelihood practice for the majority of young people. Members of Enkop have sought multiple avenues of diversification, including dramatically increasing the participation of children (and girls especially) in primary school. Parents in Enkop hold education in high esteem but, nevertheless, express a lack of confidence in the system. They make great investments in educating their children, but many obstacles – including access to school, high dropout rates, poor-quality learning, curriculum bias, and low achievement – stand in the way of translating education into livelihood security, especially for girls.

In this context, some parents continue to turn to the social institution of marriage as a means of securing their children's future. Placing daughters in trusted and well-connected families is meant to provide children (and their parents) with economic and social security. Affines share strong mutual obligations of support. They expand networks of reciprocity and facilitate access to resources, which are increasingly harder to obtain under land-privatization reforms.

From this perspective, early marriage could be significantly addressed through policies aimed at improving the viability of pastoralism, resulting in more economic security and less reliance on social institutions such as marriage for family protection. In conjunction, policy interventions should focus on improving education access and quality, particularly for girls, so that schooling for young daughters becomes a more reliable path to liveli-hood security.

The local and national discourses on early marriage confine and stabilize complex and dynamic subjectivities. The pervasive human rights dualisms of violator–victim, tradition–modernity, and collective rights–individual rights limit our understanding of social phenomena that are intrinsically unbounded, fluid, and permeable. Debunking this binary framework and recognizing the ambiguities and contingencies of social life need not result in "sloppy relativism"; rather, it can lead to productive insights. The binaries structuring popular discourses of early marriage obscure structural processes that give rise to early marriage and demand important policy attention (Cowan 2006; Englund 2006; Goodale 2009b).

Acknowledgments

This research was supported by a doctoral fellowship from the Population Council and a postdoctoral fellowship from the Social Science and Humanities Research Council pursued at the Department of Anthropology at McGill University. The writing of this research was further supported by a VENI research grant from the Dutch Academy of Sciences (NWO). I would like to acknowledge my appreciation to my many research assistants in Enkop, to Lucia Vasquez Quesada, and to the many members of the Enkop community who sup-ported this research. I am also grateful for the very helpful comments from the anonymous reviewers of AA and Editor-in-Chief Tom Boellstorff as well as Joost de Laat, Professor John Galaty, Andrea Gourgy, and the members of the McGill Writers Group.

Discussion questions

1. What does the author argue are the limitations to the conventional view of early mar-riage as a simple tension between culture/patriarchy/tradition and a girl's right to an education?
2. Why does Archambault argue against simplistic "legalistic" accounts of human rights violations?
3. What role does marriage play in terms of security for Maasai families and, in particu-lar, Maasai women?
4. How has the rise in pressure for education increased pressure on families to circum-cise their daughters earlier?

Notes

1 Given the sensitive nature of the research topic, pseudonyms have been used for all proper names of people and places.
2 The total number of rescued girls and rescue centers currently in Kenya is unknown. Research has identified at least five formal centers in Kajiado and Narok districts serving the Maasai

community. A number of boarding schools across the region also accept and accommodate young students escaping marriage.

3 The research for this chapter spans seven years of work in Enkop on issues related to human rights, specifically focused on education, social change, gender, and land-tenure reform. Much of the initial research was conducted during a two-year period of doctoral dissertation work, from 2003 to 2005. During the beginning of this fieldwork in October of 2003, I volunteered at the rescue center and was given the opportunity to formally interview eight of the "rescued girls." In June of 2007, I returned to the school and conducted interviews with five more girls, including Esther. In between these two visits, I undertook doctoral research in Enkop using a combination of participant observation, semistructured and structured interviews, and survey work. During this period, I came to know Esther's family and engaged her father, mother, and brother in numerous discussions about their situation. In 2005, I administered a survey in the three contiguous localities that comprise the field site of Enkop, randomly sampling 15 percent of the population. The survey was undertaken by local Maasai assistants, who collected de-mographic and socioeconomic information as well as specific educational data on all members of the sample households. In 2007, as part of my postdoctoral research at McGill University, I became part of an interdisciplinary team responsible for investigating the causes and conse-quences of land-tenure reform in nine Maasai communities in Southern Kenya. Enkop is part of this study, so I have been able to return to the area on a regular basis to conduct research. This project permitted me to undertake a second round of survey work in Enkop in 2008–2009 on the same sample studied in 2005. Throughout my postdoctoral fieldwork (2005–present), I have returned to Enkop two or three times a year to undertake fieldwork on various topics. The most recent period of fieldwork specifically focusing on early marriage, including Esther's case, was conducted in July of 2010, when another eight interviews were conducted with men and women of diverse ages and backgrounds. My long-term engagement with research in this community, the strong social relationships I have forged with different kinds of people in the community (old, young, men, women, educated, and not educated), and the diversity of my research agenda over the years have all been critical in providing me access to the perspectives of family, friends, and community members on the sensitive topic of early marriage. The survey data has also been important as a way to check against interview bias.

References

Anderson, David M., and Vigdis Broch-Due, eds. 1999. *The Poor Are Not Us: Poverty and Pasto-ralism.* Oxford: James Currey.

Archambault, Caroline S. 2007. *"School Is the Song of the Day": Education and Social Change in Maasai Society.* Ph.D. diss., Department of Anthropology, Brown University.

Archambault, Caroline S. 2010. "Fixing Families of Mobile Children: Recreating Kinship and Belonging among Maasai Adoptees in Kenya." *Childhood* 17(2): 229–242.

Berting, Jan, Peter R. Baehr, J. Herman Burgers, Cees Flinterman, Barbara de Klerk, Rob Kroes, Cornelis A. van Minnen, and Koo VanderWal. 1990. *Human Rights in a Pluralist World: Indi-viduals and Collectivities.* Westport, CT: Meckler.

Bledsoe, Caroline, and Gilles Pison, eds. 1994. *Nuptiality in Sub-Saharan Africa: Contemporary Anthropological and Demographic Perspectives.* Oxford: Clarendon.

Coast, Ernestina. 2001. *Maasai Demography.* Ph.D. diss., Department of Anthropology, Univer-sity College, London.

Coast, Ernestina. 2006. "Maasai Marriage: A Comparative Study of Kenya and Tanzania." *Jour-nal of Comparative Family Studies* 37(3): 399–419.

Cowan, Jane K. 2006. "Culture and Rights after Culture and Rights." *American Anthropologist* 108(1): 9–24.

Cowan, Jane K., Marie-Benedicte Dembour, and Richard A. Wilson, eds. 2001. *Culture and Rights: Anthropological Perspectives.* Cambridge: Cambridge University Press.

Donnelly, Jack. 1990. "Human Rights, Individual Rights and Collective Rights." In *Human Rights in a Pluralist World: Individuals and Collectivities,* eds. Jan Berting, Peter R. Baehr, J. Herman Burgers, Cees Flinterman, Barbara de Klerk, Rob Kroes, Cornelis A. van Minnen, and Koo Van-derWal, 39–62. Westport, CT: Meckler.

Englund, Harri. 2006. *Prisoners of Freedom: Human Rights and the African Poor*. Berkeley: University of California Press.

Eriksen, Thomas H. 2001. "Between Universalism and Relativism: A Critique of the UNESCO Concept of Culture." In *Culture and Rights: Anthropological Perspectives*, eds. Jane K. Cowan, Marie-Benedicte Dembour, and Richard A. Wilson, 127–148. Cambridge: Cambridge University Press.

Galaty, John. 1992. "'The Land Is Yours': Social and Economic Factors in the Privatization, Sub-Division and Sale of Maasai Ranches." *Nomadic Peoples* 30: 26–40.

Gasper, Des, and Raymond Apthorpe. 1996. "Introduction: Discourse Analysis and Policy Discourse." *European Journal of Development Research* 8(1): 1–15.

Goodale, Mark. 2006. "Introduction to Anthropology and Human Rights in a New Key." *American Anthropologist* 108(1): 1–8.

Goodale, Mark. 2007. "Introduction: Locating Rights, Envisioning Law between the Global and the Local." In *The Practice of Human Rights: Tracking Law between the Global and the Local*, eds. Mark Goodale and Sally Engle Merry, 1–38. Cambridge: Cambridge University Press.

Goodale, Mark. 2009a. *Surrendering to Utopia: An Anthropology of Human Rights*. Stanford: Stanford University Press.

Goodale, Mark. 2009b. "Introduction: Human Rights and Anthropology." In *Human Rights: An Anthropological Reader*, ed. Mark Goodale, 1–19. Oxford: Wiley-Blackwell.

Government of Kenya (GOK). 2001. *Laws of Kenya: The Children Act*. Nairobi: Government Printer.

Hakansson, Thomas. 1989. "Family Structure, Bridewealth, and Environment in Eastern Africa: A Comparative Study of House-Property Systems." *Ethnology* 28: 117–134.

Hodgson, Dorothy. 1996. "'My Daughter . . . Belongs to the Government Now': Marriage, Maasai and the Tanzanian State." *Canadian Journal of African Studies* 30(1): 106–123.

Hodgson, Dorothy. 1999. "Pastoralism, Patriarchy, and History: Changing Gender Relations among Maasai in Tanganyika 1890–1940." *Journal of African History* 40: 41–65.

Hodgson, Dorothy. 2001. *Once Intrepid Warriors: Gender, Ethnicity, and the Cultural Politics of Maasai Development*. Bloomington: Indiana University Press.

Homewood, Katherine, Pippa Chenevix Trench, and Patti Kristjanson. 2009. *Staying Maasai? Livelihoods, Conservation and Development in East African Rangelands*. New York: Springer.

Lesorogol, Carolyn K. 2008. *Contesting the Commons: Privatizing Pastoral Lands in Kenya*. Ann Arbor: The University of Michigan Press.

Mensch, Barbara S., Monica J. Grant, and Ann K. Banc. 2006. "The Changing Context of Sexual Initiation in Sub-Saharan Africa." *Population and Development Review* 32(4): 699–727.

Merry, Sally Engle. 2006a. "Transnational Human Rights and Local Activism: Mapping the Middle." *American Anthropologist* 108(1): 38–51.

Merry, Sally Engle. 2006b. *Human Rights and Gender Violence: Translating International Law into Local Justice*. Chicago: University of Chicago Press.

Mitzlaff, Ulrike von. 1988. *Maasai Women: Life in a Patriarchal Society*. Dar Es Saalam, Tanzania: Tanzania Publishing House.

Mwangi, Esther. 2008. *Socioeconomic Change and Land Use in Africa: The Transformation of Property Rights in Maasailand*. New York: Palgrave Macmillan.

Nyerere, John. 2009. "Technical and Vocational Education and Training (TVET) Sector Mapping in Kenya." Report Draft: Edukans Foundation.

Preis, Ann-Belinda. 1996. "Human Rights as Cultural Practice: An Anthropological Critique." *Human Rights Quarterly* 18(2): 286–315.

Roe, Emery. 1994. *Narrative Policy Analysis: Theory and Practice*. Durham, NC: Duke University Press.

Ross, Fiona C. 2003. "Using Rights to Measure Wrongs: A Case Study of Method and Moral in the Work of the South African Truth and Reconciliation Commission." In *Human Rights in Global Perspective: Anthropological Studies of Rights, Claims and Entitlements*, eds. Richard A. Wilson and Jon P. Mitchell, 163–182. London: Routledge.

Shell-Duncan, Bettina, and Owuor Olungah. 2009. "Between Crime, Faith, and Culture: Contesting Female Genital Cutting and the 'Best Interest' of the Child." *Paper presented at the 108th Annual Meeting of the American Anthropological Association*, December 2–6, Philadelphia, PA.

Stirrat, R. L. 2000. "Cultures of Consultancy." *Critique of Anthropology* 20(1): 31–46.

Talle, Aud. 1988. *Women at a Loss: Changes in Maasai Pastoralism and Their Effects on Gender Relations*. Ph.D. diss., Department of Anthropology, University of Stockholm.

Thompson, Michael, and Katherine Homewood. 2003. "Entrepreneurs, Elites, and Exclusion in Maasai-Land: Trends in Wildlife Conservation and Pastoralist Development." *Human Ecology* 30(1): 107–138.

UN Population Fund. 2005. *A Safe Haven for Girls Escaping Harm in Kenya*. www.unfpa.org/public/op/edit/News/pid/2202, accessed July 1, 2011.

Waller, Richard D. 1999. "Pastoral Poverty in Historical Perspective." In *The Poor Are Not Us: Poverty and Pastoralism*, eds. David M. Anderson and Vigdis Broch-Due, 20–49. Oxford: James Currey.

Wilson, Richard A. 1997. "Representing Human Rights Violations: Social Contexts and Subjectivities." In *Human Rights, Culture, and Context: Anthropological Perspectives*, ed. Richard A. Wilson, 134–160. Chicago: Pluto.

Wilson, Richard Ashby, and Jon P. Mitchell. 2003. *Human Rights in Global Perspective: Anthropological Studies of Rights, Claims, and Entitlements*. London: Routledge.

Chapter 31

Between a rock and a hard place

The labyrinth of working and parenting in a poor community

Sharon Hicks-Bartlett

Reproduced from Sharon Hicks-Bartlett, "Between a Rock and a Hard Place: The Labyrinth of Working and Parenting in a Poor Community," in Sheldon Danziger and Ann Chih Lin (eds.), *Coping with Poverty: The Social Contexts of Neigbourhood, Work, and Family in the African American Community* (Ann Arbor: University of Michigan Press, 2000), pp. 27–51.

It was a quiet summer night in Meadow View. The crisp air and blue-black sky were tranquil. Suddenly, the night's stillness was pierced by screams and yells of chilling distress. Shots rang out. No one could recall how many. At times like this, people move away from windows. Someone surely summoned the police. Although the station is only 2 minutes from any point in the community, the police take their time showing up. Events inside Lillie's apartment stunned the occupants and made it difficult later to remember exactly what transpired that terrible night. Things happened quickly. Everyone agreed, however, that men with guns broke into the apartment, yelling, cussing, and looking for Lillie's teenage son. When the boy refused to step forward, the gunmen threatened to kill everyone. Lillie's son finally identified himself. At this point, things spun out of control.

All the gunmen wanted was Lillie's only son. But this was more than Lillie was willing to give. A slight woman, barely 5 feet, 3 inches, Lillie leaped in front of him, shielding him, flailing her arms, screaming and pleading for them not to hurt her child. They did not. In split-second pandemonium, they killed Lillie instead. Dead at the age of 42, leaving five children and one grandchild.

Few people were able to maintain their equanimity during Lillie's funeral. Many wept openly as versions of what transpired that night circulated through the large, crowded church. A self-described longtime family friend sang a mournful rendition of Lillie's favorite song, "It's So Hard to Say Goodbye to Yesterday." The minister railed at the unsaved souls, insisting that only those who had not accepted the Lord should experience difficulty saying goodbye. His words were less a eulogy than a stern lecture to those who were "living by the sword." As sounds of sobbing filled the church, the minister bellowed at those who refused to identify Lillie's killers. The woman with whom I attended the funeral pointed out Lillie's ex-husband, who evidently had come up north to pay his respects and to retrieve his son. The community denounced the father for his son's refusal to cooperate with police. But silence, the father believed, was the only way to save his son's life. Following the funeral, father and son would be heading south to live.

DOI: 10.4324/9781003398349-35

At the funeral, people whispered about the shame of it all, how things here had gone from bad to worse, how people could not even be safe at home, and how they feared for the future. They talked about the possible fallout from the killing. Might there be a retaliation murder like the one that occurred years before, when one young man shot another, only to be killed later by the brother of the man he had murdered days before? Back then, the community's lone undertaker prepared the bodies of both men. For the community's viewing convenience, the bodies were placed in adjacent parlors at the same time. Even then, many years before Lillie's murder, people were horrified by what was happening to Meadow View. Today, people continue to shake their heads in dismay, declaring that "people have simply gone mad."

In Meadow View, families struggle to survive. Few do so unscathed. Even for those a step or two above the poorest, living in Meadow View is a merciless challenge. As residents often remark, "stuff is always happening here." The strain of rebounding from one crisis before the next occurs depletes the body and mind. Lillie's story captures the violence that can transpire here.

In discussing how we experience place, Tony Hiss explains that whether we realize it or not, we all react "consciously and unconsciously" to where we reside and work.

> [P]laces have an impact on our sense of self, our sense of safety, the kind of work we get done, the ways we interact with other people, even our ability to function as citizens in a democracy. . . . [T]he places where we spend our time affect the people we are and can become.
>
> (Hiss 1990: xi)

Meadow View is one of the nation's poorest suburbs; it is isolated from jobs, quality schools, and adequate community resources. In Meadow View, for the greatest numbers of family members to survive, space must be strategically and carefully managed, which requires a level of vigilance that burdens families and reinforces their interdependency. But despite the gloomy state of affairs here, residents are tied to this terrain and to each other in real and symbolic ways. Despite all its problems, people call this place home. The stigma attached to coming from this place engenders in many a defensive bond that strengthens intergroup relations at the same time that it threatens to rip them apart. Affective bonds are always at risk because material, social, and financial need is unremitting. Already vulnerable families struggle to fulfill each other's needs, and this very exertion reinforces a "collective ethos" that binds people together (Jones 1986: 229).

Here, people manage working and parenting by relying on loose, family-based networks that minimize risk and center on meeting immediate needs. These networks provide the only security available to families in the face of recurrent threats to their physical well-being, isolation from jobs both within and outside their neighborhoods, and meager finances. Personal sacrifices, made for the good of the family unit, strain already-limited family resources. Not surprisingly, the help of relatives who are themselves poor is never enough to change one's life situation. But when "self-sufficiency" is promoted as a policy objective without attention to the central role that family members play for one another, it is easy to overlook the fact that family and community sufficiency is required for the problems of the poor to be fully addressed.

Meadow View is a small Black suburb outside a major Midwestern city. This chapter is based on more than nine years of fieldwork in Meadow View. The daily lives of ten women were explored with an emphasis on family, community, and work. Four of the ten women were first interviewed during an earlier project; the others were added during research for this project, which took place during an 18-month period beginning in the summer of 1995 and ending in December 1996. The women, all of whom are mothers, were engaged in conversations of both a general and specific nature. Most of the interviews were tape-recorded and transcribed verbatim. Formal interviews ranged from two to more than five per person. In addition, my impromptu visits to homes produced many opportunities to talk, woman to woman, about a variety of topics.

These mothers were located through old contacts in the community, a worker at a community center, and one or two key informants. I explained to all the participants that I was interested in learning about family and community life. Consent forms that proffered more information about the study were disseminated to everyone. Participation was unanimous. Initially, no mention of money was made. Upon completion of the first interview, ten dollars was given to each informant. No mention of money was made or offered thereafter.

Interviews transpired in one of two places, with the vast majority occurring in private homes. A small number of first interviews were conducted in a vacant office at the community center. Subsequent interviews took place in the mothers' homes at their convenience. In addition, I often dropped by for informal "interviews."

All the mothers are African American. They represent a cross section of the women I have interviewed over my many years of involvement in the community. Each mother has had work experience, which tends to be part-time and low-wage. Welfare use has ranged from a few months to more than ten years. All the women acquired their first job as teens in a federally funded summer youth employment program. Two of the women later secured either part-time or full-time work as adults in the same program. The other women typically hold jobs in service, retail, or manufacturing. With the exception of Sissy, the mother with the most education and work experience in the group, the mothers often talk of desiring jobs in the caregiving fields.

A suburb in name only

Although Meadow View is a suburb situated near a once-booming industrial region, it looks like the rural south, with its unpaved roads, two outhouses, and a creek set deep in the woods. Most of its nearly 4,500 residents, whether employed or not, are low-income and Black. By 1990, 49.2 percent of the population was below poverty level. Per capita income is just over $4,500. A large stamping plant sits outside the community, but few Meadow View residents hold these skilled and semiskilled jobs. By any measure, unemployment and underemployment are pervasive, creating a community dependent on government assistance. For those 16 and over, Meadow View's unemployment rate is 26 percent. Local officials set the "real" unemployment rate higher than 50 percent. One glance around the community on any summer day gives credence to a community perception that "almost everybody is out of work."

Meadow View has always been a poor community. But not until it became poor *and* Black did it develop such intractable problems. In the shift from a poor White community to a poor Black community, Meadow View became a choice locale for low-income public housing projects. Now, 65 percent of housing is government projects. Their construction in this particular suburb, as opposed to other nearby middle-class suburbs, is a prime example of the collusion among local, state, and federal agencies to perpetuate racial and class segregation within Meadow View. This small community was particularly attractive to those who preferred suburban living but could only afford it where rock-bottom housing prices and regional housing discrimination allowed them to live.

Rajah, who is married and the mother of seven boys and an infant daughter, voices her trepidation about Meadow View; she routinely checks for opportunities to move to other suburbs.

> I've been looking and looking for a house for my kids. Looking forever! I got to get away from here before I go crazy or something happens to my boys. I'm sick of the water, I'm sick of the drugs, I'm sick of living here. This is insane! Too much stuff is happening all the time. Something is always going on.

Theoretically, Rajah's income and housing subsidy would permit her to leave Meadow View. But if she succeeds, she will most likely relocate to another overwhelmingly poor Black suburb. Her subsidy was once a ticket into a safer, more economically viable suburb in the area. Now, those who want to leave often find themselves blocked as a result of a political battle between county and local housing authorities that restricts the mobility of the Section 8 certificates in this region (Hicks-Bartlett forthcoming). Leaving the community is even more difficult for those with little income and no housing subsidy.

Economic stability, adequate community resources, healthy infrastructure, strong institutions, a robust tax base, fiscal viability, and effective local government are some indicators of community well-being. Meadow View falls short on every single one. Like other old Black suburbs, Meadow View's local government strains to keep afloat financially (Logan 1983/1988). Ironically, although Meadow View provides fewer services to its residents than its nearby suburban neighbors, its per capita expenditures are higher than theirs. This is because the local government's weak property tax base is insufficient to provide adequate services or maintain its deteriorating infrastructure. Delaying needed repairs to save money often costs more in the long run. Several times, the local government has teetered on the brink of bankruptcy. On more than one occasion, both the police and the fire department have gone on strike, imperiling the safety of residents. Except for church, few institutional supports are available to supplement and reinforce parental efforts. Community-sanctioned outlets for youth do not exist. Local services are so inadequate (e.g., years ago, the local library had to be closed due to its unsafe structure and lack of operating funds) that people must go outside the community for most things.

In the summer of 1996, more than 150 people were arrested in a series of drug busts conducted by undercover sting operations. Previous raids had done little to clean up the community's drug trade. The latest round of sweeps came on the heels of the arrest of the police chief for allegedly permitting the drug trade to flourish with impunity, which had been rumored for years. More than a decade of police "passes" have brought down not only the police chief but also six current and former police officers, all of whom now face serious charges and lengthy prison sentences. Such corruption and graft lead many parents to believe that the job of protecting children from the fallout of this destitute place is their responsibility alone.

Surviving a summer requires considerable vigilance and management of one's space. Hot homes drive people outdoors to enjoy the camaraderie on the street. At the same time, an unremitting flow of out-of-state cars scouting for drug dealers stirs feelings of besiegement and sparks endless discussions of safety, drugs, and violence. Drugs control certain streets, making them difficult to navigate. Late-model, expensive automobiles, with White people at the wheel, block traffic along some streets. These outsiders are the topic of considerable community discussion, distrust, suspicion, and anger. The mother of two young children summed up her feelings regarding these invasions:

> We can't even drive through their neighborhoods. But they can come here and do whatever they want. They don't care about nothing but getting drugs, but we the one's supposed to be so bad. We the ones *they* don't want to live by.

Often, communities like this become a market for all sorts of spillover vice. Women and young girls are propositioned by strangers hunting for drugs and sexual thrills. Although men of all types scout the community for willing females, White males, perhaps because of their high visibility, evoke the greatest ire.

The fear of getting caught in the crossfire of a drug shoot-out and the concern that one's child will either use or deal drugs or be caught up in spillover crime as a victim or participant preoccupy parents. Parents assert that "you've got to watch out for your own." Meadow View has become a place where children must learn the community's alarm call: "hit the deck" or simply "get down." Watching children here is endless, exacting work. As one mother comments:

> We ain't been doing nothing but staying inside. They been shooting the last two nights. Girl, I'm scared to look out the window. My nerves is already bad – now they really messed up. Seems like every time I try to fall asleep, racing cars or shooting wakes me up. You gotta keep yours inside – if you want 'em safe.

During interviews, mothers habitually peek out the window. This seemingly small gesture is repeated in households throughout the community. Parents survey the landscape, tirelessly scanning the environment, monitoring slow-moving cars, scrutinizing suspicious gatherings – behavior all rooted in indisputable facts of daily life. Before venturing out, people caution each other to "be careful." Some avoid going out at night altogether for fear of getting "caught" out after dark.

Young boys risk being seduced into illegal work. A field note entry describes the challenges a parent can face. Mabel, mother of eight, expressed considerable angst about her sons. Her daughters worried her less because she had more success keeping them at home. One son, a particularly quiet youth of 15 named Mark, was approached to work as a "lookout" for a local drug dealer. Fearing his mother's wrath, the boy rebuffed the offers. Later, a rather persistent drug dealer invited himself to Mabel's house to ask permission for the youth to work for him. Mabel listened patiently to the dealer's request. When he finished, she said, "Leave my son alone. . . . He can't work for you. Just leave him alone!" She was dead serious and hoped her steely glare transmitted that spirit.

Fearing that Mark would eventually turn to drug work, Mabel first thought of sending him south to live with his father's family. When this proved not to be a viable option, she tried to get him into a special program where he would leave the community to work on an out-of-state farm, safe from Meadow View streets. "For three years, I wouldn't have to worry about him getting killed or something," she sighed. The program seemed a perfect solution. One problem remained, however. Because her son had never been in serious trouble, he was not eligible to enter the program through normal channels. Only if she abdicated her parental rights, formally declaring herself unfit, could he be admitted. The logic that required her son to be in trouble before he could receive help seemed inane to Mabel. She weighed her options and declared that if giving up her rights was the only way to save her son, so be it. As she explains it:

> I don't care too much about giving up my rights, if it can help him. He knows I'm his momma, and I know I'm his momma. No piece of paper can change that. When he gets out, I'm quite sure he'll look me up, and quite, naturally he'll be grown and can understand what I had to do.

Mabel escaped having to surrender her parental rights. Her son managed to avoid drug work on his own. To Mabel, what happened seemed worse in some ways. A young cousin, while showing Mark his gun, accidentally shot and seriously wounded Mark in the head. Now, for the rest of his life, he will ingest medicines to control his seizures.

To separate working and parenting from this situational context is to fail to appreciate how bound the two are. Parents in nonpoor areas expect certain community qualities and services that support parenting. There is a vast difference, however, between the communities in which the poor and the nonpoor reside, particularly those in which poor minorities and poor non-minorities live (Wilson 1987, 1996). While protecting children is a universal parental behavior, in Meadow View, it can require extreme measures; it is labor-intensive, emotionally draining work. The need to protect children and the vigilance this requires create major barriers to working and parenting, especially when the two are attempted simultaneously. The mother of four young boys reveals what transpired one day.

> Girl, a boy got shot the other day. Right out here in front of my apartment. He couldn't have been no more than 15. They killed him right out in broad daylight. I was so glad my kids wasn't outside, 'cause usually they would be right out there, playing. But I had just made them come in a few minutes before. It took the ambulance a long time to get here. I was so scared. . . . Blood, all in the street – it's still there. I just think about my kids. Girl, what if they were out there? They coulda' got kill, too.

Frightened by her experience, she immediately requested, to no avail, that the project housing authority relocate her family to a safer area. Mothers like this woman cannot but think that if they were not at home to make their children come in, their children might be the next victims. Meadow View lacks before- and after-school programs that could engage children in constructive activities while parents work. Ironically, the luxury of such programs belongs to parents who live in neighborhoods where tax dollars can support such services or to parents who can purchase whatever care they desire for their children. But in Meadow View, where the need for such programs is so much greater, parents have neither the income nor the institutional supports to establish them.

Adults and children feel the effects of this stressful environment. Meadow View mothers often complain of "nerve problems." Some children become fearful and edgy. Others obsess about danger or being shot. Like Meadow View adults, children become extremely preoccupied with the environment and its inherent dangers. "Hypervigilance" is striking, seen in the "scan[ning] [of] their surroundings for danger and over-interpret[ing] the actions of others" (Brownlee 1996: 72). Nightmares about being chased, hurt, or killed are common. In one family, the stress on a mother and her two children, ages 6 and 10, is palpable. In discussing her children's fears, the mother laments:

> I can't get them out of my bed. You know, they are too big to be sleeping with me. But they too scared to be in the room by themselves. They got good beds to sleep in, but I can't get them in them for nothing. They sleep in here real good, but now I don't get any sleep. And my back stay hurt with one on each side kicking me, and I can't get comfortable. I really don't sleep at night. I catnap in the day, when they in school.

This sleep-deprived mother frequently complains of physical ailments. The only time she rests is when her children are at school. The many implications this would have on working outside the home are obvious.

The constancy of trauma and fear in their environment causes other problems in children. One report found that children who experience early trauma (e.g., witnessing or fearing violence) show measurable physiological and chemical changes in the body and brain (Brownlee 1996: 72). When frightened, they react in a "fight-or-flight" response. The body attempts to compensate by releasing certain stress hormones. In affected children, normal physiological and chemical reactions jump track, producing abnormal levels and imbalances in the body. The impact on learning for children in these environments has been well-documented (Garbarino et al. 1992; Prothrow-Stith and Weissman 1993). Affected children have a shorter attention span; language and critical thinking suffer. High levels of these harmful chemical changes create children who are ripe for a host of learning difficulties. Children in these environments may also misconstrue normal play as aggressive and get into physical altercations.

All these challenges influence parental decisions about work and family. This does not mean that those who face such barriers should be exempt from paid labor. When faced with objective situations that require hypervigilance (e.g., children who require extraordinary nurturing, fear management, patience, and care of chronic health problems), most mothers concentrate on performing their maternal role above all else. Those lucky enough to find others they trust to care for their children are able to work – at least on and off – because of it. Without such support, employed work is difficult and sometimes impossible to sustain. Yet money for survival is as necessary as care for children and families. The support networks that spring up to meet these challenges address this dilemma, but in ways that lessen the significance of individual achievement and self-sufficiency.

Kin matters

Meadow View families depend heavily on each other. Individuals and families expect to share with others. In addition to financial support, families provide an array of essential services, without which most would not be able to work, attend school, or enroll in training programs. All the families discussed here are involved in extensive helping networks that can buckle under the weight of a widening circle of needy members. Just how critical to survival these networks are is exemplified by one mother's family.

Wanda once lived in a two-bedroom project apartment with her two children. It also provided temporary quarters for her two brothers and two cousins, whom her parents raised after their mother died. Although she now works as a teacher's aide, Wanda received welfare for more than ten years. Throughout much of this time, she cared for her invalid mother. On occasion, Wanda received money from her parents, but this was neither regular nor expected. To avoid placing the mother in a nursing home, Wanda's father, who worked full-time at a factory in a neighboring state, sought his children's help in caring for their mother. Since Wanda had a small child to care for, she was the designated sibling to help her mother and her employed siblings who might need occasional help. Two sisters, one employed in clerical work, the other in factory work, sometimes called on Wanda for childcare. Providing care to those who need it is highly valued, particularly over low-wage work that may only slightly improve the individual's life while potentially burdening and making matters worse for the extended kin network.

Known for being able to stretch her welfare check, Wanda was often called on for a loan or a meal or a place to stay for a few days. She earned extra income by operating an in-house "store," a table set up in her kitchen from which she sold soda, potato chips, and candy to neighborhood youth; at best, her efforts rarely generated more than $30 a month. Although Wanda had her own share of money worries, she rarely refused anyone in need. For unexpected emergencies, she kept $20 stashed away. Wanda's only complaint was that she did not have anyone as generous on whom *she* could rely. Although she felt she gave more than she ever received, Wanda did benefit from some invaluable help from this arrangement.

During her second pregnancy, Wanda moved from her parents' home into a subsidized apartment. Soon afterward, an assortment of relatives moved in and out. Until they found jobs, they were neither asked nor expected to help financially. When two relatives acquired jobs at a rehabilitation center, through another relative, they began giving Wanda money, helping with groceries and continuing to babysit. Whether working or not, they babysat whenever needed. Not only did this allow Wanda respite from her children, but it also relieved the ennui of being housebound. Wanda benefited, too, from the protection and security of having men present.

> I don't mind having them here. They are good company. Plus, I know that no one is going to come in here on me when they know that a man lives here. . . . They help out just by being here. Plus, it's good for my kids to be around their uncles and cousins.

Years later, while living alone with her two children, Wanda suffered a near-fatal brain aneurysm. Her family sprang into action. During her nearly six-month rehabilitation, the extended family focused on Wanda's health. At that time, Wanda's brother Donnie had been planning to go to Mississippi for a long-awaited job. Unemployed for years, he looked forward to finally getting work – even though it required a major relocation. Because the other siblings were engaged in full- or part-time work, they were less available to attend to Wanda's needs. Together, the family decided that Donnie should move into Wanda's apartment and assume primary care of her children and her personal affairs. Other relatives helped out on weekends. When asked how he felt about having to give up his job, Donnie remarked, "You can always get another job, but you can't get another sister" (see also Stack 1990).

Wanda and her family viewed her miraculous recovery as a sign from God that she should improve her life. With the help of her caseworker, she enrolled in a community college and eventually became a teacher's aide. During Wanda's coursework, Donnie, still unemployed, continued to live with her and help out, without pressure from his family to get a job. Caring for Wanda was a job that everyone in the family valued. Donnie never mentioned going south again. Until she finished school and found a job, Donnie selflessly contributed his unpaid labor to the family and Wanda's dreams. Now and then, Wanda gave him money, but he did not receive regular pay. Without his help, her recovery would have been difficult; her schooling would have been impossible. His childcare and household work allowed Wanda to recover fully, reach a goal sparked by her illness, and obtain a job.

Most families will respond supportively to each other in times of crisis. In this sense, Wanda and her family are not unique. What is truly notable in Meadow View families is the degree to which individuals are summoned to meet the needs of others and to suppress personal goals to do so (see also Rank 1994). A great deal of working and schooling is made possible only because of the willingness of others to set aside self-interest. Many who manage to hold jobs have kin willing to defer individual pursuits for the sake of others. Because poor families cannot purchase the care their families need, they must supply it to each other.

Exploring the complicated arrangements mothers must make to work and parent simultaneously reveals how tenuous these arrangements are and how even a slight error can trigger a full-blown, snowballing crisis in families. Children's illness is a universal barrier to working that all parents face, particularly parents of young children. According to Heymann et al. (1996), fully one-fourth of all parents reported that they had no sick leave available to take care of sick relatives, including their children. But children's ailments often require them to miss school. An estimated ten million children have some sort of chronic disorder. Not surprisingly, poor children have poorer health. They have a higher incidence of chronic ailments, while their working parents have the least number of sick leave to tend to them. Sissy, a young mother who worked in retail, tells how she finally had to quit her job because of her infant's chronic respiratory condition.

> My sister was watching him, but he just kept a cold. He'd have one a couple of weeks. Then he'd be okay a couple of weeks. Then he'd get sick again. I had to keep taking off to take him back and forth to the doctor. He wasn't eating right at all. My baby was so sick! They wanted to put tubes in his ears. When he couldn't breathe, my sister would call me at work and I had to rush home to take him to the hospital. She couldn't take him because she had to watch her own baby. So I had to quit because I was taking off a lot. I wasn't making no money. They were going to fire me because I had so many problems with the baby. I don't know if they believed me. My mother said I need to think about my baby and stay at home to take care of him myself. So I quit.

A preference for family/friend childcare over other types of care derives from the conviction that only family can be depended on to deal flexibly with frequent emergencies.

In Meadow View, the importance of caregiving can compete with a work ethic that values paid labor over nonpaid caring work. Anyone trying to combine simultaneous working and parenting can identify with Darla, an unemployed mother. Darla has four sons who attend school with her sister's three daughters. Her sister, a pregnant single mother, works as a file clerk. By 7:30 a.m., the girls arrive at Darla's apartment. When it is time, they walk to school with Darla's two school-aged sons. After school, the five children return to Darla's where the girls remain until their mother arrives. When the mother is late, the girls stay over or are retrieved by another family member. Before and after school, Darla is in charge of seven children under the age of 11. She prepares snacks and sometimes entire meals for the children.

During the time we were meeting, Darla was battling cervical cancer. While often in severe physical discomfort and under medication that made her somnolent and temperamental, she took care of these children. She received little money from her sister but often was rewarded with free weekends while her boys slept at their cousin's house, a respite Darla enjoyed. Occasionally, the boys received gifts of clothing or other small items. On payday, Darla's sister brought over groceries for the children. The arrangement helped both women. As Darla explained:

> I help out my sister. She's got her hands full with the girls. And she's pregnant too! Since I got to be here anyway, I might as well take care of hers too. You can't just leave your kids with anybody. She knows I'll do right by my nieces – I wanted girls, she was the one wanted boys. She's not going to leave her kids with just anybody.

When Darla recovered from the cancer, she found a job at a department store. Immediately, her job altered her sister's childcare arrangements and created new childcare needs for Darla. Now her nieces spend their before-school time in the care of another aunt, who just happened to quit her job because of doctor-ordered bed rest due to pregnancy complications. The girls continue to go to Darla's after school; until she arrives home from work, the children are now in the care of Darla's new boyfriend.[1]

The strain that such childcare arrangements can place on families is also evident from Vicki's story. Vicki, mother of two teenage daughters, once worked nights at a local bar, in part so that she could take care of her young nephew during the day. Her childcare work began soon after she got home from work in the early mornings, forcing her to get by on little sleep. Although she did receive pay for caring for Tony, whose mother, Kelly, worked on a cleanup crew at a local animal shelter,[2] the pay was sporadic due to Kelly's variable work hours. But as Vicki explained, this far-from-ideal situation was still the best option that the family, as a whole, had.

> I took care of Tony 'cause Kelly really didn't have anyone to watch him. She was going to get him in Head Start, but someone had to get him there and go get him later. I didn't want to have to walk there and back [twice]. It was just easier to bring him over here in the morning. That way, he'd be in one place all day. . . . That's why I wasn't really looking for a full-time day job then. She'd really have a hard time finding someone if I worked full-time, days.

When Vicki was unable to keep Tony because of foot surgery, another sister reluctantly used a week of her vacation time to fill in. This help was offered more out of duty to the larger family than respect for her sister. As she tells it:

> You know, my sister and I don't get along at all! But that don't have nothing to do with Tony. I sure don't want to spend my vacation watching him. But somebody's got to watch him 'til Vicki gets back on her feet. My mother don't need to be bothered with this boy – she's too old. So I just took off to take care of him.

In a community without childcare programs for young and school-age children, someone willing and able to provide such care is highly valued. Childcare, essential to all working parents with dependent children, is especially critical here. Mothers all want their children to receive the best care, to develop preschool skills, and to be involved in constructive activities with other children. Middle-class parents can purchase this care with greater assurance that it will be reliable and responsive to their needs.[3] Being able to purchase childcare allows parents to exercise some control over the quality of that care. Quality is desired by poor mothers also. But few are fortunate enough to be able to take advantage of a program like Head Start because it fails to serve all those who want it or need it. Moreover, such programs are typically structured around a clock that conflicts with the working schedules of full-time mothers. Thus, poor mothers take what they can get. It is important to keep this point in mind when trying to understand why significant numbers of poor families' children are cared for by relatives.

Relatives can be intrinsically good caretakers, and many are. But the preference for relatives must also be understood as part of an economic reality: mothers can trust and negotiate with family and friends in ways they could not with institutions. Given a choice, it is not clear that Kelly would have chosen one sleep-deprived sister and another disapproving one to care for her son. The help they offered was better than nothing. Even if her sisters were ideal caretakers, Kelly might simply wish to avoid reliance on custodial care done out of obligation. But it is unlikely that Kelly could have found a quality childcare provider who would have allowed her to pay erratically, or one who would take her son even when doing so violated the provider's self-interest. As another mother makes clear:

> Beggars can't be too choosy. I'm grateful I got family that will help out. It's better than nothing. I don't particularly like them over there, but right now I can't do no better. And for what I'm paying, I can't be telling people how to run their house. I'm just grateful I have someone that can help me. It's better than nothing.

While limited options make one grateful for what one gets, they can place children at risk. Custodial care performed by caregivers with limited skills, poor health, little knowledge of normal child development, and unsafe homes creates anxiety for working mothers.[4] But out of a desperate need for care, mothers may pardon poor quality and disregard potentially hazardous situations. They make do, forever ready to establish new plans if absolutely necessary. High standards for the quality of childcare one will accept is a luxury few Meadow View mothers can afford if they also want to work.

The symbiosis between working poor mothers and "nonworking," "welfare-taking" mothers makes it impossible to draw moral and ethical distinctions between the two. These mothers serve as lifelines to each other. A work ethic that always defines workers as more deserving than nonworkers misses this connection (Katz 1989). Given limited education, lack of job prospects, childcare needs, and inadequate transportation, these mothers recognize their dependence on others. They realize their ability to endure on low wages is possible, in large part, because of the misfortunes of other poor women whose labor helps them with their childcare needs. Those "lucky" enough to get a job realize that keeping it most often is directly related to someone else's current unemployment. And one frequently hears, "There but for the grace of God go I."

Reliance on the family can actually intensify after a job is obtained. One suddenly needs to find regular childcare, to borrow money "'til payday," to scrounge clothes to wear to work, to borrow bus fare or endlessly pursue other transportation means; these needs can ultimately weigh on everyone. Mabel, a mother who recently secured factory work, depends exclusively on her family's services. Just as the children are leaving for school, the mother is arriving home from work. When they return home, Mabel is often sleeping before departing for her graveyard shift. An older daughter who is a student at a local community college prepares the children for school in the morning and arranges her schedule to be home when the children return from school.[5] Without this help, Mabel would not be able to keep her job. A parent working nights must maintain a schedule that is not conducive to rearing young children. Things are difficult, leading Mabel to wonder at times if she really is better off working. She comments on her ongoing struggles:

> You know, if it wasn't for [my family], I wouldn't make it. I'd be in the hole a lot. When I finish paying my bills, ain't much left. I like my job, especially getting paid every Friday, but it's hard to make it. I try to give a little to [her daughter] for helping with the kids. [Referring to the used car she recently purchased to get to her job.] I'm deep in the hole now 'cause of that piece of car. Seems like soon as I got it, it needed some of everything done to it and that ate up my little money. And the car still ain't right. It's bad when you work and still can't do no better. Girl, sometimes my brother has to get up out of his sleep and take me to work.

Life can be as tough for employed poor mothers as it is for welfare-receiving mothers who work within the home. Having a job may *feel* worse in some ways for employed poor mothers who see that working has made their lives more complicated and unmanageable than before. One mother comments on her attempts to make it:

> I don't expect nothing on welfare, so I make do with nothing. But when I was working, I expected to make it and seem like I was worse. I couldn't really stay up on it. I needed things to wear more. I needed money to pay for getting back and forth to work. The kids needed snacks when they went over to [a relative's house], and I had to send enough for her kids too. I wasn't really paid much. . . . And I could never get regular hours, and that made it hard if I had to be there before they went to school. When [the youngest child] is in school full-time, I can probably work more.

Alluding to the help she requires, another "self-sufficient" working mother states:

> I'm squeezing by. This has been a good month . . . knock on wood! I'm just gonna keep my fingers crossed – that's all I can do. You know, as soon as you think you doing all right, something happens to remind you you not. I ain't had to ask my family for nothing this month, and I hope it stays that way. I know my family gets tired of me begging, 'cause I get tired of me begging too.

Rarely does this mother get through a month without the help of relatives and close friends. Her mother "keeps a freezer full of meat," allowing her to borrow food when money is tight. Such borrowing, in turn, exacts a cost from those who may have a little more than their poorest relatives but are also living close to the financial edge themselves. In fact, a tension exists between the pursuit of individual goals and the needs of the family. One woman explains the pressures she felt at college:

> You know, I knew my family needed me. I knew they were depending on my stipend. I'd call, and they would be having problems. I felt bad being here, having all this, and

they were having a hard time. I decided to come home after my first year and get a job to help out my family. I can always go to college at home.

This woman never finished her four-year business degree. She did, however, manage to complete two years of junior college. Until she was 27, she lived with her mother and siblings in a crowded project apartment. When she left home, she moved to an apartment a few blocks away.

Even young women with the opportunity to make a better life for themselves relinquish it to meet pressing family obligations. The assumption that working makes one better off is not always true. For whom are things better off? In this context, it is questionable that children are better off. Without reliable, affordable, quality childcare for multi-aged children, it is doubtful that these mothers, who worry incessantly about the safety of their children, feel that they are better off. It makes sense to value their children's health and safety above low-wage work. When low-wage work wins out, it is in part because these mothers badly want to work and have managed to secure the support they need from others in hopes of making work pay. Many learn that work does not always pay, and that when it does, it does so primarily because of the current non-labor-force participation of others.

Some of the problems mothers face would be more easily resolved if Meadow View residents were able to work in their neighborhood. But Meadow View suffers from a lack of jobs and little transportation to where the jobs are. Family-based networks often refer workers to jobs and provide transportation alternatives. But when nearly everyone in one's network is poor, isolated from good opportunities, or dependent upon unreliable transportation, the network can provide only minimal assistance.

Finding work, reaching work

One of the ironies of employment in Meadow View is that when poor mothers exchange their informal, family caretaking roles for paid, outside employment, the employment they find often involves caring for other people. In this region, the demand for home healthcare work is high, corresponding with a Department of Labor prediction that home healthcare would have the largest job growth of any industry between 1994 and 2005 (Eisler 1997). But while people everywhere must rely increasingly on purchased care, caregiving work is low-paying and receives little credit for being important and necessary (Abel and Nelson 1990; DeVault 1991; Stack 1974; Tronto 1994). These positions tend to be low-wage, labor-intensive, and little more than a "ghetto" for women, minorities, and illegal immigrants (Eisler 1997; Statham et al. 1988). But the "soft" skills these mothers possess from years of traditional female work are usually enough to secure a job in these female-dominated fields. At least five of the ten mothers in my study have worked in nursing homes or in home healthcare. When asked what type of work they felt qualified for, all but one felt they could get a job in caregiving because, as one mother put it, "that's mostly what [she has] been doing all along."

Home healthcare has advantages that other low-wage work does not; it allows for some flexibility in work schedules, which is especially important for single mothers (Schein 1995). Because of high demand for these workers, mothers can enter and exit the field at will, depending on the availability of help at home. Home healthcare also allows for more autonomy than other types of service work. Working in private homes, women can be their own bosses. Workers also develop strong relationships with their charges and often develop a sense of loyalty to the patient. They feel positive about providing a much-needed service to those less fortunate.

Even these advantages, however, are often insufficient to compensate for the job stress and low pay. Full-time pay at some agencies is $7 per hour, a pittance for a bread-winner. Home healthcare remains a poorly regulated industry, whose profits depend on unskilled, poorly trained, and uncertified workers. Currently, the supply of workers is high, giving agencies little incentive to invest in better training for better-qualified work-ers, or to share with workers the industry's considerable profits. Without better training and industry regulations, the psychological stress and backbreaking physical demands of the job ultimately take their toll. Vicki, who has worked more than once in home healthcare, explains:

> I stayed with old man Jones for three years. Broke my heart when he died. I told them I didn't wanna work for no one for a while. I just couldn't take it. I needed a break. I had to leave.

Maggie is married, in her 50s, and mother of two adult children. She has worked as a nurse's aide and as a home healthcare worker. When asked what she does for a liv-ing, she responds, "I'm a nurse." Due to health problems, she is currently on disability. She appears clinically depressed about not being able to work and is worried about her health. She is trying to will herself back to health because she "can't afford to be sick" much longer. She comments:

> I worked in a home for years before I quit. I left 'cause it was too hard and you get so attached to those old people. I remember coming in the room and this lady I'd taken care of had died. They'd already stripped her bed and cleaned the room. Nobody told me nothing. I just didn't want to be around all that death – took me a long time to get over that. . . . No, I will not work in the old folks homes again.

Many women suffer from the physical demands of the work:

> After a while, moving people gets hard. That's dead weight you're trying to move, 'cause a lot of them can't move by themselves. You change diapers on grown people, clean up after them, bathe them, dress them. After a while, you just can't do it. You go home sore and hurting when you get through. I like the people and helping, but I was killing myself.

Like people everywhere, many people in Meadow View get jobs through family and friend networks. Those seeking work regularly interrogate others about job leads. But workers who sponsor relatives run the risk of damaging their own reputation if the rela-tives do not succeed. For instance, Wanda's brother, John, who held a respected position at a residential rehabilitation center, sponsored two cousins, a brother, and a sister for jobs. On his recommendation, all were hired, and eventually everyone quit. One resigned because he feared being fired. Because he worked a different shift than his relatives, he had to "bum" rides to and from work. Without reliable transportation, he was habitually late. The sister, who worked in the laundry, hated the drudgery of the work and claimed her supervisor was unfair and mistreated her. She left and eventually found other employment. A third quit after a disagreement with another co-worker. Of the four who terminated, one remained unemployed for more than a year. John, embarrassed, vowed never to sponsor anyone again. His sister explains why she believes things did not work out:

> They didn't really like the work. See, John has a good job there. He don't get messed over. But the rest of them . . . they caught it coming and going. And the Whites kept on John about his relatives, what they did and didn't do.

On the other hand, if an employee works out well, an employer may come to view the sponsor as a reliable source for bringing responsible workers into the workplace. In Mabel's family, job sponsoring has worked out for two siblings in their early 20s.

> Both of them work at Brown's Chicken now. Ron got the job first, and when his boss asked him if he knew some good workers, he told him about Juanda. Now they both are there. They're doing good. They like it. They get called in to do extra work all the time when somebody doesn't show up.

Many of the mothers I interviewed have acquired jobs through similar networks; they recognize their personal and skill limitations. They know that "good" jobs (i.e., full-time jobs that pay above minimum wage, with benefits) are not the jobs they will secure. For the most part, they find jobs that are temporary, part-time, devoid of benefits, and always low-paying.

The unavailability of good jobs is not the only obstacle that these mothers in Meadow View confront when they try to obtain employment. Simply getting to one's place of employment is difficult. It is widely accepted that urban communities are usually removed from suburban jobs, housing, quality schools, and other amenities. But the same isolation plagues old Black suburbs. The significance of race is an indisputable fact in suburban development (Logan 1983/1988; see also Farley 1976). Decisions regarding transportation, suburban zoning codes, restrictive racial covenants in real estate investment and lending practices, redlining, and other discriminatory practices have historically been racially influenced (Massey and Denton 1993). Meadow View is not only a community that lacks industry but is also situated in a region that is geographically isolated. Workers need to travel well beyond its borders to find work. Even though hordes of suburban workers access a highly developed transportation system that brings them to city jobs each day, traveling between suburbs in this region is much more difficult. And when Meadow View workers find jobs in the city that can be reached by public transportation, they may not be able to afford the commute. A round trip from Meadow View to the city costs almost ten dollars. To take advantage of travel discounts offered to frequent riders, one must purchase a monthly ticket, requiring a considerable outlay of money up front.

Amy, the mother of four young boys, is in her late 20s. At the age of 19, she won custody of her five siblings after her mother died and her father abandoned them. Until recently, and for ten years, she received welfare. She then got a job in a suburb not far from Meadow View and hoped that she would be able to walk the two miles from the bus to her job. The only problem she anticipated was inclement weather. When asked about arranging a daily taxi pickup from the bus, she reminded me that such luxuries were beyond her means and that the region does not have a dependable taxi service.

Instead, Amy created an elaborate strategy for getting herself and her current boyfriend to and from work, which involved a carefully managed arrangement with a former boyfriend. This man, who was considerably older than Amy, considered her four children his responsibility – although he was the biological father of only the third child. Initially, he agreed to drive Amy and her new boyfriend to work; if he was in a generous mood and did not have to work himself, he would even loan his car to her. But this arrangement was inherently unstable. When friends and other intimates are repeatedly called on for transportation, there is a good chance that personal mood and disposition will eventually get in the way. Amy tells of her experience calling on her former boyfriend:

> We were paying my ex-boyfriend to take Curtis (her new boyfriend) to work. No problems. Then he started getting an attitude and saying he couldn't take him. Now he knew there was no other way for him to get there. But because he was mad at me, he wanted to pull out.

Her new boyfriend worked part-time at a fast-food establishment. No bus routes went near his job, and a cab was out of the question. Finally, the couple agreed to pay the ex-boyfriend more money until they could find another means of transportation. Because her plan was highly unreliable and filled with tension. Amy experienced considerable anxiety each day about getting to work.

Meadow View mothers unanimously desire work. They attempt it whenever they can. But they fail often, and not because they lack motivation or a work ethic. They fall short because the demands of simultaneous parenting and working eventually spin out of control, even with family support. They fail because the jobs for which they qualify turn out to be awful in the long run and eventually clash with family demands. They fail also because they work in job markets that discriminate against female breadwinners. In response, mothers quit. They hope to return at a more opportune time. Settings like Meadow View place considerable burdens on families, making it difficult, and often impossible, to parent and work successfully.

Summary

Barriers of space and place are not unique to Meadow View. Poverty and racial segregation, conjoined with spatial isolation and disconnection from the city that it lies near, prevent this suburb from receiving many basic services. The inability to afford a quality police and fire department, for example, exacerbates many problems here. Crime and fear of random violence force parents to become hypervigilant about their children, especially because the suburb has no institutional supports – after-school programs, day-care providers – to help parents keep their children safely occupied. Parents must rely on family networks, but such networks are often strained by the demands placed on them. For people here, options are extremely limited.

Keeping children safe consumes parents and influences decisions about looking for work outside the home. Mothers, who assume much of the parenting, easily become overwhelmed by the unrelenting demands of this environment. The community is devoid of adequate resources, such as a public library, youth services, and recreation programs. Poor pay tempts some police officers and firefighters to partner with the drug economy, leaving residents unprotected and vulnerable to random violence. Consequently, considerable effort is devoted to watching and protecting children. One must be forever vigilant about keeping children near and troublemakers far, a task that is not easy.

In Meadow View, the family is key to survival. Families provide transportation, housing, food, job leads, and emotional succor. Childcare, a service that every working mother with dependent children requires, is provided by relatives and friends who are outside the labor force. Because of this, mothers' work is inextricably linked to the nonwork or misfortunes of other women who may or may not be employed. Since few can afford to actually purchase the care they need, childcare provided by industry chains is out of reach for these families, both financially and geographically. Although mothers appreciate the custodial care the family provides, they have limited alternatives. Head Start fails to reach all those who need it, and those who use it must make elaborate plans to retrieve children, whose school schedules do not correspond with a regular, full-time workday. Childcare here is prone to disruptions and is unreliable. Unexpected illnesses interrupt work, making mothers more likely to be tardy, absent, and distracted on the job.

These family networks are not without tensions. As more and more families experience hardships, the networks become increasingly stressed. It is difficult to meet everyone's needs. In some families, substance abuse has created a need to provide shelter for children and the substance abuser. Eventually, the core group of givers becomes overwhelmed, forced to make tragic choices as to who can and who cannot be salvaged.

The emphasis from both the political right and left focuses on reducing welfare dependency rather than on eliminating poverty (Schram 1995). The Right, with its emphasis on the individual as the key to achievement, sees the problem as a lack of good character, behavior, and sound morals. The liberal Left, with its stress on developing one's human capital (Gans 1995; Handler 1995), argues that with the proper schooling, job preparation, and skills, the poor can assimilate into the world of work and perform like other Americans. But neither understands the multiple effects of poverty on poor mothers (single or married) who live in a community context that manufactures major barriers to simultaneous working and parenting. Work does not exist in isolation from family and community (see McKnight 1995). What is missing from both camps is an understanding of the daily demands on families trapped in an economically depressed and racially segregated community that is also geographically isolated and lacks the most basic resources.

Over time, such conditions create deep and multiple needs in both people and institutions. Parenting in an impoverished, unsafe community forces parents to make decisions about employment and self-sufficiency based on how they can best protect their children and hold on to the coping strategies that have worked in the past. Being thrust into low-wage work, without substitute supports and services or a method for maintaining what has already been carved out, puts already-vulnerable families and children at great risk. Parents need the security of knowing that the most vulnerable among them, their children and the elderly, will be safe, cared for, and protected.

Successful work programs will need to go beyond teaching job skills to consider community issues that program participants confront regularly. At the very least, work programs should address issues of community space, family obligation, local institutional support, and how these forces, alone and together, affect parents' ability to be productive workers and effective parents. For poor people to be simultaneously good workers and good parents, they need access to the same supports and resources that other working citizens have. Policymakers must develop a perspective that incorporates the full array of forces that go into work and parenting decisions (Dickerson 1995; McKnight 1995).

Lacking this, policymakers will create policies and programs that have little relevance to the real, day-to-day world in which the poor struggle to survive.

Discussion questions

1. What are the specific challenges of balancing work and parenting for the African American families discussed in this chapter, and how might they be similar to or different from those faced by families of other ethnic backgrounds?
2. What are the consequences of the constancy of trauma and fear in children's lives?
3. Explain why the author argues that it is an assumption that working makes one "better off."
4. What are the benefits and challenges of kin networks in Meadow View?

Notes

1 Although few talked about leaving children with boyfriends for this chapter, previous fieldwork suggests that this is often done out of desperation and rarely considered an ideal situation. The risk to children left with unskilled and unwilling caregivers needs to be examined from a child safety perspective.
2 This animal shelter worker has held several nursing home jobs but found them emotionally stressful, unpleasant, and difficult to manage without a car.
3 As more middle-class families experience problems with abusive childcare workers and poorly managed childcare chains, this is less true.
4 Living conditions in Meadow View are often unsafe. Over 34 percent of Meadow View's housing is considered "substandard."
5 The daughter's need to adjust her college schedule to accommodate the childcare needs of her family could be a barrier for completing her education. The potential exists that she will leave school due to unexpressed pressures to help her family, that family needs supersede her own. An after-school program could ease this type of childcare issue. For now, the daughter's school schedule is secondary to her family's needs.

References

Abel, Emily K., and Margaret K. Nelson, eds. 1990. *Circles of Care: Work and Identity in Women's Lives*. Albany: State University of New York Press.

Brownlee, Shannon. 1996. "The Biology of Soul Murder." *U.S. News & World Report*, November 11, 121: 71–73.

DeVault, Marjorie L. 1991. *Feeding the Family: The Social Organization of Caring as Gendered Work*. Chicago: University of Chicago Press.

Dickerson, Bette J., ed. 1995. *African American Single Mothers: Understanding Their Lives and Families*. Thousand Oaks, CA: Sage.

Eisler, P. 1997. "Home Health Care: 'All the Components for Disaster'." *USA Today*, Special Home Health Care Report, March 18, Section D, 4.

Farley, Reynolds. 1976. "Components of Suburban Population Growth." In *The Changing Face of the Suburbs*, ed. Barry Schwartz, 3–28. Chicago: University of Chicago Press.

Gans, Herbert J. 1995. *The War against the Poor: The Underclass and Antipoverty Policy*. New York: Basic Books.

Garbarino, James, Nancy Dubrow, Kathleen Kostenly, and Carole Pardo, eds. 1992. *Children in Danger: Coping with the Consequences of Community Violence*. San Francisco: Jossey-Bass.

Handler, Joel F. 1995. *The Poverty of Welfare Reform*. New Haven: Yale University Press.

Heymann, S. Jody, Alison Earle, and Brian Egleston. 1996. "Parental Availability for the Care of Sick Children." *Pediatrics: The Journal of the American Academy of Pediatrics* 98: 226–230.

Hicks-Bartlett, Sharon T. forthcoming. *Kin of Mine: Community and Family Life in a Low Income Suburb*. Unpublished manuscript.

Hiss, Tony. 1990. *The Experience of Place*. New York: Vintage Books.

Jones, Jacqueline. 1986. *Labor of Love, Labor of Sorrow: Black Women, Work and the Family, from Slavery to the Present*. New York: Basic Books.

Katz, Michael B. 1989. *The Underserving Poor: From the War on Poverty to the War on Welfare*. New York: Pantheon Books.

Logan, John R. 1983/1988. "Realities of Black Suburbanization." In *New Perspectives on the American Community*, eds. Roland L. Warren and Larry Lyon, 231–240. Homewood, IL: Dorsey Press.

Massey, Douglas S., and Nancy A. Denton. 1993. *American Apartheid: Segregation and the Making of the Underclass*. Cambridge: Harvard University Press.

McKnight, John G. 1995. *The Careless Society: Community and Its Counterfeits*. New York: Basic Books.

Prothrow-Stith, Deborah, and Michaele Weissman. 1993. *Deadly Consequences: How Violence Is Destroying Our Teenage Population and a Plan to Begin to Solve the Problem*. New York: HarperCollins.

Rank, Mark Robert. 1994. *Living on the Edge: The Realities of Welfare in America*. New York: Columbia University Press.

Schein, Virgina E. 1995. *Working from the Margins: Voices of Mothers in Poverty*. Ithaca and London: ILR Press.

Schram, Sanford F. 1995. *Words of Welfare: The Poverty of Social Science and the Social Science of Poverty*. Minneapolis: University of Minnesota Press.

Stack, Carol B. 1974. *All Our Kin: Strategies for Survival in a Black Community*. New York: Harper & Row.

Stack, Carol B. 1990. "Different Voices, Different Visions: Gender, Culture and Moral Reasoning." In *Uncertain Terms: Negotiating Gender in American Culture*, eds. F. Ginsburg and A. L. Tsing, 19–27. Boston: Beacon Press.

Statham, Anne, Eleanor M. Miller, and Hans O. Mauksch, eds. 1988. *The Worth of Women's Work: A Qualitative Synthesis*. New York: State University of New York Press.

Tronto, Joan C. 1994. *Moral Boundaries: A Political Argument for an Ethic of Care*. New York: Routledge.

Wilson, William Julius. 1987. *The Truly Disadvantaged: The Inner City, the Underclass, and Public Policy*. Chicago: University of Chicago Press.

Wilson, Willian Julius. 1996. *When Work Disappears: The World of the New Urban Poor*. New York: Knopf.

Chapter 32

Madres, madrinas, mamás y más

Trans Latina mothering in and around
Chicago's sexual economies of labor

Andrea Bolivar

Original material prepared for this edition.

Katalina,[1] a 28-year-old transgender woman, regularly hung out in Humboldt Park, the park after which the historically Puerto Rican neighborhood on Chicago's Northwest Side is named. Katalina met Mariana in the park while Mariana was passing out condoms to sex workers and drug users as part of her job as an HIV tester at a local HIV organization. Mariana was a 55-year-old transgender Latina woman and former sex worker who was well-known in Chicago's trans Latina sex-working community; she was a respected and loving mentor to many of its members. Katalina lacked stable parental figures in her life since she was about 18 years old, when her biological parents violently kicked her out of the house because of her gender nonconformity. In one of our first interviews, Katalina shared that she yearned for a "trans mother." After a few months of seeing Mariana in the park, Katalina started spending time with Mariana at the HIV organization. The three of us regularly hung out there.

A few days after Mother's Day, we were sitting in the plush chairs in the waiting room at the front of the HIV organization, looking out the window at people passing by, and chatting about trivial things. Katalina seemed anxious, or as if there was something she wanted to say but was hesitant. Finally, Katalina turned to her large purse and nervously fumbled through. I was not sure what she was looking for or what she might whip out. She gingerly held out a small white envelope imprinted with the Hallmark emblem and handed it to Mariana. Mariana, who also seemed unsure of what to expect, took the envelope with her characteristic smirk. She opened it, revealing a Mother's Day card. The front of the card read: "Isn't it amazing how one little person can change your whole world?" The inside stated: "Celebrating you on your 1st Mother's Day!" In addition to the pre-printed Hallmark words, Katalina had written her own message on the inside, in sloppy, somewhat hard-to-read black ink that clashed against Hallmark's delicate light-blue font: "I love and enjoy being around you. I want to better my life because one day I wanna be like you." Off to the side she also wrote "I love you" and drew three hearts. Mariana accepted the card and gave Katalina a hug. Katalina beamed.

From then on, Mariana was Katalina's "trans mother," and Katalina was Mariana's "trans daughter." This chapter focuses on trans mother–daughter relationships, as well as other types of trans maternal mentoring I learned about during my research with

DOI: 10.4324/9781003398349-36

sex-working trans Latinas in Chicago. This chapter reveals that sex-working transgender Latinas had up to five different maternal figures in their life at once, each performing a distinct role. Sometimes, one mother embodied multiple maternal roles, and other times different women embodied different roles. Some of the mother–daughter relationships were spiritual in nature and even persisted beyond death, into the afterlife. All of them offer additional possibilities beyond normative conceptions of motherhood, family, and kinship.

Queer and trans mothering

Motherhood in the United States is highly classed, raced, and gendered. The ideal mother is White, cisgender, heterosexual, non-disabled, and middle or upper class. She is located in the nuclear family structure and is primarily expected to biologically reproduce. She is also expected to reproduce socially, though only in ways that bolster heterosexism, cisgenderism, and capitalism. The US nation was built upon, and continues to benefit from, wide-scale violence against and exploitation of those who do not meet the requirements of the ideal White mother (Gutierrez 2008; López 2008; Ross and Solinger 2017). The women in this project mother in ways that directly challenge White motherhood and exist above and beyond the limits of the White cisheteronormative nation.

Trans Latina maternal figures offer various types of support, education, and care to their daughters. Yet their relationships are not biologically determined. Trans Latina maternal figures mother within and around sexual economies of labor. Further, their mothering is possible because of sexual economies of labor and vice versa; sexual economies of labor are sustained by their mothering. Trans Latina mothers and daughter live in excess of cisgenderist and capitalist values, such as scarcity and singularity. Most importantly, both trans Latina mothers and daughter nourish "trans of color" life. Gumbs et al. (2016) queer motherhood beyond the cult of the White biological mother and define "revolutionary mothering" as "a creative practice defined not by the state, but by our evolving collective relationship to each other, our moments together and a possible future" (Gumbs et al. 2016: 29). The trans Latina sex workers in this project are indeed engaged in various types of "revolutionary mothering." While research has just recently begun to consider queer mothers and maternal figures of color (Khubchandani 2023; Molé 2021), more work is needed, especially in the current political moment.

Research on trans motherhood in the United States is urgent, given the recent increase in transphobic legislation across the country. In fact, 2023 is the fourth consecutive year in which the number of anti-trans legislation in the United States has exceeded the previous year's. Such legislation aims to attack trans people and erase trans life and, in doing so, strategically targets trans families and communities, such as those organized around drag.[2] Critical attention to trans motherhood upends the popular transphobic belief that trans people are less lovable and less capable of maintaining loving relationships, especially familial relationships. One interviewee shared that upon her coming out as trans, someone she viewed as a friend exclaimed, "But who will love you like that?" Furthermore, this research troubles racist assumptions that Black, Brown, and Latinx parents are more naturally and culturally transphobic, and thus more likely than White parents to reject their queer and trans children. Trans people of color are especially vulnerable to both discursive and legal violence.

While ethnographic research is beginning to acknowledge the various types of kinship, and attending forms of labors, that go into queer of color kin-building (Bailey 2013; Molé 2021), seldom are spiritual kinship, mentorship, and motherhood recognized (an important exception is Cáraves 2021). In fact, spirituality is often considered opposite to queerness, transness, and sex work. As I will demonstrate later, while many topics assumed to be kept from me as a researcher were not, spirituality was. It was not until many months into the research, and after they better knew and trusted me, that the women revealed their religious beliefs and affiliations to me. Thus, looking at various types of trans motherhood reveals the importance of ethnography as a methodology. Lastly, a focus on trans Latinas in particular brings together transgender studies and Latina studies, two disciplines that are rarely bridged.

Methods and key terms

I conducted the majority of the ethnographic research that informs this chapter between June 2015 and August 2016 on the West Side of Chicago, where large Latinx populations have historically resided. Most of my time was spent in Humboldt Park, which is considered the heart of Puerto Rican Chicago, and Little Village, a pillar of Mexican Chicago. I collected data across several sites, including interlocutors' homes and workplaces, LGBTQ and HIV/AIDS organizations, and streets, bars, and clubs where sexual services are sold. My methods included semi-structured in-depth interviews, life history interviews, and participant observation with 24 sex-working trans women of color. While Chicago's Latinx population has long been diverse and is increasingly diversifying, it has historically had larger Mexican and Puerto Rican contingents (Amezcua 2023; Fernández 2014). Reflecting these historic and demographic realities, the majority of the 24 participants were Mexican or Puerto Rican, and some were Cuban and Ecuadorian. Two Puerto Rican women identified as Black, and two Mexican women identified as Indigenous. One woman, who hung out with the rest of the interlocutors, was non-Latinx Black.

Before turning to the ethnographic data, I would like to define a few key terms. "Transgender" is an umbrella term referring to a variety of gender identities that differ from the ones assigned at birth and that challenge cisgenderist expectations for gender identity and expression. All the women in the study were transgender women. When referring to the women, I, of course, use "Latina," which is a feminine noun used to describe women. While there is much debate about the term "Latinx," when referring to the larger community, I use "Latinx" in order to recognize nonbinary individuals and to combat pervasive and often internalized cisgenderism within and around Latinidad. I am also inspired by Alan Pelaez López's (2008) use of Latinx "as a wound" to signify the violences of colonization, slavery, displacement, and feminicide that make Latinx identity impossible to easily articulate. "Sex work" and "sexual labor" are used interchangeably and refer to work that involves the exchange of sexual acts for money, goods, or other services. Notably, sex work requires various skills and other types of labors, such as emotional labor, intellectual labor, physical labor, artistic and creative labor – and even spiritual labor.

To capture the intersectional nature of oppression of trans women of color in the United States, I employ the term "racist-cisgenderism." My employment of "racist-cisgenderism" acknowledges critical understandings of cisgenderism that are suspicious of a cis–trans binary which can obscure more than it reveals (Agid and Rand 2012). Yet I use the term to highlight the systematic and multi-layered nature of oppression of trans peoples (Ansara and Hegarty 2011; Lennon and Mistler 2014). Moreover, my conception of "racist-cisgenderism" relies on definitions of *cisgenderism* as inherently informed by racism (Aizura 2018; Namaste 2005; Spade 2011). However, it also explicitly centers racism and processes of racialization which are otherwise at risk of being underappreciated by White, transnormative approaches to cisgenderism, and acts as a reminder that racism and cisgenderism are inextricable. Attention to the racialization of trans Latinxs in the United States begs analyses of the border industrial complex, linguistic imperialism, anti-Blackness, and anti-Indigeneity within/around Latinidad – all of which warrant more research in transgender studies.

Sexual labor occurs within a racist-cisgenderist society. Therefore, I use "racialized sexual economies of labor," which requires a longer explication. "Racialized sexual economies of labor" draw attentions to (1) the racialization of sexual economies in the United States in general and, in this case especially, where they are built around the figure of the hypersexual transgender Latina; (2) the various forms of labor the women are engaging in, including sexual, physical, and emotional; and (3) the intersection of sexual economies with various other economies, both normative and non-normative, and related social worlds.

The racialized sexual economy of labor that is the focus of this research developed around the powerful and fantastical image of the hypersexual trans Latina and intersects with extreme economic exclusion. Both transgender women and Latinas have a long history of being hypersexualized (Gutierrez 2008; López 2008), thus when combined are extremely hypersexualized. Women capitalize on the figure of hypersexual trans Latina within the sexual economy, yet they are also deeply critical of it and the larger societal structures responsible for its production and circulation.

While racialized sexual economies of labor afford opportunities otherwise denied for personal growth, kin creation, and political contestation, all the interlocutors stated that they do sex work because they cannot secure employment elsewhere. They encountered racist-cisgenderism at multiple points in the employment-seeking process. For example, Katalina, who is typically perceived as a woman, had a job interview at a factory which was arranged by one of her clients who knew the supervisor. The interview went well, and Katalina was excited when her potential boss took her identification into the next room to make copies. A wall with a large window separated the two rooms; therefore, Katalina saw everything that transpired. When the potential employer looked at her ID before placing it in the copy machine, he noticed that although Katalina has a very feminine appearance, the name on her license was still the name she was given at birth. There were a few other cisgender male workers in the room. The boss passed Katalina's ID around, and they all took turns looking at it and laughing. Katalina did not get the job.

Katalina was born in Puerto Rico and is therefore a US citizen. Barriers to employment are heightened for undocumented individuals. When an undocumented Mexican transgender woman was venting to me about her desire to quit sex work, I asked her what type of work she would like to do. She replied, "Something not too manly." As scholars have pointed out, manual labor in the United States is racialized (as Brown) and gendered (as masculine) (De Genova and Ramos-Zayas 2003; Gomberg-Muñoz 2011). Undocumented trans women, many of whom are pushed out of formal education, find themselves with two employment options upon arrival to the United States: manual labor or sex work. Domestic work is an option for undocumented cisgender women, but trans women are often unwelcome in domestic spheres because of their non-normative femininity. Between manual labor and sex work, the former may seem like the less-desirable option because of its threat to femininity. Therefore, many turn to sex work despite its criminality and the possibility of violence from various sources, including clients and police officers. Criminal records decrease employability in the formal sector and consequently create cycles of marginalization. In fact, Josefina began doing sex work precisely because she was detained for being undocumented. When she was released from the detention center, she found herself in an unfamiliar rural area, where she had no money and nowhere to go. In order to have food and, eventually, a place to sleep that wasn't on the streets, she turned to sex work. State-sanctioned and socially acceptable forms of racist-cisgenderism work against trans Latina women in ways that only reinforce their racial, sexual, political, social, and economic marginalization.

As will be clear throughout, I encourage an understanding of trans Latina sexual economies of labor that recognizes the influence of racist-cisgenderism while also acknowledging it as a space of creativity, kinship, spirituality, and love. When considering trans women of color's involvement in sex work, the former is recognized more than the latter. I argue that the failure to recognize the latter results in the hypervictimization of trans women of color sex workers, which can ultimately contribute to their dehumanization. Further, I believe that there is not anything inherently dangerous about sex work, but rather, sex work can be dangerous because it exists within a racist-cisgenderist and capitalist society. I use "trans Latina sexual economies of labor" interchangeably with "racialized sexual economies of labor" but intentionally use the former to highlight that they are political and cultural spaces created and nurtured by transgender Latina women in particular.

Lastly, I will define "trans mothers." Typically, trans mothers are understood to help only with transition; however, their role and impact is much greater (and a trans person does not need to transition to be trans). The women in my research did indeed report that their trans mothers' primary job was to "teach them how to be trans women," or "teach them how to be women." They offered support related to gender identity, including advice about gender-affirming medicine and cosmetics, such as makeup, hormones, silicon injections, and surgeries. However, they also provided various types of emotional and material care and support for their daughters, directly related to transgender identity and also related to numerous spheres of life not directly tied to gender. In the context of my research, trans mothers also taught daughters how to get started in the sex trade if they explicitly and continuously expressed an interest in sex work. If daughters had already begun doing sex work, mothers encouraged safer sex practices and shared knowledge to improve business. Interlocutors found their trans mothers on the "stroll," in clubs, and while living on the streets after being kicked out of their parents' homes. Many trans mothers offered mentorship around transgender identity, sex work, and drag, but some daughters had different mothers who offered mentoring around different things. For instance, Lucia explained to me:

> I got my trans mother, who helped me with my transition and helped me be a woman. I got my drag mother, who taught me how to perform onstage. And I got my mother, who helped me in the trade, if you know what I mean.

Lucia laughed. I use "trans maternal figures" in addition to "trans mothers" to include "madrinas," or "godmothers," in Santería. Madrinas initiate their goddaughters into the Santería religion and are also sex-working trans Latina women.

Trans mothers everywhere

Trans Latina economies, and life more broadly, transcend state and national borders and, as we will see later, the border between life and death. Some of the more successful sex workers traveled to different states for specific clients, or in hopes of appealing to new clients, especially in places with smaller Latinx populations. Many interlocutors moved to avoid violent police officers, boyfriends, and clients. Within Chicago, they often moved apartments because of housing discrimination against both trans women of color and sex workers, and because of increased rental costs due to gentrification. The constant movement was matched with new ways of connecting, illuminating the flexibility, durability, and expansiveness of trans Latina networks.

While most of the women had lived most of their lives in the United States in Chicago, a few have just recently arrived in Chicago from other cities and states. Those who had recently arrived in Illinois had trans mothers in other states who kept in touch with them and continued to offer emotional and practical support and, occasionally, financial assistance, when they could. For example, 18-year-old Alexia had moved to Chicago from North Carolina to escape an abusive boyfriend, to "start over," and to "be trans 24/7." She chose Chicago because she was accepted into a program that provides free housing to LGBTQ youth, and she hoped to be in a place with a larger Puerto Rican population, as she was Puerto Rican herself. Although her housing was free, she was still responsible for other basic expenses. When we first met, she had not started doing sex work. I asked her how she was getting by. She told me her trans mother was wiring her money from afar. I assumed that her trans mother was in North Carolina, but Alexia explained that her trans mother, in fact, lived in Seattle, and that they had never met in person. They met online while playing a fantasy video game and developed a deep relationship through the game and then outside of the game via texts, phone calls, and video chats. I asked Alexia if she felt supported by her trans mother even though they never met in person and lived so far away from each other, and she explained:

> Yeah, I mean, it would be nice to hang out in person, but sometimes I'm not that social anyways, so I don't need to hang out in person with people all the time. Virtual is basically the same for me, sometimes even better. We bonded over our love of video games. She's always there for me, just a phone call away. She gets me. And she sends me money when I need it. She supported me through this whole moving process.

Later, however, when I inquired about her hopes for her new life in Chicago, she said:

> I needed to get away from that abusive ex. I needed to start over. I needed the freedom to live as a woman 24/7. I wanted to be around other Puerto Ricans. I am sick of being the only one. And like, I heard there is a big trans Latina community here.

I asked her if she hoped to connect with other women in the trans Latina community, and she replied, "I'm looking for mentors. I am really good at seeking out support and stuff." When I asked if she was interested in finding another trans mother, she said, "Yeah, I mean, I love my current trans mother, but it would be nice to meet more women. I'm young, and this shit is hard." A few months later, Alexia decided she wanted to engage in sexual labor, and she informed me that she was developing a relationship with a trans

Latina woman who was mentoring her in sex work. In addition to teaching her about sex work, her new trans maternal figure offered various types of care and labor unrelated to sex work and based upon her experience as an older trans woman who had lived in Chicago her whole life. While physical distance did not prevent a meaningful trans mother–daughter relationship for Alexia, she also did not limit herself to one trans mother, or one type of trans maternal relationship. One relationship was virtual, while the other was in person. One mother mentored her primarily around transness, while the other mentored her around sexual labor and life in Chicago. Yet they both offered more holistic guidance and care. Alexia's experiences further demonstrate the capaciousness of trans maternal mentoring and an abundance of trans Latina love.

Biological mothers, trans mothers, and more

Importantly, many of the women also maintained close relationships with their biological mothers. Like the groundbreaking work on lesbian and bisexual Latinas by Acosta (2013), this disputes the potentially racist stereotype that Latinx parents are exceptionally homophobic and transphobic and are more likely than White parents to disown queer children. Quite the contrary, some women had up to five maternal figures, including supportive biological mothers. They had biological mothers, trans mothers, mothers related to sex work, drag mothers, and godmothers in Santería. Such kinship configurations racially, sexually, and spiritually exceed the limits of White cisheteronormative notions of family.

Brittni is a 27-year-old Mexican trans woman. Her biological mother hosted a birthday party for her in their backyard. I went and was overwhelmed by the love. Brittni's biological mother and her biological tías cooked both Mexican and Puerto Rican food, enough to fill a long plastic foldable table. Colorful balloons were scattered all around the yard, which her little cousins played with. A large white wicker chair, especially for Brittni, was also decorated with balloons and ribbons. Her family members, including cousins and siblings, were there, as well as her friends, most of whom were Latino gay cisgender men and Latina trans women. Brittni's cousin deejayed, and people danced on the grass. Brittni's biological mother bought her a large expensive cake from a nearby Mexican bakery, and we all sang "Happy Birthday" in both English and Spanish. When I first walked in, Brittni introduced me to everyone, including an older trans Latina woman and respected sex worker, named Isabella. She introduced her to me as her "trans mother," even though in our first interview months before she said she did not have a trans mother.

Before the night was over, Brittni requested that someone take a picture of her sitting on her chair/throne with both her biological mother and her trans mother on either side of her. I took the picture; Brittni smiled brightly, as did her two mothers. The next day, she posted the picture to Facebook with the following caption:

> These women mean the world to me. To my mom, I wouldn't be here without you and your love. You are my everything. To my trans mother, I wouldn't be who I am without you. I adore you. I love you both.

Even though Brittni was worried that her biological mother would not accept her gender identity when she first realized she was trans, Brittni's mom was supportive of her trans identity. She even once hosted Brittni's trans friends who were in town for an annual meeting of a national trans organization. She also cooked food for them and made sure they were comfortable in her home. In those few short days, she mothered them too. To be clear, a few women in the project were rejected by their biological mothers, and a few had more ambivalent relationships. However, the majority maintained stable and supportive relationships with their biological mothers, often at the same time as trans mothers and other trans maternal figures.

In the previous section, I showed how trans Latina kin networks defy state boundaries. They also exceed national borders. The majority of the women who were immigrants maintained relationships with biological family in their Latin America countries of origin. In fact, many proudly stated that the money earned from sex work enabled them to support their bio families, and especially their biological parents. Josefina pridefully stated, "My brothers and sister, they got minimum-wage jobs that can't help my parents in Mexico too much. I do sex work, and I can send them money every month." She was especially proud to be able to support her mom (see Bolivar 2021 for more on the complex ways money earned from sex work supports family).

Trans mothers in the club

The small dance floor at La Hueca is packed, and it is hot. Sweaty bodies rub up against one another as they dance voraciously to a Mexican cumbia. Two queer Latinas are dancing together to my left. Earlier, one of the women shared with me that she grew up near La Hueca and always heard "bad things" about the club. Her family and neighbors would often disparage it, but once she realized that she was bisexual, she overcame her fear of the place and decided to check it out. She now comes almost every weekend. Dancing there, she says, is "therapeutic." The rest of the crowd is composed of other queer couples, most of whom are Latinx.

In addition to the small dance floor, the club is full of tables, where people sit and chat, laugh and yell, and stop on their way between the dance floor and the bar. Servers – most of whom are trans Latina women – work their way through the tables, taking people's drink orders in skintight, short dresses. Other trans women lounge against the walls of the club, watching and waiting for potential clients, while others are backstage, getting ready to perform. The music cuts off, and everyone, as if on cue, immediately scatters off the dance floor and to the tables. Some are left standing, because if you do not come soon after midnight, the seats are all taken. Regardless, everyone is patiently facing the dance-floor-turned-stage. They know what is about to happen. The show was technically supposed to start at 2:30 a.m., but it is not until 3:00 a.m. that Spanish techno music started to bump from the speakers before, finally, a tall, curvy, middle-aged trans woman struts onto the stage, microphone in hand. She is wearing a tight sequined royal blue gown, and she slowly gyrates her hips as she looks out towards the crowd. The audience members cheer, and she rips the ballroom gown off. Underneath, small patches of the sequined blue fabric barely cover her nipples, and a short skirt made of frayed cloth exposes her G-string. She brings the microphone to her mouth, extends the other arm out towards the increasingly loud crowd, and belts out, "Bienvenidos al major show de Chicago!"

La Hueca is a space that is built by and for transgender Latinas. Located in a historically Mexican neighborhood on the Southwest Side of Chicago, La Hueca is one of the oldest LGBTQ clubs in the country and Latinx drag[3] bars in the nation. In the early '70s, Conchita Papaya, alongside other trans Latina women, raised money to open it by selling discos and tamales in the streets. The women wanted it to be a place where trans Latina women could perform and queer Latinxs could belong in a time of extreme homophobia, transphobia, racism, and gang violence. Conchita eventually returned to Mexico to take care of her aging parents, and since then the club has been owned by gay and straight Latino men. Its focus on trans women remains, and it is still viewed as instrumental in increasing acceptance of gay and trans people on the Southwest Side, and in Chicago's larger Latinx's community.

The club is mostly popularly known for its incredible "drag" performances and the selling of sexual services. La Hueca functions to facilitate sex work in a few ways. As the night progresses, more and more trans Latina women stand outside of the club, making themselves available to potential clients driving by. Sex workers also hang out inside the club and wait for potential clients, often telling prospective customers whom they have been chatting with online to meet them there. Because of the sex work traffic within and around the club, some neighbors have long fought to shut down La Hueca. Doing so would have a number of negative consequences for sex-working trans Latinas, their live-lihoods, safety, and well-being. Meeting potential clients in a semi-public and populated space allows sex workers to get a feel for clients before being alone with them, especially clients they have found online and are meeting in person for the first time. By meeting clients in a space that was created for and by trans Latinas, they may feel less vulnerable. If they do decide to engage clients in nearby locales, having the support of the people who work in La Hueca – people who respect trans Latina women – can be immensely helpful in dangerous situations. Grounded in the framework of La Hueca, the power of clients, which can otherwise be unrestrained, is somewhat checked. In short, La Hueca can some-times make sex work safer for trans Latina women. It is also a place where various trans Latina maternal relationships are formed and nurtured.

Brittni was 20 years old and confused about her gender when she met her trans mother, Isabella, who was 40 years old, at La Hueca. Isabella performed at the club, and before she offered to be Brittni's drag mother, Brittni spent many months helping her prepare for performances. Throughout this time, Isabella taught Brittni about being transgender and helped her transition, and thus also became Brittni's trans mother. Isabella sometimes stayed on the phone with Brittni all night as she cried about difficulties of her transition and her fear that her biological family would reject her. As I showed in the previous sec-tion, they did not. In addition to teaching her about drag and trans womanhood, Isabella taught Brittni how to be a successful sex worker. Isabella's own trans mother did the same for her. Isabella is an example of a trans maternal figure that was simultaneously a trans mother, a sex work mother, and a drag mother. Brittni and Isabella's relationship continues a long history of trans love and resistance.

Madrinas and spiritual motherhood

An additional form of trans motherhood exists, a trans feminist kinship that has not only persisted over generations but also traverses spiritual realms. In La Hueca, some women found godmothers in Santería,[4] who are also sex working trans Latina women. Santería is an African diasporic religion that originated in the Caribbean amongst enslaved peoples and that, drawing from Yoruba religious practices, revolves around santos or orishas, who are different manifestations of God. Santería allows for gender fluidity and bodily transformation amongst santos and practitioners. And as Beliso-De Jesús (2015) points out in her stunning ethnography, Santería also allows for a multiplicity of being, in body, space, and time. Brenda, 47-year-old Mexican woman, learned about both transgender and Santería – the two most important aspects of herself and her life – at La Hueca. An important aspect of trans Latina sexual economies of labor, Santería is central to trans Latina epistemologies and ontologies.

Brenda recounted to me that she first went to La Hueca in her 20s as an effeminate "gay boy" and saw the trans women performing onstage, knowing immediately that she wanted to "be like them." She got close with "all the girls," especially Sadia, who was slightly older and would become her godmother via Santería. Sadia passed away a few years before I began the research, so Brenda welcomed the opportunity to remember her relationship with Sadia. Brenda said that, before she passed, Sadia was "always there for" her. In addition to her godmother Sadia, another woman would become Brenda's official trans mother. She, too, was very present in Brenda's life. Thus, Brenda had two mothers who were both sex-working trans Latinas women, in additional to her biological mother that she maintained a relationship with.

Brenda recalled that one night at the club, Sadia received the news that a close friend, also a trans Latina woman, was arrested for drug-related activities and could go to prison for a very long time. Sacrificing opportunities to service clients and perform onstage, she rushed into La Hueca's tiny woman's bathroom and pulled Brenda with her. Sadia did an impromptu reading to ascertain her friend's fate. In a reading, the Santera communicates with the santos via a ritual of rolling, throwing, and reading of caracoles (cowrie shells). Elegguá, the owner of all crossroads, acts as an intermediary, communicating with the rest of the saints and then relaying their messages to the Santera via the shells. Sadia argued with Elegguá, yelled at and pleaded with him in English, Spanish, and Yoruba. She got sweatier, and the small bathroom got hotter. Eventually, the santos told Sadia that their friend would be charged with a crime that carried a potential sentencing of 40 years, but that she would only serve less than one year. Sadia and Brenda were relieved. The friend would go on to serve six months in prison.

It was then that Brenda knew she wanted to be a Santera. Sadia initiated her and thus became her godmother. Now, Brenda's main sources of income are sex work and readings. It is also important to note that Brenda was granted asylum, despite the fact that she had a number of drug-related charges and was deported three times. Unable to believe she was awarded asylum, I once exclaimed, "But how?" She assuredly replied that it was because of the saints. Her logic may eschew White western epistemologies, but it was accepted and lauded within trans Latina sexual economies. According to Brenda, she would have perhaps never found her gender, her faith, her two jobs – sex work and her work as a Santera – or her "freedom" if she did not start going to La Hueca. In sum, La Hueca, an example of trans Latina space-making, nurtures not only the development of the self but also various kinds of trans Latina community, in this world and beyond. Sex working, trans mothering, and practicing Santería are all interrelated community-building activities that draw from centuries of resistant queer of color knowledge and ways of being. As the women engage in ancient practices passed from generation to generation, they strive towards a more radical queer of color future.

The inclusion of madrinas in research on trans maternal relations also highlights an important methodological point. When I tell people – academics and nonacademics alike – about my research and, more specifically, whom I do research with, a common response is, "But how do you get anyone to talk to you?" It is a valid question. People put a lot on the line when talking to researchers. At the very least, research participants are incredibly generous with their time and energy. The people I work with may make themselves vulnerable in a number of different ways. They may out themselves as trans. They may out themselves as sex workers. A third of the interlocutors were undocumented, and thus, those folks may out themselves as undocumented. For these reasons, they are often considered a "hard-to-reach population." However, as Avery Everhart and colleagues (Everhart et al. 2022: 7) argue in relation to social services, "hard to reach" assumes that "trans women make no effort to meet their own needs, when in fact it is the services that may be 'hard to access.'" Everhart continues that "hard to reach" marginalizes trans people by assuming that researchers are not trans and/or are separate from trans interlocutors' social worlds. The women in my project further challenge assumptions about "hard-to-reach populations." All the women were very open about doing sex work, including on public social media profiles. They were all "out" in their trans identity, and the majority of undocumented folks were also explicit about being undocumented on public social media profiles. Therefore, while it is ethical to be concerned about the risks that members of vulnerable populations take when sharing their lives with researchers, assuming trans Latina sex workers are "hard to reach" or exceptionally vulnerable implies that trans people, undocumented people, and sex workers are hidden or "underground," when in reality they are all around us. Such assumptions hypervictimize trans women of color and may accidentally contribute to the marginalization of trans Latina sex workers.

While the women openly talked about their sex work, their trans identity, and their documentation status with me as soon as they met me, there was one thing they were cautious about making known to me. It was not until about eight months into the research that a few women shared that they practiced and were initiated into Santería. It is important to note that Santería is highly racialized, criminalized, and sensationalized. Their decision to share their religion with me was driven by compassion and care. They told me about their faith when my own family was in need of spiritual support. My younger brother was incarcerated at that time and was going up for parole. Brenda offered to do a reading for my brother, and from then it was clear that she was my spiritual superior and that I was indebted to her. In a way, she also offered me – and continues to offer me – spiritual maternal guidance.

The only other thing that some women were not forthright about until later in the research process was that they had trans mothers. For example, when I asked Brittni if she had a trans mother in our first interview, she quickly replied "no." Months later, however, at her birthday party, she happily introduced me to her trans mother as her trans mother. These two elisions highlight the importance of both Santería and trans motherhood to the women in the research project, and their desire to protect both until they knew me better and knew they could trust me. It also emphasizes the importance of long-term ethnographic research, wherein researchers slowly build trust with their interlocutors.

Mothers beyond death

I was both excited and slightly nervous when Brenda invited me to her home for the first time after months of hanging out at various activist events around the city. I had just recently conducted the interview with Brenda in which she shared that her godmother in Santería was Sadia, who was also a trans Latina woman and a highly respected sex worker in Chicago's sex-working trans Latina community. However, I had never met Sadia, because she passed away a few years ago. Yet none of this was at the forefront of my mind when I stepped off the bus in La Villita and headed toward Brenda's home. Therefore, I was surprised when, upon entering her apartment, Brenda asked me if I wanted to meet Sadia. Suspicious that she might be testing me (a completely reasonable thing to do to a researcher with whom you are sharing multiple types of incriminating information about yourself), I nervously replied, "Sure." She said, "Okay, you are gonna meet her now. She's in the back." Completely unaware of what to expect, I cautiously followed Brenda to the back of her apartment. I braced myself before crossing the threshold into the dark back room.

Brenda flicked the light switch. I was overcome by the richness of colors and shapes that filled the space. The back wall of the room was completely covered by figures representing all the santos, with altars full of gifts in front of each. For example, Obatala, who is associated with the color white, likes bland white food. On his altar were white rice and coconut meat. Yemaya, the mother of the sea, had dolphin, fish, and starfish figurines on her altar. On the adjacent wall was a long – almost life-size – poster of Sadia in a full-length ball gown. While her body was positioned sideways, showing off her petite but curvy figure, her head turned, and she gazed directly into the camera. *Oh!* I breathed a sigh of relief. *That was how I was meeting Sadia.* An altar, or boveda, sat in front of her poster. It contained candles, incenses, glasses of water, and gifts to her primary santo. Via Santería, Brenda and Sadia maintained a godmother–goddaughter relationship, not only during life, but also beyond death.

Godparents and godchildren have eternal commitments to one another, and godchildren must remember and recognize their godparents every time they pray, calling them "Babatobi Mi" (my father who birthed me in Ochá) or "Iyatobi Mi" (my mother who birthed me in Ochá). Brenda experienced Sadia's presence in a number of different ways. In her groundbreaking book *Electric Santería*, anthropologist Aisha Beliso-De Jesús (2015) describes how spirits, ancestors, and orisha are "felt" (se siente) on the body and understood as "presences" (la presencias) within electrifying circuits and spiritual networks. Copresences are sensed through chills, shivers, tingles, premonitions, and possessions, and messages from Orisha and dead spirits can be heard in one's ear or seen in visions, dreams, or other forms of spiritual communications, which are called spiritual "transmissions" (las transmisiones). Brenda regularly received messages from, and felt the copresence of, Sadia when she was home and near Sadia's altar, and when she was not. For example, when we were hanging out at an HIV/AIDS organization after hours and Brenda was telling me about Sadia, the lights suddenly flickered, and Brenda got a chill. "Sadia's there," she said. She could feel her presence, and I thought I could too. Brenda routinely communicated with Sadia, especially, but not always, in front of her boveda and was able to introduce Sadia to me. In summary, Santería ontologies in general allow for the creation of a specific form of trans Latina kinship. Beliefs about the permeable membrane between life and death, more specifically, allow Brenda, and others, to keep relationships with their trans mothers alive beyond death.

Conclusion

Legislative attacks against trans life in the United States have recently increased. As they target trans life, they necessarily take aim at and mischaracterize trans communities, which birth and sustain trans life in an already unabashed racist-cisgenderist world. Challenges to legislative violence, however, often center White transnormative experiences, further marginalizing trans people of color and other less-privileged gender-expansive people who exist outside of transnormativity and respectability politics. Ethnographic attention to the various types of kinship that nourish trans of color life is necessary, especially in realms popularly imagined as separate from or detrimental to life, family, and love. The ideas I present here expand understandings of kinship, motherhood, and maternal mentoring in general, and trans kinship, trans motherhood, and trans maternal mentoring more specifically. It also expands possibilities for care that can emerge within sexual economies of labor and, in this case, trans Latina sexual economies of labor. Further, trans people of color are often hypervictimized and associated with lack and loss. To the contrary, trans Latina sexual economies of labor house an abundance of care and love. Trans mothers mothered across various spheres of trans Latina life. Trans daughters had multiple maternal figures, sometimes overlapping and sometimes not, with boundaries between the different roles often blurry. However, the presence of one mother did not reduce or threaten the significance of another. As women challenged the deficient model associated with sex-working trans women of color, they also troubled the scarcity mindset that is central to cisheternormativity and capitalism. They lived and loved in abundance of the White cis het nuclear familial units which thrive upon isolation and singularity. Sex-working trans Latinas are at the forefront of birthing a new world beyond racist-cisgenderism. They show us that in a world beyond transnormativity, capitalism, and racist-cisgenderism, there is an abundance of love, and there is room for madres, madrinas, mamás y más.

Questions for discussion

1. What does the author argue, and what evidence do they provide in support of their argument? Are you persuaded by their argument and their evidence? Why or why not?
2. What are "trans mothers," and what are their roles in their communities?
3. What role does spirituality play in the communities that the author is writing about?
4. How does this chapter demonstrate the relationship between gender and the state?

Notes

1 All names of people, clubs, and organizations are pseudonyms.
2 https://translegislation.com.
3 Most of the drag performers were transgender women, not gay cisgender men.
4 Also called Lukumi and La Regla de Ocha but referred to as Santería by the women in the project, especially when talking to non-initiates, such as myself.

References

Acosta, Katie L. 2013. *Amigas y Amantes: Sexually Nonconforming Latinas Negotiate Family*. Families in Focus. New Brunswick: Rutgers University.
Agid, Shana, and Erica Rand. 2012. "Introduction: Beyond the Special Guest-Teaching 'Trans' Now." *The Radical Teacher* 92: 5–9.
Aizura, Aren Z. 2018. *Mobile Subjects: Transnational Imaginaries of Gender Reassignment*. Durham: Duke University.

Amezcua, Mike. 2023. *Making Mexican Chicago: From Postwar Settlement to the Age of Gentrification*. Chicago: University of Chicago Press.

Ansara, Y. Gavriel, and Peter Hegarty. 2011. "Cisgenderism in Psychology: Pathologising and Misgendering Children from 1999 to 2008." *Psychology & Sexuality* 2(3): 137–160.

Bailey, Marlon M. 2013. *Butch Queens Up in Pumps: Gender, Performance, and Ballroom Culture in Detroit*. Ann Arbor: University of Michigan Press.

Beliso-De Jesús. 2015. *Electric Santería: Racial and Sexual Assemblages of Transnational Religion*. New York: Columbia University Press.

Bolivar, Andrea. 2021. "'Nothing Feels Better Than Getting Paid': Sex Working Trans Latinas' Meanings & Uses of Money." *Feminist Anthropology* 2(2): 298–311.

Cáraves, Jack. 2021. "Trans*formative Spirituality and Self-Preservation in the Lives of Trans Latinxs." *Latino Studies* 19: 207–225.

De Genova, Nicholas, and Ana Y. Ramos-Zayas. 2003. *Latino Crossings: Mexicans, Puerto Ricans, and the Politics of Race and Citizenship*. New York: Routledge Press.

Everhart, Avery R., Hayden Boska, Hagit Sinai-Glazer, Jia Qing Wilson-Yang, Nora Butler Burke, Gabrielle LeBlanc, Yasmeen Persad, Evana Ortigoza, Ayden I. Scheim, and Zack Marshall. 2022. "'I'm Not Interested in Research; I'm Interested in Services': How to Better Health and Social Services for Transgender Women Living with and Affected by HIV." *Social Science & Medicine* 292 (January): 114610.

Fernandez, Lilia. 2014. *Brown in the Windy City: Mexicans and Puerto Ricans in Postwar Chicago*. Chicago: University of Chicago Press.

Gomberg-Muñoz, Ruth. 2011. *Labor and Legality: An Ethnography of a Mexican Immigrant Network*. Oxford: Oxford University Press.

Gumbs, Alexis Pauline, China Martens, and Mai'a Williams. 2016. *Revolutionary Mothering: Love on the Front Lines*. Oakland: PM Press.

Gutiérrez, Elena R. 2008. *Fertile Matters: The Politics of Mexican-Origin Women's Reproduction*. Austin: University of Texas Press.

Khubchandani, Kareem. 2023. "Transnational Figurations of the South Asian Aunty." *South Asia: Journal of South Asian Studies* 46(1).

Lennon, Erica, and Brian J. Mistler. 2014. "Cisgenderism." *Transgender Studies Quarterly* 1(1–2): 63–64.

López, Iris Ofelia. 2008. *Matters of Choice: Puerto Rican Women's Struggle for Reproductive Freedom*. New Brunswick: Rutgers University Press.

Molé, Talia. 2021. "Motherhood Phoenixing: Radical Conversations with the LGBTQ Community in Miami, FL and House|Ballroom Community in NYC, NY around Mother/Motherhood/Mothering as Social Practice." PhD diss., California Institute of Integral Studies.

Namaste, Viviane K. 2005. *Sex Change, Social Change: Reflections on Identity, Institutions, and Imperialism*. Toronto: Women's Press.

Ross, Loretta J., and Rickie Solinger. 2017. *Reproductive Justice: An Introduction*. Berkeley: University of California Press.

Spade, Dean. 2011. *Normal Life: Administrative Violence, Critical Trans Politics, and the Limits of Law*. Durham: Duke University Press.

Chapter 33

Advancing an intersectional politics of belonging

LGBTQ+ Latinx activism after the Pulse shooting

Nolan Kline

Original material prepared for this edition.

Introduction

At 2:02 a.m. on June 12, 2016, a shooter entered the Pulse nightclub in Orlando, Florida, and killed 49 individuals and injured 53 others. At that time, the shooting was the worst mass shooting in United States (US) history, and it occurred during Pulse's Latin night: an evening when the club played Spanish-language hits with a good dance beat. Because the shooting happened on Latin night, it disproportionately affected Latinx and Black lesbian, gay, bisexual, transgender, and other queer-identifying (LGBTQ+) people. In the aftermath of the shooting, local leaders called attention to how existing LGBTQ+ organizations failed to meet the needs of queer people of color. As one community organization leader explained, "Before Pulse, you could walk into the LGBTQ+ Center and there wasn't even a pamphlet in Spanish," pointing out how LGBTQ+ organizations were unable to meet basic needs of many people in Central Florida's LGBTQ+ community, including offering services and information in a language they understood. Similarly, community leaders noted that many Latinx-serving organizations failed to serve people who identified as LGBTQ+.

Recognizing the lack of social services for people who experience multiple forms of oppression due to their intersecting minoritized identities, local leaders mobilized to create new community organizations and a broader social justice movement that advances a politics of belonging (Kline et al. 2022). In this chapter, I describe how that social justice movement works to dismantle power inequalities associated with homophobia, transphobia, xenophobia, and anti-Blackness through harnessing the financial power of a philanthropic grant-making organization, advancing queer undocumented immigrant (undocuqueer) social mobilization, and changing local policy to be more inclusive of immigrants. Overall, the social justice mobilization after the Pulse shooting shows the importance of these movements in combatting ongoing forms of social division.

Background: Orlando, Florida – the city beautiful

On a typical year, nearly 76 million people visit Orlando, Florida. The area is well-known for its amusement parks, proximity to beaches, and even seasonal residents known as

DOI: 10.4324/9781003398349-37

snowbirds who escape colder climates in search of more comfortable temperatures and Florida sunshine. Despite being one of the nation's most visited cities, however, the Orlando area is also home to over 2.5 million people, making it Florida's third most populous city and the sixth most populous city in the US South (United States Census Bureau 2019).

Orlando is also home to a large and diverse Latinx population. Approximately one out of every three residents identifies as Latinx (United States Census Bureau 2022), all of whom represent a diversity of experiences, immigration statuses, and family histories. Central Florida's agricultural economy has played a role in Latinx migration to the region as migrant and seasonal farmworkers from Latin America moved to the Orlando area to engage in farmwork, and continue to do so (Kline 2010). Throughout the 1970s, Central Florida's Puerto Rican population grew due to an economic downturn in Puerto Rico and the opening of the Walt Disney World theme park, which inspired real estate investment and attractive retirement options for middle-class Puerto Ricans looking to relocate from the island or elsewhere in the mainland United States (Silver and Vélez 2017; Duany and Rodríguez 2006). Puerto Rican migration to Central Florida continued in the 1980s, and between 1990 and 2000, the Puerto Rican population in the area grew by 142 percent, resulting in Orlando having the largest number of Puerto Rican residents in Florida (Duany and Rodríguez 2006). Following Hurricanes Maria and Irma in 2017, the Puerto Rican population in Central Florida continued to increase, and the Orlando metropolitan area has become home to the second largest Puerto Rican community in the United States (Cotto and Chen 2019).

In addition to a sizeable Latinx population, Orlando is also home to a considerable LGBTQ+ population and hosts several LGBTQ+ vacation festivals. The city ranks 20th among cities in the United States with the largest percentage of LGBTQ+ residents (Newport and Gates 2015) and is the site of several LGBTQ+-themed annual events at Walt Disney World and Universal Studios, drawing international visitors. Despite the large Latinx and LGBTQ+ populations, Orlando's network of social service providers focused on LGBTQ+ and Latinx populations had historically failed to meet the unique needs of individuals with intersecting LGBTQ+ Latinx identities (Kline 2022). This omission from local organizations was particularly acute following the attack at the Pulse nightclub.

In the aftermath of the Pulse shooting, Florida's elected officials, including then-governor Rick Scott and Attorney General Pam Bondi, failed to acknowledge the shooting happened at a gay bar and on Latin night – a political moment of erasure and silencing of the unique identities among those most impacted (Kline and Cuevas 2018). Such silence among state government leaders reflected widespread community erasure of individuals with intersecting LGBTQ+ and Latinx identities that signaled to newly emerging social justice organizations a sustained need to advocate for, and advance the rights of, LGBTQ+ people of color.

After Pulse: the beginning of intersectional organizing in Orlando, Florida

Following the Pulse shooting, two organizations emerged as leaders focused on intersectional social justice: QLatinx and Contigo Fund. QLatinx is "a grassroots racial, social, and gender justice organization dedicated to the advancement and empowerment of Central Florida's LGBTQ+ Latinx community" (QLatinx 2021). As described elsewhere (Kline et al. 2022), QLatinx organized community-building, immigration advocacy, health equity, individual empowerment, and leadership training events after Pulse. Members of QLatinx host a number of community and organizational trainings on topics such as sexuality and gender diversity, social inequality, interpersonal and state violence, privilege, and intersectionality. QLatinx leadership routinely collaborate with local LGBTQ+ and Latinx-focused organizations to advance social, economic, and racial justice initiatives.

Like QLatinx, Contigo formed after the Pulse shooting and serves to improve the lives of LGBTQ+ and Latinx individuals, immigrants, and people of color in Central Florida. Focusing on the root causes of oppression, Contigo works to eradicate all forms of discrimination based on race, sex, gender identity and expression, sexual orientation, religion, ability, and other socially constructed notions of difference. With a focus on LGBTQ+ Latinx individuals, the Contigo Fund works to support initiatives that can correct the consequences of systemic and institutionalized inequalities that disproportionately harm people with intersecting marginalized identities. Together, these two organizations are among the key groups in Orlando to advance a politics of belonging that centers on the lives of LGBTQ+ Latinx populations and all LGBTQ+ people of color (Kline et al. 2022). Their work has intentionally been informed by intersectional social justice lens.

As feminist legal scholar Kimberleé Crenshaw has described, intersectionality considers how multiple forms of interlocking systems of oppression structure oppression and privilege in the United States (Crenshaw 1995, 1989). For example, Crenshaw describes how Black women experience oppression related to racism *and* sexism – a combination of discrimination that has consequences beyond more than just one form of oppression alone. Intersectional sources of oppression and privilege can manifest in micro-level encounters, such as direct experiences of racism and sexism, or macro-level forms of discrimination, such as systems and process that systematically benefit White individuals and disfavor people of color (Bowleg 2013).

Similarly, research on Black gay and bisexual men has shown how Black queer people navigate intersectional forms of oppression, including racial microaggressions and heterosexism, and forms of power stemming from their intersectional identities, including greater introspection and a sense of freedom from social conventions (Bowleg 2013). Further, queer critical race scholars have shown how gay Asian men are "raced" and "gendered" in otherizing ways that often uphold a power differential benefiting youthful White gay men who are physically slim, muscular, or fit, resulting in exclusionary dating practices and expectations of gay Asian men's gendered and sexual behaviors (Han 2015). Intersectionality, therefore, offers a lens through which to focus on unique forms of power, privilege, oppression, and macro-level structures as well as micro-level encounters and experiences.

Intersectionality was also the guiding framework for how organizations that emerged after the Pulse shooting rooted their activism. Following the Pulse shooting, when members of Orlando's LGBTQ+ community realized there were few spaces for LGBTQ+ people of color – including undocumented queer Latinx folks – leaders who ended up forming organizations like QLatinx and Contigo Fund sought to change this reality and squarely focus on people whose intersecting identities made them vulnerable to multiple interlocking forms of social oppression and to provide spaces to discuss sources of joy and power linked to their identities.

"A seat at the table:" advancing an intersectional politics of belonging

On a Thursday evening in the winter of 2016, I attended a QLatinx community meeting in an office building near downtown Orlando. There, one of the members of QLatinx led a crafting activity and discussion about what places like Pulse meant to community members and what the loss of such a place meant. "It just felt like it was a place where we could be ourselves," one member said. "We could go hear our music and be with our community," someone else added. One of the leaders of QLatinx noted that the organization itself is a place for community building, explaining how thankful they were for being in community with one another while working on crafts, sharing stories, and using this time to heal from a community trauma. As the evening came to a close, one of the leaders thoughtfully remarked: "This is part of our healing journey. Coming together, being in community with one another, sharing pain and love. It's all part of what we do as we chart a path forward and imagine what empowerment looks like."

Charting an empowering path forward is, indeed, what QLatinx did. Between 2016 and 2019, I was actively involved with the organization, attending community meetings, rallies, protests, and even working with QLatinx to help set up legal arrangements with other organizations. Since the time the former executive director, Christopher Cuevas, and I started collaborating to the time of this writing, QLatinx has gained prominent attention for its intersectional social justice work, climate justice efforts, immigrant rights mobilization, and health-related programs focused on sexual health and HIV prevention (Cordeiro 2016).[1] Their work, in part, was driven by a desire to be sure that all LGBTQ+ people of color, regardless of sexual orientation, gender identity, immigration status, HIV status, and ability, had a space for community and a metaphorical "seat at the table," a place to belong for those who felt they did not belong in other spaces or felt unable to be their full authentic selves.

Having a "seat at the table" not only reflects a sense of community belonging but also reflects a desire for shared power in decision-making. During a Contigo Fund meeting, Executive Director Marco Antonio Quiroga asked members of the Contigo Fund's board to examine an upcoming meeting with local elected officials and leaders of other organizations. "We want to make sure Contigo is at the table, not on the menu," he cautioned. "That's right," another member added. "Our communities are often 'on the menu,' or when people say they're 'giving us a seat at the table,' they're not really – they don't want us to actually say anything or do anything. That's not really 'having a seat at the table.'"

The phrase "If you're not at the table, then you're on the menu," along with variations of it, has been attributed to US senator Elizabeth Warren, former Texas governor Ann Richards, Planned Parenthood CEO Cecile Richards, and likely others. At its core, it refers to a person who lacks a seat at a metaphorical table and will not have their interests represented, and instead their interests will be consumed by others sitting at the table. More than being a proverb sparking reflection on power and access, however, it is a common metaphor used among leaders of QLatinx, Contigo Fund, and other Central Florida organizations. At its core, the metaphor evokes consideration of who has a "seat at the table" in decision-making and who is left out. As Contigo Fund has considered who has a seat at the table in access to resources, including financial support to carry out specific goals, it has funded organizations like QLatinx to advance its mission. More than just funding QLatinx, however, Contigo has played a substantive role in powering the intersectional social justice movement focused on LGBTQ+ people of color after the Pulse shooting.

Harnessing financial power for social change

One of the ways Contigo Fund advanced an intersectional politics of belonging was through harnessing its financial power as a philanthropic grant maker. As the largest philanthropic grant-making organization in the US South to focus on LGBTQ+ people of color, Contigo Fund provides grants to community organizations that use the grant funding to support their overall operation costs and programmatic efforts. In any given year, Contigo Fund regrants approximately $750,000–$1,000,000 to community organizations. Contigo does this through a participatory grant-making process, in which community organizations apply for Contigo funds and explain how they will use their funds.

To be eligible for Contigo Funding, applicants must submit proposals that align with Contigo Fund's overall vision and mission to advance movements that are Black- and LGBTQ+-led. Overall, they fund healing and empowerment projects, such as peer-led support groups and community organizing; efforts to advance racial equity and justice; leadership development and training for new leaders who have historically been locked out of positions of non-profit leadership; work led by Black, trans/gender-expansive/intersex individuals and women, undocumented individuals, sex workers, and Black youth; and projects that advance racial, economic, and gender justice, including projects with an intersectional focus.

As part of Contigo's grant-making process, Contigo requests information about board members and organizational leadership to see who in the organization holds decision-making power: is it a diverse group of leaders reflective of the community, or might there be opportunities to add to the perspectives of the leadership? If, for example, an organization requests Contigo funds for LGBTQ+ programing but lacks a single LGBTQ+ person on their board, or lacks any people of color on their board, Contigo might recommend diversifying the decision-making power of the organization before a grant will be made. In doing so, Contigo effectively works to diversify many of the organizations that, when the Pulse shooting occurred, had blind spots regarding who lived in Central Florida and who was part of the "LGBTQ+ community" writ large. In other words, Contigo has a vested interested in making sure LGBTQ+, Black, Latinx, and other minoritized individuals have a seat at the tables where decisions are made.

Through its participatory grant-making process, Contigo fund has been able to guide internal changes in existing organizations that have led to diversification of staff, programs, and services. For example, in the summer of 2021, I walked into the LGBTQ+ Center of Orlando for a community event. Walking into the Center, I noticed flyers, pamphlets, stickers, buttons, in English and Spanish, promoting LGBTQ+ pride, information about HIV testing, and other services that would be useful to anyone walking through the doors. Walking into the main meeting space, I saw that flags from every Latin American country were draped around the walls. "It's beautiful, isn't it?" a staff member said as I gazed at the walls. The staff member, who moved to Orlando from Puerto Rico, continued, "To think – all the flags of Latin America at the LGBTQ+ center – I wouldn't have thought this was possible a few years ago." Indeed, from 2016 to 2021, moving from "not even a pamphlet in Spanish" to all the flags of Latin America being represented, the LGBTQ+ Center had come a long way in a short amount of time.

Among the many examples of how Contigo funds organizations led by people who have historically been locked out of positions of leadership are the Bros in Convo initiative and Divas in Dialogue. Bros in Convo is an organization for Black same-gender-loving men living with HIV. It provides an important social support space that provides HIV and other STI testing services, mental health support, healthy and nutritious food programs, financial literacy and job readiness programs for youth, as well as social support for youth living with HIV. Like Bros in Convo, Divas in Dialogue is a social support group. It is a self-described "sisterhood of trans women of color empowering, building and strengthening each other for ensuring that we all have a seat at the table" (Miracle of Love 2023). The organization provides social support to members; guidance with navigating legal name change procedures, including updating drivers' licenses to reflect gender identity; HIV services, such as promoting pre-exposure prophylaxis (PREP); and guidance on obtaining gender-affirming care.

The impact of organizations like Bros in Convo and Divas in Dialogue is hard to measure, but the existence of each organization highlights a critical change in Orlando's community organization infrastructure: in 2016, when the Pulse shooting occurred, Black-led organizations for Black same-gender-loving men did not exist. Similarly, trans women of color–led organizations in Central Florida did not exist. Through Contigo's funding of these efforts, two social support organizations, and others like them, have been able to provide metaphorical seats at multiple tables of leadership and alter the tables of decision-making, influence, and service provisioning across Central Florida. Moreover, in responding to pressing public health issues like HIV, they provide important services to the most at-risk communities.

Florida is an "ending the epidemic hotspot" for the Centers for Disease Control and Prevention (CDC), meaning, it is a priority area for investing in HIV prevention efforts. Florida is consistently one of the states with the highest rates of new HIV infection; in 2019, the state had the highest rate of new HIV cases, and in 2020, it ranked second, falling behind Georgia (Centers for Disease Control and Prevention 2022). In Florida, and the United States generally, HIV disparities persist among Black and Latinx individuals. Indeed, in the US South, Black and Latinx individuals account for all new HIV cases (Centers for Disease Control and Prevention 2022). Disparities are particularly acute for transgender women; HIV prevalence among transgender women is estimated to be 34 times higher than in their cisgender counterparts (Clark et al. 2017). Between 2009 and 2014, transgender women represented 84 percent of all new HIV cases among the transgender population, and over half of this population were transgender women of color (Clark et al. 2017). Accordingly, the work of Bros in Convo, Divas in Dialogue, and similar organizations responds to pressing public health needs as well as important social and community needs.

Contigo Fund's mission and intentional effort to fund initiatives like Bros in Convo, Divas in Dialogue, and other organizations show how it harnesses its financial power to advance an intersectional politics of belonging. Specifically, it uses its financial power to combat the legacies of exclusion in many nonprofit spaces and works to combat the economic and policy-related factors in nonprofits that have historically benefited White men (Heckler 2019). Contigo arrived at this position of financial power through being awarded grants of its own. After the Pulse shooting, Contigo received funding from large nonprofits to advance its work and, in 2023, received a substantive investment from a large foundation to continue its mission. It is also slowly building a donor network to continue growing its financial capacities. Together, the grant activity and donor engagement position Contigo to continue to grow its financial power and use that financial power to change existing organizations through diversifying leadership and providing new opportunities for individuals to grow as leaders and develop new organizations like Bros in Convo and Divas in Dialogue.

Advancing undocuqueer social and political mobilization

After the Pulse shooting, staff at two community-based organizations that primarily serve Latinx farmworkers, Hope Community Center and the Farmworker Association of Florida, realized there was a gap in services they provided and who among their members felt included. Indeed, as I described elsewhere (Kline 2022), when one of the leaders of Hope Community Center learned of the shooting on television the morning after, she learned that one of the victims, Arturo (pseudonym), was part of a family involved in Hope. "I saw [Arturo's] name on the news, and I immediately went to his parents' house." When she arrived, she saw cars lining the streets as neighbors, friends, and family came to Arturo's home to mourn with his family.

> When I got there, his father came right out of the house, and he came up to me, and he said, "You know, Arturo wasn't gay." And I just thought, "Wow. Wow. Your son just died, and that's the first thing you want to tell me? Wow." And I knew then we were in trouble and needed to do something more for our LGBT youth.

In response, leaders from FWAF and Hope Community Center worked to create youth-led LGBTQ+ Latinx community groups, one of which was the Gay Farmworkers group (Kline 2019). The Gay Farmworker group met monthly, and at the time of this writing, it was unclear if they were continuing to meet due to time constraints from their members. It started, however, as a much-needed support and action group for LGBTQ+ youth who live in families with farmworkers, engage in farmwork, or live in farmworker communities. The group was entirely led by teenagers and organized by Gabi (a pseudonym), a Deferred Action for Childhood Arrivals (DACA) recipient and recent high school graduate. At monthly meetings, the group discussed issues related to LGBTQ+ Latinx people living in farm-working families, such as the challenges in finding LGBTQ+ social and health services, routine racism, and homophobia in their local communities. The group meets in Apopka – an Orlando exurb with an agricultural history that is rapidly changing as sprawl continues to reshape Orlando's metropolitan landscape (Kline 2021). Although Apopka is approximately a 30-minute drive from downtown Orlando, where numerous LGBTQ+ organizations exist, many of the LGBTQ+ farmworker youth group participants lacked a personal vehicle, and a 70-minute bus ride in one direction limited the feasibility of easily getting to Orlando and back home on a school night. Moreover, they feared some organizations might not understand concerns unique to them, including the ongoing precarity related to their im/migration statuses and the threats of family separation and deportation.

During a typical monthly meeting, members discussed xenophobia in school following the election of Donald Trump; how to navigate challenging family dynamics during the holidays as a gay, bisexual, or transgender teenager; and how to best represent LGBTQ+ farmworkers at local Pride events. The group discussed immigration enforcement matters and aggressive local police tactics and how such efforts are especially concerning for LGBTQ+ Latinx youth who experience multiple overlapping vulnerabilities.

Youth-led undocuqueer activism, including the activism of the Gay Farmworker group, shows how such groups challenge artificial social boundaries that attempt to organize people based on sexual orientation, documentation and migration status, race, ethnicity, and language ability. Rather than remaining in such silos, however, members of the Gay Farmworker group looked for ways to dismantle them. For example, at Orlando's Pride event, the Gay Farmworker group used the Farmworker Association logo to create a rainbow banner, effectively queering the organization's logo and complicating singular understandings of farmworker and LGBTQ+ identities. These efforts underscore a particular type of social mobilization that works to break down boundaries based on sexual orientation and gender identity, immigration status, and perceived racial and ethnic difference.

Changing local policy

In addition to harnessing financial power and advancing an undocuqueer-led social mobilization, the intersectional social justice movement that emerged after the Pulse shooting also worked to change local policies to make Orlando a more inclusive city for immigrants. In the United States, immigration matters are principally a federal matter, but some US states pass their own immigration laws. Some federal immigration laws encourage local law enforcement collaboration with federal immigration authorities. For example, Section 287(g) of the Immigration and National Act allows local police to enforce federal immigration laws. Similarly, another law, Secure Communities, shares fingerprints taken from local arrestees with federal immigration agents. In practice, the law can result in deportation for doing nothing more than driving to work, going to the grocery store, or taking children to school (Kline 2019). It functions in part through routine traffic stops and driver's license laws. In the United States, undocumented immigrants are often unable to obtain driver's licenses due to requirements under the federal REAL ID Act (LeBrón, Schulz, Gamboa, et al. 2018; LeBrón, Schulz, Mentz, et al. 2018). This means that they may use a driver's license from another country, one that's expired, or drive without a license. If they are stopped during a routine traffic stop and arrested for driving without a license, they are taken to jail and fingerprinted. Through Secure Communities, their fingerprints are sent to a federal database to determine if any immigration match can be found, and Immigration and Customs Enforcement (ICE) can place a 72-hour detainer on them to conduct an interview and initiate a deportation process. Overall, then, driving itself becomes a high-risk activity associated with the threat of deportation (Kline 2019).

In Central Florida, Lake County – near Apopka, and where many farmworkers who are part of Hope Community Center and the Farmworker Association of Florida live – participates in the 287(g) program. Further, Lake County law enforcement has grown a reputation of being aggressive towards immigrants (Vickers and Kline 2021; Kline et al. 2020). Recognizing the hostile climate for immigrants in Central Florida and acknowledging that change might be most feasible in Orange County, a coalition of organizations led an initiative to change Orlando's treatment of immigrants. The coalition, led in part by QLatinx, pushed elected officials in the city of Orlando to pass a "trust" ordinance (Kline and Cuevas 2018). The ordinance proclaims law enforcement will refuse to hold immigrants suspected of committing crimes longer than is required so that federal immigration authorities can determine their immigration statuses. In effect, the ordinance undermines the efforts to use routine traffic enforcement and racial profiling laws as ways to ensnare immigrants in a deportation process that divides their families, has negative health outcomes, and results in individual and community-wide trauma (Lopez et al. 2018).

Beyond Orlando: why the intersectional politics of belonging after the shooting matter

At a rally for transgender rights in downtown Orlando, a local trans leader gave a speech about inclusion of trans women of color in broader LGBTQ+ rights movements. "Let's not forget, it was trans women who threw the first brick at Stonewall!" she said, to thunderous applause and cheering. Indeed, trans women, and trans women of color, have played an important role in LGBTQ+ rights in the United States, but many feel ignored or overlooked while the interests of other LGBTQ+ people, particularly White cisgender men, are privileged. This type of exclusion is one that the intersectional social justice movement in Orlando that formed after the Pulse shooting was attempting to end. Nevertheless, in the United States, there are numerous social and political efforts that attempt to undermine the very intersectional politics of belonging that groups like Contigo and others attempt to advance.

At the time of this writing, the United States is deeply politically polarized and experiencing another political "culture wars" moment in which issues around identity have become intense sources of political debate (Castle 2019; Hartman 2019; Alfonseca 2023). The current "culture wars" moment has resulted in numerous efforts to double down on vehicles of social division and perpetuate transphobia, racial inequality through voter suppression, xenophobia, and heterosexism. These efforts represent not only the staying power of systemic oppression perpetuated through ideologies like cisnormativity and White supremacy, but also a direct opposition to social justice movements that work to advance equity, including those like the movement born out of the Pulse tragedy. Indeed, while there have been efforts to advance social justice in the United States through reforming racialized police practices (Robinson 2020), advance transgender visibility (Bockting et al. 2020), draw attention to the harms of settler colonialism (McKenzie-Jones 2019), advance Indigenous peoples' environmental rights (Dockry 2020), and other movements of inclusion, there have been simultaneous counteractions and responses that double down on harm.

One example of the entrenchment of ideologies of social difference is an effort to separate transgender people from the broader LGBTQ+ movement. For decades, trans people have felt excluded from LGBTQ+ social justice mobilizing. This has been, in part, because trans people have not benefited from the gains that gay men and lesbians have from LGBTQ+ activism. For example, the political mobilization that led to marriage equality largely advanced the interests of cisgender White gay men (Willse and Spade 2004). Despite large legal and social wins for LGBTQ+ populations, trans individuals continue to experience rampant forms of discrimination, even among sexual minorities.

Further, during the time of writing this chapter, on social media, a number of hashtags and profiles of gay men and lesbians have perpetuated anti-trans sentiment and advocated trans exclusion from lesbian, gay, and bisexual issues. Through using language akin to "LGB without the T," or "drop the T," these individuals and some organizations perpetuating similar ideas have doubled down on transphobic exclusion from LGBTQ+ solidarity. Much of this has occurred in the wake of numerous states passing anti-trans bills, with some cisgender gay men and lesbians using social media platforms to claim that transgender issues have nothing to do with gay, lesbian, and bisexual issues.

Just as transphobia continues and is perpetuated through policy, so, too, does anti-Blackness. For example, states like Florida and Texas have passed legislation banning the instruction of critical race theory – a perspective that emphasizes the root causes of racial inequality in the United States and calls for transformative change to advance racial equity (Ladson-Billings 1998; Bell 1995). These efforts may reflect altering education to deny and sanitize the United States' history as part and parcel of refusing to grapple with White privilege (Guy 2023). In Florida, the state went as far as passing the "Stop WOKE Act" of 2022, which prohibits instruction about people being privileged or oppressed based on race, gender, or national origin at all levels of education (Reilly 2022). These, and similar laws, perpetuate anti-Blackness by silencing critical discussions about the root causes of racial inequality in the United States.

These, and other examples, underscore countermovements to efforts to advance an intersectional politics of belonging. Nevertheless, organizations that came together following the Pulse shooting to advance social justice have continued to do so despite being several years removed from the shooting itself.

The fight continues

On May 1, 2023, members and leaders of over 40 social justice and community service organizations gathered at the Walt Disney amphitheater in Downtown Orlando. The theater, known for its bandshell that was painted rainbow colors after the Pulse shooting, is an iconic symbol of the city of Orlando and key landmark and gathering space. There, hundreds of individuals came together to voice their opposition to Florida legislators' and Governor Ron DeSantis's attacks on reproductive rights, immigrants, LGBTQ+ individuals, and efforts to styme racial justice through initiatives that prohibit teaching critical race theory in schools (Calvan 2021). The event included the ability for attendees to have speakers' languages translated from English to Spanish and Vietnamese, and for Spanish speakers to have their speech translated to English and Vietnamese. At the event, drag performers took the stage in a protest of legislation attempting to limit drag shows, immigrant rights leaders shared songs, and people in the crowd showed their solidarity by waving pride flags, Black Lives Matter flags, and rainbow versions of flags from Latin American countries. "It just felt like we were all in this together – I just really felt like everyone was united in these causes," an event participant shared with me. This "united in the causes" is precisely what the intersectional social justice movement that emerged after Pulse and led by organizations like Contigo has helped create.

The significance of the social justice movement advancing an intersectional politics of belonging after the Pulse shooting extends beyond Orlando and Florida, however. It represents a critical way to combat ongoing forms of inequality that persist across the United States and may become worse through increased social and political polarization. As political efforts to limit social justice continue, there is deepened need for intersectional forms of organizing. There are numerous social borders and boundaries that need to be combatted, and the organizing that occurred after Pulse can provide an example of future organizing in other contexts.

Discussion questions

1. What does the author argue, and what evidence do they provide in support of their argument? Are you persuaded by their argument and their evidence? Why or why not?
2. How does the author use the concept of "intersectionality" in this chapter? What does it reveal about the lived experience of the communities he is writing about?
3. What does the author mean by "harnessing financial power for social change"? Who was involved, what did they do, and what were the outcomes of their work?
4. How does this chapter demonstrate the relationship between gender and the state?

Note

1 For more information on QLatinx, see www.qlatinx.org. For information about their role filling gaps in Orlando, see Cordeiro, Monivette 2016. "QLatinx, a new community group for Central Florida's LGBT Latinos and Latinas, fills a need after Pulse." Orlando Weekly, accessed August 30. www.orlandoweekly.com/news/qlatinx-a-new-community-group-for-central-floridas-lgbt-latinos-and-latinas-fills-a-need-after-pulse-2531008. For information about an award QLatinx received from Equality Florida, see: www.qlatinx.org/single-post/2017/11/05/qlatinx-honored-at-equality-florida-annual-central-florida-gala.

References

Alfonseca, Kiara. 2023. "Culture Wars: How Identity Became the Center of Politics in America." *ABC News*. https://abcnews.go.com/US/culture-wars-identity-center-politics-america/story?id=100768380, accessed August 30, 2023.

Bell, Derrick A. 1995. "Who's Afraid of Critical Race Theory." *University of Illinois Law Review*: 893.

Bockting, Walter, Renato Barucco, Allen LeBlanc, Anneliese Singh, William Mellman, Curtis Dolezal, and Anke Ehrhardt. 2020. "Sociopolitical Change and Transgender People's Perceptions of Vulnerability and Resilience." *Sexuality Research and Social Policy* 17: 162–174.

Bowleg, Lisa. 2013. "'Once You've Blended the Cake, You Can't Take the Parts Back to the Main Ingredients': Black Gay and Bisexual Men's Descriptions and Experiences of Intersectionality." *Sex Roles* 68(11–12): 754–767.

Calvan, Obby Caina. 2021. "Florida Bans 'Critical Race Theory' from Its Classrooms." *Associated Press News*. https://apnews.com/article/florida-race-and-ethnicity-government-and-politics-education-74d0af6c52c0009ec3fa3ee9955b0a8d, accessed May 8.

Castle, Jeremiah. 2019. "New Fronts in the Culture Wars? Religion, Partisanship, and Polarization on Religious Liberty and Transgender Rights in the United States." *American Politics Research* 47(3): 650–679.

Centers for Disease Control and Prevention. 2022. "HIV in the United States by Region: HIV Diagnoses." www.cdc.gov/hiv/statistics/overview/diagnoses.html, accessed May 8.

Clark, Hollie, Aruna Surendera Babu, Ellen Weiss Wiewel, Jenevieve Opoku, and Nicole Crepaz. 2017. "Diagnosed HIV Infection in Transgender Adults and Adolescents: Results from the National HIV Surveillance System, 2009–2014." *AIDS and Behavior* 21(9): 2774–2783. https://doi.org/10.1007/s10461-016-1656-7.

Cordeiro, Monivette. 2016. "QLatinx, a New Community Group for Central Florida's LGBT Latinos and Latinas, Fills a Need after Pulse." *Orlando Weekly*. www.orlandoweekly.com/news/qlatinx-a-new-community-group-for-central-floridas-lgbt-latinos-and-latinas-fills-a-need-after-pulse-2531008, accessed August 30.

Cotto, Ingrid, and Adelaide Chen. 2019. "Census Bureau: Puerto Rican Population in Orange, Osceola Jumps 12.5% after Hurricane Maria." *Orlando Sentinel*. www.orlandosentinel.com/news/florida/os-ne-census-florida-puerto-rico-population-increase-20190927-lx3i6rxghzhe-hhf3md6x7hgfmu-story.html, accessed June 30.

Crenshaw, Kimberlé. 1989. "Demarginalizing the Intersection of Race and Sex: A Black Feminist Critique of Antidiscrimination Doctrine, Feminist Theory and Antiracist Politics." *University of Chicago Legal Forum*: 139.

Crenshaw, Kimberlé. 1995. "Mapping the Margins: Intersectionality, Idenity, Politics, and Violence against Women of Color." In *Critical Race Theory: The Key Writings That Formed the Movement*, ed. Kimberlé Crenshaw, 357–383. New York: The New Press.

Dockry, Michael J. 2020. "Indigenous Rights and Empowerment in Natural Resource Management and Decision Making as a Driver of Change in US Forestry." Dockry, MJ, Bengston, DN, Westphal, LM, comps. *Drivers of Change in US Forests and Forestry over the Next 20*: 76–83.

Duany, Jorge, and Félix V. Matos Rodríguez. 2006. *Puerto Ricans in Orlando and Central Florida*, Vol. 1. New York: Centro de Estudios Puertorriqueños, Hunter College (CUNY).

Guy, Mia. 2023. "Chilling Speech in the Name of 'Woke': A Critique of the Stop Woke Act." *The Reporter: Social Justice Law Center Magazine* 2023(1): 4.

Han, C. Winter. 2015. *Geisha of a Different Kind: Race and Sexuality in Gaysian America*. Vol. 12. New York: NYU Press.

Hartman, Andrew. 2019. *A War for the Soul of America: A History of the Culture Wars*. Chicago: University of Chicago Press.

Heckler, Nuri. 2019. "Whiteness and Masculinity in Nonprofit Organizations: Law, Money, and Institutional Race and Gender." *Administrative Theory & Praxis* 41(3): 266–285.

Kline, Nolan. 2010. "Disparate Power and Disparate Resources: Collaboration between Faith-Based and Activist Organizations for Central Florida Farmworkers." *NAPA Bulletin* 33(1): 126–142.

Kline, Nolan. 2019. "'We're the Gay Farmworkers:' Advancing Intersectional Im/Migration Activism in Central Florida." www.youthcirculations.com/blog/2019/2/16/were-the-gay-farm-workers-advancing-intersectional-immigration-activism-in-central-florida, accessed May 8.

Kline, Nolan. 2021. "Policing Race and Performing State Power: Immigration Enforcement and Undocumented Latinx Immigrant Precarity in Central Florida." *City & Society* 33(2): 364–381.

Kline, Nolan. 2022. "Syndemic Statuses: Intersectionality and Mobilizing for LGBTQ+ Latinx Health Equity after the Pulse Shooting." *Social Science & Medicine* 295: 113260.

Kline, Nolan, Andrés Acosta, Christopher J. Cuevas, and Marco Antonio Quiroga. 2022. "Resilience in the Time of a Pandemic." In *Latinx Belonging: Community Building and Resilience in the United States*, eds. Natalia Deeb Sossa and Jennifer Bickham Mendez, 52. Tucson: University of Arizona Press.

Kline, Nolan, and Christopher Cuevas. 2018. "Resisting Identity Erasure after Pulse: Intersectional LGBTQ+ Latinx Activism in Orlando, FL." *Chiricù Journal: Latina/o Literature, Art, and Culture* 2(2): 68–71.

Kline, Nolan, Mary Vickers, Jeannie Economos, and Chris Furino. 2020. "Academic and Activist Collaborration in Turbulent Times: Responding to Immigrant Policing in Central Florida." In *Anthropology and Activism: New Contexts, New Conversations*, eds. Anna J. Willow and Kelly A. Yotebieng. Abingdon, UK: Routledge.

Ladson-Billings, Gloria. 1998. "Just What Is Critical Race Theory and What's It Doing in a Nice Field Like Education?" *International Journal of Qualitative Studies in Education* 11(1): 7–24.

LeBrón, Alana M. W., Amy J. Schulz, Cindy Gamboa, Angela Reyes, Edna A. Viruell-Fuentes, and Barbara A. Israel. 2018. "'They Are Clipping Our Wings': Health Implications of Restrictive Immigrant Policies for Mexican-Origin Women in a Northern Border Community." *Race and Social Problems* 10(3): 174–192.

LeBrón, Alana M. W., Amy J. Schulz, Graciela Mentz, Angela G. Reyes, Cindy Gamboa, Barbara A. Israel, Edna A. Viruell-Fuentes, and James S. House. 2018. "Impact of Change over Time in Self-Reported Discrimination on Blood Pressure: Implications for Inequities in Cardiovascular Risk for a Multi-Racial Urban Community." *Ethnicity & Health*: 1–19.

Lopez, William D., Nicole L. Novak, Melanie Harner, Ramiro Martinez, and Julia S. Seng. 2018. "The Traumatogenic Potential of Law Enforcement Home Raids: An Exploratory Report." *Traumatology* 24(3): 193.

McKenzie-Jones, Paul R. 2019. "Indigenous Activism, Community Sustainability, and the Constraints of CANZUS Settler-Colonial Nationhood." *Transmotion* 5(1): 104–131.

Miracle of Love. 2023. "Divas in Dialogue." https://miracleofloveinc.org/did/, accessed May 8.

Newport, Frank, and Gary J. Gates. 2015. "San Francisco Metro Area Ranks Highest in LGBT Percentage." *Gallup*. https://news.gallup.com/poll/182051/san-francisco-metro-area-ranks-highest-lgbt-percentage.aspx?utm_source=Social%20Issues&utm_medium=newsfeed&utm_campaign=tiles, accessed June 30.

QLatinx. 2021. "Who We Are." www.qlatinx.org/who-we-are.

Reilly, Katie. 2022. "Florida's Governor Just Signed the 'Stop Woke Act.' Here's What It Means for Schools and Businesses." *Time*. https://time.com/6168753/florida-stop-woke-law/, accessed May 8.

Robinson, Laurie O. 2020. "Five Years after Ferguson: Reflecting on Police Reform and What's Ahead." *The Annals of the American Academy of Political and Social Science* 687(1): 228–239.

Silver, Patricia, and William Vélez. 2017. "'Let Me Go Check Out Florida': Rethinking Puerto Rican Diaspora." *Centro Journal* 29(3): 98–125.

United States Census Bureau. 2019. "Annual Estimates of the Resident Population: April 1, 2010 to July 1, 2018." https://factfinder.census.gov/faces/tableservices/jsf/pages/productview.xhtml?src=bkmk.

United States Census Bureau. 2022. "QuickFacts Orlando City." www.census.gov/quickfacts/orlandocityflorida.

Vickers, Mary, and Nolan Kline. 2021. "Commonplace Terror: Everyday Harassment of Latinx Immigrants in Central Florida." In *Race, Gender, and Political Culture in the Trump Era*, 118–134. Abingdon, UK: Routledge.

Willse, Craig, and Dean Spade. 2004. "Freedom in a Regulatory State: Lawrence, Marriage and Biopolitics." *Widener Law Review* 11: 309.

Part 5

Masculinities

This final section represents an entirely new focus on men and masculinities for this edition. Even though chapters throughout this book deal with the issue of masculinity as they relate to different themes, we wanted to dedicate a section to the scholarship that highlights a variety of cultural perspectives about men, how men are "made," and what constitutes different cultural scripts about "masculinity" and any particular society's hegemonic masculinity (see also Monocello, this text). It is worth distinguishing between men and masculinities, however. Writing on the influences of men on reproductive health, Matthew Dudgeon and Marcia Inhorn (2003) noted a then-recent turn of scholarship toward recognizing men as men, as "gendered agents, with beliefs, behaviors, and characteristics that are associated with but not dependent upon biological sex." While we wish to use this section to emphasize men's experiences of gendered practices and expectations, it is also true that "masculinity" – that vague and context-dependent suite of practices and expectations associated with men – is harbored by many people and at different levels of society. For instance, as we mentioned in our introduction to Part 4, the state can be masculine, but as Pierre Bourdieu (2001) adds, it is also found in our families, schools, churches, governments, and other institutions. This produces an unseen reciprocal relationship that reproduces and reconstructs masculinity generation after generation in new ways. It is in these places where men learn to be men and to enjoy masculine privilege, and where everyone else learns their relative position in society. This, in essence, is patriarchy.

The cultural construction of gender in a particular society involves definitions of what it means to be masculine or feminine, and these definitions vary cross-culturally. In his classic text, Barry S. Hewlett offers a somewhat-different perspective on the question of maternal instinct by exploring the role of fatherhood among the Aka, a group of foragers who live in the tropical forest regions of Central Africa. Aka fathers spend a significant portion of their day caring for and nurturing their children. A good father among the Aka is a man who stays near his children, shows them affection, and assists the mother with her work. Indeed, Aka male–female relations are very egalitarian. Women and men each contribute significantly to subsistence; although Aka men hold all the named positions of status, women challenge men's authority regularly and play a decisive role in all kinds of decision-making; physical violence is infrequent, and violence against women is rare (Hewlett 1991). Hewlett suggests that strong father–infant attachment among the Aka can be explained by a range of ecological, social, ideological, and demographic factors. The implications of the Aka example, especially for alternate parenting models

DOI: 10.4324/9781003398349-38

in the United States, are clear. As Hewlett argues, "[t]he Aka demonstrate that there are cultural systems where men can be active, intimate and nurturing caregivers" (Hewlett 1991: 171).

Gilbert H. Herdt's classic writing about male initiation among the Sambia of New Guinea is, unfortunately, no longer included here. However, Herdt's work remains important because he examines how masculinity is constructed in the context of ritual among the Sambia. The Sambia, like many other societies in New Guinea (Biersack 2001; Brown and Buchbinder 1976; Herdt 1982; Meigs 1984; Roscoe 2001), are characterized by a high degree of segregation and sexual antagonism between men and women, both of which are reinforced by powerful taboos. These taboos, and other facets of Sambian male identity, including that of the warrior, are inculcated during a series of initiation rituals whereby boys are "grown" into men. As Herdt observes, the Sambia "perceive no imminent, naturally driven fit between one's birthright sex and one's gender identity or role" (1982: 54). Indeed, Sambian boys and men engage in what some societies would label homosexual activity, yet they do it to create masculinity. It is precisely for this reason that an analytical distinction is often made between "sex" as a biological classification and "gender" as a set of learned social behaviors and practices. In Sambian society, this distinction is particularly explicit and, therefore, can help us examine other ways in which gender is made in a wide range of sociocultural settings, including those of the Global North. Despite the chapter no longer being included in this volume, we encourage you to make use of the 1996 documentary film *Guardians of the Flutes*, in which Herdt was involved. In the film, Sambian community members describe their initiation rites and also how the Sambian way of life was changing at that time. Provocative, yet an important example of the purposeful shaping of gendered identity, the film is an excellent conversation starter and complement to the other chapters in this section.

Touching again on themes of gender, space, and place, Broughton and Walton document the limits of the domestic–public dichotomy for explaining masculinity, fatherhood, and family relations in the context of de-industrialization. They trace the efforts of laid-off and precariously employed workers in the United States to reinvent their identities as fathers and providers and discard some aspects of the "breadwinner ideal." As they cope with unemployment, loss of benefits, lower household income, and potential dependency on a wife or partner, the role of sole "provider" becomes increasingly unrealistic. Based on interviews with male workers laid off from Maytag Corporation, they show how these men (re)construct identities as workers, fathers, and moral individuals. Fatherhood and breadwinning are closely intertwined, as examples from the daily interactions of men and their children indicate. The idealized gendered division of labor has rarely been realized, even prior to de-industrialization and the outsourcing of plants such as Maytag. Women and men have long cooperated in dividing family chores, such as cooking and childcare. Ultimately, a rigid domestic–public representation of men's and women's responsibilities does not reflect the much more flexible allocation of household division of labor in daily life.

In his chapter, David D. Gilmore takes up the question of how masculinity is culturally constructed by describing his encounter with machismo in the southern Spanish region of Andalusia. He outlines three components of Andalusian "manhood" – virility, valor, and virtue. Men must live up to the anatomical equipment with which they are born – to enact their virility. There are certain rites of passage – including the activity of *abuchear* – associated with this enactment. Real manhood implies seduction. But it also requires bravery, heroism, and hard work – the elements of valor or *hombría*. Finally, being honorable, a person of rectitude, decency, and generosity, is essential to Andalusian manhood. The behavior of Spanish men in bars (Driessen 1983) must be viewed in this light. As Gilmore argues, to stay away from the bars and to hold back one's purse are considered unmanly and effeminate.

Drawing on intensive participant observation in fraternities at a US university, Scott F. Kiesling explores the role of language in creating men's gender identity, and how men's identities differ from person to person and situation to situation. Following Pete, a fraternity leader, as he interacts with others in four contexts, Kiesling demonstrates Pete's strategic use of language to lay claim to authority, by means of insults, boasts, assertions, and disagreements. Pete's strategies are, in turn, linked to broader cultural understandings of women's and men's identities, middle-class identity, fraternity identity, and so forth. A fine-grained analysis of social interactions with fraternity brothers and other friends demonstrates how Pete uses speech acts such as complaining, insulting, and bragging to create an authoritative, gendered stance, primarily in response to the audience's evaluations of his claims.

Finally, in a new chapter for this edition, Rebecca L. Upton tells a story of gender norms and global public health surveillance in Southern Africa. Truckers (men) and trucking routes have long been scrutinized by global and public health interventions in Southern Africa as potential vectors of HIV/AIDS and other sexually transmitted infections. In this chapter, it is in the context of the early days of the COVID-19 pandemic and the adoption of TikTok as a medium of communication upon which new forms of health surveillance are installed. Upton describes the strategies that truckers who travel between Botswana, Zimbabwe, and South Africa use to navigate international borders, transnational spaces, public health interventions, and their own masculinities. She concludes that global health professionals (and anthropologists) would do well to attend to how surveillance can constrain the performance of masculine roles with regard to men's families and communities. As she writes, "Notions of care, acknowledgement of male vulnerabilities, an understanding of masculinity as emergent, contested, processual, and less of a product can all yield better, more nuanced, and efficacious approaches to understanding "health.""

References

Biersack, Aletta. 2001. "Reproducing Inequality: The Gender Politics of Male Cults in the Papua New Guinea Highlands and Amazonia." In *Gender in Amazonia and Melanesia*, eds. Thomas A. Gregor and Donald Tuzin, 69–90. Berkeley: University of California Press.

Bourdieu, Pierre. 2001. *Masculine Domination*. Stanford, CA: Stanford University Press.

Brown, Paula, and Georgeda Buchbinder. 1976. *Man and Woman in the New Guinea Highlands*. Washington, DC: American Anthropological Association, Special Publication, number 8.

Driessen, Henk. 1983. "Male Sociability and Rituals of Masculinity in Andalusia." *Anthropological Quarterly* 56: 125–133.

Dudgeon, Matthew, and Marcia Inhorn. 2003. "Gender Masculinity and Reproduction: Anthropological Perspectives." *International Journal of Men's Health*: 31–56.

Herdt, Gilbert. 1982. *Rituals of Manhood: Male Initiation in Papua New Guinea*. Berkeley and Los Angeles: University of California Press.

Hewlett, Barry S. 1991. *Intimate Fathers: The Nature and Context of Aka Pygmy Paternal Infant Care*. Ann Arbor: University of Michigan Press.

Meigs, Anna S. 1984. *Food, Sex, and Pollution: A New Guinea Religion*. New Brunswick, NJ: Rutgers University Press.

Roscoe, Paul. 2001. "Strength and Sexuality: Sexual Avoidance and Masculinity in New Guinea and Amazonia." In *Gender in Amazonia and Melanesia*, eds. Thomas A. Gregor and Donald Tuzin, 279–308. Berkeley: University of California Press.

Chapter 34

The cultural nexus of Aka father–infant bonding

Barry S. Hewlett

Despite a steady increase in the quantity and quality of studies of infants, young children, and motherhood in various parts of the world (e.g., LeVine et al. 1994), we know relatively little about the nature of father–child relations outside of the United States and Western Europe (see Hewlett 1992 for some exceptions). In general, mother-oriented theories of infant and child development have guided cross-cultural research. The majority of these theories view the mother–infant relationship as the prototype for subsequent attachments and relationships (Ainsworth 1967; Bowlby 1969; Freud 1938; Harlow 1961). According to Freud and Bowlby, for instance, one had to have a trusting, unconditional relationship with his or her mother in order to become a socially and emotionally adjusted adult. These influential theorists generally believed that the father's role was not a factor in the child's development until the Oedipal stage (3–5 years old). The field methods to study infancy reflected this theoretical emphasis on mothers. Observations were either infant- or mother-focused and conducted only during daylight hours; father-focused and evening observations were not considered. Also, standardized questionnaires and psychological tests were generally administered only to the mother. One consistent result from the cross-cultural studies was that fathers provided substantially less-direct care to infants than mothers. In fact, all cross-cultural studies to date indicate that a number of other female caretakers (older female siblings, aunts, grandmothers) provide more direct care to infants than do fathers. Since fathers are not as conspicuous as mothers and other females during daylight hours, researchers tend to emphasize a "deficit" model of fathers (Cole and Bruner 1974), that is, fathers are not around much and, therefore, do not contribute much to the child's development.

Given the paucity of systematic research outside of the United States on the father's interactions with children, it is ironic that this variable (i.e., the degree of father vs. mother involvement with children) should be so consistently invoked as an explanatory factor in the literature. It is hypothesized to be related, for example, to gender inequality (Chodorow 1974), universal sexual asymmetry (Rosaldo and Lamphere 1974), and the origin of the human family (Lancaster and Lancaster 1987).

DOI: 10.4324/9781003398349-39

Father–infant bonding

Bowlby's (1969) theory, mentioned earlier, suggested that an early secure attachment (or "bonding") between infant and caregiver (usually mother) was crucial for normal development. Lack of bonding between mother and infant led to the infant's protest, despair, detachment, and eventual, difficulty in emotional and social development. Most studies of attachment have focused on mother–infant bonding, but an increasing number of studies in the United States and Europe have tried to understand if and when infants become attached to fathers. Numerous psychological studies now indicate that infants are attached to their fathers and that the infants become attached to fathers at about the same age as they do to mothers (8–10 months of age) (Lamb 1981). But how does this bonding take place if infant bonding to mother is known to develop through regular, sensitive, and responsive care? American fathers are seldom around to provide this type of care. The critical factor that has emerged in over 50 studies of primarily middle-class American fathers is vigorous play. The physical style of American fathers is distinct from that of American mothers, is evident three days after birth, and continues throughout infancy. The American data have been so consistent that some researchers have indicated a biological basis (Clarke-Stewart 1980). The idea is that mother–infant bonding develops as a consequence of the frequency and intensity of the relationship, while father–infant bonding takes place because of this highly stimulating interaction. British, German, and Israeli studies generally support this hypothesis. This chapter examines the process of father–infant bonding among the Aka, a hunter-gatherer group living in the tropical forest of Central Africa.

The Aka

There are about 30,000 Aka hunter-gatherers in the tropical rainforests of southern Central African Republic and northern Congo-Brazzaville. They live in camps of 25–35 people and move camp every two weeks to two months. Each nuclear family has a hut, and each camp generally has 5–8 huts arranged in a circle. The circle of huts is about 12 meters in diameter, and each hut is about 1.5 meters in diameter. Each hut has one bed of leaves or logs, on which everyone in the family sleeps. The Aka have patriclans, and many members of a camp belong to the same patriclan (generally, a camp consists of brothers, their wives and children, and unrelated men who are doing bride service for the sisters of the men in camp). The Aka have high fertility and mortality rates: a woman generally has 5–6 children during her lifetime, and one-fifth of the infants die before reaching 12 months, and 43 percent of children die before reaching 15 years.

Life in the camp is rather intimate. While the overall population density is quite low (less than one person per square kilometer), living space is quite dense. Three or four people sleep together on the same 4-feet-long-by-2-feet-wide bed, and neighbors are just a few feet away. The 25–35 camp members live in an area about the size of a large American living room. The Aka home represents the "public" part of life, while time outside of camp tends to be relatively "private." This is the reverse of the American pattern (i.e., home is usually considered private). The camp is relatively young, as half of the members of the camp are under 15, and most women have a nursing child throughout their childbearing years.

The Aka use a variety of hunting techniques, but net hunting, which involves men, women, and children, is the most important and regular hunting technique. Women generally have the role of tackling the game in the net and killing the animal. Captured game is eventually shared with everyone in camp. Some parts of the game animal are smoked and eventually traded to Bantu and Sudanic farmers for manioc or other domesticated foods. The Aka have strong economic and religious ties to the tropical forest. The forest is perceived as provider and called friend, lover, mother, or father.

Sharing and cooperation are pervasive and general tenets of Aka camp life. Food items, infant care, ideas for song and dance, and material items such as pots and pans are just some of the items that are shared daily in the camp. An Ngandu farmer describes Aka sharing:

> Pygmies [the Ngandu use the derogatory term *Babinga* to refer to the Aka] are people who stick together. Twenty of them are able to share one single cigarette. When a pygmy comes back with only five roots, she shares them all. It is the same with forest nuts; they will give them out to everybody even if there are none left for them. They are very generous.

The Aka are also fiercely egalitarian. They have a number of mechanisms to maintain individual, intergenerational, and gender equality. The Ngandu villager mentioned earlier describes his concerns about Aka intergenerational egalitarianism:

> Young pygmies have no respect for their parents; they regard their fathers as their friends. . . . There is no way to tell whether they are talking to their parents, because they always use their first names. Once I was in a pygmy camp and several people were sitting around, and a son said to his father, "Etobe, your balls are hanging out of your loincloth," and everyone started laughing. No respect, none, none, none. . . . It's real chaos because there is no respect between father and son, mother and son or daughter. That's why pygmies have such a bad reputation, a reputation of being backward.

Three mechanisms that promote sharing and egalitarianism are prestige avoidance, rough joking, and demand sharing. The Aka try to avoid drawing attention to themselves, even if they have killed an elephant or cured someone's life-threatening illness. Individuals who boast about their abilities are likely to share less or request more from others in the belief that they are better than others. If individuals start to draw attention to themselves, others in the camp will use rough and crude jokes, often about the boastful person's genitals, in order to get the individuals to be more modest about their abilities. Demand sharing also helps maintain egalitarianism: if individuals like or want something (cigarettes, necklace, shirt), they simply ask for it, and the person generally gives it to them. Demand sharing promotes the circulation of scarce material goods (e.g., shoes, shirt, necklaces, spear points) in the camp.

Gender egalitarianism is also important. For instance, there are male and female roles on the net hunt, but role reversals take place daily, and individuals are not stigmatized for taking the roles of the opposite sex. If one does the task poorly, regardless of whether it is a masculine or feminine task, then one is open to joking and teasing by others (e.g., when the anthropologist chases the game in the wrong direction).

The rough joking mentioned earlier is also linked to another feature of Aka culture – playfulness. There is no clear separation between "work" and "play" time. Dances, singing, net hunting, male circumcision, and sorcery accusations all include humorous mimicking, practical jokes, and exaggerated storytelling. Aka life is informal because of egalitarianism and the playful activity that occurs throughout the day with both adults and children. Play is an integral part of both adult and child life and contributes to enhanced parent–child and adult–child communication. Parents and adults have an extensive repertoire of play and can and do communicate cultural knowledge to children through their playful repertoire.

Greater ethnographic detail on the Aka can be found in Bahuchet (1985) or Hewlett (1991).

Aka infancy

The infant lives with a relatively small group of individuals related through his or her father (unless the infant is the firstborn, in which case the family is likely to be in the camp of the wife for the purposes of bride service) and sleeps in the same bed as the mother, father, and other brothers and sisters.

Cultural practices during infancy are quite distinct from those found in European and American cultures. Aka parents are indulgent, as infants are held almost constantly, nursed on demand (breastfed several times per hour), attended to immediately if they fuss, and are seldom, if ever, told "No! No!" if they misbehave (e.g., get into food pots, hit others, or take things from other children). An Aka father describes Aka parenting and contrasts it with parenting among his Ngandu farming neighbors:

> We, Aka, look after our children with love, from the minute they are born to when they are much older. The villagers love their children only when they are babies. When they become children, they get beaten up badly. With us, even if the child is older, if he is unhappy, I'll look after him. I will cuddle him.

Older infants are allowed to use and play with knives, machetes, and other "adult" items. They are allowed to crawl into a parent's lap while the parent is engaged in economic (e.g., butchering animal, repairing net) or leisure (e.g., playing a harp or drum) activity. While older infants are given considerable freedom to explore the house and camp, parents do watch infants to make sure they do not crawl into the fire.

Extensive multiple caregiving of 1- to 4-month-old infants (Hewlett 1989) exists, especially while the Aka are in the camp. Individuals other than mother (infant's father, brothers, sisters, aunts, uncles, grandmothers) hold the infant the majority of the time (60 percent) in this context, and the infant is moved to different people about seven times per hour. Mothers' holding increases to 85 percent, and the transfer rate drops to two transfers per hour outside of the camp (i.e., on net hunt or in fields).

Infancy is very active and stimulating. Infants are taken on the hunt and are seldom laid down. They are held on the side of the caregiver rather than on the caregiver's back, as in many farming communities, so there are opportunities for caregiver–infant face-to-face interaction and communication. The infant can also breastfeed by simply reaching for the mother's breast and can nurse while the mother walks. While out on the net hunt, the infant sleeps in the sling as the caregiver walks, runs, or sits.

The study

I started working with the Aka in 1973, so by the time I started the father–infant study in 1984, I was familiar with specific Aka families and Aka culture in general. Since I wanted to test some of the psychological hypotheses regarding father–infant relations, I incorporated psychological methods into my research. The quantitative psychological methods consisted of systematically observing 15 Aka families with infants from 6;00 a.m. to 9:00 p.m. (the observations focused either on the father or the infant). This enabled me to say precisely how much time Aka versus American fathers held or were near their infants and precisely describe how American versus Aka styles of interaction were similar or different. Informal discussions while on the net hunt and in camp were also utilized to develop structured interviews. Men and women, young and old, were asked about their feelings regarding relations with their mothers, fathers, and other caregivers.

The study focused on two domains important for trying to understand father–infant bonding: the degree of father involvement and mother's versus father's parenting style. For degree of father involvement, I wanted to know how often fathers actually interact with their infants; how often fathers are available to their infants; if fathers are not involved with infants, what other activities they are involved in; and how children characterize the nature of their involvement with their father. Questions regarding paternal versus maternal parenting style included: Are there distinctions between the mother's and the father's play behavior with their infants? Do mothers and fathers hold their infants for different purposes? What do mothers and fathers do while they hold the infant? Do infants show different types of attachment behavior to mothers and fathers? How do children view their mother's and father's parenting styles?

Why are Aka fathers so involved with their infants? The cultural nexus of father–infant bonding

Although few cross-cultural studies of father–child relations have been conducted, Aka father involvement in infancy is exceptional, if not unique. Aka fathers are within an arm's reach (i.e., holding or within 1 meter) of their infant more than 50 percent of 24-hour periods. Table 34.1 demonstrates that Aka fathers hold their very young infants during the day at least five times more than fathers in other cultures do, while Table 34.2 indicates Aka fathers are available to their infants at least three times more frequently than do fathers in other cultures. American and European fathers hold their infants, on average, between 10 and 20 minutes per day (Lamb et al. 1987), while Aka fathers, on average, hold their infants about 1 hour during daylight hours and about 25 percent of the time after the sun goes down. At night, fathers sleep with mother and infant, whereas American fathers seldom sleep with their infants. While Aka father care is extensive, it

Table 34.1 Comparison of father holding in selected foraging populations

Population	Age of infants (mos.)	Father holding (percent of time)	Source
Gidgingali	0–6	3.4	Hamilton (1981)
	6–18	3.1	
!Kung	0–6	1.9	West and Konner (1976)
	6–24	4.0	
Efe Pygmies	1–4	2.6	Winn et al. (1990)
Aka Pygmies	1–4	22.0	Hewlett (1991)
	8–18	14.0	

Note: All observations were made in a camp setting.

Source: Table from Hewlett (1991).

Table 34.2 Comparison of father presence with infants or children among selected foraging and farming populations

Population	Location	Subsistence	Percent time father present/in view	Primary setting of observations	Source
Gusii	Kenya	Farming	10	House/yard and garden	1
Mixteca	Mexico	Farming	9	House/yard	1
Ilocano	Philippines	Farming	14	House/yard	1
Okinawan	Japan	Farming	3	Public places and house/yard	1
Rajput	India	Farming	3	House/yard	1
!Kung	Botswana	Foraging	30	Camp	2
Aka Pygmies	Central African Republic	Foraging	88	Forest camp	3
Logoli	Kenya	Farming	5	House/yard	4
Newars	Nepal	Farming	7	House/yard	4
Samoans	Samoa	Farming	8	House/yard	4
Carib	Belize	Farming	3	House/yard	4
Ifaluk	Micronesia	Farm-fish	13	House/yard	5

Sources: Table from Hewlett (1991):

1. Whiting and Whiting *(1975)*

2. West and Konner *(1976)*

3. Hewlett *(1991)*

4. Munroe and Munroe *(1992)*

5. Betzig et al. *(1990)*

is also highly context-dependent; fathers provide at least four times as much care while they are in the camp setting than they do while out of camp (e.g., out on the net hunt or in the villagers' fields). What factors influence this high level of paternal emotional and physical involvement among the Aka?

Aka father–infant bonding is embedded within a cultural nexus – it influences and is influenced by a complex cultural system. This brief overview describes some of the cultural facets linked to Aka father–infant bonding.

Like many other foragers, the Aka have few accumulable resources that are essential for survival. "Kinship resources," the number of brothers and sisters in particular, are probably the most essential "resource" for survival but are generally established at an early age. Food resources are not stored or accumulated, and Aka males and females contribute similar percentages of calories to the diet. Cross-cultural studies have demonstrated that in societies where resources essential to survival can be accumulated or where males are the primary contributors to subsistence, fathers invest more time competing for these resources and, consequently, spend less time with their children. In contrast, where resources are not accumulable or men are not the primary contributors to subsistence, men generally spend more time in the direct care of their children. Katz and Konner (1981: 174) found that father–infant proximity (degree of emotional warmth and physical proximity) is closest in gathering-hunting populations (gathered foods by females are principal resources; meat is secondary) and most distant in cultures where herding or advanced agriculture is practiced. In the latter cultures, cattle, camels, and land are considered the essential accumulable resources necessary for survival. These findings are consistent with Whiting and Whiting's (1975) cross-cultural study of husband–wife intimacy. They found husband–wife intimacy to be greatest in cultures without accumulated resources or capital investments. While there are other factors to consider (the protection of resources and the polygyny rate), there is a strong tendency for fathers/husbands to devote more time to their children/wives if there are no accumulable resources.

Three additional factors seem to be especially influential in understanding the extraordinarily high level of Aka paternal care. First, the nature of Aka subsistence activity is rather unique, cross-culturally. Usually, men's and women's subsistence activities take place at very different locations. The net hunt and other subsistence activities, such as caterpillar collecting, involve men, women, and children. If men are going to help with infant care on a regular basis, they have to be near the infant a good part of the day. The net hunt makes this possible. The net hunt also requires that men and women walk equal distances during the day. In most foraging societies, females do not travel as far from camp as males. Older siblings are not useful for helping their mothers because of the extensive labor involved in walking long distances with an infant. If a mother is to receive help on the net hunt, it needs to come from an adult. Most of the other adult females carry baskets full of food and have their own infants or young children to carry, since fertility is high. Fathers are among the few alternative caregivers regularly available on the net hunt to help mothers. While fathers do carry infants on the net hunt, especially on the return from the hunt, when the mothers' baskets are full of meat, collected nuts, and fruit, father–infant caregiving is much more likely to occur in the camp.

Another influential factor is the nature of husband–wife relations. The net hunt contributes substantially to the time husband and wife spend together and patterns the nature of that time. Observations in the forest and village indicate that husbands and wives are within sight of each other 46.5 percent of daylight hours. This is more time together than in any other known society, and it is primarily a result of the net hunt. This percentage, of course, increases in the evening hours. But husbands and wives are not only together most of the day; they are also actively cooperating on the net hunt. They have to know each other well to communicate and cooperate throughout the day. They work together to set up the family net, chase game into the net, butcher and divide the game, and take care of the children. Husbands and wives help each other out in a number of domains, in part because they spend so much time together. Husband–wife relations are many-stranded, that is, social, economic, ritual, parenting, and leisure activities are shared and experienced in close proximity. When they return to camp, the mother has a number of tasks – she collects firewood and water and prepares the biggest meal of the day. The father has relatively few tasks to do after returning from the hunt. He may make string or repair the net, but he is available to help with infant care. He is willing to do infant care, in part, because of the many-stranded reciprocity between husband and wife. In many societies, men have fewer tasks to do at the end of the day, while women have domestic tasks and prepare a meal. Men are available to help out with childcare but seldom provide much assistance, due in part to the more distant husband–wife relationship.

The third important factor in understanding Aka fathers' involvement with infants is father–infant bonding. Father and infant are clearly attached to each other. Fathers seek out their infants, and infants seek out their fathers. Fathers end up holding their infants frequently because the infants crawl to, reach for, or fuss for their fathers. Fathers pick up their infants because they intrinsically enjoy being close to their infants. They enjoy being with them and carry them in several different contexts (e.g., out in the fields, drinking palm wine with other men).

While the factors described earlier are especially influential, other cultural factors also play a part. Gender egalitarianism pervades cultural beliefs and practices: men do not have physical or institutional control over women, violence against women is rare or nonexistent, both women and men are valued for their different but complementary roles, there is flexibility in these gender roles, and holding infants is not perceived as being feminine or "women's work." Sharing, helping out, and generosity are central concepts in Aka life; this applies to subsistence and parenting spheres. Aka ideology of good and bad fathers reiterates the importance of the father's proximity – a good father shows love for his children, stays near them, and assists the mother with caregiving when her workload is heavy. A bad father abandons his children and does not share food with them. There is no organized warfare, and male feuding is infrequent, so men are around camp and help with subsistence rather than being away at battle. Fertility is high, so most adult women have nursing infants, and there are few other adult women around to help out. Finally, the Aka move their camps several times a year and consequently do not accumulate material goods that need to be defended.

The point here is that Aka father–infant relations have to be viewed in a complex cultural nexus. Some cultural factors are somewhat more influential than others – net hunting and husband–wife relations, for instance – but even these cultural features take place in a web of other cultural beliefs and practices that contribute to the intimate nature of Aka father–infant relations.

Father–infant bonding in the Aka and United States

Over 50 studies of European and American fathers indicate that fathers' interactions with infants and young children are clearly distinguished from mother's interactions in that fathers are the vigorous rough-and-tumble playmates of infants and young children, while mothers are sensitive caregivers. The American literature suggests that this rough-and-tumble play is how infants become attached to fathers ("bond") and develop social competence (Lamb et al. 1987). The Aka father–infant study is not consistent with the American studies that emphasize the importance of fathers' vigorous play. Aka fathers rarely, if ever, engage in vigorous play with their infants; only one episode of vigorous play by a father was recorded during all 264 hours of systematic observation. Informal observations during more than ten field visits over the last 20 years are also consistent with this finding. The quantitative data indicate that, by comparison to mothers, Aka fathers are significantly more likely to hug, kiss, or soothe a fussy baby while they are holding the infant.

While Aka fathers do not engage in vigorous play with their infants, they are slightly more playful than mothers; fathers are somewhat more likely to engage in minor physical play (e.g., tickling) with their 1- to 4-month-old infants than are mothers. But characterizing the Aka father as the infant's playmate would be misleading. Other caretakers, brothers and sisters in particular, engage in play with the infant, while holding much more frequently than fathers or mothers. Mothers have more episodes of play over the course of a day than fathers or other caretakers because they hold the infant most of the time. The Aka father–infant relationship might be better characterized by its intimate and affective nature. Aka fathers hold their infants more than do fathers in any other human society known to anthropologists, and Aka fathers also show affection more frequently while holding than do Aka mothers.

So how can vigorous play be a significant feature in American studies of father–infant bonding but not among the Aka? Four factors appear to be important for understanding the process of Aka father–infant bonding: familiarity with the infant, knowledge of caregiving practices (how to hold an infant, how to soothe an infant), the degree of relatedness to the infant, and cultural values and parental goals.

First, due to frequent father-holding and availability, Aka fathers know how to communicate with their infants. Fathers know the early signs of infant hunger, fatigue, and illness as well as the limits in their ability to soothe the infant. They also know how to stimulate responses from the infant without being vigorous. Unlike American fathers, Aka wait for infants to initiate interaction. Aka caregivers other than mothers and fathers are less familiar with the infants and the most physical in their play, suggesting a relationship between intimate knowledge of the infant's cues and the frequency of vigorous play while holding. Consistent with this is the finding that working mothers in the United States are more likely to engage in vigorous play than are stay-at-home mothers.

Second, knowledge of infant caregiving practices seems to play a role in determining how much play is exhibited in caretaker–infant interactions. Child caretakers were the most physical and the loudest (singing) in their handling of infants. Children were not restricted from holding infants, but they were closely watched by parents. While "other" caretakers were more playful than mothers or fathers, younger fathers and "other" caretakers were more physical than older ones, probably because they did not know how to handle and care for infants as well as adult caretakers do.

A third factor to consider is the degree of relatedness of the caretaker to the infant. If vigorous play can assist in developing attachment, more closely related individuals may have a greater vested interest in establishing this bond than distantly related individuals. Attachment not only enhances the survival of the infant but can also potentially increase the related caretaker's survival and fitness. Aka mothers and fathers establish attachment by their frequent caregiving; vigorous play is not necessary to establish affective saliency. Brothers and sisters, on the other hand, might establish this bond through physical play. Aka brothers and sisters, in fact, provided essentially all the physical play the focal infants received; cousins and unrelated children were more likely to engage in face-to-face play with the infant instead of physical play.

Finally, cultural values and parental goals of infant development should be considered. American culture encourages individualistic aggressive competition; Aka culture values cooperation, nonaggression, and prestige avoidance (one does not draw attention to oneself even, for instance, if one kills an elephant). Apparently, Americans tolerate – if not actually encourage – aggressive, rough-and-tumble types of play with infants. Also, due to the high infant mortality rate, the primary parental goal for Aka is the survival of their infants. The constant holding and immediate attention to fussing reflect this goal. In the United States, infant mortality rates are markedly lower, and as a result, parental concern for survival may not be as great. The Aka infant is taken away from a caretaker who plays roughly with the infant, in part because it could be seen as aggressive behavior, but also because the pervasive aim of infant care practices is survival of the infant, and rough-and-tumble play could risk the infant's safety.

These factors tentatively clarify why Aka fathers do not engage in vigorous play like American fathers do but do participate in slightly more physical play than Aka mothers (but not more than other caretakers). American fathers infrequently participate directly in infant care and consequently are not as familiar with infant cues. To stimulate interaction and (possibly) bonding, they engage in physical play. Aka brothers and sisters are also much less physical in their play with infants than are American fathers (Aka never toss infants in the air or swing them by their arms), again suggesting that Aka children know their infant brother or sister and the necessary infant caregiving skills better than American fathers do. These observations are obviously speculative and need further empirical study.

Sociologists LaRossa and LaRossa (1981) also describe stylistic differences between American mothers' and fathers' interactions with their infants. They list a number of male–female role dichotomies that reflect different parenting styles. One distinction they make is role distance versus role embracement. Fathers are more likely to distance themselves from the parenting role, while mothers are more likely to embrace the parenting role. American women generally want to remain in primary control of the children, and while fathers may show interest in caregiving, they are more likely to distance themselves from caregiving while embracing their roles as the breadwinners. LaRossa and LaRossa also suggest that fathers generally have low intrinsic value and relatively high extrinsic value, while mothers have the reverse.

> The intrinsic value of something or someone is the amount of sheer pleasure or enjoyment that one gets from experiencing an object or person. The extrinsic value of something or someone is the amount of social rewards (e.g., money, power, prestige) associated with having or being with the object or person.
>
> (64)

They use this dichotomy to explain why fathers are more likely to carry or hold an infant in public than in private. Fathers receive extrinsic rewards from those in public settings, while this does not happen in the home. According to LaRossa and LaRossa:

> Fathers will roughhouse with their toddlers on the living-room floor, and will blush when hugged or kissed by the one-year-olds, but when you really get down to it, they just do not have that much fun when they are with their children. If they had their druthers, they would be working at the office or drinking at the local pub.
>
> (65)

These role dichotomies may be useful for understanding American mother–father parenting styles, but they have limited value in characterizing Aka mother–father distinctions. Aka mothers and fathers embrace the parenting role. Generally, mothers and fathers want to hold their infants, and certainly, they derive pleasure from infant interactions. As indicated earlier, fathers were, in fact, more likely to show affection while holding than mothers were. Fathers also offered their nipples to infants who wanted to nurse, cleaned mucus from their infants' noses, picked lice from their infants' hair, and cleaned their infants after they urinated or defecated (often on the father). Fathers' caregiving did not appear any more or less perfunctory than mothers'. Aka fathers are not burdened with infant care; if a father does not want to hold or care for the infant, he gives the infant to another person. Overall, Aka fathers embrace their parenting role as much as they embrace their hunting role.

The intrinsic–extrinsic role dichotomy does not fit well with Aka mother–father parenting styles either. Again, both Aka mothers and fathers place great intrinsic value and little extrinsic value on parenting. The fathers' intrinsic value is demonstrated earlier, but the lack of extrinsic value among the Aka can best be seen by comparing Aka and Ngandu fathers (the Ngandu are the horticulturalist trading partners of the Aka). When an Ngandu father holds his infant in public, he is "onstage." He goes out of his way to show his infant to those who pass by and frequently tries to stimulate the infant while holding it. He is much more vigorous in his interactions with the infant than are Aka men. The following experience exemplifies Ngandu fathers' extrinsic value towards their infants: an Ngandu friend showed me a 25-pound fish he had just caught, and I asked to take a photograph of him with his fish. He said fine, promptly picked up his nearby infant, and proudly displayed his fish and infant for the photograph. His wife was also nearby but was not invited into the photograph. Aka fathers, on the other hand, are matter-of-fact about their holding or transporting of infants in public places. They do not draw attention to their infants. Aka fathers also hold their infants in all kinds of social and economic contexts.

Conclusion

This chapter has examined the cultural nexus of Aka father–infant bonding and has made some comparisons to middle-class American father–infant relations. American fathers are characterized by their vigorous play with infants, while Aka fathers are characterized by their affectionate and intimate relations with their infants. Aka infants bond with their fathers because they provide sensitive and regular care, whereas American infants bond to their fathers, in part, due to their vigorous play. The purpose of this chapter is not to criticize American fathers for their style of interaction with their infants; physical play is important in middle-class American context because it is a means for fathers who are seldom around their infants to demonstrate their love and interest in the infant. Vigorous play may also be important to American mothers who work outside the home; studies indicate they are also more likely than stay-at-home mothers to engage in vigorous play with their infants. The Aka study does imply that father–infant bonding does not always take place through physical play, and it is necessary to explore a complex cultural nexus in order to understand the nature of father–infant relations.

Aka fathers are very close and affectionate with their infants, and their attachment processes, as defined in Western bonding theory, appear to be similar to that of mothers. While Aka mother- and father-infant relations are similar, they are not the same. Fathers do spend substantially less time with infants than do mothers, and the nature of their interactions is different. Aka and American fathers bring something qualitatively different to their children; the father's caregiving pattern is not simply a variation of the mother's pattern. More research is needed on the unique features of father involvement in order to move away from a "deficit" model of fathering.

Finally, this chapter identifies cultural factors that influence father–infant bonding; biological forces are not considered. This is unusual in that mother–infant bonding generally mentions or discusses the biological basis of mother's attachment to the infant. The release of prolactin and oxytocin with birth and lactation is said to increase affectionate feelings and actions toward the infant. These same hormones exist in men, but endocrinologists generally believe they have no function. Is there a biology of fatherhood, or is motherhood more biological and fatherhood more cultural? This is a complex question, as both men and women have probably evolved ("biological") psychological mechanisms that influence their parenting, but if one just focuses on endocrinology, few data exist on the endocrinology of fatherhood. For instance, Gubernick et al. (unpublished paper) found that men's testosterone levels decreased significantly two weeks after the birth of their children; the decrease was not linked to decline in sexual behavior, increased stress, or sleep deprivation. Another small study of American fathers indicated significant increases in plasma prolactin levels after fathers held their 3-month-old infants on their chest for 15 minutes (Hewlett and Alster, unpublished data). The few biological studies that do exist suggest that biology can and does influence fatherhood. More studies of the biocultural nexus of fatherhood are needed.

While biology probably influences both mothers' and fathers' parenting to some degree, this chapter has demonstrated that the cultural nexus is a powerful force that profoundly shapes the nature and context of father–infant bonding. Aka father–infant bonding takes place through regular and intimate (i.e., hugging, kissing, soothing) care, while American father–infant bonding takes place through vigorous play. American fathers often do not know their infants very well and try to demonstrate their love and concern through vigorous play. American mothers that work outside the home also tend to be more vigorous with their infants. American fathers are not necessarily "bad" fathers because they do not do as much direct caregiving as the Aka fathers. Fathers around the world "provide" and enrich the lives of their children in diverse ways (e.g., physical and emotional security, economic well-being). The Aka data do suggest that there are alternative processes by which father–infant bonding can and does take place and that Americans and others might learn from this comparative approach as policy decisions about parental leave and other topics are considered.

Discussion questions

1. What mechanisms do the Aka use to promote sharing and egalitarianism?
2. How does the net hunt contribute to the husband–wife relationship and cooperation in Aka society?
3. What does the author identify as some of the key differences between Aka and American father–infant caretaking styles, and what does the author suggest may explain these different styles?
4. What cultural practices influence father–infant interaction among the Aka?

References

Ainsworth, Mary D. Salter. 1967. *Infancy in Uganda: Infant Care and the Growth of Love*. Baltimore: Johns Hopkins Press.
Bahuchet, Serge. 1985. *Les Pygmées Aka et la Fôret Centrafricaine*. Paris: Selaf.
Betzig, Laura, Alisa Harrigan, and Paula Turke. 1990. "Childcare on Ifaluk." *Zeitscrift fur Ethnologie* 114: 161–177.
Bowlby, John. 1969. *Attachment and Loss Vol. 1: Attachment*. New York: Basic Books.
Chodorow, Nancy. 1974. "Family Structure and Feminine Personality." In *Woman, Culture, and Society*, eds. Michelle Zimbalist Rosaldo and Louise Lamphere. Stanford, CA: Stanford University Press.

Clarke-Stewart, K. Alison. 1980. "The Father's Contribution to Children's Cognitive and Social Development in Early Childhood." In *The Father-Infant Relationship: Observational Studies in the Family Setting*, ed. Frank A. Pedersen. New York: Praeger.

Cole, Michael, and Jerome S. Bruner. 1974. "Cultural Differences and Inferences about Psychological Processes." In *Culture and Cognition: Readings in Cross-Cultural Psychology*, eds. J. W. Berry and P. R. Dasen. London: Methuen.

Freud, Sigmund. 1938. *An Outline of Psychoanalysis*. London: Hogarth.

Gubernick, D. J., C. M. Worthman, and J. F. Stallings. "Hormonal Correlates of Fatherhood in Men." *Unpublished Paper*.

Hamilton, Annette. 1981. *Nature and Nurture: Aboriginal Child-Rearing in North-Central Arnhem Land*. Canberra: Australian Institute of Aboriginal Studies.

Harlow, Harry F. 1961. "The Development of Affectional Patterns in Infant Monkeys." In *Determinants of Infant Behavior*, ed. B. M. Foss, Vol. 1. London: Methuen.

Hewlett, Barry S. 1989. "Multiple Caretaking among African Pygmies." *American Anthropologist* 91: 186–191.

Hewlett, Barry S. 1991. *Intimate Fathers: The Nature and Context of Aka Pygmy Paternal-Infant Care*. Ann Arbor: University of Michigan Press.

Hewlett, Barry S., ed. 1992. *Father-Child Relations: Cultural and Biosocial Perspectives*. New York: Aldine de Gruyter.

Hewlett, Barry S., and D. Alster. "Prolactin and Infant Holding among American Fathers." *Unpublished manuscript*.

Katz, Mary Maxwell, and Melvin J. Konner. 1981. "The Role of Father: An Anthropological Perspective." In *The Role of Father in Child Development*, 2nd edn, ed. Michael E. Lamb. New York: John Wiley and Sons.

Lamb, Michael E., ed. 1981. *The Role of the Father in Child Development*, 2nd ed. New York: John Wiley & Sons.

Lamb, Michael E., Joseph H. Pleck, Eric L. Charnov, and James A. LeVine. 1987. "A Biosocial Perspective on Paternal Behavior and Involvement." In *Parenting across the Lifespan: Biosocial Dimension*, eds. Jane B. Lancaster, Jeanne Altmann, Alice S. Rossi, and Lonnie R. Sherrod. Hawthorne, NY: Aldine.

Lancaster, Jane B., and Chet S. Lancaster. 1987. "The Watershed: Change in Parental-Investment and Family Formation Strategies in the Course of Human Evolution." In *Parenting across the Life Span: Biosocial Dimension*, eds. Jane B. Lancaster, Jeanne Altmann, Alice S. Rossi, and Lonnie R. Sherrod. Hawthorne, NY: Aldine.

LaRossa, Ralph, and Maureen Mulligan LaRossa. 1981. *Transition to Parenthood: How Infants Change Families*. Beverly Hills: Sage Publications.

LeVine, Robert A., Suzanne Dixon, Sarah LeVine, Amy Richman, P. Herbert Leiderman, Constance H. Keefer, and T. Berry Brazelton. 1994. *Child Care and Culture: Lessons from Africa*. New York: Cambridge University Press.

Munroe, Ruth H., and Robert L. Munroe. 1992. "Fathers in Children's Environments: A Four Culture Study." In *Father-Child Relations: Cultural and Biosocial Contexts*, ed. Barry S. Hewlett. New York: Aldine de Gruyter.

Rosaldo, Michelle Z., and Louise Lamphere, eds. 1974. *Woman, Culture and Society*. Stanford, CA: Stanford University Press.

West, Mary Maxwell, and Melvin J. Konner. 1976. "The Role of Father in Anthropological Perspective." In *The Role of the Father in Child Development*, ed. Michael E. Lamb. New York: John Wiley & Sons.

Whiting, Beatrice Blyth, and John W. M. Whiting. 1975. *Children of Six Cultures: A Psycho-Cultural Analysis*. Cambridge, MA: Harvard University Press.

Winn, Steve, Gilda A. Morelli, and E. Z. Tronick. 1990. "The Infant in the Group: A Look at Efe Caretaking Practices." In *The Cultural Context of Infancy*, eds. J. Kevin Nugent, Barry M. Lester, and T. Berry Brazelton. Norwood, NJ: Ablex.

Chapter 35

Downsizing masculinity

Gender, family, and fatherhood in
post-industrial America

Chad Broughton and Tom Walton

Reproduced by permission of the American Anthropological Association from
Anthropology of Work Review, Volume 27, Issue 1, pages 1–12, March 2006. Not
for sale or further reproduction.

Introduction

Over the past couple of decades, community-based studies of deindustrialization in the
Rust Belt have examined the devastating impact that a factory closing can have on a
blue-collar town and the people in it (Dandaneau 1996; Hathaway 1993; Linkon and
Russo 2002; Lipper 2003; Modell 1998; Pappas 1989). Likewise, broad-scale analyses
of deindustrialization (Bluestone and Harrison 1982; Cowie et al. 2003; Wilson 1987,
1996) point to the particularly wrenching financial and emotional impact of "disappear-
ing work" for disadvantaged groups. As unionized, high-wage jobs are shipped overseas and less-secure and lower-wage service sector jobs take their place, workers with
comparably low levels of education among the working class and the poor confront the
social consequences. William J. Wilson's "Marriageable Male Pool Index," which tracks
the ratio of men that can support a family to the number of women in the same age and
race group, may be patriarchal in assuming a male breadwinner, but it points clearly to
a steady decline in the number of working-class men who can "provide" for a family
(Wilson 1987). Echoing such realities for blue-collar Americans are studies that examine
the consequences of chronic job insecurity, the humiliations of downward mobility for
the working and middle classes (Ehrenreich 1989; Newman 1999; Rubin 1992; Sennett
1998), the "withering of the American dream" (Hochschild 1995; Newman 1993), and
growing income, wealth, and social inequality (Mishel et al. 2005; Wolff 1995).

The financial difficulties of coping with unemployment or dramatically lower wages, loss
of healthcare coverage and retirement benefits, and retraining and starting over mid-career all
necessitate social and cultural adaptations. In particular, for men, the loss of a good factory
job often means facing not only the prospect of socioeconomic downward mobility but also
an explicit or implicit rethinking of one's identity as a man and one's role as a father and husband. And on a larger scale, popular, and, in some cases, ideological, notions about the family, gender roles, and masculinity (e.g., the idea of a sole "provider" or "breadwinner") bear
increased scrutiny, given the structural economic changes wrought by deindustrialization.

DOI: 10.4324/9781003398349-40

A number of important works have dealt with transformations in manhood, father-hood, and family structure in American history, and the role of economic change in relation to these transformations (Coontz 1992; Demos 1986, 1997; Griswold 1993; Kimmel 1996, 2000; Rotundo 1993). As the United States industrialized, a sharpened dichotomy between public and private roles took shape and assigned distinct roles for men and women whose premodern lives had been organized around the home. The idea of the "breadwinning male" emerged as the archetypal industrial male identity – reaching its zenith in the United States during the post–World War II industrial boom. Cultural variations of the "breadwinning male" are ubiquitous throughout American history after industrialization, but as historian Stephanie Coontz (1992: 23) notes, "[o]ur most powerful visions of traditional families derive from images that are still delivered to our homes in countless reruns of 1950s television sitcoms." These archetypal understandings of the family have often lent themselves to contemporary ideological debates because of their portrayal of seemingly "functional" or "natural" breadwinner and homemaker roles for men and women in an industrial society. Nonetheless, the nuclear family (and this "breadwinner ideal," as we will refer to it) has proved to be a powerful cultural symbol and, to many in the working and middle classes, a central component of the American dream. And blue-collar workers that were able to obtain secure, high-paying jobs were able to reach at least part of this cultural ideal.

In anthropology, theorizing about masculinity has taken divergent paths. Some scholars have approached the question with an eye to certain universal masculine structures (Gilmore 1990), while others, in an approach adopted here, have sought to "document the ambiguous and fluid nature of masculinity within particular spatial and temporal contexts" in an attempt to demonstrate the fallacy of a unified masculine identity (Gutmann 1997: 387). In this sense, it is not a static, archetypal manhood with which we are concerned but, instead, the dynamics of multiple, shifting masculinities as they appear at various historical junctures.

Furthermore, this chapter heeds R. W. Connell's (1995) plea that social scientists pay close attention to gender relations among men in order to avoid perpetuating oversimplified "types" – like the myth of *a* working-class masculinity. Making use of the notion of "hegemonic masculinity," we attempt to detail the waning efficacy of the breadwinner ideal for a group of working men facing job loss.

Our work, then, is an examination of hegemonic masculinity in limbo and offers key insights into how men reconstitute and refashion once-sturdy identities in the face of global economic changes. As deindustrialization haunts the Rust Belt, we must ask: How do blue-collar workers adapt their understandings of themselves as men and fathers when paths into the middle class escape their reach? And furthermore, how do they understand this process, who do they blame, and how do they envision their future in the post-industrial world?

To explore these questions, we conducted interviews with 25 male workers (sometimes with their partners) who had been laid off from Maytag Corporation's Galesburg Refrigeration Products – a factory in Galesburg, Illinois, that employed 1,600 workers in Illinois but now makes refrigerators in Reynosa, Mexico.[1] The informants are mostly White males varying in age who have been or currently are in a nuclear family with children, regardless of actual marital status. In addition to formal interviews, we engaged in participant observation with workers from the factory at union rallies, parades, town meetings, public presentations, labor temple activities, and political events.

In this chapter, we first seek to establish how Maytag workers appeal to three elements of the "breadwinner ideal" (providing, protecting, and endowing) in constructing masculine identities for themselves as workers and as fathers – noting the symbiosis between the two roles. From there, we discuss the ways in which reaching these ideals has always been challenged by the economic exigencies of working-class life. In this section, we argue that the plant closing further necessitates adaptations among laid-off workers in pursuit of these ideals – in particular, with regard to gendered expectations about childcare and housework. In the third section, "Emasculating the American dream," we discuss the ways in which workers at the Maytag facility understand themselves as workers and fathers in the broader political and economic context – including how they already think nostalgically about American factory production and how they contrast themselves morally to "greedy" corporate executives. And finally, in "Post-Maytag possibilities: masculinity and adaptation," we explore the ways in which these industrial workers have adapted to the realities of the post-industrial world – a world based on mental labor that has downsized their jobs and, ostensibly, their opportunities for realizing the breadwinner ideal.

Providing, protecting, and endowing

In a recent study of American fathers, anthropologist Nicholas W. Townsend (2002) proposes a useful fourfold framework for the analysis of fatherhood, arguing that men gauge their success as fathers by fulfilling a set of overlapping requirements that include providing, protecting, endowing, and instilling emotional closeness (we fold together the last two facets). The descriptions of fatherhood offered by Maytag men speak to the centrality of work to men's self-worth and the interplay between work-bound masculinity and family life. By fulfilling their work obligations, men construct themselves as responsible, moral beings who have earned the right to a wage that enables fatherhood's essential provisions. These conceptions of fatherhood are informed by the breadwinner ideal that provides avenues through which men can navigate their familial responsibilities.

As working individuals, Maytag men describe themselves through a discourse that invokes the recurring moral terminology of hard work, dedication, and honesty. According to Michele Lamont (2000: 19), this moral discourse "helps workers to maintain a sense of self-worth, to affirm their dignity independently of their relatively low social status, and locate themselves above others." In this context, it is not necessarily having the job that makes the man; instead, it is a set of rules by which the job is performed that provides the barometer for the degree to which one is a "man among men." Andy, who started assembling refrigerators at the plant in 1974, had this to say:

> When Maytag was expanding, I used to work about 70 hours a week. . . . I'd say I'm way above average [compared to] a lot of the Maytag workers over there. Some of the people over there, they didn't work overtime. They liked to go out to the bar and have a few beers. . . . I like to work. I like to save my money. I like to better myself. Some of them don't even have a house, and they worked there 15 or 20 years. How are you gonna get ahead in life like that? You can't.

Such statements typify conceptions of "hegemonic masculinity" among Maytag workers. Men attain success in life by means of a strong work ethic, responsibility, and in many cases, sobriety and thrift, all of which enable moral distinctions with less-worthy "others." These understandings of masculinity in their working lives are interrelated with the ways they attend to the duties of being a father. Fatherhood revolves around a series of focal points, none more pivotal than providing. Lamont (2000: 30) writes:

> For workers, being the provider means at a minimum being able to keep necessity at bay, put food on the table, and maintain "a roof over [our] heads." It can also mean providing such luxuries as a trip to Disneyland or an above-ground pool.

Fatherhood is inextricably intertwined with breadwinning and invokes the key moral concept of responsibility, a responsibility to provide regardless of the mother's employment status (Gerson 1993; Lamont 2000). Maytag fathers conveyed an understanding of paternal duty as being partially comprised of providing material goods for the family, whether they are necessities or "extras." Informants spoke fondly of the sorts of things their wages enabled them to provide and do for their families, though the Maytag closing has forced all families to make cutbacks and has made workers question their ability to continue in these roles without significant adaptation.

A Maytag father's wage instilled a sense of security and helped foster a hospitable family environment. An excerpt from a conversation with Derrick, a divorced father of two who obtained a high-paying position on the line eight years ago, illuminates some key issues:

What sorts of things did you do with your kids when you got the new job?

> Vacations, Six Flags, and things like that. Special trips we wouldn't ordinarily have. They come out pretty well at Christmas time too, and when school time comes around, I usually give her extra money for clothes and stuff like that.

How important has that been for you to do as a dad?

> The clothes and stuff I did because they were my responsibility. But it's nice. . . . I gave my ex-wife $500 so she could give the kids a computer, and it's nice to be able to do that. A lot of jobs don't give you that luxury.

Derrick's wage allowed him not only to provide the basics but also to buy his children a computer, to offer extra spending money, and to take them on amusement park excursions. He also acknowledged, though, that he is unsure whether he will be able to maintain his current level of provision.

Similarly, Doug, a married father of two young boys and a worker with 21 years at the Galesburg factory, noted his desire to meet and exceed the provision he experienced as a boy who grew up on "Maytag money," while also recognizing the impending change:

> I grew up on that factory money. My father put 37 years into that plant. And growing up, I can't remember having to do without anything. . . . I may not have had the $120 pair of basketball shoes, but by golly, I had the $70 shoes. And I kind of expected, kind of feel like my kids deserve at least that much – and I'd like to give them a little bit more than what I was given growing up. . . . I kind of think that my kids deserve it. We work hard when we go into work. And when we are there, we work with a lot of

pride. We earn the money that we make there. And quite frankly, I believe that people deserve some nice things. But that's going to change. . . . The boys are going to have to learn – along with Annette and I – the difference between want and need.

Like others we interviewed, Doug thinks of providing in strong moral terms, but at the same time, he recognizes that his layoff will force him to adjust his identity as a provider. At the same time, however, Doug noted his commitment to a continued flow of material necessities and also a willingness to sacrifice his own material well-being – thus imbuing the character of his providing with an element of self-sacrifice and protection.

Providing can also help induce feelings of emotional closeness between fathers and children. To a large extent, according to Townsend, fathers view emotional closeness instrumentally, "as something that would make it more possible for them to protect their children from harm and to endow them with opportunities and character" (2002: 73). Whereas Townsend observed the contributions of fathers to the development of emotionally close relationships with their children to typically be indirect or mediated in some fashion, many of the men we met embraced participatory activity. Some fathers developed emotional relationships with their children through shared activities involving material goods enabled by factory wages. For example, Lou cemented emotional bonds with his son through joint participation in hobbies that would have proved implausible without the Maytag wage:

Me and the boy have always been really close, working on all the projects together. First artwork, then it was custom bicycles, and now he's into old cars. The money from working through this time has always been good; he has seven antique cars. . . . He just turned 21 in December, and there wasn't even any thought of going out and getting drunk on his 21st birthday. Most people can't understand that. The kid has morals. He knows what he wants to do in life; he doesn't want to waste it.

Lou's wages make possible the emotional connection – a shared hobby in this case – through which the process of moral endowment can play out between father and son. In this instance, the Maytag wage allowed for a father to provide material objects, but just as importantly, it opened other possibilities for masculine identity development. From classic cars to hunting and coaching sporting teams, father-and-son activities among Maytag workers enabled emotional closeness and the endowment of gendered character.

What men do as workers shapes their approach to fatherhood. Being a good worker not only facilitates fatherhood by providing wages but also, as our informants maintained, inculcates character. The capability to provide not only the necessities for their families but also the extras (like toys, computers, and vacations) bolsters the extent to which workers feel that they are realizing the breadwinner ideal and, in a larger sense, the American dream. Men use their identities as workers to inform their conceptions of fatherhood and situate themselves above others through their ability to provide, protect, and endow their children with moral character. During the traumatic and transitory period of the layoff, men cling to these ideals of provision and moral endowment but also recognize the ways in which these aspects of hegemonic masculinity are being refashioned.

Parenting and the household division of labor among Maytag families

High-paying factory work has enabled Maytag fathers access to some aspects of the bread-winner ideal. However, because of the realities of working-class economic life, full access to such an ideal has been largely limited to the White middle class, which can better afford to practice it. As some commentators note, working-class families – because of the way they piece together income and share household duties, for example – pioneered post-modern family arrangements long before the terminology describing them came into vogue (Connell 1995; Stacey 1996). For Maytag workers, strict interpretations of a gendered division of labor have proved incompatible with the survival of the family unit, which, as other studies have shown, is often rooted in cooperative efforts in both the public and private realms – though the "second shift" is surely still an everyday reality for more working-class women than it is for men (Hochschild 1989, 2003). Men uphold conventional understandings of gender roles while participating in day-to-day domestic functions by employing contextual gender strategies, capturing "the interplay of ideology and practice that is continually and subtly negotiated as couples divide family labor and make assumptions about who should do which chores" (Coltrane 1996: 52). Losing the stability and high pay of factory work further necessitates crossing traditional gender boundaries and pulls Maytag families further from the archetypal image of a nuclear family with a distinct breadwinner and homemaker – an aspect of the breadwinner ideal that, unlike aspects of providing and moral endowment, working-class families had begun to discard long ago.

Most of the men that we interviewed are, or were, members of dual-earner families with partners and ex-partners that earn salaries comparable to, if not better than, theirs. The occupations in which partners and ex-partners of the informants work include schoolteacher, Maytag laborer, X-ray technician, latchkey attendant, nurse, and after-school program worker. Thus, the act of organizing family work for these families involves much juggling and compromise. Men and women devise schedules that adapt their frantic schedules to household exigencies, often undercutting traditional understandings of the gendered division of labor along the way – though it seems that women in these families shoulder the bulk of responsibility overall.

Childcare is a central concern, and parents are forced to craft creative responses to the hindrances of relentlessly busy daily routines. Luke and his wife, Patty – who also worked at Maytag – alternate shifts so that their off-time corresponded to the times when they had to feed their children and shuttle them to and from different engagements. Luke describes a typical day (he was still working at the factory at the time):

> What we do now is she drops them off at my folks' a little before 3:00 p.m., and I'm there shortly after 4:00 to pick 'em up because they're both in school now. In fact, my wife's in school now because she's getting laid off. . . . I call her about 7:30 a.m. to make sure her and the boys are up and she takes them to school shortly after 8:00 a.m. Her first class is at 9:30 a.m. over in Galesburg, and I think she gets out about 1:30 p.m. So she just flies back here, changes clothes, and goes to work. My parents just pick the boys up from school and take them back to their house. And then she'll go to work until 12:30 a.m., come home, do some homework. It's 3:00 a.m. or 4:00 a.m. before she goes to bed, and I'm getting up about 5:30 a.m. We see each other on the weekends; we leave a lot of notes to communicate.

Luke and Patty's hectic schedule was typical of many of the workers at Maytag who, especially with the educational demands brought about by the plant closure, had to juggle and share childcare and other household duties. This example demonstrates how household and parenting decisions are often not guided by traditional gender roles, and how it is imperative for blue-collar men in dual-earner families to break with gender norms. Nearly all the spouses of the men we interviewed worked outside the home in some capacity, making childcare arrangements contingent upon work schedules and reliant on a combination of babysitters, day-care programs, kin relations, and creative time management to meet their childcare needs.

As with childcare, the men we interviewed typically would adapt to daily household demands, like cooking and cleaning, based on their schedules, though sometimes not without gendered commentary. Men like Lou claimed that cooking responsibilities were simply dependent on work schedules and said it was routine for him to make trade-offs with his wife. Luke, though, because of his wife's busy evening schedule, prepared dinner for his children every night, while breakfast and lunch were his wife's responsibility. While he says he does not mind cooking, Luke's description of his cooking abilities speaks to conventional gendered assumptions about skillfulness in domestic capacities – and he feels comfortable preparing only simpler meals. In his mention of housecleaning, on the other hand, Luke withholds gendered assumptions about the household division of labor. "She does what she can do, and I do what I can do. Sometimes it can pile up. We try to get the boys to help, but they're not real good yet." He laughs.

Don describes his involvement as trying to lend a helping hand, though he is not usually as successful with household tasks as his wife.

> Well, I like to cook a lot, and I make more labor-intensive dishes, so I do that sometimes. I try to help out. She does more than I do as far as the housekeeping, but I try to help out with laundry and that kind of stuff. It's been like that forever because we got married when I was 40 and she was 33, so I'd been living on my own for a long time and you're used to cooking and cleaning and all that. I don't do it near as well as she does, but I try to help out.

While Don is well-versed in the intricacies of housework from his days as a bachelor, now that he's married, he perceives his role within the household as complementary to that of his wife, who he believes to be much more adept. In Don's and other informants' descriptions of housework, the framing of men's essential contributions as de-skilled and supplementary allows husbands and fathers to settle the gendered contradictions inherent in their domestic participation (Lupton and Barclay 1997).

Our informants, more out of necessity than of personal choice, reject strict notions of a gendered household division of labor. Both men and women spend comparable amounts of time cooking and cleaning, and some men – especially those who are still laid off – spend large chunks of time alone with their children. One laid-off worker, Tim, said:

> I'm not a stay-at-home dad, though I have been for a while. At least I'm closer to my daughter. This is an opportunity to get closer to my daughter. Bottom line is that I'm spending more time at home with her now – other than when I'm out looking for a job or doing an odd job or something.

While resisting the label "stay-at-home dad," Tim said of his layoff: "It has a benefit. You got to look at the positives in everything."

Though this boundary-crossing would seemingly pose a stiff challenge to conceptions of manhood, Francine Deutsch argues that "it is permissible for each [parent] to expand his or her role to allow for nontraditional behavior, as long as that behavior is seen as constrained by circumstance and thus not relevant to the core of gender identity" (2002: 132). Informants recognize the economic necessity of their contributions to household-related tasks, and such obligations have, to some degree, become integrated into their normative identities. In these men's characterizations of household work and in their assessments of the value of their contributions, one can glimpse the subtle ways in which gender identities are negotiated. Masculinity among our informants is not defined by singularity; men are neither wholly Mr. Moms nor exclusively breadwinners. Instead, they appropriate elements of each role and apply them contextually – a long-standing working-class adaptation that has been stretched further in a time of job loss. Men may qualify their housework anecdotes but nonetheless participate in reworking the popularly received contours of hegemonic masculinity in the household division of labor.

Emasculating the American dream

The profound changes wrought by the closure of Maytag's Galesburg facility have ruptured the fragile equilibrium of its ex-employees' blue-collar masculine identities. If the American dream is conceptualized as a blueprint for chasing relative success requiring little more of individuals than honest, hard work, then the Maytag factory relocation is uprooting not only production but also working-class conceptions of responsibility, integrity, and survival that enable and define the attainment of this dream (Hochschild 1995). In the eyes of the industrial workers we interviewed, the corporate and political elite have shifted their ideological focus toward "free trade" policies in a move that celebrates the triumph of market forces and seeks to render debates on the ethics of outsourcing obsolete (Blau 1999; Kuttner 1997; Rupert 2000). Deindustrialization is, in effect, subverting the blue-collar discourse on the American dream by disavowing the utility of its constituent values and producing, in return, a feeling of generalized emasculation. The workers we spoke with bemoaned the advancement of free trade, which they see as not only outsourcing their jobs but, at least implicitly, also outsourcing methods for crafting gender identities that have existed for generations of Rust Belt Americans.

Katherine Newman (1999: 175) writes that masculine ideals are now conjured from an idyllic past:

> The experience of a plant closure becomes a focal point for evaluating "the kind of world" the workers inhabit. . . . Workers reflect warmly on the "good old days" when permanent shutdowns were rare. Dwelling on the past, however, is more than an excursion in nostalgia. In reconstructing their own history, remembrance becomes an act of criticism and a source of explanation for why modern America is not what it should be.

Informants raised in Maytag households or who had relatives employed at the plant fondly recalled images of a prosperous Galesburg where one could quit a local factory job and be hired at another by the end of the same day. A comment by Tony romanticizes the past in just this manner:

> I know that . . . this would've been in the mid '60s to late '70s. . . . I've heard many people, my dad for one, say that between Maytag, Gates, Butler, OMC [Outboard Marine Corporation], and Admiral, you could walk outta one factory and get another job the same day.

Renditions of a bustling industrial past occupy significant symbolic space within labor's collective memory in Galesburg. Representing the past in this manner strengthens workers' critiques of contemporary policy by asserting the agency of their occupational ancestors – and thus their own – as integral to the development of the United States we know today. Remembering a dignified past is a way for workers to remind establishment and corporate figures that the vast accumulations of wealth by the privileged and powerful have been predicated upon the efforts of men no different than themselves. To outsource their jobs is to dispense with the "backbone" of America. As Doug puts it, "they forgot who put them in the positions they're in, who put their corporations in the position they're in; because without the workers, Maytag is nothing."

In addition to situating their productive contributions historically, workers are quick to defend the talents of the average "unskilled" laborer (Halle 1987). While factory workers are commonly stereotyped as mindless automatons, most informants emphasized personal skills or collective expressions of pride in their productive effort. Andy, a machine maintenance specialist, fondly describes his job:

> I love what I do. I don't see that as a job, I see that as my hobby. I enjoy that tremendously. . . . I repair something, I want it done well. Matter of fact, a lot of the machinery – sometimes I make changes when it comes into the factory. . . . I think I would've been a mechanical engineer if I would have the opportunity to go back to school more, 'cause I can see a machine and I can see ways to make it run better, by looking at it.

Andy's application of mechanical know-how elevates his repair job to a form of skilled labor and cements his self-identification as an irreplaceable worker. The idea of recognizing skill in "unskilled" industrial labor characterizes Rick's comments on comparative work ethic. He describes the workforce at Maytag:

> Yeah, there's a lot of intelligent people, more intelligent than the company thinks. They think you don't know anything. Well, I don't claim to be the smartest person in the world, but a lot of 'em know a lot more than the foremen and supervisors do. If you tell it to [the supervisors], or explain something, or bring up an idea, they don't like it because they didn't think of it.

Rick is quick to point to the intelligence and ingenuity of his co-workers, and his remarks suggest that individual smarts and inventiveness frequently surface in an occupation as seemingly menial as work on an industrial line. As Lamont (2000: 26) puts it, "work becomes an occasion to display competence and a source of pride. Furthermore, the mastering of work . . . is one of the means unskilled workers have to gain a sense of autonomy and control in the workplace."

Corporate decision-makers have shunned the worker as craftsman model in favor of productivity-boosting scientific management measures. Workers view "lean and mean management" and "speeding-up" of production as detrimental to making "quality American products." Rick describes some of these measures:

> They call it "continuous improvement," what the Japanese did. . . . If there was 80 people on this line, they cut it down to 50. A lot of people started getting hurt, because they were doing the same amount of work in the same time. . . . We kept cutting back, more people are getting injured, more claims for lost time being off, and then . . . they're gonna push you to the limit to get all they can.

Workers commonly spoke of the devaluation of individual contribution and safety in the production process at Maytag – a company whose corporate management was steeped in Midwestern tradition and values until recently, according to both workers and local managers in Galesburg. Indeed, contemporary management in the global economy favors a cost-conscious time discipline at the expense of employee well-being and tradition (Newman 1999).

At the heart of the problem, according to the informants, are corporate strategies that deny the vaunted tradition of American business. According to Newman, workers in a deindustrializing economy place blame in a manner informed by interpretations of a shared cultural heritage:

> If we forsake our traditions, particularly those that have to do with craftsmanship, with pride in what we produce, we will reap a sorry harvest of confusion and eco-nomic disarray. . . . [T]he country must remember on whose backs the industrial preeminence of America was built, and honor their contributions by continuing to implement the values that "made us great."
>
> (1999: 197)

Luke, pinning blame on corporate management, echoes this sentiment:

> I very much blame and hold accountable the board of directors. The members that have sat on that board for a lot of years have grown up with the Maytag heritage, and for them to turn their back on that is just amazing.

For Luke, Maytag's decision to relocate to Mexico is all the more inexcusable in light of the fact that members of its board have experienced the company's historical ascent to success, sharing trials and tribulations in an indirect way with employees.

Maytag workers returned time and again to the theme of disloyal corporations that sold out their commitments not only to quality and tradition but also to their community and country. Tim, 38, who, like others, described himself as a very loyal employee, said:

> I could say that Americans stand by each other, but I can't say that no more about the business end of it, because that's the corporate world, you know; we're not in the same world no more. It's becoming the rich society part, and the lower part like me, you know. I'm the peon, and they're the people who direct the show, basically. . . . We actually make the company . . . not the execs – they don't contribute nothing into that product.

Tim's comments underscore the perceived distinction between the golden age of corporate integrity and the contemporary global paper chase that disregards the core values these men hold dear.

Related to these changes in corporate management is the decline in organized labor's power, something about which many workers commented. Indeed, Local 2063 of the International Association of Machinists and Aerospace Workers – the once-strong union of refrigerator assemblers in Galesburg – is now defunct. Before the plant closing, however, the union organized a rally at the Maytag shareholders' meeting in Newton, Iowa; staged Labor Day parades and protests; and managed to garner significant national media attention to their cause. At the events, fiery speakers, including senatorial candidate Barack Obama, derided corporate decision-makers and praised "working people" and "working families." While there was a palpable sense of solidarity at these events, the word "class" was conspicuous in its absence. Workers were clear about who and what to blame, but at the same time, there seemed to be a pragmatic recognition that Local 2063 – like many others – would soon no longer serve to focus and pursue the class interests of its formers workers, leaving them scattered and unorganized.

The ways in which workers make sense of deindustrialization through the attribution of blame sheds light upon the struggle over the definition of the American dream and working-class understandings of manhood and fatherhood. If multinational corporations and their political allies continue to erode or at least redefine the American dream, the ties between work, gender roles, and family life will have to be negotiated anew. Dave elucidates some of the anxieties associated with this new era:

> There was this covenant: I'm going to come in there, and I'm going to do everything I can for you and, in return – you know, I've worked hard and I've played by the rules – here's what I'm going to get. . . . In reality, what's happening is, while American workers are *the* most productive workers in the world – and nobody disputes that – their work is being taken away from them. . . . [Y]ou're just struggling to keep your head above water, and you can't do it.

Work at Galesburg Refrigeration Products, where wages averaged $15.14 an hour for shop floor laborers, enabled men to successfully fulfill the many obligations (as they saw them) of fatherhood, as discussed earlier in the first section. For laid-off workers, not being able to "keep one's head above water" has implications that extend beyond the loss of their job at the plant.

Indeed, the betrayal – as workers describe it – of American political and corporate leaders translates directly to specific anxieties about emasculation at home. Some informants felt the very essence of their command over the institution of family to be threatened, and all remained steadfast in their desire to preserve it. Luke commented:

> I've gotta keep my kids healthy. My kids are most important to my wife and I. My family, somehow I've gotta keep my family together. I'm not gonna close any doors. . . . I refuse to say that I'm not going to do this. There's a hog plant here in Monmouth, and trust me, it's not one of my choices to go do, but I'm not going to say that I won't. I've got to keep the family together.

To allow the family to disband in the wake of the plant closing would breach the commonly understood fatherly code and undermine a core aspect of the American dream as these men understand it. And Luke's affirmation of his fatherly charge reflects the anxiety surrounding that possibility.

Several men reported depression, increased family conflict, or irritability in interactions with their children since the layoff and directly related these problems to uncertainties related to fulfilling their obligations in their families. Tony conveyed his fears in terms of the protective facet of fatherhood:

> I started thinking I've got two kids to put through school still, and they're gonna need health insurance. . . . [H]ealth insurance is a big thing. One major accident or something like that and you're in debt forever. That was one of the biggest [concerns] as far as my kids.

While Tony is worried about his own long-term future, the loss of his protective capabilities via insurance is the most urgent concern. In fact, some workers planned to go without health insurance for themselves as long as they could maintain it for their children.

The downsizing of opportunities for masculine provision among these workers leaves some confused about the lessons that they, as moral teachers, can impart to their children. Doug reflected on the applicability of the moral lessons his father had conveyed to him about work and responsibility, saying:

> I've always taught the youngsters that if you work hard and play by the rules, then things will work out. Well, we've worked hard and we've played by the rules, and you see what's happening to us. It used to be, if you worked hard, you'd get the golden nugget in the end. That might be a fairy tale, but that was always my fairy tale.

Like others', Doug's fundamental beliefs about being a responsible worker and a "good man" have been undermined. Consequently, his status as a masculine teacher and role model for his two sons has been undermined as well – and he blames the corporate and political elite for these changes.

The feelings of loss and betrayal hint at the end, these workers indicated, of a satisfying manhood forged from the pursuit of the American dream, organized around family, and informed by the breadwinning ideal. Maytag workers invoke a shared historical memory to mitigate the vicissitudes of post-industrial life. Memories of a prosperous industrial past characterized by company loyalty and a celebration of craftsmanship (both of which engendered American economic might) stand in sharp contrast with what Connell (2000: 51–52) has termed a "transnational business masculinity" characterized by "increasing egocentrism, very conditional loyalties (even to the corporation), and a declining sense of responsibility to others (except for purposes of image-making)."

Post-Maytag possibilities: masculinity and adaptation

It is clear that the masculine identities crafted by these downsized Maytag workers require complex adaptation and negotiation as they abruptly enter the post-industrial world, left to fend for themselves in an area that is now almost completely devoid of factory work.

A "neoliberal discursive style" (Goldstein 2002: 236) that individualizes the roots of out-sourcing and shifts causality away from social and economic structures permeates post-industrial life, forcing masculinity into new spaces and conditions (Maskovsky 2002). Men are encouraged, for the good of their families, to dispense with their antiquated blue-collar identities and embrace a new "culture of the mind" (Dudley 1994) by retrain-ing for employment in work outside the factory. Though all the laid-off workers we interviewed vowed to continue to fulfill their obligations as men and as fathers, not all workers accept retraining as the means. In fact, the men we spoke with are confronting the neoliberal discourse on post-industrial work – promulgated by government employ-ment agencies, private sector employers, the media and others – in varied ways, which speaks to the flexibility and adaptability of seemingly fixed gender identities.

Ambivalence and tension regarding change surfaced often in workers' discussions of retraining possibilities. Laid-off Maytag workers are eligible for federal benefits that allow them to attend school for two years and earn degrees in "growth fields," such as nursing, radiology, and computer networking. For many, the retraining option is consid-ered "a blessing" and key to survival. Andy hopes that schooling will permit him to gain independence:

> I went back to the college before the announcement. . . . I'm taking computer classes right now. . . . I need two more semesters, then I become certified. That is gonna give me somewhat of an independence, because I don't have to rely on nobody for a job. I'm kind of going to be my own consultant. I'm gonna be working in the computer field, and I'm gonna be my own supervisor.

It has become apparent to Andy that the type of stability he has achieved over the course of his Maytag career can no longer be sustained. Though he buys into the neoliberal pre-scription for post-industrial success (i.e., increasing one's human capital), Andy claims that the lessons he passes on to his kids will be culled more from his life as a factory worker. Since the type of stability Andy has achieved over the course of his Maytag career can no longer be sustained, he accepts sole responsibility for his family and quietly plans to shoulder a heavier burden and anxiously awaits the possibility of job independence.

Though most men viewed retraining as a viable (and, in some cases, exciting) option, their nervousness over challenging mental work and competition with younger students reveals a double-edged sword (Dudley 1994; Rubin 1994).

Eric and his wife, Jodie, summarize these tensions about "starting over" in school:

Eric: People with 26, 28 years [in the factory] are afraid to go back to school and sit with young kids.
Jodie: Everything's still in [their] heads; [older workers] are gonna have to start over, kindergarten kind of thing.

Maytag workers have grown accustomed to earning a decent income through the physi-cal labor of industrial manufacturing, though they are now being forced to embrace an unwelcoming "culture of the mind" in order to survive. In this context, mental labor can have an emasculating effect as workers re-enter classrooms that have long lived only in distant, and oftentimes bad, memories to compete with younger mental workers. The ref-erence to *kindergarten* underscores this point; retraining workers are no longer men with jobs but rather "children" relearning material that they long ago discarded in favor of the security of a Maytag check. In addition, much of the training and work in government-defined "growth fields" is in traditionally feminine occupations, such as nursing. Tim, in a crude but telling rejection of the possibility of becoming a nurse, said, "I wouldn't want to wipe somebody's ass."

When considering the future prospects of Maytag employees, it is easy to lump their choices into two categories: those retraining and those seeking another factory job outside the area. Though adapting one's conception of masculinity to the evolving world of mental work may be fast becoming the normative choice, some men attempt to pursue alternative options to reaffirm their masculine selves and march into the future on their own terms. Lou, an aspiring artist, believes he has an advantage over those who choose the educational route:

> When I tell you that I'm gonna try and do all the artwork I can, I'm not gonna rely on her income and be the starving artist. I worked construction for 25 years before I went in there. I've got an advantage over most of the people out there that're gonna go retrain. . . . I'm in contact with enough people in construction around the area that if that's what I have to do, I'll do it. . . . I'm not a 30 worker [at Maytag]; this isn't all I've ever done. . . . This retraining is a stalling thing for some.

Instead of relying upon retraining, Lou is satisfied that his diverse work history will enable him to find gainful employment. Though his wife has a stable job as an X-ray technician, Lou would feel remiss in his family obligations if the calling that most appeals to him – art – does not provide an income comparable to his factory work. Lou's future success is contingent upon his deployment of a versatile masculinity, one that seizes upon his resourcefulness to earn a living without having to retrain.

Tony, also resisting the demands of the post-industrial world, said this:

> I've got a heating and air-conditioning background; I started doing that in '85 and did that all the way up to '96, when I went out there. . . . I enjoyed the type of work I did before that better because there was more challenge to it. I had my own crew, and I would basically figure out how we were gonna run the wiring, the gas piping, the ductwork, the whole nine yards. It was more challenging than standing there, putting screws or shelves in a refrigerator all day long. . . . I like working with my brain. I don't want to be stressed out about what I'm doing, but I at least want to have a challenge.

For Tony, manufacturing is a last resort, something he was forced into by the circumstances of his life. Tony's preferred brand of mental work is, at the same time, a far cry from the white-collar norm. Positioning himself as a blue-collar mental laborer, Tony redefines the parameters of the "culture of the mind" as they have been presented to the laid-off workers. As these examples demonstrate, post-industrial "hegemonic masculinity" need not depend on white-collar aspirations and is often shaped by resistance to imposed change.

The workers with whom we spoke are intimidated by their return to education because they have been away from school for so long, may have done poorly in school while there, and often were not encouraged by their parents to take it seriously. They were expected to pass their classes, graduate, and then get a job and have a family. In fact, many workers spoke of the strong resistance their parents *still* have to higher education, which they see as a way to avoid work, wasteful of time and money, and even self-indulgent. The current generation of laid-off factory workers – if our sample is representative – contrasts itself to the preceding generation and uniformly claims to promote educational values among their children – even if the parents are just learning those values themselves. One man, George, a laid-off forklift driver (and a self-proclaimed "troublemaker" when he was in school), noted the changes:

> That's where the future is headin' for these kids. It isn't, well, I can get out of school, and I don't have to worry about college. I don't have to worry about anything other than [getting] out of school and [going] to work – like I did – to start earning a paycheck. They're going to have to have education also. And education is not going to be a matter of associate's degrees. They're all going to have to have bachelor's degrees. . . . [Companies are] going to take the people with all of the education; the guy that can sit there and [solve] this problem in the least amount of time, he's the one that's going to get the job.

Fathers spoke often of having renounced the traditional idea of encouraging their children to follow in their footsteps at the factory (as they had been encouraged when they were young) in favor of ensuring their children the best education they can afford (see also Weis 1990).

Due to financial limitations, however, Maytag fathers spoke frequently and hopefully about college athletic scholarships for their children. By applying their blue-collar ideals of hard work, dedication, and persistence, many see these scholarships as viable avenues into college and back into middle-class respectability – a way to reverse the downward mobility of their families. Andy told his children, even when he was still employed at Maytag, that they would have to seek athletic scholarships to go to college – advice made all the more urgent given his layoff:

> I explained to them that I wasn't gonna be able to send them to college with my wages at Maytag. I said the only way was to get a scholarship. My older son, he played football. I told him he's gotta become the best football player if he wants to be picked up by these schools.

The informants continue to endorse the same moral discourse used to construct their identities as blue-collar workers – hard work, "playing by the rules," sobriety, and responsibility. But given new post-industrial realities, they teach their children to adapt and apply these still-useful traits in new ways in order to forge new identities in the future – and new paths into the middle class.

Prior to the plant closing, Maytag workers aligned their identities as workers and fathers with the hegemonic norms ascribed to the breadwinning male. While rhetorically successful, these identities, if framed as attempts to fulfill hegemonic imperatives, were always substantively incomplete manifestations of the breadwinner ideal (as discussed in the second section). Whatever the organizing principle that passes for "hegemonic masculinity" at a given moment (in our case, the dutiful provider), it is inevitably contested and undermined just as it is reinforced. The flexibility of identity is evident as individual fathers mold masculinity's commandments to the complicated, often contradictory conditions of lived experience. As deindustrialization hits home, a chapter closes on the forms of masculine identity that carefully intertwined work and fatherhood, but new strategies and adaptations point to the historical fluidity of what constitutes a gendered identity. Global economic restructuring has left men laid off to contend with the ascendancy of neoliberalism and a work regime notably lacking in high-wage, full-benefit manufacturing jobs or similarly compensated work. The response has not been, as some might expect, an invigorated masculine fundamentalism. Cut adrift from the regulatory functions of the breadwinning regime, some men choose to embrace the individual-oriented, free market dogma of retraining, while others seek college degrees or entrepreneurial alternatives – and some relish the opportunity to simply be dads to small children, if only for a short while. What is clear, however, is that the new regime of work doesn't have a place for these men if they do not refashion themselves as both workers and as men.

Discussion questions

1. How are the roles of a man as worker and father related for the men in the study?
2. In terms of emotional bonds with their families, how did the men's role as worker enable them to fulfill the roles of protecting and endowing for their children?
3. According to the authors, how has the strict gendered division of labor played out in working-class households?
4. How did the men in the study adapt their notions of masculinity and gender roles in order to cope with the changing circumstances in terms of employment?

Note

1 We use the actual names of the city, the factory, and the workers who gave us their permission to use their names. For other workers, we use pseudonyms. The interviews and fieldwork used for this chapter are part of a longitudinal, fieldwork-based project in both Galesburg, Illinois, and Reynosa, Mexico.

References

Blau, Joel. 1999. *Illusions of Prosperity: America's Working Families in an Age of Economic Insecurity*. New York: Oxford University Press.

Bluestone, Barry, and Bennett Harrison. 1982. *The Deindustrialization of America: Plant Closings, Community Abandonment, and the Dismantling of Basic Industry*. New York: Basic Books.

Coltrane, Scott. 1996. *Family Man: Fatherhood, Housework, and Gender Equity*. New York: Oxford University Press.

Connell, Raewyn W. 2000. *The Men and the Boys*. Berkeley: University of California Press.

Connell, Raewyn W. 1995. *Masculinities*. Berkeley: University of California Press.

Coontz, Stephanie. 1992. *The Way We Never Were: American Families and the Nostalgia Trap*. New York: Basic Books.

Cowie, Jefferson and Heathcott, Joseph. 2003. *Beyond the Ruins: The Meanings of Deindustrialization*. Ithaca: IRL Press.

Dandaneau, Steven P. 1996. *A Town Abandoned: Flint, Michigan, Confronts Deindustrialization*. Albany: State University of New York Press.

Demos, John Putnam. 1986. *Past, Present, and Personal: The Family and the Life Course in American History*. New York: Oxford University Press.

Demos, John Putnam. 1997. "Oedipus and America: Historical Perspectives on the Reception of Psychoanalysis in the United States." In *Inventing the Psychological: Toward a Cultural History of Emotional Life in America*. eds. Joel Pfister and Nancy Schnog, 63–78. New Haven: Yale University Press.

Deutsch, Francine M. 2002. "Halving It All: The Mother and Mr. Mom." In *Families at Work: Expanding the Bounds*. eds. Naomi Gerstel, Dan Clawson, and Robert Zussman, 113–138. Nashville: Vanderbilt University Press.

Dudley, Kathryn Marie. 1994. *The End of the Line: Lost Jobs, New Lives in Postindustrial America*. Chicago: University of Chicago Press.

Ehrenreich, Barbara. 1989. *Fear of Falling: The Inner Life of the Middle Class*. New York: HarperCollins.

Gerson, Kathleen. 1993. *No Man's Land: Men's Changing Commitments to Family and Work*. New York: Basic Books.

Gilmore, David D. 1990. *Manhood in the Making: Cultural Concepts of Masculinity*. New Haven: Yale University Press.

Goldstein, Donna Meryl. 2002. "Microenterprise Training Programs, Neoliberal Common Sense, and the Discourses of Self-Esteem." In *New Poverty Studies: The Ethnography of Power, Politics and Impoverished People in the United States*. eds. Judith Goode and Jeff Maskovsky, 236–272. New York: New York University Press.

Griswold, Robert L. 1993. *Fatherhood in America: A History*. New York: Basic Books.

Gutmann, Matthew C. 1997. "Trafficking in Men: The Anthropology of Masculinity." *Annual Review of Anthropology* 26: 385–409.

Halle, David. 1987. *America's Working Man: Work, Home, and Politics among Blue-Collar Property Owners*. Chicago: University of Chicago Press.

Hathaway, Dale A. 1993. *Can Workers Have a Voice? The Politics of Deindustrialization in Pittsburgh*. University Park: Pennsylvania State University Press.

Hochschild, Arlie R. 2003. "The Fractured Family." In *The Commercialization of Intimate Life: Notes From Home and Work*. ed. Arlie R. Hochschild, 161–171. Berkeley: University of California Press.

Hochschild, Arlie R. 1989. *The Second Shift: Working Parents and the Revolution at Home*. New York: Viking.

Hochschild, Jennifer L. 1995. *Facing Up to the American Dream: Race, Class, and the Soul of the Nation*. Princeton: Princeton University Press.

Kimmel, Michael. 1996. *Manhood in America: A Cultural History*. New York: The Free Press.

Kimmel, Michael. 2000. *The Gendered Society*. New York: Oxford University Press.

Kuttner, Robert. 1997. *Everything for Sale: The Virtues and Limits of Markets*. New York: Knopf.

Lamont, Michèle. 2000. *The Dignity of Working Men: Morality and the Boundaries of Race, Class, and Immigration*. New York: Russell Sage Foundation.

Linkon, Sherry Lee, and John Russo. 2002. *Steeltown, U.S.A.: Work and Memory in Youngstown*. Lawrence: University of Kansas Press.

Lipper, Joanna. 2003. *Growing Up Fast*. New York: Picador.

Lupton, Deborah, and Lesley Barclay. 1997. *Constructing Fatherhood: Discourses and Experiences*. Thousand Oaks, CA: Sage Publications.

Maskovsky, Jeff. 2002. "Afterword: Beyond the Privatist Consensus." In *New Poverty Studies: The Ethnography of Power, Politics and Impoverished People in the United States*. eds. Judith Goode and Jeff Maskovsky, 470–482. New York: New York University Press.

Mishel, Lawrence, Jared Bernstein, and Sylvia Allegretto. 2005. *The State of Working America, 2004/2005*. Ithaca, NY: Cornell University Press.

Modell, Judith. 1998. *A Town without Steel: Envisioning Homestead*. Pittsburgh: University of Pittsburgh Press.

Newman, Katherine S. 1993. *Declining Fortunes: The Withering of the American Dream*. New York: Basic Books.

Newman, Katherine S. 1999. *Falling From Grace: The Experience of Downward Mobility in the American Middle Class*. New York: Free Press.

Pappas, Gregory. 1989. *The Magic City: Unemployment in a Working-Class Community*. Ithaca, NY: Cornell University Press.

Rotundo, E. Anthony. 1993. *American Manhood: Transformations in Masculinity from the Revolution to the Modern Era*. New York: Basic Books.

Rubin, Lillian B. 1992. *Worlds of Pain: Life in the Working-Class Family*. New York: Basic Books.

Rubin, Lillian B. 1994. *Families on the Fault Line: America's Working Class Speaks about Family, the Economy, Race, and Ethnicity*. New York: HarperCollins.

Rupert, Mark. 2000. *Ideologies of Globalization: Contending Visions of a New World Order*. New York: Routledge.

Sennett, Richard. 1998. *The Corrosion of Character: The Personal Consequences of Work in the New Capitalism*. New York: Norton.

Stacey, Judith. 1996. *In the Name of the Family: Rethinking Family Values in the Postmodern Age*. Boston, MA: Beacon Press.

Townsend, Nicholas. 2002. *The Package Deal: Marriage, Work and Fatherhood in Men's Lives*. Philadelphia: Temple University Press.

Weis, Lois. 1990. *Working Class Without Work: High School Students in a De-Industrializing Economy*. New York: Routledge.

Wilson, William Julius. 1987. *The Truly Disadvantaged: The Inner City, the Underclass and Public Policy*. Chicago: University of Chicago Press.

Wilson, William Julius. 1996. *When Work Disappears: The World of the New Urban Poor*. New York: Knopf.

Wolff, Edward N. 1995. *Top Heavy: The Increasing Inequality of Wealth in America and What Can Be Done about It*. New York: The New Press.

Chapter 36

My encounter with machismo in Spain

David D. Gilmore

Original to a previous edition of this text. Courtesy of David D. Gilmore.

Let me begin with a disclaimer: When I first went to Spain as a novice anthropologist in 1972, I did not choose machismo to study. On the contrary, machismo chose me – I had no choice. This happened during my dissertation fieldwork in the southern region of Andalusia. Being a child of the '60s and influenced by the then-fashionable mix of Marxism and do-goodism, I originally went to Spain with the intention of studying (and possibly ameliorating) the "objective realities" of what I saw as oppression under the Franco dictatorship. I envisioned a scholarly thesis on weighty matters like class consciousness and workers' rights, with an emphasis on the clandestine labor organizations that were springing up as Franco breathed his last (he died in 1975, and the dictatorship fell soon afterwards). However, while collecting data, I soon ran into a practical problem. While conducting informal discussions and interviews, I was constantly bombarded by verbal static emanating from my subjects. By "static" I mean background noise, chatter – talk about tangential topics. Since this noise struck me as irrelevant, rather like radio interference, I largely ignored it. As I soon learned, this was a mistake.[1]

One person's noise can be another's symphony. When interviewed, people would get bored talking about politics and, to liven things up, would launch into gratuitous pronouncements about more interesting subjects. The most common detour was the subject of sex, perhaps not surprisingly, since most of my informants were unmarried youths. Usually, these impromptu digressions would lead to colorful accounts about the nature of male and female, about what a "real man" should be, "being macho," and so on. Often, the talk would segue into mild boasting about how they, the Andalusians, were superior to other Spaniards in matters romantic, and certainly better than benighted foreigners such as myself. As often happens to anthropologists – and despite my intentions – I became sidetracked by the "subjective reality" of sex talk, and eventually, the static took on a life of its own. After returning to the United States, and for years afterward, I tried to avoid thinking too hard about it, dismissing it all as youthful braggadocio. But after having written some dull treatises on politics, I returned to what had imposed itself upon me so urgently in the field. In what follows, I will explain how – and what – I learned about Andalusian "machismo."

DOI: 10.4324/9781003398349-41

Of course, I learned other things. For example, I learned to appreciate the good old anthropological "culture concept," about which I had been indoctrinated in graduate school. While this hoary tenet has been questioned recently by some postmodernists (see Abu-Lughod 1993), it has withstood the test of time. As anthropologists have said, *culture* consists of shared understandings and standards held by a group: a body of mutually agreed-upon values, norms, and beliefs that work as a nonverbal grammar and also as a source of identity, of ethnic pride, and of group unity. As I quickly learned in Andalusia, people's notions of manhood (and of its converse, femininity, too, of course) were very different from my own and, indeed, contrasted starkly with what I had read about other cultures elsewhere. Moreover, these ideas about gender were not only widespread but were also enthusiastically shared by both sexes, were consensual among all ages, and were repeated by different people in different settings. Ideas about what a "real man" was, especially, were cherished by virtually all the men I knew and by many women as well. These ideas made up a very substantial part of Andalusian culture.

It is also important to point out that whatever discrepancies might exist between these ideas and my own cannot be ascribed to differences in social class between me and my informants, as a critic has meretriciously alleged (Pina-Cabral 1989). Nor are these differences due to a deficient understanding about working-class culture in my own Native America. I can say this because most of my informants in Spain were not, in fact, working-class at all. Rather, they were similar to me in status, being mainly middle-class professionals, and they possessed an impressive vocabulary to articulate their ideas. Some were college graduates; one or two, like me, were in graduate school. Among them was a sprinkling of high school teachers, menial workers, and farmers. A few were peasants, and one or two were illiterate landless laborers who joined our almost-nightly talk sessions. So I was dealing with a decidedly cross-sectional sample, with an emphasis, if anything, on the middle classes – a social setting rather analogous to my own in America.

As these nightly gabfests would gather steam, many of these friends and acquaintances would join in until we were often 20 or more guys chewing the rag, or "cutting the cloth," as they say in Spain. The conversations took place during long walks in the village park or in the bars where village men relax for hours, sipping wine or coffee, playing cards or dominoes, and of course, chatting. Sometimes, the men who were absent at one occasion would confirm my written notes later. All this continual affirmation led me to conclude I was dealing with a "cultural fact," because when one encounters a point of view so widely and repetitively expressed, it constitutes something objectively real, a fact. There was, of course, some variation of opinion, as there is in any society, but such variations were of degree, not of kind. Agreement on the main principles of a proper manhood was virtually unanimous.

Virility, valor, virtue

Let me provide some ethnographic context. The largest region of Spain, Andalusia makes up most of the southern part of the country. In many ways, it is similar to America's "Deep South," or the Mezzogiorno of Italy, being a largely agrarian region, socially and culturally conservative compared to the rest of the country, and having its own distinctive accent, a "southern drawl," and well-known for cultural peculiarities, in this case peculiarities from which other Spaniards often disassociate themselves as being backward or dubious. In the northern regions of Castile or Catalonia, for example, many people say that Andalusians are lazy, carefree, given over to wine, song, and sloth – the usual prejudices about "southerners" one encounters in Europe and America. Andalusia is also the region most closely identified with the stereotypical Spain of the travel posters: bullfights, flamenco music, raven-haired maidens with roses in their teeth, perfumed gardens, mantillas, and of course, Don Juanism. Remember that the original Don Juan story was set by Tirso de Molina (1571–1648) in Seville – the unofficial capital of Andalusia.

First, before recounting my experiences, let me emphasize my main point: *machismo* and *manliness* are not synonymous in Andalusia. Although this region has been identified in some accounts as the epicenter of so-called Hispanic machismo, supposedly transported thence throughout the Spanish-speaking world by Andalusian immigrants (see Gonzalez-Lopez and Gutmann 2005), nevertheless, the manhood code here is complex and cannot be reduced to a single factor. What I propose to do here is to explain how the bundle of manhood traits imposed itself on my ethnographic radar in Spain, then to describe the components of the manhood code, "machismo" being just one, and finally, to compare this package briefly with such codes elsewhere. The reader will immediately gather that the so-called machismo so tirelessly invoked in social science in actuality represents a wide diversity of forms, all of which have something in common and are therefore amenable to comparative analysis. What is needed here is what Ward Goodenough, borrowing from descriptive linguistics, has called the method of "componential analysis." This method involves breaking down a semantic category into its constituent parts and analyzing each independently before putting the whole together again as an overall pattern, a Gestalt. Goodenough (1970: 72) explains:

> [A] linguistic expression may be said to *designate* a class of concepts or images. It may be said to *denote* a specific image or subclass. . . . And it may be said to *signify* the criteria by which specific images or concepts are to be included or excluded from the class of images or concepts that the expression designates. What is signified consist of the definitive attributes of the class, the ideational components from which the class is conceptually formed. Componential analysis is a method for forming and testing hypotheses about what words signify.

Briefly put, the main components of Andalusian "manhood" (that is, the subclasses constituting native ideas) are three, which I will here gloss as *virility*, *valor*, and *virtue*. Each has its own linguistic label in standard Castilian, which will be discussed in turn as we proceed. I begin by describing some eye-opening experiences from my first few months in the rural town of Fuentes de Andalucía – my research site in Spain since 1972. Fuentes is a small farming pueblo (population 7,500) located in Seville Province, about equidistant between the provincial capitals of Seville and Cordoba. The ethnographic present used here is the decade between 1972 and 1982. Since then, of course, it has all changed with modernization – but that is a subject for another study.

Virility: the macho

Attending to my original research program, I made friends with a number of young men (and a few women), usually seeking them out in their favorite bars or taverns. When one meets regulars in any bar in Spain, one is very soon introduced to a large coterie of friends and friends of friends – a kind of spontaneous expanding network that makes fieldwork in Spain both easy and pleasurable. I found that, very often, my queries about subjects of concern to me would be sidetracked by more immediate interests of my friends, as I suppose is true in any social setting. But I found this to be true especially where a comparison or analogy, often invidious, could be drawn between their own self-image and what they attributed to *forasteros*, outsiders. The latter term included not only strangers from other parts of Spain but also foreigners from what they referred to as "the north," meaning, northern Europe and North America. Such exotics were referred to as *nórdicos* (Nordics) in what anthropologists nowadays call an invocation of "the other," that is, the formulation of a stereotype as a straw man. Although not a *nórdico* by ethnic persuasion, I became their resident representative from this mysterious world, which was to them an unofficial sounding board for their native Andalusian habits and customs.

One evening, I was sitting in a bar with about ten friends, talking as usual about why Spain "is different," as the travel posters say, when the conversation turned to the influx of European tourists on the Costa del Sol, that is, the Spanish beach resorts – a hot topic and one that gave grist to the mill for judgmental comparison. The ensuing conversation turned on the point of supposed characterological differences between the nórdicos and the Andalusians. Something they had noticed keenly was the behavior of the foreign men on the crowded resort beaches. The nórdicos, they observed, would sit quietly amongst scantily dressed tourist women and "do nothing" – an egregious act of omission which proved the inherent superiority of the Andalusians. The logic went as follows.

My friend noted that the northerners who visit the Costa del Sol beach resorts (mainly British, Germans, and Scandinavians) go out to take the sun and swim in the company of beautiful blond women who wear virtually nothing. "Those men," he scoffed, "do nothing. Are they men?" This lack of any reaction at all to the unclothed female he found both notable and bizarre. An Andalusian man would not let such an opportunity pass. A real man must "do something"; a real man answers the call of his manhood. My friend repeated: some remark must be said, some sort of pass made, "something, anything" must be done to acknowledge the opportunity for a *lio*, or romantic connection.

Now, occasionally, the Spanish men observing all this at the beach resorts would converse in broken English with the foreigners in some bar, and this subject would come up. My friends said that the nórdicos would explain that they were "just friends" with these naked girls, a concept that incited incredulity and scorn from the Andalusians. To get the point across, my friends would recite one of their favorite aphorisms. "A man and a woman," they would say, "cannot be friends, unless the woman is very, very ugly and the man very, very foolish (*tonto*)." Explanation: to neglect one's manhood not only qualifies a man for contempt as inert but also, as my comrades emphasized, stupid, "foolish." A shy man is not only unmanly but also brainless and unnatural. Another term they used in this context is significant: weak men are called *flojo*. In Spanish, *flojo* means inadequate, flaccid, weak, or soft. Literal dictionary definitions also include *flabby*, *lax*, *loose*, *slack*, and *sluggish*. Andalusians of both sexes use *flojo* liberally to describe a flat tire, a broken tool, or anything that does not work, often with derisory connotations of debility and perversity. The analogy to sexual impotence is, of course, obvious: a man who "can't get it up," like a dead battery or a punctured tire, is *flojo*. But more, such a man is said to neglect his natural duty to inspire romance and make a *iio*. So even more than merely signifying inadequacy or inutility, *flojo* carries with it a strong whiff of moral disapproval and opprobrium. I detected in all this not only contempt for the moribund nórdicos but also an invidious judgment and a not-so-hidden self-congratulation. There were nationalistic overtones to all this. This piqued my curiosity and naturally provoked further discussions.

I learned that the quality being adjudged here is "being macho" (*ser macho*). Although *machismo* is a perfectly good Spanish word (Castilian nouns take an *-ismo* ending as with the cognate *-ism* in English), it is never used in everyday speech in Spain, except nowadays as an epithet by university feminists. As elsewhere in Hispanic countries, "macho" simply means "male" (Gonzalez-Lopez and Gutmann 2005). It connotes explicitly anatomical maleness, the possession of a penis and testicles. When a child is born, or a farm animal calved, for example, the first thing people ask is, "Macho o hembra?" (Male or female?) "Hembra" means both female and, literally, womb; so the sexes here are initially distinguished by reproductive physiology, as is the case in many societies. But for a postpubescent male in Andalusia to "be macho" (*ser macho*) has a special connotation of living up to the qualities attributed to the male physiology. In Andalusia, being macho means using your anatomical equipment in the expected ways, or at least giving the impression of doing so. Further concrete examples and some colorful illustrations flowed from my friends. Telling the poor deluded nórdico anthropologist about "being macho" was becoming a cottage industry in Fuentes.

A few days later, I was out walking at dusk with a few friends. We came upon a group of about 12 boys, 13 or 14 years old, milling about in one of the central squares of the pueblo. These youth packs are called *pandillas* (cliques or gangs). While there was nothing unusual in that male *pandillas* are often seen lurking outdoors at any time of day or night, my ethnographic alarm bell went off and told me this group was poised for some mischief, which might be of interest. So I made inquiry to my companions. They told me the following. What I was witnessing was the first stage of a traditional adolescent activity called the *abuchear*, a word I later found translated loosely as *shouting, jeering*, or *hooting*. My informants immediately understood what was going on because they had participated in such rituals themselves in their teens. The boys were in fact lying in wait for some unsuspecting and, more importantly, unaccompanied young girl to pass by. When one did, they would rush after her, hollering obscenities, jeering and grasping at her clothing, driving her crying to her home, at which point they would relent and reorganize to repeat the process with another victim. The boys did not physically molest the girls (physical abuse is against the rules), but their victims were usually shaken up and frightened. In one famous case of abuchear, I was told, a girl ran home in tears, her clothes in tatters, and told her father that she recognized the persecutors. Angry and insulted, her father then went to the boy's house to extract an apology from the boy's father; some words were exchanged. But the response of the hooting boy's father remains a classic piece of folklore in the pueblo. Rather than being chagrined or apologetic, the father coolly replied, "Why, thank you for telling about this: that means my boy must be a real macho." He took it as a compliment.

Obviously, the central theme in "ser macho" is the erotic element: by *virility* here I mean pure sexual potency, sexual assertiveness. *Ser macho* implies an adventurous, probing, phallic sexuality that is both predatory and peremptory. My friends consistently defined "macho" in terms of a quantifiable energy stemming from the *cojones*, testicles. When I asked a friend what *macho* meant in a fly-specked bar (he was a university-educated youth), he pointed to two copulating flies on the counter and said, "You see that fly, the one on top? That's what we mean by *macho*." A refrain I heard often touted in these discussions was this: we, Andalusians, are more highly sexed than forasteros – this was offered often as a scientific fact. Andalusians are more potent, more irrepressibly sexual than others; they have larger penises and heftier balls (a legacy, some said proudly, of the Moorish occupation of Andalusia). Indeed, this was the only instance I heard anything complimentary said about "los moros," the generic term Andalusians use for Arabs and Muslims. One of my friends added, "You know, Don David, that's how we Spaniards conquered the Americas: one hand waving the sword, the other the penis!" (I learned later this was a common saying in Spain.) So *macho*, then, means being a sexual conquistador.

The piropo

Further conversations ensued as my friends continued amplifying on what they meant by *macho*. I heard many other local sayings. For example: "Dress a shovel in a dress and we *fontaniegos* [male residents of Fuentes] will gladly make love to it: that's macho." Then there is the venerable tradition called *el piropo*, which remained strong in both rural and urban Andalusia until very recently (Pitt-Rivers 1971: 92). This requires a brief digression. The word *piropo* means a complement or an offering given by a man to a passing woman in public (literally, it means a "ruby"). It can mean a gift or a gallantry of any sort, but in modern-day usage, it refers to a linguistic tradition of cavalier flirtatiousness. In Andalusia, the piropo is a verbal "something," "a spoken gift" or symbolic acknowledgement that a man offers to a comely woman passing by. If a good-looking girl walks by unaccompanied by a man (piropos are off-limits when the girl has a man with her, for obvious reasons of prudence), her sexual allure must be commented upon, even in some abstract sense – "something, anything," as my informants repeated, "must be done." To fail to do something is to be egregiously *flojo*, to be deficient in masculinity. Piropos are expected especially when men are in groups, as each outdoes the other in expressing appropriate lust. I recorded some of these piropos from Fuentes and some from other pueblos; they range from the chivalrous and polite to the ugly and vulgar. For example, a youth, bowing slightly or raising his cap, will say to a passing girl, "I salute your mother, to create such a beauty as you." He may then pucker up and offer a kiss, make lurid lip-smacking noises, or pantomime a dance step. Or if less courtly, he may shout, "Hooray for the brunette [or blonde, or whatever]! Let me hold you in my arms, let me make passionate love to you." The girl always ignores the comment and walks on. If the boy feels he has been insufficiently forceful, he may pursue the girl down the street, issuing further pronouncements, and these can get aggressive and lewd (see Suarez-Orozco and Dundes 1984 for some crude Latin American examples).

Sometimes, when boys from Fuentes traveled to the next town or to a big city where they were less known, their terminology would indeed degenerate into aggressive witticisms and obscenities. However, whatever the words, the symbolic communication of the piropo was always the same. The men told me that the verbal dart was not directed so much at the woman, who, unless an actual prostitute, was always immune and never reacted, as to the general *male* audience: its purpose was to "show that you are a man," to demonstrate virility. A man, they said, needs to show his manhood constantly, to show that he never fails to appreciate feminine pulchritude and that he has no hesitations about it. Otherwise, there may be doubt.

Another American anthropologist, Irwin Press, who was working in the city of Seville at about the same time I was in Fuentes, found much the same thing among relatively sophisticated urbanites. Press notes that a man in Seville feels it necessary to make a piropo in order to express his masculinity publicly, to show "his nature verbally" (1979: 133). Other anthropologists in Spain have collected hundreds of these pronouncements, once again from the poetic to the uncouth. Press collected some colorful examples in his entertaining book on Seville (1979: 133–134). His remarks on this subject are worth repeating at some length:

> Traditionally, the piropo was a statement of admiration to a woman as she walked by. Piropos ranged from the elegant ("The stars and moon are at your feet, along with I, your slave, my pretty!") to the ludicrous ("I worship the mushroom that grows in the shade of the tree which you grace with your presence, beautiful!"), from the simple ("I salute your mother, my beauty!") to the complex. Today's [1979] piropos are more direct. . . .
>
> Jose Maria the painter, thirty-seven years old, married but a year, stands with his buddies at the bar when two shapely but very heavy young women walk by, arm in arm. "Wow! Look at this!" he cries to his friends. "Real juicy!" They run to the door of the bar and José Maria calls out to the girls, "Oh, how sweet this meat is, fitting sepulcher in which to bury myself!" The girls continue on, pretending to hear nothing. "Ooooooo, but I'd like to suck your cunts," he hisses loudly after them, and returns to the bar stool with his approving friends, whereupon the conversation shifts to the vulval virtues of fat versus thin women.

The corollary to such lechery is recognized outside Spain as Don Juanism, personified in the image of the Latin lover, a deathless stereotype which figures prominently in folklore about all the Mediterranean peoples (for vicissitudes of the Italian variant, see Reich 2004). Stereotype it may be, it nevertheless reflects a real, self-appointed, and certainly unapologetic aspect of the masculine self-image in Andalusia. My friends insisted that a real man takes advantage of sexual opportunities regardless of context, and he does so because this is his God-given nature as a man, which he has a sacred duty to heed. So it is often said that one is not a real man who does not at least attempt to seduce an available (unattached) woman, and thus, in consequence, a man and a woman cannot be Platonic friends, unless, as they say, the girl is very ugly or the boy is very foolish. My friends adhered to these sexist sentiments without any self-doubt or squeamishness.

While in Fuentes, my friends would often resort to the abundant local poetry to get certain points across when I was being obstinate or dense. There is an old tradition in Andalusia of reciting oral poetry to hammer home a point, especially that which reflects community themes and concerns. In Fuentes, for example, many local bards (all the poets are men) composed raunchy ditties every year to be sung during February carnival, and they would march around the village with accompanists and shout their lyrics in exchange for drinks. So in keeping with this tradition, my friends decided it would help illustrate local attitudes by reciting salacious carnival songs. I repeat one such exemplary poem in what follows, composed in the 1960s by a most famous carnival poet. In it, a nameless everyman encounters an unchaperoned young girl, called Isabel, out at dusk, seeking to buy milk. Confronted by such a rare opportunity, and being too wily to settle for a mere piropo and too mature for the abuchear, the hero of the piece performs what is expected, maneuvering the maiden into sex in a dark doorway:

Y en la Alameda me preguntó una criada,
Me dijo que si vendía
La leche merengada,
Y yo le dije: 'eso no lo vendo yo,
Pero aquí tengo un tubito
Que apretándole un poquito
Echa leche pa' los' dos.
Vamos ligero que aquí no estamo' mojando;
Vamos a una cada puerta y me la sigues topando.
Y ella me dijo, dice la niña Isabel:
"¡¿Porque me siento un chorrito
Que me coje del ombligo
Hasta la punta de los pies!?"

Once in the park I happened upon
A serving girl, who asked me
If I sold fresh milk.
I answered no, this I do not sell, But better still, I have little spigot here
Which when squeezed a little bit, Will make "milk" enough for both of us.
So let's not tarry here, we might get wet.
Let's go to some doorway
So I can give you what you need.
And then she cries out, does the maiden Isabel: "Oh why do I feel a gushing that
Shakes me from the navel to the toes?!"

– composed by Juanillo El Gato

The song repeats a common analogy made between male "milk" (semen) and breast milk. Perhaps it also reflects the universal male fantasy of the willing rape victim, but despite the crude metaphors, the ditty evoked amusement and approval among my male friends. The innocent young maiden Isabel, not knowing what she wants, must be seduced by the cunning, tricky male. His high-voltage sexuality is uncontainable – a life force that gushes and spurts. It is no coincidence that the original Don Juan story is titled "The Trickster of Seville" ("El Burlador de Sevilla"). For the macho, any means, fair or foul, are acceptable to make a conquest.

A final anecdote will conclude this account, then we will look at other ingredients in Andalusian manhood. When I first went to Spain, I was with my wife, and she frequently accompanied me during fieldwork. One week early in our stay in Fuentes, she returned briefly to the States. She was gone only for about a week. During this time, I was conspicuously alone in the pueblo. My friends regarded this as a trial, for it is thought that without a woman to take care of him, a man is helpless and pathetic. Soon my friends became concerned for my well-being. They conferred among themselves, debated, and finally sent a delegation to my house one evening. "Don David," they said, "now that your wife has been away all this time [three days], you must need a woman. So we have agreed to take you to Carmona [the nearest big town] and to get you a nice, clean whore." When I told them this was unnecessary, they professed disbelief: "No grown man can last for more than one day without a woman. Come on, we'll take you in your car. You drive." They were being merry, of course, but not facetious.

This erotic fixation is the phallic component of manhood, and for simplicity's sake, I call it *virility*. It constitutes the first and most flamboyant symbol of manliness. As well as providing a unitary and global theme to the subject in Andalusia – a shared understanding – it deviates somewhat from other instances of "machismo," such as the North American, so far as I understand it. For most Andalusians, physical power, feats of strength, and bravery are not considered part of "being macho." Indeed, pugilistic prowess, fighting, issuing challenges, or taking silly risks with life and limb, and so on, are highly devalued. In Andalusia, men cherish a deep culture of civility which preludes displays of bravado or belligerence. Similarly, toughness and athleticism, which seem to loom large in America, are scorned as childish and vulgar. Rarely does one see physical confrontations among Andalusians – a fact that other ethnographers working in the area have noticed. In the pueblo of Almonaster (Huelva Province), there exists "a total pro-scription on all expression of overt hostility. There are no angry shouts, scuffles, offenses to property, or even stumbling drunks on the streets" (Aguilera 1990: 13). In Santaella (in neighboring Cordoba Province), "the actual use of fighting is rare and people strongly devalue fighting" (Driessen 1983: 129). The same is true in Fuentes. In 20 years of work-ing there, I never witnessed a single physical fight or even a brief scrap among men. The idea of a "barroom brawl" is anathema to these genteel, courteous folk.

Other "machismos"

Given the preceding text, we should perhaps pause here to take note of the very sali-ent discontinuities between Spanish machismo and the so-called machismos of other places and times. First of all, we have a semantic problem. In my opinion, the ethno-label "machismo," like other sociological words such as "unilinear" or "matrilocal," is in danger of becoming reified aprioristically into a pigeonhole, an example of lexical "butterfly collecting." There are many variants of hypermasculinity codes throughout the world. All of them have something in common, perhaps (because men have to "do some-thing" to prove themselves, there are tests of manliness, etc.); but all have widely different emphases and nuances. It is true that cognate forms have been reported throughout the Spanish-speaking world, especially in Mexico, and so a supposedly monolithic "Hispanic machismo" has been held up as a kind of classic model for comparative purposes (see, for example, Lewis 1961; Ingham 1964: 96). One must point out, however, that even the model of Mexican machismo has been subject to its own critical scrutiny lately and come in for a drubbing as being ethnocentric (Gutmann 1996, 1997). There is also, for example, the Sicilian *maschio* or manliness code (Giovannini 1987: 66), the *rajula* com-plex of swaggering Moroccan youths (Mernissi 1975; Geertz 1979), the violent *wand-nat* concept of Ethiopian tribesmen, and the bellicose *pwara* masculinity cult of the Trukese islanders in the South Pacific (Marshall 1979; for more examples, see Gilmore 1990; Gutmann 1997). Most of these male codes have been explicitly likened to "Mexican machismo" by their observers, and indeed, the ubiquitous use of the Spanish term tends to conflate variants under that vague rubric (for a review, see Gilmore and Uhl 1987).

In most of these variants of machismo, of course, fighting and violence play a big role. For example, in the Truk case, the youths demonstrate their manly *pwara* by kung fu combat and in weekend fistfights, and some Ethiopians show their *wand-nat* in whipping battles and by beating each other up (Levine 1966; Reminick 1982). In Sicily, Sardinia, and Greece, men may engage in violent vendettas and feuds, and may they steal each other's sheep or compete in singing and dancing contests, or engage in verbal duels, and so on (Campbell 1964; Herzfeld 1985; Sorge 2007). But in the Andalusian variety, for whatever historical reasons, violence is specifically excluded from the ideal, and as we have seen, "ser macho" is fixated purely upon erotic prowess and is directed only at women (possibly, the same historical actors have militated also against the violent mafias that one finds, for example, in southern Italy). In other words, an Andalusian man cannot act "macho" with *only* other men present. To be macho in Andalusia is to need a woman as sexual object, a *tertium pro quid*. All this brings us to the second component in manliness, which I call "valor." Here, physical bravery, and, in some extreme cases, even fighting, may play a role. But such behaviors are not part of the Andalusian meaning of "macho."[2]

Valor: bravery

An emphasis on civility limits belligerence in Andalusia to a degree unknown among men in many places. But civility notwithstanding, men in Andalusia are expected to stand up for what they believe in and to show determination in the face of danger, even if this means a fight. But this is a different matter from machismo. It constitutes a totally distinct semantic subclass of manliness, one analogous to what we might call "heroism." In Spain, in casual conversation, they call a man "strong" (*un hombre fuerte*) if he stands up for himself and, specifically, protects his dependents. When a man shows moral courage, they call it "valiant" (*valiente*). Valor constitutes our second component of masculinity. The qualities connoted add up to charisma. Together these criteria have their own name: *hombría* or, simply, "manhood." A man can be valorous and thus have hombría and not be a "macho," and vice versa. *Hombría* was a subject that men were somewhat less enthusiastic to talk about, but it came up in discussions later in my fieldwork, some of which are described next.

First, when my friends and I began conversations relating to courage as opposed to machismo, many resorted to a concrete example of the bullfighter (matador). One must note, the matador does not fight other men but shows – as Hemingway put it in his Spanish stories – grace under pressure. Perhaps the difference between North American machismo, as I understand it, is that for most Andalusians, bravery is not played out in contests with rivals but, rather, against the inimical forces of nature, against injustice, or against adversity in the workplace. An important ingredient here is the sense of duty or obligation. This theme is often conveyed when my friends (male and female) would say that a "real man" was one who worked hard under harsh or perilous conditions and who never complained, never ran away, who was "a hard worker," and who made "sacrifices" for his family. When I spoke to women about masculinity, they often referred to this abstract quality: a real man works hard, they said, never complains, and brings home the bacon. We hear such sentiments in working-class cultures in America and in many other places around the world where men are expected to do their duty (a man's gotta do what a man's gotta do). The word "dignity" (*dignidad*) is often invoked in this context.

Men sometimes compete about hombría, so it can indeed involve contests between men. As a form of heroism, hombría is shown off in multitudinous ways. For instance, in Fuentes, a group of young men, usually after a few late drinks at a bar, will meander down to the municipal cemetery to exhibit their disdain for ghosts and goblins. On their way, the boys will acquire a hammer and a nail or a metal spike pinched from some garbage heap or borrowed from someone's toolbox. After arriving at the cemetery and climbing over the 5-foot-tall wall, they posture drunkenly for a while, then one of them pounds the spike into the cemetery's stucco wall while reciting the following formula:

Aqui hinco clavo	Here I drive in a spike
Del tio monero	Before goblin or sprite
Venga quien venga,	And whoever appear,
Aqui lo espero!	I remain without fear!

The last man to flee wins the laurels as the bravest. Occasionally, I was told, young men may challenge one another to spend the night in the cemetery, but otherwise, hombría is non-confrontational, as in the preceding instance, in which the threat is displaced onto a supernatural object. Men and boys do not fight each other in shows of athletic prowess or even compete much in aggressive sports or games, although young boys do play soccer. One-on-one competition among older men is confined largely to dominoes, cards, competitive drinking, and ironically, generous barroom "inviting," as we saw earlier. The Hollywood "tough guy" had little resonance in Andalusia. "Only Americans and Germans shove each other around like that," the men told me dryly. Of course, Spaniards slaughtered each other during the Civil War, but a line is drawn between the unavoidable violence of war and the civility of peacetime.

Hombría and "honor"

Julian Pitt-Rivers, who worked in Andalusia in the 1940s and 1950s, has perhaps depicted this quality of valor/hombría best: "The quintessence of manliness is fearlessness," he writes, "a readiness to defend one's own pride and that of one's family" (1971: 89). Perhaps the best way to get the idea across is to quote an old Andalusian saying which conveys the image both metaphorically and ironically, in a typical Andalusian inversion: "El hombre como el oso, lo mas feo, lo mas hermoso." A rough translation: "Men are like bears: the uglier they are, the handsomer." What this means is that, unlike women, men are not supposed to be pretty or charming. Rather, a man should be strong, resolute, and determined, and even perhaps a little feisty (I call this "the beauty of the beast").[3] Masculine "beauty" is a moral, not an aesthetic, value, consisting of a man's ability to inspire respect – even fear – in the observer, rather than sympathy or love.

Unfortunately, the emphasis on valor has sometimes been, mistakenly, I believe, conflated with the obsolete notion of a belligerent "honor." For Pitt-Rivers, for example, honor in Andalusia, as elsewhere in the Mediterranean world, is a gender-bound quality, or "sex-linked." Only men have honor. The most important attribute of honor, in this traditional view, is that it forms the main public arena for a competitive masculinity based upon the sexual modesty of one's kinswomen. As Pitt-Rivers (1977: 45) remarks, "[t]he honor of a man is involved . . . in the sexual purity of his mother, wife, and sisters." Another expert on Andalusian male norms and the author of *Metaphors of Masculinity* (1980), Stanley Brandes, seems to concur in his study of a pueblo in nearby Jaen Province. He points out (1980: 75) that

> a woman's sexual purity must be maintained lest her entire family's image be tainted. It is the husband's prime responsibility to control the conduct of his wife and daughter. If the females should go astray, their behavior reflects as much on him as on them.

I found that in Fuentes, it was the mother, not the father, who policed the sexual moral-ity of her daughter, but no matter. One finds similar statements in virtually all the works on Andalusia, rural and urban. Men are like bears in this regard: fierce in defense of self and kin. Most important in all this is the defense of ones' women. This is the one arena in which violence may be acceptable. One recent and well-reported incident will perhaps illustrate this.

In February of 2000, hundreds of men in and around the Andalusian pueblo of El Ejido (Almería Province) went on a violent rampage, attacking immigrant North Africans who had come to their district to take low-paying jobs in agriculture that the newly affluent Spaniards had rejected. This riot was not altogether spontaneous. The men had organized their attack days before and, armed with sticks and clubs, chased, beat, and pummeled Africans throughout the region. The depredations went on, savagely, for three days: one Moroccan man was beaten to death, and many others injured, before the national police intervened to stop the riot. What triggered the incident, according to local accounts, was the rape and murder of a Spanish woman a few days earlier, after which a Moroccan immigrant had been arrested and charged with the crime. Interestingly enough, tensions had been running high between the Spaniards and the North Africans for months, even years, before the riot, but these had never erupted into a full-scale lynch mob attack. Interviewed later, some of the rioters spoke openly about their motives, saying that eco-nomic competition played no role in their anger, but that it was the violation of a local woman by the outsiders that caused them to react. "They can't abuse our women and get away with it," one of the men said with heat, "we're men: we have to do something." Apparently, such motives still play a role in Andalusian male culture.[4]

I finish this section with a final comment about manliness-as-valor. In Andalusia, hom-bría has one additional element, which is probably a political legacy of the Franco dicta-torship. In the waning years of Franco, hombría could be demonstrated by active defiance of the regime, by standing up to the secret police or the paramilitary Civil Guard. It was often shown among workers who organized the clandestine unions and who refused to back down in labor disputes – these acts were praised not only as politically correct but also as manly. Heroes of the labor movement (of whatever class) were called *valiente* and were said to be *muy hombre* (very manly). Charismatic labor leaders, especially those jailed and tortured under Franco, like Marcelino Camacho, the head of the underground Communist Party, were highly praised in this regard, almost as icons of hombría. I found it of interest that, no matter what a man's political viewpoint, most would admit the manliness of an opponent who showed courage in the face of overwhelming odds.

One concrete instance from Fuentes may help. During the years after the Civil War (1936–1939), a famous ex-Republican lived in Fuentes and was known throughout the village by his nickname, "El Robustiano" (his real name was never used as far as I knew). Literally, this moniker means "The Robust One" but can best be rendered as "Hero" or, perhaps more colloquially, as "The Big Guy." He was so called for his height (he was almost 6 feet tall in a land of smallish people) and known for his political savvy and physical courage. After serving in the Loyalist Army and serving a prison term afterward, Robustiano returned to Fuentes and began the militant labor agitation that made him famous. Even while he suffered fierce persecution during the Franco dictatorship, he continued to defy the police again and again, serving numerous prison terms, undergoing torture, both physical and mental. But all the beatings, threats, and blackballing had no effect on him. After each jail term, he returned martyr-like to the struggle. He was also known never to have betrayed a comrade, to have taken beatings with equanimity, and indeed, he won admiration from all sides, including his jailors, one of whom I actually met, who effused about his erstwhile victim. Robustiano developed a huge and active following in the town until his death in 1969 and is remembered to this day (2007) as a "man among men." My friends told me he represented the ideal of hombría, and it was great pity that I never got to meet him (I arrived in Fuentes three years after his death). It also helped his reputation that his wife and three daughters were beyond reproach – chaste and virginal, respectively. Also in his favor was that he had fathered nine children in all, and, most importantly, six sons – a sure sign of virility, because having many sons is, for reasons always unclear to me, a crowning glory of manhood. So here, the man personified both attributes of Andalusian masculinity discussed so far: the sexual and the moral, a paragon of both the machismo and valor components of manhood.

Virtue: manhood and courtesy

Finally, we come to the third and last ingredient in the Andalusian masculinity ideal, which I will call, for simplicity's sake, *virtue*. As I mentioned earlier, the notion of a classical "honor" has little resonance with men in Andalusia today. Nevertheless, townsmen do speak of an analogous criterion, a moral formality, which they reckon to be as important to a man's status as being virile and valiant. This final quality is what they call being "honrado," which literally means honorable, but having the connotation in Fuentes of rectitude and personal probity, that is, it means taking one's obligations seriously and paying back one's debts, and doing so with promptness and dignity. It relates to character and also what we might call "attitude." For example, early in my fieldwork, when I asked my friends if a certain man I knew in town was "honorable" (using the term that Pitt-Rivers made so much of), I was informed that if I meant "honest," then yes, this man measured up. They said, as far as they knew, he paid his debts and he returned favors reliably and courteously. Going further, they noted that, for example, in his regular bar, this man would routinely enter into exchanges of drinks and do his fair share of what they call "*invitas*" (invitations), that is, if someone bought him a drink, he would reciprocate ("invite") them back sooner or later. Honesty of this sort is crucially important to a man's standing, and especially in his circle of peers, wherein lies community judgment. The true measure of virtue in this sense is communicated in what Brandes calls "the estimates of personal decency" (1980: 48). In this sense, it differs little from the standard English "honest" or "creditable." It has little to do with one's sexual prowess and nothing to do with bravery. Nevertheless, it is intimately bound up with manliness and forms a third, independent variable of the Andalusian manhood jigsaw puzzle. The negative pole of honorability is *vergüenza*, or shame. If a man has the requisite quality of shame, that is, has a decent respect for the opinion of others, he complies with expectations and is therefore honorable. The unethical, dishonest man has no shame and callously ignores obligations, thumbing his nose at public opinion. He has a "hard face" (*cara dura*), they say. In this regard, Andalusian notions of decency can be elaborated further as an integral aspect of character. Its internal mechanism and social (thus measurable) manifestation is a punctilious reciprocity, which is usually balanced and predictable. Whether monetary or not, repayments of goods and services are often calculated to an amazing degree of exactitude, but just as often, they are vague and approximate. In any event, returns of favors are carried out on the community public stage, in public places like streets and bars, conspicuously, but always in the spirit of nonchalance, without ostentation, as though the matter were but a trifle. Obviously, reference should be made here to what Michael Herzfeld and others have called "Mediterranean hospitality" (Herzfeld 1989), a common denominator around the Mediterranean and known to the ancient Greeks and modern Arabs. These rituals of generosity are exclusively male. Women never enter the bars except for holidays and are always accompanied by a man. Women do not "invite" in bars or anywhere else; given the conservative sexual code in rural villages like Fuentes, women are not "invited" by unrelated men. Bar invitations are thus entirely male and an integral part of a man's "connectedness" to society and his public face.

Having observed these exchanges and begun to participate in them, I soon became aware that there were many contexts in which men were expected to get involved and, in so doing, to publicly demonstrate trustworthiness. The main context is the arena of the public house (bars, taverns, coffeehouses, casinos, and clubs). Every man in Fuentes has a neighborhood dive where he hangs out for at least three or four hours a day, meets with cronies, palavers incessantly, and does business. Thus comfortably ensconced, he participates in the requisite rituals of exchange. These exchanges look and "feel" casual to the first-time observer yet are deadly earnest. Always accompanying bar convivial-ity are serious rounds of what anthropologists call "tournaments of value" (Appadurai 1986). In Spain, these tournaments of value consist of offerings of drinks and cigarettes, usually accompanied by much backslapping and glad-handing. Although seemingly dis-interested, barroom exchanges are governed by a subtle but ironclad etiquette. While no one would ever say so openly, it is a crass transgression to accept more than a drink or two without reciprocating. As the evening proceeds, everyone makes out more or less evenly in the long run. In the circular movement of commodities, what counts most is the display of disinterested generosity and "playing the game," that is, not holding back. For a man to withhold, to hesitate, to stint, or to respond grudgingly is to court opprobrium as a cheat and a rogue. If a man continually fails to play his part, he is quickly labeled a *sinvergüenza*, a shameless guy. Worse is the *sinvergüenzón* (a big flagrant shameless), someone who is notorious for toadying, no better than a thief. Considering the pervasive-ness of bar gossip, such labeling quickly leads to general censure, and this can sometimes result in social ostracism. Hence, most men voluntarily abjure a calculus of personal aggrandizement in bar society, for it can lead to economic paralysis, since no one wants to cooperate with a *sinvergüenzón*. If a man is niggardly in bars, the logic goes, he will be equally, if not more, untrustworthy in business deals. How all this relates to judgments about manliness is explained next.

When I inquired about what motivated all these little offerings, I was told that the point was not the object given to another but the generosity so evidenced, and that, indeed, generosity was the gold standard by which character was judged. The operative principle involved is "personality." The *fontaniegos* evaluate a man's personality once again on a binary scale as either *abierto* ("open") or *cerrado* ("closed"). Although there can be degrees, I quickly noticed that most men considered the open/closed measure in absolute and oppositional terms, either/or. So when speaking of an absent party, people would usually say that he was either of an "open" or "closed" personality. Such judg-ments were, again, often consensual, rigid, and immutable. One, of course, could be "very open" or "very closed," but not slightly open or closed. (Incidentally, women were never judged by this idiom, as these words would have devastating sexual connota-tions for a woman in a pueblo.) An "open fellow" (*un tio abierto*) is generous to a fault, convivial, gregarious, rapidly reciprocating a favor. A closed guy is sour, stingy, evasive, furtive, louche. Decisions were based largely on simple degree of *social participation*. A man who "gets involved" in the raucous conviviality of the bars and who pays back debts was open; one who kept himself apart, refused to engage, or failed to reciprocate was closed.

All this may seem axiomatic: one finds similar judgments in most societies where men cooperate. However, it soon became clear to me that such evaluations went deeper than character assessment and touched upon a man's reputation as manly or not. A man who stayed away from the bars or who held back his purse or spent "too much time" indoors, avoiding male society, was regarded not only as closed and delinquent, a *sinvergüenza*, squalid, but also as unmanly, as effeminate. One unhappy example will demonstrate this connection between personality and manliness.

There lived an odd fellow in Fuentes named Alfredo Tissot, a commercial broker. I got to know him rather well, since he lived on my street, but he was scorned by my other friends as a recluse and a miser (the Catalan-sounding name did not help). What made him really repugnant was his avoidance of the bars and of men's circles in general. Alfredo was that rarity in Andalusia: an uxorious homebody, a sit-by-the-fire. In consequence, he was a virtually friendless man. Although aware of men's expectations, he resisted them, because, as he confided to me, such goings-on were not only a waste of time but also expensive: he watched his pennies and hated the profligacy of the barroom. So he preferred staying at home with his family – a wife and two adolescent daughters – reading books, watching television, or going over his accounts. I should add that he was a relatively successful businessman, indeed, quite affluent by local standards, and therefore, all the more susceptible to demands and expectations for generosity.

Walking past his house one day with a coterie of my friends, I was treated to a rare tirade that intensified into a crescendo of abuse. "What kind of man is he, anyway," said one, nodding at his sealed and cloistered home, "spending every second at home like that?" The others took up the cue, savaging the loner for his defects, likening him to a "brooding hen" and to a "mother cow" and other female animals. They insinuated a number of character flaws, most egregiously stinginess and furtiveness, misanthropy and avarice; but beyond these surface defects, they alluded to something worse: a failure at man-acting. Intensifying the character assassination, my friends left the domain of the observable and ventured into the realm of speculation, which is common when a man is judged faulty. We proceeded up the street, and the men offered their suspicions about this pathetic scapegoat. It all boiled down, they said, to his failure to be a man. This was demonstrated by his shadowy introversion, his hermit-like, withdrawn lifestyle. When I asked if his self-removal could be attributable to business requirements, I was hooted down with denunciations of "A guy who will not invite, who never goes to the bars!" "He's the worst closed," they continued, "hoarding, never participating, selfish, petty." The others seconded this and began scurrilous speculations as to the deviant's sexual preferences, some insinuating homosexuality or some sordid clandestine perversion which might explain his evasion of manliness. In all this, Tissot was paying the price for his withdrawal from the man's world. Being "closed," he must also be self-protective, introverted, guarded – traits associated with women, who must protect their chastity by social withdrawal and evasion, hence the comparison to hens and cows. One may, of course, appreciate the Freudian symbolism here of the open-closed metaphors with their anatomical suggestiveness without being psychologically reductive about it.

Summary and conclusions

When I first went to Spain, like many foreigners, I was duly impressed by displays of machismo. I soon noted, however, that Andalusian machismo differed from notions of masculinity in my culture (middle-class America) and in many others in its erotic intensity. But the main lesson I learned is not that machismo defines manhood in Spain but, ironically, that one cannot speak of "manhood" in Andalusia by reference just to machismo. Machismo is a necessary, but not sufficient, ingredient in the Andalusian code of the real man. As I have tried to show, being a real man signifies (in Goodenough's term) a complex bundle of behavioral subclasses, the interplay of which results in a carefully cultivated dynamic – a multi-layered system of checks and balances. As I came to understand it, the measure of manliness in Andalusia is a three-fold package, a triumvirate of dos and don'ts.

The first component is *virility* (this is what the Andalusians themselves mean when they speak of macho). It connotes sexual potency – a sexual fire in the belly. Although Americans might call this "machismo" and leave it at that, in Spain it has none of the American overtones of belligerence and risk-taking. The second component is what I have called *valor*. Valor implies intestinal fortitude and tenacity – doggedness in the face of adversity. The final piece in the jigsaw puzzle is a more ambiguous concept which I call *virtue*. In Andalusia, this is measured by a man's enthusiasm in public dealings: his generosity, his honesty, his courtesy, and his participation in masculine pursuits. If a man wants to be truly manly, seducing women is not enough. He must adhere strictly to rules of civility and must engage in lavish public generosity. These rules tend to prohibit or at least limit confrontations among men and put a damper on sexual competitions and misdeeds, so there are built-in inhibitors against antisocial behavior. Each of the three components, virility, valor, and virtue, plays its own necessary role in the evaluation of a "manly man." Each component operates alongside, and in tandem with, the others.

What all this complexity shows, perhaps, is the obvious conclusion that gender evaluations in places like Spain are part of a broader moral calculus which men negotiate on an everyday basis and in a variety of contexts. From this we can conclude that in many societies, Hispanic or otherwise, anyone who wants to understand gender codes must be aware of the context in which judgments are made and must also understand the rules governing personality assessment. Even in a famously macho land like Spain, men do not live by machismo alone.

Discussion questions

1. What does the author argue are the three major components of Andalusian "manhood"? How does each play into being a man?
2. Why did the Andalusian men see the foreign men as "unmanly" for not having some sort of obvious reaction to the scantily clad women at the beach resorts?
3. How do Andalusians define "macho"?
4. Why did the men feel it was important to make a "piropo" in order to make their masculinity publicly apparent?

Notes

1 My fieldwork in Spain, conducted intermittently between 1971 and 2003, was supported by grants and fellowships from the following institutions: the National Science Foundation, the

National Endowment for the Humanities, the H. F. Guggenheim Foundation, the J. S. Guggenheim Foundation, the American Philosophical Society, the Council for Exchange of Scholars, and the Program for Cultural Cooperation between Spain's Ministry of Culture and US universities. I thank these agencies for their generosity.
2 The best monograph on Andalusian machismo is that of Stanley Brandes (1980). For a comparative view from neighboring southern Portugal, see the interesting book by Vale de Almeida (1992). Matthew Gutmann attempts to debunk "Hispanic machismo" as an ethnocentric fantasy or a sexist conspiracy, with varying degrees of success (1996, 1997).
3 For more on the notion of masculine "beauty" and its relationship to concepts of manliness in various cultures, see Gilmore (1994).
4 The riots were reported in all local papers, in the Malaga paper *Correos de Andalucia*, in the Madrid daily *El Pais*, and in the *New York Times*. The quotation is excerpted from interviews taken by the author in October 2006 in El Ejido.

References

Abu-Lughod, Lila. 1993. *Writing Women's Worlds*. Berkeley CA: University of California Press.

Aguilera, Francisco. 1990. *Santa Eulalia's People: Ritual, Structure and Process in an Andalusian Multicommunity*, 2nd ed. Prospect Heights, IL: West Publishing Co.

Appadurai, Arjun. 1986. "Introduction: Commodities and the Politics of Value." In *The Social Life of Things*, ed. Arjun Appadurai, 3–63. Cambridge, UK: Cambridge University Press.

Brandes, Stanley. 1980. *Metaphors of Masculinity: Sex and Status in Andalusian Folklore*. Philadelphia: University of Pennsylvania Press.

Campbell, John. 1964. *Honour, Family and Patronage*. Oxford, UK: Clarendon Press.

Driessen, Henk. 1983. "Male Sociability and Rituals of Masculinity in Andalusia." *Anthropological Quarterly* 56: 125–133.

Geertz, Hildred. 1979. "The Meanings of Family Ties." In *Meaning and Order in Moroccan Society*, eds. Clifford Geertz, Hildred Geertz, and Lawrence Rosen, 315–386. New York: Cambridge University Press.

Gilmore, David. 1990. *Manhood in the Making*. New Haven, CT: Yale University Press.

Gilmore, David. 1994. "The Beauty of the Beast: Male Body Imagery in Anthropological Perspective." In *The Good Body: Asceticism in Contemporary Culture*, eds. M. G. Winkler and L. B. Cole, 191–214. New Haven, CT: Yale University Press.

Gilmore, David, and Sarah Uhl. 1987. "Further Notes on Andalusian Machismo." *Journal of Psychoanalytic Anthropology* 10: 341–360.

Giovannini, Maureen. 1987. "Female Chastity Codes in the Circum-Mediterranean: Comparative Perspectives." In *Honor and Shame and Unity of the Mediterranean*, ed. David Gilmore, 60–73. Washington, DC: American Anthropological Association, special publication no. 22.

Gonzalez-Lopez, Gloria, and Matthew C. Gutmann. 2005. "Machismo." In *New Dictionary of Ideas*, ed. M. C. Horowitz, Vol. 4, 1328–1330. New York: Thomson Gale.

Goodenough, Ward. 1970. *Description and Comparison in Cultural Anthropology*. Chicago: Aldine.

Gutmann, Matthew. 1996. *The Meanings of Macho: Being a Man in Mexico City*. Berkeley: University of California Press.

Gutmann, Matthew. 1997. "Trafficking in Men: The Anthropology of Masculinity." *Annual Reviews in Anthropology* 26: 385–409.

Herzfeld, Michael. 1985. *The Poetics of Manhood*. Princeton, NJ: Princeton University Press.

Herzfeld, Michael. 1989. *Anthropology Through the Looking Glass*. Cambridge, UK: Cambridge University Press.

Ingham, John. 1964. "The Bullfighters." *American Imago* 21: 85–102.

Levine, Donald. 1966. "The Concept of Masculinity in Ethiopian Culture." *International Journal of Social Psychiatry* 12: 17–23.

Lewis, Oscar. 1961. *The Children of Sanchez*. New York: Random House.

Marshall, Mac. 1979. *Weekend Warriors*. Palo Alto, CA: Mayfield.

Mernissi, Fatima. 1975. *Beyond the Veil: Male-Female Dynamics in a Modern Muslim Society*. New York: Schenkman.

Pina-Cabral, João. 1989. "Mediterranean Studies." *Current Anthropology* 30: 399–406.

Pitt-Rivers, Julian. 1971. *The People of the Sierra*. Chicago: University of Chicago Press.

Pitt-Rivers, Julian. 1977. *The Fate of Shechem, or the Politics of Sex: Essays in the Anthropology of the Mediterranean*. Cambridge, UK: Cambridge University Press.

Press, Irwin. 1979. *The City as Context: Urbanism and Behavioral Constraints in Seville*. Urbana: University of Illinois Press.

Reich, Jackie. 2004. *Beyond the Latin Lover*. Bloomington: Indiana University Press.

Reminick, Ronald. 1982. "The Sport of Warriors on the Wane." In *Sport and the Humanities*, ed. William Morgan, 31–36. Knoxville, TN: Bureau of Educational Research.

Sorge, Antonio. 2007. *The Free Highlands: Honour, Identity, and Change in Central Sardinia*. Unpublished Ph.D. diss., Department of Anthropology, University of Calgary, Calgary.

Suarez-Orozco, Marcelo, and Alan Dundes. 1984. "The Piropo and the Dual Image of Women in the Spanish-Speaking World." *Journal of Latin Lore* 10: 111–133.

Vale de Almeida, Miguel. 1992. *The Hegemonic Male: Masculinity in a Portuguese Town*. Providence, RI: Berghahn.

Chapter 37

"Now I gotta watch what I say"

Shifting constructions of masculinity in discourse

Scott F. Kiesling

Reproduced by permission of the American Anthropological Association from *Journal of Linguistic Anthropology*, Volume 11, Issue 2, pages 250–273, December 2001. Not for sale or further reproduction.

Introduction[1]

Recent work in language and gender suggests that gender should not be thought of as a presocial, unidimensional, bipolar category but as a fluid, cultural construction by social actors who use language to "do gender" (see West and Zimmerman 1987; Hall and Bucholtz 1995; Bergvall et al. 1996; Coates 1997). At the same time, research on masculinity has emphasized that there are different kinds of masculinity (Connell 1995) and that the term *masculinity* is itself a culture-bound concept (Hart 1994). Though comparatively little work has focused on the role of language in creating men's gender identity, or how men's identities differ from person to person and situation to situation (see Cornwall and Lindisfarne 1994, Johnson and Meinhof 1997 for exceptions), the new emphasis on gender fluidity suggests that focusing on the variations within "masculinities" and "femininities" may provide a better understanding of the relationship between gender and identity.

This chapter investigates the linguistic strategies that one man uses to create a multitude of identities and shows how these strategies are connected to wider cultural understandings.[2] "Pete" shows authority through expressions of certainty, boasts, taunts, insults, and disagreement. However, these linguistic forms are not static repetitions of a single strategy but creative responses to moves by his interlocutors, their identities, and the speech situation. By investigating how Pete's gender identity shifts as he deploys these resources, this chapter illuminates the processes by which language is used to perform identities.

A theory of gender relations in society and the relationship between language and gender must provide a model of how the tension between structure (or the regularity and expectations of gendered behavior) and practice (the performance of gender) is resolved. There is an emerging consensus that the nexus between structure and practice is located in what Hymes (1974) has called the speech activity or speech event. This view has been illustrated in analyses of language in cultures around the world, including the Kuna of Panama (Sherzer 1987), the Kaluli of Papua New Guinea (Schieffelin 1987),

DOI: 10.4324/9781003398349-42

children in south Philadelphia (Goodwin 1990), police officers in Pittsburgh (McElhinny 1993, 1994), and experimentally in the United States (Freed and Greenwood 1996). Ochs (1992) has theorized more generally about the ways that language indexes gender through the speech activity and its constituent acts and stances. "Indexing" is a kind of meaning that is based on experience of use; for example, since we experience hearing men using low-pitched voices, we make a meaningful connection between masculinity and low pitch, and anyone can make their voice sound more masculine if they lower their voice. Ochs, then, points out that cultural norms for appropriate stances, acts, and activities mediate the cultural norms for how gender identity is "appropriately" constructed and the kinds of language used by women and men.

Stance is thus the location of the coupling between performativity and structure; it is in stances that identity performativity takes place. *Stance* is defined here as "the specific interpersonal relationship constructed by talk in interaction." This definition subsumes traditional sociolinguistic constructs such as power, solidarity, intimacy, and politeness, and at the same time, it can also describe more specific relationships constructed by speakers, such as "kind but firm father." The structural regularities of stance mean that interactants know what kinds of stances are possible in an interaction and expect people to take particular stances. The more permanent kind of identity is, in fact, a *repertoire* of stances, where people of the same gender, for example, tend toward similar kinds of stances while leaving space for individual variation.

The men in the fraternity in many cases did their best to act at the top of some hierarchy, although what that hierarchy was changed from interaction to interaction. This focus on hierarchy is related to the cultural ideology of *hegemonic masculinity* identified by Connell (1987, 1995), which orders identities, and especially men, into relatively subordinate and dominant masculinities:

> "Hegemonic masculinity" is not a fixed character type, always and everywhere the same. It is, rather, the masculinity that occupies the hegemonic position in a given pattern of gender relations, a position always contestable. . . . *It is the successful claim to authority*, more than direct violence, that is the mark of hegemony.
>
> (Connell 1995: 77; emphasis added)

This "claim to authority" is accomplished not only through structural societal relationships (for example, a hierarchy based on potential violence to enforce hierarchy itself) but also through face-to-face encounters.

Two main types of authoritative stance can be found in the following interactions: (1) simple assertion of dominance, and (2) expression of confidence. The repertoire of linguistic strategies Pete uses includes boasts, taunts, insults, disagreement, and direct comparisons between himself and others, though the most important strategy is the expression of certainty. The hierarchies Pete uses in taking these stances can be classified as follows: (1) positions in an institutional structure; (2) physical or mental strength, skill, or endurance; (3) knowledge and experience; (4) economic wealth. All these stances are hierarchies, in that they implicitly order people by some criteria. Crucially, however, the social alignments within which Pete might take authoritative stances are constrained by the speech situation and negotiated by Pete and his interlocutors. He must therefore shift the kind of hierarchy through which he constructs his authority as he responds to the changes of setting, his interlocutors' expectations, and his goals for the interaction.

Method and background

Research for this chapter was carried out within a fraternity at a university of approximately 13,000 undergraduates in the Northern Virginia suburbs of Washington, DC.[3] The members of the college fraternity that became the focus of my research are overwhelmingly European American,[4] and non–European American members were often marked explicitly (e.g., through jokes and nicknames such as "Punjab" and "Turk"). Because I was a "brother" in the same national fraternity, I was accepted by the members as an insider.[5] I was included by the men in all aspects of the fraternity, from serious business discussions to parties. I spent over a year attending different events and hanging out with the members throughout their day, resulting in a corpus of 37 hours of interaction.

The college fraternity provided an ideal site to investigate forms of men's identity. Fraternities are all-male social groups at American universities and colleges. They are dense, multiplex networks, with members usually drawn from similar societal groups. Fraternity men are generally stereotyped in a number of unflattering ways with regards to drinking, casual sex, and hazing.[6] But if we consider gender and identity to be fluid, the fraternity becomes an excellent site for understanding the tension between cultural norms and individual creativity.

Relations within the Greek world also constitute a pattern of hegemonic masculinity. First, there is a strict binary organization of fraternities and sororities, separate organizations for men and women, respectively. The ideology and structures of competition between fraternities and sororities order "authorized" identities: the motto of Gamma Chi Phi is "Be Men." Gamma Chi Phi was continually concerned with its standing with respect to other fraternities. For example, one aspect of the fraternity of which the members were most proud was its dominance of intramural sports: for several years, they had won the trophy for the most successful intramural sports team, and they prided themselves on "making enemies." Competition came in other forms as well: which fraternity had the best parties (i.e., well-attended by attractive women), and how well they did in rush (i.e., how big their "pledge class" was).

There is also a hegemonic masculinity structure within the fraternity. Once a student joins, he becomes a probationary member, or a "pledge." Pledges are treated much like soldiers in a boot camp: they learn the customs of the fraternity and are treated as if they have little individuality or autonomous rights and are often "feminized." The full members are thus put in a dominant position, with the pledges in a subordinate one. After becoming full members in the fraternity, members are still considered to be unknowledgeable and in need of more instruction in the ways of the fraternity. As they become older, they move up in a fraternity hierarchy based on experience. There are thus several intersecting and related hierarchies that are important to fraternity members. Among these are age, offices held, how much service ("hard work") a member has given the fraternity, sports ability, competitiveness, hetero- and homo-sociability, and intelligence.

As discussed later, these hierarchies are constituted through linguistic practices, such as name-calling, boasting, and insulting. This interactional style signals the men's closeness with each other through the lack of any attention to politeness. The competitiveness thus co-exists with a sense of acceptance and camaraderie that the men value. They have already "proved themselves" to be in a hegemonic position by passing through rush and pledging and can relax with their "equals" in an arena where they know they are accepted. The fraternity also provides a way of expressing homosocial closeness without worrying about homosexual connotations, which would threaten the men's status in middle-class America.

The four faces of Pete

Pete – a short, stout, middle-class Italian American from Virginia Beach, Virginia – was vice president of the fraternity when I began my research. A former wrestler, he carries his body with bent elbows and arms to the side, as if he is perpetually ready to take on an opponent. He moves and changes positions little when he sits. This body image suggests solidity and a physically powerful identity; his often-combative demeanor fits with this type of identity. Pete's demeanor also suggests a relaxed ease with accomplishments, as if success will come about through natural talent. Pete is part of what might be called the fraternity's "establishment," since he has taken the path up the hierarchy through hard work, culminating in his election as vice president.

Election meeting

The first excerpt is of Pete speaking in an election meeting. He is at that time the vice president of the fraternity and is commenting on the candidates running for vice president. As such, he has an obvious claim to power based on his position and as an expert with knowledge about what it takes to be the vice president. Pete makes salient his positions in the structural and experience hierarchies of the fraternity and creates a confrontational stance with other fraternity members, castigating them for doing less work in the fraternity than he does. This "hardworking" stance is also authoritative in the fraternity: a member who dedicates himself to the fraternity and works hard in its service is regarded highly. The stances that he takes imply his status at the top of the fraternity hierarchy, both in age and in title. They do not go unchallenged by members of the audience, however, who question whether the claims Pete makes about the vice president position are claims about himself.

Elections in the fraternity are held once a year and follow a generic format: after nominations, all candidates leave the room, each returning for a short speech. After the speeches, while the candidates are still out of the room, members discuss the strengths and weaknesses of the candidates. This discussion itself has a structure: each member raises his hand, and the president, in this case, Hotdog, notes his name down. The president then recognizes a speaker, who then theoretically has the floor indefinitely. However, in practice, each speaker has a tenuous hold on the floor and does not hold it exclusively; there is constant intrusion as members react to and evaluate what is being said.[7]

What follow are Pete's comments on the vice president candidates. He begins by explicitly making his position and his authority salient (his speech will be presented in three parts to facilitate analysis).[8]

(1)

1	Hotdog:	Pete.
2	Pete:	OK. (2.5)
3		As vice president I will tell you who I would like. (2.1)
4		'Kay this jo:b entai:ls a fuckin' hell of a lot of stress
5		#lemme just tell you that right now#
6	?:	(???)
7	?:	Jesus.

This brief section shows that Pete is explicitly putting himself in a hierarchical position of both structure (he holds a high office) and knowledge (he has held the office for the past year). In addition to baldly highlighting his official position, Pete's comments in line 3 (and *OK* in line 2) perform a prefacing function. This prefacing gives his comments more weight by delaying the speaker's actual argument, much the way extended pauses give more drama to award announcements. The long pauses (2.5 and 2.1 seconds) following lines 2 and 3 also add to the dramatic effect of this preface. This prefacing and pacing are characteristic of older members who hold offices and thus allow Pete to take an authoritative stance from the outset by indexing this group of members.

One common strategy employed by members high on the explicit hierarchies of age and office-holding is to make claims without any citing evidence for them (Kiesling 1997). Another strategy used here is an iconic separation of Pete from the audience, through his "lemme just tell you that right now" in line 5. This statement distances him from his audience through a separation of pronouns – "me" telling "you" – and emphasis on his expert, knowledgeable position – the form of the utterance echoes the lecturing of a teacher. This statement situates Pete in opposition to, and as more knowledgeable than, his audience.

Next, the audience intervenes and provokes Pete to make his confrontational, boastful stance even clearer. Pete takes it a bit too far, however, and is castigated by several members.

In this excerpt, Pete uses speech acts such as complaining, insulting, and bragging to create an authoritative stance, primarily in response to the audience's evaluations of his first claim.

Finally, Pete moves to the next stage of the structure, the comments about the candidates, and returns to an authoritative stance based on his status as an older member. He again begins with a kind of preface in lines 25–26. Notice the audience's relative silence during this portion of his comments, which suggests that Pete's stance is acceptable to the audience.

---

(2)

8	Pete:	OK. and | I can't see |
9	Pencil:	| (He'll eat | his way) He just eats the stress up
10	Pete:	I-I eat eat it dude
11	Mack:	| (I-I could fuckin'?) |
13	?:	| (hell of a lot of aggression) |
14	Pete:	Ask-Ask Connor dude
15		| | I suck in some stress |
16	Hotdog:	| ((bangs gavel)) | | SHUT UP
17	Pete:	You guys don't realize the fuckin' work I have to do for you=
18	Hotdog:	=Gohead.
19	Pete:	And you guys don't do SHIT
20		And now you're fuckin' (takin')
21	?:	COME O |:N
22	Tex:	This isn't about you Pete (this is about?)
23	?:	| Shut up du:de stop feelin' sorry for yourself.
24		((several others speak at once, unintelligible))

---

(3)

25	Pete: I'm tellin' you dude
26	I'm telling you right now OK
27	Saul, the only reason he wants this,
28	Is 'cause he wants a fuckin' titlehead (.)
29	*or figurehead whatever* he wants a title.
30	Doesn't deserve it.
31	Can't do the work.
32	There's no way in hell.
33	Speed, (1.8.) h- he's not a fuckin'–
34	Rush he did great a great job,
35	It's a week long.
36	And he was fuckin' stressed to hell over rush,
37	Last fall he had his chick do it.
38	And he didn't do anything to change rush, I mean
39	He spoke about how much he was gonna change #this do this do this#
40	We've done the sa:me fuckin' thi:ng every semester.
41	No one's changed rush.
42	OK?
43	That | leaves |-
44	?: Except for| the stripper.
45	?: Shh chu chu chu chu
46	Pete: That leaves Paul Sutton and Brad Waterson.
47	And out of those two,
48	I think Paul Sutton is the only person qualified for the job,
49	'cause Waterson is just a little too young.
50	and needs to hold a position,
51	and prove himself,
52	before he does anything else.
53	Paul Sutton is fuckin'–
54	He's done his job.
55	I mean he- he has done his job
56	and he's done it well.]
57	I mean yeah he fucked up on times here and there.
58	But he fuckin' got us some fuckin #Patriot Centers when he got the opportunity.
59	Y'know.
60	And he fuckin' tried to organize philanthropies that (we) didn't go to.
61	So, y'know, if he didn't do his job it's my fault.
62	Y'know.
63	And I think he did a good job.
64	*He's #the only person I see qualified to do this job.#
65	Hotdog: Don Conner.

In this excerpt, Pete uses several devices to index his place at the top of the fraternity age and structural hierarchy. In the prefacing comments in lines 25–26 ("I'm tellin' you, dude, I'm telling you right now, OK"), Pete iconically separates himself from the audience using first- and second-person pronouns. Furthermore, the verb he uses creates an asymmetry, with him as the active, instructing subject, and the audience as a passive, naive experiencer. This sets Pete up as more knowledgeable than his listeners and demands their attention.

Another device that demands the audience's attention is the lack of mitigation in any of his statements, which creates an air of certainty that helps construct an authoritative stance. Notice especially his comments about Saul in lines 30–32: "Doesn't deserve it.

Can't do the work. There's no way in hell." Pete is also unmitigated when he discusses Paul Sutton in lines 54–56: "He's done his job. I mean he-he has done his job and he's done it well." In lines 34–41, he displays his knowledge of fraternity history, which, in turn, indexes his age and authority. In fact, the statements about Rush in lines 40–41 are irrelevant to Pete's actual argument about Speed; they serve almost exclusively to mark his status as an authoritative elder in the fraternity.

Two more aspects of this excerpt help Pete create this authority. First, in line 61, Pete takes credit for Paul's mistakes: "So y'know if he didn't do his job it's my fault" (it is Pete's fault because one of the jobs of the vice president is to get members to attend functions). This line indexes Pete's authority because it puts Pete in a leadership position over Paul. Finally, in Pete's last line (the summary), he uses a syntactic frame often used by the older members in these statements: *I see X as Y*. The *I see* creates an authoritative stance through the metaphor of being able to see clearly and wisely, as if looking into the future. Moreover, it implies that simply because *Pete* believes this to be the case, others should see what he sees.

In excerpt 1, Pete uses a confrontational and boastful stance to create a hierarchy with the audience. In excerpt 2, he constructs authority through his ability to handle stress and work hard, while in excerpt 3, he takes the stance of an older, wiser member, with knowledge of the candidates, the job, and the fraternity. The next situation finds Pete in a much more fluid, and less serious, situation, although he still manages to stay at the top of any hierarchy he is challenged with.

Monopoly game

It is a Sunday afternoon at the townhouse where Pete lives, a center of social activity for Gamma Chi Phi. Several members of the fraternity have come over to watch football. Pete, Dave, Boss, and I are sitting at the dining room table (within view of the television), and the three members are playing the board game Monopoly.[9] In the first excerpt, Pete lands on one of Dave's properties and, after some negotiation, does not pay rent because he has a free pass.[10,11]

(4)		
1		((Pete rolls, moves))
2	Dave:	Nice. Pay me. (2.3)
3	Pete:	I can't. Aren't you in jail or something? Don't I not have to
4		pay you this time?
5		| Free pass. |
6	Boss:	You | got a | free pass. He's got one more.
7	Dave:	No that's your last one.
8	Pete:	I have one more.
9	I've got one left.	
10	Dave:	No that's it
11	Pete:	I have one left. I've only used two.
12	Dave:	That's right. And these over here. OK.
13	Pete:	The deal was for fi:ve.
14	Dave:	God damn I needed that money too you son of a bitch.
15		((Dave rolls))The deal was for TWO.
16		(4.3)

This excerpt is presented primarily as context for the next two, but there are a few aspects to note as the players position themselves. Dave and Pete have a dispute about whether Dave has to pay, and Pete "wins" the dispute, as his interpretation of the state of affairs holds sway. This ability to determine the outcome of events is the very definition of power, and Pete is therefore at the top of a hierarchy. In the next excerpt, he takes up a fictional "game identity," drawing on the fact that he is metaphorically staying at Dave's property rent-free:

---

(5)

17	Pete:	Hi: hi: hi: honey I'm home.
18	Boss:	I'm gonna blow by Dave right here.
19		((Boss rolls))
20	Dave:	Fuckin' so awful.
21	Pete:	I know its fuckin' t-turnin wheels and shit in your parking lot.
22		(2.5)
23		((Pete makes car squealing noises as he moves the car marker))
24	Boss:	Go Pete.
25	Pete:	And my horse has left a big shit right on your property.
26		Big tur:d right there.
27	Dave:	Alo:ng with the money.
28		((Pete moves))
29		(9.0)

Pete's taunt in line 17 constructs and reflects dominance relations in the larger society, especially domestic relationships between heterosexual partners. Pete uses the phrase "Hi, honey, I'm home" to take on a fictional role of a stereotypical American husband greeting his housewife upon returning home from work. I informally asked several of the men, including Pete, what the phrase suggested to them (without telling them the context), and almost all suggested this interpretation. A smaller majority said the phrase brought up a picture of a 1950s husband arriving home from work, and cited the sitcom *Leave It to Beaver* as the paradigmatic example. Within the game, this move focuses attention on Pete's game status (he is staying rent-free on an expensive property, so Dave is an unpaid servant). By assigning roles in a well-known cultural script, with himself in the authoritative husband role and Dave in the subordinate wife role, Pete achieves a dominant hierarchical position over Dave. This practice of assigning subordinate women's roles to others is common among the fraternity men, especially in this kind of competitive camaraderie (see Kiesling 2002). Pete's statement thus reinforces societal gender inequalities, since his statement makes little sense unless the interlocutors share the cultural model. As Hill (1995) has shown, jokes are often powerful, if covert, vehicles to perpetuate hierarchical relationships in society.

In the exchange which follows, we see Dave admit that this event puts him at a disadvantage in the game. Pete builds on this game situation and figuratively creates other mini-narratives in the game world, using the shapes of the game pieces (car and horse) as cues. In this world, Dave is again put into the subordinate position; Pete claims a dominant position for Boss by saying that Boss's car is turning wheels in (i.e., vandalizing) Dave's parking lot, thereby creating a stance for Boss against Dave (in line 20). Thus, we can see a social structure being created by the talk around the game, both in meta-comments about the rules (as in excerpt 5) and in elaborated images of the game world, as in excerpt 6. Pete exemplifies a hegemonic masculinity in all these fields, while Boss presents what Connell (1995) calls a complicit masculinity (not hegemonic, but benefiting from dominance relations and allied with hegemonic masculinities), and Dave a subordinate one.

Although Pete is consistently boastful and confrontational in these excerpts, he shifts the hierarchy on which he bases his boasts a total of at least three times. First, he is dominant in a dispute about the state of the game, but then, with single phrases, he creates entire imaginary worlds, based on the "game world," in which he is dominant. The differences in language use are heightened by the differences in body, voice quality, and role in the fraternity. Dave is tall and thin and speaks more softly than Pete. He thus does not immediately project a physically powerful image, which Pete does. He is also not as loquacious as Pete. For example, whereas Pete often speaks in meetings, Dave speaks only occasionally. Dave admits to setbacks, such as when Pete does not have to pay rent. And instead of threatening or taunting back, he calmly suggests that he is going to get some money despite the actions of Pete's horse.

In sum, Pete deftly changes the field on which he takes an authoritative stance as he negotiates his position with Dave. While the genre I have investigated is play, it nevertheless gives us a window into more "serious" genres. Compare Pete's boasting in the meeting with that of the game: in the former, his claim to authority using boasts was unsuccessful, while the latter was successful. But in the meeting, Pete still managed to create an authoritative stance through other means. In addition, we have seen that the identity that a man tries to create can fail to be authoritative. In the monopoly game, Pete successfully creates a powerful identity at every turn. Dave cannot say anything that Pete does not turn into an opportunity for boasting, even though Dave takes several lines of "attack."

I played this excerpt for another member, Mack, whose comments upon hearing it provide telling insight into what is going on. First, Mack commented that this type of competitive, boasting, and insulting banter is central to the social life of the fraternity, noting that it goes "only skin-deep." He noted, however, that some members get picked on more than others because they are perceived as targets: "People get relegated to a position because they can't stand up in the beginning." Dave is one of these members. Mack said that Dave is a "designated welcome mat" who "gets stepped on the most." Dave seems to have a fraternity role as the one who gets picked on, largely because he is not skilled at this particular speech genre.

When he listened to the monopoly excerpt, Pete found the conversation to be normal and, indeed, very humorous. In contrast, he was serious and even regretful about his behavior when he listened to the tape of the meeting. Even though he is confrontational in both activity types, Pete recognizes that boasting and insulting are more appropriate for "just hangin' out." This fact suggests that Pete may have been simultaneously indexing another activity type besides the meeting (or trying to reframe the activity type; see Tannen 1993). The role he indexes, while creating a confrontational stance and a competitive role, also indexes the competitive camaraderie typical of the men's discourse when they socialize with each other. In fact, Pete may have considered Pencil's sarcastic interrupting statement in line 9 of excerpt (2) ("He just eats the stress up") to be an opening to one of these boasting contests, and thus continued in this vein. Pete's boasting in the meeting can thus be explained by a momentary mixing of activity types. However, the mismatch and negative reaction of the audience to his boasting show that different ways of manifesting powerful identities are appropriate for some situations, but not others, and that strategies cannot be chosen from a list at random.

Maggie's bar

In this section, we see Pete shift discourse strategies during an activity because of a change in the participants. Pete is sitting in a bar with me and another member's friend from home. After a short time, a woman (Jen) comes in, and Pete's language changes dramatically. In these excerpts, we get a view of the different identities Pete constructs for male and female friends.

In the first episode, which takes place before Jen enters, Pete is subtly confrontational by playing down the significance of Dan's utterances. The excerpt begins during a conversation about a party at Pete's house later that night.

(7)		
1	Dan:	(You got) a keg?
2		(?)
3		BYOB? ((Bring Your Own Beer))
4		IS it really?
5	Pete:	That's what it always is at our place man
6		except for once in a whi:le.
7		An' everybody just comes over there gets wasted.
8		fuckin' sits around,
9		plays caps or whatever. ((caps is a drinking game))
10	Dan:	I love playin' caps.
11		That's what did me in last-| last week.
12	Pete:	| that's- |
13		Everybody plays that damn game, dude.
14		(1.5)
15	Dan:	Y'know who's good is: Nell?
16		(1.0) *Is good uh*
17		(1.3) ((snapping))
18		What's his name.
19		The marine guy.
20		What's his name?
21	Pete:	Griceman?
22	Dan:	Yeah.
23		He's good. (0.8)
24	Pete:	Everyone's: (.) all right.
25		Everyone's pretty good.
26		|Just depends on how |wasted you are.
27	Dan:	|(?? awful)|

Throughout this excerpt, Pete takes a stance of "informed native," saying we always do X (line 5), or everybody does X (lines 7 and 13). He thus creates an authoritative insider role, putting himself at the top of a social hierarchy (which, in this case, is an "inner circle"). Pete continually plays down Dan's comments through his use of *everyone, everybody*, and *always* (lines 5, 7, 13, 24, and 25). This use of *everybody* and *just* implies that these practices are common occurrences, and that Pete (or at least his house) is at the center of a social milieu.

A short time later, Jen, a sorority member, walks in. After greeting Pete, she goes to talk with some friends at another table and then returns to our table. As she returns, Pete remarks, "Now I gotta watch what I say." After Pete introduces me and Dan to Jen, Jen and he begin a conversation. Pete continues his nonchalant stance, but his intonation range becomes narrower, and his utterances shorter.

(8)		
93	Jen:	God I haven't been here in a long time.
94		Um, what time do have to leave?
95		Do you really have to go to class?
96	Pete:	|Yes.
97	Dan:	|Can we have another glass? ((to waiter))
98	Jen:	You do?
99	Dan:	No rush. ((as if to waiter, who had been slow))
100	Pete:	What time is it?
101	Jen:	I'm parked over there is that OK?
102		(?)
103		Six twenty-five
104	Pete:	Forty-five?
105	Jen:	Twenty-five.
106	Jen:	What time do you have to leave?
107	Pete:	I have to leave by seven.
108	Jen:	No: Seven fifteen. (.)
109		Do you have a test in your class?
110	Pete:	Yes.
111	Jen:	Oh well then OK (?)
112	Pete:	I'll leave at (.) ten after.
113	Jen:	Greta's coming here too.
114	Pete:	Greg?
115	Jen:	No.
116		Y'know what-?
117	Pete:	Greg was s'posed to come.
118	Jen:	Alex called, was like
119		Can you tell Greg to um
120		he owes us a hundred an twenty dollars for his bills.
121		I was like he doesn't live here now.
122		(3.1)
123	Pete:	(Guess that's Greg's problem.)
124	Dan:	You want another one?
125	Pete:	Yeah I want another one. Huh.
126		(3.7)
127	Dan:	I told him to get you a glass.
128	Jen:	(I got kicked outta here one time)
129	Pete:	Why? Were you being obnoxious and rowdy?
130	Jen:	Oh: my God. I can't tell you how drunk I was.
131		Don't even remember anything.
132	Pete:	Shouldn't drink so much.
133	Jen:	Are they gonna card me? (.)
134	Pete:	Huh?
135	Jen:	Are they gonna card me?
136	Pete:	Pro | bably.|
137	Jen:	| I'm | nervous. he ha
138	Pete:	I wouldn't worry about it too much.

Because of Pete's comments, we know that Jen's presence will make a difference in the way he talks. Pete told me that he and Jen had dated in the past, so each was likely to be performing identities which they hope are sexually desirable to the other. Pete now shows the inexpressive face that Sattell (1983) discusses. Notice in line 96 Pete's very short answer to Jen's question about him going to class. Later in the conversation (lines 109–110), we find out that he has a test in his class. But in line 96, Pete does not volunteer this information. He just says "yes," indicating that the decision is final, no justification needed. Compare this answer to Pete's answer to Dave's question about BYOB in line 5 ("THAT'S WHAT IT ALWAYS IS at our place, man"), which provides much more justification.

Pete takes a paternalistic stance toward Jen. His question in line 129 is paternalistic because the utterance has a singsong intonation, with an exaggerated final rise, as well as a more precise articulation (less coarticulation, deletion, and vowel reduction) than his other utterances. These qualities give the utterance a "parentese" quality, which positions Jen as a child, and Pete as the father (the authority in a stereotypical middle-class American familial hierarchy). After Jen's explanation, Pete quietly, and ironically, tells her she should not drink so much (as he drinks several glasses of beer before an exam). Pete also creates this paternalistic stance with his reassurance in line 138, another speech act that indexes a parent–child relationship. All these statements create an impression of paternalistic protection: confidence, knowledge of the world, and suggestions for better behavior.

This excerpt parallels some of the meeting speeches made by other men (see Kiesling 1997) in an intriguing way. In the meeting, one of the strategies members used to create an authoritative identity was to appear as a wise elder or father figure, displaying knowledge about the fraternity and using that knowledge to give advice. Here Pete is creating a similar identity with Jen. The stance Pete creates is also similar to the stance of problematizer and primary recipient, roles most often identified with the father in Ochs and Taylor's (1995) study of family interaction in White middle-class America. There is thus a connection here between the "father knows best" cultural model and Pete's interaction with Jen.

Another device Pete uses in this excerpt with both Dan and Jen is the dropping of the subject of a sentence (lines 26 and 132). This device adds to Pete's inexpressiveness by using the minimal amount of words to express his ideas. Both instances are used at points where Pete is creating an "in control" identity. In line 26 ("just depends on how wasted you are"), Pete is an expert on caps. In line 132, he's a counselor ("shouldn't drink so much").

Upon hearing this excerpt, Pete was tentative about his motivations for his "inexpressive" behavior with Jen, saying, "I guess I didn't want to have a conversation [with Jen] in front of you guys." But Mack characterized Pete's behavior as typical for Pete, who, said Mack, is always different around women. Mack believes Pete's voice becomes a little deeper, and Pete goes into "shutdown mode," in which he tries to act like a "calm, cool, got-his-shit-together guy." This observation suggests that this stance is one in a repertoire of stances for Pete and is used only in a particular speech setting.

The two parts of this excerpt illustrate the ways in which this man uses language to modulate his identity with respect to the audience. In both parts of the excerpt, though, Pete is the expert. He creates a stance in both situations that puts him at the top of a hierarchy, based on his superior knowledge of a group (his social circle) or the world at large.

However, with Dan, he has more intonational range and more discourse particles, such as *man*, *dude*, and *fuckin'*. With Jen, he uses a narrower intonation and uses fewer modifiers of any kind. Thus, he is "authoritative" throughout, but he is "inexpressive" when speaking to the woman. Jen's role in keeping up a steady stream of questions and comments allows Pete to interject minimal amounts of information (a pattern also discussed by Fishman 1983), underscoring how interlocutors help co-construct a complementary stance and identity. This difference between excerpts (7) and (8) shows that the hierarchies at the top of which Pete places himself are different with each interlocutor. With the man, he shows his knowledge of – and central position within – his social group, but with the woman, he orients himself towards the world at large and presents himself as a wise, authoritative, unemotional (father) figure.

Interestingly, there are parallels between Pete's syntax when speaking to Jen and when speaking to the fraternity in a meeting. Both times he uses bald assertions without justification or elaboration, which suggests that Pete is creating similar stances in terms of knowledge and authority. Indeed, in both situations, he seems to create an identity based on worldly wisdom and experience. This similarity may at first seem paradoxical, since the two settings are so different in terms of formality, but when we consider society's ordering of women and men in terms of authority, it is not surprising: such an ordering is identified as the most important aspect of hegemonic masculinity, and central to the hierarchic ideology of the fraternity, which puts the men of the fraternity at the top. Pete's everyday identity construction thus reproduces on a local level the ideologies of the fraternity and society as a whole.

Conclusion

In these four situations, we have seen Pete deftly shift the hierarchies on which he creates a dominant, or hegemonic, identity. But this microscopic window into Pete's "doing gender" has also revealed how this fluidity of identity is restricted: Pete's attempts to create authoritative stances were not always accepted by his interlocutors. In addition, he continually shifted his stance within a conversation as the social alignments of hierarchies were negotiated (e.g., in the monopoly game and in the bar with Dan). His stances were thus responses to the speech situation and the reactions of his interlocutors.

But while the identities presented by Pete were fluid, there was also a remarkable consistency in the way Pete relentlessly put himself at the top of a hierarchy. This consistency suggests that we must find some way to reconcile the local and interpersonal fluidity of identity with the cultural constraints placed on identities that lead to probabilistic similarities among members of culturally defined identity types. Thus, we have to understand that while gender is, in theory, infinitely fluid, in the practice of most people's lives, it is constrained by cultural models: for men's identity, women's identity, middle-class identity, fraternity identity, etc.

The hierarchies created by Pete can all be connected to cultural models of men in North America: the corporate or military leader implicates a structural or economic hierarchy, a "working-class hero" implicates a physical strength hierarchy, a "father knows best" model implicates a knowledge/experience hierarchy, and a sports star implicates a skill hierarchy. These models can also, in turn, index other hierarchies: Pete created a structurally authoritative stance when he created husband and father-like stances in the monopoly game, and with Jen. We thus see how this system of language-stance-hierarchy-cultural model creates feedback loops within interactions so that the cultural models are not simply something "out there," which speakers invariably index, but something which speakers help create. For example, by using the "Hi, honey, I'm home" phrase to index a specific kind of family, Pete keeps this model alive and makes it valid. Here, then, is the connection between structure and practice: the fact that the indexing of a cultural model is not ever wholly a presupposing one (see Silverstein 1976), because through its very use, the model is reinforced and (re)created. This is the feedback loop that allows the structural coupling between gender practice and gender structure to happen.

What we characterize as "masculinity," then, can be thought of as a repertoire of stances connected with hierarchies and cultural models. Speakers select from this repertoire depending on the speech activity and their interlocutors. Gender identity is a performance which is understood in a complex context which includes not only the immediate speech event but also knowledge of cultural expectations for gender and knowledge of social structures. This detailed analysis of a portion of one man's identity repertoire has yielded some answers to the nature of the relationship between language and gender, and the tension between structure and practice in that relationship. We need to see more such studies, perhaps of less-hegemonic identities, in order to understand more fully how we can characterize the differences in stance repertoires that lead to the probabilistic differences in language we find between different genders.

Discussion questions

1. How, according to the author, is gender performed and actively created through the use of language and posture (stance)?
2. How does Pete use language to exhibit his authority in the fraternity?
3. How does Pete's behavior change when he is around women, rather than just other men? Why does the author suggest Pete make these changes?

Notes

1 This is an abbreviated version of an article published in 2001 (Kiesling 2001).
2 I will use the term "identities" and "men's identities" rather than "masculinity" because of the problems of the latter term, identified earlier. In addition, "identities" captures the fact that gender interacts fundamentally with "other" aspects of a person's identity, such as class and ethnicity.
3 The student body of this university is composed primarily of state residents (89 percent as of 1990), specifically residents of Northern Virginia (81 percent). Most students live off campus (85 percent), and informal discussions with students suggest that approximately half of these students live at home. All figures are from the 1993–1994 student handbook; all names (school, fraternity, and people) are pseudonyms.
4 Of the 33 members as of Fall 1994, four were from Middle Eastern backgrounds and one from a Korean background.
5 Members from other chapters are always outsiders to some extent, as they do not have the close personal connections of other members and have not participated in the local initiation rituals. The initiation ritual boundary marker was made clear to me when one brother suggested that their initiation practices were "harsher" and more difficult than I was subjected to in my local chapter.
   I was thus doing ethnography largely in my "native" environment. As a number of ethnographers have pointed out, there are both positive and negative aspects of doing "insider" ethnography (see, particularly, Eckert 1989, Dunk 1991, and the papers in Messerschmidt 1981).

I entered the fraternity (which I will call Gamma Chi Phi) as a middle-class European American male member of the same national fraternity. However, there were also a number of significant cultural differences between these men and me. I was at a very different life stage, being between five and ten years older than the men and engaged to be married (and later married). Second, I was in a fraternity at a private university in a big city, as opposed to a state school in the suburbs. I was also a graduate student, while none of the men in the fraternity ever expressed an interest in academia as a career choice. Thus, when I began the ethnography, I found their world quite different from mine, and it took me a while to get over this slight shock and to learn the interactional norms of their culture.

6 *Hazing* is the practice of putting a potential member in danger of mental or physical harm or requiring illegal activity during initiation activities.

7 The rush process for sororities is somewhat different, but the differences are not relevant here. See McLemore (1991) for a description of the rush process in Texas, which is essentially the same as at the university where this research was conducted.

8 The election is between four members: Speed Farmer, an older member who has held the position of rush organizer; Saul Larousse, a second-year member who has held a few offices but who has a reputation as being "belligerent;" Paul Sutton, another second-year member who has held the jobs of philanthropy and fundraising chair; and Brad Waterson, a newly initiated member who has held no positions. Sutton won the election.

9 Transcription conventions (a slightly modified version of those introduced by Gail Jefferson for conversation analysis) are as follows:

| |	Bounds simultaneous speech
=	Connects two utterances produced with noticeably less transition time between them than usual
(number)	Silences timed in tenths of seconds
#	Bounds passage said very quickly
TEXT	Uppercase letters indicate noticeably loud volume
–	Indicates that the sound that precedes is cut off, stopped suddenly and sharply
:	Indicates the sound that precedes it is prolonged
,	Indicates a slight intonational rise
?	Indicates a sharp intonational rise
(text)	Transcript enclosed in single parenthesis indicates uncertain hearing
((comment))	Double parenthesis enclose transcriber's comments

10 Monopoly is a game in which players move pieces around a square board, landing on squares which are "properties" (modeled after Atlantic City, New Jersey). A player may buy the property if no other player has yet done so, using play money each receives at the beginning of the game. If the property is bought, the player who lands on it must pay rent to the owner. Properties are organized into colored groups; if a player acquires all properties in a group, then he has a monopoly. A monopoly raises the rent on all properties in the group and gives the owner the right to buy houses or hotels on the properties, which increases the rent of the properties still more. The object of the game is to bankrupt all the other players. It is thus very competitive, and players can evaluate how well they are doing by the amount of money they currently have.

11 Free passes are agreements between players that exempt one player from paying rent on another's property, usually given in exchange for a property.

References

Bergvall, Victoria, Janet Bing, and Alice Freed, eds. 1996. *Rethinking Language and Gender Research*. Harlow, Essex: Longman.
Coates, Jennifer. 1997. *Women Talk*. Oxford: Blackwell Publishers.
Connell, Robert W. 1987. *Gender and Power*. Stanford, CA: Stanford University Press.
Connell, Robert W. 1995. *Masculinities*. Berkeley, CA: University of California Press.
Cornwall, Andrea, and Nancy Lindisfarne, eds. 1994. *Dislocating Masculinity*. London: Routledge.

Dunk, Thomas W. 1991. *It's a Working Man's Town: Male Working-Class Culture*. Montreal and Kingston: McGill-Queen's University Press.

Eckert, Penelope. 1989. *Jocks and Burnouts: Social Categories and Identity in the High School*. New York: Teacher's College Press.

Fishman, Pamela M. 1983. "Interaction: The Work Women Do." In *Language, Gender and Society*. eds. Barrie Thorne, Cheris Kramarae, and Nancy Henley, 89–101. Rowley, MA: Newbury House.

Freed, Alice F., and Alice Greenwood. 1996. "Women, Men, and Type of Talk: What Makes the Difference?" *Language in Society* 25(1): 1–26.

Goodwin, Marjorie Harness. 1990. *He-Said-She-Said: Talk as Social Organization among Black Children*. Bloomington, IN: Indiana University Press.

Hall, Kira, and Mary Bucholtz, eds. 1995. *Gender Articulated*. London: Routledge.

Hart, Angie. 1994. "Missing Masculinity: Prostitutes' Clients in Alicante, Spain." In *Dislocating Masculinity*. eds. Andrea Cornwall and Nancy Lindisfarne, 48–65. London: Routledge.

Hill, Jane. 1995. "Junk Spanish, Covert Racism, and the (Leaky) Boundary between Public and Private Spheres." *Pragmatics* 5: 197–212.

Hymes, Dell. 1974. *Foundations in Sociolinguistics: An Ethnographic Approach*. Philadelphia: University of Pennsylvania Press.

Johnson, Sally, and Ulrike Meinhof, eds. 1997. *Language and Masculinity*. Oxford: Blackwell Publishers.

Kiesling, Scott Fabius. 1997. "Power and the Language of Men." In *Language and Masculinity*. eds. Ulrike H. Meinhof and Sally Johnson, 65–85. Oxford: Blackwell Publishers.

Kiesling, Scott Fabius. 2001. "Now I Gotta Watch What I Say: Shifting Constructions of Masculinity in Discourse." *Journal of Linguistic Anthropology* 11(2): 250–273.

Kiesling, Scott Fabius. 2002. "Playing the Straight Man: Displaying and Maintaining Male Heterosexuality in Discourse." In *Speaking of Sex: Language, Desire, and Sexuality*. eds. Kathryn Campbell-Kibler, Rob Podesva, Sarah Roberts, and Andrew Wong, 249–266. Stanford, CA: CSLI.

McElhinny, Bonnie. 1993. *We All Wear the Blue: Language, Gender, and Police Work*. Ph.D. diss., Stanford University.

McElhinny, Bonnie. 1994. "An Economy of Affect: Objectivity, Masculinity and the Gendering of Police Work." In *Dislocating Masculinity*. eds. Andrea Cornwall and Nancy Lindisfarne, 159–171. London: Routledge.

McLemore, Cynthia. 1991. *The Pragmatic Interpretation of English Intonation: Sorority Speech*. Ph.D. diss., University of Texas, Austin.

Messerschmidt, Donald A., ed. 1981. *Anthropologists at Home in North America: Methods and Issues in the Study of One's own Society*. Cambridge: Cambridge University Press.

Ochs, Elinor. 1992. "Indexing Gender." In *Rethinking Context: Language as an Interactive Phenomenon*. eds. Alessandro Duranti and Charles Goodwin, 335–358. Cambridge: Cambridge University Press.

Ochs, Elinor, and Carolyn Taylor. 1995. "The 'Father Knows Best' Dynamic in Dinnertime Narratives." In *Gender Articulated: Language and the Socially Constructed Self*. eds. Kira Hall and Mary Bucholtz, 97–120. New York and London: Routledge.

Sattell, Jack. 1983. "Men, Inexpressiveness and Power." In *Language, Gender and Society*. eds. Barrie Thorne, Cheris Kramarae, and Nancy Henley. Rowley, MA: Newbury House.

Schieffelin, Bambi B. 1987. "Do Different Worlds Mean Different Words? An Example from Papua New Guinea." In *Language, Gender and Sex in Comparative Perspective*. eds. Susan U. Philips, Susan Steele, and Christine Tanz, 249–262. Cambridge: Cambridge University Press.

Sherzer, Joel. 1987. "A Diversity of Voices: Men's and Women's Speech in Ethnographic Perspective." In *Language, Gender and Sex in Comparative Perspective*. eds. Susan U. Philips, Susan Steele, and Christine Tanz, 95–120. Cambridge: Cambridge University Press.

Silverstein, Michael. 1976. "Shifters, Linguistic Categories, and Cultural Description." In *Meaning in Anthropology*. eds. Keith H. Basso and Henry A. Selby, 11–55. Albuquerque: University of New Mexico Press.

Tannen, Deborah, ed. 1993. *Framing in Discourse*. New York: Oxford University Press.

West, Candace, and Don Zimmerman. 1987. "Doing Gender." *Gender and Society* 1(2): 125–151.

Chapter 38

TikTok, truckers, and travel bans

Digital disease surveillance and the scrutiny of masculinity in Southern Africa

Rebecca L. Upton

Original material prepared for this edition.

Introduction

This is a story about gender in Southern Africa. It is a story told in several parts and from several perspectives, all of which offer insight into how gender, masculinity, and health are understood and surveilled across particular time and spaces. In Part 1, I describe the impact of COVID-19 on the lives and livelihoods of many of those along border communities in Botswana, Zimbabwe, and South Africa, introducing several of the truckers that I have worked with over the past several years. In Part 2, I turn attention to how many of these individuals communicated during the pandemic, both with me as a researcher and with one another in efforts to provide care, strategize for success, and safety. Lastly, I consider how, in the seeming aftermath of the pandemic, global health organizations continue to draw assumptions about gender and use surveillance techniques as we consider the future of global public health in Africa. Throughout the story, I draw upon ethnographic narratives, highlighting the tales of three men, men who traverse the complex, contested, and often invisible boundaries of masculinity and health that undergird the lives of truckers in this part of the continent.

Across Southern Africa, transnational movement during the COVID-19 pandemic was largely limited to "essential" travelers. For those who provide goods across national boundaries, such as long-haul truck drivers, surveillance of their bodies has steadily increased as suspicion and stigma surrounding the vectors of the spread of the virus continue. Concurrently, over the past several years, the social media app TikTok has taken on an expanded role as a means to communicate, connect, and even provide care as these essential, mostly male, workers traverse these challenging social and even physical landscapes. As truckers have been subject to increased surveillance, scrutiny of their cargo, and of their lives, the use of the app to forge connections (both personal and professional) has been critical and remains central to their discourse about how to navigate (pandemic) borders. Additionally, with the Africa CDC efforts to enact "digital disease surveillance," men, and male labor force migrants in particular, find themselves somewhat unintentionally at the forefront of innovative global public health interventions. In this chapter, I use data from several truckers, migrants, and TikTok users to draw parallels between

DOI: 10.4324/9781003398349-43

historic migration and the renewed, persistent, and heightened scrutiny of the potentially "threatening" African body in this geographic region during the COVID-19 pandemic. In particular, I examine the position of men, their movement across borders, and the meaning of masculinity in these contexts. Their narratives illustrate the precarity of personal connections and professional boundaries in a public health crisis.

Methods and motivations

Beginning in 2016, I have been traveling along various trucking routes and studying in Southern African border communities, interviewing and learning from long- and short-haul truck drivers. My motivation has been an extension of prior research in different contexts, a way to bring together various threads of my scholarship on the negotiation of gender, health, masculinity, religion, and identity in the United States (Upton 2016) with my long-term ethnographic work on fertility, HIV/AIDS, migration, and movement across borders in Southern Africa (Upton 2010a, 2010b, 2011, 2019, 2022). I have been curious about how truckers themselves were both literally and figuratively cast as some of the main vectors for the spread of HIV/AIDS over the past several decades. Particularly in border communities, in urban centers, and along transportation routes, I have been interested in, and asking questions about, perceptions of gender, health, and access to care and medicine. As a medical anthropologist and public health practitioner, I ask questions about health-seeking behaviors and remain fascinated by what people tell me in terms of how those behaviors are assumed to vary by gender. As an older woman in the city of Francistown in Botswana told me once:

> Men are moving, they are always moving, women are the ones who remain, who take care of things, take care of others, so the men they move around, they bring the diseases back to the villages and women have to take care of it.
>
> (cf. Upton 2003)

Given the long history of out-migration by men in and across Southern Africa, such observations have been important in tracking and surveilling patterns of exchange (economic remittances) as well as mapping the spread of HIV/AIDS over the years.

The construction of health and the medicalization of migrant workers in this region (Packard 1993) mean that there is a history here of studying the intersections of gender, health, and the movement of bodies. In the past several decades as well, studies of therapeutic clientship (Zhou 2019; Nguyen 2010) have emerged, where the provision of medicine by NGOs and others was often regulated and cast as coincident with community or national identity across Africa. Such research helped shed important light on the limits to health care and the role of global public health institutions in tracking who was "sick" and how we might "care." Other research on the contestations over hegemonic masculinity have also been important as I embark on this project, from studies of "stuck men," those who have "failed" to achieve status in adulthood through "traditionally" masculine means (for example, in the past, young men may have been expected to migrate in search of employment and to send remittances to their families back home, whereas today those same men are oversaturating the informal sector and labor market in urban areas, largely unable to earn enough money to support themselves or family members) (Momoh 1999; Utas 2005; Honwana 2014), to the impact of prior pandemics, such as

Ebola and HIV/AIDS, on male mobility (Hoffman 2016; McLean 2019), both literal and geographic, form the springboard for this larger research project. This particular chapter emerges from the more recent COVID-19 pandemic, where these intersections became all the more salient as moving bodies were forced to sit still. Discourse about what it means to be an essential worker, a trucker, who is both subject to critique and scrutiny and yet lauded for transnational supply of goods, provisions, and care, ran rampant on social media and later CDC surveillance, reminding us, as Maina et al. (2022) do, that social media and messaging about masculinity and cultural norms shift over time and terrain.

With me as an ethnographer, the typical research landscape and methods used in this project shifted as well; much of the data found here are drawn from virtual ethnographic approaches, as tools such as TikTok, social media, photo- and video-sharing apps, and WhatsApp all became (and remain!) invaluable ways for communities to connect (and ethnographers to learn and participate) across cultures. I highlight some of the central themes that emerged through daily discussion, shared social media, and constant (albeit virtual) companionship that I have experienced in the lives of three of the many male truck drivers with whom I continued to work during the height of the pandemic.

Part 1: "You must be carrying COVID"

The line of long-haul trucks seems endless, stretching several miles from the South African border; a few engines idle, but most are switched off in the effort to conserve fuel and are tacit recognition that no one will be crossing anytime soon. The air is hot and dusty. It is September 2020, and medical workers in hazmat suits make their way down the line of trucks, swabbing throats and noses, distributing masks, and checking cargo. Frustrations are running high, as the usual backups along the Tlokweng border have been exacerbated by confusing COVID-19 protocols and delays that put drivers in precarious positions, weighing personal health and safety with the need to deliver freight across the region.

So for Ernest Bongaka, the border patrol officer's words struck fear, illustrated stigma, and perhaps worst of all, meant that he would not be delivering his load of produce and perishable goods from Polokwane to Mmankgodi and then Dukwi and on to Francistown that week. "You must be carrying COVID," argued the border patrol officer, a refrain that would become, over the course of 20 months, ubiquitous at any number of borders in Southern Africa. In South Africa, where better testing capacity captured more incidence and prevalence, the focus on truckers, the disruption of the supply chain, the flow of goods, people, and services across borders and to neighboring communities were profound. The impact of those closures was arguably worse in some ways (though not to diminish by any means the number of deaths and health issues caused by the highly infectious virus) than the impact of the pandemic. Not just on the movement of goods, but on the accessibility to people and the creation of precarity in social relationships that may extend well beyond this particular global outbreak.

Ernest Bongaka and Macdonald Nthebe

Ernest is a 35-year-old long-haul trucker who has been driving for almost ten years but who has never encountered anything like the traffic backup along the border. He works for a large local company, headquartered outside of Gaborone, Botswana, and transports everything from building materials to perishable goods, traveling across multiple borders several times each week. Ernest and his friend Macdonald Nthebe, also 35, and who drives for a different company based in Gauteng, South Africa, grew up together in the small village of Malolwane along the border of the two countries. Fascinated by engines and trucks of all sorts, the friends became certified drivers and worked locally in Botswana for a beverage distribution company in Gaborone before finding jobs in the international long-haul industry. As Ernest shares via text as they sit in the same, seemingly interminable line of trucks that day, "The border control think we are all carrying COVID, they don't see the rest of the cargo, or the reasons we need to move, they just see us as sick." Both Ernest and Macdonald have been accused of being vectors of the virus, border officers and even their family members shouting suspicions and sharing concerns that truckers were, and are still, spreading disease across the continent, fears of COVID-19 mapped onto the drivers themselves. As Macdonald describes sadly one day to me:

> My family was very proud of me when I began as a driver. They knew I was good at this, and I was going to make a lot of money. I do have a stable job, but now they are afraid, afraid of me, of the virus, and that those will meet, that the Macdonald they know will be someone with bad blood or who will be shamed. . . . [M]y sister was telling me that everyone in the village was talking about me.

Certainly, public and online commentary about COVID behavior has been ubiquitous. In 2020, the MTV Staying Alive Foundation, in response to the outbreak, developed an educational entertainment series (approximately 70 episodes that were disseminated on YouTube) called *MTV Shuga: Alone Together*. The series, like many "edu-tainment" strategies in Southern Africa over the years (Upton 2020), was envisioned as a mechanism of peer influence, online support, and "powerful public health tool" (Baker et al. 2021), and despite the recognition that not all have equal access to digital technologies, the show and subsequent online discussions were largely successful (ibid.), fostering ongoing awareness and social "norming" around COVID-19 behaviors. Plots were drawn from characters in challenging pandemic-related situations across several countries (mainly African, though some episodes were set in the United States for comparison) and were freely available on social media platforms, and viewers were able to comment in real time. Macdonald and Ernest were both avid watchers of *Alone Together*, sharing links to episodes with family members, friends, and fellow truck drivers during some of the long stopovers and quarantine queues. Ernest shared with me that at one point, one of the episodes sparked some of the most heated debate that he had encountered while driving during the pandemic:

> There was a young man on one of the episodes. He wanted to keep partying, to keep playing, so even though he knew he had been exposed to his aunt who was very sick – she definitely had the virus – this guy, he went out to a big party. The episode showed him going to a club, even though it was outside, and you saw him greet all the people. He was playing *so much*, but the thing that made everyone talk was that then he was getting ready to go up north, so he wasn't even staying at home. He was trying to leave, to go to his home village up north, and everyone just knew, they knew he was going to spread the disease, and everyone we knew was breaking lockdown. But there were some on the road, not our families as much, but some drivers who agreed, that

he should be okay to drive, to travel home, they felt so upset that the lockdown was so limiting. They needed the money from driving, and the blocked roads, the lockdown, it made it impossible for so many men like that. They argued with us all the time when we said we had to be careful. They saw that character suffering because of the government and the global health people.

In many ways, of course the global health concern was warranted: cross-border traffic and travelers were significant factors in COVID-19 transmission throughout Africa and, in particular, along borders in the eastern and southern regions (Emeto et al. 2021). In Kenya and Uganda, along with Botswana and Zimbabwe, truckers tested positive at rates much higher (Dube 2020) than those in the general populations (though lack of access to regular testing may explain some of those data) and were characterized in the news (Lichtenstein and Baerendtsen 2020) and conversation as literal carriers of the pandemic. International borders were closed or tightly restricted. Fear led some to close before any cases had been reported, and by 2021, it was clear that long-distance truck drivers were having an impact on the spread of COVID-19 infections and were among those considered highest risk (Malinga et al. 2021).

Early in the pandemic, as conditions varied across the continent, initial reports on social media suggested some real barriers to movement. As Ernest described:

> One day, Tlokweng was at a standstill. Nobody moved. It was like we were statues. On my regular route, I would go through there many times, at least once a day. They knew me there, but then, full stop. That border would close for a day, close with no warning, with nobody telling us anything.

Prior to the pandemic, some trucking companies in the region advertised that with their own in-house clearing operations and bonded transfer agents, drivers and clients would easily move through customs without facing delays, VAT, or unexpected fees. As Ernest told me:

> If you work for one of those companies, you get a nice cab and an easy haul. Things would be pretty seamless, no penalties for anyone. They weren't stuck hanging around Beitbridge or Kazungula [border posts with notoriously long lines for truckers and tourists alike] . . . but after COVID, everyone became the same . . . all of the drivers, all of the trucks, nobody moved.

Other barriers to movement were even more profound. Macdonald and Ernest both described days-long quarantine periods while awaiting test results and without sufficient running water, toilets, or adequate space to socially distance from other drivers, adding to the public health crisis. As Ernest says, "It was so ironic. We were treated like we were carrying the disease, and yet they had no ways to keep anyone safe. We had to figure it out ourselves, take it into our own hands to stay healthy." According to the SA Long-Distance Truckers Facebook page, in May 2020, trucks were queued for nine days or more, and "police . . . escorted trucks into Lusaka and parked off. . . . All the drivers were loaded into a bus and taken to a university building and left there under heavy police guard to quarantine in inhumane conditions." This despite drivers not showing any symptoms of the virus. Trucks were also not allowed to off-load for that fear of "carrying COVID."

The vilification is reinforced in varied national testing and contact-tracing policies. For instance, instead of general community testing, Botswana implemented a "sentinel testing" strategy, with a focus on points of transit, villages close to its borders, and points of entry, meaning, that truckers and other migrants were tested most routinely. Tswana officials also implemented a color-coded permit system where holders could only cross into certain geographic zones during certain times a day to keep contact and the coronavirus at bay. Eventually, and similar to reports (cf. Clottey 2020) of what was happening in eastern Africa, Ernest and Macdonald began to follow posts online offering drivers negative COVID test results for sale, bribes to bypass the restrictions, lengthy interviews at customs, decontamination processes, temperature monitoring, and later, vaccination status checks that were disrupting the flow of goods as well as individual driver paychecks.

None of this, however, is new. Suspicion of, and scrutiny over, some bodies, and not others, particularly in this region, has deep roots. Male out-migration for labor movements meant that their patterns of behavior, remittances, and sexual encounters have all been fodder for scholarly and policy observers alike. The current stigma attached to and enacted upon liminaly situated male truckers reminds many of the position of young men who were described as *lehetwa* (literally, "those better left on the shelf," unattached "players" with multiple concurrent partners who, if seronegative for HIV, became the "go-to guys" when trying to safely fulfill fertility desires) at the height of the HIV epidemic, who were regarded as responsible for persistent prevalence of this virus (cf. Upton 2010a, 2019). HIV has shaped masculinity in ways that are complex and required navigating responsibility, monogamy at times (embedded, for example, in early and largely failed global HIV and AIDS awareness and prevention strategies that insisted upon the ABCs of "**a**bstinence, **b**eing faithful, and **c**ondomizing"), voluntary circumcision, and now central figures in navigating the new landscape of multiple concurrent pandemics. Much of medical anthropology and global public health literaturae over the past two decades have, in fact, examined the interactions of men with various forms of medical or public health interventions across the African continent, highlighting how masculine norms and practices as well as ideas about bodily and community health are represented and contested.

Macdonald, for example, relayed a story of how certain ideas of gender and health were taught in his secondary school during a time when HIV and AIDS incidence and prevalence rates were high. In the early 2000s, the numbers of those infected and living with HIV and AIDS in Botswana were estimated to be around 35 percent of the population, though data varied across geographic, urban, and rural regions and were largely a result of sentinel testing and surveillance of women at antenatal clinics in Gaborone and Francistown, along with other peri-urban communities (UNAIDS/WHO 2004). AIDS awareness campaigns were in full swing, funded largely by external donors and international aid agencies, and as Macdonald recalled:

We knew the ABCs of HIV. There were signs everywhere about knowing your status and preventing the spread of the disease. We were kids, so we heard about AIDS everywhere. We knew people dying in our families. There were funerals all of the time in Malolwane. My aunt ran a burial service. My uncle was a welder for those memorials you see on top of the graves. They did really well during that time . . . so it wasn't as if we didn't have knowledge of that [pandemic]. People were dying everywhere, but I can remember sitting with my friends at the football pitch. It was December and really dry and hot, the sand blowing around, and someone asking about whether the dust could give us HIV. . . . I'm sure we'd learned otherwise, but for some reason, we had it in our heads that only girls could get it, they were the ones who we thought were at risk. . . . There was a lot of risk, we knew that, but somehow as boys, *we didn't think we were the ones* who were going to catch it.

These cultural assumptions and masculine privilege in Southern Africa are perhaps nothing new, but with those advantages came expectations that men would provide, would send remittances and familial support. As McLean (2019) points out, those expectations have become exceedingly difficult to achieve amidst rising economic and global health instability, and African men are often cast as "in crisis," responsible for toxic, deliberately harmful, uncaring forms of masculinity (cf. Decoteau 2013). But in pandemic times (Ebola, HIV/AIDS, COVID-19), we have seen the emergence of myriad other forms of masculinity and care. For Ernest and Macdonald, their choices to press on in the face of unsanitary conditions, stigma as potential virus vectors and border-crossing drivers, to deliver necessary goods meant that they could claim status as "essential," as "providers," and as rising to challenges posed by yet another kind of pandemic. There was and is a dynamism to the kind of masculinity that men like Ernest and Macdonald embrace, and this became an emergent theme, voiced by many on social platforms and media.

Part 2: TikTok

Even with COVID restrictions in place, informal cross-border trading activities continue, and people communicate. Borders are porous along these transportation corridors, and images such as those of financially strapped Zimbabweans crossing the Limpopo River near the Beit Bridge border post into South Africa, exchanging cigarettes and beer for groceries and other household items with Musina residents, were shared widely on social media. For Ernest and the other truckers, these images sparked wide debate and their own social media (mostly Twitter and TikTok) discourse. For them, these informal crossings (framed as "illegal" by law enforcement officials) fed into the continued, problematic, and growing narrative that *anybody* crossing the borders, including truckers, were dangerous COVID-laden criminals. As Ernest says:

We had to do something. That's not an image we wanted to persist, not of being criminals, and not the idea that people couldn't get what they need. The whole reason behind driving is to help people survive, to bring their goods.

Truckers often frame what they do on the road – their jobs – as a responsibility to protect others. For example, bokangbokang935, a South African trucking industry TikTokker, posts often about the need for truckers to help track down and even punish thieves who steal cargo off flatbeds.

Since its launch, TikTok's popularity has grown rapidly across Africa (The Rise of Tik Tok in Africa 2022). In October 2018, it was the most-downloaded photo or video app and currently has over 500 million monthly active global users. In Botswana, the number of people using social media for daily news doubled in the years just prior to the pandemic; from 2014 to 2019, over a third of the population gained access to those news sources. And throughout the continent, TikTok's popularity and usage grew exponentially during the first two years of the COVID-19 pandemic and continues to grow. As Ernest and others told me too:

> Yes, it is something that you think of with youth, but here we men are using it, older men, we grew up with SMS so it is familiar but now you see a lot of men on here doing what we do and using it this way.

Truckers claim this technology as something of their own. Ernest and Macdonald and many other truckers on social media leveraged their own growing social networks (once the purview of CB radios, most drivers now communicate and share information on social media platforms) to speak up against unfair treatment at the borders and, in the process, created a more effective distribution system of essentials, COVID information, personal protective equipment, food, and water. As Macdonald proudly describes:

> We are the essential workers now. We can move – even its difficult – we can move when everyone else has to sit still. We tell other drivers what load we're carrying, what extras we can take, and where it all needs to be. So if I know I have a free pallet and can take water, cans, and masks that are meant for Polokwane but might be held up back in Pretoria, then I will. All I have to do is post something on #southafricatruck-drivers and things will move.

During the first year of COVID, when personal protective equipment was hard to find, when supply chains stalled and even simple masks were limited or nonexistent, particularly in remote areas, Ernest made certain that boxes of sanitizer, hand wipes, and soap were included in his load. In Francistown, Botswana, along the eastern corridor of the country and a highly trafficked route for transport throughout the entire region, much of the local population were without reliable boreholes or plumbing and using "tippy taps" instead. Made by attaching a jerrican of water to a stick, dowel, or branch and operated by a foot pedal connected by a rope, tippy taps are ways that even those without running water could increase handwashing and contactless cleaning. But in Francistown and villages outside of Dukwi, near the border, it became clear that cans, soap, and twine were in high demand and low supply. Ernest and two of his colleagues brought a load of cans (there are often excess jerricans in Gaborone or NGO headquarters, as they are seen as an essential yet easily donatable item), Sunlight soap, and rope to the community. As Ernest describes it:

> We got the idea from those local guys on motorbikes – kids, really – who were selling drinks, cigarettes, snacks. . . . They'd bring you takeaways, any kind of food – *seswa*, *pap*, *biltong*, or chocolate, sometimes beer, and definitely Fanta – while you were in the border queue. . . . They were weaving in and out of the trucks as we were lined up, delivering it all, since we couldn't move. You could yell to them to stop if you needed something, but mostly, they began to just deliver things to people from online. . . . Nobody wanted to be face-to-face then, anyway . . . so TikTok, Insta, WhatsApp, if you were in a group, the motorbike delivery guys would get your message and find you in the queue. . . . Sure, they made money, but it was the *idea*, that they had organized all this to help bring us things when we were stuck. . . . We liked that, and so did the same on a bigger, international scale.

In this way, the rise of TikTok as a traveler's or trucker's aid is a necessary means through which communities of care, safety, and supplies continue to travel even as physical cross-border movement grinds to a veritable halt. Technologies such as this are familiar as social movements and political organizations, from the 2011 Arab Spring to Kenyan artisans entering a global economy using iPhones (Mahoney 2017), are facilitated through such tools. Mobile phones are essential, and it is not surprising that the uptake of social media and mobile apps has been so tremendous in Africa. In Botswana, landline technology has been quickly outdated, eclipsed a decade ago by mobile phone usage. As Ernest reminds me, "If I didn't have my phone, I wouldn't have family, nobody would have food, and I'd be lost [laughs] literally." The "family" he refers to are mainly other truckers and people on the road with whom he connects along the way each week (girlfriends, friends, business partners). Ernest does not use the phone to actually make calls; like many in the continent, he uses SMS, TikTok, or Twitter to communicate.

With their physical mobility restricted, drivers use other hashtags, such as #truck_driver_south_africa, #truckersofsouthafrica, #africantruckdrivers, among others, as ways to update people on their well-being, travel status, and road and border closures. Truckers and their communities create social networks of care and encouragement and even help one another combat disease through sharing resources and bringing them to hard-to-reach communities. Where once truckers used CB radios to connect, they now deploy TikTok to broadly (and visually) share experiences and information, voice opinions, and film the impact of the pandemic on personal and professional lives.

Lawrence Kgosikwena: pills and precarious borders

Lawrence Kgosikwena is a career trucker who I first met over five years ago when I first began research into the lives of truck drivers and the management of health along Botswana's border with Zimbabwe. We had met while I was working at the University of Botswana one year and Lawrence had come to a public seminar sponsored by the Center for the Study of HIV/AIDS. He was interested in community responses to the then-current rollout of AIDS awareness strategies. He had a sister who was a teacher in one of the local city secondary schools where children were learning about health, and he soon became a friend, confidante, and my entrée into a community of transportation experts. Like Ernest and Macdonald, Lawrence has long been fascinated by working with engines, learned at a young age how to build and repair any kind of motor vehicle seemingly from scratch, and joined a trucking company as a young adult, rising through the ranks of employees and becoming a recruitment manager, overseeing new hires. Unlike Ernest and Macdonald, however, Lawrence had mainly spent his early career driving *within* Botswana, his company covering routes from the capital city of Gaborone in the south, along the eastern corridor of the country, to Maun in the northern district of Ngamiland.

I spoke with Lawrence one day in 2016 while we were at a truck stop in Francistown, Botswana, a city along the border and, at that time, the site of the growing Dukwi refugee camp, home to immigrants and refugees mostly from Zimbabwe and fleeing from then-president Mugabe's administration. I was beginning research on how truck drivers and transportation routes were functioning as vectors for the spread of infectious disease, primarily HIV/AIDS in this region, and was talking to Lawrence about what he saw as the role of truck drivers, the tensions in the community, as well as the revolutionary new policy in place in Botswana to support anti-retroviral (ARV) pill therapy for all citizens. At first, Lawrence described for me how the government policies were indeed innovative, setting the bar high in a region where ARV care was the true magic bullet in the prevention and care for HIV/AIDS. As he remarked:

> Everyone says that Botswana will have an AIDS-free generation soon, that our kids, they won't have it, we'll know how to prevent it, not just with people's decisions, but with pills. . . . We should all be proud of what the government and [aid agencies] have done.

Gradually, however, it became clear that Lawrence was a bit more skeptical and critical of the country-wide programs being rolled out. Specifically, given that only Botswana *citizens* can access the subsidized ARV therapies, Lawrence observed that such health inequities

> will make it so not all of those children have the same opportunities to be healthy – if you are a migrant, a refugee here, you don't have access. If you have a child, like many [of those in Dukwi], it doesn't matter if the father is a MoTswana (a citizen of Botswana). You and your child, there is no guarantee, no rights to health or to access those pills.

As Lawrence concluded back then: "There are some great policies that you are writing about, but there are many who are invisible, many people who will still be sick that you do not see."

Around the same time that Lawrence and I first met, he had begun attending some local men's groups in southern Botswana that were geared toward raising awareness of gender equity and challenging toxic masculinity. As Lawrence described:

> Nobody used those words, but it was basically about talking with other men about our lives, our wives, girlfriends, daughters, sisters, mothers . . . the women in our lives, and how we needed to remember how important respect is. When you are a young boy, you are always taught about *botho*. We all are, everyone in school, at home, you're taught the expression. In Setswana it means "I am because we are," and so you respect and recognize why we should care for one another. It is basically about learning how to care for the community because they care for you . . . but as you grow up, there is competition and caregiving, and I think that for me, and many others, we were told that boys do one of those things and not the other. . . . You compete, you don't want to be the caregiver; that's for your mother, grandmother, aunties, and the older women in the community to do.

When I pointed out that, for years, male out-migration, remittances from men were not only *de rigeur* but also the subject of myriad historical analyses about providership in Southern Africa, Lawrence agreed but reminded me too that "they were moving for certain kinds of jobs. They didn't have to be at home; they just had to *think* about it. The women were the ones acting on it. They were the ones who were there." In his own family, for example, Lawrence's father, uncle, and cousins all worked for mining corporations in Botswana, Angola, and South Africa as drill operators, metallurgists, mine safety engineers, and managers. When I asked why and how he became a driver instead, Lawrence said directly, not mincing any words:

> I was *not* going to be a *lehetwa* [a young man who was seen as useless, aimless, and not yet having achieved male adulthood]. I was going to make money, use my mind and muscles, but in ways that were smart. I love mechanics, and this way, I could be more of my own boss, at least on the road. I've always worked for a company, but the regulations don't bother me. I always feel safe, I follow the rules, and this was a way to do my part for others.

Long before the COVID era, therefore, Lawrence and those with whom he worked were navigating complicated terrain about what it meant to provide care and seek companionship as men, as intimate partners. They were not alone. In 2018, CNN reported on similar groups of men in South Africa in Mpumalanga province who were gathering to discuss, debate, and redefine masculine gender roles in the country (Gbadamosi). These Young Men's Movements (YMM), as they were called, grew out of concern over the lack of "care" for cultural values, respect, and reports of rising rates of femicide in the region (Maluleke 2018).

Thus, while HIV has long been an omnipresent risk in Botswana, along border communities, and in places like Dukwi with large numbers of migrants and refugees (where non-citizens were not granted access to ARVs or even primary care), there were movements afoot to address perceptions of a "care crisis" among men several years before the advent of COVID. For Lawrence, tackling the gendered assumptions as to who would and could provide health care became focused on the provision of anti-retroviral pills to all (without consideration of citizenship) in the communities he was traveling to, such as Francistown. He said:

> I've been called a *ngaka* in disguise, a doctor, even a nurse. There were some young children in Dukwi, and they told me that their mothers were talking about me as a nurse, an angel even, and that they were able to live because of what I could bring them. They felt left out, and I could help, so I did.

In the years that followed, Lawrence would regularly bring ARV therapies to vulnerable individuals living along the borders. While hesitant to reveal all his strategies for navigating the electronic health record systems in the country (Botswana chemists, or pharmacies, have an extensive national system for tracking pharmaceutical adherence) and accessing additional refills of pills, Lawrence shared with me that he would stop along his trucking routes on a regular basis to share those much-needed and efficacious medicines with those he'd come to know. While Lawrence was unusual in that he was the vector for *medicine* along his route while, he has this to say:

> My friends, they were having sex with the ladies there. They were working against me. I would talk to them, but there was no breaking that chain [a euphemism at that time used by UNAIDS and others to refer to multiple concurrent partnerships in one's sexual network].

There were numerous stories of how people were beginning to share ARV pills, medications, and to stem the spread of that virus in informal ways. In 2019, the government of

Botswana formally extended free HIV treatment to foreign residents and all people living with HIV/AIDS in the country (UNAIDS 2019), and goals of reduction in incidence and prevalence have been very successful. By 2022, the government reported (BAIS V 2021) that, in fact, Botswana had achieved the UNAIDS 95–95–95 goals (95 percent of people with HIV aware of their status, 95 percent of those aware on ARVs, and 95 percent of those on ARVs achieving viral suppression) for people living with HIV shortly thereafter. These goals were heralded by many; even Lawrence, an exceedingly humble man, acknowledged that he played an important role in helping spread awareness, as well as access, in the name of informal health care. He said, "I got other guys [truckers] to help. We were literally carrying the message about medicine and the meaning of staying healthy for others in the community, and it worked, better than some of those national policies."

Part III: The last mile and the meaning of masculinity

So what do the movements and caregiving motivations of Lawrence, Ernest, Macdonald, and others have to do with masculinity? Scholars of transnationality and social networks throughout this region often cite or refute notions of migrants as carriers of culture, and such discussions are far more complex and nuanced than I can do justice to here today. But for Ernest, Macdonald, and others that I continue to work with, the conversations about "carrying COVID" have shifted. There is a sense that they, like long-haul truckers I researched in the United States, are carrying important messages alongside that cargo. That what they perceived as precarious masculinity in some cases and unsettled financial times with a range of health challenges in others might actually offer some personal success and stability, as well as a more nuanced notion of caregiving. Particularly in moments when national governments or international organizations impose systems of surveillance and restrictions on mobility, the limits that are placed on the performance of masculine roles with regard to families and communities should be examined. Self-concepts such as autonomy, independence, agency, and bodily integrity usually associated with masculinity may be challenged and reinterpreted in these circumstances, and highlighting men's responses can shed important light onto academic as well as applied discourse.

As Ernest said on WhatsApp the other day:

> The current viral surveillance program is going well. There's good uptake, guys are joining, and there is a sense that we are doing this better than much of the world – that is a good feeling for those guys who were seen as *lehetwa, or in danger of being left behind, getting sick, or not pulling their weight.*

Ernest's observation was echoed by a text from a CDC colleague in Gaborone who sent something similar, stating, "Yes, from the surveillance perspective, these men are the pieces of the puzzle about how to solve pandemic problems, the people who are in place, and they can be empowered to act as protectors of regional health." They continued, "It's interesting that you suggest that this might have implications for gender, power and other outbreaks. . . . I think we need to think even more about that and hopefully not reinforce old stereotypes."

In a region where HIV/AIDS has been part and parcel of everyday life for generations, there are roadmaps for how to protect communities through behavioral change. Donor agencies and governments have long strategized how to best disseminate medicines and improve health literacy. HIV awareness strategies are far from the early "ABC" (abstain, be faithful, and condomize) campaigns of the Bush and, later, PEPFAR (President's Emergency Plan for AIDS Relief) eras and recognize the role of gender and sexual decision-making in negotiating perceptions of risk that surround health and illness. Edutainment strategies, like *Alone Together* and the wildly popular *Magkabaneng* radio soap opera in Botswana, work well in addressing the impact of HIV in everyday life. Yet national, international, and NGO supply chains are fraught with challenges that continue to make the provision of medicine, care, and consistent messaging to people in their communities persistently difficult, a concept in global public health that is captured by the idea of going "the last mile." In 2016, "Project Last Mile" (PLM) was rolled out by USAID in partnership with Coca-Cola in the effort to draw on best practices in the private sector, coordinate community health efforts, and achieve medical access for all in Africa.

The question driving the development of PLM remains; "If you can find a Coca-Cola product almost anywhere in Africa, why not lifesaving medicines?" With the aim to "leverage" Coca-Cola's best practices in providing products and creating "pickup points" for medications, their efforts have been successful (Project Last Mile 2019). More recently, in 2021, and drawing upon these strategies, PLM has implemented COVID-19-specific efforts that reached over 27 million people in South Africa in just the five months through a mixed-media campaign about the importance of vaccinations. From September 2021 to January 2022, vaccination rates in South Africa increased from 10 percent to almost 30 percent, considerably greater than across the continent as a whole.

It appears that the informal, social media–driven (and literally driven) goods and information that truckers in Southern Africa are bringing to communities mirror much of what larger, international, and ministry of health offices are trying to do. The strategies that truckers are using are fodder for those thinking about how to reach the millions of African populations without access to vaccines, PPE, or communication about COVID-19. For example, in early 2022, the director of external communications for the South Africa Department of Health, Nombulelo Leburu, stressed the need to continue these efforts and shift the focus to "identify more innovative, nontraditional communications approaches to motivate vaccine uptake, especially among the youth." Ernest is therefore understandably proud when he talks about how the USAID and Coca-Cola partners "had the same idea that [they] did" and describes the latest "viral" (he always puts it in air quotes, a nod toward humor in otherwise-painful pandemic times) TikTok video about vaccine uptake, viewed over six million times in one month. Today, Project Last Mile is focused on exploring other strategies to motivate vaccinations and health precautions and improve awareness, mostly through incentives such as airtime for mobile phones, electricity, or cash vouchers. Ernest and Macdonald, on the other hand, continue to carry COVID-related goods (tests, vaccines, medical equipment, PPE, sanitizer, wipes, and masks) alongside their regular loads. They are literally closing that gap, going that last mile so that others (local community members, NGOs, volunteers, practitioners, and others) may not have to.

Thus, while PLM requires some opting in, they push out the information, but agency and responsibility largely still rest with those in precarious positions and those seen as moving targets. In that sense, programs that track, surveil, and continue status updates via social media may be better positioned to address vaccine uptake and health inequities by meeting men (and women) where they are. Certainly for Ernest, Macdonald, and

Lawrence, the sense that this was their duty, their emergent tasks as men in positions of mobility, reinforces an idea of masculinity as constructed and in response to (and not defined by) crisis.

The era of digital disease surveillance

Lastly, how do we track those shifts and crises? While disease surveillance is not new and measures to track infectious, reportable conditions have long been in place, digital and online sharing of surveillance data creates a new kind of terrain. Digital tools and the use of online sources to collect information and maintain databases about health conditions and potential threats are rising in high-income contexts around the world. In parts of the continent, however, the gaps between high- and low-income settings can be tremendous. With the Africa CDC efforts to enact "digital disease surveillance" (CDC Africa), truckers like Ernest and Macdonald find themselves somewhat unintentionally at the forefront of innovative global public health interventions. The CDC site describes their next efforts as the "aggregation and analysis of data available on the internet, such as search engines, social media and mobile phones, and not directly associated with patient illnesses or medical encounters," but rather an approach to tracking behaviors and movements of people. The goal of the pilot program is to develop digital surveillance indicators and online disease dashboards based on social media to inform infectious disease surveillance in Africa. It is expected to strengthen real-time surveillance of infectious diseases in Africa, guide interventions, and build capacity in "Big Data" approaches for outbreak prediction, analysis, and prevention. Through the program, Africa CDC is supporting member states to evaluate the use of Google search engine, Twitter, and other digital sources to monitor cholera, Ebola, influenza, plague, and yellow fever and building their capacity in digital surveillance. Things that arguably, as I note earlier, Ernest and others are already doing in real time.

Yet the CDC is not asking about gendered notions of care, communication, or communicability. A cautionary tale exists alongside the story that these men are telling, and that is that we should be wary of reproducing myopic perspectives on COVID-19 in the same ways that Nguyen (2010) and others (Epstein 2007; Petryna 2004; Zhou 2019) have suggested occurred with AIDS exceptionalism and the construction of "therapeutic citizens." As Lawrence pointed out when talking about Dukwi and the line between the literal "haves" and the "have-nots" when it came to healthcare:

> It came down to who you knew, how you could reach them online, and their willingness to take care of you. . . . [T]he government sees the COVID numbers, but I think it is going to be the people themselves who have to shift their thinking about who is a healthcare provider and who is not. There's not a special set of drugs for a special set of sick people. . . . [T]his hit everyone, but not everyone had the same success.

He wondered further, "Who is going to get ongoing care? If AIDS goes away and COVID is over, what is next, and who will step up to care for Botswana people?" In May of 2023, as the global pandemic was officially ended by the World Health Organization, the role of surveillance systems will undoubtedly become of even greater importance. While case fatality rates in the continent only accounted for 4 percent of all deaths that were reported globally and many lauded the approaches of Southern African public health professionals, COVID-19 tracking and tracing systems, and the ongoing efforts of the CDC Africa organization (CDC Africa 2023), the risks associated with lack of care, and just exactly *who* is at risk, remain. There is clearly interest in developing digital surveillance strategies for public health actions worldwide, and arguably, the informal networks and strategies of long-haul African truckers may again provide the best insights about how to create community, combat disease, and move essential consumer goods where they need to be. But what of the individuals, the ethnographic stories and lived experiences – the making of masculinity in many ways that is happening across these borders? Identities and infections are not co-terminus with citizenship, and masculinity studies of this community might very well be a much-needed complement to culturally competent global health research.

Finally, with this ongoing research, I return often to the notion of precarity as it defines not just lives during the pandemic but as a term that can be useful in thinking about masculinity in cross-cultural context. If precarity suggests uncertainty and a kind of contested, flexible state, then certainly it applies to the narratives and lives we see here. At the same time, however, it describes well the more fixed notions of masculinity as dangerous and risky, in sharp contrast to security and care. As men like Ernest, Macdonald, and Lawrence all share, all those things can be true at the same time and in their own lived experiences as men. In this chapter, therefore, I have attempted to highlight a few key moments in their precarious trajectories – arguing that social media and the rise of TikTok, in particular, as a traveler's or trucker's aid has become a new (and necessary) means through which communities of care, safety, and supplies have grown. Moreover, it seems logical to suggest that if official public health interventions fail to acknowledge the role of seemingly informal communication strategies and the surveillance of bodies only serves to create new and different forms of stigma, then we all run the risk of new variant waves, transmissible beyond the obvious borders. Recognizing the uncertainty of masculinity may, in fact, be necessary if we are to adopt better global public health interventions. Indeed, as McLean (2019), Musariri and Moyer (2020), Ahikire and Mwiine (2020), and Wojnicka (2021) all suggest, ethnographies about men in Africa during the COVID-19 pandemic reveal a constant (and not "crisis") refashioning of masculinity in response to shifting circumstances. It is not, as Ernest tells me, "[a] one-off moment; we're not just going to be providers now during the pandemic and then forget what we've done. I think people everywhere will see how valuable this work is and how we care." Renegotiating roles, as breadwinners or mobile community health providers, the stories of truck drivers like Ernest, Macdonald, and Lawrence offer templates for how we might understand the dynamic and innovative options for gender and health care going forward.

Conclusions

There is perhaps no single conclusion to be drawn from the intersecting stories of COVID-19, TikTok, and the meaning and making of masculinity in Southern Africa. Rather, as scholars such as Mkhwanazi (2016), drawing upon Adiche's (2009) powerful critique, remind us, solitary stories are not only incomplete but are also the "antithesis to anthropology." "Anthropology endeavors to document the complexity, richness and diversity of lives lived" (Mkhwanazi 2016: 194), yet I suggest, following Mkhwanazi, that it is key to move beyond a "single story of medicine, health, and health-seeking behavior" in

Southern Africa if we are going to craft better health responses in the future. Particularly in moments when national governments or international organizations impose systems of surveillance and restrictions on mobility, global public health professionals (and anthropologists) would be well-served by thinking about the subsequent limitations placed on the performance of masculine roles with regards to family and communities. Notions of care, acknowledgement of male vulnerabilities, an understanding of masculinity as emergent, contested, processual, and less of a product can all yield better, more nuanced and efficacious approaches to understanding "health." Whether in person or virtual, rich ethnographic data, individual narratives, and social media analyses can help complete the incomplete and sometimes precarious stories from and about men and masculinity and help improve healthcare mapping in the future.

Discussion questions

1. What does the author argue, and what evidence do they provide in support of their argument? Are you persuaded by their argument and their evidence? Why or why not?
2. According to the author, what does the COVID-19 pandemic have in common with HIV/AIDS for truckers in Southern Africa?
3. How and why do truckers in Southern Africa use TikTok?
4. What does this chapter reveal about the relationship between men, masculinities, and global health?

References

Adiche, Chimamanda Ngozi. 2009. "The Danger of a Single Story." *TEDGlobal*. July. https://www.ted.com/talks/chimamanda_ngozi_adichie_the_danger_of_a_single_story?language=en.

Ahikire, Josephine, and Amon A. Mwiine. 2020. "COVID-19, 'Nested Newness' and Changing Masculinities in Uganda." *Gender and Covid-19*. www.genderandcovid-19.org/research/covid-19-nested-newness-and-changing-masculinities-in-uganda/.

BAIS V. 2021. *Botswana AIDS Impact Survey V*. Gaborone, Botswana: Government Statistics Office.

Baker, Venetia, Georgia Arnold, Sara Piot, Lesedi Thwala, Judith Glynn, James Hargreaves, and Isolde Birdthistle. 2021. "Young Adults' Responses to an African and US-Based COVID-19 Edutainment Miniseries: Real-Time Qualitative Analysis of Online Social Media Engagement." *JMIR Form Res.*, October 29 5(10): e30449. https://doi.org/10.2196/30449. PMID: 34596568; PMCID: PMC8562417.

CDC Africa. n.d. *Digital Disease Surveillance*. https://africacdc.org/programme/surveillance-disease-intelligence/digital-disease-surveillance/.

CDC Africa. 2023. *The Transition Beyond the Acute Phase of COVID-19 Pandemic in Africa*. https://africacdc.org/news-item/the-transition-beyond-the-acute-phase-of-covid-19-pandemic-in-africa/.

Clottey, Peter. 2020. "East African Truckers Pay Bribes for Negative Coronavirus Tests." *VOA*, October 19. www.voanews.com/a/africa_east-african-truckers-pay-bribes-negative-coronavirus-tests-official-says/6197325.html.

Decoteau, Claire Laurier. 2013. "The Crisis of Liberation: Masculinity, Neoliberalism, and HIV/AIDS in Postapartheid South Africa." *Men and Masculinities* 16(2): 139–159.

Dube, Mqondisi. 2020. "Landlocked Botswana Truck Drivers Face COVID-19 Dilemma." *VOA News*. www.voanews.com/a/covid-19-pandemic_landlocked-botswana-truck-drivers-face-covid-19-dilemma/6193637.html.

Emeto, Theophilus I., Faith O. Alele, Olayinka S. Ilesanmi. 2021. "Evaluation of the Effect of Border Closure on COVID-19 Incidence Rates across Nine African Countries: An Interrupted Time Series Study." *Transactions of The Royal Society of Tropical Medicine and Hygiene*, October 115(10): 1174–1183.

Epstein, Steven. 2007. *Inclusion: The Politics of Difference in Medical Research*. New York: University of Chicago Press.

Gbadamosi, Nosmot. 2018. "The All Male Group Tackling Toxic Masculinity." *CNN Inside Africa*, December 21. www.cnn.com/2018/12/21/health/south-africa-male-group-toxic-masculinity-intl/index.html.

Hoffman, Danny. 2016. "A Crouching Village: Ebola and the Empty Gestures of Quarantine in Monrovia." *City & Society* 28(2): 246–264.

Honwana, Alcinda. 2014. "'Waithood': Youth Transitions and Social Change." In *Development and Equity*. Leiden, The Netherlands: Brill. https://doi.org/10.1163/9789004269729_004.

Lichtenstein, Amanda, and Pernille Baerendtsen. 2020. "Truck Drivers Blamed for Spread of COVID-19 in East Africa." *Global Voices*, May 15. https://globalvoices.org/2020/05/15/truck-drivers-blamed-for-spread-of-covid-19-in-east-africa/.

Mahoney, Dillon. 2017. *The Art of Connection: Risk, Mobiliy, and the Crafting of Transparency in Coastal Kenya*. University of California Press.

Maina, Beatrice W., Yandisa Sikweyiya, Laura Ferguson, and Caroline W. Kabiru. 2022. "Conceptualisations of Masculinity and Sexual Development among Boys and Young Men in Korogocho Slum in Kenya." *Culture, Health & Sexuality* 24(2): 226–240. https://doi.org/10.1080/13691058.2020.1829058.

Malinga, Thobile, et al. 2021. "A Scoping Review of the Impact of Long-Distance Truck Drivers on the Spread of COVID-19 Infection." *Pan African Medical Journal* 38: 27. https://doi.org/10.11604/pamj.2021.38.27.26691.

Maluleke, Risenga. 2018. "Crime Against Women in South Africa." *Statistics South Africa* Report No. 03-40-05 (June). Pretoria, SA.

McLean, Kristen E. 2019. "Caregiving in Crisis: Fatherhood Refashioned by Sierra Leone's Ebola Epidemic." *Medical Anthropology Quarterly* 34(2): 227–242.

Mkhwanazi, Nolwazi. 2016. "Medical Anthropology in Africa: The Trouble with a Single Story." *Medical Anthropology* 35(2): 193–202. https://doi.org/10.1080/01459740.2015.1100612.

Momoh, Abubakar. 1999. "The Youth Crisis in Nigeria: Understanding the Phenomena of the Area Boys and Girls." *Conference on Children and Youth as Emerging Categories in Africa*, 4–6 November, Leuven, Belgium.

Musariri, Linda, and Moyer, Eileen. 2020. "A Black Man Is a Cornered Man: Migration, Precarity and Masculinities in Johannesburg." *Gender, Place & Culture* 28(6): 888–905.

Nguyen, Vinh-Kim. 2010. *The Republic of Therapy: Triage and Sovereignty in West Africa's Time of AIDS*. Durham: Duke University Press.

Packard, R. M. 1993. "The Invention of the 'Tropical Worker': Medical Research and the Quest for Central African Labor on the South African Gold Mines, 1903–36." *The Journal of African History* 34(2): 271–292. www.jstor.org/stable/182429

Petryna, Adriana. 2004. "Biological Citizenship: The Science and Politics of Cherobyl-Exposed Populations." *Osiris* 19(2): 1–17.

Project Last Mile. 2019. "What is the Role of Coca-Cola Within Project Last Mile?" *PLM_Admin*. February. www.projectlastmile.com/what-is-the-role-of-the-coca-cola-company-within-project-last-mile/.

The Rise of TikTok in Africa. 2022. 18 March. www.indiablooms.com/life-details/L/6415/the-rise-of-tiktok-in-africa.html.

SA Long-Distance Truckers Facebook. 2020. May. www.facebook.com/salt.co.za/.

UNAIDS. 2019. *Botswana Extends Free HIV Treatment to Non-Citizens*, September 24. www.unaids.org/en/resources/presscentre/featurestories/2019/september/20190924_Botswanatreatmentnon-nationals.

UNAIDS/WHO. 2004. *Report on the Global AIDS Epidemic*. 4th Global Report. https://files.unaids.org/en/media/unaids/contentassets/documents/unaidspublication/2004/GAR2004_en.pdf.

Upton, Rebecca L. 2003. "Women Have No Tribe: Connecting Carework, Gender and Migration in an Era of HIV/AIDS in Botswana." *Gender and Society*, special issue on Global Perspectives on Gender and Carework, April 17(2): 314–322.

Upton, Rebecca L. 2010a. "Promising the Permanent Condom: Fertility Fears and Fatal Outcomes as a Result of Voluntary Adult Male Circumcision in HIV/AIDS Botswana." *PULA: Journal of Research in Botswana* 24(1): 101–117.

Upton, Rebecca L. 2010b. "Fat Eggs: Gender and Fertility as Factors in HIV/AIDS Prevention in Botswana." *Gender & Development* November 18(3). Special Issue on Food: 515–524.

Upton, Rebecca L. 2011. "Sterility and Stigma in an Era of HIV/AIDS: Narratives of Risk Assessment Among Men and Women in Botswana." *African Journal of Reproductive Health* 15(1): 95–102.

Upton, Rebecca L. 2016. "Fat Eggs and Fit Bodies." *Contexts. Journal of the American Sociological Association* 15(4): 24–29.

Upton, Rebecca L. 2019. "Illness and Healing: Africanist Anthropology." In *A Companion to the Anthropology of Africa*, eds. Roy Richard Grinker, Stephen C. Lubkemann, Christopher Steiner, and Euclides Gonçalves, 97–117. Hoboken: Wiley-Blackwell.

Upton, Rebecca L. 2020. "Global Health at the Local Level: Innovative Approaches for Preventing HIV/AIDS Among Adolescent Girls in Botswana–Evidence from an Evaluation Study on Perceptions of Cross Generational Sex and Edu-tainment Strategies." In *Reinventing and Reinvesting in the Local for Our Common Good*, ed. B. Hoey, 99–123. Knoxville: University of Tennessee Press.

Upton, Rebecca L. 2022. "TikTok, Truckers, and Travel Bans." *Anthropology News*, September 14.

Utas, Mats. 2005. "Building a Future? The Reintegration and Remarginalization of Youth inLiberia." In *No Peace, No War: An Anthropology of Contemporary Armed Conflicts*, ed. Paul Richards, 137–154. Athens: Ohio University Press.

Wojnicka, Katarzyna. 2021. "Men and Masculinities in Times of Crisis: Between Care and Protection." *NORMA* 16(1): 1–5.

Zhou, Amy. 2019. "Therapeutic Citizens and Clients: Diverging Healthcare Practices in Malawi's Prenatal Clinics." *Sociology of Health & Illness* 41(4): 625–642.

Index

Please note that page numbers in *italics* indicate a figure and page numbers in **bold** indicate a table on the corresponding page.